Talking Art 2

Talking Art 2

Interviews with artists since 2007
Edited by Patricia Bickers

Art Monthly | Ridinghouse

Contents

Preface

The purpose of this preface is to thank all those without whom this project would never have been possible, beginning with our collaborators on the live Talking Art series at Tate Modern, curator Marko Daniels and writer and curator Gabriela Salgado, formerly of Tate, some of which are published here in edited form for the first time. Also Frederika Whitehead, former assistant editor of *Art Monthly* who liaised with Tate.

Thanks also go to Sally O'Reilly who organised the Duelling Banjos event at the Whitechapel Art Gallery, and to Gilda Williams and Julian Stallabrass, who agreed to debate the merits of the interview format, along with their nominated 'seconds', Lisa Le Feuvre and Marq Smith respectively, an edited transcript of which forms the introduction to this second volume of *Talking Art* interviews.

Thanks too, to Kita Roos, who transcribed many of the Tate live interviews with phenomenal speed and accuracy, and to present and former colleagues at *Art Monthly*, including former deputy editor Andrew Wilson and current deputy editor David Barrett, for his work on the interviews originally printed in the magazine, and especially to *Art Monthly* associate editor Chris McCormack, for his patience and care in preparing all the edited transcripts, for his work liaising with artists and interviewers, as well for steering the production process, and lastly to our peerless proofreader Penny Williams.

Thank you Mark Thomson, former deputy editor of Art Monthly and ace book designer, who not only designed this volume, but also both editions of *Talking Art* Volume 1. Thank you everyone at Ridinghouse, past and present, especially Doro Globus and Daniel Griffiths, and above all Karsten Schubert, publisher of both volumes of *Talking Art*, who has been such a staunch supporter from the outset.

Finally, thanks are due to all the artists who generously agreed to be interviewed, to the interviewers who undertook the interviews with such skill and insight and to all, including the estates of artists, who agreed without exception to the interviews appearing in this second volume of *Talking Art*. Thank you.

Patricia Bickers
7 August 2017

Banjos at Dawn

'Banjos at Dawn' was a debate that took place at the Whitechapel Gallery. It came about as a result of a conversation with Sally O'Reilly when, during her writing residency at the gallery, she suggested collaborating with *Art Monthly* on an – unspecified – event. Two years earlier *Art Monthly* had published *Talking Art: Interviews with artists since 1976*, volume one of what was always intended to be a series. The suggested event seemed a good opportunity to review the idea of the interview: is it really an invaluable tool for historiography or does it simply perpetuate the cult of celebrity? O'Reilly proposed that the debate be presented in a dramatic form as an intellectual duel between two protagonists, each of whom could call upon 'seconds' to support their argument, using clips from a series of live interviews with artists commissioned by *Art Monthly* in collaboration with Tate Modern.

I invited art critic Gilda Williams to argue 'for' the motion and art historian Julian Stallabrass to put the case 'against'. Williams nominated curator Lisa Le Feuvre to act as her second, and Stallabrass nominated academic Marq Smith to act as his second, while O'Reilly oversaw the event to ensure fair play (the services of a surgeon would not it was hoped be required). The date and time having been agreed between all parties, 'Banjos at Dawn: for and against the interview', was launched on an expectant audience on 24 September 2010.

The publication of volume two of *Talking Art*, to coincide with the 40th anniversary of *Art Monthly*, seemed an appropriate time to publish the outcome of the duel by way of an introduction: what follows is an edited transcript of the original debate.

Patricia Bickers

SALLY O'REILLY   This is a discussion intended to introduce some controlled friction into the auditorium. I thought this friction was necessary, since spectators and participants can frequently be overheard voicing their weariness of panel discussions where those convened to talk on a subject start politely at the point they have been asked to address, but soon wander off into their own fields of interest, perhaps absentmindedly or through habit or, less generously, for safekeeping. The consequence is often frustratingly diffuse, a wide-open terrain of vague thematics lacking the sort of triangulation of perspectives that provokes sharper thought and more vigorous discussion. So the discussion has been configured to make a series of benevolent *dérives* from a vague starting point impossible.

Two speakers who have been known to take opposing views on a subject are invited to state their position, which hopefully guarantees if not two opposed forces in full battledress, then at least some contrary stances, contentious refutations and inquisitorial stabs. Art critic Gilda Williams and art historian Julian Stallabrass respond to the question of whether the interview is a dynamic, constructive format or a received genre that perpetuates undesirable constraints and assumptions. Gilda and Julian have both written extensively on modern and contemporary art in formats that include the editorialised interview, and both have been interviewees themselves, so they will be speaking, I think, historically as well as personally on the subject.

The proceedings will run like this: firstly, Gilda will present her argument for the interview, then Julian will present his argument against it, but without responding specifically to what Gilda has said. It will be an exercise in establishing clear positions rather than dialogue up to this point. Gilda will then be invited to take issue with Julian's views, followed by Julian taking issue with Gilda's. As is the tradition in duelling, after this initial parry if either party feels so inclined they may call on their seconds in the audience to contribute to their argument. After that, it is a free-for-all.

GILDA WILLIAMS   I am going to start with defining some terms, because I think that is crucial here. The interview is one of the many forms of writing that have proliferated in contemporary art, among them catalogue texts, reviews, artists' writings, and so forth. We are going to concentrate on this text form, the artist's interview, which for now I will define – though this probably will broaden as the discussion goes on –

as a dialogue between two people, at least one of whom is an artist, whose voice is prioritised.

We all know that this model – this very conventional model – has been riffed on in every possible direction: multiple voices, round-tables, mock interviews (artists interviewing themselves, critics interviewing themselves) or the 'in-conversation' model which isn't really a Q&A – short 'Q' followed by a long 'A' – but a format in which each voice is given equal weight. It seems to me that the interview was invented mostly to serve four purposes – most of which are now in crisis – which is why, I think, we're having this debate right now.

The first purpose is a kind of fact-finding exercise, asking the artist: what did you do? When did you do it? When did you show that first? What is it made out of?

Secondly, there is the idea of a general public gaining access to some kind of 'insider' talk. What is the artist really like? What do artists and critics or curators, for example, talk about behind closed doors? However much we know it is a fiction, there can still be the illusion or fantasy of that kind of authentic access, which, I think, is as seductive as it ever was.

Thirdly, there is also the idea – and this is probably the expectation that is most in crisis – that the interview will help you read or understand the artist's work; that there is some kind of primacy in the information – the motivations or the sources and images behind the work – that only the artist can reveal, and that is somehow going uniquely to enrich your experience of the artwork. I think most of us probably indulge in this, even though we know that that kind of belief in artistic intentionality has been very much challenged.

The fourth purpose that needs to be considered is the interview as performance – as part of an artist's practice. The Andy Warhol interview would be the most typical, for example where he would reply only with 'Yes' or 'No' – no matter the question. The interview is an occasion to perform an artistic persona that fuels the 'character' behind all the artist's art. We all know of artists for whom the interview is very much a performative event – Jeff Koons, Gilbert and George or Tracey Emin, for instance – but there are others, I think, who are more subtle, like Paul Chan. Are Chan's interviews a part of his practice? Arguably, yes.

These four purposes seem to me to be why the interview was invented in the 1960s in art and why we have sort of stuck with it. For those reasons – because it can do those four particular things – the interview has a special status within art writing. What I'm now going to look at is why and how the interview might have lost that status, and what power the interview still holds.

First of all, we are all aware that a printed interview is a fiction. We are all aware that artists know that they are being taped, that they are not necessarily 'being themselves', and that the interview is edited, re-edited and reworded. We also question the very need to locate the artist solidly behind the work, as representing the most authentic subjective experience of their art.

So, why do we still love interviews? My first reaction when Sally said, 'Would you be "For" the interview?', was 'of course I will!' I got the easy side of this debate – right? Interviews are easy to love, easy to read. The language is easier. If you need to accomplish something difficult, what do you do? You break the job up into pieces. Writing about art can be hard, and interviews break the text into pieces – Q&A. Artists often end up telling stories, which readers love. We like interviews for the seductive fiction of eavesdropping on a conversation. A conversation enlivens proceedings, however much we might know that it is potentially a false enlivening. Novelists bring a story to life by adding dialogue. The back-and-forth of the interview still makes this kind of text more pleasurable than many other types of art reading.

Certainly, if I open an art magazine, the first thing I do is read the interviews. If I'm doing research on an artist after seeing the work, the first thing I will look for is the interviews. Why is that? We can all think of dozens of great interviews that we know and love. For me, the interview Warhol did with Benjamin Buchloh in 1985 is unforgettable almost despite itself – despite being a failed interview in many ways. Buchloh is trying to salvage Andy Warhol as a kind of conceptual artist, and position him as 'better' than the 1980s figurative painters whom Buchloh despises. But Warhol won't budge – even if Buchloh is in many ways trying to save the by then faded Pop artist, as he was considered at the time. Something emerges that is bigger than the questions and the answers – some larger text emerges, about Warhol's steadfast conviction about what he's doing, even when the chips are down and a powerful critic is offering a kind of rescue. Warhol sticks to his story, and his dead certainty in what he's doing amazes me every time I reread it. Some third kind of result comes out of that pairing.

I'd like to read not an artist interview, but the beginning of *Interview with a Vampire* by Anne Rice from 1976. The vampire says:

'I would like to tell you the story of my life, then. I would like to do that very much.

"Great," said the boy. And quickly he removed the small tape recorder from his briefcase, making a check of the cassette and the batteries. "I'm really anxious to hear why you believe this, why you … "

"No," said the vampire abruptly. "We can't begin that way. Is your equipment ready?"

"Yes," said the boy.

"Then sit down. I'm going to turn on the overhead light." […] the vampire moved towards the table and reached for the overhead cord … At once the room was flooded with a harsh yellow light. And the boy, staring up at the vampire, could not repress a gasp … "Dear God!" he whispered, and then he gazed, speechless, at the vampire. The vampire was utterly white and smooth, as if he were sculpted from bleached bone, and his face was as seemingly inanimate as a statue, except for two brilliant green eyes that looked down at the boy intently like flames in a skull […] The boy shuddered, lifting his hand as if to shield himself from a powerful light.

"Now," [the vampire asked,] "do you still want the interview?"'

The reason I bring that up is because it's an important date, 1976. It is the year that *Avalanche Magazine* ended, one of the legendary magazines that came out of New York in the 1970s. It consisted solely of interviews, producing a series of great interviews with the good and the great of – mostly – Conceptual Art from the period. It is also the year that *Interview Magazine* – Warhol's *Interview Magazine* – really took off, moving from being underground to being mainstream. I think Rice's opener here examines the original idea of the artist's interview in which a mysterious figure who has not spoken in centuries – a vampire, an artist – is now, with the aid of technology, able to talk. And they are able to reveal something that no one else has known until then. They can give their side of the story. And this, I think, is how the artist's interview really began, when artists were first asked, in the late 20th century, to speak.

It was a political issue, about power distribution in the art world, to allow the artist to take control, to have their own voice, to offer a kind of transparency about what they do. They can fully articulate meaning for their own work, no longer reliant on the critic to supply the words like an inspired but mute maker, lacking speech and intellect.

I don't want here to go over vintage highlights from the 1960s and the 1970s. Instead, I'd like to read you part of an interview between Maurizio Cattelan and Peter Coffin from 2007. It is an artist interviewing an artist, although Coffin is very much the subject. Cattelan asks: 'Should we challenge existing conventions of art that limit how we think about and make art? What do you think is important about how artists are working today?'

Coffin replies: 'The value of particular artists after Duchamp can be weighed according to how much they question the nature of art, which is another way of saying, what they added to the conception of art, of what wasn't there before they started.' He goes on in that somewhat MFA-ish way for another three sentences. Then Cattelan asks: 'But what is the truth? How should we be true artists?'

Coffin replies: 'Thou shalt be the messenger of freedom. Thou shalt fight and form and reinvent life. Thou shalt give thy love. Thou shalt grab the soul and give something back. Thou shalt have a sense of purpose.'

Cattelan responds 'Really?'

'Well I don't necessarily agree with everything I say.' says Coffin.

Cattelan says: 'OK, well what's a good working method?'

'Do one thing at a time. Know the problem. Learn to listen. Learn to ask questions. Distinguish sense from nonsense, accept change is inevitable, admit mistakes, say it's simple, be calm and smile.'

'Is this how you work?', asks Cattelan.

'I like the idea that even as I sleep or play the work is moving towards its completion.'

Now, what we have there is ventriloquism. Coffin is totally aware of the fiction of the interview and puts on all these different voices. First, the dutiful artist and the art student: 'I know my Duchamp, but I can talk the talk. Here I go.' Then, he puts on this curious biblical voice, reciting some kind of holy truth. Finally, he assumes the voice of managerial newspeak, you know, 'do one thing at a time' – all that. Then he takes off the last mask only to reveal another mask. Finally he is going to 'be himself' – which, again, we doubt. But the thing that is interesting about this interview – and it's a good interview in my opinion – is that, despite all the play-acting, towards the end Coffin stops playing games. Ultimately he gets to something about what he thinks an artist does and what he's after:

'I really feel there's a kind of dialogue of imminence, that certain questions become demanding and potentially answerable and that everyone involved on a particular level of asking questions – whether a physicist, a philosopher or an artist – is essentially involved in asking the same questions. And if at some point we look at the world and feel that things are not resolvable by logical thinking, we have to develop an antithesis and that's really what contemporary art is in our culture: it is an antithesis.'

I think this is an interesting idea in and of itself, whether spoken by an artist or not: that there is a post-post-enlightenment moment outside familiar logic that may encapsulate what art is after; that the interview is still a place where an artist is willing to start doing crazy things like defining 'art' or 'an artist'. When I started looking at a lot of interviews through this exercise, I noticed how many artists are willing to go out on a limb and start saying the kind of things you could never address in any other context, asking big questions like: 'What is art? Why are we making this?' They're terrible questions that we are usually too embarrassed to ask or put into writing.

Lawrence Weiner says in an interview of 1997: 'I'm just an artist. I don't have to be right all the time. I'm not giving out medical prescriptions to people; I'm not flying an aeroplane – I'm just this person putting things in the culture and that thing can change the culture.' Or Lynda Benglis, in an issue of *Frieze*, who talks in an interview about the bounds of materials and the unbounded nature of the universe and imagination – and how in her work, she is trying to mark time. These are big issues. It is hard to find a place in the art world where we can safely grasp at big questions, which really are important to revisit periodically.

One last example – Dennis Cooper, in an interview with Tom Friedman that I edited myself. In this passage they're talking about 'the purpose of art', and they're laughing about the impossibility of the question, because you have to laugh about it.

Cooper says: 'But, ultimately you believe [art] is important.'

Friedman responds: 'I don't know. I think in terms of ideals. If I were to think about what the ideal art would be, that would be an art that gives viewers an experience that they take with them. And it causes them this incredible revelation which they, as enlightened people, turn towards society. They would do these amazing things that penetrate other people. And then they'll all come together and live in harmony. And there's peace, and we're all transcendent individuals.'

Friedman ends with: 'It sounds like a comedy.'

Under the cloak of the interview the artist can change voices. Friedman can start with the non-committal 'I don't know', and then move towards his greatest, almost inexpressible aspirations, a move which is hard to pull off in straight prose. Friedman can go way out on a limb, expressing his ultimate hopes and dreams: ideally, art will promote world peace, harmony, universal transcendence. This is difficult to express or even admit to in other texts where it would sound ludicrous, unsayable. The lightness of the interview becomes a place to play with hyperbole, to push possibility. And if you accidentally go over the top in the interview, you can always resort to humour, and laugh it off – save face, as it were.

If we look at its history, the interview is part of an overall bigger idea about deskilling. The artist became deskilled; the critic became deskilled. Anyone can shove a mike at somebody's mouth and get an interview. But actually, make no mistake – a good interview is a really, really skilful thing and it needs to be prepared for probably as much as any serious text. Like any good text, the printed interview needs interesting and varied language. It needs smart questions. It needs good listening. It needs a beginning, middle and an end. It needs ideas that are brought into the discussion. But what is particular about the interview is that those ideas are actually tested with the artist – 'live' – as it were.

SALLY O'REILLY   Julian, do you want to come straight in against the interview?

JULIAN STALLABRASS   I'm not going to be just against the interview. I've done some of them myself, for one thing, and I've been interviewed many times myself. Gilda has laid out the case for them very eloquently. We get enjoyment from them, we get insight from them. They are an accessible and informal public dialogue. So what could be wrong with interviewing?

Two issues give me a certain kind of pause. Firstly, their dominance in art discourse, which is a historical matter. It has not always been the case, so that might be something we ask questions about. And secondly, there is their general character. Gilda has laid out for us towards the end of her talk the ideal of what the interview could – and should – be, but if we look at the reality of the regular run of interviews, I think a rather different picture emerges. There are some problems that all interviews have, I think, and this is especially true if we're thinking of the interview as giving the reader access to an insider discourse or to some sort of truth.

Our problem is the general unreliability of memory, about which a great deal of work has been done in the sciences. We should be extremely suspicious of anything that deals with retrospection. There have been good, long-term studies of people revisiting their student years, for instance, and being asked about their political opinions and forgetting entirely – and it's not lying, necessarily, but forgetting – what their early opinions were, what their early perspectives were, and simply assuming there is a much greater coherence in a life trajectory than there really is. This is something we all do.

Then, of course, there's the issue of honesty. People lie, they lie a lot – especially about things that really concern them. There are things which may fall short of lies, but which may be propagandistic statements, statements designed to alter a reality. Many politicians' statements fall into that kind of category. Their statements are speech acts, though not quite a formal speech act in the J L Austin sense – for example, 'With this ring I thee wed.'

I don't know how many of you have seen or remember *The Phil Silvers Show*, where Silvers plays Sergeant Bilko. Bilko's statements are almost always like that. They are statements which seek to transform reality around him, and to change everybody's perceptions. It is often perfectly clear that Bilko doesn't believe what he is saying, but he manages to convince everybody else that the world around him is different from what they might otherwise imagine it to be. Such speech acts are also an exercise of power, which is perfectly clear in the case of politicians, but which I think is also true of many interviewees. What you have here is a rather unequal set-up. Of course, there are exceptions, but you have somebody seeking access to a supposed truth from somebody else. The interviewee is immediately given a special status, and in that case these forms of speech acts and propaganda – and perhaps lies – are exercises of power.

So, I think we should treat all interviews with a certain amount of circumspection, but I think that when it comes to artists, we have another set of particular problems that you can add to these general ones. One, I think, comes out of a cult of celebrity which is also another historically contingent matter which surrounds many artists today, and which has led some critics like Isabelle Graw in her book, *High Price*, to describe the artist as an ur-celebrity – a founding celebrity. Some of the most successful artists live their lives very much in the media and here the interview form is, of course, crucial, along with the profile. There is a general cosiness that these interviews degenerate into. They are fundamentally a form of promotional literature. As such, I think we should be extremely suspicious of them, and of the status of any statement that is made within them.

A separate problem is the predominance of the interview in the

general literature on art, and the overproduction of interviews. The fact
that they so much dominate what passes for critical discourse about the
arts – one might think about Hans-Ulrich Obrist's various productions,
the monumental productions of interview books, and the marathon
interviews that he conducts.

Then, again, artist's statements are not like politician's statements,
or statements by other people in interviews. They are a peculiar class of
statement, because they often come across as somehow ineluctable or
unchallengeable, particularly if the artist is famous.

I've been looking at the work of Jeff Wall lately. He is an interesting
case. In his early career he wrote many highly intelligent critical pieces
about photography and Conceptual Art. He's been interviewed many,
many times and this discourse forms a block which, it seems, is extremely difficult for people who write about his work to move around. In his
catalogue raisonné, many of these texts are reproduced and they are cate-
gorised as 'primary' texts, which I think is interesting. So, any statement
by Wall is a 'primary' text; any statement by anybody else is a 'secondary'
text. Now, the issue of what constitutes a primary text in the study of
contemporary art is a rather delicate and interesting one, and you might
think that contemporary art criticism is entirely primary. So, this is an
ideological naming. But perhaps what is interesting is that we can see
the work and these texts as part of a unit. They are all, in a sense, part
of the oeuvre.

The remarkable thing about this is that many prominent art historians support Wall and they frequently cite these texts as if they're a kind
of gospel. So, if they're seeking to make a point, often they'll go back to
Wall's writings and interviews and make this point. But if you read these
texts, Wall changes his mind really radically, especially over political
issues – from early bleak, Adornian, leftist, melancholic and elegiac
writings through to something quite conservative in later texts, where
his leftist views are entirely disposed of.

That kind of trajectory is not often registered and these critics and
art historians will reference a text from 1978 and another text from 2002
as if they're the same thing. So there's something strange in the way in
which interviews are often handled as ineluctable truth. I think that they
are dangerous in a certain way and that they can harm critical discourse.
In Wall's case, I think what you have is a real deformation of the writing
about him. He has successfully managed to bend that writing around
him in a particular direction. Wall studied for a PhD at the Courtauld

Institute, and part of his study was about Marcel Duchamp, who was, of course, another master of making textual interventions to determine and perhaps over determine the interpretation of his work. Then, of course, there's the issue that artists are interested parties. Stephen Farthing, when he was the Master at the Ruskin School, once told me – and this was something that stuck in my head – that artists are liars, cheats and scammers. Well, this might be a slight over exaggeration, but I think it is very different from the way that the interview encourages us to think about artists.

So, plainly, as Gilda has said, there's a lot going on in the interview, which is about a certain form of self-presentation. Artists lie – and quite a lot. And some of them have been caught out. For instance, to go back to some famous cases about long-dead artists, Giorgio de Chirico predated many of his paintings in an attempt to show that he was more innovatory than he really was. Joan Miró claims that many of his surrealist works were automatic paintings, done in daylong trances from which he would emerge to find an elaborate painting. Of course, the problem of painting for surrealists was a deep one given their attachment to automatism. You could just about imagine that a drawing might be automatic – but a large painting? This is a problem – right? The art historian David Lomas discovered many preparatory drawings for these paintings – so Miró was plainly lying for ideological reasons.

Another point, I suppose, is whether the proliferation of interviews is at all interesting. Once an artist has been interviewed maybe five times, do we learn anything more from further reiterations of these things?

There's an interesting issue of *Art Journal*, from 2004/05 I think, which is devoted to the issue of the artist's interview. Tim Griffin thought that he and Jeff Koons had a good exchange; Koons seemed to be very open and revealed all sorts of interesting things. But shortly before his interview came out in *Time Out*, he opened the *New York Times Magazine* and saw another interview with Koons, in which almost exactly the same material had been reproduced. So, Koons is plainly giving a standard off-the-peg performance. And this isn't new either.

If you read Henry Moore interviews, for instance – and, again, there are many of those – it becomes apparent that he has a particular kind of schtick, and he will say the same thing over and over again. As with many artists, there are things he won't talk about – he won't talk about contemporaries and he won't talk about his relationship to Barbara Hepworth. If he's asked about influences, he always goes back to

Michelangelo for pretty obvious reasons. Similar things can be said about photographs of Moore, who had his own official photographer. The way in which Moore poses reveals how he carefully considered the presentation of his image and his work. It is not a matter of Postmodernism but of publicity, which is a good deal older.

The sculpture assistants who used to work at the Moore Foundation were very amusing about some of these photographs, taken when Moore was in his 80s and showing him standing beside some enormous piece of marble with a chisel and a hammer, when he was plainly physically incapable of doing that work any longer. The sculptures were, in any case, mostly completed by Italian craftsmen in Carrara. But the pictures tell a different story – another kind of lie, if you like.

I think that this is also part of celebrity culture, and many artists participate in this – they appear within the same kinds of circuits, the same kind of mass media, and act in ways that are very familiar. It is a kind of simulacrum – a hall of mirrors. In this realm, the interviews are also, in a sense, contentless. We know as much or as little, in a sense, about Amy Winehouse or Madonna as we do about Koons or Damien Hirst. As in the discourse of spying, you can't be sure that any statement that you read is remotely straight – everything can be manipulation, bluff or double bluff.

There's a deeper problem though, which is that artists don't really know what they're doing in their work. They may, in a sense, know what they're doing in terms of how they think of their practice, and interviews can be useful in illuminating that, but in terms of making interventions in a wider culture, they don't know what they're doing. We often don't know what they're doing either. In an understanding of that intervention, there's no reason why an artist's opinion should be any more valuable than anybody else's. Gilda mentioned an interview between Buchloh and Warhol, and I want to mention another of Buchloh's interviews, which is an extraordinary one that he did with Gerhard Richter, also I think in the 1980s.

Now this is a magnificent interview and, again, it is a failure in a certain sense in that the two are just ships passing in the night. They have little to say to each other. In fact, there are certain points at which Richter is aghast at Buchloh's interpretation of his work as an affectless repetition of elements of mass culture, a reflection on the impossibility of originality, or of art-making as an original and significant intervention in a scene. For me, Buchloh's powerful interpretation of Richter's art is much more interesting than Richter's. So, again, there is no real reason why we should privilege artists' statements. There has been some good work done on the success or failure of movies and movie producers. It is clear from this work that you can quantify these things in market terms: that no one in the movie industry really knows what they're doing, and that successful producers and directors and actors and so on are merely lucky. Basically, you're launching a cultural work into a deeply complex and fractal environment. You have no idea how it will be received – and that's as true of artists as it is of anybody else. It is true of writers, too, incidentally.

Now, as Gilda mentioned, positions for or against the interview do have historical dimensions. It becomes clear from *Avalanche Magazine*, which Gilda also mentioned, that the interview was pitched as a weapon against the dominant authoritarian and powerful formalist art criticism of the late 1960s and early 1970s. But we do not live in those times, and we do not have that kind of criticism. If anything, we might say that art criticism is too weak and the interview, along with a profile-linked form of art publicity, is pretty dominant.

Some people claim that interviews build community through formal dialogue, but as I say, although there are many variations on the form, the fundamental character of it – this interviewer/interviewee relation – seems to be unequal. It is also usually one-to-one and it is a broadcast medium and form. I think that the current dominance of artist statements and interviews feeds into a cultic elevation of the artist and, in that sense, I would like to see it dissolving in a wider egalitarian and participatory culture.

SALLY O'REILLY   Thanks. I understand we have slightly equivocal positions here – for and against – but I think there are lots of points of elision and contradiction.

There's one surprising point, in terms of what I understand from both your writings, which is the reverse of what I expected you would both want to find in an interview: the concentration on the idea of truth and lies, the veracity of the information that an interview contains and the delight in the illogicality of an interview. Do you want to pick up that point about truth and lies?

GILDA WILLIAMS   I spent many years transcribing and editing interviews with artists, when I worked for *Flash Art* for five years and then at

27

Phaidon for over a decade. The original tape was always incredible. There is always this absent centre which is the transcribe, and the editor who creates the fiction, and I can tell you hilarious stories of things that go in and go on and go out of an interview. I'm going to tell you one – this is a true story – about a transcription I did myself.

When Raymond Pettibon was interviewed by Dennis Cooper, Cooper asked him an excellent question: 'Raymond, your work really changes at the end of the 1970s. It goes from being really magaziney, cartoonish to something much more serious, much more literary. Did something change?' And Raymond says – and I heard this myself, on the tape – 'Yes. I read the books of Anne Tyler and they completely changed my perspective on literature; they completely changed my work.' So I'm hearing this and I'm thinking – really? Anne Tyler changed Raymond Pettibon's life? I felt I needed to check this. 'You *do* mean Anne Tyler, author of *The Accidental Tourist* – even though she was mostly writing in the 1980s? Really?' and I email him but he never gets back to me. I finally have him on the phone one day, and I say, 'Raymond, you do mean the novelist Anne Tyler? Should we mention some early book of Tyler's that was especially important for you or something?' And he says, 'I don't know what you're talking about. I've never read Anne Tyler in my life. She is of no interest to me. Stop asking me about Anne Tyler. She means nothing to me.' So, of course, we just took this whole strange moment of the interview out, and it's gone, replaced in print with something like, 'OK, well, let's change the subject'. Next question! It was probably the most curious thing in the interview, but it disappeared from the text. It vanished – our little secret.

What I mean is that the fiction of the interview is something we all need to admit to. We know that it's a fiction, and that's what artists do – they invent things.

Buchloh did great interviews. I will champion him because he is worth it. Buchloh is so prepared. He can go head-to-head with Richter the way Julian describes well because he is as engaged and knowledge-able and interested in Richter's work as Richter is. So the text is not a failure. The only place for that kind of documented confrontation and debate is an interview. For me, it happens in the Warhol interview mentioned from 1985. Art-historically speaking, Warhol at that point was a dinosaur. He was dead in the water. He was supporting street art. He'd sold out. Everyone hated him. He was dying and Buchloh throws him a life preserver by saying, 'Andy, you're different. You're better than these guys. You're not like David Salle and Eric Fischl and all those guys. You're a conceptualist. You're making fun of these Rorschach tests and working with seriality and stuff.' Not hard to see that Buchloh is really saying, 'Andy, wake up! I'm helping you here!' But Warhol will not budge. He's like, 'No, I don't know what you're talking about. I love these guys – Jean-Michel Basquiat and Keith Haring – they're all great.' And Buchloh says, 'What about Lawrence Weiner?' 'Oh, he's great too. Is he doing the same thing? That's great.' I'm paraphrasing here, of course, but my point is he will not 'take his Warhol off' for even two minutes – even when he's drowning – and it's an amazing thing, a strange third text. It gives me the shivers. Only an interview can do that. You couldn't put that in any other kind of art writing – Warhol's rock-solid commitment to his particular sense of his purpose as an artist.

So interviews can be wonderful and unique things. And I have to say, in Obrist's defence, that having commissioned dozens of monographs at Phaidon, almost every artist, when I asked, 'Who would you like to interview you?', would answer, 'Hans-Ulrich Obrist'. Eventually I had to say, 'No more Obrist', because he can't do all the interviews in our books. He is extremely beloved as an interviewer, at least by that generation of artists, by and large, though I'm sure there are exceptions. Obrist only does interviews. Some critics who do interviews will not write. Obrist is one of them. Kasper König is one of them. The interview is the means chosen by these curators to 'write', to exist in print.

JULIAN STALLABRASS   He has students who write for him.

GILDA WILLIAMS   Perhaps, but he does the actual interviews. I think we can admit the fiction of the interview and allow for that as part of the instability of the interview itself. I worked with Jeff Wall, and yes he is cautious in interviews – very, very careful. He usually does interviews in writing and doesn't do face-to-face, so I have to agree with your point there. There's laziness among critics too. The interview is a shortcut whereby you let the artist do all the talking and have them do all the work by email – those interviews don't work. That method kills the interview and is usually not worth the paper it's printed on.

JULIAN STALLABRASS   I think that I would see that laziness, if that's what you want to call it, as a structural feature of the scene. I think that is the problem, and Buchloh is an extreme outlier in this. As you say, he is fantastically well-prepared and knowledgeable, and not only that, he has well-developed and thought-through opinions of his own which he is prepared to pitch against the ideas of even famous artists – but I think that's an extreme rarity. They are absolutely revealing and extraordinary pieces, and I think you're right that the interview is the only place where you would get that kind of confrontation. Most interviews are not like that, they're tied up with an industry of publicity and celebrity which I've tried to examine.

In a sense, this business about logic or the lack of logic and instability – ambiguity – is linked with that proliferation of discourse too. Someone once said to me, in some frustration about art-historical discourse but it could apply equally to art criticism and art discourse generally, 'Is no matter ever settled?' Of course it can't be, because the discourse must continue. In that sense, it is very much unlike science. It has to continue because we have to continue to fill art magazines. We have to continue to fill art catalogues. We have to continue to make these texts, which are counted by state bodies for assessment exercises to judge our research and so on. There's a definite link, I think, in academia and outside in the mass media, too, between an often lazy, postmodern attachment to instability, to deconstruction and so on, and this endless proliferation of publicising discourse.

Gilda was saying at one point that there were all these statements which were plainly sorts of masks and seemed to come out of the persona, but there seemed to be a point at which Peter Coffin stepped out from behind all those masks, and said something which seemed to come from the heart, or something of that sort.

GILDA WILLIAMS That's the illusion.

JULIAN STALLABRASS That's the illusion. I think that applies pretty much to any artist interview that you read.

GILDA WILLIAMS Sure.

SALLY O'REILLY You've both spoken about the interview from the position of the artist and interviewer – the producer of this material. What would you say about the responsibility of the reader towards this information, because there's a commonsensical idea that curiosity is good and healthy, and that a comprehensive understanding of lots of things is to be supported. But then there's the opposing view. Terms like 'spying' and 'eavesdropping' can be seen negatively as shallow, pond-skating ways of dealing with epistemological content. What are your hopes for readers of interviews in terms of what they do with the knowledge that can be gleaned from them?

GILDA WILLIAMS The kind of laziness we are talking about is really in the service of a particularly undiscriminating or uninformed reader. You know that the interview is the quickest, most readable way to know everything about an artist because you've got it straight from their mouth. But Buchloh's interviews – and let's keep that as our paradigm – you can't just absorb them passively. They are full texts. They are treated like finished texts and you have to read them like complete texts from the beginning to the end. So I think there is a sense of obligation from the reader – a more attentive reader would certainly be the beneficiary of a better-made interview, which is what I'm suggesting.

JULIAN STALLABRASS I think there are plainly many ways to read interviews, and I wouldn't want to prescribe one or the other, but it is important to bear in mind as you read them that they are the production of an industry, and to see them as a part of that would be one step towards having in mind a critique as you read. Another thing that Gilda said which struck me was that interviews seem to be the place where big ideas are raised.

GILDA WILLIAMS Potentially.

JULIAN STALLABRASS Potentially. I think it's often true that people punt these ideas – but isn't that a curiosity in itself that the big issues should be expressed in this most skimpy, skittish and insubstantial of forms? If you want to address those big issues, go and read something serious.

SALLY O'REILLY Do you want to call upon your seconds at this point?

GILDA WILLIAMS I'd like to call upon Lisa Le Feuvre, my colleague at Goldsmiths.

LISA LE FEUVRE I am here to second the 'for-the-interview' argument. I think that Julian's last comment, 'Go read something serious', is indicative of the position that Julian has taken in arguing against the interview. I think he is defining the interview as something shallow, intellectually insignificant and descriptive that doesn't really get anywhere at all. But to my mind, what you've described, Julian, is 'the bad artist interview' in the same way as we have the bad critical piece of writing or the bad piece of critical theory. Not all interviews are rigorous.

Gilda has argued for the status of the artist interview within an intellectual discourse around artistic practice. The artist interview is a moment for generative thinking. There are good artist interviews, there are bad artist interviews, but as a mode of writing it does do something that a monographic text does not. The artist interview gives an opportunity for the artist's voice. The artist may well be a liar, a scammer and a cheat, but it is still of interest to hear the artist putting that position forward.

Secondly, there is this sense of generative thinking. The interview, as Gilda has argued, is the product of three people: the artist, the person who the artist is in discourse with and the editor – and together those three people create something that is generative thinking. It also taps into Julian's comment about unequal power. You mentioned the Buchloh example of an interview where Buchloh was much more interesting than Richter. Great. That's not a problem. I think the artist interview is not just about the artist's voice, it's about the voice of the person interviewing the artist, too.

The third point that I want to raise in seconding the importance of the artist interview is that the interview always takes place at a particular time and place. So when you read an artist interview, you are performing some kind of time travel that has not been mediated by what Julian described as a retrogressive, fictionalisation of the past. So, to return to *Avalanche Magazine*, if you read those interviews you can find, for example, Bruce Nauman struggling with what it is to be an artist at a completely different point from where we recognise his artistic practice now. It is the moment of getting a sense of a particular time and place.

So I'd like to second Gilda in stating that the artist interview is a site for productive intellectual discourse. It is not a site where we are merely presented with something that passes as critical. It is a site where we can have something that really does contribute to discourse. We should accept that artist interviews that are poorly researched and badly written are just plain bad. We must not denigrate the interview as a genre – it is a way of thinking, listening and articulating sets of ideas.

JULIAN STALLABRASS   I'll call on my second, Marq Smith, who, among other things, is editor of *Journal of Visual Culture*.

MARQ SMITH   I can happily start by saying that in principle I'm a hundred per cent unconditionally supportive of Julian Stallabrass's position. It is my role as his second, after all.

I do, though, feel slightly ambivalent about this: there are lots of bad interviews out there – lots of bad interviewees, and bad interviewers. Lots of bad – which is to say unthought through, uninteresting and unproductive – interviews. That said, I've conducted lots of interviews with artists and academics, and it has always been a joyful and generative process – the interviews have always shown themselves to be smart, thoughtful and engaging. I've been lucky, I guess. I'm also of the opinion, having worked as an editor for over 20 years, that the editor really is (or at least needs to be) a most sophisticated 'curator'. As commissioning editor at MIT Press Roger Conover put it in a 2006 copy of *Art Journal*: 'I think of publishing as a fundamentally curatorial practice, that is to say, it is about the selection and placement of texts and ideas in relation to other texts and ideas. Someone once said that the best editors are the authors of their authors – framing, shaping, conceiving, commissioning, and creating lines and encounters between books rather than merely processing manuscripts. The curatorial, authorial role of the editor as a cultural producer is under-articulated in our society.'

The first thing to say about the interview is that it is an invention of 19th-century journalism and I think that if we've lost anything since its founding, it is the responsibility that goes along with the understanding of what it means to conduct interviews. This is, then, the fault of the interviewer, not necessarily that of the interviewee, and concerns how one prepares for and conducts an interview or facilitates a conversation. What is involved in doing a good job, a proper job, of this?

The second thing is to draw attention to the etymology of the word 'interview' which takes us back to the French *entre vue*, to 'see between'. I think this is key. I think this is integral to what both Julian and Gilda have been saying. It's the possibility of interviews generating something above and beyond what the two participants could possibly have imagined in advance, what Gilda called 'the third result', which I believe is absolutely vital.

So it's disappointing to admit that, having carried out extensive research in this area, I can say with conviction that 84% of interviews don't actually do this. My data confirms that 84% of interviews are actually rubbish and not interesting – and I think that there is correlation between interesting-ness and generative-ness.

I think there are issues, which are frustrating and need to be acknowledged, around laziness (a lack of preparation) and boredom (a lack of interest), masks and facades (obfuscation, playing the fool, wilful obscurantism etc), and lies and more lies and damn lies that make interviews way, way less interesting than they should be. I think that artists can be bad interviewees, and I think that this is not unconnected to the deskilling question that was raised by Gilda earlier.

Oh dear, I have ended up supporting both sides, which wasn't the plan at all, but I'm doing my best to play devil's advocate. On behalf of the interview, I'd want to add that interviews are wonderful for foregrounding the figure of the artist. If they're not just talking for the sake of talking, such discourse can be incredibly generative. As I noted before, something might emerge that is unanticipated, different and pleasantly surprising. Also, the medium of the interview itself might offer affable, personal insights into making, thinking, doing, process, and so forth, as well as the things that drive and motivate. In addition, as an encounter the interview presents what I'd call 'thoughts-in-formation', a snapshot of current thinking.

Finally, and connected to all of the above, the interview is 'live', or at least performs live-ness. For me, there is something extraordinary about the immediacy of conversation: a series of genuine acts in real time. The apparent naturalness and veracity of improvised exchange. The sound and materiality of the voice – its resonance, its cadence, the hurried or unhurried qualities, and its urgency. The pauses, the noises we make as we formulate our thoughts before we're ready to put things into words – over speaking. And yet, this live-ness is unreproduceable. Of course, I'm not trying to fool anyone: the raw material, the conversation – whether face-to-face, via the telephone, email, Skype or whatever – is subject to editorial mediation too. The material is transcribed and edited and re-edited, and sometimes 'live-ness' is 'injected' into it after the fact.

Let me just bring up an issue that wasn't raised earlier: where an interview is published, the publication itself. There is obviously a difference between working on an interview for *Time Out* or *Frieze* and an interview for an academic journal. I think that interviewers and interviewees prepare in very different ways. I think that the way that those interviews are received and read and engaged with are given very different kinds of credibility, and I think one just needs to draw attention to the limitations of certain kinds of publications.

There is a question of quality – the quality of discourse, of conversation, of debate in general – which rarely gets addressed and one has to acknowledge a certain dissolving or flattening-out of the question of quality, of there being just 'so many words' – I think this might have been the phrase you were looking for when you were talking about Obrist. Often, there are too many words, and if one is going to curate words, one needs to attend to their quality, one needs to be selective or economical about what it is that words do, what words mean and what they have the capacity to do. So, in supporting Julian, overall I guess I'm really saying this: fewer interviews, please.

SALLY O'REILLY   We can open it up now to the whole room if anyone would like to pitch in. I think I'll start on one question. Julian, I was intrigued by your brisk outro in which you reiterated the monolithic celebrity culture aspect that interviewing appears to perpetuate, and said that you'd like to see something in its stead that was more participatory. Is this the internet that you're pointing at here, or is there some other model?

JULIAN STALLABRASS   The internet is certainly a part of it. As I say, the interview seems to me to be fundamentally tied up with old media and there's often – not always – an unequal relationship between the two participants, although it's true that Gilda's point about the editor is absolutely right. Of course, the editor often has considerable power over the way the interview is sculpted and structured and made into an apparently coherent text.

One of my main suspicions about it, I suppose, is this privileging of the artist's discourse, not so much in the description of process because, surely, they do have something to say about that because they are the ones who are doing it, but, when it comes to reception, what a work of art does within the world. Then I think that anyone's opinion is as valid as anybody else's.

The dominance of the interview form is a problem especially because it's not just that interviews sit there, but that they are then taken up by the critical literature and used, very often, over and over again to make the points that the artist wants to make. So it's a way for the artist to dominate the discourse about what they're about, and that's a power relation that we should be clear about.

35

SALLY O'REILLY   Do you want to come in here Gilda and maybe talk about your point at the beginning about there being something beyond the text that's being discussed? It makes me think of stained glass windows where you can read the picture or where the coloured lights can have a sensory effect on you. Is there something in that dual nature of the text that could be used in refutation of that didacticism of the artist that Julian is talking about?

GILDA WILLIAMS   What we haven't touched upon is the potential of the interview for parody. There are a lot of interviews that are fakes. There is a great interview that Jimmie Durham wrote called *The Interview with a 10,000 Year Old Artist*. It is wonderful. It is a parody of himself as a Native American Indian and it is very funny about his assumed place within a marginal culture. He asks the 10,000-year-old artist: 'Well, what were things like 10,000 years ago?' And the artist replies, 'Well, it was really hard. There weren't that many artists and there weren't that many galleries ... Well, no galleries you would want to show in', and he just goes on like that. He uses the interview as a format, as a structure to get at another kind of critique. So I think there are ways in which that kind of manipulation actually can be taken advantage of in interesting ways.

By the way, I think there's something about that 84% statistic – I loved it – but you could do that with anything, 84% of all reviews go unread, 84% of all art is soon forgotten.

SALLY O'REILLY   Also, 84% of people love statistics.

GILDA WILLIAMS   Yes. There is a kind of defensiveness in the art world, and worry about taking a position. When I was editing at Phaidon, the part of the book that artists were most interested in was the interview. In fact, many of the artists weren't that interested in the rest of the book. And there was a lot of defensiveness: 'Oh, no, get rid of that because that makes me look a little bit funny.' There was a lot of this sort of censoring, improving and face-lifting that went on in the interview and I think that's where this self-adjusting takes place more than in many other kinds of text. So I would give Julian a bit of ammo here, because I think the interview is a place where artists can invent a position which may not really have been part of their practice until then, and may not really continue.

In response to the question from the audience about artists who refuse to give interviews, I have a literal example of that. I was working on a book about On Kawara and, as you may know, he does not do interviews – never has. He leaves no mark of his physical existence to the extent that he wouldn't even sign the contract for the book. It's wonderful to meet him, by the way, because he takes no phone calls, has no mobile. He's got none of those distractions. He just talks to you the whole day about life and consciousness.

Our monographs at Phaidon had a certain format, which always started with an interview. We had to get around that and decided to create this kind of 'tribute' in which people who know On or have worked with him – people who he nominated – would write short texts about whatever they wanted: an experience, a memory, a work of art. So there are ways around the standard interview, and I think this solution was part of On's conceptual practice in that case, and so it was very coherent. On loved it, and that's probably my favourite book in that whole series.

JULIAN STALLABRASS   Ideally one would hope that, for artists who refuse to talk about their work, it would liberate the discourse around it and you could get a greater proliferation and variety of interpretations. I'm not sure that that actually happens. It will be interesting to see whether that is the case. I do know of some cases of artists who famously don't talk where, certainly, academics are wary of venturing into that territory because they are not sure whether they can get any special access. They're a bit frightened by it I think, by that very freedom which speaks indeed to the ideology – the powerful, old and current ideology – of the author as originator.

The discussion took place 25 September 2010 in collaboration with *Art Monthly* to mark the reprint of *Talking Art Vol. 1.*

Sally O'Reilly is a writer. O'Reilly presented 'Banjos at Dawn' as part of the Writer in Residence programme at the Whitechapel Art Gallery, London.
Gilda Williams is a writer and a lecturer in the art department at Goldsmiths, London.
Julian Stallabrass is an art historian.
Lisa Le Feuvre is head of sculpture at The Henry Moore Institute, Leeds.
Marq Smith is editor-in-chief of *Journal of Visual Culture*. Smith is also research leader and head of doctoral studies at the Royal College of Art, London.

2007–2016

Hans Haacke

interviewed by Patricia Bickers

Plain Speaking

PATRICIA BICKERS *This has been a remarkable year: to mark your 70th birthday, there has been a two-part retrospective – the first you have had in Germany – in Berlin and Hamburg. Although there was a single catalogue, the shows were not identical.*

HANS HAACKE They complemented each other.

PB *And this year has also seen Documenta, the Münster Sculpture Project, and the Venice Biennale all fall in the same year. You have long been associated with all three but especially with Documenta, not only because you have participated in so many – the first time, arguably, in 1959 – but also because you studied in Kassel, though not art.*

HH I studied Art Education.

PB *In one of those serendipities that an editor dreams of, while research-ing in the Documenta archive for your catalogue, Walter Grasskamp came across some small, unsigned, black-and-white photographs that focused on the reactions of people in front of the art rather than on the art itself. In one photograph for instance with a work by Kandinsky in the back-ground, a boy is reading a comic with his back to the art, while in another a couple, heads down, are reading a hand-out. There were other photo-graphs of works being installed – the kind of behind-the-scenes museum business that the public never sees. It was only when he showed you an article he'd written about them that he discovered that you had taken them when you were a student in Kassel, working as an assistant for 'Documenta 2' in 1959. Grasskamp suggests that, in a way, these photo-graphs prefigure your future work. Would you agree with that?*

HH There may be something to that. Like the other visitors, I saw most of the works at Documenta for the first time in my life.

But I also had an opportunity to look behind the scenes and learn to understand what kind of an operation such an exhibition is. All sorts of interests are at play. It requires cleaners as much as collectors, art lovers and money or, in the case of Documenta, extensive public funding. In short, it is not just about beauty on the wall. There is more to it.

PB *At what point did this awareness of the system that underpins the aesthetic experience start to play into how you thought about making work yourself?*

HH I think that began at the end of the 1960s, when my generation became politicised by the Vietnam War and by pervasive racial conflicts and poverty in the US. We became aware that exhibiting in a commercial gallery – in a museum, or wherever it may be – is to be part of a larger social engagement. Such seemingly rarefied contexts can affect what you present there and may have consequences elsewhere. There is no object, no painting, no photograph, nothing that is immune to the socio-political implications of the environment in which it is viewed.

PB *Later this awareness of context was subsumed into 'institutional critique' but even before the term was coined you went beyond it in the sense that you not only showed a way out of the museum but also legitimate ways back into the museum. It was never simply about critiquing the institution from the outside because you were also part of it.*

HH Yes, I *was* and remain part of it.

PB *As Rosalyn Deutsche put it in her catalogue essay, you have developed your own democratic model of an audience's relationship to art and to the institution. Famously, in the 1970 'Information' show poll, you asked visitors to fill in a questionnaire. This is now common practice, particularly in marketing, but when you initiated this audience profile – which was completely voluntary – it was the first time anyone had actually asked themselves who their visitors were, let alone why they visited the museum. Was there any resistance to this idea when you proposed it?*

HH When I was invited to participate in the 'Information' show, I told the curator that the question that I was going to pose in my *MOMA-Poll* would be about a current issue, without spelling out what exactly that issue would be. I arrived with my question the night before the opening, fearing – and for good reason – that had it been seen earlier something might have happened to prevent it from being installed; it asked:

'Question: Would the fact that Governor Rockefeller has not denounced President Nixon's Indochina policy be a reason for you not to vote for him in November? Answer: If "yes" please cast your ballot into the left box; if "no" into the right box.'

In order to fully understand the implications of this question one needs to know that David Rockefeller, the brother of Nelson Rockefeller – then the Governor of New York State – was the chairman of the board of trustees of the Museum of Modern Art. Nelson was also a member of the board, as was their sister-in-law Mrs John D Rockefeller 3rd. The museum's treasurer was an executive vice president of the Chase Manhattan Bank, of which David Rockefeller was the chairman. As I heard later, John Hightower, the director of the Museum resisted a demand from his boss to censor my poll. In his autobiography David Rockefeller says that, this 'failure', together with other examples of Hightower's admitting of critical voices inside the museum, led to Hightower being fired shortly afterward.

PB *Soon after that incident came the infamous cancellation of your solo show at the Guggenheim – an extraordinary opportunity for an artist still only in his 30s at that particular institution. You must be tired of talking about it, but it is such a key episode that I would like to go over it again because the work that was rejected relates to the* MoMA-Poll. The Shapolsky Project, *or to give it its full title,* Shapolsky et al. Manhattan Real Estate Holdings, a Real-Time Social System, *as of May 1, 1971, charted the connections and property holdings of a slum landlord in New York, installed in a quasi-conceptual manner. Among the people who are excluded from museums – and from so much else besides – are the poor, the very people who are forced to live in such slums. Thomas Messer, the director of the Guggenheim, made the following statement: 'To the degree to which an artist deliberately pursues aims that lie beyond art, his very concentration upon ulterior ends stands in conflict with the intrinsic nature of the work as an end in itself.'*

HH If you were to accept what Messer postulates, we would have to wipe out much of art history. With the exception of that extremely brief period of Formalism, and arguably not even then, artists always referred in and through their works to the world outside the studio. Religiously motivated or not, they promoted certain understandings of the world as they saw or were made to represent it.

PB *In solidarity with you, many other artists came out in support.*

43

The list is very impressive including, in alphabetical order, Carl Andre,
John Baldessari, Robert Barry, Mel Bochner, Daniel Buren, Dan Graham,
Douglas Huebler, Neil Jenny, Sol LeWitt, Brice Marden and so on. It's a
long, long list. I wonder if this would happen today when the market reigns
supreme and artists tend rather to be set against each other.

HH As I mentioned earlier, my generation of artists came to 'maturity' at a time when in the US, and also in Europe – in Paris as we know, in Germany, and also in the UK – young people in general and also young artists, became much more socially engaged than they had been before. They actively participated in what was happening politically around them. As you know, this is also what triggered the Art Workers Coalition in New York, which challenged museum trustees' connections to the political establishment. The de facto exclusion of non-white artists became an issue, as was the very low representation of women artists in the museums' programmes and collections, as well as broader artists' rights. It may have helped that there wasn't the kind of art market we know today. Taking a political position didn't risk ruining a young artist's 'career' – a term unknown at the time.

PB *Speaking of the 1960s and 1970s Seth Siegelaub has said 'There was no possibility of artists selling out. No one wanted to buy'.*

When you represented Germany at the Venice Biennale in 1993, your installation, Germania, *included a scaled-up one Deutschmark coin above the entrance of the German pavilion where formerly there had been the Nazi emblem, removed in 1945. At the time the gesture was understood as representing the triumph of capitalism since, following unification, the former East German economy became tied to that of a booming West Germany. Since then it has come to seem prescient because from now on it will again be officially permissible for works from the Biennale to be sold openly, though most of us think of it as an art market anyway.*

HH The Venice Biennale was, in fact, founded late in the 19th century, specifically as an art fair.

PB *It is interesting that selling was suspended in 1968 – that pivotal year in a highly politicised decade. Have you ever allowed your work to be represented at an art fair?*

HH No. I saw the Cologne Art Fair in the late 1960s. It was the first of the fairs as we know them today. The founders were two art dealers from Cologne. I got to see the fair because I was visiting my parents who lived close by. I was so disgusted by this experience that, even though I could have stayed a little longer, I took the next plane back to New York. Since then, I have told every gallery that has represented me, that they should not present my works in an art fair. In such a setting, everything is viewed exclusively in terms of monetary value.

PB *Teaching was obviously a crucial part of your career as an artist. What has teaching meant to you?*

HH It was my economic base. It may have been as early as Documenta, where I had the chance to look behind the scenes, that I said to myself: 'I do not want to be dependent on the sale of my work.' I had studied art education. Teaching and dealing with young people was attractive to me. For a few years I taught in various types of schools before I landed a job at the college level. You do not have to go to work every day. That leaves you some time to do your own work, and you get long vacations. Teaching paid the rent, as one says, and it gave me a degree of independence. But – back to the other part of the question you pose – as I said, I really did enjoy dealing with young people. I learned a lot from them. It allowed me to be in touch with other generations and to get a sense of where their heads were at, what they have to contend with. It also challenged me not to engage in art-speak or using academic jargon. I had to speak plainly, a very good discipline to be subjected to.

PB *I did notice that, at the time you were selected to represent Germany in the Venice Biennale, only two works of yours were owned by German museums.*

HH A significant one has since been added.

PB *The Akademie der Künste in Berlin, the venue for the first retrospective, is located right next to the Brandenburg Gate, in what was formerly East Berlin, while the Deichtorhallen in Hamburg was a market hall in the middle of what has always been a very powerful commercial centre in western Germany. Both of these sites are very evocative, especially in Berlin.*

HH As you say, the location in Berlin on Pariser Platz, across the square from the Brandenburg Gate, is politically highly charged. This geography is soaked with history. Less than a five minutes' walk away, you have the Reichstag, where the German Parliament meets and where it did meet until Hitler shut it down after the Reichstag fire in 1933. You can see its dome from the upper floors of the Akademie. Across the square is the French Embassy. The British Embassy is around the corner, and the new American Embassy is going up practically next door. Only a bank separates the Akademie from the American embassy. Immediately adjacent on the other side is the rebuilt Adlon Hotel, where Hitler used to hang out. And, leaving through the back door, one faces the Holocaust Memorial.

I had the option of exhibiting in the second location of the Akademie amidst the greenery of the Englischer Garten. But I said, 'No, I don't want to be in the park – if I am going to exhibit in Berlin at the Akademie, it should be in the centre of the city, where Max Liebermann was its president until he was ousted by the Nazis.' Unfortunately, the rebuilt building is a bit of an architectural disaster. The entire facade of the new building facing Pariser Platz is glass, set in a regular grid of thin frames. One of the things I find very upsetting – particularly in Germany with its racist history – is that people who do not look like natives have to watch out. Ethnic discrimination, of course, also exists in many other regions of the world. Since the reunification of Germany in 1990, 48 people have been killed, simply because they didn't look German. Using the grid of the façade as a ledger, I posted brief data on the murdered: where he or she was born, how they were killed – stabbed, clubbed, run-over – the location, and the date. In recent years, Pariser Platz has become sort of a theme park with organ grinders, 'living statues', men dressed as Russian soldiers and other 'exotic' figures, surrounded by busloads of tourists – into this charged environment I introduced this jarring account, an ugly reality of the present.

PB *There used to be makeshift memorials to people who'd been shot in the killing zone along the old wall separating East and West which were removed when the wall came down.*

HH Let me speak about another work that was fitted into the building's interior architecture and, in an oblique way, related to the installation on the façade – and which also has something to do with London. I covered the wall that separates the large entrance hall from the interior exhibition spaces entirely with a blown up photo of an arrangement in a showcase I had assembled in my 'Mixed Messages' show at the Serpentine Gallery in 2001, an exhibition of items selected from the collection of the Victoria & Albert Museum. It was the image of an 'exchange doll' from the Bethnal Green Museum of Childhood in London, which is part of the V&A. The doll dates from the early 20th century, and there is a black boy's head and the head of a blond, white girl, as well as interchangeable black-and-white limbs. I would love to know the historical background to this unusual doll – 'exchange doll' is the title given to it by the museum in Bethnal Green – and whether it might have been an early attempt to overcome racist attitudes. The visitors in Berlin passed through an image of this 'exchange doll' into the exhibition.

PB *Speaking of memorials, you have also recently completed one to Rosa Luxemburg. Made from inlaid brass letters set into into the ground of Rosa Luxemburg Platz in Berlin, the work flows over the pavement and onto the road. The texts you quote are taken from a variety of sources including her diaries, love letters, polemics and political speeches. By giving us this multi dimensional view – albeit in a two-dimensional form – of Rosa Luxemburg, who has been heavily co-opted by factions within the left and elsewhere, you allow her to speak for herself in all her complexity. What was the experience of being commissioned like for you?*

HH I was surprised to be invited to this competition for the design of a permanent, public installation to commemorate Rosa Luxemburg. It was a lengthy process. In the end, my proposal was chosen. Then there were the usual problems: would the money be sufficient, would I get all the necessary permits, and a lot of other bureaucratic stuff that always accompanies politics. As I had expected, none of the Rosa Luxemburg factions – and there were many – were totally happy. Mine was not the picture postcard version of Rosa – it included contradictions and a number of her misjudgements. As we all do she made predictions which didn't pan out. But there are also pronouncements that are still topical today, for instance, her assessment of the repercussions of the American War in the Philippines. I selected a few of these statements that are pertinent to the war in Iraq, without changing a word. Neither have her critical comments on ideological orthodoxies and the suppression of dissent lost any of their validity. I also chose entries from her diary and personal exchanges that give us a sense of her as a warm and loving woman.

PB *Do you sometimes feel weary of being, in a sense, the art world's conscience? I understand that on 9/11, when the World Trade Centre was destroyed, the phone rang continuously with the media asking you to respond in some way.*

HH I certainly don't want to be viewed as the art world's conscience, as you say.

PB *You have tackled some very powerful characters in your work. I compiled a list and it is pretty much a rogue's gallery ranging from Ronald Reagan and Margaret Thatcher to Peter Ludwig, in* The Chocolate Master, *and Josef Abs in* Josef Abs at the Wallraf-Richartz-Museum, *which is concerned with the dubious provenance of Manet's painting of a bunch of asparagus, now in the museum's collection. Abs was a trustee of the museum, and instrumental in the work's purchase. In this work, which was also rejected, you simply put a version of the picture on a stand with, alongside it, the history of the work's ownership.*

HH That was in 1974, the 150th anniversary of the Wallraf-Richartz-Museum, a major municipal institution. In the brochure celebrating the anniversary, the Manet painting was highlighted as a significant, recent acquisition, with a photograph of Herman Josef Abs presenting it on a studio easel, in memory of chancellor Konrad Adenauer (the dedication is still on the frame today). Several layers of German politics are imbedded in this still life. I had been invited to *'PROJEKT '74'*, the exhibition of works by contemporary artists that was mounted on the occasion of the anniversary. The museum censored my work – which comprised a provenance of the painting with extensive biographic information on the owners and its transfers – apparently because it thought it could not afford to offend Abs, one of their benefactors. During the Nazi period, Abs was an upper level executive of the Reichsbank and a member of 44 boards of directors. In 1974, the year of the museum's anniversary, Abs was not only the head of the museum's board of trustees, he was also chairman of Deutsche Bank, the biggest and most powerful German bank then, and perhaps still today. The museum's director made a remarkable statement in a letter to me: 'A museum knows nothing about economic power; it does indeed, however, know something about spiritual power.'

PB *This latest rejection prompted another instance of artistic solidarity, did it not?*

HH Daniel Buren and a number of other artists who were also in *'PROJEKT '74'* either withdrew their works and/or participated in a public protest. Daniel asked me for a facsimile of my ten panels, which he pasted on his striped papers on the wall – and so, in a way, the work was smuggled into the exhibition. The chief director of museums of the city of Cologne then had the facsimiles ripped off. Depending on how one defines a work of art, he damaged and, in effect, censored one or two works of art: Daniel's and mine.

PB *Just what you want as a museum director – a vandal.*

HH Daniel had also pasted on his stripes a provocative statement with the title 'Art Remains Politics'. With this he pointedly commented on the slogan 'Art Remains Art', a quote from Goethe with which the exhibition was advertised.

PB *Inevitably this act of vandalism, or censorship – or both – received so much publicity that he might have done better to have quietly allowed the work to be shown.*

HH It's hard to tell whether the museum benefited, at least at the level where it believes that it counts, namely, by attracting donors, and bringing in money. Whether it lost or whether it gained, I'm not in a position to evaluate. More than 25 years after this incident, another director of the museum, Kasper König, acquired the *Manet-PROJEKT '74* for the museum's collection.

PB *Publicity is a difficult animal to manage, if you seek to control it you will almost certainly fail.*

HH It's difficult to manage – very tricky, and it can backfire badly. Whatever you do, irrespective of how the press may react, your actions should be able to stand on their own – not as a means to get PR.

PB *The piece you made for the courtyard of the Reichstag is in part a deliberate riposte to the words 'DEM DEUTSCHEN VOLKE' – 'To the German People' – which are carved on the portico of the façade of the Reichstag. Instead your work spells out in white neon the words 'DER BEVÖLKERUNG', which translates as 'To The Population', deliberately avoiding the word 'German'. The words sit in a bed of soil comprising samples taken from all over Germany containing wildflower seeds from the locations where the soil was collected. The work thus brings a wild, unpredictable element into the pristine precincts of the new, or renewed building. Given your history, were you surprised that you, of all people, were asked to contribute a work for the Reichstag?*

HH Yes, I was surprised, particularly after *Germania*, my installation in the German pavilion of the Venice Biennale in 1993. As you may have noticed, I am often surprised. But, even though the Bundestag's arts committee had overwhelmingly accepted my proposal, it became quite controversial when the only dissenting member of the committee started a nationwide campaign against it. To non-Germans the dedication DEM DEUTSCHEN VOLKE sounds innocuous. However, when you consider that, during the Nazi period, the word 'Volk' had taken on an exclusive and racist meaning, I thought it was necessary to put that in perspective by an additional dedication to the BEVÖLKERUNG, to the residents of the country, irrespective of their national origin. The laws passed by the Bundestag, of course, also affect their lives. Presently close to 10% of the residents of the

49

country do not have German citizenship. Based on a provision in the Bundestag's by-laws, a full house debate and a vote by the entire parliament is required to adopt or reject the art committee's decision. In 2000, the project was finally approved in the Bundestag by a majority of two votes.

The ultranationalist tenor of much of the opposition's speeches surprised me. In fact, it was quite shocking. It did, however, have an unintended salutary effect: many MPs who had originally planned to abstain because, as they said, one does not vote on art, eventually felt that, under these circumstances, they could not permit the defeat of this proposal. They therefore voted for it. I think it is noteworthy that the two votes that helped to pass it were cast by two members of the conservative CDU/CSU party, who did not join their fellow party members who all voted against it; both dissenters were women and both were members of the arts committee. One of them, Renate Süssmuth, had been the president of the Bundestag in 1995 when it made it possible for Christo to wrap the Reichstag (at the time the German parliament was still meeting in Bonn). Helmut Kohl, the leader and chancellor of her party, had been against it. Since my project's inauguration things have calmed down. Even a number of MPs of the CDU/CSU have brought soil from their constituencies as their tribute to DER BEVÖLKERUNG. Since 2000, close to 300 MPs have participated. As I stipulated, there is to be no gardening to tame the wild growth of a great variety of plants that has developed over the years.

PB *I can't help wishing that the arts in this country mattered enough to warrant being debated in Parliament.*

HH I could never have imagined that the media would pay attention to the issues raised by this project for almost half a year, debating on whether something of this nature should be allowed in the Reichstag building and on how it reflects on the nation's sense of itself. For the inauguration, Wolfgang Thierse (SPD), the successor of Rita Süssmuth as president of the Bundestag, had collected soil from the Jewish cemetery in his Berlin district. An MP from Solingen contributed soil from the site where five Turks had lost their lives in a racist arson attack. And a newly elected member of the conservative Bavarian branch of the CDU/CSU brought an apple tree from his district and planted it next to the dedication DER BEVÖLKERUNG. I don't know whether he did so thinking of what Martin Luther is reported to have said: 'Even if I knew the world was to come to an end tomorrow, I would still plant an apple tree.'

This is an edited version of an interview which took place at the Starr Auditorium, Tate Modern on 23 June 2007

Martha Rosler

interviewed by Iwona Blazwick

Taking Responsibility

IWONA BLAZWICK *I first came across your work in the 1980s as part of the exhibition 'Issue' at the ICA when I was a young curator. Yours was a very remarkable series of works in a very remarkable show. I've been looking through this work again in the past few days and it looks as fresh and relevant today as it did 27 years ago. What this opens up for me is a particular theme, one of four themes that I would like to talk to you about now. They are 'Modes of Address' – in which I think you have created a paradigm shift in the kind of methodologies you use, 'Space', including public, domestic and institutional space, 'Gender' and 'Labour'. Last year your work was in an exhibition at the Hugh Lane Gallery in Dublin called 'The Studio'. When one thinks of the studio one immediately thinks of the Pollock-esque splattered, hermetic space of the protean painter. By contrast your studio is very ordered and very cerebral, I would say. What do you think your presentation says about your methodology?*

MARTHA ROSLER That presentation was a highly idealised picture of my space, which of course is messy and horrendous. But the basic honest and true element is that it is an office. One of the shockers for me as an artist is, as I used to say, no one ever told me in art school that I would be a secretary to a mythical artist called Martha Rosler. Further, nobody ever told me – because they could never have imagined it – that I would be the digital assistant to an artist who literally no longer exists.

I was interviewing in the spring for an assistant and the person said 'So, would you say that 90% of your work is done at the computer?' and I became quite indignant until I realised that was probably an underestimate. So the fact that my studio, with its rows of slides and tapes and so on, is nevertheless centred on a computer, and of course the indispensable radio, is what the Hugh Lane conveyed. Unfortunately this is a dangerous thing to say, especially in the States when the art market dictates that everyone be a painter and a dumb one at that.

IB *The work that I saw in 'Issue' at the ICA in 1980 was a series from 1974 called 'Tijuana Maid' and it took the form of postcards, so that was an early form of address for you. What made you decide to use that mode?*

MR My practice is to a large degree rational and text-based; even if the outcome is an image, there is still a basic framework of textuality. I was sitting in some graduate class in the early 1970s and thinking about ways to address the public – because the topic of the moment was of course artists attempting to seize control from the gatekeepers of institutions, magazines and so on. Trying to get rid of the middle person and address the public directly. And my friend Eleanor Antin had done her '100 Boots' postcard series, and we were living at that time as exiles from New York in a very small town called Solana Beach, California, and I was thinking about postcards as a mode of address. I realised that I would like to do a serial postcard 'novel' that had no images at all. So this idea really bypassed not just the actual modes of distribution of art to the public but also the expected, which would be that art be based on images, be they incidental or descriptive. I wanted to produce a series of false autobiographical works, or at least start with one about my subject of the day, which was women and food. First I sent out a text card on another subject, which was complete on one card. Then I cobbled together a mailing list from nowheresville and sent the food novels.

IB *Who did you send them to?*

MR Partly I used Ellie's [Eleanor Antin's] list, partly I sent them to a bunch of alternative galleries, younger curators all over the country and to friends. Then the first card novel, *A Budding Gourmet*, was picked up by the *Village Voice*, and it turned out that there was a recipe network – which by the way is alive and well online – and people then wrote to me. So people collecting recipes, who had no interest or involvement in art, also came to be on my mailing list.

IB *It strikes me as a kind of viral strategy. It comes unannounced through your letter box.*

MR Spam.

IB *Yes, spam. Do you think that the internet is an analogy for that today?*

MR I do, yes. You may be surprised to know that some people were offended by the appearance of a postcard in their mailbox unbidden and saw it as an intrusion, and I said, 'Well, why is that more offensive than, say, a flyer trying to sell you furniture?' And of course they had no answer, but I guess it was because it was too close to something they might have been interested in.

IB *It could be because postcards are always celebratory, they are news from a holiday, or news from somewhere pleasant …*

MR … with a picture.

IB *One of the most important and influential aspects of your work is your lens-based work, your use of photography and video. Some of your best-known works – also shown at the Whitechapel in 'Inside the Visible' – are your rephotographed collages where you juxtaposed images of Vietnam with domestic interiors. Can you say something about how you got to that methodology and why?*

MR The methodology of montaging?

IB *Yes, it's so different in a way from Dada collage, for example.*

MR Yet, it's a direct outgrowth of Dada – actually Surrealism; Max Ernst was my first model on this and a Californian artist named Jess who worked with what subsequently we would call clip art and made them into elaborate tableaux. What interested me about those practices, as opposed to the Dada photomontage of which we saw very very little in the US in the mid 1960s, was the rational space – they weren't flying off at all angles. I was very taken by the idea of giving a viewer a place to stand, and therefore the photographic became the obvious choice because photography tends to suggest the possibility of a real space, if you don't just cut it up and ignore the idea of perspectival relationships. I was very much interested in the picture of the world that our culture propagated, one that suggests that there were numerous 'worlds', none of which quite intersected with one another or, if so, in some arcane way. I wanted to suggest the unity of the world and therefore our – at least putative – responsibility for what went on within it, and that in particular related to the space of representation in which women were inserted, and which we disclaimed as being actually about us. Also of course it was to do with the notion of a war elsewhere, on others' territory, which we could say was happening 'over there', 'outside somewhere' although we could hardly disclaim responsibility. So that was my aim.

IB *To a certain extent both the sources you use could be regarded as*

*not quite readymades but found images, so was there something about
authorship in there as well? You took what was already out there in the
world.*

MR Even the postcards, you had to work hard to find my name anywhere – there was just a tiny little rubber stamp with my name and
address on the back of the card. Authorship was also in question in
the 1960s, and how we arrived at it. I think Pop Art very much revo-
lutionised the notion of who created what and what the nature of
a work of art might be in a culture so dominated by corporate culture
and a culture industry.

IB *Again there is a difference I think, quite a radical shift from Pop Art.
One thinks of Richard Hamilton, in the UK, or Claes Oldenburg: their
relationship to the everyday and popular culture is essentially – dare
I say it – apolitical, except in its refusal of the idea of great master art and
the masterpiece, and in its juxtaposition with Abstract Expressionism.
In your work you intercepted something unpalatable and shocking, a
woman whose arms have been blown off in a deluxe sitting room – that
jarring effect takes it away from these ravishing, beautiful but kind of
hilarious interiors.*

MR Well, first I never accepted that Pop was apolitical. In fact I still
have some long screed that I penned in the late 1960s or early 1970s
about the absurdity of trying to read Pop as though it had no deep
political meaning just because the people who made it said so. Clearly
Pop was about the nature of the world, and the social world that's its
subject, and therefore it could hardly refrain from being 'political'.

I would also like to offer something of a gentle corrective about
what you said, because frequently people in thinking about these
images of the Vietnam War retrospectively give them an expressionist
content that they simply don't have. The image that you appear to
be describing was of a young girl, a 12-year-old girl, who is missing
a leg and part of her arm, and you can see them bandaged in the
foreground of a black-and-white photograph of quite a nice lounge.
But everything in these images is quite still. In fact I was an anti-
expressionist but it is inevitable that when we see these confrontations, especially for the first time, that the horror comes first, and
that is a legitimate emotion. But I don't think that horror is my genre.
I really prefer to stay quite cool, even to the point of stasis, rather than
showing a lot of blood or providing some kind of moment of shock.

IB *When did you first pick up a video camera?*

MR I didn't actually. My video work had an entirely different origin. I was a graduate student at the University of California, San Diego, and David Antin, who was my professor, made friends with Charlie Cox, who ran a medical school facility where they were doing something a little bit new, which was videotaping autopsies and operations. It was in the basement of the medical school. He suggested to me and three guys that we should learn to do video, which actually was already an art world practice because this was 1973. We all went, and I learned how to use a studio camera and a switcher, and to study the electronics of wave forms, and to read the wave form monitors and so on. A few years later David Ross, who was the director of the Long Beach Museum, said, 'I want to give you a show but you have to make new tapes, so here's a camera.' He gave me a Hitachi 3030 which is a big, clunky, not very good – but at the time a state-of-the-art – portable colour camera, and I made four tapes in two weekends and that was my first use of portable equipment. A couple of years earlier I borrowed a portable black-and-white tape deck from an artist equipment collective in New York, Film/Video Arts, and I made *Semiotics of the Kitchen*.

IB *What year did you make* God Bless America?

MR 2006. It was part of a show in which I had a 3.5 metre high blue prosthetic leg that slowly kicked and a number of invisible sound fields that you walked through. As you probably know, the traumatic amputation of limbs, particularly legs, is one of the signature wounds of the war in Iraq because of the improvised explosive devices that the opposition uses. There is another work about war that I called *Fascination with the Game of the (Exploding) (Historical) Hollow Leg* in which I use legs as a metaphor for phallocentric emptiness and of course missile power. In *God Bless America* you have a child's toy in a home environment which opens to something larger, and it is derisory.

IB *In terms of the presentation of video where did you want it to appear? In a gallery? On a monitor? Or did you have ambitions to get it on to television? What was its route to the public?*

MR In the beginning there were only monitors. Then there was some artists' cable – very little but some. Even in the mid 1970s my work was on some artists' cable networks. PBS showed some people's work, but I knew it would not show mine, particularly with its use of appropriated imagery. It was sort of in the Allan Kaprow model of small audiences – one after one after one, rather than mass audiences. The thing about video was that it was cheap and cheap-looking. It had no 'standards', you didn't have to make things that looked like high production value film; and it was easily transmissible in various ways to various audiences, most of whom who were quite eager to see it. Though most of the audiences were of artists and art publics, that was by no means all: there were frequently other groups that were interested in seeing things, especially once there were small players available, then it could be seen anywhere.

IB *What did you feel about the restaging of* Semiotics of the Kitchen *at the Whitechapel Art Gallery?*

MR Well, you invited me to do it as part of 'Performance 2' and I said that it was never meant to be a live performance but that I would be happy to do it as an audition. So we put out a call for young women. Twenty-six young women saw the tape and we rehearsed a bit. I told them what I would like them to do, which was to be expressive, with-out harming themselves or others, with kitchen implements. We staged it in groups as a round. The first group began and then another and another and then we got together at the end and enacted the semaphoric ones. It really was a terrific experience. I very much enjoyed working with that diverse group of women on what became a theatrical performance.

IB *Are you making a tape?*

MR Yes, we are working on it.

IB *All of the works that we have spoken about draw on the world of mass media, popular culture, magazines and television. Was that initially inspired by the cookery shows?*

MR Absolutely. There were no projections in the mid 1970s, so everything would be on the same kind of box – the telly – that you would watch at home. So all the gestures are throwing things outside of the box, and everything is in fact quite small. It's meant to be quite small as was *God Bless America*, which is meant to be seen even smaller. It was indeed inspired by the late Julia Child who was our great inspiration.

IB *Another form of address has been your work as a writer and teacher, but there are a number of publications that you have been involved in both as a writer and as an editor – curating in a sense. Has that gone all the way through your practice?*

MR I wrote stories as a schoolgirl. I considered myself an artist but

I was actually an English major in college, although I also studied painting, especially at the Brooklyn Museum School. It wasn't at all clear to me, when I finally settled down, what it was that I was going to do.

Writing is a tremendous chore. It often feels like a big distraction. I often think if only no one asked me, I wouldn't do it. But that of course is a self-serving lie, because I even respond to blog posts. Why am I doing this? That shows that I really am demented! Because that is really a mistake. I don't mean posts about me, I mean on political subjects.

IB *A book that we were looking at earlier published by the Dia Foundation called* If you lived here *focuses on urban space, on the city. When did you move from California back to the East Coast?*

MR 1980.

IB *What* If you lived here *brings together is a number of different voices talking about the city. I wanted to use that to talk about your Bowery piece. Can we just talk a little bit about that, the move and the inspiration behind the* Bowery Project?

MR I'm from quite a large island off the coast of the US and from the westernmost tip of it, which is Brooklyn, New York – the island being Long Island in case you were wondering. I then moved to southern California and I became immersed in the local American culture. I made quite a number of works, one of which was a garage sale. What I discovered was that much as I liked living in this strange, countrified environment, I dreamt of sidewalks, which was quite chilling for somebody who had long imagined that they were a country girl at heart but trapped in the city. In 1974–75 I graduated and moved back to New York for a year. That's where I made *Semiotics of the Kitchen*. I walked down the Bowery every day, and I just had this idea that I would like to make a work that is about documentary, about the city and particularly the Bowery, which is an archetypical skid row. And about how these representations are inevitably stereotypical. They are always of the 'bums', not of the streets.

I was keen, unlike all the other work that I had been doing, that it be a museum work or a gallery work. I meant it to hang on a wall with other works of documentary, to ask questions about the tradition of documentary. I arrived at its title a bit late. It's called *The Bowery in two inadequate descriptive systems* – the reason being that there are more images of words than there are of the spaces, and there are no images of people. I didn't want the viewers to think that I was saying 'no, pictures are not privileged above words, words are privileged above images', but let's remember that when we are talking about representation, they will always betray their subject, and that includes any form of representation. This is a commonplace now, but it wasn't such a commonplace then. And as so often with artists I had to work my way there.

The images are of the Bowery; it is a walk down the Bowery. The words I put together by asking people 'what are the words that you use for "drunk"?'. I also consulted a slang dictionary because I particularly wanted historical and even outmoded Elizabethan words for drunkard so that the words switched from a series of metaphorical, adjectival terms to outdated and contemporary noun forms.

IB *Looking back at it now, there is an unexpected sense of it as an archive of something that has disappeared, which is the Bowery itself as this kind of space. This is in a way a kind of a memorial from 30 years later to a streetscape that doesn't exist any more. In Manhattan, as here in London, the massive force of money and gentrification has even eroded what were once no-go streets which have become a shiny developer's dream. There is a sense of something that has gone but not been replaced by something better.*

MR I will have to be, once again, slightly rude. First of all as I was walking here, along the bank of the Thames, I was acutely conscious of the fact that, both late last night and today, one could hardly be unaware of being in a kind of Disneyland of history. That one could walk through Southwark, through the alleys and byways late at night, without there being anything to be scared of. The Bowery is similarly being gentrified.

When I teach photography I begin by showing a documentary image to my students and saying, 'What was the photographer thinking about?' Invariably they say 'about history' and I say, 'that's probably the last thing on the mind of the photographer'. Photographers don't work like that. Photographers by and large take photographs for immediate purposes, not to create an archive of what may not be the same in 30 years.

So I would say that you are fulfilling your role as a museum person. But I really must say that I had absolutely no interest in creating an archive. I was very interested in the systematicity of recording. I would say that my influence was, even at some remove, Pop. It was

Ed Ruscha. The idea that if you want to take a picture of a street you have to picture every element on the street of every shop window and that it could not be a random selection.

Obviously when you see the work itself, it is not every shop window, but the rolls of film show just about every shop window. What I was thinking about was documentary as a social practice and as a museological object.

IB *Were you thinking about the great historical photographers, Walker Evans, for example?*

MR How could I have failed to think about Walker Evans? New York was a very vibrant documentary photography city and the abstract painters fulfilled their desire for pictorial narrativity by taking pictures in their off hours. We very much appreciated documentary. I wouldn't have said Walker Evans at the time, but looking at it now it clearly is in the Walker Evans tradition. But I would also say Ben Shahn and Robert Frank and other photographers, so it was a particular tradition more than a particular author.

IB *In Documenta this summer we saw something quite different, we saw parks and gardens in Kassel itself, often punctured by molehills. Can you say something about that?*

MR It was called *Kassel Gardens (from the Perspective of a Mole)*; there was a tiny joke in this because 'Something Gardens' is a typical name for a neighbourhood in Los Angeles that is in distress, the opposite of a castle garden. It was mole season when I was in Kassel taking the pictures, and I was struck by the fact that molehills are tolerated all over the beautiful well-kept public gardens. I did a little research and found that moles are protected. What protected means is that you have to get permission to kill them. Which means, finally, that you can kill them. One of the themes at Documenta was 'bare life', and the whole question of 'bare life' relates exactly to the classes of people who are stateless but are protected by the king, which means in effect that they can be killed. Their protected status actually leads to their end, which is very interesting – I know that I am vulgarising the concept a bit.

I was asked to show flower photos at Documenta along with *The Bowery* and I thought about what this would mean to the viewers. It is a body of work: I am an avid gardener and I take photographs of flowers. I think the curator wanted to show my range from the deplorably political, which of course she liked, to other images of communal life.

But I was not going to be the mature artist who shows *The Bowery* from 1974 and flower photos from 2005, because I thought the viewers will think I am dotty, especially people who have seen me embroidering flower tapestries on stage. Something's wrong. So I thought I have got to do more than this. They arranged local tours for me with a man named Achim Vorreiter, so that piece is 'Kassel from the viewpoint of Achim Vorreiter'. I wanted gardens that represented neighbourhoods in every class. But I also wanted historical landscapes. Kassel is one of those reinvented German cities after the bombing of the Second World War. Kassel was, and remains, a large military manufacturing town. So you had not only the gardens of every class, starting at the castle – many of these aesthetic images punctured, as you say, by moles – but also the greenhouse and the conservatory down to the working-class park, which, as Achim said, is largely a dog run. But also the landscapes that are now nothing but hillsides of mostly greenery with occasional little smashed tiles on the sites where the slave labourers, who were primarily from Russia, Poland and Yugoslavia, were forced to live and to take cover during the bombing, which means that they were killed in mass numbers. Because this hillside was between the tank factories, it's called the Black Path; it's right between the main train station – which is not the one that visitors to Documenta use – and the munitions factory. Some of the bullet-shaped shelters that the local people were allowed to use, but not of course the slave labourers, are still located there, in private gardens. Finally there are the very beautiful landscapes of the Rose Hill. The Rose Hill is a very large artificial construction right between the Documenta Halle and Aue pavilion, where all the rubble from the downtown area was shoved over the edge of the cliff. The town fathers then threw dirt on the new hill and planted a rose garden. It is a series of landscapes which is both exactly of the moment in May when the golden chain laburnum is blooming and the first flowers, and also of the history of Kassel ...

IB *Inevitably the molehills – one couldn't help reading them as the return of the repressed ...*

MR ... the history of Kassel coming up, through the agencies of the mole, itself a well-known political symbol ...

IB *... Yes, making visible the invisible seems to be the leitmotif throughout so much of your work.*

61

Audience questions

Q *How much planning went into* Semiotics of the Kitchen? *There are certain stages when it looks as though you have made a split-second decision. The first few times that you move the nutcracker there is silence, but the last three times there is a noise and it is almost as though at that moment you decided that you wanted there to be an audible crack. There are a few other instances where you change your movement half-way through. To what extent did you plan this?*

MR Well, it was many years ago, but it is not the first take and I am a sneaky person. It is true that there is no sound with the nutcracker but it would have been nothing to go back and insert a sound, nothing. But I decided to leave it alone. And whatever is crossing my face at the time, I can't say, but I had already gone through it at least once on camera. We didn't save the first take so I have nothing to compare it to. So there are spontaneous elements but there were also things that maybe were mistakes – I can't remember whether the sound of the nutcracker was a mistake or not – that could have been repaired, but I decided not to. I am untrustworthy, as far as what seems spon-taneous.

Q *I want to ask about the scale of your work. There seem to be certain choices made about a particular take on scale. At the moment there seems to be a certain giganticism in art, that perhaps this museum embodies to a certain extent. I wonder whether the issue of scale is something that you make a conscious choice about.*

MR I think scale is something we can't evade. One of the favourite gambits of the powerless – and artists are always alternating between maniacal self-aggrandisement and feelings of marginality – one of the favourite gambits is to treat something as a miniature. So you make a model of something, you shrink it, or you change it in some way. I think that I am constantly manipulating the scale, or the idea of scale, by changing the size of the things I am replicating or making some reference to. I don't think I have a single strategy but it is something that no artist can avoid and perhaps, as you say, the institution, the art market and the institution – we know already in Abstract Expressionism that the easel painting became a mural-sized object – demands large objects. The public demands objects to worship. There is always a need for something, a sun to be wor-shipped or something of that order. We can hardly fail to comply. It may be odd to remember that the standard size of a photograph used to be 8.5 × 11.5 inches and nobody, who wasn't doing this as a conscious postage stamp-sized image now, would dream of presenting 8 × 10 inch photographs, unless it was a 'signature' thing to do. So the scale is something that comes at us as a problem and something that we need to address.

I am interested also in scaling down large concerns, which is slightly less about actual scale than about conceptual scale. Talking about the microcosm of world events within the home, the micro-politics of home and domesticity and also things like driving in your car, or going through the airport as a traveller, or riding on the tube.

Q *I have been studying the work of Wilhelmina Barns-Graham. Barns-Graham felt that her early success overshadowed her later work, and while the success of her early work did put her on the map it also made her feel as if she had died when she was young. What do you feel about the success of* Semiotics of the Kitchen *in relation to your current work?*

MR I was a success as a young person only ten or 20 years after I was that young person. Everybody hates my work when it's made. Except the feminists – I have my audiences. But mostly the audience sneers at whatever it is I do. You can't imagine that anyone wanted to show *The Bowery* when I made it, or *Vital Statistics*, or *Semiotics of the Kitchen* or *Losing* or any other tapes that I made. I have the luxury of being a success at an early age only in retrospect.

Now that doesn't get rid of the question of how annoying it is when you have to be constantly looking at *Semiotics of the Kitchen*. The answer is that in 20 years maybe you are going to want to see *God Bless America* or the works that I did in Documenta or Münster. So I am annoyed in two ways. But I do understand that this is what institutions do, they write history. And one thing that really annoys me is the way that institutions and art historians rewrite history. What annoys me is not about me at all: it is the rewriting of the history of video to create a completely false picture of how video began, who was doing it, what it looked like, and what it was about and also the rewriting of the history of Los Angeles (of which San Diego is a largely unnamed addendum). Both of those annoy the daylights out of me. I can say this in full voice because I am one of the lucky ones. I am actually mentioned in these early histories but in fact they are fabrications. I think that art historians usually do better than museum people because they are less involved with objects and more involved with stories.

Q *I was wondering about your decision to reprise* Bringing the War Home. *Could you just talk a little bit about that, was it a similar experience or a very different experience?*

MR It was a meta decision, and it was one that I knew would get me in trouble for the following reason. I haven't made montages really – except for one or two random ones – since the early or mid 1970s. I decided to go back to the exactly identical form in order to say that this is exactly the same situation, there is no difference. To say to you in the art world who knew those images, and who have the reprehensible habit of fetishising them as though they were either attractive or glorious at the time they were made, that this is about something happening that you are responsible for. I made a decision. I knew I would be criticised for repeating an old form, but I wanted very much to use the same form of address.

This time something happened that is different from the last time, and I knew it would be different. This time they began in the art world; the first series was never in the art world. But this time I knew, now I have made a name for myself as an artist, that if I did this they would be in the mass magazines immediately, and they were. So my route to getting them into, say, *Der Spiegel* magazine or in *The San Francisco Chronicle* was to put them in the art world. The art world itself has metastasised in the interim and draws in a mass audience. So I felt that I was doing the same thing but at an entirely different moment and the message was, 'What's different? Not much'.

As to making the images, what's different is that I did cut and paste them, but they are digitally produced. I decided not to use Photoshop but nevertheless to print them digitally because at the moment our technology of image production is much more sophisticated, and these new ones of mine are much slicker and depend on different types of imagery than before.

Q *I find myself writing an essay on art for society's sake – are you transforming, or just commenting on the social and political issues of contemporary life?*

MR Much as we like to think otherwise, I have never believed that art transforms society. All social movements are social movements and they all involve the imposition of a political will, either on the basis of social currents, or on the basis of revolts from below. Whether they take the form of a literal revolt or not I won't say. But to put it as simply as possible, social change depends on social movements, and all that artists can do is be a partner to a kind of concentrator of ideo-logical currents. I do see myself in that role if possible, but I certainly do not see artists as literally leading. I think it's important because on the one hand artists are belittled for an unfulfillable messianism, and on the other they are chastised for abandoning utopianism. We may have a messianic propensity, we may suffer from utopianism, but still it would be a mistake to believe our own press. I would like to be a part of whatever it is that people are doing to move us to a better place than this one.

Q *It seems that a lot of your practice has a political bite to it. You tackle issues of gender, of sexuality and of domesticity. Do you want politics to be a part of your work?*

MR Yes. In the past I used to be criticised by feminists for mucking up my feminist critiques by simultaneously referring to issues of geopolitics. I'm not so good at agit-prop. I would always like there to be something else going on, but I am allergic to saying 'and now we will all rise and salute the flag' or something of that order. I am at base a conceptual artist, and what I mean by that is that I would like to engage you in the arena perhaps of the visceral but also of the rational. I would like, perhaps, for you to leave the work with a question, and not just an answer. I am always arguing with people. I am arguing with someone at the moment about what the newer photomontages mean and what the older photomontages meant, because they may mean one thing at the first level, but inevitably there is always something else going on. I don't think that we are as compartmentalised as people might think we are. I do think that they tend to take on various instantiations of the political because I am from that generation of feminists who said that everything is political, and that there are macropolitics and micropolitics. That applies not just to the politics of gender, but to all locations of power, and I am postmodern enough to say that it is not useful to talk about victims and victimisers necessarily, but about other issues as well.

Q *Writing in 2004 in* Artforum *you discussed the responsibility or duty of art as a specific zone of art activism. How has this changed since the early 1970s? What chance is there for bona fide art activism now, bearing in mind the market and other conditions?*

MR I am always the world's worst prognosticator. I wrote an article called 'Post-Documentary?' just as documentary became the genre of the moment. So you are asking the wrong person. However, we can dust off our old homilies and say that it is always darkest before the dawn, and there is plenty of potential for art activism as a result of the market. This is from direct experience. I teach in two places: at the Städelschule in Frankfurt and at Mason Gross School of the Arts at Rutgers University in New Hampshire. I have seen a sudden attachment to the notion of art as activist practice, art as a performative industry, art as guerrilla action, art as viral, art as aggressively public – especially on the part of young women artists – and as cerebral, in a way that it's not supposed to be. All those things at once, a tremendous resurgence of interest in every form of art that is not painting or sculpture. So I would say that the question is not whether there is possibility, but whether there is a will and a desire. And judging from the Städelschule, where students are not doing this in reaction to the school's imperatives, and from Rutgers, where they are, there is tremendous potential.

The problem is that – actually I just wrote something about this for *October* magazine – the question is not to blame artists for their lack of engagement, but to blame the general public. I don't think that artists are any more guilty than any of us sitting in this room for the continuation of engagement in Iraq. I think that social movements have difficulty gaining purchase in a world which is such a 'Society of the Spectacle'. So it is difficult to maintain focus. Yes, there is the possibility. It just requires people to be determined to hang on with something.

This is an edited version of an interview which took place at the Starr Auditorium, Tate Modern on 29 September 2007. Published Issue 314, March 2008.

Joep Van Lieshout

interviewed by Marcus Verhagen

The Master's Plan

MARCUS VERHAGEN *Most people are familiar with the work of Atelier Van Lieshout, either with the earlier work, the living units, often made out of shipping containers, including various facilities – toilets, kitchens, beds and so on – or with the more recent work, much of which consists of models through which Atelier Van Lieshout has imagined the functioning of large communities – essentially totalitarian communities run along fairly insane lines.*

A few years ago I was doing research on utopianism in contemporary art. This was around the time of AVL-Ville when you and your collaborators declared your studio in Rotterdam a free state. At the time I thought this was a utopian project. I'm less certain about that now. Perhaps you could start by explaining why you went from working under your own name to founding Atelier Van Lieshout in 1995.

JOEP VAN LIESHOUT Actually, I was educated as a sculptor in Rotterdam and started working as an artist after that. Around 1994 I changed the name to Atelier Van Lieshout for two reasons: one was conceptual because at that time I was questioning the position of art by making furniture, by making artworks in limited editions and, to reduce my role as an artist or designer, as a contractor. I said to people: if you want to have an artwork like a toilet or a bathroom or kitchen, just tell me how you want it and I will make it for you. To change the name of the artist into the name of the company was a conceptual move.

The other reason was pragmatic. At that time I was working on a commission in France. I collaborated with Rem Koolhaas, the architect, but the French clients didn't like Koolhaas and they didn't like me so they said, 'No, no. We don't work with artists. We only work

with real companies.' So I said, 'OK, I'll start my own company.'
That was the pragmatic reason for using a company name.

MV *Given how interested you are in organisational structures and how communities are managed, I was wondering how you manage Atelier Van Lieshout.*

JVL During the time of AVL-Ville, the Free State, you could say there were two parts – a very structured part and a very anarchistic part. One of them was the atelier – Atelier Van Lieshout – which was my studio and which was structured as a company with me being the boss, and it had rules that everyone had to start work at nine o'clock and so on. Basically it was organised very much like any other company. Then there was this piece of land in front of my studio that I declared a free state and I told my people, 'You can do whatever you want there. If you want to build a house, you can build a house. There are no rules – no aesthetic rules, no technical rules. You can have parties. You can have intercourse with animals if that is one of your desires.' There were no moral rules whatsoever. That was the anarchistic element; you could say the non-structured part.

MV *Since we're there already, let's talk about AVL-Ville. It is the culmination of a certain line of development in your work. Over the five-year period before AVL-Ville, you consistently showed an interest in self-sufficiency. Then you created something a little like a free state with a currency and a constitution. Could you say something about how it worked during those nine months?*

JVL Right from the beginning I had always been very much interested in functional artworks and, basically, in creating worlds. You could say that by making certain groups of objects or mobile homes you create a world. Then, at a certain moment, I just said, 'OK, I have all the stuff I need to start a free state – so let's do it.' Holland has this tradition of allowing things – as long as it doesn't pose a huge problem – and makes a point of its laws not being applied too strictly, a 'soft' law in many ways. There is a lot of liberty unless you make a big mess. So, that was why I started with this idea that I'd make a nice place with art and lots of people and little parties that everyone would like. But, at exactly the same time, there was a political change and a lot of people began to oppose these 'soft' laws that allowed certain drugs and prostitution and so on. We found ourselves being published in all the newspapers and being featured on television, so we were the ones sticking our necks out.

MV *You were scapegoated?*

JVL Yes, absolutely. The authorities were not very co-operative.

MV *So what exactly happened?*

JVL What happened was that we had constant inspections. We had
a bar and restaurant and, of course, we didn't have a building permit
or a restaurant permit or an alcohol licence. And we had a farm and
the European farm inspectors came and said, 'You have two pigs, 20
rabbits and chickens' – it was nothing, it was almost like a petting zoo
– but they said, 'Oh, no. You have to have concrete here and special
tanks for the shed and then you have to do this, and you have to ster-
ilise that'. We had this heating system with renewable energy, and
they said, 'No, no – it should have a filter'. There were a lot of rules.

MV *This wasn't the first time you had a run-in with local authorities, was
it? A couple of years earlier the mayor shut down your show 'The Good,
the Bad, and the Ugly' in Rabastens. You showed* Mercedes with 57mm
Cannon *which is both the title and a description of the work, and it was
on account of that piece the show was closed down.*

JVL Yes.

MV *Do you set yourself up to have these confrontations?*

JVL No, no – not at all. I'm always surprised when it happens –
especially this thing at Rabastens which was like a normal exhibition.
There weren't any dirty pictures or anything like that. It was quite a
decent show, I would say. I was completely surprised that it happened
and I think it had much more to do with the mayor thinking, 'OK, a
lot of people don't like the show, so I will be the hero of the town and
close it down'. So he did. There was a lot of publicity, which was good
for the show. Actually, I think the mayor was fired by the minister.
I prefer to just do my thing and to create artworks and have fun.

MV *Were you hoping that AVL-Ville would last?*

JVL Well, I always expected it would first grow to the size of one
thousand people, and then would exist for 1,000 years!

MV *So there was a master plan?*

JVL There was a master plan. I didn't expect that I would have so many
problems. But I was also a little bit naive, probably I still am.

MV *Well, perhaps that naivety is enabling, in a way. I wanted to ask just
a little bit about the specifically Dutch context of your work. There's
obviously a strong libertarian impulse behind a lot of your work – behind
AVL-Ville for a start. There's a sense that you're pushing against barriers,
trying to break them down, trying to find new areas of personal freedom.*

There is a sense that you're offering a kind of critique of a highly regulated environment – that you're proposing a less regulated environment. I was wondering whether there's a commentary there on the Dutch model in which there is this tradition of social tolerance – but yet the state is ever-present. Is that right?

JVL Yes, I think there is a hate/love relationship towards that. On the one hand I like complete freedom to do whatever I want, wherever and whenever I want, and on the other hand I think a certain control is necessary. I mean, for example, for the environment and urban planning. Holland is a country with extreme urban planning but that means, for example, that where I live in Rotterdam (and Amsterdam as well) you can take your bicycle and within five minutes you are in the kind of landscape that looks as it did 600 years ago. A lot of people also say that there are too many rules, while other people say, 'No, it's good like this'. It is an important discussion point.

MV *So, among other things, AVL-Ville was trying to give a new impetus to that discussion?*

JVL Well, yes. People often make a rule which doesn't really function, so they make a new rule and a new rule and a new rule – so you get a rule on top of a rule on top of a rule – and that means there are too many rules.

MV *That makes sense in the context of more recent work. I'm thinking here specifically of* Schiphol Skull *which is this red box with a big bed where you can rest in or near the airport. In a sense it plays on this tradition of social tolerance since it looks not just like a resting place, but also a place where you can go and have sex.*

JVL I also make soundproof boxes in museums and many other places. I think every public place should have a place to relax – to do what you want. So I did the same thing for the airport – but, actually, it was never used.

The thing was, when they gave me the commission, I asked them: 'Now are there any rules?' They said, 'No – no rules. Only two things: no sex, no pigs. For the rest you can do whatever you want.' So I made something without sex or pigs, and then I installed it, and they said, 'But it should be fireproof as well.' It was not fireproof, so people weren't allowed to go in. But maybe they were just lying. In reality they didn't want people to go inside.

Another interesting story is that until a couple of years ago there was an anti-prostitution law in the Netherlands but then prostitution was legalised: they said, 'If you want to be a prostitute, that's fine with us. You can create your little company and you can have all the benefits – social benefits. You have to pay tax, of course.' So prostitution became a legal job. Immediately afterwards, one of these big entrepreneurs from Amsterdam wanted to open a big nightclub and striptease bar in Schiphol Airport, and that made me very proud. I mean this is something that, if the Netherlands had done it, it would have been a beautiful place. But, of course, they didn't allow it.

MV *It is interesting to me that a lot of your early works consist of structures on wheels –* La Bais-ô-Drôme, Modular House Mobile, *the* 3M Mobile *– a lot of these structures are made to move around. Tell me about that. Why wheels?*

JVL I think there are many reasons for it. One is that you can move the work; another reason is that it gives freedom – it's like creating a capsule with which you can move around the world. Another reason was legislation. Basically, if you build a house, you need a building permit; you have a lot of rules that you have to comply with. However, it is a mobile home if you put some wheels under it, and then there aren't these rules any more. As long as you put some wheels under it, it's a vehicle – an object. That was the reason, of course, to find a way around the rules in order to do what I wanted to do. It doesn't have much to do with the Dutch national hobby of camping.

MV *I'd like to talk a little more about sex in your work. I could mention any number of different pieces, but I'm thinking of the* Sonsbeek Raft *you made which is a restaurant in the form of a raft. There's a phallus at the front that acts as a kind of signature. Why the phallic objects?*

JVL I don't know. Louise Bourgeois – I think she uses even more phalluses than me, so I don't feel so guilty any more. I don't know why I do it. I work in an intuitive way and, basically, once every couple of months I have the urge to make another phallus. Why? I think it is a personal thing – very primitive – it has to do with the origin of man, with masculinity, with reproduction, power, domination, enjoyment, sex – all of that. I never ask myself this question of why or should I do it, because I don't care about that.

MV *Let's talk about masculinity then, in a broader sense. I'm thinking of the emphasis on technological mastery in works like* The Technocrat, *the militarism of your* Workshop for Weapons and Bombs, *or the sexual bravado of the* Modular Multi-Woman Bed. *Why this display of masculinity?*

71

JVL Again, there is not really a reason for that. I think it is just my style. You could say it's the thing I'm intrigued by. The only thing I can say, maybe, is that I'm very much interested in power at all levels. Power used to be about physical strength, maybe now it is about intelligence, money – economic power. I think it really has to do with that.

MV *So the phallus, or this masculine dimension, is part of your looking at power?*

JVL Yes, and it's also about sex, of course, and that is something nice to do.

MV *About power, are you advancing a critique of power? Are you looking at how it works?*

JVL I'm looking at how it works. I think it is inevitable. Also at AVL-Ville, in a way I withdrew myself but on the other hand I used the tools and mechanisms that our world uses – so I'm not against power. I just know that the world functions – people function – around power, the use of power. It's not really a criticism, more a registration of that.

MV *In a lot of the more recent works you isolate body parts or organs –
in* BarRectum, *for instance, or in* BikiniBar, *or in the series of enormous internal organs. Why isolate them?*

JVL I think there are a couple of reasons for those organs. One of them is that the body is a system. For instance, *The Technocrat* was a very technical work about the recycling of biogas and force-feeding, so there was a complicated machine in which the human was reduced to a small particle and the machine was the master. It was also a digestive system of gas, biogas, shit, food and so on. Your own digestive system is also a system but on a personal level, so you have the big system – the group or society – and the individual. This juxtaposition interested me a lot.

There were other reasons for it. It is about design. Design plays a big role in my work. I use design as a palette for creating my artworks and the design of organs is beautiful – you don't know how they work and why they look the way they do. I mean, why don't they look like stuff we would make ourselves? And then you can ask yourself, 'Who was the designer of this? Is this evolution, is there a higher creature?' It goes back to larger questions about life itself.

Another thing: I used those organs to create functional objects, like *Wombhouse* or *BarRectum* and that, again, has to do with design. I wanted to turn my back on contemporary design and to create something where the form is completely independent of the function, the materials, or the design, or fashion, or trends. I just wanted to make beautiful forms and then I cut a door in them and some windows and then they became a house.

MV *Isn't there a risk that people will say you're looking at the body as a kind of convenience? I'm thinking, in particular, of* BikiniBar, *which is a woman's body – isn't there a risk that people will say, 'Look, you're treating a woman's body as a facility or a series of facilities?'*

JVL I've never heard this criticism. It's the only body you can enter without asking. Of course, there's that freedom.

MV The Technocrat *is a phenomenally complex work and, as I understand it, it's not just one work. It has generated a series of works, all relating to the same overarching idea. It seems there's a real shift in your practice at the beginning of the 21st century. There's a movement towards making objects that can be used for thinking about models and systems – much larger social forms. There's a shift, too, from bottom-up systems to top-down systems and from the self-contained community as a kind of refuge to the self-contained community as a totalitarian state. Basically, it seems there's a movement towards more megalomaniacal work and, in my view, more pessimistic work. Am I imagining this, or do you agree that there is a shift?*

JVL Yes, there is definitely a shift. I think the shift has something to do with AVL-Ville, or the end of AVL-Ville – the breaking of the big dream, you could say. After that I made, you could say, contrary works. I started to work more on systems or something that is controlling or oppressing. Yes, that's absolutely true.

On the other hand, I always try – within this kind of system – to find something nice or something beautiful. For example, in *SlaveCity*, there will be a huge museum, beautiful buildings, nice urban planning and good healthcare – so it will be environmentally friendly. It is like reformulating good and bad.

MV *The way you've just described it,* SlaveCity *sounds wonderful – but it's also a place where many people are processed and composted, basically, if I understand rightly – so it is not a utopian society.*

JVL The idea was to make a concentration camp for 200,000 people – 100,000 men, 100,000 women. The idea was to make as much money as possible with this concentration camp, so that all decisions would have an economic basis. That means that people would have to work like slaves for seven hours in high-tech jobs, or on the land, or in supporting roles, followed by seven hours of sleep and three hours of spare time.

But the idea was to make as much money as possible which, in this case, I calculated at €8bn a year which is an awful lot of money and, with this large amount of money, you can do many good things as well. You could be as powerful as Microsoft, for example, or, if you had a couple of these slave cities, you could generate enough power and money to change things in the world – for the better.

MV *While maintaining people in a state of slavery?*

JVL Yes, but just 200,000 people! I mean, 200,000 people for a better world – that's a good sacrifice.

MV *So it's a dystopian community that has a kind of invisible utopian hinterland?*

JVL Yes – except that it has renewable energy, self-sufficiency in food and energy, no carbon dioxide – but also, everything is recycled, even the slaves if they are not efficient enough or not healthy enough. In that case they are not composted but digested as biogas. But before that you harvest them – you can give the heart to someone, or the liver, or the kidneys. So there's a big transplant industry that also could save more lives. Basically, it's very much about morality – about good and bad. I think it is also a little bit of a warning about the economic power of international capitalism, which could become uncontrollable. On the other hand, I think the world in which we are living now will soon need a system that organises the world because there will be too many people – too much consumption.

Maybe the scenario of a slave city within 50 years is not as unimaginable as it was 60 years ago – at this very moment there are slave cities all around the world. I mean it is not something new that I invented.

MV *It is intriguing to me that a lot of the people in* SlaveCity *work in a giant call centre – so I wonder if* SlaveCity *could be understood, in some sense, as an allegory of a certain kind of corporatism today. We think of a call centre as a paradigmatically contemporary corporate form related to the spread of offshoring, delocalisation, and the advent of globalisation – so I was wondering if you could take* SlaveCity *to be, among other things, an allegory?*

JVL Well, when I invented my little concentration camp, I was unaware of this outsourcing of technology jobs. *SlaveCity* is not a criticism of this practice.

MV *What about the timing? I want to come back to this shift towards work like* The Technocrat *and* SlaveCity. *Both works were made during a crisis period in Holland that saw the rise of Pim Fortuyn and the hard right. It completely upset the Dutch political landscape and then, of course, there was the assassination of Fortuyn in 2002, which, if I remember rightly, was the year* The Technocrat *was finished. So is there a sense that this shift towards work that imagines totalitarian conditions is in some way an engagement with current conditions in Holland?*

JVL Of course the things that happened around me have an influence on my work, but not that literally.

MV *Where does the interest in concentration camps come from?*

It's an interest I've had for a long time. Why did the Holocaust happen in a country that is very close to my country with a language that is very close my language in a time that is very close to the time I'm living in at the moment? It happened 60 years ago and it could happen again. I've always thought that.

Then I was also interested in the system behind it – how it was organised. How it was possible. How they built it. How they designed it. And then you discover that it was much more rational than you might think. For example, the way a concentration camp is designed is very modernist and very rational.

MV *Where do you stand on that kind of rationalism? How does it fit in your work – in your way of seeing things?*

JVL Again, it is a difficult or sensitive point because rationalism is useful in creating a culture, in creating a society, or in creating wealth. Without it there is no structure and there is no advancement. On the other hand, rationality can be restrictive as well – especially today because the tools to control and to check rationality or profits are very accurate and very fast. So, on the one hand rationality is good – I use it in my own company in the production of my work and how I think and travel and work – but on the other hand it is something that I absolutely do not like. I like the craziness of people and the unpredictability of people.

MV *This rationalism is what connects the fascist model of the concentration camp with the drive for profit that is very much a part of the rhetoric around* SlaveCity. *Does that make sense?*

JVL Yes, I think so.

MV *Tell me about the cultural budget.* SlaveCity *has an arts budget of €78m. Any idea how that's going to be used?*

JVL Well, actually, I think it's not enough. I think when I come to recalculate the whole financial plan I will look at more money for the arts. The idea was that with lots of money you could create fantastic museums and theatres and so on, so you could also have the best artworks, operas and everything. Not only in the *SlaveCity*, but in many systems when culture is used to promote a country and to win ...

MV *Legitimisation for a certain political system?*

JVL Yes.

MV *Finally, I wanted to ask a little bit about your interest in circularity. I'm thinking in particular of* The Technocrat. *The idea behind* The Technocrat *is that you get a lot of people together, and the people produce waste, and the waste is used to produce biogas. The biogas is then used to produce alcohol and food, and then the cycle starts all over again.*

JVL I think it's interesting because it can be interpreted in lots of different ways. You could see the circularity as a way of shutting out the outside world, or you could see it as a way of lampooning the environmentalist movement. I'm not sure how to read it.

The origin of *The Technocrat* was basically AVL-Ville. During the AVL-Ville time I was interested in infrastructure and in finding ways to produce energy from waste. So I first started to make compost toilets because that gives you independence from the existing sewerage grid. And then I thought, 'No, no, no. We should make a biogas installation – that's the best way to recycle shit.' At that time I still had the idea of the 1,000 Free State for 1,000 years, so I designed this biogas installation – the first in the world for human waste – for a thousand people.

MV *That was in Venice, wasn't it?*

JVL That was in Venice – yes. I designed it originally for AVL-Ville, but since AVL-Ville no longer existed I said, 'OK, I want to continue with this biogas installation'. So that's why I created the rest of the system, with bunk beds where 1,000 participants, slaves and prisoners lay while being force-fed with food – cheap food for a maximum yield of gas – and also alcohol to keep them happy or suppressed – just enough for them not to start a revolution. Then the gas produced is used to cook the food and to make the alcohol. This idea is to make a perfect system – an environmentally friendly, highly advanced technology system. On the other hand, it's completely idiotic to make something like that because you reduce the human being to a small cogwheel in this machinery, so the recycling is perverted.

MV *This is why I said it could be understood as a satire of a certain kind of environmental model.*

JVL Yes, but it is also about technology. There are many new technologies that I dislike. I mean, I'm not really happy with email or mobile phones – I can remember a time when you could disappear from the world for a month. There are many times when technological advancement means slavery. But you could also see *The Technocrat* in parallel with the existing world where we also produce products and consume products, where we are kept alive and kind of happy, but society expects us to be as profitable as possible.

This is an edited version of an interview which took place at the Starr Auditorium, Tate Modern on 20 October 2007.

Siobhán Hapaska

interviewed by Hester R Westley

Another Way to Say It

HESTER R WESTLEY *This new body of sculpture is startlingly different from the work you last showed in the UK over ten years ago. Do these objects represent a new departure in your working practice?*

SIOBHÁN HAPASKA I've always had a clear idea in my mind of what my work is all about. It's very difficult to abandon the preoccupations that make me the person I am but it has also been necessary to rethink the ways of manifesting those ideas. If you can say it this way, can you find another way to say it?

For me, in the beginning, the process of making sculpture was about reduction. It became an economy of means. I remember when I did my work to get onto Goldsmiths MA I had three sculptures that constructed a narrative. They were all there like guests around a dinner table. They all had their part and place but I realised that not everyone all the time understood the significance, meaning, or the role play of those individual elements. So I thought 'I need to simplify things', and that's where this process of reduction came from. I remember a significant moment at college during a studio visit when there was some debate about whether my objects had been reduced too much, whether they were disappearing into nothing and how they functioned in terms of language. Jean Fisher, one of my tutors at the time, said: 'I think these objects function in the space – if you could call it a space – where the sentence ends with a full stop and a new sentence begins.' So my work has stuff happening on either side, but it's also this thing that happens in the middle with them.

I guess now in a way this process has changed or reversed, and it is now about addition. I have always really loved materials but over the last ten years my sculpture was pushing things to their own internal limits: if you take anything more away it collapses and its meaning disappears. Now I'm having a great time being completely free, and the making process is a lot more intuitive. The one thing that you never lose is your sensibility. That part rarely changes – rather the means of how it comes about simply adapt.

HW *Where has this new-found freedom come from?*

SH I don't have to look over my shoulder as I've been left to my own devices for quite a while now. The dull people, with their clichéd responses, say, 'God, your stuff is strange' or 'your stuff is weird' but I think they must have had a very sheltered visual existence if that's the case. My particular language is particular to me, trying to make it more 'normal' is like hearing those phoney accents that make me think, shit, is that really necessary? So I've got past that and it's now just an advanced case of doing my own thing.

HW *You mentioned your intuitive working processes. Do your ideas come from the materials or are the materials subordinated to the idea?*

SH It changes. I think that materials can have the potential to be very emotive. With the work *Lung*, I absolutely knew that I wanted to use loofahs, but I had no idea how to use them. I bought 200 from a store on the internet and when cut open and turned inside out they reminded me of an interior of a lung. I wanted to say something personal, so it is best to be quite formal. It is an imposing work, standing larger than human height. A lung's need is to process oxygen, but it is being constricted. You don't know if it is being constricted by the channels which contain it. The colour of these channels is a fluorescent orange, it almost pulses and appears to dissolve the solidity of the constricting channels. So I'm interested in the push and pull and all the maybes that exist within those two elements and how they function together.

HW *How consistent are you with your working practice and studio habits?*

SH I rarely do sketches. I keep a library of ideas in my head and occasionally I note down titles which will jog my memory. I used to start off with a very fixed idea of what I wanted to say so the idea has always dictated what the object will eventually look like. It's now a hybrid, and that has been really exciting for me. When I used to make the big fibreglass pieces, they were designed in advance on a computer program and I would work on one shape for days on end. When I eventually arrived at a shape that somehow resonated with the feeling or the idea that I was trying to get across, I would stop. The image was printed off, gridded up and in the studio I would transpose the shape onto a massive block of polystyrene.

The initial fun in that process was the rapidity with which I could find the form inside the polystyrene and the snowstorm of debris which resulted, but after that it just descended into months of endless sanding. During that, you would be mulling over the next pieces or what to cook for dinner or the things you forgot to do or whatever, so in a way you weren't even giving that particular work much attention because as soon as you'd got the polystyrene object that was it, done. The next wave of excitement was when a production mould had been made and a first positive object would then have to be sanded down – and the final wave of excitement would come when the work was being sprayed. The only thing that changed was the possibility of what colour it could be. I couldn't sustain that way of working.

I love those works and I would always stand by the process, which was necessary. But the frustration was that no one understood how time-consuming the process was, how laborious it was to eradicate any trace of their making. I didn't want to leave any traces of me in those works; that is one reason why they had to be smooth and perfect. The impersonal surfaces were also important to me because they do not have the same associative power. Fur or wood or loofahs or leather or any of those porous materials seem to almost have a built-in cultural and historical memory so they can mean something to a person immediately. In my earlier works I wanted to remove that and it was almost like my fibreglass surfaces had no memory, they had amnesia – a bit like a Teflon surface where memory and experience slide off, ending up like a puddle on the floor. I think, in a way, while people were attracted to these surfaces they were simultaneously repelled because there was very little they could bring to it from their own experience. I found the push and pull of those two scenarios interesting but I ran out of enthusiasm and besides, I started to look like a wrestler from all the sanding!

HW *Duchamp thought the title of a work of art was everything, but Picasso thought it was of little significance. How important are the titles to your works?*

SH I tend to title my work at the last minute because you can never fully understand what the thing is before that. As much as you try to understand it during the making, you can't, because the meaning of an object is not just within itself but also what people bring to it; the discourse that builds up around it fully gives it its function and place in the world. That's why I find it difficult to title my work before or during its construction, or even when it is just made.

One day I was sitting here in the studio and listening to the shipping forecast and the lady said in her lovely voice 'Becoming Cyclonic'. It seemed so appropriate, because it suggests a change and that something is changing for the worse, a volatile situation with an end result that is potentially catastrophic. That is why I called it *Becoming Cyclonic*. I always try to keep the titles of my work quite short. I guess how you choreograph your works in a show affects how the titles will work with each other. For me, each work can function entirely by its own means, but what is lovely about an exhibition is how you choreograph the objects, because within that you can construct paragraphs and within that you might get a text or an essay.

HW *You mentioned this idea of an approaching change. Can you describe the nature of the change?*

SH I think the works I made then were very much of the thinking that there can be progress, we can go forward and it can be a linear thing and that there is hope at the end of everything. But I've since thought that maybe that is not the case and that notion has been directly manifested in this new version of *Far*. Because this is my first solo show in London since 1995, it became important for me to have a piece of work in this show that related back to earlier works and which maybe described why this change in my work had come about. Rather than it being the shiny optimistic thing *Far* once was, it has completely changed its identity and its appearance; so it's become thoroughly animal-like, barbaric and it's armoured. You don't know whether that gleaming surface is still under there because it is certainly concealed now, and it has become demonic in a way. It almost resents its former self. It resents its former self so much that that identity has been killed off and it is dragging its carcass behind it. It's up to you to make your mind up about what is happening to this object but it is basically the same object with two identities and what has became of one and what will become of the other, we don't know yet.

HW *Why do you insist on fabricating all your work yourself?*

SH Because I can. Well, that's not quite true. Marouf Al Barnawi sprays my work and Bill Roberts makes my big moulds. I do small ones. Beyond that, yes, I do everything. There was no man in my home when I was growing up so if anything needed doing, like tiling a bathroom or worse, I did it. I did the bathroom when I was eight. My legacy and my plight, self-sufficiency!

HW *Can you explain some of the ideas informing this new work?*

SH *Dry Spring* is about eight feet tall and it refers to a spring as a source of water rather the season. It is again quite a personal piece, representing the dualism of spirits contained within the same thing. I guess it is a relationship: this object came about from me staring at the dysfunctional stopcock or water valve outside my studio. *Dry Spring* looks like a craggy old maid with all its stuffing coming out but also possesses a male part where water should come out and it's only held together by this intricate hessian webbing. But because it is miserable and rotten and it displays this residual notion of being a water valve, it is frail and incapable of releasing anything. So there is a copper pipe which twists around the craggy thing and just yearns to have water flowing through it but it doesn't, and out of sheer frustration these flowers have sprung up on the surface of this pipe, and maybe this is the reason why this object is the way it is. I guess it is a binary thing again. Within this awful situation there are these little flowers which are so obtuse in their desire to be beautiful but equally, with the pipe, they act like a boa constrictor.

Another work, *Looped linear thinking pac thing*, developed from memories of my grandma knitting at night, she never slept. She would be sitting in her rocking chair by the fire and I would be assisting in the endurance game of holding the skein of wool for her as she worked. It was the memory of this process, doing this repetitive thing with your hands and staring at the fire, which left your mind completely free, which has stayed with me. I wanted to describe this because it became very much about how I think, my own thought processes. My grandmother also made me knitting nancies – a thread bobbin with four pegs in the top. Passing wool over each, you got a knitted wool cord. I never knew what to do with the cord. In this piece, the eight pegs become like mental options or choices, and the thronging tube is like my unformed thought. The sledge-like feature functions as a sort of repository that would have held this material to make thought. Sledges, of course, are normally on a slippery surface, and thought itself is on a very slippery surface until you actually put stakes in the ground to stop it passing beyond you. You need to anchor yourself for a time in order to understand the complexity of what it is you are thinking. But these sledges are black and made out of pony skin, so they are also a contradiction in terms. And I haven't stared at a fire in a long time.

HW *You seem concerned with the expression of emotional subjectivities. How does this awareness figure in your work?*

SH It would be impossible not to make objects without thinking about what constructs you as a person. *Speaker* resembles a very crude ape and from the gaping hole of its mouth comes this protrusion which is like a flower and is painted in a very refined way. Within that flowering there are always two binary elements again. The first is very open, free-flowing, organic and imaginative, which expresses both potential and possibility. The second is found in learned responses that are nearly always black-and-white, almost fascist. So on the peripheral parts of these petals there are black-and-white areas which represent fixed thought and narrow-mindedness, necessarily co-existing with their free-flowing interiors. It is a graphic depiction of how my understanding of understanding is structured.

HW *Just as you constantly juxtapose familiar objects and images with those that are utterly bizarre and foreign, so you seem always to ground highly personal responses within a much broader frame of reference. Is this the sort of interplay that your current work explores?*

SH They are all linked. There are endlessly repeated patterns and any particular cycle of events can almost always be transcribed onto a larger framework. At first I was troubled by the notion that I might be making stuff that came from a personal source. I then started to realise that it really doesn't matter so long as it's not overtly played up and directly autobiographical. There is enough that has drifted into it that keeps me satisfied that I have addressed something that is of a very personal nature but it also has an external existence which is open.

I think these works come from some deeply restless part of me. This feeling, in part, comes from the memory of an experience I had as a very small child. I lived with my mum and grandmother in the centre of Belfast in a big Victorian house, at the back of which was an alleyway which connected the backs of the houses. At the entrance to the alleyway was a black stone courtyard which never got any real sunlight. I remember standing in the middle of the courtyard looking up and noticing how the wall of the courtyard formed this perfect black perimeter against the extremely blue, blue sky. It was exquisite.

I remember how this deep black line met this blue line – or was it a blue line meeting a black line? – and at the precise bottom corner an aircraft entered the space. I watched it move diagonally across the blue square until it disappeared out of precisely the same spot on the top corner. All the aspects – like the moment the aircraft entered the blue square and the time I had to fantasise about where it was going, like the formal aspect of how this image was constructed and seeing that aircraft disappear – seemed to set up this residual longing to be somewhere else.

Issue 311, November 2007

Eva Rothschild

interviewed by Ian Hunt

They Don't Unpack

IAN HUNT *You were saying that you almost felt militant about sculpture.*

EVA ROTHSCHILD Militancy is probably overstating it. But I feel strongly
that it's sculpture and not anything else. I didn't go to college to do
sculpture, I studied printmaking, but at a certain point I became uninterested in making work in any other way. Some of the first things I
made, the black Perspex pieces, were essentially flat things that stood
up, whereas now there's a different dimensionality in the pieces.
Some of them are flat but most have no other way of being. They don't
unpack. They don't reduce. That is new. And I guess there's been an
introduction of what's termed organic form – which to me means
things without corners.

IH *But they still don't have much mass.*

ER They have volume but they don't necessarily have mass. Except for
the boulder, which is specifically created to be the only solid object in
the whole body of work. I'm interested in objects that take up space
while not having much materiality.

IH *There are a great many three-dimensional things that artists contrive
according to their needs, which may be quite legitimate, but they aren't
necessarily or even very often sculpture.*

ER Someone like Glenn Brown, who makes his sculptures out of
paint? He is very much a painter and yet those objects are so sculptural. But they are clearly paint, they seem to be paint the whole
way through, even though there must be an armature. They are
ambiguous as objects.

IH *The Glenn Brown works play with viewpoint, you find a particular view
that seems to work more. One of the defining things about sculpture is how*

85

it makes you circumnavigate. The new pieces on the stands – do you call them stands?

ER I do call them stands ...

IH *I mean the one called* Garlands. *In the circuit you make around it a form appears and disappears, a kind of crashed star form.*

ER Because of its whiteness and blackness as well. It is physically attached to the stand, woven to it, it's like a growth from it. The lines, because they're angular, are like a continuation of the stand. Then equally they're not. The piece is made out of circular section softwood and the stand is made from square section steel. They're disharmonious in that way. People often think that the works are all steel, even when they look quite close, but they're mainly wood.

IH *Often it is clear – the grain of the wood shows through the black gloss, but you are forced into a particular alertness about materials used. What governs the choice of materials?*

ER It's partly to do with the degree of finish. With wood you can never get it perfect. There's a warmth to wood, too. Also I have complete control over it – as I'm working I can change it. I can't work steel so I have a very different relation to it. I choose to use timber to make a lot of works it might be assumed would be made of metal. To use metal might give a different kind of integrity but it would take away from the sense of touch, the sense of craft. In terms of materials, *Jokes* was specifically made of oak, initially because the floor of the South London Gallery is oak. But after it was painted, it could have been made of any other wood.

IH Jokes *is an intriguing work from the point of view of spectator movement, the way the green-painted edges of the cubes disclose themselves.*

ER The green interrupts the idea of the cube. For me the cube is not authoritarian exactly, but there's a canon of artists who have worked with cube forms: Mel Bochner, Robert Morris. It's only this year that I've made work with cubes. I'd never used any square forms before. They just seem very masculine. I wanted to use the cube but as a totally unsound construction, expressing the opposite of weight and heaviness. Then it is also interrupted by the green. Painting the objects is really important to me, how you paint an object changes the perception of its form. Something as simple as a stripe or a coloured line on a very thin, light structure is enough optically to interrupt the planes you're viewing. That's been in the work a long time. In the past, in college, I was always interested in camouflage. Now those principles are applied to geometric forms.

ɪʜ *But the cubes are liberated from a geometric, rectilinear order in the way they occupy space. They make a notional sphere of interest.*

ᴇʀ Because of how you perceive them as a whole being, perhaps. The title is *Jokes* – I wanted to make something that seemed impossible, something very light. It's also the tallest of the pieces on stands: it's 330cm. And I didn't know if it could work with five cubes but I didn't want four. I wanted the height from that thin material. The stands are made with similar heights but always in relation to viewpoint – I work from my own viewpoint and add a few inches. I don't make things in relation to the body so much, but to the eye: I always think about where the eye will be in relation to them. The piece called *The Inside of Your Head* is made specifically so I can put my head inside it. I was making it at a table standing up, and this specific possibility of interaction became important in deciding where to place it – but I don't think it fully became an artwork until it went into the space.

ɪʜ *It wouldn't be a sculpture when on its stand in the studio?*

ᴇʀ It kind of is but it definitely resonates differently. The ideal place for me to show work is a gallery. There is something about being able to see an object separated from other objects that is really important to the idea of sculpture. There is always going to be a relationship between the sculptures in the studio and the chair and the other objects, which all stand in their particular ways. And these works were all made with a particular large space in mind: the South London Gallery has that high ceiling, and that strong single viewpoint on entry. The conversations that can be had between the works in the gallery can't be had in the studio.

ɪʜ *How strongly are they designed for that gallery? One of the commitments to the making of an individual sculpture is that it will travel to another space.*

ᴇʀ You have a certain amount of control over your work the first time it's shown, after that it's very often out of your hands. You can see work terribly installed and that is galling. But when you're making a body of work to go together, although you are aware of how each piece can exist separately, it's impossible not to think of that first showing as its best possible existence.

ɪʜ *Which in this case meant thinking about* Higher Love, *the tall piece with three circles at the entrance, and* The Rock and the Arch *positioned not as a triumphant entry but near the end of the gallery.*

ER I was really clear from the start where I wanted those pieces, they never moved very much.

IH *Thinking about* The Rock and the Arch *in relation to how you described earlier work as flat things stood up – the arch is a flat form that has a direction, an axis implicit in it, but the rock insists on being circumnavigated.*

ER The arch is a line, and the rock is a complete mass.

IH *Made from black bathroom tiles. And the title makes it sound like a fable.*

ER It just comes from what we were calling it in the studio when we were making it. I had grand titles for it but in the end it just had to be titled in a lumpen, rooted way, named as what it was.

IH *The arch has tree-like aspects, in common with works like the upside-down tree form of* Weeping Willow *of 2005, but this is odd in an arch – it reinforces the sense of downward movement.*

ER An arch doesn't have to be a built arch. It can be an organic arch, a tree or a fallen tree. I prefer that. The Roman arch is weighty and academic, a bit like the cube. I like the idea of something that has a potential to be broken, that could end at any of those points. Also there is so little you have to do to give something a narrative or pictorial sense. Just by adding a strut of metal it becomes branch-like. You need so little to bring something into language.

IH *You use the word broken: the alternation, the banding of colour in these works is in graphic terms a broken line.*

ER I couldn't imagine these pieces without the stripes. They suggest a hesitancy about the line and where it could go. It also allows colour to come into the work – though obviously I'm never going to be known for my great colour palette, it's important, it interrupts the sense of something continuous. That's there in all the work. In the woven pieces it's a discontinuous surface, an image made of parts. There's never a sense of a unified whole.

IH *What interests me is the hesitancy that colour brings into the perception of form doesn't imply disbelief in sculpture as a specialist form of knowledge, knowledge of things that don't easily disclose themselves.*

ER It may be a different thing, but we were talking earlier about making and when you commit to making an object. When people don't make anything, not necessarily just art, or start but give up because they can't see an immediate result, something is wrong. When you're making you get more confidence about whether something might work or not, you learn perhaps to give something a month, or six months to see where it goes. There's a commitment in that way, I suppose, but that's a very pragmatic aspect of it.

IH *The reason for asking about a commitment to sculpture is that your work has been explicit, especially in the woven works, in its interest in forms of belief, spiritual, political and so on. Sculpture has represented one small form of belief through the last century.*

ER And what do you think that belief is?

IH *Partly about finding things that communicate to us physically and humanly in a world where engineers and architects, new image technologies, are making the running in defining our experience.*

ER That's true but all art doesn't have a large role to play in terms of what we take in visually now. To be a photographer now, when each day we see hundreds of photographs or photographically created images, means you face incredible competition. To be a sculptor is an easier option. We aren't confronted with so many objects that don't have a use. Sculpture may have a rarefied position, but to me it seems to be one of the last uncolonised areas of making. There isn't much access to it but there isn't the same kind of competition from the real world either. Maybe this does mean sculpture is elitist somehow, but in a way I'm happy that it isn't catered for popularly.

I think it's specialised rather than simply elitist, but it would take all day to hash that one out. I want to ask about the corner piece. It's another work that relies on us noticing materials – the struts are black-painted wood, against the use of reflective Perspex. And for a sculpture to occupy a corner is disconcerting.

It is disconcerting, and it's quite big – 2 metres, bigger than a person. I like the idea that you look into the corner and the corner looks back at you. It's the most illusionistic piece in the show, it creates an infinity of space. It doesn't deny the architecture, it doesn't deny the corner, it is obviously two-dimensional, just with these forward struts. And while you know what it is, materially, your eye doesn't operate on the same level as your brain. I called it *Riches* because I wanted it to have a generous title – and it's also seductive, this big black diamond is almost welcoming you into it.

IH *You say the corner looks back at you – as I was standing looking, it definitely didn't give me back my own reflection, which appears in two places if you face the corner.*

ER There are tricks that occur in the pieces, physical tricks, but I want those tricks to be simple. In *Higher Love* the supporting metal strut is lost among the long strands of leather. There's something unbelievable about what you're seeing in relation to what you know must be true. It's like the stripes as well – there's nothing complicated, but your eye can't simply follow. What I'm concerned with in all the work is the interaction between the object and the eye. I want you to become aware of looking. There's almost a kind of hardness in your looking, as you try to understand what it is you are seeing – an object that seems confusing. I think about confusion and materiality when I'm making the work, and how to combine them in ways that aren't really a trick, but a fact of the physical objects that exist there in front of you.

IH *Part of this is a wish to make sculpture, to make objects, that are not exhausted by one angle of view, that make us come back to look again.*

ER They have to make you aware of looking and continue to want to look, in a different way than when reading a text or grasping a narrative, or even looking at a photograph. I want there to be something experiential, a quite tough interaction between the viewer and the object. We were talking about things that are catered for in society, or over-catered for. The interaction with forms as forms, as forms without function, it isn't anywhere in our general dealings with things.

IH *We should talk a bit about meaning, about the role of referential aspects of the work. In* The Narrow Way, *those are snakes aren't they?*

ER They're just woven leather, which is a bit like snakeskin, with one end slightly thicker. In terms of figuration, that's it, but of course they are snakes – I call them snakes – with all the obvious malign connotations from the Judaeo-Christian tradition. And then I also did the photographic project of people holding real snakes for this show, which allowed me to work in a completely different way. Only one of the people had held a snake before. It's odd what happens when people hold snakes, because the snake doesn't really know you're a person. The snake doesn't care. You could be a tree. And then quite apart from the fact that people have such phobias about them, and their associations with the Fall and loathsomeness so on, there is something about the being of the snake that fascinates. The whole mode of movement and being is so alien to our way of interacting with objects and spaces. The snake is like the least-lived form: there's a disdain for it and equally a fascination. There's something about the form of the snake that is so untrustworthy.

IH *I wasn't going to ask, but there are no snakes in Ireland. Is* The Narrow Way *set in the Wild West, as there is a work nearby called* Cactus?

ER I'm Irish, but I had never thought of that. I thought everyone might think *The Narrow Way* was named after the street in Hackney, but I was thinking of the religious context when titling it.

IH *You use leather as form and structure. The leather fringes in your work have been over-identified with those on leather jackets. Have they shed those associations a bit?*

ER I hope so! I don't really mind them being there though, I make the work, I know those things are there. The single woven work in the show is derived from an image I've used before, of a naked, breastfeeding hippy. I wanted that strong, humanistic image, but it's one I've used before so it does have specific associations.

IH *How loaded is your preference for black?*

ER These things wouldn't work without it. It does something very definite in visual terms, it completes the work. And because of the way black works, it is completely different when manifested as absorbent leather, or reflective Perspex, or wood, in how it interacts with the eye. In a way black is one of the primary materials of the work.

IH *In terms of the quest for connection with life outside the gallery that any time has, that any artist wants, one thing that strikes me is that your works have sometimes seemed to act as placeholders for some social action that is anticipated or blocked.*

ER That's interesting. But what do you mean by that?

IH *I was thinking of one of the earliest works of yours widely seen,* Burning Tyre *of 1999, with the burning joss sticks. That seemed to be an eloquent way of talking about how art aims to have some kind of social connection but also admits its own limits.*

ER I think that work really did do that. It's one of those works where you think – OK, I wish I could make another one like that. It just found its right moment. It did have that social aspect. The recent work doesn't have that social or political aspect so explicitly. *Burning Tyre* was also reactive, it was made for a show about protest, something I'm still strongly interested in. You find moments when your art coalesces with that, but you can't be always co-opting one to the other.

Issue 311, November 2007

Christian Marclay

interviewed by Gilda Williams

On The Right Track

GILDA WILLIAMS *The first thing I would like to reflect on is the fact that because you are so specifically associated with the crossover between music and art, the variety of your art-making – which goes well beyond the overlap between these two media – is often overlooked. By variations on your art-making I don't just mean the distinction between the performance work and the gallery work, but the many strategies you use, which include using readymades (whether in records or in music or in film); collage; video; installation; seriality and repetition; grids; and themes that include gender; race; language; politics – I think, to some degree – and archives. And you borrow from so many different sources of sound, from taped sound, to telephones, film sound, musical instruments, improvised music, white noise – particularly the sounds that music-making machines make themselves – and silence. Do you sometimes feel pigeonholed?*

CHRISTIAN MARCLAY No, I don't feel pigeonholed. The sound aspect is very much central to my work and people see me as the artist who deals with sound in visual ways as well as using the actual sound. I just use whatever form and media that I need and that I find is appropriate for what I'm trying to do and, in that sense, I don't feel stuck in something because I'm not going to the studio and thinking, 'How am I going to paint that canvas today?' I'll invest in different technologies because they best express what I'm trying to do – be it video, be it just a sound recording, a performance, or a sculpture, or even a painting – that's fine.

But it is an important question – especially now that I've just moved to London and I have to kind of find new ways of working because I don't have my New York infrastructure – my studio. Not that I am very much of a studio artist per se, but one finds ways to create work within a environment and access to certain people, to technology or to certain media is easier for me in New York.

GW *You allow for a lot of improvisation in your work. Are there any examples of works that you attempted but which you felt didn't work out, and that you had to abandon?*

CM Not really. It's more that I don't want to be pigeonholed as a video artist, for instance. I have a touring show which originated in Paris at the Cité de la Musique and focuses on my work in video, and even though the medium of choice there is video, I don't think of it as a video show but more as a kind of music show where I'm using video to create musical compositions. It just happened that video allows me to have an image at the same time as the sound. The show went to Melbourne in Australia and everybody there thinks that I am a video artist because that's all they see. So now, if I've been doing something for too long, I try to do something different.

GW *The number of times image and audio unexpectedly overlap in* Up and Out, *which combines images of Antonioni's* Blow Up *with the soundtrack to Brian de Palma's* Blow Out, *is quite extraordinary. I feel that you really understand the ebb and flow of film – you know when it's time for a love scene and when it's time for action. Is your work always planned in advance, or are you sometimes surprised by what results from the combination of sound and image?*

CM Well, this project, in particular, is a simple edit. It's the simplest video I've made. I just took the whole visual track of *Blow Up* and added the sound track of *Blow Out* just randomly – just starting the two films at the same time so you see *Blow Up* and you hear *Blow Out*. So, it's a perfect combination because *Blow Up* is a very visual film. It's about a photographer trying to resolve a crime and trying to find clues in images while in *Blow Out* John Travolta is a sound engineer who is trying to do the same thing – resolve a crime using sound and trying to find clues in a sound recording. So, those two seemed to be a perfect kind of marriage of sound and image and this interesting juxtaposition, which is purely chance, is now fixed in this video, so it's always the same relationship.

That interest in the chance element is something that, of course, has been exploited by people like John Cage and this relationship is something I've experienced first-hand watching Merce Cunningham's company dance with the sounds of scores by Cage. The idea was that you could start the dance and the music at the same time and they would happen at the same time, but they looked to be totally unrelated. Our brains are so used to trying to put sound and image together that we do it automatically, and we find connections between things that are unrelated, and that kind of surprised me the first time I experienced that kind of juxtaposition, I think I was inspired by that. I eventually did get to work with Cunningham and experienced that really by making music with the dancers, not expecting anything. At the end of the show audiences would come and say, 'That must have taken a lot of rehearsals to get those synchronisations just perfect', but it was pure chance.

So, yes, I definitely believe very much in how chance can happen in a very positive way and, being a musician and an improviser musically, I've also experienced that a lot when playing with other musicians. You're trying hard to be in sync with them, but sometimes accidents happen and you find yourself doing something that you weren't quite happy with, but the combination ends up being very good. The tension exists between what you're trying to achieve and the circumstances – the medium, in some cases. It's just like if you make a sound with a record and it skips a certain way – those are interesting moments where you kind of lose control while you're trying to accomplish something.

I think that's just life. We try hard to follow a track, but things happen and one has to be alert to take advantage of those little incidents.

cw *Which verge on the miraculous at times. At the end of* Up and Out, *the soundtrack finishes with a long gap of silence while we watch the last scene of* Blow Up, *which is, of course, players miming a game of tennis – which is, obviously, silent.*

cm Yes, perfect – I couldn't believe it. When the imaginary ball goes above the court and falls on the ground and the music stops… I knew, when I saw that, it was just like I knew this was the right thing. There are these moments when you know you're on the right track when it just happens. You start with an idea and you don't know if the end result will be as attractive as the idea.

cw *I have this fantasy about the 'Body Mix' series, which is that you'd thrown all your record covers on the floor and somehow noticed, 'Oh, my God! Cat Stevens's hand is Sheena Easton's leg' or something. Were those combinations accidental, somehow – hybrid bodies that somehow emerged from your record collection – or did you seek those collages out?*

CM I don't remember what the spark for that was, but I used to buy
records every day and my studio was filled with records, and a lot of
times the records would come out of the covers and never go back
in because of what I do with the records – either in performance or
in using them for recordings or for art – but I never threw away the
covers because they're such interesting artefacts, so much thought
went into the design – not always, but most of the time. If you think
of how many records were published, there's so much creativity there
– so I held onto them for a long time. I think it came out of constantly
going through bins of records and seeing patterns in the way the body
is used to sell music and to see how that 12-inch square was used to
create either an identification with the buyer – so, just the face of
the artist which is almost life-sized – or this kind of cropping which
ended up in chopping up the whole body.

CW *Lots of decapitated women in particular.*

CM Yes, and it was interesting to see this kind of cut-up that already
exists, and that limitation of the square and how the body kept re-
appearing. At some point I was shopping for body parts. I would go
through the record bins and look for an arm, for a leg, for something
that would match what I already had. I did that for two years. I had
to stop after a while because it became too obsessive. I had this giant
sewing machine in my studio and I was just kind of sewing these body
parts like …

CW *… Frankenstein.*

CM Frankenstein – yes. It was also an interesting process where I
wanted these to remain record covers as opposed to just being collages, like two-dimensional collages. It wasn't only about the image,
it was really about the cover and that it was originally a sleeve that
contained the record, so that sewing them – that kind of rough stitch-
ing – allowed me to keep these in the realm of objects, not just collages
in two dimensions but almost like a three-dimensional collage.

CW *There is also their recognisability in the new context that you're
creating for them. In fact, a lot of times you ask your audience to do two
things at once – not just in* Up and Out *where the audience listens to
one thing and watches another. You are also asking your audience to
remember the place where they originally saw the film or heard the music,
to isolate that memory and then reconnect with it. Is that something
you're interested in: having people pay attention to their senses and keep*

in mind two things at once?

In Video Quartet, *for instance, part of the pleasure of seeing this collage of four screens of films – showing splices of films that we recognise – is that moment of recognition.*

CM Yes, I think so. I mean, with the record covers there is this idea that, once you recognise something, you get more involved with it and then, if you change the context, you're right away more involved because of that recognition. It kind of forces you into the work. When I started using records – mixing records on multiple turntables – I would often quote things, so people had that sense, 'Oh, I know what that is. I can recognise that', and then I would kind of make something with it: play it at the wrong speed or play it backwards or overlap it with other things that would transform it and make it unrecognisable. There's this kind of weird tension between what you recognise or think that you recognise and what's really happening. Sometimes the fact that it is recognisable is more of a distraction, I think. With the *Video Quartet*, on the first viewing, most people play that game of recognition and say, 'Oh yes, I know. What was that? What was this?'; it takes a few viewings for them to allow themselves to just kind of let go and enjoy it for what it is instead of for what it triggers in your memory. But I think the triggering of memory is definitely an important aspect of my work.

In general I like to work with things that people are familiar with – so, in that sense it's not something completely abstract, but comes from everyday life. It comes from our lives, from our experience. It is the fact that it is very grounded in our daily life that, I think, allows the audience to get into it and then reach other layers of meaning.

CW *Having seen* Video Quartet *a number of times, I now watch the overall form more than the specifics of each film – until I get to the duelling banjos bit from* Deliverance. *Suddenly I can't forget the emotion of that, and I'm back to just remembering and watching the movie.*

CM They trigger these emotions that are based on memory, but also, I think, in that short fragment, that sample, there is also a kind of emotion that we understand. Of course, the music tints the mood of the image, but also we recognise an image that is dramatic over an image that is sentimental or humorous. We're quite used to how cinema is constructed so we recognise those emotions with very little information. There is a kind of musical composition going on that has these different emotions and different momentums, but there's also the visual narrative – so it is as much a sound composition as it is a visual composition.

cw *I think that is what is unique about your work. Other artists are associated with music, like Jackson Pollock with jazz and Andy Warhol with pop and so forth – but you're interested in the overlap between art and music. The images in* Video Quartet *actually produce the music. It's not an overlay of the soundtrack. The work is really about the image producing music.*

cm That is, for me, really important – that this composition is edited the way sound is edited. Video allows me to edit the image and the sound at the same time. It is not so much like film where the tradition is to overlap the soundtrack over images and rework the sound. I just grab that visual soundtrack and use it as one so the image and the sound become one in video. The challenge of making a piece like *Video Quartet* was to create a composition that would hold together visually – how the four screens would relate from one to another – and how, musically, it made sense as well. So, sometimes I would find a perfect image, but it had the wrong sound or vice versa.

cw *One thing also characteristic of your work is that it is so enjoyable. Works like* Video Quartet *or* Telephones *are perfect to show someone who is unfamiliar with contemporary art or who is resistant to contemporary art. The work is meaningful to specialists but it is also enjoyable for those who are not necessarily versed in art. Is that important to you?*

cm Yes. I think the work is accessible because a lot of it is grounded in very common things and comes out of pop culture.

cw *You seem to have more faith in your music, or you seem more daring in your music performances than in your visual art. Do you, in a way, have more faith in music specialists than in your art audience?*

cm No, I don't think so. I think what I'm doing with records now is not so cutting edge as it was 10, 20 years ago. But it's less accessible – yes. The music is more difficult – but that's questionable too. I think if someone comes into a concert and experiences the music first-hand and understands how it's fabricated from old records, they usually get into it. But sometimes listening to a recording and not understanding the process might drive people crazy – keep them away. So, in that sense, yes, it is maybe less accessible and more specialised. But, you know, that's very subjective.

I don't want to distinguish these two things as two different activities. I can take a record and make something visual as well as

97

something audible. A record is this interesting object that is very physical but can magically produce this immaterial music.

cw *Kim Gordon, in the interview in the Phaidon monograph, asked a great question. She divides your work not so much between music and art as between the laboured works like* Video Quartet, *where there is a lot of synchronising, and the works that are ephemeral like* Record without a Cover, *which is exactly that: a record without a cover. It has been subjected to all the scratching and all the destruction that an unprotected record can endure, or the* Sounds of Silence, *which is the Simon and Garfunkel single in a frame.*

cm It is a photograph.

cw *It is a photograph – yes – and so it instantly evokes a memory of the song. Is that a more accurate way of looking at the different ways in which you work – between works that are extremely labour-intensive, and those that are basically readymades?*

cm Well, every type of work requires a different process and some is more labour-intensive than others. I don't think it is the labour that makes the work good or bad – it is the result. I think it is better if you are not conscious of the labour when you look at some work.

cw *But a work like* Tape Fall, *which is a reel-to-reel just pouring down onto the floor, creates a waterfall sculptural form and its simplicity is its beauty. You can immediately tell how it was made. It is a different way of looking than in* Video Quartet, *where you enjoy it because of how well or unpredictably things go together. Is it more, perhaps, in the reception of the work that this difference becomes apparent?*

cm You try to think of what makes a work successful or not, and how much the process becomes integrated into the end result, and how that influences your perception of it. I mean, of course I love work that is simple like a haiku where there's no need to add a word or anything – it's right there. But I can enjoy a poem that is 50 pages long, that's laboured, and I don't think one is superior to the other.

I think there are times when one has that kind of drive and energy as a creator to get started on a project like *Video Quartet*, which took me a year. After it was done I thought, 'I'm never going to touch a video again.' It's too much effort and too much work. It is unhealthy to sit there at the computer day in and out – I mean, it's just insane. But in the end you forget about all that and then, a few years later, you find that strength in yourself to go back and get started on a similarly humongous project. The simple work that only requires a little sketch, on the other hand, may appear simple, but it might take many years for it to kind of click.

In the same way I enjoy playing music because it is very much about the instant – improvisation is great because you don't know where the hell you're going to go, but you just move forward. You play with other people and it just develops. That kind of instant discovery is very satisfying. Sometimes I need that, and at other times I like to be more reflective and spend time thinking about a project, and it might just be that technically it requires skills that I have to learn, or I have to get help from other people. In music I have that choice, which is great, to do something very direct and simple – simple is maybe the wrong word, but very direct – and then works that require more time and reflection.

cw *But, for example, the kind of collaborations that you do in music – do you ever work the same way in visual art? You seem mostly to remain the sole author behind your artworks – could that be a difference between them?*

cm Yes, it's different. Most people today don't necessarily work in a studio by themselves. My work is so varied that often I need the expertise of other people. The demand is quite different than in the past where artists tended to work more by themselves. I think making art today is a very collaborative effort.

In music it is more direct. You play with other people, but you also have the technical aspect which requires engineers and a certain know-how. I'm not always interested in the technology. I mean, I edit video, but I know nothing about computers. I hate computers. I wake up and I turn on my computer. I can't get away from it.

cw *You might resist this, but I find a fair amount of nostalgia in your work, for instance in the Christmas music – the kind of music we heard as children – and all the Hollywood films. Also the kinds of instruments you choose – for instance accordions, which always scream '1950s' to me. There is nostalgia not only in the images and the graphics, but also in the art-historical precedents – Fluxus and Duchamp – and a certain approach to making art which is experimental, like the early Avant Gardes. Do you look backwards that way?*

cm When you're dealing with readymades – with found objects – yes, things become objects of the past very quickly. I mean, the record is an obsolete medium now. When I made these things it was the medium of the time and most recordings were on vinyl – so people had a different relationship to those objects. Now they look more nostalgic than they did then and maybe some people have absolutely no connection to these objects. Give it another generation and nobody will know what these things are.

Nostalgia is a little bit on the other end of what's contemporary and fashionable. It has that same kind of lightness and uncertainty about itself. There are a lot of artists who deal with things of the moment – very fashionable, very in, very cool – and you don't know what's going to happen with that. When you deal with pop material – pop culture – you don't know what the use-value of the object will be in five months, five years, ten years down the line. But nostalgia is not a bad thing. Everybody thinks that it is a slightly negative-sounding word – 'nostalgia' – but we're all suckers for nostalgia. It is reassuring and that maybe is why I use these things – like the accordion. Now it is kind of more hip.

CW *There is a gradual dematerialisation in your work – from big gramophones and big horns to albums and CDs. Your work chronicles that process, whereby the reproduction of music has lost its material presence. I still miss looking through big 12-inch cover images of music to inspire me. Is the iPod workable for you? Can digital media function in your work?*

CM I think so, but it's maybe too new for me to have enough distance to be critical of it. I'm still trying to figure out what it is. DJing came about at a time when it was just on the cusp of records becoming obsolete. Looking back DJing kept that medium alive longer than was necessary.

If you look at art history, there are these moments when something has been around long enough that you can actually get at it critically because there's enough distance from it and you're not just sucked into it because of the novelty of it.

CW *But it is also looking at the rituals of listening to music and how that changes.*

CM Yes, it's really interesting. It is a cultural revolution – computers and the fact that music is being consumed differently through these objects – records, tapes, cassettes – and now you're just plugging your iPod into the computer and downloading data. It has again become this immaterial thing that it was before. It is a interesting moment where suddenly the music industry has lost grasp of this thing that they could sell through recordings – how music became an object that can be traded. I think that is happening more and more for all media – not just for sound but for images as well – and maybe we'll feel more comfortable with having fewer things.

cw *Do you ever work with an iPod?*

cm I don't have an iPod.

cw *You don't have an iPod?*

cm Yes, it's confession time. I'm not a huge consumer of music – strangely. People think that I just have this incredible knowledge of music and film, but I know nothing. Like everybody else I just turn the radio on. It is just that this stuff is around and you can't escape it, of course. A lot of my musician friends constantly listen to music. I moved to London and still don't have an iPod. I have a radio.

cw *I just assumed that you were super-specialised, and seriously up to date with music ...*

cm No, no – I'm not. I think that also, maybe, allows me more freedom.

cw *I find in your work that there's a certain romantic longing for a particular America: the open road, as with* Guitar Drag; *or a certain old Hollywood film; and certain vintage rock 'n' roll record images. You seem to me more influenced by New York punk than British punk, for instance. I know that you are not completely American but not completely European either.*

cm It is hard to escape the media barrage from the us and the kind of romantic image that you described is everybody's kind of idea of America.

cw *Does American image- and music-making work better for you?*

cm Well, you know, I don't feel necessarily very American. Like you said, I grew up in Switzerland, I lived in Europe and in the us, and now I'm back in Europe. I go back and forth. I'm confused. I don't really speak French any more, or English very well. It is this weird thing which I resisted for many years because I felt a grounding was very important but, in fact, the older I get, the more I realise that it is so unimportant and that motion – movement – and having that incredible chance as an artist to constantly be moving and confronting a lot of different cultural environments is really positive. Yes, *Guitar Drag* has a very American quality to it, but you could argue that the electric guitar is an American invention and that this kind of road movie aesthetic is also very much an American thing, but it's such a cliché. It is also universal – who doesn't know about rock musicians destroying their instruments? It's become another kind of cliché and I think the piece works more on those kind of clichés than traditions.

I think it is interesting to be in this kind of in-between position culturally. I think it is a huge advantage. It's partly to do with distance – if you're too close to something, you can't be critical of it. I try to think of it as something positive.

So now I have to reinvent myself here in London and, like I was saying, I spent all this time in New York trying to pass for an American and now I'm here and I open my mouth and I'm a foreigner. It is an interesting position to be in. I think more people should be in this position then we'd be living in a better world.

cw *One subject that you look at that interests me is easy-listening music. You use the covers of easy-listening records in a interesting way. For instance in* The Road to Romance, *which is a series of record covers – all of girls holding sometimes palm trees, sometimes guitar necks, that together create this long, long collaged road. Adam Scrivener of the London-based artist group Inventory has written about easy-listening music as the 'bad conscience' of the music industry – which opportunistically put together everything that the audience was meant to like, and came up with something that nobody liked. What is it about these kinds of covers – that particular kind of kitsch – that you are looking at?*

cm Well, I think, as bad as it can be, there are a few gems. I like it as a contrast. Musically I will sometimes throw in a little bit of that kind of music or a kind of relief. It's always been interesting, this kind of idea of easy-listening because it's there – almost everywhere. Now music has changed. Now easy-listening can include a beat and it doesn't disturb people the way it did 20 years ago. This kind of background music – elevator music, or Satie's *musique d'ameublement* – you're not supposed to be too conscious of it. It is background music and bringing it to the foreground is interesting – but also, just because it's so much part of this kind of ambient noise. We don't even pay attention to it at all. In that sense it's kind of interesting.

cw *One thing that easy-listening does, often, is to dispense with the lyrics, and lyrics seem to me one part of music that is relatively little explored in your work. There is language in your work, and there are sometimes plays on words in titles, but do you look at lyrics? Are lyrics less interesting to you?*

cm I thought you were going to remark that I use very few lyrics in my music work.

cw *Yes, but also in the visual artwork.*

cm I think lyrics are a little bit like image. If you sample a tiny bit of a lyric it is usually easy to identify where it came from – maybe because of the words or the recognisable timbre of the voice – the kind of grain and quality of the voice, or something.

CW *Do you ever play the guess-the-lyric game, where you say one line of a song and everyone has to remember the song? It's a good game for a long drive.*

CM I would be terrible at that game. Whereas if you take one frame of a film, you know exactly what film it is if you've seen it once. It's a lot more recognisable – harder to disguise in a way. Being between two languages and two cultures, I don't rely on words as much as other people do, maybe. Growing up in Switzerland and speaking French I never paid much attention to lyrics in British or American pop music. I always misunderstood the words. So then I built up this kind of reflex of just listening without understanding the words, which I can't do in French because I can understand the lyrics better – and still to this day it is very much like that. I don't pay as much attention to the lyrics in English as I do in French. Maybe it is just a reflex – an old habit – I don't know.

CW *But there is language in your work, for example in titles like* White Noise *or* Screenplay.

CM I like words and I like language. It is the way we communicate – so I do use it. It's interesting, this idea of translation and how language is difficult. There are certain things you can express with language, but not everything. Music is a good example of something that is hard to translate into words. I've done pieces that deal with that – in particular *Mixed Reviews.*

I think there is one where somebody is reading a line of text on a wall. It is a composite text that I made based on descriptions of sounds found in music reviews from newspapers and magazines when the reviewer would attempt to describe the sound. Most musical reviews don't talk about the sounds in a very specific way. They kind of make reference to other sounds or use metaphors.

CW *When talking about music, Americans tend to tell you an anecdote about what happened during the recording, or where and how the song was written or something, whereas the Brits tend actually to talk about the music itself. Americans tend to tell more stories in their lyrics too – maybe because American rock 'n' roll came straight out of the blues. That's my theory, anyway.*

CM I'll have to read the British reviews.

CW *I prefer how the Brits talk about music.*

CM Well, they're more literary, maybe. But that kind of impossibility, translating something from one medium to another, is something I'm interested in. The text for *Mixed Reviews* doesn't exist as a published text. It gets installed in various exhibition spaces but, depending on which country it's exhibited in, it is translated into the local language – but it gets translated from the last installation, so it always changes. So the original text, which was that original attempt by someone or many people to describe sound, gets lost somewhere.

The only fixed version that exists is a video called *Mixed Reviews* where I had a deaf person sign it in sign language. There's a person who's born deaf describing these sounds.

CW *But is that failure a big issue in your work – the failure of music to translate into the visual, and how we use memory and other triggers to compensate for the impossibility of translating the sensations of music into visual experience?*

CM Yes, I think 'failure' is one of those bad words, but it is a good thing. Failure is like a step backwards and hopefully will help you take a couple of steps forwards. I think there is something interesting in the failure – something potentially positive.

CW *This goes back to language. So much language in music has to do with the body, like the 'jacket' of a record, and 'licks'. The body comes up over and over in your work. The guitar in* Guitar Drag *seems a kind of prosthetic body, but there's also* Prosthesis *and there's* Body Mix *and* Your Weight in Records.

CM I think the reason it is impossible to really define or translate music into something else other than music is because it is so much to do with the body, with the senses.

CW *You said somewhere that one kind of music you don't work with is dance music, which perhaps most literally involves the body. Is it perhaps about a different way of looking at the relationship between music and bodily experience, one that isn't dance?*

CM As I said, I don't make dance music in that sense. I don't have the skills, maybe, for it. I would, if I could, but I haven't tried. But I've worked with dancers throughout my career. I worked with dancers in the early 1980s and have done scores for dancers, for contemporary dance. It is not dance with a beat because that's the traditional kind of way of making music for dancing. I mean, that's the main kind of pop music that drives the sale of records – and I'm not interested in that. My work is more critical of records and of the music industry.

cw *But you can do it with a lot of humour, which is quite wonderful. You can get your point across without sounding preachy in terms of gender, for example.*

cm Humour is good because you can be pointed and still be light about it. Stand-up comedians do that all the time. It appears funny and light. It is often sharp.

This is an edited version of an interview which took place at the Starr Auditorium, Tate Modern on 24 November 2007.

Lawrence Weiner

interviewed by John Slyce

I Am Not Content

JOHN SLYCE *I thought we might begin with a line which I either remember or misremember coming from you which is, 'We are of our times as we are trying to figure out who we are.'*

LAWRENCE WEINER I thought that the basic reason for the making of art is an attempt to find out who you are, or where you are, or why you are. But as far as being from our own time, that is exactly the same thing as saying art only exists when it is made for a public and when the public interacts with it. This nonsense about art being of the 1980s, the 1970s, the 1960s, or 1950s – I entered the art world in the 1950s and now it is 2008 – are you going to tell me that there's been a hole in time that we've fallen into?

JS *The point I was trying to tease out is that we're always of our times if we engage with them.*

LW I come from a generation that entered the scene in the 1950s. If you remember the people that were supportive of me – surprisingly, and nice people like Willem de Kooning and Franz Kline – most of that group died in their 40s. Nobody really lived very long. I never thought I'd make it past 35 or 40, and I wasn't being romantic. There was a joke when I was a kid that, if you didn't show by the time you were 24, you may as well forget it because you're not going to get your 11 years.

We have to discover what the purpose of art is. It has become an industry. It has become a national football team – practically. Are there artists roaming around the world (which seems to be the necessity now in order to be able to make anything) all wearing baseball jackets or football jackets or rugby jackets that have national colours on them? This was not what it was all about to begin with and it wasn't what it was all about for me.

JS *Isn't that what you would refer to, or have referred to, as the ambience that the marketplace injects into that?*

LW The market can make your life comfortable, it can make your life uncomfortable; it cannot make your work enter into the world. So the market is not at fault.

The work that I tried to design was work that even if somebody were responsible enough to buy it before they used it, they could not tell anybody about it without them knowing exactly what it was. You could not lock it in a vault. You could not tell somebody what you have. You couldn't say, 'I have The Green Painting', because The Green Painting does not make any sense. They'd have to tell somebody what it was and that was an interesting idea to me – to make art that, even in its rejection, was being propagated. That's why I take the trouble and break my balls to make exhibitions to put the art out in the world. When somebody attacks it, they have to say what it is so you've already covered your bases.

That is really not a trick or anything, it's just – make work that's accessible to absolutely everybody and then you don't have to talk about populism. You don't have to talk about the market. You don't have to talk about those in power in a situation. You can talk about the work itself, non-metaphorically, and as what it is – an object.

JS *Because part of that proposition is already an ethical model of culture – a democratic model of culture.*

LW I don't like the words 'democratic' or 'ethical'.

JS *A participatory model of culture?*

LW It is an interactive model of culture – OK? You know bad people make good art and good people make bad art. I try to make work that cannot be used against what my basic philosophy is and, essentially, it is the reason that, when I'm in a group show, I rarely even ask who else is in it – unless a person is sexist, racist, or fascist – there's absolutely no reason to. I learned this from musicians: if the people that you're showing with are lazy and don't get it together, then you just do your job and don't show off – you'll look OK – and, if they happen to be fabulous, you'll look even better.

Seriously, it gets back to your reference to the 'practice' of an artist. That's bullshit. Artists are not practising; they're doing. When somebody asked Duke Ellington (this is the favourite quote of the woman I live with), 'How do you determine who's a musician?' his answer was, 'Somebody who practises every day.' Well, that's practice. What you see once an artist puts something out is the performance. That's not practice. (The other thing they asked Duke Ellington which is fabulous was, 'Why are the people that you're working with so loyal?' He looked at them – and this is not a joke – and said, 'I pay them.')

It is what you show and how it's used, and how it's laid out in a way that's possible for other people not to know anything about you, and still use it.

I was so touched recently. I was showing with another artist at Lisson who is a rather interesting artist – and he told me that he grew up in a city where I had a public work and that most of the people in the city had absolutely no idea who did it or even when it was done, but it has entered into their culture, and they've all developed their own individual metaphor from it. That's a win. That's fabulous for me.

JS *And that space was created because you didn't bring a metaphor?*

LW I think that if you bring a metaphor into your work and you use it as a metaphor, you're telling the other people that in order to use it they have to accept your moral structure and your values and, in fact, your faults. The great joy I get from the Whitney retrospective is that it is in my own city. As a general rule I'm showing in places where the initial language is not English and the work is translated. When people say, 'Oh, I get it!', it doesn't mean they accept it, they get it because they don't have to be somebody else in order to get it. They can be who they are and figure what that means to them. It's like graffiti.

All graffiti has a right to always be there – they say – but in fact it's not true. Graffiti has to say something. It has to say either, 'My children are hungry', or, 'The sky is blue'. Those are non-metaphorical things, and art is all about 'The sky is blue'.

We spent the past 40 years trying to integrate art into 'the public' and everybody forgot there is no public and there are no artists. Artists are the public as well. They pay taxes, they take their kids to the dentist. It is just another way that people enter into the sphere of things. It's not special.

I'm proud of being an artist. I don't like art schools, but I like art students because the greatest compliment is that they've chosen the profession that you have chosen yourself. The academy does something else to it – but that's their problem, not mine. The whole point is not to be socialised, it is to be social. I had ideals and I have aspirations, but the work itself is what it's all about. It's not about me.

JS *Are you not content?*

LW All of my friends are really rather successful. But, although I have total access – I can show any place – I'm not making a lot of money. I realise that the reason I didn't like expressionist art was that the content was the artist. I am not content – it has a double meaning in English. I am not content and, in fact, I was not content with my lot – but I wasn't angry with anybody.

JS *But useful art can come from anger.*

LW All art comes from anger. You wake up in the morning, you go into whatever working space that you're thinking of – it could be mental space too for some people though I require materials as I'm basically stuck with being a materialist – and you're discontented with the configuration that the society is presenting you with. You ain't happy with it. It doesn't satisfy you. It ain't right – and you try to present something that's going to change the configuration. If that's not anger, I don't know what is.

You take a big risk when you make art. The making of art is especially about the relationships of materials to materials, and no matter how much you pooh-pooh it (and I'm using this in a meta-phoric sense), you take the risk of losing the love of your parents – whether your parents are your culture, your country, your whatever it is – and you might just find yourself with something that doesn't fit in. Maybe that's the romantic part of being an artist. I don't think it's special for artists, but it is part of the profession.

I don't know where this all came from. We've been sitting here for ten minutes and we haven't talked about art. Not one word – not what I think constitutes art or what might constitute art. We don't get to it, do we? But that's your responsibility. Not mine.

JS *But that choice between, say, virtuosity and competency …*

LW Virtuosity is not bad. I like people to do things real well, but it is not a necessity. Every once in a while I've got it real right. Most of the time it is just pretty much workaday making art and trying desperately to maintain a conversation about the real world, and the material world, with people that I don't know in a way that's accessible to them.

JS *As a form of show and tell?*

LW More as a form of 'show' rather than 'tell'. SHOW (&) TELL was an unfortunate title. It sounded great when they were doing it – a *catalogue raisonné* of films of mine up until the 1980s – but no, it's really just 'show'. I don't have anything to tell. I'm serious. I wouldn't be continuing to make art if I knew all the answers, would I? I'd be in that position of being a guru or something and sit there and let people bring fruit to me.

JS *But it's not your job to know the answers. It's your job to question.*

LW I don't know what my job is. I make it up. I made up the fact that artists are supposed to ask questions. The role of the academy – that's art historians and art people – is to provide answers to people when they don't have answers or, at the very least, to provide solutions. I have no idea if that is right. For all I know art is about giving answers, but I don't have them OK? I'm not trying to be funny.

You'll have to understand that we're talking about a situation for the past 40 years where artists have found themselves in unknown territory – very much like mathematicians and very much like people trying to deal with the way the world is changing.

I don't assume anything when I start to work. It makes it hard to make art, but it makes it satisfying when you get something that even basically looks like art.

I don't mean to be offhand. It's just that I'm sorry you're getting me at the tail end of having made a show in my own city and being a little bit distressed that it was popular. Taxi drivers would stop and ask you questions because they'd gone with their kids to the museum and they'd seen the picture outside of me without a shirt cutting a hole in a wall. OK – maybe artists then can be role models for people if you basically take the trouble to try to have a conversation. There are people who will listen to you.

JS *And what was the nature of those taxi cab conversations?*

LW Whether you really could objectify desire. It was the piece that I did in Iceland which was for me, as a United Stateser, an extremely important point. The Declaration of Independence is the only document in the world that says that the pursuit of happiness really means something and objectifies it by calling it 'a' pursuit of happiness; then it becomes an object – it's a sculpture. It intrigued him because the guy was learning English, and he was also working 18 or 19 hours a day in order to keep his kids in school, so it was a big deal: can you really objectify desire?

And that is what art is about. It is about setting up these signposts for people to understand where they are and, at the same time, you figure it out for yourself – but it doesn't last. Times change. The world turns.

That's why I'm reluctant to talk about history. My memory, surprisingly, is good. I remember exhibitions I've seen. I remember essentially who was there and what they said – but there is no pattern. Anything that I might have done to enter into the art world in the 1960s is of no use in 2008.

JS *Can you remember the kind of experiences you had in New York – like that cab driver – that showed you …*

LW Oh, the manhole covers, that came about because, by chance, I drink in a bar – a local bar where I live – where there are a lot of people who work for the company that made the manhole covers. I think people were attracted to the fact that it was my drinking route when I was a kid. I started drinking on the Lower East Side when I was like 14 in what they called checkerboard clubs, and then I went through to Union Square and next it was Max's Kansas City – so it's basically the history of people. City people don't look up to find out where they are. They look down. You remember fire hydrants and you remember manhole covers.

Once they allow me to get work into a public sphere, it seems to function – that's all I can say – maybe because it is of some use and maybe because you don't have to know anything.

JS *I've always been taken by your work in the public sphere – largely because of the aural component that your public pieces take on outside the gallery.*

LW Do you mean the records and things?

JS *Yes, I mean the music – sound pieces like* NOTHING TO LOSE *– but I'm really talking about the way the public pieces are infused by all the sounds of the city.*

LW I did a tape for the Whitney where I remixed a radio programme for them. Instead of talking about the work, I mixed in sound works I had done. I got nice feedback from musicians and actors who I like, but I haven't heard whether it worked with the public or not.

When I go to a gallery obviously I'm looking for something that really excites me like a Barnett Newman or a Piet Mondrian – quite frankly – then I'm in seventh heaven. I'm in another world, and you hear everybody around you. That's all part of it.

I must explain that the work all comes from bringing shit into the studio, stuff like concrete. I have no idea sometimes why I'm interested in concrete. I have done manual labour, but I didn't particularly like it – but you bring in concrete, you bring in wood, and you deal with it. As a sculptor you move it around and you do whatever you do with it. You go out in the field if it's too big and you do something in the open or you go across a glacier and you try to find your relationship to ice and snow and things – but then I translate it into language and then I'll clean it up.

That's my failure, in fact. That's my little bit of expressionism. That's my way of trying to make the work as beautiful as possible because you want the work to be as attractive as possible to get somebody to take the trouble to basically say it out loud to themselves, and once they do you've got them. They really, actively, have to either reject it from their psyche and from their use, or just let it come in.

Well, isn't every artist doing a trick like that? The whole point of it is to get it into somebody's psyche and then let them choose to reject it. I mean, just because somebody doesn't want to use what I do doesn't mean they don't understand it.

I've never understood this waste of time of signage in museums explaining something to people. People are not stupid. They're thinking that if people understand it, they will like it. That ain't the point. In disliking it, it could be of its own use – but whatever it is, most people are quite capable of understanding anything that any other human being can do.

JS *Can we talk a little bit about some of those early journeys – voyages – not the bar-hopping. That's the kind of prototype of a series of voyages that you've embarked on.*

LW You mean going from place to place? That's what a guest worker does. That's what a person does when they're looking for a public or looking for employment. Also, you're interested in seeing something else.

JS *Yes. I mean, you didn't begin as an itinerant worker in the service industry that you are in now.*

LW No, I began as a person who worked to get myself through school and I maybe learned a lot from it but generally didn't enjoy it. But you mean, why did I go to San Francisco?

My god there were people in San Francisco – The City Lights

Bookshop and all of those – I thought they were just the cats' pyjamas. They were fabulous and I wanted to go there and tell them what I did because I was as egocentric as everybody else. When I got there and I told everybody what it was that I was doing, which was wanting to do these explosions in the Mill Valley, surprisingly, some of them listened. They thought it was funny but, as I don't know how to drive, they got a car and drove me there.

JS *What possessed you in 1960 to stick those charges in Mill Valley?*

LW I got it wrong – that's what's so funny. I thought each one was an individual, specific sculpture. That would possess me. I would make a thing out of removing something from something by force. It was just a matter of how much damper you put in to make what size hole you're going to get. I thought each one was a specific sculpture and until about 1965 or 1966, it didn't occur to me that it was the whole idea of blowing a hole in the ground that was interesting – far more interesting than each specific sculpture.

JS *In retrospect, Mill Valley doesn't seem as interesting as* WHAT IS SET UPON THE TABLE SITS UPON THE TABLE (STONE ON TABLE).

LW In fact, perhaps it's not. *STONE ON TABLE* was a desperate attempt of mine to enter a world that I was desperate to enter into – into a conversation as an artist without cheating. I went and stole the stone from a bridge and built the table and set it up. It was a way of engendering a conversation and that conversation seems to be continuing.

But you're looking back in retrospect. They were all part of a conversation.

JS *The aspect of it which seems right to me in retrospect is the fact that you may have taken the trouble to trim the limestone a little bit.*

LW Oh, no, no. I thought I was going to make something that was going to look like something.

JS *But you didn't.*

LW Well, in the end I didn't. But let's not give myself credit for things that are after the fact. After about three months of teaching myself how to use stonecutting tools and pushing it around the table and cutting it down, it got rather diminished. It reminds me of the Joyce Cary movie, *The Horse's Mouth*, because, by chance, I often live on a boat and I do live a reclusive life and I remember he couldn't get into his own show at the Tate. There was a sculpture in the movie that started off as an enormous block of stone but by the end was whittled down to the size of Picasso's *Glass of Absinthe*.

But I tried. Luckily it engendered a conversation with artists who I respected who would come by the studio to see what was going on or drop by the studio to smoke a joint or have a cup of coffee. Everybody in those days was reasonably broke and there was no real market – so people had a little more time on their hands. The realisation came to me that it was moving it around the table, and the placement of it on the table that meant something, and this came out of conversations with other artists.

I make exhibitions so that I can talk to people about something besides what whisky I like or who I think is pretty. We talk about something else, and that's why you make an exhibition. That's why every artist that you ever meet makes things and shows them – it is to be able to talk about that specific thing.

JS *You are often surprisingly enthusiastic about painting.*

LW I love painting. I think painting is a beautiful means of communicating with people. It's essential. It's direct. I stopped painting – and the paintings were functioning quite well – because it had reached the limits, for me. But, at the same time, people like Robert Ryman and other painters were continuing, and they were having conversations with the world that were making sense to some part of the world. I just stopped because it was the limit for me. Why shouldn't I be enthusiastic about it?

My idea about this Whitney retrospective, and all the others that I've ever done, is when a society either aids and abets you or allows you to get away with working as an artist within the society, a certain amount of work develops and it builds up. There's no signage in that show, and there's no direction of where to start or anything else, and there won't be at the show at MOCA either. As I said, people are not stupid. They can walk in and they can figure it all out and, in fact, what difference does it make?

We're confronted with a stage within art in 2008 where a large majority of the art is self-reflexive. This isn't about Expressionism. But then you stand back and you look at the 1980s or you look at the early part of the 1960s – there was an enormous economic bubble, and all this hype. Then it disappeared and we don't even remember the artists who were on the covers of magazines for three or four years – not because we rejected them, we don't remember them. They were of no use because self-reflexivity has little to do with the making of art.

JS *Isn't that what we're not content with?*

LW I don't know you. I read your articles in *Art Monthly*, but I don't know what you're not content with. I know what I'm not content with but, again, you can't read it from my work. You're not supposed to be able to read it from the work. You're supposed to be able to read from the work something that is a fact. I make this strange work that is a specific object that has no specific form – I don't know how you deal with that. I can, but it's a matter of habit. Maybe I'm used to it. I realise the difficulty for a lot of people.

When it has no specific form, how am I supposed to judge what you are discontented with? I'm just content with the fact that people don't quite realise that objects are only objects in relation to human beings; it is non-phenomenological. We're not getting into the wonderfulness of art and all of the things that make it wonderful. After a while you realise that all the stuff that we use to learn things changes your whole attitude towards things just as art is supposed to do, and when art doesn't do that it just becomes a nice object of desire.

JS *But at the same time, as Ludwig Wittgenstein's infamous proposition in* Tractatus Logico-Philosophicus *states, it is a ladder that you kick away once you've climbed up it.*

LW I don't know why you have to kick it away. You can leave it for somebody else to climb up.

JS *Yes, but you kick it away for yourself.*

LW Why don't you just leave the ladder? That is what museums are for. They're not to validate. They're to leave the ladder and let somebody else climb up.

Art is aggressive. Yes, you attack what somebody took for granted, something that was their dream – their sense of satisfaction. That's the anger. But it is for the people at the moment that you're showing it. It is not about worrying about how you're going to affect the generations to come.

My concept of a social world – of socialism – goes totally against the grain of the way it all worked out. The point is not to make a world where your children could live their lives better than you do. It is to make a world where it doesn't matter how your children live their lives. You don't know. It's supposed to be a surprise, and art is supposed to be a surprise. You're supposed to be looking for situations that, in fact, have not yet encountered the logic structures that you're putting out. Then it becomes the old in and out. They're pushing it out, and you're pushing it in. An awful lot of people call that sex.

JS *Which brings us to your films.*

LW Does that bring us to my films? I guess. My films are home movies. They're non-Straubian. They use the language of film as if it were a normal language that everybody who watches a movie knows. I don't know what it is going to be like, by the way, when you look at a film on a 1-inch × 1-inch iPod. I can't quite figure it out. I've been sitting with my camerawoman and we're trying to figure out how somebody reads subtitles when it's that small, which means it then precludes, and we're back to the old American/German/English model where there's these five people that make all the sounds in all the movies because it's too small an image.

I find a situation that is a small premise and sometimes it's like building Lego. Sometimes it is talking about the world that I live in – sexuality and avarice and things like that are all part of it – so I just build this in. I put the work within that structure to see how that is going to develop.

I'm lucky enough to have found people of my own class – meaning people who know what I do (they may not like it, maybe, but they know it). They'll play in these things – they're always called 'players', they're not actors. The objectification of the actor is a fantastic thing. It doesn't mystify anybody. Somebody is asked, 'Can you do that? Can you do a pirouette here? Can you walk across the room?' They say, 'Yes, I can. I'll do it.' You don't have to know anything about them. You don't have to identify with them. Empathy is not necessary.

JS *The films were screened at Anthology Film Archives in New York as part of the retrospective …*

LW Yes, but happily there have been in screenings in Vienna in a public theatre, and in Jerusalem and in Paris, places like that – so, they get out. I mean, I think that people are a bit perplexed but, hey, you are on an airplane and you're watching a cartoon from the 1940s. You'll be perplexed too, but you'll watch it.

This is an edited version of an interview which took place at the Starr Auditorium, Tate Modern on 2 February 2008.

Gustav Metzger

interviewed by Andrew Wilson

Waste

ANDREW WILSON *You are one of a group of artists who turned away from traditional ways of making art at the end of the 1950s, evolving new ways of making art – art that would abolish boundaries between disciplines and activities, that would be more about process or event rather than object, art that has inscribed in it a social or political function as an action. The first lines of the lecture you gave to the Architectural Association in 1965, in a sense, codified the theory of auto-destructive art that you talk about as being a coherent theory of action. What is it that made you effect these changes, not only within your work, but in the way you led your life as part of your work?*

GUSTAV METZGER That goes back to the early stages of my actual involvement with art. I felt that art could be a force for change – for social change – and, of course, that is the case. The idea of thinking about art, making art and social realities – going towards an art that would directly interact with society, and hopefully for the better, was present at the age of 18 when I moved into the idea of working in art.

AW *What made you decide to be an artist in that sense?*

GM Before that I was concerned with social change as such, and I thought I could be active in politics – possibly revolutionary politics – in order to effect social change. Around that time of involvement with politics, I was also reading the writings of Eric Gill who was an artist – a Catholic and a socialist – very concerned with society, and he had a quote which I can more or less recall: 'The artist is not a particular kind of man. Every man is a particular kind of artist.' This, of course, is a forerunner of that famous Beuys quote. So, you see, from the age of 16 or 17, I was involved not just with the possibility of politics but

117

with art and particularly with craft. I was working as a furniture-maker. I studied furniture-making and so I was close to Gill, in a sense, but also to work – to workers.

AW *Did you see yourself also, in any sense, as part of an arts and crafts tradition?*

GM Many of the arts and crafts people were, in fact, socialists or communists. So, it goes back very far. It isn't that suddenly I got involved with nuclear disarmament, for instance. It was a fairly logical step from the early phase of my life.

AW *But then the step from working with paint on canvas or board to evolving an idea of art that might be auto-destructive – that is quite a big step, isn't it?*

GM Yes, that's right, and very difficult – a painful, wrenching, experience.

AW *What led you to make that move?*

GM I think that directly relates to history. When I started thinking of being active in social change, it was during the war – when I was 16, 17, 18. It was a major experience moving me into the future and, when it came to the dropping of the atom bomb, the whole world was totally shaken up and, no doubt, I was too. That is another step, I think, towards the idea of interacting with society, hopefully for the better.

AW *Also, that does refer back to your early life as well and your move from Germany to the UK just before the war started, and the fact that your family was lost in the Holocaust.*

GM Yes, in Poland, or thereabouts. But to come back to art: when I got involved with art I was soon concentrating on avant-garde art, and with that kind of direction I almost immediately came to London at the end of 1945. Avant-garde art is the desire and the need to go beyond the existing, and so ever since starting as an artist – or after a year or so – I was feeling my way towards the point where I could break with the past and where I could build on the past and make something new. It happened at a certain point in the autumn of 1959 in London. Again, having been away for five or six years in King's Lynn, I came back, I think, with another kind of energy and an openness to change in the great metropolis.

AW *So, from 1959, you evolved this theory of auto-destructive art. You published five manifestoes that have shifting emphases within three principles underlying auto-destructive art – that it was an art that was concerned with a reaction to the nuclear threat; it was an art that was*

concerned with and reacted to an ecological and environmental threat;
and it was also an art that was an attack on the art market and on the
capitalist system as a whole. Destruction can often be thought of as nega-
tive, but auto-destructive art does not necessarily have that thrust of
meaning, does it? In a sense, it is positive.

GM That is actually the point. What I was after is the comprehension
– the bringing together of actual social and intellectual and artistic
aesthetic realities into one formula, into one whole. That was the
aim. The first three manifestoes – all published between 1959 and
1961 – concentrate on these directions. The lecture at the AA in 1965
that you referred to was a summary of the experience that I had had
and an attempt to present it in a comprehensive manner. That is an
attempt to respond to actuality. Contemporary life then and now is
extremely complex, it is full of interactions, so this was an attempt
to comprehend large chunks of the world within a theory and a
framework of ideals and practice.

Now, the problem – my problem, and it is ongoing – is that the
monuments that are at the centre of the theory were never made, and
there is no prospect of them being made, though they could be made
and would, in fact, be large. They would be in a public sphere and
they would disintegrate bit by bit in a time not more than, say, 10 or
20 years. They would then be gone. All that is a kind of shock/horror –
horror/shock – my God, what's happening? But it didn't happen and
so there is this theory that aims to change the world, but it has never
been tested except in talk and on paper.

AW *Do you feel frustrated that the monuments haven't been built so that*
they can fall apart?

GM Yes, it is a constant burden which of course one suffers from.
But also, to be realistic, you expect to work and get paid, and I had
expected to get paid like an architect – you get a percentage of the cost
– so, as an artist I haven't had the income that I could have had which
would, of course, have been extremely useful and necessary.

AW *Could you define a bit more how you understand the idea of public*
art, because you do see these as public art. They're not for individual
consumption; they serve a collective purpose.

GM Yes. That again goes back to my reading of Gill and others – that
art is for the public and the public interacts with the art without
paying, without formalities, and that is an ideal of art that goes back
thousands of years. I was in that tradition – a long tradition of making

art for the public in the public sphere.

AW *Obviously, auto-destructive art does not deliver commodities that can be traded, and so you were attacking the art market on that point, but you also wanted to use that as a microcosm.*

GM That's right. Art is not meant to be traded and bartered, and certainly not in the manner that we have become used to during the last few decades and especially now. There was an article I came across in the *International Herald Tribune* discussing a work by Jasper Johns. His paintings now start at a million and recently one was sold privately for $80m – well, I don't think that is the way art should be treated.

AW *Do you have a solution, in your own mind, to the way the market works?*

GM Yes. As you know, in the ICA catalogue *Art into Society* I proposed what is now called 'the Art Strike' and I still, after all these years – or especially after all these years in view of the present developments in the art world – believe that the turning down of the art gallery system is an essential path in the development of contemporary art. I think we are getting bored with these auction results. We are bored with picking up an art magazine which is 80% advertisement, and we are becoming more intelligent, in a sense – and so I believe the time is ripe for the disbandment of the art galleries and I would vote for that. I exclude, of course, public galleries. I'm speaking of the commercial galleries and auction houses that function through all kinds of devious machinations to artificially achieve crazy results. I think these two institutions can be attacked intellectually and historically and certainly morally, and I believe the time is ripe for artists to take power into their hands and readjust the whole system so that we do not have art galleries except, of course, if some individual is desperate to have an art gallery. We won't say, 'you mustn't', but in general we can phase them out. They can be phased out as from now – at any time – and I believe that art will flourish as a consequence. Artists will exhibit as groups and work with institutions such as this. That is my feeling now. I haven't given up this idea of tearing down the art system through the action of artists and we can certainly reconstruct and recreate the essential spirit, the essential necessities of art.

AW *By the time of The Destruction in Art Symposium in 1966, certainly from about 1965, your interests were shifting towards a concern with science and technology and what their effects might be. You were involved with organisations like The British Society for Social Responsibility in*

Science as well as The Computer Art Society. I was wondering if you could,
perhaps, describe a bit how you understood this change that your work
and your interests were undergoing at that time.

CM Yes, that is not difficult. It was on the basis of a deep experience
that I went through at the beginning of 1965 when I realised that
science and technology are not accidental. They don't come about
by chance or merely through historical accumulation. Science is
generally linked with technology – with telescopes, with machinery,
with optics – and I felt that all this activity which I sensed had to do
with destructive elements in the human being – in the individual
human being and in groups – needed to be uncovered if you are going
to get away from endlessly building armies and atomic bombs and
other weapons. So the ten years – from 1965 – were essentially about
my inner understanding and concern for such questions and, again,
that of course links with auto-destructive art. Auto-destructive art is
destructive and leads you to think about destruction.

AW *I think what also ran parallel to this period of your increased interest*
in science is what you have retrospectively described as a political phase.
I wondered what could be more political than the work you had been doing
in the early 1960s with the Committee of 100, and the way that interfaced
with your art, so what made your activities in the early 1970s, leading up
to the declaration of the years without art in 1974, more political?

CM Can I just go back to the 1960s and say something about the other
side of this quest to understand the development of science and
technology through history? There was the clear vision that we need
to transform the kind of science and technology that we had.
There are two strands: one is the attempt, in my mind, to discover
– to uncover and to research – how science and technology got to
the stage up to, say, the atom bomb with destructive energies going
through individual physicists, for example, Einstein or Niels Bohr –
physicists in particular, but also other scientists – so that they moved
in directions that will end in destruction through physics or through
biology or through chemistry and whatever in this range.

At the same time there is the vision of a science that goes the other
way, which uses nature, which engages with water and wave. There
was an article published in 1969 in *Studio International* in two parts,
'Automata in History', and the first part ended along the lines that we
can move into the technology of paradise – living as primitive people
do, surrounded by nature, using nature and the sun to survive.

I think that is the point which later on led me to write in 1992 the essay 'nature demised resurrects as environment' which was published in 1996 in the book in which you are a contributor, *damaged nature, auto-destructive art.*

AW *Do you feel that you need to engage with those ideas even more urgently now than then?*

CM Yes, yes, of course. The problems are there – but we are in a new situation. The world has never been so open to fundamental change as now, which is, of course, very positive.

AW *One way in which you have talked about auto-destructive art is that you have described it as a 'facing-up to history', whether it is your own history or the history we find ourselves living through. When you came back to London in the mid 1990s you evolved this idea of a strand of work that you termed 'historic photographs', in which you covered the photographic image and forced the viewer into much closer bodily contact with it. What led you to make these works?*

CM There is certainly a clear cutting-off point and starting point which was an image that was on the front pages of the world press in 1990, of the so-called 'Massacre on the Mount' where Israeli police killed 20 or more Palestinians on the site of the Al-Aqsa Mosque. This was an outrage that swept through the world. There was one image of two Israeli soldiers guarding 20 Palestinians who were lying on the ground as if they were dead. They were in fact not dead. This image shook me and I came up with the idea of 'Historic Photographs' – that is to say that the image is so horrific that you can't face it.

This was the first idea for the 'Historic Photographs' and it took five years before the first historic photographs were made with work for an exhibition at workfortheeyetodo, coinciding with the publication of *damaged nature* where the first two historic photographs were exhibited in its small book space. The first photographs that were produced were of the boy in the Warsaw ghetto – a child coming out of the cellars with his hands up. So this photo was enlarged and, in front of the photograph, there are wooden shutters stacked on top of each other so that you do not see the photograph at all. The second photograph that was made was of Adolf Hitler addressing the Reichstag in July 1940 after the fall of France. Again, this was totally covered. You couldn't see the photograph.

From these beginnings 12 historic photographs have been made. It is a principle, but again, there is a theory – an extensive theory –

behind this development and it is ongoing. Not all the historic photographs are completely sealed off from sight – some you can go into. Then there is a tactile element. Some historic photos can be touched – have to touch you physically.

AW *You talked about the horror of the image and the need to cover it over, but also the fact that some of these images are so well known we almost can't see them any more and so you have to cover them over to, as it were, think about them and remember them. You know the image but you don't see it any more.*

CM Yes. That is one strand of the principle. The other is physical contact, not just eye contact. It is a way of shaking up existing rigidities in relation to art. Again, this is the point of avant-garde art, to change the relationships between the viewers, the public and the work of art to be looked at.

AW *Thinking in terms of this idea of facing up to history – the subject matter of the historic photographs ranges from recent history and past history to reflections on your own personal history. There is one image in particular, of Twyford Down, which signals this idea of a renewed interest and importance for you of dealing with the way in which the ecology and the environment have been dangerously degraded. From this perspective, the 'Historic Photographs' are also an attack on capitalism and capitalist growth. Does this attention to ecology restate the tenets of auto-destructive art?*

CM Auto-destructive art, certainly, is an attack on the economic political system known generally as capitalism and I was anti-capitalist from the age of 17 or 18 onwards. We have heard the word 'waste' repeated here today more than once and it is a major concern of mine in the past years and, I think, for all of us. It is estimated that one-third of food in this country is actually wasted one way or another. On personal experience, in wartime a paper cup would be preserved because you would need it, whereas now it will go straight into the waste bin.

Waste is a principle of capitalism. Capitalism couldn't exist without waste. The wealth we've got now in western societies is based on waste – on the deliberate production of waste – so that the factories can endlessly be in production and so that money can be made and circulated. Waste is the most important word in the English language, I suggest, and it all has to do with a system that deliberately attacks and denigrates and destroys and subverts not just material values, but also moral, intellectual, religious and aesthetic values.

That is how I see the art world. It is a waste to sell something for £20m when it's just a bit of canvas and it is wasteful to spend time and energy on making that £20m and the divisions that are involved – the artificial, fake and often unjust divisions between the so-called successful artists and those who are not successful in that way. That's why I feel that we are at the historical point when artists and the art world can take over the art world and eliminate this 'waste'.

If we had co-operatives where we build exhibitions, everybody – most people, at least – would have a chance to show what they can do. I think we are all clever enough now. In society we are at a point where almost everybody has enough to live on and often even to spare for the activities that would be required in stepping from a gallery system to a non-gallery system.

AW *Your idea of reduced art flights fits into this view of waste that you have described.*

CM Recently we've had endless reports and letters on flights – on the dangers of aircraft emissions and the noise that aircraft make. It was at the *Skulptur Projekte Münster 07* and the curator of my exhibition in the Kunstverein, Carina Plath, agreed that we could hand out a leaflet which said, 'Reduce art flights', and we had a German text on the destruction of Münster. This poster was lying freely at the entrance to my exhibition, and 5,000 colour leaflets were taken over by a group of artists who were showing in Turin.

'Reduce Art Flights' was a concept that would appeal – that does appeal – to the art world to fly less from one place to another (a biennale or art fair) and send goods and works of art less by plane. Of course, I support this. I think it is a perfectly valid form of development that I think will take off in other places. 'Reduce Art Flights' will be an activity that moves from place to place for the next few years, I would expect.

AW *This was suggested to you, in a sense, by the Basel Art Fair in 2006 which proposed that anybody who went to the Basel Art Fair and then on to Miami Basel, could get half-price flights.*

CM Yes.

AW *You don't have a telephone, a mobile phone, or a computer. What you are suggesting here is more about slowness than speed and yet, as an artist, I remember you talking about visiting the Tate Gallery in 1946 with David Bomberg and saying what you wanted was an art expression that was to do with speed. Is your desire for speed, and your suggestion to go not back to nature, but to cast off the concerns of a modernised, industrialised world, a contradiction in your mind or not?*

CM If it is a contradiction, I won't mind because I believe contradictions and interchanges and complexification are all very, very important. So that's one side, but the other is, I do object to the modern world which, again, is totally integrated with and totally dependent on waste, on unnecessary consumption, on showing off – and on and on and on.

So many of us now are behaving in a totally artificial manner – showing off bodies, showing off dresses, showing off handbags, showing off shoes, showing off wealth, money and power – and we are over using technology. I suggest that 99.98% of mobile phone calls are unnecessary. It is a logical statement because we can prove that 30 years ago we were as happy as now and as sufficient as now. That's the other point. We can prove now, again and again, that what we've got is wrong. What we've got is surplus. What we've got is dangerous because the figures are there – the statistics are there. We can call them up on our technology and prove what we are doing is wrong, wrong, wrong, wrong.

This is an edited version of an interview which took place at the Starr Auditorium, Tate Modern on 29 March 2010.

Glenn Ligon

interviewed by Patricia Bickers

A Body of Work

PATRICIA BICKERS *I first encountered your work in this country in 'Double-take' which was at the Hayward Gallery in 1992 where you showed a work from the 'Dream Book' series begun in 1988. Soon after that you were included in 'Mirage' at the ICA, where you showed one of my favourite works,* Rumble Young Man Rumble *of 1995.*

The 1980s, when your work emerged, was a period in which appropriation was the dominant mode, a quintessentially postmodern critique of issues such as authenticity, originality and authorship. But I am not alone in thinking that in your work, although you use appropriation and quotation, it is not precisely a critique – although of course it contains critique – but it is more, as Wayne Baerwaldt put it rather elegantly, about 'the presence of the past in the present'. It struck me at the time how valuable it was that you brought history – and this is not just because I am an art historian by trade – back into the mix, into the present, but because this was at a time when Francis Fukuyama famously declared that history had ended. Did you feel a mission almost to reinstate history, or the importance of histories?

GLENN LIGON Well, in the beginning my text work was about, as Wayne said in the quote, the idea of bringing the past to the present. I think, looking at what one would call appropriation artists and thinking about their work, that in some ways you have to have a text known before you can deconstruct it, so my approach to texts in the early paintings was really about making them known. I remember a formative moment: I was in the Whitney Museum Independent Study Program, which is a postgrad programme for young artists, and I was sharing a studio with someone who was working with photographs by

Charcot and was very deeply into psychoanalytic theory and making work that was beyond my comprehension. My studio mate asked me what I was working on and I said 'Well I'm not really working on anything because I've got too much reading to do, but as a palate cleanser I have been reading James Baldwin's essays', and she said 'Who's that?' and I thought 'Ah! Here's the problem'. It was not so much that she had never read Baldwin – a lot of people haven't read Baldwin – but the fact that the name was totally unfamiliar to her, a name which I thought, in an American context, was canonical since from the early 1950s he had been writing very cogently about race relations and American identity. So the fact that that name was totally unknown to my studio mate prompted me to rethink my painting practice.

I'm fairly literal, as opposed to literary. When I started using text for paintings, I was looking at things by Jasper Johns, Robert Rauschenberg, Cy Twombly, people who had some kind of text in their work, and I thought, 'How do I get these things that I'm reading – Baldwin essays, or Zora Neale Hurston, Walt Whitman or Jean Genet – how do I get ideas from those texts into the work?' And I thought, 'well I'll just put them in there.'

The work touched on those questions of authorship, too, because the early painting always had an address to the viewer: 'I feel most coloured...', 'I am an invisible man...', so there was this presumption by the viewer that the text was being written by the person who made the painting, even though it was quotation.

PB *You ceded authorship, in a sense, since the 'I' wasn't you. That was a very generous strategy. You were reaching out, nevertheless you were doing it in a form that was regarded, for instance by Darby English, as 'difficult'. It seems that from the first you decided to complicate, or rather recomplicate, the issues.*

CL We have talked before about first and second generation feminism or gender studies which largely focused on the work of recuperation – just as you recuperated James Baldwin who should have been known but wasn't. But although there is still work to do there, perhaps because we are from the third or, in your case, fourth generation, it was possible to be more critical, more ambivalent towards the sources that you used. Would you agree that that was a shift?

Well, yes. Certainly other people had been inspired by someone like Baldwin and made work in relationship to his essays and his writings – maybe not directly text-based in the way that I did – but it seemed like I was at a different moment. When I started making text-based work I was looking at artists like Barbara Kruger, Jenny Holzer and thinking about the strategies that they employ in their work, but at the same time I was very invested in painting. We are talking about mid to late 1980s, so in New York there was a distance from painting, there was a lot of painting going on, but the text work that I was looking at was in a way a critique of painting, a critique of the aura of originality.

All of these things influenced the way I used quotation and is why the paintings – the early paintings – have a systematic approach: a sentence repeated over and over again – that is from Sol LeWitt. I thought from very early on that it was important to me to be in dialogue with the things that were happening around me, as well as in dialogue with work that had come before.

PB *So that is another layer of history. But repetition doesn't just extend to the use of repeated phrases that are overlaid over and over again, but also, as Judd said, there need not be a linear history, you can return to works, you don't have to constantly go on to something different. For instance, I am thinking of the series of works referencing the Million Man March that you have returned to periodically. That is a way of denying a linear trajectory and of offering both to yourself and to the viewer the opportunity to rethink your situation vis-à-vis a work that you made earlier or a position that you held earlier.*

CL I am always interested in having a practice that is a bit more than simply a painting practice, which is maybe not good for my career but it is good for my mental health. Because I think that at a certain point painting can get boring and you need to move on to other things but I am still deeply interested in painting. So these other projects were initially a way to get myself away from the painting process and to try other things. But I think that now they are more integrated and investigations that happen in a painting, or a neon, or a video, are related – they are different because of the materials but they are related. If I had a more linear practice – I am a painter and this is what I do – then maybe some of these investigations could have been 'finished' earlier. But it is just as interesting for me to still be using oil stick and stencils after all these years and to find something new in that.

PB *The use of the stencil is an obvious distancing device and in that sense people have linked it with Minimalism, in that it is a pre-existing form. But although stencilling is very impersonal, the layered use of it – the blurring and the smudging – makes it very painterly and somehow very personal. So you have squared the circle: you have made painting that is text and you have made painting that is apparently distanced but that becomes very personal and very textual and sensuous. What led you to add the glittering coal dust to the mix?*

CL It was in thinking about Baldwin again. He is a key figure in this work. Baldwin writes like a preacher. In fact he was a boy preacher. An essay that I have used a lot is titled 'Stranger in the Village', and it documents his time spent in Switzerland in the mid 1950s. He is trying to deal with a lot of stuff in that essay: his relationship to America, the fact of being a stranger in Europe, his relationship to colonialism and European history, the fear and fascination that a stranger in any context creates; all of that is within a ten-page essay. So the gravity and weight and panoramic nature of that work inspired me – again literally – to think about how to use the text from that essay in a way that reflected that gravity and weight. And the addition of the coal dust seemed to me to do that because it literally bulked up the text. Coal dust is a very beautiful material but it is a waste product.

PB *You say quite often that you are literal minded and that metaphor comes subsequently – and the metaphors do flood in; to the viewer the metaphorical layering of the work is so rich. One of my favourite works is one that I haven't actually seen in the flesh – and I say this as someone who normally insists on the importance of seeing work – but such is the conceptual strength of the work that it is still possible to talk about it. The work I am referring to is the diptych* Untitled *and* Untitled (Contact) *of 2002 comprising one very heavily worked oil stick and stencil painting that was pressed against a second, naked white canvas, leaving an impression of the text in reverse on the surface. Though there is no single reading, this sticky contact, which is incredibly sensuous, is metaphorical: it is obviously sexual and represents the literal intermixing of black and white.*

CL I started using black text on white canvases because that's the way it appears in books. It has taken on this racialised meaning but for me it was simply how text appears. Those two paintings in particular use Baldwin's essay, 'Stranger in the Village', and were part of a cycle of paintings that were done for Documenta 11 in 2002. Those paintings were interesting for me because they were trying to do what the essay was doing. What the essay was talking about was the contact between different things, so I took one canvas and pressed it against another painting. But of course it makes a mirror image because the text was backwards. That was interesting to me because a lot of what Baldwin talks about in that essay is the question of mirroring: how he sees the villagers, how they look at him and how he uses them as a mirror to see himself. That is what that painting was about. Its meaning comes from experimenting and figuring out what things mean.

Maybe why I cycle back to things is because I am slow and I need time to figure things out. Sometimes three or four years later I think 'Oh, that's what that was about' and it sparks an interest in continuing my investigation.

PB *Sometimes you return to things when times have changed. For instance it was very interesting that you started to make the Richard Pryor joke paintings – Pryor's live shows really skated on the edge, they were so daring, it was like a tight-rope walk. You made a series of paintings starting in 1994 of Richard Pryor jokes and then you said in an interview that you backed off from them, that you were scared. Can you say more about that? It is rather different from returning to interrogate an earlier work.*

CL I think the thing for me about those paintings is that if anyone knows Richard Pryor's routines, they are very tough in lots of ways: there are critiques of American society, there are critiques of sexuality, and the jokes are very harsh. The initial series was shown at the Whitney in an exhibition called 'Black Male' in 1994, which was an exhibition about masculinity and contemporary art. A friend who was a docent at the Whitney was giving tours of that show. The paintings are rather small and a lot of them have the word 'nigger' in them and he didn't feel comfortable reading these jokes aloud. But because the paintings were so small and the groups on the tours were so large, people from the back of the group kept saying 'Read the joke', because they were too far away to read it themselves. The docent ignored them and kept talking about issues of narration, about text in art and things like that, but from the back it kept coming: 'Read the joke', 'Read the joke'. Finally someone pushed their way to the front, pushed him aside and read the joke, and all hell broke loose. Someone said 'This was supposed to be a show about the representation of black men in contemporary art and here are these nasty Richard Pryor jokes.' 'Don't you like Richard Pryor?' 'I love Richard Pryor – at home, on my stereo, not on the walls of the Whitney Museum.'

What was interesting for me about that story – and maybe this is a side thing, in some ways it had nothing to do with the paintings, but it maybe has something to do with my reticence about the series – is that that half-hour debate where they pushed the docent aside happened because of the paintings. It happened because of the issues that were brought up in those paintings. It was almost too much for me. So I backed away from them. But when I was listening to Pryor again years later, I thought, there are very interesting critiques of masculinity in these jokes, there are incredible political critiques, and it seemed very timely. Even though those jokes were from mainly the mid 1970s, they seemed right now. If Pryor can make a joke about having gay sex in the mid 1970s, when the dominant representations of black masculinity were *Shaft* and *Superfly* – images of hypermasculinity – I thought it would be interesting to return to that in these times, when rap and hip hop have also returned to these modes of representation.

PB *It was so interesting that the person that pushed the docent aside didn't mind Richard Pryor at home but objected to him in a public sphere. In a way there is an analogy here with a work you made back in 1993, To Disembark, which is about Henry 'Box' Brown who literally boxed himself in a crate – or had himself boxed in a crate – and had himself posted to freedom in Philadelphia, an amazingly courageous thing to do. You made a series of these boxes, built to the same dimensions, as part of an installation. Some observers have said that this was a way of smuggling yourself, the black artist, into the museum. Do you agree with that interpretation?*

CL I think that work came out of the paintings in some ways because I was interested in voice, and one of the things that I was curious about when I heard this story about a slave in a tobacco factory who mailed himself – or was mailed – in a crate to an anti-slavery society in 1849, was that one of the things that would have given him away when he was in this crate on his 25-hour journey would have been voice. So this made me think about what it means to speak and what it means not to speak. It dovetailed with the text work that I was doing. Also, my work is autobiography, but autobiography filtered through other people's texts. Using Henry 'Box' Brown's narrative to generate my piece was a way of relating his story to my story, not to say that they are the same but to tease out the connections between them.

I was less concerned about the critique of the museum, in the way that someone like Fred Wilson has used material like that as a way to critique the unspoken narratives of the museum. It was more about the question of voice and where does voice appear and disappear.

PB *I'd like to go back to those 'Dream Book' paintings in the 'Doubletake' show. People might not know – and I certainly didn't until I saw the show – that dream books were used in the numbers game, that interpretations of dreams – word association, or what was associated with that type of dream – each had a three digit number and this was used in the numbers game which was a kind of illegal lottery. So black people in particular were basically betting on their dreams. This is very much a Native American culture, isn't it?*

CL It's not so different from people betting on the lottery using their kids' ages and their house numbers and things like that. But what interested me is that these dream books implied a whole set of beliefs. Also there is a secret autobiographical element in there because my father was a numbers runner; he worked for General Motors during the day but worked in a numbers parlour on the side.

PB *There was one work from the series in particular which was about voice:* Speechless, No 348, *'To dream that you are speech is a sign of adversity and shame. To regain your voice denotes that others will no longer speak for you.' This idea of being forcibly silenced, of the suppressed voice, you have returned to many times. You don't always enable the voice yourself, on the contrary sometimes you deliberately obscure the words, silencing the voice. But then perhaps you have the right to do that?*

CL I think the text in my work is often difficult to read because the ideas in the text are difficult. And so that struggle to read is a parallel to what those texts are about. The difficulty of, say, Baldwin trying to decipher his place in the world. It's hard to make that explicit, it's hard to explain that. So I think the difficulty of the texts is about that. Text demands to be read, so that frustration and the failure of language are interesting. To stage that – and to make the viewer frustrated that there is not an easy access to any explanation of culture or identity – is the work.

PB *You said earlier that the work was autobiographical in a way but that you refused the 'I'. You said in an interview that you resisted solipsism, that you don't want to refer only to yourself, so other people's narratives are overlaid with your own. This is very much the case in your work* Annotations *on the Dia website. When each photo is clicked on, suppressed images emerge – scrawls on the back of images, little*

autobiographical passages, singing, other, hidden, images, pornographic
and erotic ones – there is this idea that the photo album is where we
understand ourselves –

ᴄʟ – Yes, it is where the family represents itself to itself. In that
representation I am always interested in the things that cannot be
said in the photograph. Things that may be known if you are in the
family, things like 'oh that's uncle so-and-so's "friend"', it is not
spoken about but it is there. So part of that project is about unveiling
those things by having the footnotes. Clicking on the photograph
takes you to a text or another image, images that don't necessarily
explain what you are seeing but give you some sense of background
and context. The project is half found photographs and half family
photographs so there are differing levels of fiction in there.

ᴘʙ *Also people can construct their own narratives because we all have*
photographs like that.

ᴄʟ I was also interested in it formally because – I don't know if
everyone's family albums are like this – mine are not chronological.
Sometimes my parents put in a photo because it was a certain size
and it fitted in a space and the time between adjacent photos may be
20 years. I was really interested in how that worked as well, clicking on
the photo would take you somewhere else, but also on the page itself
there were these jumps in time.

ᴘʙ *Could we go back to when you emerged in the 1980s. It was very*
interesting that you felt an immediate connection with some of the things
that were happening over here – I am thinking in particular that you
met Isaac Julien at 'Doubletake'. I taught Isaac at St Martins, as it then
was – though actually I rather think that I was a student of Isaac's – and
the first work of his that I saw was his student film Young Soul Rebels,
which knocked us all sideways. Soon after that in 1989 came Looking
for Langston *which, as Darby English points out, blurs the past and*
the present, using actual footage combined with film of actors playing
Langston and there is this dream-like melding of history with the present.
You have acknowledged the influence of some advances in cultural studies
in this country, people like Stuart Hall from the Open University, which
was something of a refuge for people who had missed out on education
but also for academics like Hall who were challenging the way we thought
about postcolonialism in this country. Meanwhile slavery and slave
narratives were being addressed in the ᴜs. *There seemed to be a moment*
when these things met.

GL   When I came to visit London I always thought that these debates were way further along here than in the US. That there was a sophistication to the debates about the nature of images and how one deals with historical material, debates that had just really gotten started in the United States or, if it was present in the United States it felt like it was present in very constricted ways. A work like *Looking for Langston* was really important to me and I spent a lot of time thinking about how that film was constructed, how one uses the archive, how one might bring the archive to the present, how you fill in gaps in things that cannot be represented. Langston Hughes's estate would not co-operate with the making of the film, so many things had to be filled in, imagined and that was really interesting.

My interest in text came about in part as a result of reading Stuart Hall and debates about the body, how the body – particularly black bodies – had been represented. It was also about using text as a way to refer to those debates: there is a body reference in the paintings because one has the word 'I' in it, it's a text on a door-sized panel and the panel is shaped to the body, but it sidesteps figuration. However, I am not strict about that, so fairly soon after that I was doing a body of work which was from images of a march in Washington DC – the Million Man March. The images were of a moment in the march when there was a pledge by black men to the black family. I don't think I have ever adhered to a strict party line in terms of the way my work had to appear.

PB   *Absolutely, that's what makes you part of the next generation. You literally deconstructed Louis Farrakhan's Million Man March: referring to the Day of Absence, when women were told to stay at home and watch the march on television, you said that that already rendered the event into an image; you then silkscreened the image, reworking it over and over again until eventually the image of solidarity literally breaks down.*

GL   All of the images in that work were from the newspapers. When newspaper images are blown up to a scale of say 7 × 10 feet, all the information starts to drop out. The images got darker and darker and less distinct and, as they became less distinct, they became less about a march on Washington and more a sea of hands – they became decontextualised and I thought actually this process of disappearing lets other things appear.

PB   *You are, as you say, at heart a painter: you think like a painter, and your work came out of a love affair with Abstract Expressionism and with*

De Kooning in particular. Jackson Pollock denied the accident in his work, but you do not: you start something aiming for one thing and end up with something else. Paradoxically that takes a lot of control.

CL Well you need to recognise when you have had a good accident, one that is productive. We were talking earlier about my use of stencils and when I first started making stencil paintings using oil sticks I was trying to not have the letters smudge. I thought that I could use oil paint and plastic letter stencils and produce perfect letters but you can't. It took me six months to work out that the smudged letters were the most interesting thing about the paintings.

In any body of work that I have worked on there is always this moment when something goes really wrong that turns into something much more interesting than what I had intended. The first video project started as a sound project – I did a tape recording of me talking to a therapist about losing a painting. Then I realised that it was a video project so we did a couple more sessions – it cost a lot of money, therapists don't charge their normal rates when they are on camera – where it was videotaped. But I had this great first session on audiotape and I thought 'I have fucked this whole thing up'. But then I thought it's kind of interesting because if anyone has ever been to therapy you know it is sort of discontinuous, it doesn't make sense and there is a disconnect between what is being talked about and what is meant. And there is a further disconnect because a therapist appearing on camera is performing for the camera as well as trying to do a session for you. And so the accident became incorporated into the piece and it was a richer piece because of that.

PB *Also you were performing, because it is your voice, you were supposedly the analysand, the subject. It's your voice, but you are performing your-self, so it is not really you. Or is it? I understand that for the first half of the interview you really didn't know the whereabouts of the painting in question, which was a painting of Malcolm X derived from a school colouring book aimed at African American children to raise their under-standing of their heritage. You reused the works that resulted in a project at the Walker Art Gallery in Minneapolis: the children coloured in these pictures with no idea that it might be dodgy to put lipstick and eyeshadow on Malcolm X's face. And in fact one child thought it might be you because he had no idea who Malcolm X was. So again there was a job of recuperation to be done there, like there was in the beginning with James Baldwin. So one is always having to work at this according to different*

135

levels of awareness. In the video you had lost the painting and then you hadn't lost it.

CL That became a discussion in the video: 'I am ruining the art by telling you that I found this painting because the whole premise of this video is talking to you about this lost painting.' And you can't say that to a therapist and not talk about it. So it became very circular and then I left her.

PB *Why is it called the* The Orange and Blue feelings?

CL There is a long story in there about the first moment when I thought maybe I was an artist. The story is that I was eight or nine years old and we were in art class making papier mâché boats. I was obsessed by *A Night to Remember*, a movie about the sinking of the Titanic which used to come on at major holidays in the United States. I loved that movie and I was obsessed by the Titanic so I made an ocean liner with four smoke stacks. The teacher was going around the room looking at our boats and she said this is great, it is really beautiful, now you should paint it. So I painted the hull blue and the deck and the smoke stacks orange. The teacher came back and she said, 'Oh my god, those are such ugly colours why don't you paint it something beautiful.' And I painted the boat black.

PB *Your first political act.*

CL My first political act. Actually orange and blue were a good colour combination. That was the first moment when I thought: I have ideas. And she's not right and I know she's not right.

This is an edited version of an interview which took place at the Starr Auditorium, Tate Modern on 24 April 2008. Published Issue 317, June 2008.

Cornelia Parker

interviewed by Lisa Le Feuvre

Stuff

LISA LE FEUVRE *Cornelia, you have done so many interviews and conversations – there are countless exchanges in which you talk through many varied aspects of your works. It seems to me you attach great importance not just to the experience of what we see, but also to the 'how' of it. So I wanted to ask you about the importance of the conversations that happen around your work – to me this seems especially apparent with* Chomskian Abstract *which you showed at the Whitechapel Gallery in 2008.*

CORNELIA PARKER Conversations are important to me. In 1989 I did a three-month Rome scholarship, and I realised for the first time that my work is quite aural, that the way I go about making work is very much to do with conversations – not with people from the art world necessarily, but with all kinds of people who I might collaborate with. When I was in Italy, making work became really hard for me because I didn't speak Italian. I always had to go to somebody else to interpret, a lot got lost in the translation. What you don't see when you witness my work is the conversations. The work is almost like a waste product as a result of those interactions or journeys I've had.

LLF *I like the way you talk about a product from a conversation. It seems to me that so many of your works have a generosity of spirit: rather than being full stops they are commas – it is as if they are initiating another conversation. Yours is almost a continuous practice: there is a continuous temporality to each artwork.*

CP When I came up with a title for my exhibition at the Ikon, I called it 'Never Endings' – plural, because I just felt that there was all this unfinished business going on, that one thing leads to another and you make a work which is not necessarily a full stop, but, as you say, a comma. I am always thinking about the next thing but sometimes, having an exhibition is like stopping and pausing for breath. There are these little concretions that go on, which is the work. There are so many different threads that lead off to other places. I work in so many and various mediums because I'm endlessly curious about stuff.

LLF *What is interesting for me about* Chomskian Abstract *is the way the film is constructed. I think it is a conversation taking place rather than an interview because, in an interview, one assumes that someone is asking and someone else is answering. Here you present a conversation where we don't know what you are saying. I kept on thinking when I first saw that work that it was as if you are inhabiting the spaces between listening and telling – this condition runs throughout your practice. Could you tell us a little bit about how you came to develop the conversation with Chomsky? I understand you invited him first to go over to the Sharjah Biennale as your contribution.*

CP Yes. The theme of the Biennale was 'Still life: art, the environment, and the politics of change'.

LLF *That is a paradox.*

CP Yes, especially as the Biennale is located in a country which has a huge fossil fuel economy. I was very conflicted about being part of this Biennale and about what I could possibly do to engage with that issue. I showed a couple of existing works – like my burnt forest piece *Heart of Darkness* – and then I wanted to do something new, more head-on, something more confrontational, I suppose, because I was feeling so worried about things that were happening in the world at that moment. I had seen Chomsky speak in 1992 and again during the second Bush era and his voice seemed increasingly important. There is an incredible bravery and clarity and uncompromising 'truth to materials', as it were, in what he says. I was burning with a desire to ask questions. I wanted to hear his thoughts about the possible end of the world vis-à-vis environmental disaster. He never really talked about that eventuality; instead he talked about other possible – perhaps nuclear – apocalypses. Although he couldn't come, I asked if I could go and talk to him at MIT in Boston. I didn't expect him to say yes.

I was given 45 minutes to talk to Chomsky and thought, 'Oh! What a tiny window of time!', so I had to think hard about what questions I was going to ask. It became almost too important. In the end he gave me an hour. His secretary kept coming in and interrupting the interview and saying, 'Your time is up', and he just carried on. He didn't bat an eyelid, but you could hear her voice, and so we had to cut some of that out, but perhaps we should have kept it in. My time for questions seemed to melt away.

When I came to editing the film, I didn't want that 'me' in it. But I did not want lose this space where he's listening and trying to think how he can respond – which I left silent in the film, so that's where the 'still life' element came in. When you hear eminent people speak, you're not necessarily watching them listening and thinking.

LLF *It becomes a portrait and as such it links to the wider series titled 'Abstracts' which you have described as being 'forensic forays into the minutiae of iconic thinkers' – which is a wonderful phrase. Other works in this series are 'Marks made by Freud', which includes a photograph of the creases made by Freud on his leather seat, 'Einstein's Abstracts' and 'Brontëan Abstracts'. I think, for me, it comes back to the importance of the 'how' as well as the 'what' in your work, this sense of picking up minutiae – these things that don't matter.*

CP It is trying to unearth the unconscious of these famous places, the underbelly of the monument. So, with Chomsky, it was about allowing yourself time to look at him thinking, somehow, not just concentrating only on what comes out of his mouth. It's like the inverse of an image I made of Emily Brontë's quill pen nib, with an electron microscope. You can see the worn-down edge of this natural object that she's been scribbling away with, or a highly magnified pinhole made in Charlotte Brontë's pincushion. Somehow you can tell more about them through those details than you can through their writing.

LLF *It is as though you are, to put it simplistically, showing 'evidence of thought' or 'evidence of activity'. But it is more complex – it is not simply evidence, which implies some factual content, but rather it traces encounters that we – including you as the artist – project our own ideas onto.*

CP I remember, years ago, I was on a panel discussing 'Intention in making art' at Tate Britain. I found that idea terrifying, intention is very hard to describe. There's an Eastern saying about how you can describe a hole. The hole is not made of wood or marble, but the [material] around the hole is what defines it because you can't quantify what the hole is because it's a negative space. In the same way you never see your true self, only a reflection in a mirror or by how people react to you. Somehow intention can only be described by its

139

opposite; if you try to focus on it, it falls away. I've just been in Lima and I gave a guided tour of my museum show there and somebody in the audience said, 'What's the punctum – the punctum of the work?' I said, 'I don't do punctums!' It's not pointless, but somehow, that's not the point.

LLF *It makes me think about John Cage's advice to people to pay attention to the spaces between words. It is as if you are pointing to the stuff around the thing. We never know what the thing is, and if we did – if we could place it within language – it would disappear in some way.*

CP A lot of my work alludes to words or the absence of words. The idea of giving the Brontës imagery that can be associated with them that's quite raw and primitive, quite different from their literature, replacing their words with physical evidence of their presence.

LLF *They stand in for not a collective consciousness, but a kind of collective act of perception?*

CP Yes. I think we nominate people to represent certain things like Freud or Chomsky or the Brontës – these people are legendary for a good reason – but it's as though they become catalysts for something that is much more subterranean in society.

LLF *Of course, it's not just people – you're looking to language as a structure too. In 1992 you made* Words that Define Gravity *in which text cast in lead appears in the form of handwriting – something very personal – yet it's not.*

CP It was a definition of gravity made in lead in my handwriting. I cast all these words which I had modelled in clay. The dictionary definition of 'gravity' has a couple of meanings: one about the gravitational pull, and another which is 'gravitas' – grave things. I took these definitions and literally threw them off the white cliffs of Dover. Real gravity made them completely illegible – little tangled lumps of lead that you couldn't read afterwards. I liked the idea of real gravity trumping man's literal definition of it.

Also, I have terrible vertigo, so standing on the top of the white cliffs of Dover with a rope round me and two people on the end of it – cleverly hidden in the photograph – was a real physical act of containing my fear. It was not about destroying language, but more about the tussle we have with everything that's man-made versus nature.

LLF *Your work often engages with gravity. Not with gravity as empirical fact, but rather it is almost as if you're slowing down gravity, drawing attention to its speed and its pace by suspending objects.*

CP Obviously, nothing gets really suspended. The reason that things hang towards the earth, as it were, rather than float around, has to do with this gravitational pull. This is why the idea of sending a meteorite back into space appealed to me because that really would defy gravity. The idea of a star that has fallen – pulled in by the earth's gravity – being set free again.

LLF *Meteorites keep coming back in your work. You seem to be quite fond of them.*

CP I do love the idea that there are hundreds of thousands of meteorites that have fallen to Earth. Very few people seem to have been hit by one. I've seen a photograph of a woman in Alabama who had a big bruise on her leg from a meteorite that fell through the roof into her living room, bounced off a piece of furniture and hit her leg. But this is one of the rare recorded instances and I just think, 'How come?' It's very reassuring, somehow.

LLF *Yes, and you also bought meteorites from eBay – it seems completely nuts that you can buy meteorites.*

CP Even before eBay, I used to buy them from geological suppliers in London. More recently I've been more interested in buying moon rock. I love this idea that you can buy a piece of the moon. I looked at the first piece of lunar meteorite I bought through a microscope and you could see tiny impact craters in it. It looked just like the surface of the moon, as a little microcosm.

For the first Japanese expo in 1970, as men had just been to the moon, they exhibited a tiny piece of moon rock and people queued around the block to see it. So, for my piece at the same expo in 2005 I bought a piece of moon rock and threw it in the garden and let it disappear. Then I put up a sign in the garden saying there had been a moon landing.

LLF *You also dropped a piece of moon rock to the bottom of a lake in Boston.*

CP There was a sign that announced *At The Bottom Of This Lake Lies A Piece Of The Moon.* My work is very literal – really.

LLF *It is that literalness that demands belief. For example, placing a piece of the moon at the bottom of a lake, or the fact that you have bought pieces of the moon off eBay. I have no doubt, of course, that this is what you've done, but it requires our trust or belief, which in turn elicits that generosity I mentioned earlier.*

CP People often ask me, 'Is it true you did this or did you just throw any old rock into the lake?' It's all to do with me wanting to hold an actual piece of the moon. I have a desire to touch things, to run my finger along the blade that chopped off Marie Antoinette's head, for example – which I've done. In a way it's a kind of nosiness. I get a prurient delight out of the physicality of these things and being able to touch them – being able to lie on Freud's couch. So it is to do with satiating some sort of curiosity I have about the world and the work is residue of that.

LLF *Perhaps your work is not concerned with abstract or invented narratives, but rather is about presenting actual facts. It is a fact that real meteorites have been exploded in a firework. It is a fact that a steamroller has rolled over those objects. That literalness enables these spaces to open up – these spaces at the edges or the middle.*

CP I went to art school in the 1970s where 'truth to materials' was the mantra especially when you're making sculpture. You just go with the flow with what that material does naturally. Somehow I've applied that 'truth to materials' to all kinds of things – the feather from Freud's pillow, for instance, which I put in a glass slide and projected at an angle across a wall so that it looks, because it's being projected anamorphically, like it's been shot from a bow and arrow. But that's what a feather does – it flies, it defies gravity, it is used for bows and arrows or darts or whatever. I just like this idea of giving it back its original quality of apparently defying gravity.

LLF *There is also the truth to the material cultures around objects. I'm always fascinated by the piece of work called* Blue Shift *from 2001. It is a nightdress but it's not just any nightdress. It is a specific nightdress with a specific history.*

CP Yes, that nightgown, which I bought when I was pregnant, was worn by Mia Farrow in *Rosemary's Baby*, which is a film that I saw snatches of on TV through my childhood and found terrifying. I thought of it as being a horror film about an innocent girl giving birth to the devil – but if you watch that film (especially when you're pregnant), you realise it's much more complex, more psychological than that. The horror could be all in her head, a hormonal imbalance caused by her pregnancy.

I remember, I was doing a show in a museum in Turin at the time and I wanted to make some kind of diptych for the Turin Shroud. I was scouring online auctions trying to find a contemporary relic from somebody famous – and I saw this nightgown which Mia Farrow put in a Sotheby's auction for Unicef. I thought, 'Wow that's it! Perhaps I could wear it when I'm giving birth!', and then it became an artwork. I just loved the idea that it was a garment associated with the fictional birth of the devil while the Turin Shroud is supposedly the shroud of Christ. The death of Christ and the birth of the devil, there's a nice parity there.

The work was somehow about fact and fiction. I didn't allow people to see the nightgown. You could only see it through frosted glass. Sharon Tate was an extra in the film and she was pregnant at the time, and a few weeks later she was murdered by Charles Manson. There were all kinds of reasons for me to make this piece of work, not least me being pregnant and being fearful of the idea of giving birth aged 45. All this stuff is just anecdotal, but that's how that work came to be made and when it's on view, people will invest whatever they want to in it.

LLF *And that's where the power of the work is – it's asking all these difficult questions about how we understand our place in the world and how our assumptions are built on perceptions that are quite often built on fiction.*

CP I just like the idea that we're surrounded by stuff – materials, objects and conversations – and we struggle through life using these as orientation points.

LLF *I love the idea that you can make a work that refers to a fly in relation to a Donald Judd sculpture. There's just something wonderfully silly about that.*

CP I went out to Marfa in Texas to see the Chinati Foundation and there's this aircraft hanger full of these beautiful minimal stainless steel cubes. The Chinati Foundation asked me if I'd make a print for them, and I asked them to collect and send me the dust and flies that have to be cleaned out of the sculptures every week because it is a very dusty desert location. I scanned them and the result looks like some kind of gothic horror show of all the detritus that's collected inside Judd pieces – the very opposite of Minimalism. I titled the print *Dust Breeding (On Judd)*. Afterwards I remember coming here to the Tate and seeing the Judds upstairs and noticing all the little dust balls that had collected on them, and thinking 'I could have used them instead'.

LLF *You have this eye for detail. There are these tangible and intangible co-ordinates that keep on returning – the white cliffs of Dover, the meteorites, pearls and breath. You mentioned that your work refers to bodily processes – exhaling and inhaling – and there are early works like* Exhaled School

House *of 1990 that use breath as well as more recent works like* Perpetual Canon *of 2004.*

CP I realised that I could categorise my work either by inhaled works or by exhaled works. For me *Cold Dark Matter: An Exploded View* is an exhaled work and I made a piece called *Inhaled Roof* where I lined an attic with copper because the dome outside had a copper roof. Then there are lots of quiet inhalations, like my series of wire drawings. The process of making wire is called 'drawing' – you melt down an object like a silver spoon and then you pull the silver ingot through what is called a draw plate, which silversmiths use, which has holes of various sizes that go down in size. They keep on drawing the metal through until it gets finer and finer. I did this with a load of bullets that I had melted down and made into various gauges of wire. Then I'd make a drawing – a net, for example – out of the wire, the idea being that a bullet was able to catch something. I like the idea of the trajectory of the bullet being compacted and then made into something quite deliberate like a grid, which seems a perverse thing to do.

LLF *You have also drawn out wire from a gold cross that was deposited in a pawnshop. This object, which is completely invested with belief, is not redeemed by the owner and then someone else purchases it ...*

CP ... and melts it down to wire and uses it in a piece called *Beyond Belief*. They call pawned objects that their owner never comes to back to retrieve 'unredeemed pledges', which is sad, but I love the term. There are all these pawnshops all over the country full of unredeemed pledges. I've bought wedding rings and engagement rings and all kinds of things in pawnshops because I like the fact that they have histories. You have to destroy the object to make the drawing.

There's an earlier piece called *Measuring Liberty with a Dollar*. That is made with a silver dollar that has been drawn into the height of the Statue of Liberty, so it is the literal measurement of a famous monument using a dollar, but it could also be about how you can measure liberty with money. I like playing around with those literal and metaphorical meanings.

In Lima I wanted to show this piece called *Exhaled Cocaine* which used burned cocaine that UK Customs and Excise had given me. But I couldn't import it into Peru because they have a strict drug protocol. So I asked the museum if they could liaise with the Customs there to see if they would give us some cocaine. There was a comic quality to the bureaucracy needed to obtain it. I think the president of the country had to sign the form to release it but we got this big mountain of cocaine for the exhibition. I donated it to the museum there because I knew I wouldn't get it out of the country.

LLF *Following the work you did around the Brontës, you took some hair to Nelson's column.*

CP I tried to have strands from the three sisters – their real DNA – inserted into Nelson's hair on Nelson's column, when they had scaffolding up around there to make repairs. There was this programme on TV about them restoring his hair and I was working with the Brontë hair and I had this great desire to unite them because I thought the Brontës hadn't got a monument of their own and perhaps they could borrow Nelson's. Their name comes from Nelson because Nelson was made the honorary Duke of Brontë in 1799. Brontë is on the banks of Mount Etna – the volcano – and Brontë means sound of thunder. The Brontës' father was originally called Brunty, which is far less exotic. When he came over from Ireland to study at Cambridge he wanted to reinvent himself and had his name changed by deed poll as he hero-worshipped Nelson. I didn't know if I'd known this by reading it somewhere many years before, but I had this intuitive need to unite them.

And then I worked out that the column (which took about 15 years to build) bookended all the literature they wrote – the Brontës – and they would have seen it being built – a couple of them, at least – because they visited Trafalgar Square to go to the National Gallery during its building. I liked this idea of impregnating Nelson – this phallic symbol – with real Brontë DNA, but I think it was all too much for the different bureaucracies that protect that monument. Nobody would have seen my interaction; it would just be a myth. I haven't given up on it. I might train a carrier pigeon to go up there or get one of those protesters to climb up on my behalf. I still have faith in the idea.

LLF *On the subject of literature, you have made reference to a famous poem by Philip Larkin in a project in Frome, Somerset, in 2008.*

CP Yes, and it caused some consternation. It is a public project called 'Intervention, Decoration'. Frome has a lot of nonconformist chapels that had broken away from the main church in Victorian times when mill owners weren't allowed to join the established church. Both my parents died last year, ten weeks apart – it was quite an emotional year – and in conversation with my sisters about what to put on their gravestone, Philip Larkin's poem – you know the phrases, *they fuck you up, your mum and dad*, from *This Be The Verse*, came ringing in my head. Of course, we couldn't put that on the gravestone. They wouldn't allow that in the churchyard, because there is etiquette about the kind of language you can use. You realise that almost every gravestone has the same sentiments; there is no deviance from 'dearly beloved' or 'deeply cherished', no note of dissent. So for my project in Frome, all I did was have this poem carved in stone in Courier script, the typewriter font that Larkin would have written it in in 1971, and I put it up on the side of a schoolhouse which borders onto a graveyard. It is not part of the graveyard but it's on a footpath so you could see it from the grounds. It's just there temporarily, but it has caused a lot of debate in Frome.

LLF *And carving it in stone monumentalises it.*

CP It's very discreet, quiet and formal. When we bury relatives we think we're burying a lot of stuff, but you can't bury it. It carries on with the living, somehow. There's all this respect for the dead, but somehow there's not as much respect sometimes for the living. People are much more respectful of somebody when they've 'moved on'. There are lots of ambivalences that death throws up and I think they're all part of this gravity thing that we deal with throughout our lives. So many friends of mine are going through the death of their parents at the moment. It is something we're all talking about and the feelings that releases.

LLF *And the language cements, once again, perceptions. I'd like to ask you about one specific piece of work that (rather selfishly) I want to hear about which is* Latent News.

CP 'Latent news' is a surrealist term. The surrealists used to cut up newspapers and make up new sentences to create a kind of . unconscious of the news. We're bombarded with newspapers; the underground trains are awash with them.

When buying silver for my 'squashing' fetish I went to a lot of street markets and antique markets, and when they're packing up objects in the market they use newspaper – they unwrap then wrap things up again at the end of the day. There are all these screwed up pieces of newspaper everywhere and I found myself photographing them and then using the found headlines to make cut-up phrases.

My almost seven-year-old daughter, Lily, is having to practise her writing and spelling and I decided to ask her if she could write out these phrases: she would try to write the word 'consequences' and I'd describe to her what it meant. She could only do short ones – 'The world is on the brink of tricky small print' was one; 'A sweeping gesture is struggling to stop' another. Lily started off writing 'A sweeping gesture …' and struggled to stop before she went off the edge of the page. I liked the idea of somehow allowing Lily to grapple with these words when she doesn't yet know what they mean, but which she will understand soon enough.

LLF *Almost in the same way as when you were talking to Chomsky, there's this sense that he is saying, 'Don't believe what you think is around you.' You are drawing out or unravelling language to the point where it becomes impossible to describe experience.*

CP Yes, and I think somehow these phrases were just intuitive little groupings of words which weren't really about anything – 'The world is on the brink of tricky small print' – what does that mean? We're going to drown in the news, it is stuff that we absorb all the time – informing our beliefs whether we like it or not.

This is an edited version of an interview which took place at the Starr Auditorium, Tate Modern on 31 May 2008.

Susan Hiller

interviewed by Richard Grayson

Only Connect

RICHARD GRAYSON *Let's begin by talking about* The Last Silent Movie.

SUSAN HILLER People are concerned about the disappearance of certain British songbirds, and about the reduction of species in the plant world and so forth due to the way we use our planet, but less is made of the disappearance of languages which, to me, is much more important. This is something I have been brooding on for a long time because language has been a central focus of my work for quite a while. The piece uses, as basic material, the recorded voices of people speaking languages that either no longer exist or are on the verge of extinction – that's the basic material of the work.

I don't know what else I can say about it because I don't want to anticipate people's reactions but, like all my work, it starts with what I've always called 'cultural artefacts'. That is, it starts with things that already exist. It doesn't start with a blank canvas. In fact, I don't think any artist starts with a blank canvas because the notion of a 'blank canvas' is itself a cultural artefact – this is a kind of paradox.

The materials in this work are, of course, immaterial in a sense, but sound is an important means that I have used in quite a few pieces. The reason I like sound – and this is a sound work, primarily, although it takes the form of a so-called silent movie – is because it gives you an intimate connection with the source. In this case, we're listening to the words of people who are already dead but, because sound physically touches our ears in the way that something that you see visually doesn't literally touch your eyes, I think it sets up a kind of close relationship with the people who are speaking. And that's important for the work because I'm not making a didactic presentation about language death. I'm simply – I hope – creating a situation for audiences where they can have this close sense of connection to other people.

RC *Do we actually get to understand what the sounds are saying?*

SH Yes, that is why it is structured like a movie because I've used subtitles. It is just a series – on the screen – of blank screens with subtitles that translate what the people are saying, but I think what happens as you progress through the piece is that you realise that the translation is inadequate. Like any translation it is never really giving you exactly what's been said. A lot of what's coming through has to do with different rhythms, textures, speech and sounds. All these different languages have a repertoire of different forms of vocalisation and sounds, some of which we can't even begin to represent. We can't make those sounds ourselves – we don't know how to. All those things feed into the meaning of somebody's speech when they talk to you. It is the expression of the individual. The subtitles give you one level of meaning, but the actual experience of listening gives you other levels.

RC *This does seem to be something that happens in the work constantly, which, in a way, is to do with a gap between what we understand it to signify and also just the material – the matter of the experience.*

SH Yes. In this case, the difference between the translation of these languages and what actually comes through the voices of the people speaking the languages. So that's what got me started.

RC *Which is the earliest recording?*

SH I think the earliest is from the 1930s. It was recorded on wax cylinders. It is a particularly poignant recording that was only rediscovered recently. What I've learned through doing this piece is that anthropologists and linguists, when they feel a language is endangered, will begin to make a series of recordings supposedly to preserve it. These recordings then go into these academic archives where, I think, they're silenced again because once they are archived that's it.

It is also very odd that all this care and attention is devoted to archiving the traces or remnants of these languages, but the people are dead, and nobody is doing anything about the disappearance of the people who speak the languages. Why have the people gone? What has happened to them? That is of more concern to me, but I'm only addressing those things obliquely in this work.

RG *How did you actually access these archives?*

SH I didn't go to all these individual separate archives but to what you might call the archives that archive them, like the British Library Sound Archive, and found these examples. I've only used very, very few examples out of the hundreds and hundreds of examples that there are of languages that are gone.

Of course we know that languages disappear. Latin disappeared in a sense, but Latin turned into many other languages. With micro languages, that is languages which are spoken by small groups of people, they don't usually go anywhere. They just end. And they are not just languages from ethnographic groups. I've gone to quite a lot of effort, or I paid attention to the fact that there are languages in Europe that this is happening to as well. There are two or three from the British Isles: Jèrriais is a language of Jersey and Manx which died in the 1940s – the last speaker died on the Isle of Man. There is one Romany language from Wales which is extinct – recently extinct. What we hear on the soundtrack is quite often the last person able to speak the language that has been recorded.

RG *But then there is also that element from what the anthropologist, Benjamin Whorf, says about how each different language encapsulates its own world.*

SH Yes, I'm glad you mentioned that. There is also something more important to us about the death of languages which is, as you said, the death of an entire worldview or a construction of reality. Whorf started off as an insurance investigator and he investigated a case where a fire was started in a factory because someone threw a 'dead' match into an empty gasoline cylinder. The factory was empty but it was full of fumes – you see, this is a language issue – and the thing exploded and started a huge fire. He left off being an insurance investigator and eventually became an ethnographer. Based on this experience Whorf began to investigate languages in a way that was slightly different: instead of recording the phonetics and translating them literally, he began to think about the worldview that was being conveyed by different languages.

He went further than that. He maintained that each language proposed a view of reality that was distinct. For the Hopi, a new sun rises every day because they have that many words for the sun. There is a different word for every day. That's strange to us because we think of it as the same sun rising, and they see it as different every day.

There's a whole idea there about change and flux and so forth that we don't have.

And he talked about the Navaho – another Native American group who also live in the south-west. If you give them a formal test where they are asked to arrange colour samples in some order, instead of putting what we would call all the greens together or all the reds together, they arrange them instead by intensity, not by hue.

RG *So that it is not just the way language contains the world, but also that language is the expression of a different perception of the world.*

SH It's a different set of perceptions, isn't it? Our whole culture is built up on the idea that the world out there is the same for everybody and the little differences in the description are irrelevant – but he felt that was wrong. Artistically, I found that whole idea very stimulating and very important because what it implies is that the world as constructed through the English language isn't necessarily the final answer to what the world might be.

RG *Building on from work to do with languages that are dead, you have also used what you might describe as sounds that purport to be the languages of the dead, in particular reference to Konstantins Raudive.*

SH Yes, and actually you are reminding me that I do a lot of things that seem to relate to representations of death. Raudive was important to me because of his strange insights about the nature of reality. He was a Romanian scientist (this is in the 1940s and 50s) who left tape recorders going in empty silent rooms – you can see the relationship to Whorf, in a way – and he discovered that, if the tapes were amplified, they had recorded sound on them. In a way this relates to John Cage also. I think all the recent work in sound art, which is becoming an important element of contemporary art practice, comes out of Cage's idea about silence, but Raudive's idea about silence is equally fascinating, though perhaps a little more peculiar. Raudive took these crackles and hisses that he heard on recordings of silent rooms, and he amplified them, and he said that he obtained the voices of dead people speaking. It is also interesting that all these mechanical recording devices have their uses as tools for the occult, if you like, which is another thing that I'm interested in. When you listen to the recordings that Raudive made of these amplified silences, you do hear voices. Whether that's because he messed around with the mechanics of re-recording or whether he somehow tuned into radio stations and things nobody knows, but he was never accused of cheating. The most rational explanation is that these are some sort of artefact of the process of recording, re-recording, amplifying, and so forth. Another possibility is that when you listen to his samples as they exist now, you are always told in advance what you are going to hear.

RG *You have used his recordings in different ways in different pieces.*

SH There is a soundtrack to *Monument*. You sit on a bench and you listen to it if you want to. I was trying to imagine a time in the distant future when I would be dead and someone might be listening to this tape and I would be this ghost voice speaking, and one of the uncanny things about all these recording mechanisms is that we listen to the voices of dead people all the time. The dead speak to us, but we don't even think about how very, very strange that is – that we have these physical traces of them in music, sound, on film, whatever. Anyway, I was very aware of that strange fact.

Magic Lantern is another piece which marries the Raudive voices with a clean scientific optical demonstration of the kind that some of you may have seen in school where you take three coloured discs – red, yellow and blue – and you combine and recombine them to make many other colours. The thing that interested me more than that – in fact, that element of it is meant almost as a distraction – is that you also see after-images which is something that people who aren't painters usually never think about. So, when a red disc comes up in a slide projection, you see a green one. Now where is the green one? It's real – visually real – as real as the red one, but is it *out* there? It is that combination of what's out there and what's in the mind that creates the reality that we live in. People tend not to think so much about what is in the mind.

I realised when I was nervously thinking about what we were going to talk about today that, really, a lot of my work is about trying to retrieve the idea that what you might call 'the human imagination' or 'the subjective perceptions' of a person have a kind of life that is provoked by art practice. That seems to be the thing that interests me the most, to revive that awareness.

RG *Your work seems to place itself at a point of rupture, where there is the possibility of both transmission and the interruption of transmission.*

SH I was once angrily accused by a British art critic – nameless – of being a modernist rather than a postmodernist. I don't know what the distinction might be, but it is true that there is a utopian hope in

Modernism that the past and otherness of all kinds can be resolved. I know that I make work that looks backwards, somewhat, but I also think it is looking forward.

RC *Coming back to language and different worlds: in* Witness *you used many different languages. The work referred not to a singular world, but to a world that is shaped by an experience.*

SH Yes, *Witness* is a piece that I did with hundreds of stories of people talking about having seen UFOs or visitors from other spheres, and I discovered that these stories exist all over the world. That doesn't surprise me because it is a kind of construct of people's imaginations. People have always had extraordinary experiences – let's just call them 'visionary experiences' – and, in our secular world, it seemed to me having collected all those stories, that the only way they can find to describe those experiences is just to put them into the language of science fiction. It is interesting to me that they exist cross-culturally. For example, some of the African stories seemed to me to be marrying older folk stories about visitations by strange creatures with science fiction. I think that, with a lot of the stories from this country and from the US in particular, there is an older kind of Christian thing that underlies the stories.

I think there's a lot of work for some anthropologist to do on that – but what I was really interested in was the sounds of the people talking, filling a room with these many, many hundreds of voices all going at once. It is the way I experience being in the world, with so many conflicting stories and conversations going on all around you all the time – and that was the set-up I wanted.

RC *What I loved about that piece was the way that it wasn't editorial in any way. You took no position, but at the same time, the listener/ viewer/ spectator was made very aware – again – of this world-building function of language. I walked into this cloud of speakers and put the speakers over my ears, and I heard the story of somebody driving down a desert road and seeing a bright light – and it became very, very clear that the world that these people were in is a world which allowed for the possibility of alien contact. You take a risk in not editorialising, in not maintaining a distance.*

SH I make art – I think – for myself, in the first place. To put myself clearly in a position I know I'm already in and, if other people share that position and understand the ambivalence, and the ambiguity, and the paradox – then I think we're getting somewhere. Maybe that is the way I structure the pieces – to lead people to certain conclusions.

RG *I do think it is significant as well because I know that in commentary about your practice this approach confuses people to an extent.*

SH The subject matter, if you like, the cultural artefacts – or, as I would say, the social facts – that exist are only the starting point for the work and the work has different, but always, I think, considered formal aspects, and it is in the relationship between the subject matter and the form that anything that you could call the content of the work might emerge. That is harder for people to get because one does a piece that seems to be dealing with UFOs, then people immediately get hung up on the whole UFO thing, and that's what they want to talk about. That is only the starting point, as far as I'm concerned.

RG *In, say, something like* Psi Girls *or* Wild Talents, *these non-central discourses, belief systems, etc are obviously of great interest to you.*

SH This is an example of something I shouldn't be saying – but I did say this already in the 1970s – that I was interested in things that are marginal or considered to be trivial and so forth. And the reason I said that was because in the early days of conceptualism – I consider myself to be a second-generation conceptualist – there was a lot of criticism of my work because I was dealing with trivia because the first major piece I did in that genre (the first piece, I think, that was really my work) used postcards and postcards, in those days, were considered to be kitsch and more like Pop Art than anything worthy of an artist's attention. I realised then that I was, indeed, interested in things that tend to be overlooked and not taken very seriously.

One way of getting rid of doubt within any society is to mock it – so, people who are opinion-makers will mock the whole UFO phenomenon, for example, and I'm suggesting that there is more to it than that. That's all. That's why I'm interested in these kinds of things. I don't want to sound too utopian, but I also think that if people don't feel there are possibilities other than those that are laid down in official culture, a sense of despair and a lack of progressive development will occur in societies. I think there are other things too that people like to play around with in their heads as ideas, like the fact that there might be intelligent life on other planets. Perhaps it would be quite hopeless if people didn't have those kinds of ideas to play with.

RG *You were just now talking about working in the 1970s – I presume there was another sort of political discourse and directive going on to make*

this necessary. In preparation for this interview I read a review of The
Unknown Artists *that compared it to the contents of a handbag.*

    sʜ Yes. I just need to go back and say that at that time – in the early
1970s – I was doing two kinds of work. I was doing these rather strict
minimalist paintings and I was making events and choreographing
group situations investigating things like dreams, ᴇsᴘ and so forth.
So there were these two things – the completely rational, and the
totally irrational, studio practice and non-studio practice – and I felt
quite split. In fact, I used two names at that time to work under.

ʀɢ *There's a thesis out there for any student …*

    sʜ Shortly after that I realised, or stumbled on, this other way of
working with cultural artefacts and doing installations and videos
or drawings or whatever the work required – not being bound to
one kind of approach. It did coincide with the beginnings of the
Women's Movement. I think one of my commitments to working with
language was strengthened by the Women's Movement, and by my
understanding of myself as a female in culture with this difficulty of
articulating perceptions which might seem slightly different in some
way. That was very important.

ʀɢ *Looking through your body of work, there is this moment where you
visit an incredible amount of violence on what you've been doing, when
you cut up your old paintings and built them into cubes, or burnt them and
put the ashes into light bulbs.*

    sʜ I don't see that as violent. When you bury someone or cremate
them, are you really doing violence to them, or are you simply trans-
ferring their physical remains into a different form? I mean, I was
always interested in taking works past the point where they're thought
to be finished. This is one of the strange things about having work in
a collection like the Tate – that you're never allowed to change it or
revise it. It has to stay like that. Whereas if you keep a work in your
studio, you can come back to it years later and do whatever you want
to it – so I like the idea of taking paintings further and changing their
form.

    With the cubes, which I call *Painting Blocks*, I was changing surface
into mass, in a way, and changing a painting into a sculptural thing.
That was what interested me about that. I also made books out of
paintings because the thing about a painting is that, if you segment it
into a book, then you can actually touch it, which, in theory, you can't
do with a painting. All these different ideas are about process so that

the painting itself didn't have to be the final step.

RG *In the 1960s and 70s there was an extreme interest in alternative constructions and social facts on a level that was clearly oppositional – ie, it was in opposition to the constructions of capitalism or whatever, and the constrictions that it was presumed to have upon our imaginations – so these other discourses have a certain loading. Do you think that loading has changed now?*

SH I think we oversimplified very creatively in the earlier periods. People made some very bold intellectual moves which are still being reproduced – over and over again. There may be some new moves, but I haven't seen many.

There was also, of course, a completely different economic climate and I don't think we can underestimate that. When I came to England at the end of the 1960s, not only was it the lively scene we've all read about endlessly, it was also extremely inexpensive to live here and this attracted a lot of artists. It is completely different now. London now is probably the most expensive place that an artist can pick to live in – possibly other than Hong Kong. So, there was a sense of relaxation about earning money and that affected the way a lot of artists here practised and there was a relaxed view of money too. It was possible to be against the capitalist system in the sense that you did not want to show in galleries or whatever, but you could still get on. People could live from a part-time job, which is hard now. They could support a practice. They could have a place to live, maybe with a big front living room where they could work.

The two things went together. I suppose I'm a little bit of a social determinist. I don't think ideas just occur out of the blue. I think they're brought about by the environment that we all live in, and I think the fact that it was easier to live financially had a lot to do with it, plus the sense of possibility that people had. People could drop out of the mainstream job market and not become homeless and desperate. It was different. That fed into a lot of experimentation and a sense of freedom in the arts.

RG *What was your take on this world that you had arrived in – as somebody not from England – as an American and, I suppose, as a woman?*

SH Oh, love. We came to this country and it was just a terribly exciting time to be here. It was very different, less materialistic in many ways and much more conservative in other ways. It was stimulating, and it was a fascinating time for the reasons that we all know – that the different creative worlds were coming together. I guess that's why there is still this nostalgia for that period because it seemed as though anything was possible.

Another thing was that there wasn't the dependence on the notion of a market or on authority figures – curators, critics, etc. We had few serious art critics here. Most of the people who wrote for the newspapers were ridiculous, pathetic.

RG *Where did the 'handbag' comment come from?*

SH The handbag was from an English art magazine, but I treasure it. It was the first review I had in this country. The kinds of things that now happen in museums like collaborative group events or audience participation events or events of long duration – somebody living in a gallery for six months or whatever – all those kinds of things used to happen, but they happened in someone's living room. Nobody bothered the Tate with things like that. The Tate, in those days, didn't even collect photographs, let alone performances or videos or anything like that. It didn't stop them from happening, but they happened in other contexts.

There were a few interesting galleries. I think there were four: Jack Wendler had a gallery, Nigel Greenwood and there was the Lisson Gallery and the gallery at the Goethe Institute which was run by an ex picture-framer – one of the most international programmes that has ever existed here in London. That was about it. There were other galleries, but they seemed to be caught in a time warp of some kind. It was a small, intense group of people who went around to events and performances and poetry readings and concerts and films and so forth. In a way, that took the pressure off, too.

RG *How do you think your position as an outsider shaped your experience of living in the UK? Was it a problem? Was it empowering?*

SH I never wanted to be an outsider, and I certainly never wanted my work to be considered odd or peculiar, but it was difficult and gender, of course, entered into that, although at first I wasn't aware of it. Again, I do thank the Women's Movement for making me realise that 50% of the people in the art world felt the same way. The American thing was a problem because there was so much anti-Americanism and I was often told things like, 'Well, if things don't work out for you, you can always go back', as though I had anything to go back to. I didn't.

Artists benefit, I think, from the sense of 'outsiderness' – as we know – and I think there's a moment in the life of most artists where they leave the place that they're from, and they go to someplace else, whether they come to the capital city in their own country or they go abroad. Those things are very, very important to give one a sense of distance from the work and to see how the work operates in different contexts. So I think I benefited from that. Retrospectively, I would say I benefited from all those contradictions although, at the time, they were painful. I always wonder what men feel when I say this thing about gender. Do you feel bereft because you're of the dominant gender?

RC *Well, there's a level of victimhood that's been denied to us.*

SH Anger is not a bad motivation. I think that there is consolation in the history of art for anybody who feels neglected, marginalised, peculiar or whatever within the art world. So many of the 'great' modernist artists were outsiders of one kind or another. This is always given as a tale of how you achieve success – by having something to fight against. I think, to a great extent, it is an encouraging experience. Yes, obviously, there's a backlash – but I still feel that to know oneself is important and there are many ways of finding out about oneself and one way is to examine the consequences of your placement in language and culture through gender. That's why I say it is one of the most valuable things I have ever gone through.

RC *You have said that you have a personal sense of inhabiting a museum – a historically specific museum of culture and permeable boundaries which might as well be called 'The Freud Museum'.*

SH I visited the Freud Museum in Vienna and it only has photographs of all the things that are here in London, which is interesting – poetic justice, I think. When Freud had to leave Germany, he was allowed to bring most of his art collection, his library, his famous couch – everything – it is all here in London in the last house he'd lived in.

I was invited to do an installation there which was an important opportunity for me. As I was working there I realised that practically every single thing that I was working with for *From the Freud Museum* could be traced back to something in the work or life of Sigmund Freud because he was not just significant for giving us a whole vocabulary and way of looking at human beings, but he was also a collector, a writer, a traveller – a multifaceted individual whose life spanned an incredibly important period in human history from the end of the Victorian period through to the Second World War.

I realised that if we were going to sum up the world that we live in, you could call it 'The Freud Museum'. Practically every little thing that we have has its roots in that particular historical period and we've learned to look at everything – whether we like it or not – through some kind of psychoanalytic perspective, no matter how incredibly superficial that is. That is why I say we live in a Freud Museum.

RC *He is also a representative of, or indicative of another sort of movement – which is literally a movement in many ways – which you touched on in a major piece dealing with the destruction, erasure and fleeing of the European Jewish population during the middle of the 20th century.*

SH *The J. Street Project* is an example of looking backwards and forwards because the situation in the Middle East, to a large extent, would be very different now had it not been for the Nazis' attempt to exterminate all the Jews in Europe. Our whole world would be different now were it not for what the Nazis attempted to do.

RC *Can you describe how this work came about?*

SH I was exploring Berlin with a street map in one hand, and looking up at the street signs to see where I was going, and I saw that I was on a street called 'Judenstrasse' which means 'Jew Street' and I was completely taken aback, as is practically every foreigner who goes to Germany. I didn't know what to think. Was this some sort of commemorative thing or was it an old street name? What was this about? I then went back to our flat and looked in the A to Z of Berlin under J, and there are five Judenstrassen scattered around Berlin. I then became interested in how many there are in Germany and started this project, which I didn't really want to do. I knew it would be melancholy – to say the least. In the end I travelled around Germany and photographed and filmed all the remaining Judenstrassen and it turned out that there are 303 of them. It documents – in a rather straight-faced way – each of these places. Of course, it is more than that because it leaves a space. As you said earlier, I don't editorialise, and so simply by listing or assembling all these places a big hole is left in the middle for an explanation which is filled in by the viewer. In a sense that's how the piece works.

And to answer a question that usually comes up when I mention this: all these street names are old. They go back as far as the 11th and 12th centuries, and they come up to recent times. There were streets that we visited where people recollected their neighbours being marched off in 1938. They are all over Germany, all over the country – most of them are in the countryside, actually – not in urban locations at all.

[In answer to a question from the audience Susan Hiller replied]

SH When the Nazis took power they, of course, changed many street names – just as every new political regime changes names like 'Martin Luther King Boulevard' when that becomes possible. After the war, as part of the de-Nazification of Germany rather than with any particular intention to commemorate these streets or the Jewish people, the old names were put back on the street signs. Then it came to be seen as though retaining those names was some form of respectful commemoration but, in fact, the street names are the result of a history of segregation and racism – so it is an ambiguous situation. And so it is uncomfortable because, as somebody said to us, 'It is not a very nice name'. No, it is not a very nice name: 'Jew Street'. It is not like saying 'Jewish Street'. It is 'Jew Street'. Sometimes it is written with an umlaut over the 'u' which is a kind of slang. It is an unpleasant way of saying 'Jew'. The existence of this artefact is uncomfortable, and I give the Germans full marks for retaining it because of that uncomfortableness. But who pays attention to the names of streets? I mean, we have Old Jewry in London, and there's a Jew Street in Brighton – who cares? It is only in Germany that it has this special meaning, because of the horror of that history.

RG *Of course, in different periods of history, it would have the same meaning here.*

SH Exactly.

RG *I don't know if there is a Jew Street in York, but there were an awful lot of Jews killed in York.*

SH No, there isn't. The first pogrom in the world was in York. Yes, England has a very good history.

This is an edited version of an interview which took place at the Starr Auditorium, Tate Modern on 14 June 2008.

Adam Chodzko

interviewed by David Barrett

Bad Timing

DAVID BARRETT *I get the impression that your show was conceived partly in relation to the specifics of the Tate St Ives building and its position above Porthmeor Beach.*

ADAM CHODZKO The building and its situation are really unusual. The gallery was designed to reflect the peculiarly confusing structure of St Ives itself: it seems to have no stable orientation points, the ways in which we feel we can reliably access one part of town from another are confounded, and there is a breakdown in the usual sensing of which direction is inland and which is seaward. That experience of instability and surprising arrangements certainly guided my choice and layout of works for the show.

DB *The first space in the Tate that visitors encounter is the loggia, which is a kind of open-air amphitheatre with a domed roof. This is the focus of your* Tate Etc *magazine-insert piece,* Memory Theatre, *2008, which consists of a diagrammatic collage of images depicting an imaginary event in the loggia itself.*

AC The gallery's architecture as a whole appears fantastical. It seems to grow out of the radioactive granite beneath it, and I sensed that there was some kind of hidden alignment to the structure – as if the loggia's design had a particular, but unknown, purpose. My *Tate Etc* page proposes that an event occurs at the moment when two natural events coincide: the sun reaching one specific position, and an extreme high tide.

DB *A proxigean tide – the title of the show.*

Exactly. So in this work, my fantasy is that the sun is magnified by a lens in the aperture of the loggia roof, and, for a fraction of a second, this beam of light is powerful enough to ignite something – probably a gallery visitor – in the space below.

DB *As if the architect was secretly worshipping a sun god and looking for a sacrifice?*

AC Maybe the architect, but just as easily it could be a recent intervention, such as a glazier repairing a damaged panel in the skylight – who knows! It could be a conscious intervention or an accidental one. I also wondered whether it is meant to create an annihilation or just a moment of ecstasy because, 'according to the calculations', at the exact moment of combustion the extreme high tide should rise up and extinguish the fire.

DB *But in the work there is a pile of ash that gets washed away into the sea.*

AC But if you scrutinise that image, you'll see that the ash is actually suspended on ice. So all these events seem somewhat out of control. An extreme moment is apparently contained within one image, but the peculiarities of its constituent elements spin it off into other directions. It's not clear if ecstasy or violence was the intention. Was it bad timing, so that the two natural events didn't quite coincide? Or is the coincidence simply between a series of shapes and materials which happen to be in close proximity? Whatever the sequence of elements, this narrative is haunted by the notion that the gallery has the capacity to consume or absorb its visitors.

DB *Similar to your work,* Hole, *2007, for* MAMbo *in Bologna.*

AC Yes. Again I imagined someone disappearing inside the gallery to become embedded within its fabric, and somehow fulfilling the museum's unconscious aspirations. I was exploring the idea of museums performing powerful supernatural roles as part of the mediation of artworks. With a lot of my recent work my ideas stem from imagining an extreme or urgent form of people's expectations. Here it concerns those of both the gallery and its audience. So *Memory Theatre* applies the same technique to Tate St Ives. I was also interested in how the shape of the loggia appeared to relate to the carousel of a slide projector, which itself is a kind of memory theatre: a space, real or imaginary, that consists of illuminated chambers, functioning as an aide-memoire for tellers of long, complex stories.

DB *And this connects with the piece that you refer to as the end of the Tate St Ives show, your slide-talk performance,* Longshore drift, early Detroit techno, and other processes of erosion, *2006–.*

AC Both pieces are about catalysing memory, whilst also exploring the instability, complexity and fluidity of this process. In *Longshore drift* the 'memory' shifts depending on what the consecutive slide is. The piece begins with an observation that on certain stretches of coast you can find in one area of beach, say, all the fragments of washed up glass, and in another will be all the driftwood. So the implication is that the tide sorts material from a variety of different periods and sources – but that there's a hidden logic to this sorting, an archiving process. *Longshore drift* is based on my supposition that what constitutes the image on a 35mm slide, the particular placement of emulsion on the celluloid, would create different degrees of friction, and so from one image to another there would be a different amount of drag determining how far an image would float before ending up being deposited along the beach. The order of images in *Longshore drift* follows this logic; in the performance I try to give a lecture with a narrative that connects these otherwise disparate images, believing that the action of the tide has actually created a completely logical ordering that I need to try to follow.

DB *This idea of a high tide continues in the gallery; upstairs there are the* Mask-Filters, *2004-, which look like fishermen's detritus, and the driftwood-like* This is it, *1992.*

  AC Yes, it's as if the deposition of works within the gallery are ordered in relation to the deposition from a huge wave. But this was more a private vision that I utilised in order to arrange the works rather than it being a crucial element for understanding the exhibition.

DB *It's not, 'Adam Chodzko, Tidal Artist'.*

  AC Yes, exactly – that's quite enough aquatic content! Although I live by the sea in Whitstable, there are many other things (the rest of life, for instance) that continue to be a much more fundamental influence on me than, say, tidal flow. However, the idea of a strange shift in weather is built into the collective unconscious now; we regularly see footage of people canoeing down their high streets. Also, British science-fiction narratives often start with someone noticing a minor change in the weather patterns, or the usual levels of, say, sand or traffic or whatever. These observations bring about a sense of isolation (because they're usually solitary insights) and foreboding, and they precipitate some other change, like a breakdown in a community. They're little observations and anxieties about a transition in the ordinary: 'Have you noticed how everyone is walking faster recently?' There is an awareness that some previous normality has now gone,

163

and it forces a heightened perception; now we all start studying
tiny details in order to divine what the changes might mean for us.

DB *The first interior space in the gallery is the Heron Mall, which contains Patrick Heron's large stained-glass piece,* Window for Tate Gallery St Ives, *1992-93, and also hosts your new work,* Borrowed Cold Lodge, *2008. This piece, in which you display different kinds of heavy winter clothing that you have borrowed from the local community, also suggests a disastrous shift in weather patterns, particularly for summer visitors coming in off the beach. There's a lot of specialist survival or rescue gear, which is unfamiliar and disquieting, and suggests catastrophic events, but the room is also like a cross between a cloakroom and a tomb.*

AC I wanted the first interior space of the gallery to become a threshold questioning the contract between the individual viewer and the institution, the guest and host – what are their expectations for each other? Like with *M-path*, 2006, or *Sowmat*, 2007.

DB M-path *was your piece for the British Art Show.*

AC Yes, where I sought donations of hundreds of pairs of old shoes and then offered them to visitors at the start of the show, so they could view the exhibition wearing other people's shoes, changing their movement through the gallery space and therefore their perception of its contents. *Sowmat* was similar in that I made a trough of mud and wormwood seeds as a kind of 'welcome mat'. Visitors tramped this mixture – it stuck to their shoes – around the gallery and then out onto the street with the potential that much later this would accidentally create a wormwood forest in Malmö, with the gallery at its centre. But the challenge of showing in the Heron Mall is of course the dominance of Heron's *Window*.

DB *It acts as a keynote for the rest of the displays.*

AC And it literally overshadows, or colours, that space. So I wanted to pervert the assumption that we should be reading this abstraction in an 'appropriate' way and did so by implying that Heron's artwork here is actually very pragmatic and functional: a diagram for dividing up the winter clothing as it is returned to the owners at the end of the show. The *Window* still has a critical importance, but now as a useful map. Yet in some ways the contradictions inherent within *Borrowed Cold Lodge*, with all of its disparate allusions to use-value, serve to create an even bigger abstraction. There is an abundance of material to look at, but as viewers we're also conscious of a number of indications that the work does not expect our gaze. It is a museum cloakroom! It is to be looked past on the way to the art. Certainly *Borrowed Cold Lodge* is temporally displaced for viewers; it is set in the wrong season (more bad timing: a winter event, held in high summer) and the gaze it is directing us towards is of the unviewable, a private process still to come (the removal and dispersal of the clothes back to their owners a few days after the show has ended during the deinstallation period when the gallery is closed).

DB *Similar to* White Magic, *2005, when you switched groups of red and green items of clothing between charity shops in Kent and Brooklyn.*

AC Yes, here again seeing is deferred to events outside the work: the imagining of the colours slowly disseminating into the two respective communities as people slowly buy up the transferred clothes.

DB *The strange, subdued architecture of the Heron Mall loads a religiosity onto the abstract formalism of* Window *– appropriating its intentions – and yet you puncture this by reappropriating the work for yourself, giving it another use.*

AC Like those Rodney Graham works that looked like Donald Judd sculptures, but then you notice that they have a copy of Freud tucked inside, annexing the abstract sculptures so that they became display cases, perversely and literally giving Minimalism a psychology. Yes, the Heron work is turned into a key for *Borrowed Cold Lodge*. Within much of my practice is the idea that somewhere in the work is embedded, or secreted, a key to something, but it is never clear what this key will reveal or where exactly it is located – it certainly isn't where you would expect to find it.

DB *It also seems that the works are trying for something that may not ever happen. The randomised video,* Plan for a Spell, *2001, appears to have the ingredients but just keeps bashing them together until hopefully something is transformed.*

AC A lot of the works have this sense of deferment in the titles: 'Plan for ...', 'Pattern for ...', 'Design for ...'. They're all preparation, or working towards potential events. The question is whether the preparation is simply part of a process that leads to an event, later, offstage, or whether this preparatory work actually constitutes the event itself. I'm intrigued by the tentative and intimate interactions that make up these explorations, because it seems to me that these exchanges both describe and connect societies much more than rigid plans that emerge more centrally through broad consensus. The 'beginnings' I like to work with are much more precarious –

filled with the potential to spin off in a million different hyperbolic directions at once. Most of the time they don't, of course, and reality remains familiar!

DB *There are so many ways that humans can interact with each other, it's amazing how societies don't collapse all the time.*

AC I think that beyond our normal daily activities we sometimes need these other kinds of spaces in which we negotiate each other, when established hierarchies are overturned and we can enter another reality. Alternatives are provided in many different ways through, for example, religion, drugs, carnivals, raves, sport, crime etc. In a lot of my work I'm wondering how this form of 'heightened' social interaction can occur between viewer and art object. In the reflexivity of an artwork – in the exchange of looks – can we momentarily join a social space that is carnivalesque? Hence with *M-path* the idea of a symbolic, physical transformation, a costumed parade, when entering the gallery.

DB *And that piece made viewers self-conscious, heightening their perception as they studied each other's shoes. 'Is everyone walking much faster these days?' This sense of heightened perception also relates to the strong sense of place in your work, for example in the paired billboard series,* Better Scenery, *2000 –*

AC The texts were written as if someone was giving you directions to a similar sign in a completely different location.

DB *– or the two video pieces,* Around, *2007, and the Folkestone Triennial piece,* Pyramids, *2008. These last two were part of regeneration schemes;* Around, *for example, was commissioned by Breaking Ground in Dublin for the notorious Ballymun district. How do you negotiate the expectation that you'll bring a new sense of identity to a place like Ballymun?*

AC I think we're all somehow working in someone else's regeneration scheme ... The attempts to transform Ballymun are on a massive scale and it is an extraordinary place. Strangely, it didn't matter which direction I set off in to explore its territory, I always ended up back in the centre. It was like there was no escape. I'm familiar with a number of estates in south London and many have diffused edges. I know that you can wander through them and easily permeate different residential areas beyond, but in Ballymun I always found some form of boundary on its margins diverting me back into the centre.

DB *Like in some computer games, if you cross the edge of the screen you just come back on at the other side, or perhaps come across an invisible wall that is the limit of the game world.*

AC Yes, exactly, I was thinking about these gaming borders where the designers rendering them decide that they've gone far enough in creating the fictional space and equally I'm fascinated by that invisible blockade in Buñuel's *The Exterminating Angel*. In *Around*, which was one of the works I made in response to Ballymun, I imagined that the barrier around the estate would produce a series of small phenomena, such as causing Tamagotchis to die if they crossed it, or make kites plummet from the sky. Historically, Ballymun was the name for a much bigger district, but then this housing development was constructed and it quickly gained a bad reputation for drugs and crime. Eventually the inhabitants of the residential areas beyond the estate's periphery thought the best way to distance themselves was to change any street names that contained the word 'Ballymun' and get their postcodes switched.

DB *So estate agents renamed the surrounding areas West Hampstead?*

AC Something like that. The massive regeneration has transformed the appearance of the estate but, despite acknowledgement of the social problems, the physical ghettoising of this housing estate has somehow been retained, or perhaps even enhanced. I wanted to question the existence of that barrier through suggesting that it was created and maintained because of some other force – one where it was ambiguous as to whether its powers were benign or malignant.

DB *Like ley lines, or the forces involved in dowsing?*

AC Yes, some unknown power. But going back to your remarks about regeneration, in the promotional literature for the Folkestone Triennial it explicitly states that the event is part of the regeneration of the town. And for me that context, and its implicit hopes and anxieties, became the subject of the work as I followed the existing evidence to its logical (and perverse) conclusion. Located within Folkestone's social and cultural change, *Pyramid* tries to catalyse a framework for its own mythology; the need for regeneration was not because of economic decline due to the collapse of the ferry, mining or fishing industries, but because of a 'curse' on the town caused by the fact that the new support structures added to a cliff-side concert hall 'accidentally' created four huge inverted pyramids!

DB *So you have taken something that already existed in the town and then transformed it with a new narrative. In the Bologna video, Hole, you took footage of huge diggers working in the gallery when the museum was being*

*built, but then treated it as if these were demolition crews looking for a
missing visitor years after the museum's completion.*

AC Yes, I like repositioning or reversing the time at which documents
are supposedly generated and then misreading them in a new location. More bad timing! In this way, images of making appear to be
those of destruction and vice versa. In the 2005 video *Yet*, when the
narrators think all the plants are dying 'in early summer', they've
actually just misread the timing of the scene. It is in fact winter.
Everything is as it should be, but in the meantime, through this
misunderstanding of 'when something happens' there is a panic,
a lurch into crisis management and hyperbole. *Hole, Around* and
Pyramid form a trilogy and all three share this hyperbole through the
impossible arrangements of time, the misplacement of documents
and the misreading of the ruins that evolve from this.

DB *You often combine your questioning of a sense of place with similar
questioning of a sense of belonging. For example, the text in the billboard
work,* Looper, *2003, announces a 'reunion of the most perceptive', so
viewers have to ask themselves if this is a group to which they belong. But
what allows you to ask these questions is your use of mythical narratives
to shape perception.*

AC They're not existing myths – that's important. They're premature
myths that might exist in the future, or could become commonplace
in a parallel reality. Yet they emerge from very ordinary relationships
and objects in the present. A lot of my work is divided into two types:
things that are either too early, such as 'plans for ...', or too late, such
as reunions. The myths straddle both of these bad timings (being
both too early and too late), which sounds a little painful, but through
what occurs as a result of this dysfunction they actually become a
quite joyous opening up of new possibility!

DB *They give the viewers clues, pieces of jigsaw, but each piece seems
to be from a different jigsaw. In a whodunnit you would normally start
with very broad suppositions and every clue narrows your focus down
to one correct answer, but in your work viewers start with a supposition,
or what they think is reality, and then each clue takes them further from
that reality, expanding the picture. This technique of connecting disparate
narratives – do you see that as something that builds a sense of place,
belonging, community?*

AC Well, that sense of belonging or place happens if we each take
an equal role in creating connected narratives. Each of my works

offers a suggestion of a relationship that we could be having with our environment.

DB *So you see your artworks as facilitators?*

AC I wish. I see them as having that potential. But art would have to have a bigger (or at least different) role in society for this to be fulfilled. But each work is a process where I communicate a proposition as a response to the world and lay it open for the next person's suggestion. And this is how we can engage with our world – with multiple understandings, built collectively, beginning over and over again, as a form of play – rather than maintaining a more passive acceptance of a singular linear reality.

DB *At least one series of your works is about puncturing myths. In the 1999 piece,* Inverter (Clearance Sale) (No. 2), *you sell off in* Loot *the items from a luxury ad in* Harpers & Queen, *with both adverts appearing in their respective magazines simultaneously – although on different shelves in the newsagent. You expose one kind of fantasy by dismantling it with another one.*

AC Yes, these advertising images are built up through a tacit agreement that we'll understand their content and respond with desire because we all share a common aspiration for glamour, sex, wealth, respect and so on. *Inverter* is made by a very 'innocent' narrator (selling the items in *Loot*) who misunderstands the whole set-up of the original ad because they've somehow missed out on being indoctrinated into those consumerist constructs. They understand that the source image is an advertisement and that it's about selling, and they're trying to help! But they misread the visual language of the glamorous photograph, instead seeing bizarre items and damage: the enlarged diamond-encrusted tiara is misread as a huge 'wing made of broken glass', the carefully sun-dappled dress is seen as having 'faded patches' and the seabird that stands with its reflection on the horizon is misread as a 'double-duck' ornament. The narrator is without the visual knowledge that we build up, apparently naturally, so that we become adept at reading images very quickly. *Inverter* is like going right back to the beginning again with an image – having no expectation – and failing to understand the most basic presuppositions about scale, hierarchy or two-dimensionality.

DB *When I last interviewed you, one thing you said about* Flasher, 1996-, *was that 'the work is imagining it appearing somewhere else', as if it was a purely conceptual piece. And while there exists a tradition of conceptual*

production, you have a rather idiosyncratic way of making these, some-
times modest, objects; they're usually conspicuously handmade and
often include your distinctive handwriting, as opposed to being typed up
or printed out. For example, each poster that makes up Meeting, 1999 –
where you invite stammerers to describe fire – includes a different drawing
of a fire.

AC It's to create a balance between thought and act. As you say, there
is an expectation for particular kinds of conceptual artworks to be
made in an emotionally detached way, but for me the act of making
is more an opportunity to engage with and empathise with certain
states of mind. With the *Mask-Filters*, 2004, for instance, I really
wanted to work with sculpture again after a gap of over a decade.
I am always amazed by what hands can do, especially when our
thoughts are elsewhere; they sometimes produce amazingly complex,
improvisatory negotiations with the world as if by themselves, absentmindedly toying with whatever items are around. In some of the
videos there are shots of hands weaving, making lace, using divining
rods, drumming, manipulating magnets or dental floss. So I want
the *Mask-Filters* to look a little like the hands have made something
'by themselves', from a collection of material 'that came to hand'
– was found under a bed or in a gutter – rather than as if I have had
something fabricated to a set of instructions.

DB *This technique slows the viewer down. You can't just clock the concept*
and move on. If you want to read 1999's Cleaner *(a story), for instance,*
it's hard work because of the way it is written; as a viewer you have to
struggle if you want to grasp it.

AC It's not just an aesthetic thing; it is also to do with the fact that
they are laborious processes. It is to equalise an expenditure of
energy. I'm imagining how long it takes for the people with stammers
to describe a fire, the organisation of this event, and the witnessing
of its poetically perfect articulation. (I used to stammer, by the way.)
I want to put an equivalent amount of energy and time into my
articulation through the artwork. So it is important that the posters
are not just objects repeating one thought, describing one vision, but
that these posters themselves are participating: they are stammering,
each suspended within a flickering struggle to communicate.

DB *This is similar to your commission for the Frieze Art Fair,* Night
Shift, *2004, for which you produced a carefully drawn and decorated map*
that plotted the paths of various folkloric animals through the fair at night.

AC I remember at the first art fair in 2003 there was a commissioned piece by Pawel Althamer, and I overheard someone ask a dealer if he had seen it. And this dealer dismissively summarised the piece by saying, 'I don't know, he's living up a tree somewhere in the park.' And he said it really matter of factly, because of course this is art and nothing amazes anyone any more. In fact the piece wasn't like that at all (he was 'living' in a tent attached to the main pavilion, creating an access point to it) but by a process of Chinese whispers, allied to an expectation of the absurd, there was this very accelerated consumption of a piece that few people actually saw, because no one has time. So I wanted to make a work that would be experienced by being based within that intense art environment but that would also, more importantly, develop in a dream space beyond it. It was a map offering an audience a path for looking within the fair, and after they had left the fair – and were in bed drifting off to sleep – could perhaps begin imagining these animals moving around the fair in this nocturnal parade. It's like the 'regeneration' context; you're trying to make an artwork within a particular situation, a situation that is loaded with contradictory histories, politics, constraints and high expectations. I'm interested in the point where you just give up on trying to make a rational sense of it all in order to do the 'right thing' and so drift off to sleep, and at this point all these separate pieces of information finally coagulate into an irrational, surreal form. Somewhere they retain their roots as situation, documents, historical artefacts, observations and so on, but from this half-sleep state their relationship to each other seems suddenly, briefly, both unified and truthful from a state of being fantastically – and productively – 'wrong'.

Issue 318, July-August 2008

Dennis Oppenheim

interviewed by Lisa Le Feuvre

Exorcisms

LISA LE FEUVRE *There is always a real temptation in conversations with artists to try to reduce their work to something that fits within language. It seems that, throughout your career, your work defies explanation in terms of a signature style. I wonder if you could talk a little bit about this sense of constantly shifting registers in your practice.*

DENNIS OPPENHEIM I think it could be the case that individuals who do have a signature style, who continue on a certain level or on certain pathways for a long period of time – perhaps their entire career – are able to do it, while those of us who may have tried to stay with a certain idea, a certain strand – and continue it, repeat it, extend it, elongate it – have found it difficult or impossible to do so. I think that I would probably fall into that category.

I have tried to sustain interest in certain things long enough to have a consistency, but for some reason I have always found it difficult or impossible. If that is the case, one then has to invent excuses for what occurs – a seeming dislocation – which suggests to some that you may not have come up with anything yet that you feel is important enough to sustain. It plays havoc with your career because the support system is usually looking for evidence of a certain sort of discovery on the part of the artist, and they equate this discovery with the ability to keep doing it.

If you look closely at the landscape in which such consistency evolves, one could say that, once you have discovered something, repeating it is not necessarily going to extend it. I think that there is some sort of catalytic device that occurs when I land on something that has a certain potential, like Land Art. As an area to find yourself involved with, Land Art seemed to be of such substance that you could continue with it for the rest of your life. So there is a mechanism in you that short-circuits it – you purposely bring it to a close so that you can move on.

LLF *That for me is one of the wonderful things about your practice – you are constantly asking questions in order to move towards an answer but, as soon as that answer comes into sight, you shift to a different register.*

Last week you took part in a symposium that looked back at the 40th anniversary of the 'Earth Art' exhibition organised by Willoughby Sharp in 1969. It brought together a number of artists and, retrospectively, it has come to be seen as the moment this became named as a tendency in art marking. I am intrigued to know how it feels to talk about this work that is now nearly four decades old.

DO Earth art and body art are falling under the equation of Conceptual Art. I don't think I know of a movement that has permeated art as much as Conceptual Art. It seems to still be among us and it is 40 years old – at least. I was talking to some students and they kept bringing up Conceptual Art, and I said, 'Why are we talking about something that is 40 years old? Let's talk about the present.' Forty years ago, most of the people in the 'Land Art Show' were unknown. It was a point where you come out of oblivion into visibility and so that early period is always extremely important for anyone who experiences it.

Talking about the evolutionary vicissitudes involved in a career, if you are always moving from one place to another, you can find yourself going from radical art – truly a sort of new window – and then back into areas that are more conventional. I think that is what I would have to bring into the conversation: the fact that Land Art was a relatively radical departure from making objects really did usher in this whole state of dematerialisation. It is sort of paradoxical because it took its cues from Minimalism and was trying to become so minimal that you excluded the substance from the work which opened the doors to the outside world. It was almost like music trying to do away with sound.

It was extremely adventurous to go out on that pathway. A lot of the work I'm doing now – particularly the public art – you would have to say is comparatively conventional. That is uncomfortable because you want to believe that there is some sort of authentic extrapolation from one period to the next – unfolding, but yet expanding. But if you trace some of these pieces from one to the next, you see instead a kind of moving backwards into a region that has almost been rejected by the work prior to it – so it is convoluted and perverse.

LLF *I think the work that you are producing now is informed by this earlier practice. There is something quite radical in your public art – it is taking an extreme risk in its pretence of conventionality.*

Risk-taking characterises all of your practice – from Land Art, to body art, to the museum-based 'Fireworks' series. It feeds into something that you have investigated right from your earliest work where you interrogated the art system itself. There are two series of works in particular that I would like to talk about: 'Variations on Gallery Structures' from 1967 and 'Gallery Transplant' of 1969. Not much has been written about them but to me they are very important works.

DO They go way back. In fact they go back before any works were executed out on the land. There was a period in 1967 when I made proposals which were all extrapolated from minimal art and dealt with negative space. It's funny, in the summer of 1968 when a lot of this outdoor work was just beginning and was generated by Robert Smithson and Michael Heizer and so on – we called it 'The Summer of the Hole in the Ground' because there seemed to be so much wrapped up in the idea of a hole – the work seemed to carry this idea of Minimalism further because, if you dig a hole, you are creating a question about where it ends. The supposition was that the hole activated the periphery, which created this whole horizontal situation. Probably one of the major breakthroughs of this art is the fact that it countered the verticality of sculpture with a horizontal activation, and that just opened the floodgates.

Now, the 'Gallery Transplant' works, which were done in 1969, are an indication of the fact that you never forget where you came from and, even though you open the doors and you are outside – and you are working in real time and you are working in deserts and you are working on the land – you don't really forget the gallery. You want to attack it. It wasn't a direct objective but one constantly wants to refer back to the gallery or museum, so the 'transplants' were simply about taking the floor plans of these spaces and putting them outdoors.

LLF *From that early period – 1967 to 1968 – you utilised other structures within a gallery. For instance, lectures were a staple element in the kind of art conventions you explored. Also, in* Recall *of 1974 you looked at the art school system. You were not necessarily attacking these structures and systems in these works – I think that is a very romantic reading of them. Rather you were highlighting these systems and, in doing this, questioning them.*

DO If you work the way that I do, where your guard is down sometimes, you can become captive to certain impulses and, in making art in the mid 1970s, it seemed that, as you directed it towards an outside entity, you became more a captive of the mechanism that you were engaging with. In other words, the psychological, physiological, philosophical matrix that made up the pathways that you are engaging in order to attack became the very pathways where you wanted the art to be directed to. You cannibalised your methodology so that it became what you wanted to illustrate or to objectify.

In the 1970s – and it lasted for four or five years – most of that work had this autobiographical element where it was surreptitiously uncovering one's own mechanism and it was very seductive. Sometimes the stuff you do is what seduces you, and sometimes the seduction is intellectual, and sometimes it is a combination of the intuitive and the intellectual.

LLF *Documentation seems really important at this moment, though the photographic documentation was more a trace of what had happened rather than being a substitute or a surrogate for the artwork itself.*

DO Well, there was a lot of suspicion about the early use of photography, particularly by individuals who were claiming to be sculptors, particularly if you were doing Land Art, for instance, and relying on photography.

However, it is strange that photography became such a primary art form because, before the mid 1960s, photography was a relatively minor art form. Then, since it dovetailed with Conceptual Art, it became major – in fact it is probably on the same stratum as painting. That came forth through this usage, it was just another by-product of the whole engagement.

LLF *That is something I want to come back to: the way your work seemed to shift throughout the 1970s. There are some very particular works in which you put yourself in a position of risk. For instance in* Rocked Circle – Fear *of 1971 you stand in the centre of a circle and someone throws rocks at you – which seems the craziest thing to do. It is a work that is both a performance and a film. Then, through the 1970s, you began to introduce what you have described as 'machines' into the gallery space which later developed into the 'Fireworks' series, and from your use of flares. I wanted to discuss your interest in this quite literal risk that you have worked with so often.*

DO It seemed to show itself overtly in body art. It seemed that, in going along the journey of body art, it materialised from one of the more radical places where an artist can find themselves functioning as both subject and object. It was truly a period when you really didn't have to entertain outside material – that you could almost count on some sort of action where the body was psyching back into itself, and that was enough to constitute an artwork. In the beginning it was questionable whether a work that relied so much on performance could be considered sculpture.

A lot of these things you test. If an action had a certain element of risk, a certain element of, maybe, danger, it seemed to me better than the one that didn't. You had to internalise that. You had to try to understand that. Was it always true, or was it simply a kind of dramatic mechanism that you were engaging simply for the added result or effect on the viewer? It did seem that works that had this edge came out better.

LLF *You are emphatic about describing your work as sculpture. Are you thinking about sculpture in a similar way that an artist like Lawrence Weiner does – that sculpture is simply a relationship between a subject and an object and that it will inevitably take a three-dimensional form, whether it is something that has materiality or not?*

DO That is one of the conditions, I think, that became exposed through Conceptual Art – the fact that substance seemed to be able to traffic itself through non-material forms. But it had to be accepted. It had to make sense. When you ask people to extrapolate meaning and substance from a photograph that was of a physical situation – like a Land Art piece – you are testing the possibilities for people to engage in a kind of dematerialised, more atmospheric state or concept. You could wade through that almost as if it were physical – a physical space.

It had to have finally evolved – the fact that this could be felt in the gut as sculpture. But there is something kind of antiquated about the notion of sculpture. I mean, it implies something heavy and big and very visible. The thing about the kind of work we are describing here, the concept-based work, was that it was diaphanous and liquid and dematerialised – and particle-like and energy-laden. It was truly a transcendental form in which sculpture could find itself. And the artists who operated in that kind of liquid desert were really operating in an elevated consciousness and also with an elevated understanding of the evolution of sculpture and art.

The work that I am doing now, although it is addressing a totally different context, is back within the physicality of sculpture as we knew it then.

LLF *How did the shift from your machine-making to the super risky firework pieces come about?*

DO The fireworks pieces that were done in the late 1970s – I think I had worked on them for about four years (I made a lot of them) – came partly from an interest in architecture but also, not forgetting early Conceptual Art, from the fact that these works were generated through a cerebral engagement, an idea.

You would start simply with nothing in your hands. You would start basically with your mind. So it wasn't difficult to become involved in a sort of cerebral mapping – almost drawing in the mind. These fireworks machines were physical counterparts to some sort of conceptual action, and the shooting of the fireworks became what I would call exorcisms – almost re-enacting a kind of cerebral mapping that was extricated through fire into visibility. They became more and more hazardous, more and more out of control. It became a lesson, in my mind, in how the artist can become like a mad scientist and find themselves mixing things without really knowing what the outcome will be.

LLF *Some of these works were actually set off inside the museum.*

DO Yes, well, that was a little stupid. It is interesting that Land Art is very well known and body art is very well known, but these firework machines went into oblivion. Yet they were so in your face. They were extremely large and, when they were ignited outdoors, they reached extreme crescendos. But as an idea, they are strangely unreported. They never seem to find a way into the pantheon of art history.

I'm just remarking that, for me, they occupied a very important period in the early 1980s because they were physical and they were transactional. They were about drawing and thinking. In other words, they were diagnostic and they were interpersonal and they were autobiographical, and they operated within this sort of important substance zone that I think is really what artists want to work with. They want to work with the mechanisms that make their art – particularly the cerebral mechanisms.

To see them manifested in physical terms was like standing back and saying, 'I am creating a kind of architectural counterpart to the mysteries of the creative process'. Although this statement is impossible to justify, you could say that is what I was trying to do in these pieces. At that time it was hard to think of anything more important than to have an artwork be a physicalisation of the very mechanisms that you think are behind your functions. Why they are so obscure I don't know, but it's OK, it's all right.

LLF *There is another period of work that I think is overlooked even more than the firework pieces. It is a series of works that took place within the gallery, again. In one particular work,* Galloping through the Wheat *of 1993, a set of miniature bronze horses, with stilt-like knives attached to their legs, appear in a very literal way to have cut their way through a loaf of bread and are heading straight for the gallery wall. That is one of those works that, as soon as you place it within language, sounds the most ridiculous and crazy proposal to make.*

DO I'm not a real fan of that work. I think there is something about the very nature of this profession that can disarm the practitioner, and sometimes you are simply not in possession of the kind of acuity that you know you need, but you do the work anyway.

That can be problematic. I think this could be a condition that a lot of artists relate to. Lots of people say, 'Well, artists are afraid to stop working because they may not start again.' Not a bad statement. I don't know how true it is with everyone, but I think people have experienced backing off for periods of time and finding that starting again could be a problem. It is like treading water. You aren't really going anywhere, but you are moving.

LLF *And now you are mainly working on commissions that you describe as public art. This term, I think, reduces it to something that relates to an idea of monumental, bombastic sculpture.*

DO Public art is an extremely troubled area, a sort of problem zone in which to practise art.

LLF *Yet you choose to do it.*

DO It is this sort of zone that you have to be a little bit perverse to engage in because, coming from fine art, it is like a cold shower. Coming from your own laboratory and going into public art is like going into an arena that is laden with juries and codes and limitations, but some people think – and I wish I had this sort of perspective that they have – that this operation in the public arena is operating at a higher coefficient than fine art. In other words, they think the most advanced art now is coupling with architecture and allowing in functionality, once considered such an evil in art.

I'm not sure if I could relinquish all of the attributes of fine art to that degree and usher in this kind of democratic art or believe in it to the same extent. But yet I would like it to happen. I'd like to finally be overcome by this sort of realisation that, yes, we have shifted on to this other plateau where there is a fusion – a morphing – of all these other art forms that have, for years, been sort of relegated to subservient positions in relation to fine art. I guess you are talking about some sort of a social context or functionality in art.

LLF *What you have said suggests that you are not one of these people – yet you are somehow engaging with this curious practice of public art.*

DO Yes, but I wanted to be the first to talk about the perversity of moving from an extreme, close engagement with fine art – in all of its ramifications – into this other region and I am trying to survive this repositioning. But sometimes I look back at fine art and say, 'God, why did I leave that? That's such a neat area. You can do whatever you want.'

LLF *There is one particular work that I keep thinking about:* Lead Sink for Sebastian *of 1970. I wonder whether you could just tell me a little bit about that work.*

DO That's a good piece. It's from the area of body art and it's from a period in a six- or eight-year spectrum in which I was engaged in that type of work. This is probably the richest area. *Lead Sink for Sebastian* is a performance about body proximity to material – so it is extremely engaging and pertinent to the sculptor. When you think of the sculptor the way you did back then, you were thinking of hands, you were thinking of pliability and of the mechanism of the hands forming materials. *Lead Sink for Sebastian* uses an exterior agent, it uses a performer who happened to be an amputee who had only one leg. I spent a long time trying to find this person who I could do this performance with. It sounds macabre, but it was dealt with in a very strict, formal way. We actually put a lead pipe where his leg support was – in other words, we substituted a lead pipe for a wooden peg – and this was melted using a butane torch that was attached to his leg. This operation that I'm describing was filmed with a video camera focused just on the butane torch and the lead pipe. He was leaning against the wall.

In the video, the performer's body movement was dictated by the fact that he was melting lead where a leg should be. So the whole thing about the work is simply that melting lead is a reductive sculptural procedure, like carving, which is one of the major characteristics of traditional art – carving wood, carving marble. Pieces like *Lead Sink for Sebastian* at that period were all intended to preface some aspect of traditional art and to show how it has moved along. It operated within this combative engagement with performance and sculpture and materiality.

LLF *This sense of art as a transaction runs through your work. There is a series in which you worked with your children. You have described them as being 'extensions of your own physicality'. In one series, drawings were transferred from you to the back of one of your children who then transfers them again. Once more there is this sense that you are constantly pushing at the limits – of the physical in this instance – to find out what happens when you extend your own physicality to someone who can be linked to you genetically.*

DO You are talking quite simply about the profession of generating concepts and making them physical and profound. I think that is what artists are trying to do, and in so doing we are trying to seduce ourselves through ideas into making objects.

You can lighten this up. You can say that artists occasionally find themselves in a more relaxed and temperate period where their works seem to be enjoyable – that they are doing pastoral works that show a certain proximity to the sublime. But by and large I think we are doing nothing less than trying to come up with formulas as profound as those of James Joyce or Albert Einstein.

It occurred to me back then that there could be this genetic thing: if I work with my children it is going to bring in another element of possibility, of justification, in the artwork. It is going to imbue it with more substance and it is going to make it more profound. You never really know how, but you are trying to combine all these inputs into this unusual discipline of art, which is unlike any other discipline, in order to materialise something that is extraordinary.

This is an edited version of an interview which took place at the Starr Auditorium, Tate Modern on 25 October 2008. Published Issue 373, February 2014.

Martin Creed

interviewed by David Trigg

Time and Motion

DAVID TRIGG *You mentioned that installing your show at Ikon has been hard work.*

MARTIN CREED I find it really hard to decide where to put things in a show with more than one work, to decide how to place things in relation to each other and to decide what not to put in. I used to have a rule that I would never show more than one work at a time because when I make works I make them to work on their own. In shows where there's more than one artist's work, instead of there being a relationship between the work and the viewer, or the work and the rest of the world, there's a relationship between works. If you're there with one work, it's just you and the work, but if you're there with two works, it's like you're not actually needed because there's a dialogue between those works.

DT *Tate Modern once paired your neon piece,* Work No. 232: the whole world + the work = the whole world, *2000, with Carl Andre's* 144 Magnesium Square, *1969, which set up an interesting dialogue.*

MC I was happy with the pairing – partly because he's a hero of mine. I think he's a great artist and his work has been an inspiration to me, so in that way the pairing was very exciting. But I think you could just about pair anything with anything and it would make something.

DT *Some meaning would inevitably get attached to it?*

MC Aye, though I do think my neon text and his floor piece make a great combination. I've always liked that you could walk on Carl Andre's floor pieces – you can walk on his sculpture and it just becomes part of the rest of the world, which fits with my text.

DT *That neon was originally made for the façade of Tate Britain. More*

181

recently you've made another work for Tate, Work No. 850, 2008, *which comprises runners sprinting the length of the Duveen Galleries.*

MC That work was an experiment to do with this idea that all experience is kinetic, happening in movement and time. One of the ideas with the running was, instead of having the usual situation where the work stays still and the people move past, to have the work moving faster than the people – a simple reversal.

DT *There's a fairly rigid structure to that piece: it happens every 30 seconds and it's always down the length of the Duveen Galleries. You made another running piece,* Work No. 570, 2006, *which was shown at the Palazzo dell'Arengario in Milan. There the runners were dressed in ordinary clothes and they appeared less frequently – the viewer encountered that piece in a very different way from the work at Tate Britain.*

MC That was, in retrospect, an early version of the work at Tate. They would run through the show and out into the piazza and round the building and back in again. They constantly ran that loop, so the frequency was determined by the time it took them to go through the show and out and round and back in again. They were middle- to long-distance runners who would maybe do a one-hour shift so it would be like a cross-country run. Doing that work made me realise that the runners needed to be more frequent. Also, having them in normal dress wasn't quite right; they really needed to be in running gear.

DT *So you think viewers were confused about whether or not it was actually part of the show?*

MC Aye. And I'm not really interested in whether the viewer wonders about what's happening like that.

DT *You feel it strayed a little too far over that line?*

MC Yes, I do. I think it's more generous to the viewer if they can rely on the work always being there to look at. So with *Work No. 850,* even though it is this sudden flurry of activity, you can rely on it happening every 30 seconds. I wanted to try and make the work like a natural event rather than an artificial one. One of the big models for that piece in my mind is the sea; you can rely on the waves coming in every so often and you can enjoy it – the audiences are like people walking on the beach.

DT *I hadn't thought of it like that – the runners only run one way.*

MC I decided that having them only run one way was to make it more reliable and less confusing.

DT *Were you aware of Jean-Luc Godard's 1964 film* Bande à part, *which features a scene where the protagonists attempt to break the world record for running through the Louvre?*

MC No, I've never seen the film but of course you can be influenced by things without realising. I think I was more influenced by my own experience of running through a museum near to closing time, finding it exhilarating and thinking it was funny.

DT *These running works have an element of theatricality to them. In the past you've spoken about art galleries as being like theatres.*

MC I find it more and more helpful to think of it that way. If you're doing things in galleries all the time – like I often am – you start to wonder about what exactly their function is. In my mind, the best way to describe a gallery is as a theatre for looking at things. If you expand that idea you could say that an exhibition is just a really long, slow piece of theatre that lasts for two months instead of two hours and in which the audience come and go as they please – they dip in and out of something which is already there as opposed to sitting there while stuff happens, concentrated into two hours. Every experience happens in time and in movement; although objects may be static on the wall, or wherever, the experience of looking at art is always a live one because people are alive and always moving – the heart's beating. But if you're completely still, you're dead, in which case you presumably can't appreciate art – but we don't know that for sure!

DT *The regularity of the runners at Tate Britain creates a particular rhythm, which is an integral element in many of your works, particularly* Work No. 160: The lights going on and off, *1996, which you're showing in the Tower Room at Ikon. There are several versions of that piece aren't there?*

MC Yes, the difference is the timing. The timing makes a huge differ-ence – *Work No. 160* is the one-second version. It's a very different work from the five-second version. I'm a very slow worker and I find out about my work over years. After making a 30-second version of the lights going on and off I made the one-second version, then a few years later I made a five-second one because I was trying to figure out a frequency that worked with people entering and leaving the room, giving just enough time for them to realise something was happening – a bit like trying to decide how frequent the runners should be.

DT *The frequency has to be palpable, otherwise if you go too far one way* or the other it's going to be either a strobe or completely imperceptible.

MC Exactly.

DT *You also re-presented the one-second version in your old flat in Brick Lane.*

MC Yes, in the back room – it's a permanent installation viewable from the street. When I lived there I thought it would be a great place to make the lights go on and off – I thought it'd make a good public work. When I moved out I didn't want to sell the flat and I haven't been sure what to do with it since. I'm doing projects with different artists in the front room and in the back room there's the lights going on and off 24 hours a day. It's a kind of gallery. Maybe it'll develop into something more – like a project space – but it's still a flat and people stay there sometimes. It's all just a bit of an experiment rather than an official thing. We're planning some shows, one's going to be curated by Tess Jaray, my old teacher from the Slade.

DT *You studied painting at the Slade, which you later rejected. I was interested to see that you have returned to making paintings.*

MC Well, I don't think I rejected it at all. I stopped painting because I wasn't happy with the paintings that I made, so I tried to rethink what I was doing and started making things on the wall as opposed to paintings on the wall. But I've never thought that I really got away from painting. I think a lot of my earlier work came from thinking about painting – trying to do this thing that I couldn't do. Like those wall protrusions upstairs – the white ones – they come directly from painting, from thinking of trying to make a thing for a wall, taking away the object and making the shape of the wall come out and do something. In a way they were like little experiments, trying to make a new kind of painting.

DT *And in fact they are painted.*

MC Absolutely. One of the problems with painting I always found was the relationship between the painting and the wall – you can't really see the painting without seeing the wall around it. I couldn't handle the difference between the object and what's around it – I don't know why but I couldn't. When I stopped painting I tried to make these wall works that solved the problem. One of the ways of solving it was making works that were seamlessly joined with their environment: from the lights going on and off to the door opening and closing, in all of those pieces you can't say where the work finishes and the rest of the world begins.

DT *But you've now returned to a more traditional approach to painting –*

working with paint on canvas.

MC I think it comes from accepting that it can actually be helpful to draw distinctions between things. With those earlier works there was no frame, no boundary between the work and the rest of the world – they were seamlessly joined. To make a painting on canvas you have to accept that there is a boundary because you can't make a separate object without one. A world where there are no boundaries, no rules and no clear divisions is more difficult to live within because you never know where you are or where anything begins and ends. I think it can be helpful to draw these lines.

DT *What about the figurative drawings, the portraits you've been making?*

MC Well, *Work No. 657: Smiling Woman,* 2007, first, that was how the figurative drawings started. That came from a photo I had in my studio of a woman smiling. I've been working on this series of photographs of people smiling for a few years and I always liked this particular smiling photo. One day when I was away in Italy I was on my own and I was just feeling really lonely. I think I started making the drawing of this woman to keep me company – I didn't think that at the time but it's what I think now. I wasn't trying to make a certain type of drawing or anything, I just was seeing if I could copy the picture. I was just trying my best, as usual. Then I did a few more.

DT *Did* Work No. 753: Holly, *2007, come about in a similar way?*

MC Whereas the Smiling Woman drawing just kind of happened, Holly was more a self-conscious set-up, done from life. Again, I wasn't trying to make a certain type of drawing, I just thought I would try to make a portrait. Most of my work is planned over weeks and months and done in private and then exhibited in public. One of the reasons that I like doing talks and live things with my band is that I find I can learn from doing things in public. I realised that life drawing is a similar situation – you're sitting in front of someone, drawing them, and that person is your audience, you're effectively making work with an audience.

DT *That's an intriguing concept – the life model as the artist's audience, or 'audient' perhaps. But when the work is exhibited that process and those thoughts become hidden, that meaning is lost – all people see is a figurative portrait.*

MC Exactly, and that's always been something that bothered me. I think that's why I started making the kind of work I made because it bothered me that the process was not necessarily evident in the final work – I thought the process was the important part. In other words, if I could tell someone the story of my attempt to make this thing – including the final product – that would be something worth seeing, whereas just seeing the final object might not be. I often think of the final work as actually being the bit left over, after the artist has finished working.

DT *I think that notion relates to* Work No. 610: Sick Film, *2006, which marked a radical departure from your previous work, in both form and content.*

MC That came directly from doing slide talks about my work. Over the years, as I was doing more and more of these talks, I realised that the slides were a kind of escape route for me, a way of avoiding actually talking about something, away from a dialogue. So I started doing talks without slides and I decided that the best way of talking about making work was to try and make a work in front of people, using words.

DT *Like a piece of performance?*

MC Aye, but I was just talking about my work without slides – I was trying to make a work using words. I would improvise, there would be questions and often it would just end up as a bit of a conversation, but it was to try to take away some of the conventions in order to make it more of a direct experience. It just happened that in those talks I kept talking about vomiting as being a good example of what I thought making work is like – getting from the inside out, trying to make something on the outside of me that rhymes with the inside of me. Vomiting is a convulsion, it isn't a thought-through process.

DT *It's involuntary.*

MC Yes, well at that moment it is – maybe beforehand you can make yourself sick but at the moment you're actually being sick you are out of control. So in a way it is vomiting as an example of true expression – you can't have a fake vomit. More and more I feel that my ability to think things through gets in the way, I want my work to be more like a vomit than a rumination. That idea led to the thought that I could perhaps film people vomiting – if vomiting is such a good example of making work then maybe I should make a film of people vomiting. The final product wasn't planned at the beginning. First of all, I just wanted to film people vomiting but then I thought, how can I do that? I'm really scared of vomiting!

DT *You didn't want to appear in the film yourself then?*

MC I thought I could try but I don't think I would have been able to. I find it really difficult to make myself sick, even when I'm feeling really sick. I was also directing behind the camera on the day; it was a one-day shoot so it would have been impractical. The positioning of the camera in that film was very important: the camera was fixed, to show the performer's whole body. There are no close-ups. It was important to me that the performers chose to go in front of the camera and decided for themselves when to leave the shot. They knew where the camera was and it was very important that the camera didn't follow the performers around.

DT *Did you edit the footage much?*

MC No, but the editing I did do is quite precise. For instance, the amount of time before the performer enters the scene and the amount of time the pool of vomit is left on the floor before it cuts to the next scene, those cuts I spent a lot of time on – it's all unedited apart from that. One thing to say about it is that *Sick Film* is not a gallery work – though there are various gallery versions – it's actually a 35mm film designed for theatrical presentation.

DT *I saw it when you showed it at the Arnolfini in Bristol; I found it extremely uncomfortable to watch.*

MC I used to find it very difficult to watch the footage; now I'm totally immune to it, it doesn't make me feel sick. Now I think they're just like portraits of people, you know; that it's just a film of ten people and the reason they're good portraits is because at an extreme moment like that your character is revealed – their characters do come out very much in the film.

DT *For me it evokes Stuart Brisley's visceral performances from the 1970s, the ones where he would make himself retch.*

MC He was a teacher at the Slade when I was there. He didn't teach me but I am familiar with his extreme performances, like when he would sit in a bath of offal.

DT *Had you considered the formal similarities between Sick Film and some of his performance work?*

MC No, not really. But whenever you do anything there are often similar things that other people have done, there are crossovers everywhere and it can really stop you doing things if you think about it too much. The first time I used neon indoors I was worried that people would think it was like Bruce Nauman. But I wanted to use neon because you can switch it on and off. It's a way of saying and not saying something. Then of course, as often happens, after you do something like that, you realise it's actually quite different from the work you were so worried about.

Issue 321, November 2008

Christian Boltanski

interviewed by Rikke Hansen

Wait and Hope

RIKKE HANSEN *The first time I really encountered your work was in one of the 'Do It' exhibitions, curated by Hans Ulrich Obrist. This particular show was in 1997 in Denmark. The concept behind these exhibitions consisted of instructions given to the curators at each museum where the show was going to take place, so that at every venue a new work would be produced – not by the artist as such, but by curators. Maybe we could start by talking a bit about your contribution to that?*

CHRISTIAN BOLTANSKI First, let's speak a little about this show, 'Do It'. Sixty percent of my work is usually destroyed after a show but it can be remade. In such cases I send instructions and the curator, or anybody else, makes the work.

Since the second half of the 20th century there has been no need for art to be touched by the artist, so there is no need to transport a work from Los Angeles to London, for example, it is better to simply remake it – it's a question of economics. In the future it is possible to imagine a museum with only rules and plans so that each time a work is shown, it is a facsimile of the work – you wouldn't need any more guards.

For this reason, I decided to do this show. After that we did *Home Do It* – so that you could also 'do it' at home. In fact it would be possible today to make a copy of Vincent van Gogh exactly the same as the original, so each museum could have the same number of possible paintings because they are identical with the originals.

On the other hand, it is good is to make this kind of ideological pilgrimage. I think it is important to make the trip to see the original. Besides, if it was possible to see all the best art pieces everywhere in some kind of perfect collection, it would be really very boring. So for this reason I think it is important that we have to make the journey.

Most of the cities in Europe were founded on somebody's bones – on the relics of a supposed saint. They would then build a church dedicated to the saint, and people would come and pray, and then there'd be a fair, and eventually there would be a real city. Now it is the same with art, for instance in the case of the museum in Bilbao. Bilbao was a really poor city and they put some relics in a big cathedral, and a lot of people went there to pray, and now the city has become rich with plenty of restaurants and so on. In 'Do It' we tried to show that there was another way to make art.

I remember, a very long time ago the Tate bought one of my works, *The Reserve of Dead Swiss*, from 1990. When I came to London to install the work the curator said, 'The white cotton is going to turn yellow in time.' And I said, 'That's not a problem, we can change it.' Then he said, 'You know, the photos aren't very good quality and they are also going to turn yellow in time.' I said, 'If they disappear, you can change them because there are always new dead Swiss.' Finally, the curator said, 'This shelf is good for this room, but if we put it in another room perhaps we could change the shape of the shelves?' Then he said, 'What did we buy?' And I said, 'You bought an idea of dead Swiss with white cotton on shelves. But it is not *this* dead Swiss or *that* dead Swiss. There are so many dead Swiss – I really don't care.'

RH *I guess this is related to what Dick Higgins called 'intermedia'. There's a kind of score for the work, but there's also the dependence on having to continually reproduce the work, to 'act it out' again and again. The work exists in the tension between these two 'states'.*

CB What seems to be important when you make an art piece, whether traditional or not – I am very traditional, sometimes I feel myself to be a very conservative artist – is to ask questions and to provide emotion. What is also very, very important to me – and I think that is art what art is – is to speak about my own problems but that each person looking at the work will think it is about their problems.

There is something between the more personal and individual and the more collective. When people are looking at the same movie in a cinema, each person is in fact looking at a different movie. I think that what you can do as an artist is to send out some kind of a stimulus. It is the audience – the person who looks at the art – who makes the finished art piece. If I show an image of a child on a beach, each person knows this image, but each person can say, 'Oh, it looks like someone I know. He looks like my grandfather'. Everybody sees another image, but it's the same image.

For this reason I try to use very common objects in my work. A biscuit box, for example, is a minimal object, but it is also something that everybody can recognise. I mean, if I tell you (it's not true, I hope) that I have a diseased pancreas nobody can understand that, but if I tell you I have a headache, a lot of people can understand because a lot of people know what a headache is.

RH *Speaking of the fragile body, maybe we should also talk a little bit about the theme of loss and mortality. You very often return to the issue of death in your work. Clearly death is the one thing we all have in common, yet suffering is something that is singular.*

CB We are all of us going to die.

RH *You have said that there are only three or four themes or topics in art and that death is one of them. But even when your work deals with matters of death, it also seems to touch upon other issues. So what is it about death that seems to open up to other things? And what are those things?*

CB First, I don't know what I'm doing. We never know what we are doing. That's the beauty of art. I believe that everybody is unique and very important and, at the same time, everybody is so fragile. I mean, after three generations, there is no memory any more. The memory of somebody goes so quickly. We can speak about our grandmother, but not about our great-grandmother. It is something strange. We imagine that everybody is so important; everybody knows so much but, at the same time, everybody is going to disappear so quickly.

At the beginning I was trying to show what I call 'the small memory'. There are big memories like wars, but small memories are what we are and what we know. These kinds of things are going to disappear with us. We try to preserve them but, in fact, it is totally impossible to preserve everything.

I always knew that I was going to fail. I try and I try, but I fail all the time because you can't hold on to life. Also, if you try to preserve a life, you kill a life. If I put these glasses in a vitrine in a museum, they are not going to be destroyed but they are not going to be glasses any more. They are going to be imaginary glasses. Every time you try to preserve something, you kill it.

For this reason what I was trying to do was impossible, and I knew it. But perhaps it was important to me to try. I'm not Alberto

Giacometti, unfortunately. I love Giacometti, but I'm not Giacometti. What I love about Giacometti is that he tried every day to make a portrait of his wife or his brother but he was never happy with it, so he tried again and again. I think there is something about the act of making art; it is a way of fighting against the fact of death and disappearance, a way of trying to catch a life, even though it is totally impossible.

For me, art is about asking questions, and often when you ask a question it leads to a new question. I have not answered the question, but I have a new question. These questions are not new – they are the same questions that were asked in the 17th century. The way we speak is a little different, but the feelings are more or less the same. We may work with sound and videos and photos, but these kinds of things are, in fact, not so important because we are trying to ask the same questions, but I speak with the language of 'now', of my time.

RH *But then, at the same time, there must be some important cultural and historical differences, for instance when we talk about issues like death.*

CB I think that dying now is much more terrible than 200 years ago. In the past, especially in the country, when a grandfather died, the father took his place, and the son took the place of the father – but what was important was the land which was passed on. When you are a worker, you teach a young person to do a task and tell him that you are going to die, but he is going to take over after your death. Now, I think it is rather terrible that there is no idea of transmission from one generation to another.

But, to be optimistic – and I am somebody who is a very optimistic person – what is beautiful is your face. You are full of dead people – you have the nose of your great-great-grandmother; you have the ears of a great-great-uncle. I think it is so marvellous to imagine that we are full of dead people! Somebody told me, though I don't think it is true, that I was part Tartar. My family comes from the Crimea and there were many Tartars in Crimea. In any case, I was so happy to imagine that part of me was Tartar. Everything goes on – that is what is so marvellous.

RH *That's really interesting because, when people become interested in genealogy, it is often a way of rewriting their own identity, something which is also an issue very central to your early, more autobiographical work.*

CB But if we read Marcel Proust, he is not speaking about himself, he is speaking about the one who is reading his books, and each time we read Proust we recognise ourselves. When I spoke about my family, I spoke about a very normal family – just normal clichés – so that everybody can think, 'Oh, yes – mine was the same'.

In my work I am really trying to make archives of people. There are a lot of people in my work. There are a lot of names of people because I think it is very important to name names. I work a lot with images of people – photos of people. I have thousands of images of people. I work a lot with used clothes and for me a used jacket is like a portrait of somebody. Now I am making archives of heartbeats – but it is the same thing. Each time you have something, it reveals an absence; you have an object in relation to its subject, but the subject is missing.

RH *But is there not also a case in which the subject is present: there is a wonderful passage in Maurice Blanchot's* The Space of Literature *where he says that we're used to thinking that when life stops everything stops, but that strangely enough the corpse is still there. He describes this in terms of a presence, which is why we have to have all these funeral rituals because the corpse represents a kind of a delay. Is there also not a sense of presence in the clothes which remain?*

CB Sure. I think a body, or used clothes, or a photo is maybe the same thing. It's an object in relation to a subject that is missing. There was somebody.

RH *But there is also something left of them even though they have gone.*

CB Yes. For a long time I bought my shoes at a flea market, but now I can't do that any more because you can feel the feet of the person who used the shoes before. I made several works with clothes because there is something so touching about them. When you are at the flea market you see a jacket which belonged to someone who loved it and who died or who decided he didn't like it any more. In any case, the jacket is there with no memory. If you buy it you are going to love it. You are going to give that jacket a second life, a new story. I think you give life when you look with love.

I once bought a jacket and in one of the pockets there were two tickets for a theatre in New York (a comedy). It felt very strange to me to find a little part of the old life of the jacket. I've made a lot of work with lost property. A lost property office is a terrible place because there are, I don't know – 200 keys – but nobody knows which doors they can open. For this reason all these objects are waiting for love or waiting for somebody to say, 'I know you. You can come with me'.

That is so depressing.

I made a piece for the Louvre, which has so many visitors that they have a lost property office, and I took 100 objects over one month and put them in the medieval section of the museum. I asked one of the curators who was an archaeologist to write the labels, but to write them as though she did not know what kind of objects they were, as though she had found them. If it was a camera, she might say – I don't know – 'An object coming from Asia; end of 20th century; perhaps a religious object'. It was amusing to insert the object directly in to the Louvre collection.

RH *Did anyone come and ask to have their objects back when they saw them on show?*

CB Not in the Louvre because I think they had mostly belonged to tourists. At one time I made a show in the Haus der Kunst in Munich in 1997 and we transported the contents of the Munich lost property office to the museum, together with the staff, so that the museum became like a lost property office for one month.

RH *There's also something about putting something in a display cabinet that kind of elevates everything to the same sort of level, which is a little bit like what you do. For example, your photographs of the children from the North Westminster Community School are all framed the same way, exactly like a school photograph, but in fact they are not all from the school – so in a sense everything is given the same value in that context.*

CB You are referring to the piece I made for the Lisson Gallery in 1993, which was funny to me because it is really a little too much like Duchamp. I made two copies of the photo: one was for the school, which was located directly opposite the gallery, and was sold to the parents of the children, if they wanted to buy it – for £3 or £4 – and another copy was made for the gallery, but was sold (or not sold, in fact) as a group. For the school I wanted the photos to be useful, but in the gallery it served as an *exemplaire* of a school in London at the end of the 20th century. It was not the real thing.

Ten years later we tried to find these children. It was very difficult. Out of something like one hundred children we found only about twenty and it was very depressing to see them because, when you see the photo of the children, they are full of hope, but after ten years of living in a poor part of London, it was a bit sad.

I work with the subject of childhood because I think it is the first part of us that will disappear. A Polish theatre director once said that

we all have a dead child inside us. When you are an artist, you try
to preserve this a little longer – this dead child. In any case, it is
always there.

Like all artists, I have very few moments of inspiration. In any case,
the first was when I was about 23, I understood that my childhood
was finished. I remember it perfectly well: I was with my parents in
a car when I realised that my childhood was finished. It was such a
big shock. In fact, all my work began from that day. Another such
moment was when my parents died and I realised that I was getting
old. In any case, these moments of inspiration are always very
important in your life, but mostly you do nothing. You wait.

RH *I guess it is also to do with the fact that when your parents die you
cease to be the child of someone.*

CB You become your father. I physically changed in one year. In fact,
in my life I don't work so much as I used to. I almost do nothing.
I have a very happy life for this reason. I'm very proud of the fact that
I do not have an assistant, or a secretary, in an age where most artists
have both. You know, normally I just wake up, look at the TV, go to
my studio and do nothing. That's how I pass my day as an artist – and
that's good. But if I were to have an assistant at my studio, he would
need to have something to do, and I have no idea what that would
be. The more you have assistants the more you need money, and the
more you must produce – and if you produce too much, it will always
be bad.

I have time – I have time to look at the TV, to do stupid things.
Sometimes it is difficult to think of anything when you are totally
empty, so you pass the whole day looking at the TV and you become so
depressed. It's worse than a drug.

RH *That's what you occasionally end up doing as a student – watch TV
all day.*

CB I sometimes teach at an art school in Paris – in France it's not like
here, you can go when you want, both the students and the teachers –
and I always say to my students, 'The only thing you can do is to wait
and to hope'.

RH *Let's talk some more about your current work. Recently, you have
turned to sound as an artistic medium.*

CB I work a lot with sound. I made a piece last summer for a very
big room in a very small village. When you arrived in this big room
there were plenty of seats and whenever you sat on one, a voice would

ask, 'What did you do with your life? Who are your friends?' And you would leave feeling a little destroyed. Outside there was an old truck with a very big loudspeaker, which gave answers – hundreds and hundreds of stupid, contradictory answers. It was a kind of clarion call: what I wanted to say is that there are many questions but no answers.

RH *You mentioned earlier that you have made work using the sound of heartbeats.*

CB I think of myself as a painter, even though I don't care so much about the medium. I just try to find the best medium to say what I want to say. For instance, there are two ways to use video: there's one way that is close to film, and one way that is close to sculpture. In fact, it is not the medium that's important. It's the fact that you have a beginning and an end, and that you can move around in the space. If you have to sit, and if you have a beginning and an end, I think you are in the art of time like music, theatre, or film. If you can move around, you are in the art of space.

For this reason the choice was not whether to use video or not but to choose to be in the art of time or in the art of space. If I have a major show like a retrospective, I try to make a work with a beginning and an end. I have made many musical spectacles in which I try to make art to do with time and space. A work can run for six hours, but people can stay ten minutes or one hour – just as they like – and move around: they are not in front of something, they are inside something.

When you use time you have something marvellous – suspense. Very often the emotion comes from what I call '*reversement*'. I don't know if you have seen *La Dolce Vita* by Federico Fellini, in particular the moment when, after so many sad and awful things have happened, he goes to the beach and sees this young girl and everything is changed. You can do these kinds of thing only with time – not with space. What I am trying to do now is to make something like the beginning of a novel, but something that is at the same time totally real.

I'm working on two projects at the moment. One is a permanent installation on the island of Ejima in the Sea of Japan. It is a very beautiful place. What I want to do on this small island is to create some kind of a foundation and to store a million heartbeats there. It is going to open in two years and it will be possible to go there and say, 'I want to hear the heart of Mrs Smith', and the technicians will make it possible for you to hear the heart of Mrs Smith. Now I collect heartbeats. I already have something like 7,000 heartbeats but each day there are going to be more and more. For me it is like the beginning of a novel: 'There is an island in the Sea of Japan with millions of heartbeats … ' But if it were only a novel, it wouldn't be very interesting to me. What is interesting is that it is real. You can actually go there.

The other project is with a man I met who is from Tasmania. He is a very, very rich man because he is a thief: he plays at the casino and wins a lot of money. He never loses because he can remember millions of numbers. He came to see me in Paris and I told him I wanted to play with him. We decided that I would sell him a piece, which he would pay for every month by instalment, over a period of eight years. If I die in two years, he is the winner; if I die in ten years, he loses money. He told me that he never loses, but we will have to see.

RH *He didn't ask for a health check before investing in the piece?*

CB We have a contract: if he dies before me his daughter must give me the money until I die. What I sold him is my life. There will be several cameras in my studio and he will be sent a video of my life. He can keep the DVD of my life, but he can only use it when I am dead.

In that event, he will have lost nothing because if he had paid me for two years, he would have two years of my life, but if he had paid me for 20 years he would have 20 years of my life. It is like the beginning of a novel: 'There is a very rich man in Tasmania who knows the future, or pretends to know the future. He doesn't really know the future, but he could kill me …'

This is an edited version of an interview which took place at the Starr Auditorium, Tate Modern on 6 December 2008.

Francis Alÿs

interviewed by Anna Dezeuze

Walking the Line

ANNA DEZEUZE *The piece you present at your first solo show in the UK in 1999, 61 out of 60, was related to the Zapatista movement in the Chiapas. How was it displayed?*

FRANCIS ALŸS It was simply presented on a table. It was only shown once, at the Lisson Gallery, in the late 1990s. I had made 60 plaster figurines of guerrilleros, which I broke into hundreds of pieces, and then I reused the material to create 61 figures. It was like the small miracle of the multiplication of the Zapatistas at the time. There was a laptop next to the work which allowed visitors to be in direct contact with the Zapatista website in the Chiapas, a Zapatistas internet site where you could chat. It was intended to draw attention to the existence of the Zapatista movement because I realised that it was practically unknown in England; I'm not sure whether it's better known now. The relations between the UK and Latin America are practically non-existent, since it did not form part of the British Empire. This is beginning to change because contemporary Latin American art has opened internationally, but it remains a bit of a caricature – especially in the UK because I think it belongs to another history.

AD *In terms of your relation to Mexico, and your thoughts about Mexican society in which you live, how would you position the Zapatistas?*

FA Zapatism is directly linked to 1994 when there was a clear fracture in Mexican society. 1994 was a year of great disillusionment in Mexico, and Zapatism was probably the event that attracted the most media coverage. In terms of my personal experience of the city, and of my artistic trajectory, 1994 was probably the moment when I shifted from the role of an observer to one that sought to get involved in a more political arena – I mean 'political' in the sense of 'polis', 'of the city'. Also, everyday life in the city changed considerably at that time. When I arrived in the 1980s, you could walk around the city at night without any problem. The government's complete loss of credibility really happened in the mid 1990s, when the neoliberal programmes and promises collapsed, and the state lost all control over the situation. It has not really been able to recover ever since. Somehow that period also marked a clear shift in my relations with Mexico. People realised that the promise of 'progress', of entering the 'First World', was a complete fraud, and the reaction that followed that deception was quite violent – disgust, and rejection of all political power and representation and, later on, a reaction against the whole US model of society. So it was really a turning point in local history, and in my own personal history. To go back to the Zapatistas, they probably stood for this rupture, although their own discourse was completely different. They remain a kind of barometer of the national health.

AD *What about your more recent work, exhibited at the Vincent Award in Amsterdam,* The Lynchings? *This kind of imagery seems unusual in relation to your other work.*

FA Yes and no. It's not fundamentally different from other projects where I want to flag up a phenomenon which is becoming increasingly common. In this case it is the phenomenon of lynchings that emerged in the early 2000s, as a way of saying ...

AD *There is no justice?*

FA Yes. It was also a crude manifestation of the disillusionment of indigenous communities in places like Guatemala or the Chiapas, which were utterly frustrated by the ineffectiveness of the state legal system and saw in such methods – lynching is a very generic term – means of reintroducing a code of justice that could escape central government authority, and of regaining an autonomous space, some kind of identity in the age of globalisation. It is an ongoing phenomenon that is not covered much beyond the front pages of the local newspaper, and which is not really analysed outside of the immediate local context. It's a phenomenon that seemed to me nevertheless quite revealing of a general state of things in Mexico and in some other Latin American countries today. I wanted to translate this horror – a little like Goya's images of war.

AD *So they're paintings based on newspaper photographs?*

FA No, no. They're paintings – there are only three or four of them, very few – based more on echoes of events that I heard or read about: of undercover policemen in Tlahuac who were burned alive, or others elsewhere who were hanged by the mob. In general, the images that make it into the papers are very poor in quality; they are usually taken with mobile phones in the middle of great confusion. So my images don't have a precise source – they come largely from the description or rumour of the events. They are – I don't think 'allegorised' is the relevant term – reduced to the essence of the scene. In Amsterdam they were presented alongside a series of texts that I had found in newspapers and on the web around this phenomenon.

AD *It is a surprising type of imagery, since this kind of violence tends not to be present in your work as a whole.*

FA Is it any more violent than taking a photograph of someone sleeping in the street? I'm not sure.

AD *You are referring to your slide show, 'Sleepers', begun in 1999, which shows images of people and dogs sleeping in public spaces. Do you ever fear that this kind of image, like the ones in the other slide shows – 'Ambulantes', ongoing since 1994, or 'Beggars', ongoing since 2000 – might be interpreted as voyeuristic, or even sentimental?*

FA Certainly it's always a risk. It's like walking along a tightrope. I'm constantly involved in damage control because the documentary series can be read as paternalistic, naive, sentimental or judgemental, especially when they're exported outside their original context. I'm always aware of this risk, but when you address a certain sphere of society – a kind of sub-society – that risk is an unavoidable collateral effect. Yet all these people who live around my studio in the historical centre of Mexico City remain the principal inspiration for many of my projects, and they are a constant reminder of the crude reality of the metropolis.

With the 'Sleepers' series, what interested me was the use of public space in such a private way. It was this 'private within the public' sphere that I was interested in. There are few activities as private as sleeping, and it's this way of appropriating space – whether it's 2sqm or the hidden-away places in the city – and the way this is completely integrated within the urban system, that I'm interested in. It's not a marginal activity any more, it's something that has become part of what the city offers.

It's the same with the 'Beggars', and the way they beg at subway entrances: it's this appropriation of this particular space, for this specific activity, that I'm interested in.

AD *So you're not that interested in the question of whether they have a choice in the matter or not?*

FA I'm interested, of course, but I don't think it's something I could translate in the work. If I did I would fall precisely into a more patronising reading. I believe my role as an artist – with the advantage of being always a little out of sync with the reality of my adoptive home, even though I'm losing that distance lately – is to witness how this society in which I've decided to live since 1990 works, how it is evolving, and how it manages to maintain its own identity throughout this evolution. That's the dimension – which isn't necessarily only the artist's privilege – that I'm interested in personally, in relation to both the city of Mexico and other places where I've found myself.

AD *Can a witness be a force for change?*

FA There are different levels. There is a kind of consciousness-raising, which is the first stage – to awaken a reaction which might help improve the reading of the situation. That's the small miracle of the contemporary art scene: it has been opened to a wider public, and I think at that level the artist's potential to act and to intervene is certainly much bigger now than 20 years ago. Up to what point can the artist influence the course of local history? I don't know. It is impossible not to react to urban aggression in Mexico City. It is a personal need to constantly position yourself in relation to a changing urban entity, and to record these changes, as well as an urge to make people aware of what is being lost, and what may be gained eventually. But of course I'm not talking about a social programme for on-site interventions. Let's say that I'm more at a recording, flag-waving stage.

I think the artist can intervene by provoking a situation in which you suddenly step out of everyday life and start looking at things again from a different perspective – even if it is just for an instant. That may be the artist's privilege, and that's where his field of intervention differs from that of an NGO or a local journalist.

AD *This kind of poetic rupture is of course at the heart of your 2004 work,* Sometimes doing something poetic leads to something political and sometimes something political leads to something poetic, *also known as 'the Green Line'.*

FA   Yes, in this case in particular, the action had to be borderline ridiculous for people to start talking beyond stereotypical discourses on the left or on the right, whether Palestinian or Israeli. It was about recreating spontaneity in a situation which is not spontaneous at all, which has become so weighed-down by its own inertia, its 'impasse'.

AD   *Is this why you chose to make the piece on your own, rather than make a collective work like* When Faith Moves Mountains *in Lima in 2002 or* Bridge/Puente in Key West-La Havana *in 2006?*

FA   I didn't consider the option of doing a collective piece, maybe because someone had to take on the responsibility in order to provoke a shift, and in this specific case this responsibility had to fall on one individual rather than on a collective body. But it was the collective action of *When Faith Moves Mountains* that raised the question of the extent to which one can play between the poetical and the political, and which triggered the piece in Jerusalem.

There were specific reasons why I chose Jerusalem as the site for that project. It wasn't a commission, it was a project that I sought out, and I think I chose Jerusalem because it was – in terms of an intervention within a conflict situation – the one that was the most archetypal, the most historically representative of a conflict situation that was ...

AD   *Extreme?*

FA   It's extreme because – to use a cliché – Jerusalem is the cradle of western civilisation, and that's a large part of the reason why it has such international resonance. But it is a minor conflict. I'm afraid to say this, but as important as it may be – and of course any human life that is lost is the most important thing in the world – if you look at the numbers, I would say that since the beginning of this year [2008] there must have been around a maximum of 100 victims or so, whereas the narcotics conflict in Mexico has so far claimed the shocking figure of almost 3,000 victims. Does the British press talk much about this internal gang war? I doubt it. In terms of casualties only, the Palestinian-Israeli conflict is a minor conflict, yet it is a millennial conflict, and perhaps one of the most representative today of the clash between two cultural models. It has incredible international resonance, although in comparison with many conflicts taking place on the planet today, it is a small conflict. It's this paradox that I found interesting.

AD   *It's a conflict that's very violent at the level of discourse, too.*

FA   I was criticised for interviewing mostly left-wing people, whether on the Palestinian or Israeli side. The reality was that because of my personal sympathies, my contacts naturally happened to be left-wing, so it was very difficult to approach right-wing people who would agree to talk. We tried to approach the Rabbi of Jerusalem, but we got nowhere. The closest we got in terms of centre-right was Shimon Peres – we had three meetings scheduled with Peres, which were all cancelled at the last moment.

The action itself was a pretext for the commentary. In a way there were 15 potential actions, and I chose the most obvious, the most immediate one, in order to provoke a reaction. My intention was not to intervene within the space of a conflict situation, but to generate, through this act, a commentary about that situation, the opposite, if you like, of what I do here in Mexico, where a given situation exists, and I try to – I was going to say 'exploit it' – to transcend it, to translate it. In the case of Jerusalem, I first had to interact with the situation in order to trigger the discourse, whereas here it is the existing situation that triggers the discourse.

AD   *And in terms of your practical experience, did you have problems intervening within the city – at the checkpoints perhaps?*

FA   Very little. In fact, one of the interviewed people – Rima Hamami – said when she saw the film: 'You are a real sneaker, you walk fast, like a Palestinian in the crowd.'

AD   *But another of your interviewees, Eyal Weizman, criticises this ease. He says it's not easy for a Palestinian to walk around.*

FA   The action was made easier by the fact that a lot of people did not identify the route, or the action, and that has something to do with the issue of memory, the fact that history is forgotten more quickly than we think. And I certainly played on the tactical margin described by Meron Benvenisti when he recounts how Moshe Dayan drew the original green line with a green wax crayon and the 3-4mm line on the 1:20,000 scale map represented, on the ground, a 60-80m-wide strip of land equivalent to a whole city block. This allowed me to avoid the checkpoints in advance by walking along the other side of the block, while remaining within the width of the green line.

AD   *So you were able to avoid checkpoints. But there is one at the end of the film.*

FA   Yes, it was the exit, it was inevitable – it's the only road in that place.

AD *But if you'd been Palestinian you may not have been allowed to pass.*

FA That's true. Maybe it's something similar to what happened with my revolver work, *Re-enactments*, 2000, in which I walked down the street with a gun until the Mexico City police stopped me. Perhaps because of its ridiculous or absurd quality, an artistic action becomes excusable, and sometimes it can make its way through unlikely situations because it simply cannot be taken seriously. Humour – or a humorous dimension – often allows you to bypass situations that would not otherwise have been allowed to happen if I had taken, for instance, a militant attitude.

AD *The ease with which you walk through the city makes me wonder about something more general in your work. What I like a lot in your work is that you manage to speak of a general human condition through your own individual narratives. Obviously this is very different from the discourse of 'identity politics' where one talks less of the human condition than of 'the Palestinian problem', 'the condition of women', or of gays ... How would you situate yourself in this context?*

FA If there is a possible field of action it must pass through an acceptance that the human condition is the most immediate, the most tangible of spaces. I'm not going to speak of a space of 'intervention', because it's not intervention so much as conviviality. Intervention would imply that I am external to the situation, whereas I think in the collective actions I attempt to erase that distance by creating a space of conviviality.

AD *And solidarity?*

FA It is a kind of solidarity, but even the term solidarity may be somewhat condescending. By conviviality, I mean being in the same place at the same time for the same goal or reason – even if three hours later everyone has gone back to their own private world. I think that it's possible to achieve this conviviality through – and I'm going to use a term that's a bit outdated today – through endurance. I think here we go back to the discourse surrounding work as a space of conviviality, but I'm speaking of physical work. When I was a student for some time I used to be a demolition contractor, and that was a fantastic space of conviviality – to destroy a house with a group of ten people is one of the most intense collective experiences. I don't want to fall into sentimentality here – I don't come from a working-class background, and on average my activity is probably more intellectual than manual – but in my experience, activities that involve a highly physical component, and are collective, lead to a degree of complicity that is much more difficult to achieve in intellectual activities.

I have been thinking about this as Raphael Ortega and I were working on an event in the Straits of Gibraltar this summer. It was a rather straightforward project, an image of a bridge of boats between Tarifa and Tangiers.

AD *Did you use the same system as in the* Bridge/Puente *you made between Florida and Cuba?*

FA Yes, it was similar, but in the Florida/Cuba project I was left with the feeling that I hadn't exploited the full potential of the action.

AD *Why?*

FA Because I think I focused too much on the Havana side, thinking that it would be immensely difficult to make something concrete happen over there, so I left the Florida side somewhat behind. These projects are fuelled by the organisers' convictions – in this case those of Taiyana Pimentel, Cuauhtémoc Medina and myself – and the im-balance between the responses on each side was more a consequence of our degree of involvement with each side than a true manifestation of each side's intention. The end result was misleading, in a sense – we ended up with too many boats in Cuba, and not enough in Florida, which led people to conclude that Cubans are eager to leave and Americans are not. This reading, which happens to correspond too neatly to the general expectation, did not necessarily reflect the reality of the situation, but was largely influenced by the logistics of the project.

AD *So, did you manage to resolve the problem in Gibraltar?*

FA In Gibraltar we changed the mechanism. Instead of fishermen, we worked with teenagers, and with models of boats – shoe-boats, as we called them. It became much more of a celebration of the passage in between, a ritual of sorts. The metaphorical dimension was present, but in a more ludic way. There's a section where the action turns into a children's tale, or a fable, soon after the two lines of kids, coming from each shore, meet up on the horizon.

What I was interested in – and that was largely a lesson from the Key West-Havana project which had turned out a bit like a military operation in terms of the logistics involved – was getting back to a project that would be more playful, where the viewer had to provide, through his or her imagination, the missing fragment that would unite Europe and Africa. That missing stretch on the viewer's horizon became the *conditio sine qua non* for an artistic operation to take place. Since the distance between the two continents is only about ten miles in some parts of the Straits, we could have imagined the possibility of gathering enough boats to make a real bridge joining both sides. But to do so would have turned it into a military operation, recalling the way in which such bridges get built during floods or wars. The political connotation was so evident that there was no need to insist on that aspect.

Anyway, the reason I'm bringing all this up is that it was an occasion where conviviality through collective effort was really achieved. It was a collective effort geared towards making a gesture. It's not easy to document, however. The direct record of the action can only suggest something of the emotion of the moment and most often simply recording the event will not be enough to translate that emotion. The documentation becomes another chapter of the story, which cannot compete with the event. Each chapter represents a specific life of the project, and you should not let one take over from the other. It is very difficult to find the right balance: when you do the event you shouldn't be influenced by its documentation, and when you do the documentation you shouldn't be presenting the facts so much as conveying to the viewer your memory of the emotional dimension of the facts. Each time, you have to reinvent a language to tell the story.

AD *I like that very direct, very open relationship to reality in your work. But I get the feeling that in some works this relationship gets lost precisely because you're too concerned with this issue of documentation. For example, in* The Rehearsal II *of 2005, which involves a female striptease artist who stops and backtracks in the course of her act according to an audio recording of a singer rehearsing a Schumann* Lied *with her pianist, it felt very …*

FA … theatrical?

AD *Yes, especially in comparison with* The Rehearsal I *of 1999–2004, in which the Volkswagen Beetle tries to go up a hill, also following a rehearsal recording, in this case of a Mexican brass band.*

FA Yes. The striptease in *Rehearsal II* is much colder. I would almost say that it's a flat image. I saw it as an episode in a larger narration, as part of a whole. The seduction game and the linear progression inherent to the striptease offered the ideal situation for what I wanted to illustrate: the feeling of frustration provoked by an endless postponement of any conclusion. The striptease literally embodied the temporal space that I was looking for, and I didn't really question the space of representation. Yet it is possible that the connotations of the situation itself take over from the temporality that it tries to represent. It is different, in its aesthetic, from my other works. Were you also wondering about this relation between reality and representation in *Gringo*, 2003?

AD *I like this work very much because in it your relation to reality is very direct, and the vulnerability that this involves becomes visible.*

FA Yet this suggestion of vulnerability happened by accident. We had wanted to stage this a lot more than we were able to. Originally we were in fact working with a trained dog and a dog handler who was going to help us film the scene. But there were other dogs on the road where we had chosen to shoot. They had been calm when we had started, but after the first and second takes they got restless and they attacked and bit the trained dog because they probably felt that their territory was being invaded or threatened. The dog handler got really upset and left in a rage, and we ended up working with the street dogs, so we were driven right back into a field of operations that involved a direct intervention in a given situation.

AD *But you didn't get bitten, did you?*

FA Oh, I got bitten all right!

AD *Oh dear, it isn't exactly Chris Burden's* Shoot, *but it's not that far off …*

FA Thinking of that work, I think there's a space of direct relation to reality, of sincerity and emotion, that's related to youth. Often works by young artists are poignant in their – I wouldn't say naivety – but certainly in their ingenuity, their absolute conviction. And because I'm no longer 'young' – you know, when they're doing a mid-career survey of your work like the one planned for Tate in 2010, then that's it, it's one foot in the grave, one way or another – I have become more sensitive to youth and to what artists whom I respect and admire did when they were young. Often there is an emotion – and I'm not talking about nostalgia here – a kind of emotion that gets lost little by little with maturity, sometimes in line with the artist's growing confidence, ambition, or doubts. It's slippery territory. I think this is an inevitable phenomenon – and this is why I say it's a personal worry.

AD *What about your paintings? I have a feeling that your paintings and your drawings are the most personal side of your work, the most hermetic in the sense that they appear to relate to your personal preoccupations and obsessions.*

FA   My paintings are always created in parallel with the actions. It is a way of taking a certain distance from the logistical problems involved in a project like the one in Gibraltar, for example, which concern production, managing unions, permits, transport, etc – they're very, very concrete problems that are not poetic at all. So drawing and painting are my way of thinking about a project without thinking about – of thinking about it in a different way, from another angle. The Gibraltar project generated lots of drawings because it was such a long project, and because it was a project that somehow lent itself to images. It's a therapeutic activity. It's really a way of processing ideas.

The paintings and drawings are also what finance my other projects. I don't systematically lose money with these projects – though I often do – but they're definitely not projects that generate profit, or at least not the profit that would help produce the next project. They break even at best. So there's certainly an internal logic in my mode of functioning.

AD   *To go back to our discussion regarding reality and representation, I have the feeling that the paintings occupy a purely …*

FA   … imaginary space? Yes, absolutely.

AD   *A space which in fact allows you to return to reality in a more direct way once you've finished the paintings.*

FA   They certainly clarify my discourse. But they're really a way of going forward without thinking about it. Painting is such a slow activity. It's not like writing, because there's a point where you let go. And because it's so easy, and so irresponsible – unlike real action.

AD   *And it's a more sensual activity.*

FA   Yes, but it's a real space for thinking, which I need, and a kind of step back from the speed of the other projects where once the production is launched, everything has to go fast. Drawing and painting are the opposite: they involve stepping back from this rat race. But of course it's a space that I question a lot with regard to the other side of my production. Are they compatible? It's a necessary process, let's say, in my own practice, but is it necessary to disseminate them? Sometimes yes, sometimes no. I'll tell you one thing: I've saved you from a lot of paintings. Most of my paintings are painted over two or three others, so there's always a process of natural selection going on.

AD   *I'd like to ask you about your axiomatic formulas, like 'sometimes doing something leads to nothing/sometimes doing nothing leads to something' or 'sometimes doing something poetic leads to something political' (and vice versa). This way of thinking in terms of pseudo-mathematical axioms, where does it come from?*

FA In the case of the 1997 'ice piece', *Paradox of Praxis I*, which corresponds to the axiom 'sometimes doing something leads to nothing', and involved pushing a block of ice around the streets of Mexico until only a puddle was left, there is actually a counterpart that I am still working on: 'sometimes making nothing leads to something'. I wanted to relativise each axiom through its opposite, even if it sounds complementary, in a way. That helped me take away any kind of real positioning. If you make two proposals that cancel each other out, it is also a way of saying that neither is primary, neither has more weight than the other in terms of the proposition.

AD *So we're back on that tightrope again?*

FA Yes, we're back on the tightrope.

Issue 323, February 2009

Lorna Simpson

interviewed by Alison Green

Mirror Images

ALISON GREEN *I am interested in* Photo Booth *of 2008, a work which comprises photo-booth images plus small ink drawings, particularly because it has to do with your appropriation of an archive, and because certain strategies it uses resonate with other ways that you approach work.*

LORNA SIMPSON Yes, I've always had an interest in photography – not only in what the photographs declare or how we might read them, but also in the viewer's desire in relation to those images. The photo-booth image is really a self-portrait and all these images that I found were from the 1920s up until about the 1960s. What is uncanny about them is the posing that occurs because the sitters are really posing in front of a mirror in order to have the image taken, so it is a very direct gaze. The gaze at one's self reveals a particular kind of facial expression represented in order to evoke a desired expression – as opposed to just having your photograph taken by a photographer. The portraits are quite intense in terms of the way the sitters gaze at themselves. On the wall these small bronze-framed images seem dispersed, but as you come closer to them, they become these miniature, intense portraits.

The drawings – the ink stains – are, to me, like the back of a photograph when you rip it out of an album and part of the black paper is stuck to it, or the way a photograph deteriorates chemically so that stains are created over the course of time. So I used the stains to mimic a set of images that are already there, or thinking of them just in terms of the way that photographic images deteriorate.

AG *These images are really interesting. There are all sorts of issues that emerge to do with the relationship between the person posing not to a*

photographer but to a mirror, given the structure of the photo-booth. I was
thinking, also, that the figure in that relationship is the intended audience
because, in a way, when you go into a photo-booth, most of the time the
picture is made for a purpose. It is maybe for the purposes of identification
for an audience or it is a memento –

LS – or just to have some kind of visual communication about how
well you are doing or how things are going. A lot of the images were
taken during the time of the Jim Crow laws – segregation laws in the
US. It is portraiture during a particular time in American history
but also of individuals who were leaving the South and going north.
There is this kind of necessity to show that you are safe or to show
that you are doing well having left what was home. I don't believe that
it necessarily means that all was well; but to be able to project how
one might want to be perceived.

AC *And it turned out not all of them were of men …*

LS I was given a handful of portraits of men but, looking through
them, I realised that they were not all men. So, again, this idea of
gender, and the way that gender plays and is read within a spectrum
of race was apparent just in my dealings with these sorts of images.

AC *This draws out one of the issues that you are working with – how the*
social body is defined through photography or through an archive or
any kind of bureaucratic system that organises and categorises, where
representations become inadequate or fall apart or misrepresent or
subjugate. There is a series of drawings you made after the invasion of
Iraq – could you talk about 'The Interrogation Drawings' *from 2008?*

LS The series is about people who were 'detained' for interrogation
and the way that information is conveyed in the media and how
certain rights that we have as individuals are suspended.

One is of a blindfolded Iraqi businessman who has been detained
and held for interrogation by American soldiers. There is a kind of
acceptance of what we see in such images, which come to be seen
as the norm.

AC *That is an image that appeared in the* New York Times *of a top Iraqi*
official held at the Baiji refinery who was suspected of skimming profits
and having ties to insurgents.

LS Although he is blindfolded and handcuffed – I mean, his name
is Ghalib Ali Hamid and details are published as part of the caption –
who is he being blindfolded from? It becomes an interesting prospect. It is more about the assumption on the part of the American

public of what you accept as responsible interrogation practices –
like holding and detaining individuals during a time of war.

I did some research about interrogation rooms. There are these
places that repurpose rooms like gymnasiums, bath-houses or derelict buildings temporarily to interrogate or torture, but then there
are also these instant pop-up plywood maze-like structures that are
constructed by the military for the same purpose.

AG *Structures that can be moved and rebuilt?*

LS Exactly. Easily dismantled – they disappear.

AG *The original image is a documentary image but you are involved in a
kind of representation of that through a different medium in an attempt
to reorient or reconstruct our vision about what that is. Part of what
photojournalism does is that it leads us towards a particular interpretation
of something, but it also normalises the looking at something. The photograph doesn't actually prove anything but, with the caption and within the
context of a newspaper, for instance, it is there as evidence.*

LS It also develops a kind of apathy, an unquestioned acceptance
after a certain point.

AG *Was this after the Abu Ghraib photographs, after the controversy
around those events?*

LS Yes.

AG *I still have a memory of seeing those images for the first time and not
understanding how horrible they were because, in some respects, they
looked like pranks.*

LS What is also interesting about that is the situation of the soldiers
coping with their day-to-day life and having no boundaries in terms
of how they accomplish what they felt they were there to accomplish
and the obvious beliefs that they held about ethnicity and religion.
So living within that hell, the response is to create a mirror. The
photographic evidence is trophy-like. The images really speak to what
they are doing day after day and what they were capable of on a day-
to-day level.

AG *Let us go back to an early, iconic work from 1986,* Waterbearer.
*In a way it could serve to orient us towards your particular use of text
and image and also to the way that you were using photography as a move
away from documentary. You started out as a documentary photographer
but made a break with that and started to pursue photography in a
particular way with particular purposes that were quite different.*

LS I have to say, in terms of my education, probably experimental film had a lot to do with looking at the way that I made these kinds of images – taking away the background completely, turning the gaze away from the viewer, and giving the viewer something else to think about rather than supplying the viewer with visual expression or emotional details or personality traits in terms of the reading of the images. Eliminating all of those desired aspects of the way that we read photographs allowed the text to talk about something else.

I think my frustration with documentary photography at the time was how the same tools were used to read each photograph regardless of photographer, regardless of subject, and in some ways I wanted to take away those tools. Thus what viewers expect from a photograph would be slightly circumvented.

So, this kind of image, which is ten years' worth of work, had this sort of structure: the figure, actor and text. In particular, the text in *Waterbearer* speaks about memory – memories that are denied or not accounted for, or recognised – but not in a nostalgic way, rather in terms of the consequences of one's memory.

This is an example where the work is more, I would say, poetic. But then again the text – and other works – were created in a manner more like concrete poetry, where lists of things start appearing or an accumulation of lists or alliteration that creates a sense of a particular time or story. So, within my relationship to text there was a lot of back and forth and playing with words, playing with language and double meanings.

AC *You stripped away a lot of information from the image so that it is in an apparently neutral space.*

LS Well, it is a constructed image.

AC *The white dress in* Waterbearer *– is it a shift or some form of institutionalised garment that she has been made to wear? In the text and in the image, she has been pulled out of a specific time and place that, say, a documentary image would give to you. But that isn't to say that it lacks a politics. The text directs us towards a certain interpretation of what we are looking at. She has witnessed something. There is a connection to the interrogation rooms in a certain sense of the way memory is suggested.*

LS Or the silencing of memory. I didn't think about those connections back to the earlier work, but it's true. I think I have found the junction of memory with regard to political contexts of silence, erasure and revision compelling. It is the moment those things collide that I find to be visceral.

AG *I read an early text about your work by Bell Hooks who talked about this work in terms of countering the racist and sexist stereotyping of African Americans in photography. She read this as the first positive image of a black woman she had seen.*

LS I think my effort was to think about the 'who' pictured in photography and what assumptions are made about the portrait or the individual almost regardless of race. The way that, for instance, Diane Arbus's work is interpreted and so much is interpreted – about her personal life and suicide in terms of looking at those images in a kind of timeline of her own destruction – in some ways, I think, takes away from the power of the work in and of itself. Being immersed in the history of photography, all those things seemed to be for the pleasure of creating a biography about the photographer in the reading of the images, which I found too neat a structure. The reading of the work and the narrative about the photographer feed on each other. I think that maybe I did not assign a specific narrative to the subject in a manner that was the usual linear binary relationship of image and text.

AG *Arbus's pictures always had a subject – that is what they are about – whereas you have put the subject to the side. In a certain sense one is always thinking about the relationship between Arbus and her subject in those pictures – that is the dynamic and that is the fascinating part of them. The images in your work function in a completely different way. I think that is a great demonstration, in a way, of the difference. In* You're Fine, You're Hired *of 1988, the use of text is very different.*

LS On the left side it reads: 'Physical exam, blood test, heart, reflexes, chest x-ray, abdomen, electrocardiogram, urine, lung capacity, eyes, ears, height, weight.' And on the right it reads: 'Secretarial position.'

It was made at the beginning of the AIDS epidemic. When I got out of graduate school I quickly got a job as a secretary in one of these kinds of corporate offices. The text lists the things that they said they were testing for, but in fact they were testing for drugs; they were testing for AIDS; they were doing all kinds of tests to see whether or not you were actually a viable candidate to work within their company or if you were a liability. If you were fine, you were hired; if you were not fine, you were not hired. The law has now changed but it was one of those discriminatory practices in terms of using healthcare as a way to sort the potential employees.

AG Wigs *is another text-image piece that I would like to discuss because again the text is used very differently.*

LS Most reviewers assume, 'Oh, it is about the way black women wear their hair', but it is nothing to do with that. In fact, the piece has to do with gender and how we think about gender in this culture and the kind of binary sense of the boundaries of masculinity and femininity. It is to do with different moments in history and how on a day-to-day level people choose to live their lives in terms of their appearance and their gender. It is really to do with transgendered politics. The piece was done in the 1990s but it is much more part of the culture now than it was then.

There is one text which is about a man named William Craft and his wife, Ellen Craft, who were fugitive slaves and wanted to escape slavery from the South, going to the North and New York. She was light-skinned, so she pretended to be an elderly white man and her husband, who was a slave and very dark-skinned, pretended to be her slave. So it was a mimicking of the very social structure that they were trying to escape, which in disguise they embodied, that allowed them to escape. This is one example of the necessity of changing the roles of gender and sexuality.

Another text in *Wigs* is about cabaret acts by Gladys Bentley which created this institutionalisation of anti-cross-dressing laws in Los Angeles in the 1950s. It is to do with the social and public obsession of trying to limit or control someone's sexual or gender identity at the time of their death, as though by post-mortem evaluation or examination you can determine whether someone was a man or a woman and then that becomes fact and creates some sort of social closure that is acceptable. The piece, really, deals with that.

AC *By pointing to historical examples, the text gives these issues a sort of grounding. You seem to explore the issue as being concretely experienced or historically experienced.*

LS It is multifaceted. I appropriated the text of a discussion between a mother and a sociologist. She is talking about her son who is maybe five or six years old. In that conversation the dialogue goes back and forth and it becomes very clear that the mother is completely obsessed with her son's behaviour in terms of his liking for stockings or mannequins. It is her concerns about the appropriateness of his behaviour that is really what is at issue rather than anything to do with 'fixing' or changing the child's behaviour. So it is to do with a personal construct of masculinity.

I live in Brooklyn, where there is one very long mall with maybe 60 – I don't know how many – different wig shops in one section. I just bought as many different kinds of wigs as I could. There was one wig I bought that was a kind of natural afro and was made from real hair, but generally they are all highly stylised and completely different from one another, which I found fascinating.

AG The Park *of 1995 is another lithograph on felt and maybe this would be the context to talk about the change from, say, a silver gelatin print to this very soft surface. Felt is used in printing as a buffer, not normally as a surface to print on.*

LS This comes from a series that I called 'Public Sex'. I always used to carry a Hasselblad camera with me when I travelled. What was funny about that was I thought that if you carry a big, heavy camera as opposed to an instant camera you are absolutely bound to take photographs – like you have to if you've lugged this through customs in a separate, heavy bag.

I was in New Mexico reading a book by Pat Califia called *Public Sex*. This is a really interesting anecdotal historical account about how people choose and transform public spaces into sexual spaces. In thinking about that I realised that I had all these empty photographs of different public spaces that I had taken over the course of the year without any intention – really as a way of assigning myself something that doesn't have a purpose. After reading that book, I was like: 'Wow. This is a perfect solution to using those images in a certain way because they are anonymous and they don't have individuals in them, but they are of public spaces.'

The Park, which is of Madison Park in New York, was taken from a friend of mine's apartment. On one side there is a text from a sociologist named Laud Humphreys who documented the sexual activities of men in public toilets. He is an intriguing character because his ethical way of being a sociologist and a participant was very interesting, but also because his subjects were viewed at the time as engaging in degenerate behaviour. Humphreys wasn't well respected nor was he seen as being qualified in terms of his choice of subject matter. It was the subject matter that others wouldn't even look at.

What I found interesting about him was that he would position himself as a lookout within these bathrooms and then he would casually exit, maybe even engage in a conversation with a subject, and then watch them walk to their cars and write down their licence plate numbers. Then months later he would go to the DMV (the Department of Motor Vehicles) and request their addresses and then, two or three years later, he would request an interview as a sociologist about lifestyle with the subject. He would then interview the same men at home with their families. So it became this kind of binary or double life that he was trying to express.

That is a lot for a little piece of text. On the other side are the machinations of someone who has just got hold of a telescope to look as a voyeur at the goings-on in the park or in the buildings across the street.

A lot of the works from 'Public Sex' aren't so much about the kind of sex that is performed, but really about how one occupies public space and thinks about one's behaviour. When does that space become a park space during the day and a sexual space at night?

AG *The second text, which talks about looking through a telescope, implicates the viewing that the camera does because the camera also gives this position of distance. It is a voyeuristic position as well. This is a sort of lead-in to* Easy to Remember *of 2001.*

LS This is an early piece, a piece that I went back to. When I'm sometimes stymied as to what I should do next, I look back at the threads of my work. I had been making videos for about four or five years at that point. I wanted to do something that had not a narrative connection to my work but rather a kind of visual connection to what I had done previously, and that was easy to remember. In this video I shot maybe ten different individuals with the camera very close to their mouths. I did a casting call in Columbus, Ohio for singers and, in doing so, I got a bunch of people who could sing amazingly well. I had them wear headphones with John Coltrane playing the ballad *It's Easy To Remember*, the Rodgers and Hart composition. Because it is jazz it really threw the participants off because you have to choose a particular octave and you have to choose a particular part of the melody that you are going to follow. I grew up listening to a lot of jazz. That's me. I understood completely, because of my familiarity with that particular song. So although everyone was really experienced, the looped melody really threw the singers. I had certain singers that were freaked out, like: 'I can't start there! I'll start here and try to figure out how to hum this particular tune.'

AG *So it is a translation in itself.*

LS   Exactly. This piece and another video, *Cloudscape* from 2004, had to do with music but also had to do with the production of sound or melody from the body. Terry Adkins performs, whistling a phrase of *I Could Not Hear Nobody Pray*, a spiritual hymn. I wanted something that had to do with the body and the emotion of sound.

It was quite interesting to work with someone who was a baritone, or an alto, because there was a huge range in terms of the vocal quality and levels of people that participated. It required really going into a studio and editing all of them together in such a way that you get that range of the voices that were participating.

AG   *They are singing individually, so they come together as a chorus in post-production, as it were. It is simple in that way, but there is something quite complicated that happens when watching it which has to do with the slippages between looking and listening. It reminded me of those Bruce Nauman videos from the 1960s where he repeats a word over and over again so that you lose track and the meaning starts to change.*

LS   I think it has more to do with the listening. As participants, they are listening to something that is more abstracted, so therefore their participation is so much more tentative in terms of how they get through this song and, when you put it all together, it has a completely different feeling than if it had been just a straight-out melody.

AG   *This seems to embody certain issues that we know, but need to have demonstrated again, about the difference between, say, a fixed meaning in language versus how it gets used in speech. That leads fairly well to something else I wanted to discuss. You once mentioned that film allowed you more spontaneity than working with photography. I would have thought that it would be the opposite.*

LS   When I am in the studio by myself, photography fulfils a particular idea that comes to fruition and it is just a process of carrying it out. The process of film, however, is collaborative and means negotiating the many variables that collaboration always involves. I have a clear idea in my head of what it is that I want to accomplish, but the process of making shifts it and turns it, and different things happen – if you are open to that. I like the shift and change and collaboration that happens in film as a process, almost to the point that I don't care about the end product. The process is such an interesting one in terms of what I have in my head – how it gets made and the negotiation that I experience. I find this really interesting.

AC *Can you tell me about the 2006 work* Corridor?

LS It was a work commissioned by Mass MOCA and the Society for the Preservation of New England Antiquities in Boston, Massachusetts. At the time, the institution that was sponsoring it, and where the show was going to be held, allowed each artist 2,000sqft. It was a huge factory that they had turned into an exhibition space. Some people like large spaces – the more square footage the better – but just filling a room was really not of any interest to me. But what I did realise in going through their catalogue was that they owned a lot of property, and one of the properties that they owned was a house by Walter Gropius in Lincoln, Massachusetts, and another was a house that is called The Coffin House – it's a 1640s house. In Brooklyn, I live in a house built in the 1860s and I always thought it would be interesting to make a period piece because these houses almost reflect the pre-emancipation era in the US. But vernacular American architecture is changing all the time with additions and revamping, and the fascination with the Victorian era – a lot of that is lost.

So, it was a great opportunity to have these 100-year time periods in terms of character. I worked with Wangechi Mutu, who is an artist in her own right but who, at the time, had just finished working for me compiling images and information for a Phaidon monograph on my work. I asked her if she would be in the project playing two roles – a woman from the 1860s and a woman from the 1960s, showing their day-to-day lives. One woman is an indentured servant or slave in terms of her duties and takes care of the house during the day, and the other woman lives in her own architecturally modern house, prepares for an evening and gets stood up.

Nothing happens in either video. I think it is more a moment-to-moment chronicling of a certain number of hours from day to night. The soundtrack is by a composer named Blind Tom, or Tom Higgins, who was an enslaved African American who had an amazing gift of being able to hear a tune once and play it exactly. But because he was a slave, and because he was blind, he was paraded in a circus-like manner as a kind of idiot savant when, in fact, he was an amazing musician.

AC *Do recordings of his music exist?*

LS The compositions exist, but he died in poverty in 1908. Although the phonograph had been invented by 1857, I believe there are no recordings of Higgins, only of the manuscripts of his compositions, which include a lot of Americana and European music, and which have a dark quality that comes through in the music.

I paired his music with that of Albert Ayler, who was a concrete, experimental jazz composer during the 1960s. What is interesting – because you can hear it in Ayler's music – is that a lot of what is early American melody is part of his repertoire. It doesn't sound like that at first, but the playing of them together, mixing those two forms of composition – the similarity and the cadence of Americana plays through both of them. It was an idea that I had years before, but it created this physical opportunity to be able to create the piece.

AC *And there are all sorts of interesting things filmically, moments where one woman passes out of the screen and the other one comes in. Narratives are set up between the two screens and between these two time periods. Each woman has a kind of autonomy, but both are also stuck there in that house.*

LS You can think of the late 1950s or early 1960s in terms of the roles of women and the household. Also, in terms of timing, the other screen reflects the pre-emancipation moment: what the woman on the left must be thinking about her interior life, and how the advent of emancipation changed her interior life and will change also her day-to-day life. This echoes through to 1960, towards the end of the mid-part of the Civil Rights era and what is going on in a more middle-class woman's life in terms of the structural changes to both our routine and emotional lives.

This is an edited version of an interview which took place at the Starr Auditorium, Tate Modern on 7 March 2009. Published Issue 377, June 2014.

Liam Gillick

interviewed by John Slyce

Recuperating Modernism

JOHN SLYCE *Shall we begin by looking at the retrospective? How did things come together at the Kunstverein in Munich? I understand you staged a play?*

LIAM GILLICK The Munich aspect of the show is really the production part of the retrospective project. Everything else – in Zurich, Chicago and Rotterdam – had a somewhat dark quality, and I didn't get my hands dirty or get deeply engaged in the execution of the structures. In Zurich, Chicago and Rotterdam I gave back 50% of the space to each institution to deal with and use to address the work over the last 20 years. For Munich I thought it would be a good reflection of my practice to make one part of this retrospective absolutely production-orientated. And, of course, a play is literally a production. It's the aspect of the retrospective where I asked for certain elements to be put into place, including people – I worked with 15 actors. I had a basic outline of what this play would be and I had a basic structure in the gallery, but beyond that I didn't know the precise details until I got there.

That's taken me back, really, to my original way of working, which is a developed form of the Seth Siegelaub idea of sending artists to shows and not art. I put myself into the position I was in back in 1990 when I'd go to Nice and I'd work out what to do when I got there. It put me somewhat on the spot. I had to find a way to stage a play – in German.

JS *To produce a production in a post-production mode?*

LG Yes, exactly. It went on for two months or so, a longer run than a lot of real plays get.

The idea was to use the play as a way to introduce various

characters I have worked with over the years. I've often used the idea of the person who carries a narrative, or carries an ideological component within the work, and in this case I saw each of the characters in the play as potentially having multiple functions. They were, in a way, a group of people that I might have worked with over the years (or certain curators and artists), but at the same time they were also all one person – and they were also all me.

JS *And what is the historical time of the play?*

LG It is set on the day of the birth of the main character. Not a birthday but literally the day of birth. But it is also set in the present, in a bar next to a Volvo factory – hence the title *A Volvo Bar*. Some of the locations are also the Kunstverein, Munich itself. So the director's office, for example, is one of the locations – not literally; it is just one of the places that gets talked about. The basic outline is: there's a bar next to a Volvo factory and a man arrives on the day of his birth and interacts with various characters in the bar. They describe power relationships and locations which are those of the play. At the same time the discourse is generated from the perspective of a bar in Sweden.

Structurally, it makes perfect sense in relation to my work – the idea that you are forced to address the current surroundings (because that's where the work is), but you also have to accept, at some level, that the focus of the work is displaced. So you have a doubling of reference points in relation to the site and this causes tension that mirrors the way my work often functions. There's a concern, sometimes, in the way that people deal with the physical work that I make – that the work doesn't match my rhetoric, or the work doesn't seem to match the words. I've always wondered in which period of history art has literally matched what was said about it, in a precise way. I mean, that's what is interesting about art: the attempt to constantly redescribe the artwork, or redescribe what it is doing.

JS *Can we look more closely at the issue of avoiding the transparent message or direct access to meaning in the work. I've never had the sensation that there's a mismatch or disconnect between word and object in the work. In fact, that's the relationship set up. Can you talk about your wish to avoid that kind of transparency, even as far back as 1990 when you were looking at documentary forms?*

LG There are very clear reasons for this apparent avoidance. On an idealistic level, the only way you can use art is as a fragmented mirror of the complexity of contemporary society and you try to produce a system of art production that is just as multifaceted and potentially misleading, based on a series of parallels. This was my main revelation at art school – the idea of art production as a series of parallels. Michael Craig-Martin used to talk about the idea that instead of his work having a style within a trajectory of late Modernism, he – the artist – would be the common factor in his art. This would free him up; allow him to do many different things. Now, of course, his work has become more consolidated and recognisably his – but initially it jumped around a lot.

Yet, if you emerged during a period of difference – of revised forms of identity and new understandings about relativism in relation to cultural meaning and social structure – then of course you wouldn't be happy with just saying, 'Well, I'll be the common factor and I'll let the work find its own way'. You must also dissolve a little bit, too, as an author. While the work is always heavily authored up to a point, the sense of responsibility for authorship, or the level of authorship, is questionable. The location of the art moment does not reside with my consistent presence. It can exist at different moments within the work.

In early Modernism you can see a quite urgent exchange between the process of modernity and the critical reflection of Modernism but, as time goes on, these processes get further and further apart. And it's that gap that I'm interested in: the gap between modernity and the critical potential of Modernism and Postmodernism.

And that's how I might end up designing a shelf, for example, which is what I have been doing recently. It is not because I'm interested in design alone, and it is not because I'm interested in art and architecture. It is because the act of designing a shelf has a very particular meaning if you are operating in this gap between modernity and Modernism. This explains a lot about the work, I think.

I always used to say that I was more interested in Anni Albers than Josef Albers, and this remains true. I am more interested in the applied forms of Modernism, the attempt to have a much more functional role in relation to daily life; but I also want to operate in an art context. I don't want to operate in the textile world or in the world of applied art. I was quite influenced – even as a student – by Swiss artists like Richard Paul Lohse, who might make posters for the public transport system and produce reductive abstract paintings, both as equal aspects of his practice. This seemed extremely interesting to me: the idea that you could operate in a terrain where it might be normal for you to be doing these different tasks but operating from the perspective of being an artist.

People describe me – as they did during the Vincent Award at the Stedelijk Museum – as 'critic, writer, designer, artist'. And I think this is odd because these things they are referring to are all part of my art production. The problem, historically, is that this might be a big claim to make. So I don't necessarily mean it in a profound way. I just mean that my artistic practice includes these approaches as different forms not supplemental activities.

JS *Yes. But it is a condition of that polymathic existence that people have to understand what one does – if you do multifaceted things – as a hyphenated kind of entity. Maybe it is related to the problem of why people feel that they have to 'get it', or at least should be able 'get it'; that there should be a one-to-one relationship with what is before the viewer – whether that be Liam Gillick as artist or the work that Liam Gillick produces.*

LG Just for the sake of argument, if you try to describe what art could be – drawing only on extremes of artistic practice now – and you cut out all the bits that are ambiguous and annoying, the extremes would be a kind of transparent documentary form on the one hand, and a form of super self-consciousness, super subjectivity on the other. When I meet with my graduate students in New York, for example, they seem to be loosely divided into these contemporary camps.

JS *Neither pole of the art practices you describe dodges the problem of 'getting it'.*

LG Yes, because I make use of both strategies, in a way. There's an acute super-subjective element to the work and there is also an extreme clarity about certain things, but the work as a whole is not intended to fulfil either of those two extremes of contemporary art fully. It steps a little outside simple binarism.

I've just been writing a text about the idea of the discursive as the basis of dynamic art production in the last few years. I think this is a better way of describing relational practice than talking about some kind of interactive or social component. The idea that art comes out through negotiation, not through sitting alone at home with a piece of paper and how this discursive potential of art can be sustained over time.

JS *I think there's more access to the subjective content in your work*

through your writing. Maybe the real interest of this play is that it will
make visible, in a non-writerly way, exactly those kinds of writerly
activities and subjectivities. It strikes me as a kind of Erasmus Is Late
proposition, but as a play, not directly as a text.

LG   Yes, and it has shifted to the recent past because I am looking at
the idea of 'the moment' that could have been – the ultimate postwar
moment. For example, take a random date like 17 June 1974, when the
mode of production in the Volvo factory was perfect, when the idea
of new forms of teamwork hadn't yet turned into a form of flexibility
that led inevitably to redundancy. I am interested in 'setting' my work
on the day before this all dissolves into a neoliberal farce.

So my play is set on that day. It is set on an ideal day in Sweden
when Calvinist, good, hard-working, low-church values have produced a system that is viewed as exemplary, as a way of retaining
forms of honest capitalism, good production, teamworking and
flexible working practices. But the action takes place in a bar. And
they don't have bars at Volvo factories.

I've been thinking about this a lot, the idea that certain modes
of thinking and certain modes or models of art production – even
curating and critical writing – are really deeply steeped in some of
the postwar structures that led to Volvo's teamwork and flexibility.
Starting at playgroup, through to the way you're taught to work in
teams at school, and on to the workplace with its projects and projections. I am trying to look again at some of these questions. If we
assume that the postwar period is a completed moment – historically
– then how do we re-engage with the better aspects of ameliorated
working conditions? How can we continue to work in a discursive
manner if its basis merely prepared everyone for redundancy?
Can we find a way to accept difference and work collectively?

JS   *Those are fundamental and very heavy questions. How would you*
describe your strategy or approach to posing – let alone answering – such
questions?

LG   Most of my work on these questions came from looking through
Brazilian academic papers about progressive working practices in
Scandinavia, which tells you quite a lot about my working method.
In a fairly undirected way, I just read South American academic
papers about innovations in Volvo car production in the 1970s. The
work was made while thinking about these things. Sometimes works
are produced under the influence of thinking about something when

I made them, though this influence never manifests itself in a direct, didactic way.

JS *Yet it doesn't come forward as a decoy? Many practices position work as research, but what comes forward is fundamentally a decoy that even sends you back to the original research, only to spiral off somewhere else.*

LG Yes, but in the press release for my show in New York – I quite enjoy writing press releases, they're getting more and more ludicrous – I mentioned some of this stuff and in the more mainstream reviews of the show, of course, people simply didn't get it. I didn't say that it was an exhibition illustrating the conditions of car production in Sweden in the 1970s – far from it. I said the work was made while considering these ideas – that's a totally different thing. Even then, however, you are faced with shiny metal objects and overreaching statements, which in my mind is quite a precise parallel to car production and consumption.

JS *What is the function then of the original research material, or even a press release, or critical writing on the work by yourself or others, if not an extension to the experience of the art?*

LG It is interesting. There's always a subtext in the work – and it is not just in my work, I think you see it in the work of some of the other people of my age – there's a mixture of clarity and … almost a petulance at some levels. It is connected to a fear of being sucked into an instrumentalised art practice. It is a suspicion of being sucked into a responsible Habermasian art practice that is all to do with everyone having perfect information and contributing to an even-handed dialogue about how to produce a better society.

I am also interested in artistic autonomy. I think that people like myself, who were born in between the end of the Second World War and the fall of the Berlin Wall, saw a lot of other things happening that made us not entirely 100% sure about anything. The period of the IRA, the Red Brigades and the permanent threat of nuclear annihilation led to a distrust of transparency. It was a time of subterfuge and conspiracy and the last thing you might want to do is telegraph your intentions to the dominant culture by merely parroting or mirroring the worst of it. We wanted to make use of the products of the postwar period as social spaces and spaces for art and so on, but not necessarily to go along with that completely. We wanted an interventionist strategy, whereby sites both literal and metaphorical could be appropriated. Production would be the focus of critique, not consumption.

I wanted to look at all this and to make the complexity of the built world and its manipulation the subject of the art. And I think that's true throughout my work from the beginning – even when I was collaborating with Henry Bond in the early 1990s on documentary photos in response to daily updates from the Press Association. We used our self-consciousness about our backgrounds, gender, appearance and access to higher education to get into closed events. We didn't want to separate ourselves from the production of events within society in a postmodern way. We were always silent at these events. We never asked any questions. I remember at the time think-ing that we were not happy to just go away and make art that was purely an ironic response to the ecstasy of communication or the imploded quality of signs within the culture. We were very conscious of the fact that things were still being decided. Countries were still being formed. Governments were still collapsing. People were still getting poorer. Other people getting richer. People were still being jailed for their beliefs. We wanted to go and check.

As artists we did not take up the accepted role in society, which was to go away and be involved in increasing diversity and increasing production of difference. Instead, we wanted to go – for a short while – to what might be called the centres of power and to see who was still there and how they were working. And of course we found that the power structures were rolling along quite nicely thank you and hadn't succumbed to the 'matrix'. We were also of course following on from people like Allan Sekula and others, who had already been working in this way for a long time. But we were doing it without the structural integrity that they might have had in connection to critical theory.

JS *It's important to clarify that you weren't attempting to reinvent a documentary mode.*

LC No, not at all.

JS *Nor to facilitate the implosion of Modernism.*

LC No, and it is very significant that at the time Henry often viewed himself as a photographer, and not as an artist using a camera in order to carry out an agenda. He had an interest in, and knowledge of, the history of photography – of modern photography – and this was crucial. But of course he is also an artist with specialist knowledge and we spent a great deal of time arguing about art while attending a video link between Bill Clinton and the TUC or waiting for PLO in the Russian Embassy. We wanted to be there at nine o'clock in the morning at the PLO Headquarters in London finding out what was happening, so we needed a photographer – and we had one, as it were.

I'm not trying to totalise the work. I've tried hard to avoid a clear-cut trajectory. But I do think there are some common and recurring factors within the work, and they are connected in equal measure to some scepticism and to some enthusiasm for the products of the postwar period.

JS *Do you think that this mode of life is signalled through these elements of soft modernism that you access in the work?*

LG Yes, because I'm interested in applied modernism. But the thing that doesn't get talked about very much is the idea of autonomous art. Obviously this is a big area, but I'm interested in the potential of art as an exception within the culture. I'm also interested in the production of something that does not necessarily carry enormous claims within its resolved structure, but still occupies a similar territory to things that, in the past, have done that.

I have always been interested in how to be an artist when you don't have any ideas at the beginning – or when you don't have any work to show. I didn't see why that should be an impediment to being involved in the art world or functioning as an artist. The same thing applies to this retrospective. Because the further you go back with some of my work the more unclear and collaborative it gets, and the less you're going to find an originating moment – which is normally what you need for a retrospective. Just because there is no original revelation or breakthrough doesn't mean I can't have a retrospective, but I want one that looks at things structurally rather than historic-ally. I still retain an interest in the art system. The systems of art dissemination and the spaces for art interest me just as much as the spaces for building a Volvo 240. I view them as another form of construction within the society that also needs to be looked at.

JS *As spaces structured by capital?*

LG The machinations of global capital and social structures, in my adult life, have been centred on capitalising the near future and the recent past. This has been a constant subject of my work. If you can find a way to recuperate and recapitalise the recent past, you're onto a winner. If you can keep recuperating the recent past, you can get closer and closer to the present and find a way to really sell it again – just after it has happened.

This is not about nostalgia. It is literally about recuperating and reorganising. And, of course, the near future is also the terrain of contemporary capital and contemporary organisation, which is why they don't bother building a new building any more unless there's a real boom. Instead you renovate the foyer or you re-signify the building but you leave the structure the same. You can exchange spaces this way. These are the terrains that I'm really interested in. How the near future is controlled in a chaotic, displaced socio-economic environment. Even the work with Henry was about getting a fax from the Press Association at nine o'clock saying that at eleven o'clock today Margaret Thatcher is expected to resign. We already knew that the press – with Henry and me tagging along – were going to gather in two hours' time to wait for her to resign. And it is that speculative zone – and a reclaiming of it away from people who use speculation purely to capitalise on things in an antisocial way – that I remain interested in, stretching those two hours into something more complex. I didn't see why only certain people should be left alone to address ideas of projection, speculation, and the near future. I realised that this could be the subject of my work.

JS *Those are the strategies that lead, in some way, to the criticism of your work as being corporate.*

LG I can understand that. As a student I was always a big fan of Donald Judd's artworks. I've read the reviews from the time he was working and of course he was constantly criticised for echoing late Modernism and for being conveniently in sync – or even in cahoots – with the aesthetics of corporate modernism. I'm very conscious of that. It's a proximity that I want. It's not a mistake. For the last ten years I've lived in Midtown Manhattan – that's what I look at every day. I operate in proximity. The work doesn't necessarily sit comfortably in the spaces that you would imagine it should do, nor does it necessarily sit comfortably with a reductive late Modernism like Judd and Carl Andre and so on.

JS *Can we talk about the Venice Biennale? What is your take on being thrown into the national model of the pavilion just as national brands decline?*

LG Well, my first shows were as the Berlin Wall was coming down and I was on the boat as quickly as possible. I made use of the European context as the last of the old soldier presidents and chancellors were trying to leave it as they'd imagined it – to put it back together again for the first time, as it were. I was very conscious of that negotiation between President Mitterrand and Jack Lang, the way they decentred cultural policy. I was also conscious of the legacy of the federated model of Germany. These were very generative terrains for me to operate in. It meant a lot to get away from a centred culture and go to places that were decentred, where they have repetition and multiple iterations of similar things.

The interesting thing about Venice is that it tells you more about the curator than it does about me. Being selected to work in the German pavilion is a gesture by the curator Nicolaus Schafhausen to make a point. In the recent coming together in Berlin of a new international art community and a consolidated identification of a new German art that is complex, professional, successful and public, there have been people who decided to operate within that system without living there. Living there – being a resident – does not make you a German artist. What do we do with the people who operate within this terrain without living here? What do we call them?

I think for Schafhausen, this question of whether you live some-where is one of the complicated issues of instrumentalised postwar society building. The desire to accept the people that come and live among us is a very strong drive of progressive people in Germany – that we accept our Turkish or Kurdish brothers and sisters as our neighbours and that they should be here and be welcomed. Yet I think he was trying to confuse things even further.

The correct thing to do would be to ask a Turkish or Kurdish German art collective to do something. But to ask a straight white Anglo-Saxon man to do something means I have to take on board the idea of showing in this building on behalf of another country, I have to ask myself questions about how to continue. Maybe I have to ask myself questions I should have been asking all along. It is a test and a challenge that I cannot answer with my symbolic presence alone. I have to do something. But on another level the invitation does reflect something precise. The very fact that it is tolerable, or it can even be done, shows that in the last 20 years there has been a shift. You could say that, in a way, all the major pavilions of Germany since 1960 have really been about the postwar period. But maybe now … it is not that we think that the past is hidden but that to continue in that trajectory might become parodic. To put Neo Rauch in the pavilion or Jonathan Meese – they're both artists who are deeply attractive to the system – would be to continue the endless renegotiation of the postwar period: in Rauch's way, by jumping backwards to a kind of pre-war condition on an allegorical field in the middle of nowhere between Frankfurt Oder and Łódź, and, in Meese's way, by both parodying and making fun of earnest postwar performance art while forcing us to keep remembering something.

I'm thrown into that still quite tense discussion. And of course Berlin, for example, is also peopled by a large number of successful, well-known, non-German artists who choose to live there. But I'm not one of those either. I think it is a deliberate act on the part of the curator and it's a test. It's like: 'You've worked here a lot and you've continued to be productive here, so here's another German space, see if you can continue in these conditions. Here's a 1938 Nazi building. Are you going to have a discussion or something? What are you going to do?'

And of course the problem now is showing in Italy. This is difficult. If you want to be really tough, you do something about Italy, now. While I was in Venice for the architecture biennale, there was a Lega Nord rally on the waterfront. So while looking around the German pavilion, I could hear someone ranting about immigrants and gypsies – and this is disturbing. So, whether it is a situation where I can continue as normal, or whether this has to be an exception is very hard to say. This is why I think they asked me – because I have to make a decision about how to function. In a way, I have to ask myself whether I should emphasise the interest I have in the legacy of modernist autonomy that I don't think is complete – an almost Adorno-like belief that you should continue to produce a form of heightened art, a kind of melancholic art of refusal and abstraction – or do you use it to try to continue a dialogue in a place that maybe requires a little silence?

Issue 324, March 2009

Glenn Brown

interviewed by David Trigg

Painting Paintings

DAVID TRIGG *Your paintings are all derived from reproductions of other artists' work. It must be strange seeing your own work reproduced.*

    GLENN BROWN That's why it was difficult to decide which paintings should be in the Tate Liverpool exhibition. I only have photographic records of my paintings and some works look great in the photographs but in reality aren't as good as I remember them, and for others it's the exact opposite, so there were a few surprises when I saw the paintings again. The whole printing process is very crude compared to painting, which is very, very precise. It's why as a technology painting is fantastic and nothing comes anywhere near it.

DT *You once revealed that as a student you would break into the college's painting studios after dark so that you could paint all night.*

    GB I'd have to deny that. And anyway, I'm sure the security is much better in Bath now. When I was at Goldsmiths I had my own studio, so there was no need to break in.

DT *It clearly demonstrates how much passion you had for painting – an obsession that is part of your subject matter. Do you still feel the same compulsion?*

    GB I still love painting, it's a fantastic game to play – difficult but enjoyable. Painting is a set of puzzles – you know there are answers but sometimes you just can't find them, then you have to go to other paintings and figure out how other people have solved various problems.

DT *The first painting you made of another painting was* Atom Age Vampire, *in 1991, which was copied from a reproduction of Frank Auerbach's 1973* Head of J.Y.M. *and rendered his thick impasto brush marks completely flat. Was that made while you were still at Goldsmiths?*

CB   Yes. Most of the paintings in the first room at Tate Liverpool were made when I was at Goldsmiths. That first painting came after a very arduous studio critique; I was making the moonscape and modernist building paintings at the time and people were saying: 'Why are you painting? There's no point, just rephotograph them.' Painting was considered extremely archaic at Goldsmiths in the early 1990s but I knew I wanted to paint, I liked the process and its subtlety. Therefore, without changing my work incredibly radically, I tried to answer that problem by making a painting of a painting.

DT   *That work represents an important turning point in your career – why isn't it included in the exhibition?*

CB   There are other paintings made just after that which are very similar and make the same point slightly better. There's a painting called *The Day The World Turned Auerbach* from the same year which has greater detail and the sense of obsession is slightly stronger.

DT   *It is perhaps more resolute whereas the first painting was more of an experiment?*

CB   Yes. The first one is slightly more blurry, it's more Richter-looking whereas *The Day The World Turned Auerbach* has a sharper, more photorealist look to it.

DT   *When you started making paintings of paintings were you aware of Mike Bidlo's project from the 1980s, where he made copies of works by Picasso, Warhol and Pollock?*

CB   Yes, absolutely. But Sherrie Levine was more of an influence – at the time I was completely in love with her work. Also artists like Simon Linke with his *Artforum* paintings and even On Kawara; that certain dry, conceptual form of painting is really what I was after.

DT   *There's a room in the Liverpool exhibition that juxtaposes several other paintings derived from Auerbach's* Head of J.Y.M. *– it's a motif you've returned to many times. What is it about that particular painting that made you want to revisit it so frequently?*

CB   It's quite a camp image; the pose is very theatrical and the figure has her head turned to one side while still looking at the viewer, so it appears to be quite self-conscious but also very ambiguous. I realised therefore that I could twist the image in various different ways because of its ambiguity; I could make the painting recoil, or come forward and be more aggressive, or I could make it pitiful or grotesque – I knew there was a lot of mileage to be had from that one painting.

DT *In the same way that the first Auerbach painting signified a new direction in your earlier work, I think* St Anthony Returns to the Womb, *painted in 2000, perhaps marked the start of another shift in your practice – a move towards a more inventive, freer and fluidic approach, rather than slavishly mimicking existing brush marks.*

GB *St Anthony Returns to the Womb* is based upon a Georg Baselitz painting – one of his feet paintings from before he started turning them upside down. I think that's when I became more interested in building a figure that was fairly unrecognisable from the original. I made other paintings after Baselitz which also encouraged me to be far more playful – inventing brush marks for instance. Two paintings in the exhibition, *Seventeen Seconds* from 2005 and *International Velvet* from 2004, are both based on the same Baselitz painting but one is turned upside down.

DT *Those works seem to be worlds apart from your earlier paintings. The heads have evolved into these weird, grotesque biomorphs. Do you still think of them as portraits?*

GB Yes, absolutely, I always see them as portraits.

DT *Hanging opposite them is* The Asylums of Mars, *2006, which is an astonishing work – to quote Clement Greenberg, it has a 'hallucinatory vividness'. It also recalls Dalí's double images as well as evoking Arcimboldo's portraits.*

GB It was meant to be similar to the paintings based on Baselitz, which is why I put them in the same room. It was meant to be a large, ambiguous comic head – it's actually based on a Fragonard painting.

DT *The central female figure?*

GB Yes, but then there's an old woman's head looking down and there are other faces and things in there too. It took a long time to complete. To start with, the female figure in the middle was very recognisable, then I got rid of her and you really couldn't see that there was a figure. People would come into the studio and I'd ask if they could see the figure and they couldn't, even when I pointed it out to them, so I started painting her back in again. It's very difficult to gauge what people are going to see in a painting – sometimes people come into the studio and say, 'oh I like that face there, that's interesting', assuming it was my intention when I've never even seen a face there before.

DT *I had wondered how much of that was intentional and how much found its way in there subconsciously.*

CB I think some of it is genuinely subconscious, but I do like to try and make the other small characters within it very ambiguous so you don't quite know whether you're making it up yourself or whether it was my intention.

DT *In an unusual move you've painted the top right-hand corner green. A similar device is also used in* Suffer Well, *2007, where the top left corner is painted black, recalling Sigmar Polke's painting* The Higher Powers Command: Paint the Upper Right Corner Black! *of 1969.*

CB I see those corners as operating slightly differently in each painting. In *Suffer Well* I see it as being like a Russian constructivist sense of depression just about to move into the painting to threaten the figure, as if it could take over the painting. In *The Asylums of Mars* it's more of a comic irritant that you don't really want to look at – it's irritating because every time you look at the figure your eye bounces back to the green triangle. That green isn't anywhere else in the painting. Every time you look at it and then go back to the central figure again you see it in a slightly different way.

DT *I've noticed something similar appearing in other recent works too, where you've inserted these Baldessari-style coloured discs. Do you intend these to function in a similar way?*

CB I always think that narrative in painting is most strongly developed by the way your eye moves across the surface, rather than what any particular character is doing. It's about the route your eye takes around a painting. The circles or the green corner are compositional devices to make your eye move in a very particular direction and bounce between different shapes; they make the painting more dynamic and keep you looking at it for longer, as well as simply being very odd visual moments.

DT *You have also given several of your figures halos and your titles often feature religious references.*

CB I love art history and a quick wander around the National Gallery will make you aware that Catholicism dominates the history of western art; to ignore its influence would be like saying, I'm going to speak using the English language but not use the letter 'a' – it is part of the vocabulary of painting.

DT *Religious imagery is also used quite explicitly in your series of prints, 'Comfortably Numb', 2008, where you've combined Guido Reni's* Head of Christ Crowned with Thorns *with one of your Auerbach paintings.*

CB I like Reni's over-the-top sentimentality and the rather ridiculous sense of drama that he imbues all his figures with, especially the Virgin Mary and Christ figures. The lighting and the posing in his paintings are very theatrical and, as I was saying earlier, this particular *Head of J. Y. M.* is also very theatrical – the pose is very Reni. I see a clear relationship between the posing of the figures and also the use of colour; I think Auerbach's use of colour has become much stronger, especially in the paintings he's making now – it's more acidic and far more late Renaissance. His paintings aren't depictions of reality; his colours aren't realistic – they're far too lurid. It's an artificial world and therefore I think Reni's late Renaissance paintings fit in very well with Auerbach. I wanted to put them together to suggest that they share the same view of the world.

DT *Auerbach's paintings have also had a significant influence on your sculptures. When did you start making them?*

GB In 1995; the first one, *These Days*, is in the Liverpool show. To me they are fundamentally paintings, it's just that they are paintings on three-dimensional surfaces.

DT These Days *is the one sitting on the floor?*

GB Yes, the intention was to put them all on the floor. The initial ones were based on Auerbach paintings and they were meant to be like abject heads. I still think they are very abject looking objects, sort of dirty and grotesque. To me they are head-like in the way that Brancusi sculptures can be head-like, and also like the moment in the film *Eraserhead* when the character's head suddenly drops to the floor, or perhaps a pile of guillotined heads.

DT *Why did you start putting them into vitrines?*

GB Well, when I first showed them in an exhibition at Karsten Schubert people kept kicking them.

DT *Tripping over them?*

GB No, intentionally kicking them. At the private view someone kicked one right across the room. That was interesting because I realised that this notion of the abject worked so well that somebody actually felt that all they wanted to do was kick it. As they became more intricate I realised that I just couldn't put them on the floor because they'd become so dirty and dusty that they'd only last for a few days – that's why I started to put them onto tables. But I quickly realised that people then wanted to poke them and try to break bits off. It became virtually impossible to show them without the perspex covers on.

DT *There is something about the vitrines that makes the sculptures become more like museum artefacts.*

CB I could have vitrines that are far more beautiful and overbearing. For instance, Sherrie Levine's vitrines are clearly part of the work and they're far more museum-like with their little brass fittings and nicely finished wooden corners. I don't want my cases to be too obvious and articulated so I've kept them relatively light and simple – I want the sculpture to dominate, so the case is just a frame to hold the work.

DT *Although your paintings have evolved enormously in recent years, the sculptures have developed more slowly and continue to reference back to Auerbach.*

CB It's partially because I've made so few of them; I think on average I make one every two years. They borrow a very particular language from Auerbach in that he just uses one size of brush to make his paintings. My sculptures are always painted with the same size of brush; the size varies from sculpture to sculpture but it keeps a certain uniformity to it – that's the kind of thing I think I should be playing with more. I haven't developed the language of them very much and ideally there should be as much difference within them as there is in the paintings.

DT The Sound of Music, *begun in 1995, is a very uncharacteristic sculpture. I'm assuming this paint-encrusted table started life as a piece of studio equipment?*

CB No, it was always meant to be a sculpture. It started with photographs I'd seen of Auerbach's studio – everything was absolutely covered in paint and his palette spread across the entire table with the paint slowly building up. Also I visited an open studio once where somebody had this table in the middle of the room that they used to mix paint on. It was so encrusted with paint – it was an absolutely beautiful object. So that's why I started making that work. I worked on it for years and years, although for about five years of its life I gave up on the idea of it being a sculpture and it just became a table that I used to mix the paint for the other sculptures on. It was only later that I actually thought I would make it into a sculpture again.

DT *The paint is like a fungus colonising the table.*

CB I never could decide if it was finished – it did seem to be like this organic thing. When it was first shown it was in a vitrine but that killed it because it was too high. In Liverpool we could just use a barrier.

DT *But you've kept it on a plinth.*

CB The plinth was only made a couple of days before the opening. Initially I wanted it sitting on the floor but it just didn't look right. Had it been a wooden floor or even concrete I would have put it on the floor, but because it's a painted floor there was a relationship between the paint, the table and the floor which I didn't like so I put it on a base.

DT *For your exhibition at Karsten Schubert you've produced a new series of etchings that superimpose reproductions of etchings by Rembrandt, Urs Graf and Lucian Freud. These pitchy amalgams are strikingly different from your other work.*

CB I wanted them to be monstrous. Again, I see them as portraits and I wanted them to be like the Auerbach or Baselitz paintings. I wanted to create these ambiguous images, something that was between states of mind, and one of the best ways of doing that was to combine different elements together to get a schizophrenic portrait. We all have multiple personalities and we can shift from one mindset to another very easily. They're meant, in some sense, to be poetic representations of the human psyche.

DT *That notion is particularly evident in some of the layered Rembrandt images, where you can see a double head, for instance – other prints, however, are almost entirely black.*

CB I think the highest number of images laid on top of each other in a single print is 16, so it gets pretty black. It represents that depressive point at which you can't stop thinking about things, where there's too much information flooding into your head and it just turns into this black oppressive darkness.

DT *Existential angst?*

CB Absolutely – things being too real and too present. That's why a lot of the etching plates were overly inked up, to make them very dark and foreboding. The whole image is starting to decay and degenerate from being overly reproduced.

DT *What drew you to those particular artists?*

CB Rembrandt obsessively drew and painted self-portraits and whenever he painted somebody else they also ended up looking just like him – it's like everything he did was a self-portrait. Freud is one of the more famous contemporary artists who makes etchings. There are certain compositional devices that he repeats, so when you overlay them you get the idea of a single coherent character being formed; they still feel like Freud and that essence doesn't go away, no matter how many layers you put on top of each other.

DT *And what about Graf?*

CB When you see a Graf etching everything is distorted and over the top – there's something depressive about them. Everything is just filled with this squirming, overly detailed decay, which is what I like in my paintings too – this sense of everything decaying, killed off – and I wanted to emphasise that, by layering them to the point where they're unrecognisable. It's that sense of putrefaction, although when you start to putrefy you do not become any less complex.

DT *You lose form.*

CB You lose form but you start to turn into something else. You don't just disappear, you migrate into maggots and bacteria and move into a different world.

DT *These notions of decay and the grotesque seem to be important themes.*

CB We are obsessed with the grotesque and things that we find fundamentally debasing and uncomfortable – you find it in Graf and you find it in painters like Jean Dubuffet and Willem de Kooning as well. With De Kooning you always feel like you shouldn't be seeing these paintings, they're embarrassing and you don't know whether he was in his right mind when he painted them. There is a certain point at which paintings do become enlivened with a sense of embarrassment because they are overly intense, overly emotional or just slightly wrong in a way that becomes very intriguing. You want to stare at them like you want to stare at a car crash – you can't not look. That same feeling is there within great art as well – a strangeness that makes you want to stare.

Issue 325, April 2009

Elizabeth Price

interviewed by Paul O'Neill

Mad Love

PAUL O'NEILL *When I first saw your work in the mid 1990s, there was an interest in the legacy of late 1960s conceptualist practices, and how time and its performative aspect could be made material in the resultant artwork. Can you tell me about your interest in this period of the so-called 'dematerialisation of the art object' and the relationship between acting out time and its material formation?*

ELIZABETH PRICE I think that the desire to dematerialise is a problematic aspect of Conceptual Art, while the annotation of bodily time is an interesting one, and I have pilfered from and mimicked both of these projects.

I used conventions of acting out time to help me think about a certain kind of work: the banal administering, exchanging, repairing, packing and polishing which is required of the 'completed' art object. This is where my interest in administrative ephemera and the archive came from. I used, adapted and produced such materials to reveal the continuous work of production, the embodied time of that labour, the world of material and social forces to which the art object belongs.

I've always been interested in how dematerialised art relies upon administration just as materialised art objects do. I think it's very funny. We don't reference Robert Barry's 'empty gallery' using an image of the empty gallery, but through an image of the notice fixed to the gallery door informing you of the gallery's emptiness. This is because the object can't just disappear. Its absence has to be administered otherwise we wouldn't perceive it. So we are left with a receipt, a certificate, a proxy. In Conceptual Art this proxy might be a more austere thing – a page of type. But this isn't an effective economic dematerialisation – after all, a bank-note works on the same principle.

It's clear now that so-called 'dematerialisation' constituted little resistance to processes of commodification: there was always a range of materials and information that stood in for the singular art object, which could still be commodified. Yes, it did explode the art object and that's been very important to me – the idea that an artwork might be constituted in the configuration of a range of things: objects, texts, documents, photographs, drawings etc – but that's dissolution, not dematerialisation. Which brings me to the big, political problem with dematerialisation as far as I am concerned, and that is the idealisation, the notion of transcending material. I don't want to transcend material. I'm interested in, and part of, a world made up of unredeemed, sensual debris.

PO'N *Is there a particular tension between the failed object and this post-autonomous producer?*

EP I work very episodically and artworks are rarely completed definitively; they are usually revised by subsequent episodes. I am currently making a series of videos in which each episode establishes a room within a fictional institution. I have been working on it for four years and two rooms have been 'built'. More will come, but a finite architecture will never be established. Many of the object works operate similarly; TROPHY, begun in 2000, is engraved with the details of each occasion of its public display so that it is clear from looking at it that it has a provenance – it has its own history inscribed on its surface. As entries accumulate I hope that the potential of an ongoing, repetitive and promiscuous narrative is suggested.

PO'N *I remember Seth Siegelaub saying how he became disillusioned with Conceptual Art, particularly the artists he was working with in the late 1960s when, in spite of their interest in replication, the work was becoming too repetitional in its form, too formulaic, leading to a dearth of new possibilities for a different conceptual form. In your own work there is an element of repetition, particularly in how you act out time. In your first video work,* HELP *– that's what it says,* made in 2001, you handwrote every invitation for a show, a process documented in a five-hour video and presented in the gallery.

EP Working in the same way for years is sometimes given credibility as rigour, when in fact it's often merely intellectual complacency or career-based pragmatism. And you're right that there is a particular version of this problem with conceptual art methods because of their ascetic logic. If an aspect of a work seems problematic or suspect, it's simply excised. This is valorised as critical virtue, but intelligent reduction is incredibly difficult to sustain. HELP – *that's what it says* was a slapstick endeavour. I was disconsolate in art. I saw myself as a stooge and did sincerely want some help.

PO'N *You mentioned* TROPHY *earlier, and then there is* Boulder, *which you began in 1996 along with* Hearse Attending ... *Many of these works are cumulative and demarcate time through an evolving process, akin to a slowly unfolding narrative.*

EP Yes, but the processes are of degeneration or dissolution as well as accumulation, which allows for a more contingent narrative potential. TROPHY is engraved each time it is displayed and it will continue to be made in this way until its entire surface is exhausted. Right now, it records its history coherently, but it will become an increasingly baffling document when the inscriptions run over the uneven surfaces of the body, lid and handles of the trophy. With *Mummified Dog with a Mummified Rat in its Mouth*, begun in 2004, the principle of never wrapping the plinth during transit or repairing any resulting wear may one day generate a defining moment of critical damage. What will I do then? I'm not sure. Exhibit the debris of the former plinth and balance the mummified remains of the dog on top?

PO'N *There is pathos to this irresolvability of the art object and the implicit possibility that you might never be happy with it.*

EP The ongoing objects allowed me to work faithfully with apparent purpose while waiting in expectation for something more interesting to happen. Who could be happy making a huge boulder out of brown tape? I wanted the persistence of making it to have dramatic suspense as well as slapstick pathos, not to mention a certain teen-anguish.

PO'N *Talking about being angst-ridden and adolescent, the last time we met you mentioned a piece of work that you made for* Platform *in 2004,* This Record Belongs to Jenny England, *as being a turning point in your career. You may have meant it flippantly at the time, but was it a key transition point in your practice?*

EP I found the Jenny England record around about the same time that I found the will of Alexander Chalmers, and it really informed my response to that document. It is a 7-inch single wrapped in a white paper sleeve that I bought in a charity shop. The previous owner had written information on the sleeve. I've seen lots of records labelled in that way but this one had more detail than usual. It included the exact date of purchase in 1978, the shop where it was bought, reiterated the artist's name and song titles, along with the underlined statement: 'This record belongs to Jenny England.' I was familiar with strategies of *détournement*, but this seemed different to me. Maybe it was because of her name, which seemed like a punk name, an invention. Perhaps it was because her name was the last in a temporal succession of producers inscribed on the record: songwriter, publisher, artist, record company, distributor, retailer. It made me wonder about an appendix, about secreting something in the archive, inventing another episode to accrete to the existing story of an artefact.

PO'N *A number of your projects question what constitutes an archive. I'm thinking of your early curatorial project 'The Dot Archive' – a year-long cumulative archive-as-exhibition-as-archive of other artists' work and material.*

EP   This was an expanding archive with a soft system, so its principle was that it would adapt its physical structure and system of cataloguing to accommodate whatever was added to it over time. I was interested in how it wasn't possible to hold a sovereign view of this archive because it could mutate.

A similar concern influenced my work with the Chalmers Bequest, but in this instance I was adding material to a closed history – exhuming it and adding to it. Through reviving the bequest I generated new administrative documents and materials that I literally added to the existing archive. As I said, I was very interested in the idea of the appendix, but more precisely that the appendix would corrupt the integrity of the original as a complete story or body of material. And for me this corruption was the means to move between social history, fiction and fantasy.

PO'N *Your response seems to highlight the fragility of legacies and inherited histories, but also how the past can be intentionally misconstrued in the present.*

EP   My understanding of those things evolved throughout that project. When I found the will of Alexander Chalmers in the Hackney Archives I had all kinds of questions about authorship, power and politics that I couldn't seem to resolve. I decided to undertake the instructions of the will to stage this dilemma: I would satirically perform the impossibility of my own authorship by following the instructions accompanying a paternalistic art legacy. (The will left a collection of art and a capital fund to the former London Borough of Stoke Newington, along with ten instructions regarding the expansion and use of the collection.) I thought, OK, I would give myself the problem of this legacy.

The bequest was completely moribund when I found it; it was defunct, the funds frozen, the collection buried in permanent storage. The local authority to which it had been given no longer existed and every single body, role or institution specified in the will had been superseded. I exhumed this collection and its institutions and restored them to an administrative half-life for a while. I asked artists, writers, council officers and councillors to fulfil all the various roles, and I carried out each of the ten instructions over a six-year period.

At the end of that project I was a different artist. I think that in baldly addressing the principle of inheritance, I was able to find a more productive expression for my inability to assume authorship in any way that seemed politically credible. In 2006 I made a video, called *A Public Lecture and Exhumation*, to tell the story of the Chalmers Bequest. The video started out like a local history lecture but ended up more like a gothic romance, and that trajectory mirrored my own move from a post-conceptual artist to an inventor of ghostly fantasies.

And I do see a relationship between principles of inheritance and the form of the archive, that's what was important to me in dealing with the Chalmers Bequest – and then in 2007 the Stanley Picker Trust for *At The House of Mr X* – the bringing together of art objects and all the administrative materials that they generate. They were gathered together into the body of a bequest, under the name of its male donor, and instituted upon the occasion of his death. The body of material could clearly be seen as a proxy for the lost body of the donor. What interested me about this (and led to *A Public Lecture and Exhumation*) was that I could exhume an image of that male body and reveal an archaeology of its idealisation. I saw this idealisation occuring primarily in the body of the gift itself, but also in the organisational body of the recipient – the local government. Well, anyhow – in the final stages of the video a body is exhumed, but it is a zombie: corrupted, fractured and incomplete. Both horrible and comic.

PO'N *Many of your works involve organising things, arranging objects and exploiting a falsity of their systems of classification. How do you think these systems curb or curtail what we experience of the past and how we might know it?*

EP I reorganise objects by recognising contingent properties that might link them. I find a materialist premise for a departure into fantasy, so that both social history and fiction are employed in knowing the past. I think Surrealism has informed this. In *Mad Love*, André Breton relates how he finds an object at a flea market, an elegant metal helmet with slatted visors, but he can't precisely identify it; the strange visors seem to impede vision and it is difficult to detect their purpose. In the absence of other knowledge, he imagines that it's the highly evolved descendant of a helmet flirting with a velvet mask. Later he discovers its use. It was a military helmet of disastrous design, which so impaired vision that it contributed to terrible casualties. So through the course of the text the literary image of a refined velvet mask is succeeded by images of blundering violence. I know there are problems in the conjunction of fantasy and social history, and I'm interested in them. I like Georges Bataille's caustic observation that the problem with Surrealism is given away in its literal meaning 'above-realism'. But at the same time, in Surrealism it's clear that fantasy is a way to form desire, and desire is a political force.

PO'N *Recently, you moved away from more conceptually driven object-based productions into making videos. I was wondering whether there was a new-found interest in evolving narrative structures around objects rather than making the objects themselves.*

EP With the object-based work there was a central object that drove the narrative, but I was more interested in the digressions or contingencies the object could generate. Many of the works have produced quite complex archives, including drawings, texts and photographs. But one of the things that exasperated me was the way in which those configurations of material always ended up looking rather familiar in their presentation – they looked like Conceptual Art.

PO'N *One could say the same thing about videos that are accompanied by music with texts encoded onto the image: they always end up with the look of pop videos – for good and bad.*

EP Yes, but I was frustrated by the rather exhausted relationship between the particular concerns that I had, say, with authorship, the archive and taxonomy, and classical conceptual art language. So the prospect of exploring these ideas through things that may resemble car adverts or pop videos offered a different trajectory, although I do still regard it as a conceptually driven one. The videos were not really informed by other video art; they were a solution to bringing text, image and narrative together, so they resemble advertising, the infomercial, corporate and pedagogic uses of PowerPoint. A big influence is the work of Barbara Kruger. I should probably mention that the narration in my videos is always textual: it is silent, graphic and runs across the screen. While Kruger is didactic in ways that I consider untenable, she does offer a compelling ventriloquism of that silent, aggressive voice of print that fills our public space.

The move into video was also to do with a different relationship to the stories that objects generate. In the videos, I write the stories. They are derived from an archive or a body of texts, but I definitely invent a narrative. For example, *At The House of Mr X* features a house that was built to contain a collection of art, and an archive relating to it. That archive included architectural specifications, curatorial inventories and details of the cosmetics manufacturing business that funded the collection and the house. I conflated the different vocabularies and forms of these texts, mixing up the precise, scholarly finesse of an art inventory with the sexy innuendo of make-up advertising, to generate a suggestive story of a sensual inhabitation, an erotic dissolution in and of that house. So in the videos I perform a rather extreme form of authorship. Through them I become the author of a supernatural story, the author of a zombie story, the author of sci-fi erotic fantasy – the most preposterous, insinuating author you can be.

PO'N *There is a shift in how the fragment is being employed. In the more sculptural works the object is a fragment gathering its complete form over time to make up the whole. With the films, however, the narratives are insistent and, while they play on the authorial nature of voice and its didactic language, you use image, sound and textual fragmentations to create an episodic story, which is defined by this insistent filmic language.*

EP That's exactly right. I bring many disparate elements together, and use storytelling and video-making to bind them. The videos are all structured as tours led by fictional narrators – collective entities (committees or human resource departments) that are simultaneously didactic and unreliable. I use this unified/divergent voice as an excuse for all kinds of digressions and connections. This is important because I consciously work against the idea of reduction in building a video. In USER GROUP DISCO from 2009, I combined a melody from A-ha with a bastardised quote from Borges over a series of images of erotic tableware.

PO'N *There is such a conflation of references and sources that the work creates an occasionally confusing cacophony of fantastic, compulsive, hallucinatory and sometimes repulsive imagery. Are these intended to collapse into one another, or are they about a deliberate lack of intentionality?*

EP I always bring things together around a point of contingency. It is conceptual bricolage, but it is not absurdist. In USER GROUP DISCO and 2008's WELCOME – the Atrium, which are the first two episodes in my attempt to build a fictional institution, I don't use an existing collection or archive but have selected the objects and texts that feature in the video. In organising them through the form of video, I produce categories and establish categorical relationships between things. For example, I relate the image of a rotating phono-graph record with an excerpt from an Edgar Allan Poe story about a whirlpool. They come together around the image of a spiral. The spiral becomes the basis for a category that will allow me to bring things together – things that share few other common properties in terms of form, material production or social history. So you have a moment of coming together, but also a temporary dissolution of other things, other categories and institutional or cultural provenances.

But to come back to the cacophony, I think that partly emerges out of a heterogeneous idea of art. Is John Carpenter's *They Live* satirising Kruger's critique of advertising through a sci-fi movie, one in which the protagonists understand the real message of advertising only if they wear Lou Reed-type sunglasses? Art isn't a separate, inviolable category; it's porous and part of the world. My first book on art was the *Marks and Spencer Book of Great Masters* and that has clearly shaped me – along with the first art I loved: post-punk records and Kafka.

And talking of post-punk and cacophony – pop music is very important to me. The soundtrack to USER GROUP DISCO, which was created by Jem Noble, employs the same method of bricolage as I use to formulate the imagery. It uses bastardised melodies from the

Cure and Desmond Dekker. It borrows from Carpenter's film music, but it also shapes an interior architecture for the fictional institution using sound. I wanted to create a sense of being inside taxonomical categories, as though they were a crumbling, dripping architecture filled with litter and debris. I loved working with this soundtrack – it gave me a ground-plan, a set for the drama.

PO'N USER GROUP DISCO, *which is in your current show at Spike Island, brings the viewer through an episodic series of rooms, objects and their spaces and structures of display. Set in what you call the* Hall of Sculptures, *it presents a museum of fictions, entropy and decay. But in spite of their apparent seductiveness, the objects themselves are pure artifice and surface.*

EP They're spectral, I think. One of the things I thought about in making in this video was the history of recording technologies, from analogue to digital. This video is emphatically digital, it uses motion graphics and the soundtrack is digital, so there is a sense of the featured materials and objects being converted into information, into data. A part of the video draws on the ideas that accompanied the emergence of the phonograph record, of it being a medium for access to a ghost world. Edison promoted his invention as a means of retaining the voices of people who had died. I think the *Hall of Sculptures* is a place where material is dissolving into something spectral. Things dissolve into stories, but also into images – into a sparkling, glistening display. It's not the wetness of material, though, but a different shine. I think the technology of high-definition video is significant here. Its clarity in recording the surfaces of objects is very strange – acute and toxic. I'm fascinated by it.

PO'N *There was a particular phrase that struck me in* USER GROUP DISCO, *'you too are an appearance'. It seems to suggest that, while recognising the instability of the fragmented image of the object, you are also manipulating the viewer, or suggesting to the viewer that he or she may be a human resource to be manipulated by the authorial voice and become part of the same system of representation and consumption that the objects occupy.*

EP My videos draw the viewer into an imagined institutional structure where they are both consumers and consumed. This dynamic becomes particularly violent around objects from domestic interiors. During the final stages of *At The House of Mr X* the viewer is invited to imagine adding their own bodily materials, as a kind of shimmering décor, to the already lustrous materials of the house. So the body of the inhabitant is expended as a material in the consumption of the house's luxurious domestic ideal.

USER GROUP DISCO has a similar denouement. It concentrates upon a group of objects that all combine domestic functions with eroticised images of the human body. For example, there is a nutcracker that takes the form of a naked woman who cracks nuts between her thighs. This is informed by zombie films and my interest in the relationship between the zombie of cinema, which is an unconscious devouring consumer, and the zombie of voodoo, which is a slave that cannot be liberated by death.

PO'N *Are you creating your own taxonomic system, even though you are quite critical of taxonomy – most evidently in* USER GROUP DISCO *– as being non-neutral systems of organising?*

EP This whole video is a series of perverse organisations of shitty objects. Of course the point is that my organisation is to do with contesting power. Disturbance in the archive allows the fiction to happen, but it doesn't really reconfigure the taxonomy. So it's an important gesture, but it is only a gesture. It makes me think of the dark enlightenment of Gothic novels, and how Gothic had both radical and conservative aspects. I'm really digressing now – I was going to start talking about Frankenstein.

PO'N *I think that the disruption of any taxonomic system exposes the original classification system upon which that taxonomy is based as being equally constructed and dysfunctional.*

EP I agree with that, but knowing that it's fictional doesn't count for much in terms of real politics, and I suppose that's why the notion of moving something into the wrong place in the archive, and precipitating a fantasy, has pathos. What can you do with what you inherit, what you are given as culture? It is an already organised legacy.

PO'N *The last time we spoke you seemed quite keen for your work to be seen as institutional critique, and this is particularly evident in the video works where there is at least a soft critique of the ways we function as consumers within our inherited spaces of display – the museum, the archive, the collection, the atrium. It's no accident that my videos present dilemmas of power and desire in which I am implicated. My critical position is not 'hard'; it is in formation, unstable. But I won't apologise for that. Criticism seems to have become a way of professing, rather than a way of thinking, and I believe I'm right to be wary of its manners. But if by soft you mean mild, I would be very disappointed at that. I hope that my videos express argument with scorn and heat.*

EP   I don't want my work to be seen as institutional critique, but perhaps as one of its descendants. I'm interested in working with it not as a failed project but as an unfulfilled narrative. I certainly don't have the same reserve about institutional critique that I have about dematerialisation. I'm party to its politics. But I am interested in picking up the threads of things like that, in taking them somewhere else. Institutional critique aspires to make the institution transparent, in the hope that the mystique of its power will shatter – which of course it never does. My work doesn't continue that attempt but rather it accretes more weird, byzantine, shiny, viscous stuff to the edifice of the institution, not cleaning it up but doing the opposite. So Catholic!

Issue 326, May 2009

Pipilotti Rist

interviewed by Patricia Bickers

Caressing Space

PATRICIA BICKERS *We first met at the Venice Biennale in 1993, in what was to be the last Aperto, and, some 12 years later, you represented Switzerland in the Biennale, at the deconsecrated baroque church of San Staë where you showed* Homo sapiens sapiens – *a sumptuous contemporary version of a work made in di sotto in sù. I'd like to ask you about this work since it is characteristic of your immersive sound and video pieces. What was it like working in that space?*

PIPILOTTI RIST The Swiss government helped pay for the renovation of this church, which is why it is now used as a second Swiss pavilion. I was extremely interested to work in this space. The way I normally work in a space is that I adapt to it. In this case, I decided that I did not want to take over the church, but rather to be almost not there.

The work was made with four projectors placed on the ground projecting upwards onto the ceiling so that, when you lie down on the cushions and look up, you can't see where the video image begins or ends because of the capital frieze. The computer image had to be compressed so that it became square, distorting the perspective. It has to do with the idea of the spirit rising up into heaven. It was how I imagined Paradise to be before the Fall of Man.

PB *In your vision of Paradise you refuse to surrender to the idea of the mind and body split. Instead you bring body and mind together in some notional, gloriously guiltless, prelapsarian space.*

PR I appreciate that you see it like this. Sin is so much linked to images. The idea is so deeply ingrained in us that we are full of sin from the moment we are born, that life is only a test and that the real life is the afterlife. I wanted to create something that would wash out our old pains.

PB *You may not have wanted to 'take over' San Staë, but with this piece, which is uplifting with its Tiepolo-like colours so appropriate to Venice, the space will always be associated with your work. I am sure I am not alone in wishing that it could be a permanent installation.*

PR Actually the church was closed down after four of the six months. Although it is not used as a church, a priest collected signatures to send a petition to Rome, but in the end there were only 40 signatures. They hung a sign on the door: Closed for technical reasons. I wrote to them, 'You should not lie!' The people of the Portuguese pavilion next door collected more than 2,000 signatures to open it up again, but it didn't help.

PB *Another major work after the Venice piece was* Pour Your Body Out (7,354 Cubic Metres), *which you did for* MOMA *in New York in 2008. You created a similarly immersive environment in which people could lie back and 'lose themselves' in the work. In other works, however, like* Open My Glade, *2000, for instance, in which the body is pressed against the glass, you deliberately remind the viewer of the limits of the medium – the fourth wall – creating the opposite effect, that of entrapment.*

PR Let me first say something about 'immersive'. You are right, I try to work as immersively as possible because I think we always try to frame everything behind and within the square format and it affects us strongly. It is a kind of remedy to make the work as huge as possible – it becomes like our skin. In life you are often alone, but when you come together in imaginary rooms you become a common body.

But the problem with electronic media is that it is not like looking in a mirror because you can always decide, 'Ah! It's only pixels'. You see all the mistakes, the shortcomings of video. When you think of old standard-definition media, which we once regarded as so sharp – and now we are going over to high-definition media which maybe one day we will also not think so sharp – you realise that no media – whether photography, film or video – will ever be as sharp as real life. But our super brain compensates for all missing information as we take in only 10% of impressions and 90% is generated individually. So close your eyes and watch the afterburn.

PB *So works like* Open My Glade *express a kind of frustration with the limits of the medium because the human eye will always be sharper than any camera?*

PR You would have to jump into the other's eye, or live on the retina of the other.

PB *I remember a lovely quote in which you said, 'The eye is like a blood-driven camera.'*

PR Yes. Video technique is just a poor copy of how our eye works.

PB *Unusually for you, you made an outdoor installation in St Gallen, Switzerland, called* Stadtlounge *– also called* Redbloodmonstersculpture *– in which you covered every available surface, including furniture, a car and a fountain, with red tartan so that everyone could have the privilege of walking on a red carpet – it was like entering another world.*

PR This was a collaboration with the architect Carlos Martinez in a city close to where I grew up. The basic concept was to pretend that the outside space was an inside, private one.

It was a competition for a combination of landscape architecture and public art in 2005, and I didn't really want to win it. They asked three artists to collaborate with architects, and architects with artists. We thought about what would we do if it was our space. The jury just said, 'Let's do it', and in 18 months it was realised because everybody involved pulled together.

PB *You certainly won the public's prize.*

PR Yes, that was surprising – nice. It has become a widely accepted permanent work – it's been there for several years now and was recently even enlarged. I think it became very popular because people felt welcomed by the soft material, making it like a collective playground, and because the colour in all of us is red. It was not more expensive than doing it with ordinary tarmac.

PB *The awkwardness of the space in St Gallen takes me back to* Pour Your Body Out (7,354 Cubic Metres)*, which was commissioned by* MOMA *for its vast atrium. It is a very difficult space, not as difficult as Tate's Turbine Hall, perhaps, but 7,354 cubic metres is still a huge volume to tackle.*

PR Each room has its own condition, at MOMA the room was not supposed to be dark – I don't like dark rooms anyway and I don't ask for them. Of course they expected me to do something with moving image and sound, but when it is for a space where people meet like in an atrium, the content should not be authoritarian. Usually if you make a mistake, you do it better next time – but you can't do that with architecture, you need to get it right.

PB *There is a white column in the space but you managed to bend the video around it. I suppose after San Staë it was probably easy for you.*

253

PR Actually, this column takes up only a small area – the whole work combined consisted of seven projections.

PB *And you modelled all this?*

PR Yes. For San Staë I had three models. Also for MOMA we worked on a model in the scale 1:3 in the studio beforehand.

PB *In the centre of this experience – and people never say they have 'seen' a Pipilotti Rist work, they always say they have 'experienced' it – you created an 'eye' with a circular blue 'iris' where people sit and gaze at the floating projections. This suggests a kind of reciprocity between viewer and viewed, between the human eye and the mechanical eye of the projector.*

PR Yes, I couldn't say it better, thanks. People took over the space, and even some yoga people came up with the idea themselves and used it on a couple of Sunday mornings for their sessions. I was very proud.

PB *You have said that your work 'caresses' the museum, that you are not interested in attacking it, that you are not interested in institutional critique in the manner, for instance, of Andrea Fraser.*

PR I meant 'caresses' also in an architectural way. I could have decided to try to destroy the space, or to fight against it. I decided instead to caress Taniguchi's space. It is a very elegant space, so, in a formal way, I tried to melt into it. And it was said that I have changed the gender of the MOMA. I am just doing a service to make the space as positive as possible so that through that relaxation deeper reflections can take place.

PB *You referred earlier to the idea that we are marked by sin, a very Catholic view of the world. This darker aspect is more overt in your earlier work, especially in* (Absolutions) Pipilotti's Mistakes *of 1988 – it is there in the title, and in the frighteningly ambiguous scene of the girl who is apparently being drowned in the swimming pool, or is she being baptised? In this work total immersion is the very opposite of the 'blissed-out' experience of, for instance,* Sip My Ocean.

PR It goes backwards and forwards, like life.

PB *Yes. And the girl in the sinful red dress repeatedly falls over – literally, a fallen woman – but she gets up each time.*

PR I always try to accept mistakes as an offer of life.

PB *It was filmed in Super-8?*

PR No, it was already a video but still analogue. With digital mistakes, if something fails, it fails much quicker. But in this work, I used 22 ways of analogue disturbances that shows us to be –

PB *Human?*

PR Yes – the truth, where we should go and what we should decide in life. It is astonishing to me how much we get hurt in life, and by other people. But we always get up again and accept the hurt and turn the other cheek. It is about this energy, this exorcism. It is a kind of exorcism that raises us up, not down.

PB *You dare to reference all those things that are associated with the feminine – nature, earth, water – particularly water. In fact, you celebrate them uninhibitedly.*

PR Yes, I understand what you mean in terms of feminism but for me my figures stand for the human, not only for women. It is a question of language: when there is a naked man – aha, it must be about the 'human'. But when there is a naked woman, the assumption is that it is to do with sexuality. We came out of water – and maybe that is my superstition again – but I think we are still very much like fish. We have developed out of the water and later became mammals. When I use water, there is also the wish – for example, in *Sip My Ocean* – to float with the other, or to flow freely for a short while – and sometimes it happens.

PB *Of course, music – singing – is a crucial part of your work, reflecting your background as a member of a band.*

PR Yes, it is the band's 23rd anniversary. I first joined them only to work on the staging – the projections, the slides and the Super-8 films – then they took me into the band. After six years with them I was still very much afraid to go on stage. I prefer to work backstage, to work on the sound in the basement until it's ready for the performance.

PB *In the Venice Biennale of 1997 you were awarded the Premio 2000 for* Ever Is Over All, *one of your most popular works. It shows a woman behaving transgressively – blithely smashing car windows with the smiling approval of a passing policewoman.*

PR In this case, the lady imagines that the obstacles in life are much smaller than we expect them to be.

PB *She wields an oversized flower with a long stalk known in this country as a Red Hot Poker – a wonderfully phallic image.*

PR Hmm – I would call it clitoric. Not everything nice is phallic! This work is linked to a longer feature film and it is actually about daring to do something, about daring to do more, to do the unexpected. When people see this piece they go out happy, rather than not.

PB *It is strangely empowering.*

PR I would not say I have a clear ideology or message. As I get older I am less sure what is right and wrong. There should be a certain mildness coming from my work because the reality is always much more complex than any ideology, not to speak of the irrationality.

PB *The feature film you mention is* Pepperminta, *which you described, when you were still working on it, as more like a novel than a poem, so, presumably, you think of your video works as more like poems. What was it like for you to work on a feature film?*

PR I worked for four years on this feature film. I finished it in 2009. It was a very good experience to work on this film. Usually we work with a low, low, low budget, but to film a longer story you have to work with professionals so that you can hold everything together – and professionals are very expensive. Working with a whole crew was like playing in a sport – everybody knew what to do. The idea of the film is to free the world from all the unnecessary fears – not necessary fears, but those fears that lead us into daily self-censorship. That is what the film is about.

PB *Is the little girl based on your own persona?*

PR You're right – it is a little bit close – the name 'Pepperminta' is close to my name – I realised that too late. But it is not me, it is just how I would like to be – without all those unnecessary crazy fears that I have too.

This is an edited version of an interview which took place at the Starr Auditorium, Tate Modern on 6 June 2009. Published Issue 350, October 2011.

Seth Siegelaub

interviewed by John Slyce

Part One: The Playmaker

JOHN SLYCE *Could you say something about the particular context of New York in 1965–66?*

SETH SIEGELAUB Firstly, a rich, developed, capitalist country exports its culture more easily than a poor country. I mean, that's part of its power, to be able to impose its vision of the world on the rest of the world.

There were other, contingent factors: the rise of technological communication media in general – an important new sector in capitalist society which was in the process of replacing manufacturing. Much of the international success of, say, Abstract Expressionism and postwar American art had to do with the success of the US. Europe was battered by the war and the need to rebuild, and the US was able to exploit that. Its cultural institutions, which include the Museum of Modern Art, were in a position to export art and a lot of the exhibitions that came over to Europe from the US were encouraged, in one way or another, by fiscal incentives or subsidies during the Cold War.

These were some of the factors backgrounding our activity, or my activity. Another one, of course – quite conjunctional – was the Vietnam War, and the student uprisings in the US and Europe which created a critical atmosphere that opened up the possibilities for what is today called 'institutional critique', concerning the role of institutions and to what degree, if any, artists should collaborate with them in a world that divided rich and poor, oppressors and oppressed. So my art world activities all fitted into that framework or context.

257

The questions opened up by these contemporary problems were reflected in responses to, for example, concerns about art as object and as commodity, the permanence of the art object, the one visual canon, and what makes a work of art 'ownable' or not 'ownable'.

One should keep in mind that it was the period of Marshall McLuhan's 'the medium is the message' and the idea of the 'global village'. This is something that is, in a way, in the process of being realised today with the internet, and with the same kind of images of a free world with everyone communicating – happy, happy, happy – when in reality it is controlled by very few people, but it is made to seem like some kind of revolutionary possibility. Which, to a certain degree, it is: but in a way that is similar to Bertolt Brecht's analysis of the radio as a medium of propaganda, as opposed to a medium of communication between people.

So all these questions were floating around in the air and each artist, in his or her own way, took the ball and ran with it.

JS *How did you come into contact with what would become your 'stable': Robert Barry, Douglas Huebler, Lawrence Weiner.*

SS That's a relatively easy one – particularly in retrospect. I met Lawrence Weiner, then I met Joseph Kosuth through Lawrence, and then Carl Andre and then Bob Barry and then Doug Huebler. Curiously enough, by way of history here, Doug was introduced to me via Dore Ashton.

And so this nucleus developed, little by little. Each artist in his own way. But obviously the interaction between them led to a breakdown of what their work had been before. It was the beginnings of that kind of art: there was Daniel Buren in France, Germano Celant and Arte Povera in Italy, so what we were doing wasn't totally unique. It is just what we did. All I would do is try to organise interesting exhibitions, and I usually had very close connections with the artists I was working with.

I had a gallery for a while on 56th Street in New York. 'For a while' means about a year and a half. One should remember that at that time the art world was relatively small, there was relatively little gallery traffic. It was barely possible to make money making art unless you were very rich to begin with, or your father was Matisse, or you were connected to a very rich or well-known family or something.

So, besides the fact that it was hardly a way to make a living, it was extremely boring because you just sort of sat down and did an exhibition, and then you'd have an opening and give people drinks and all that stuff – and I really didn't like it. Although I did some interesting exhibitions – this isn't an auto-critique or something – I wasn't cut out to be a salesman. I really didn't have a feel for that, and I really didn't want to approach my relationship to art as that of a dealer.

Although I was still closely attached to a small group of artists, after the gallery closed in the spring of 1966 my role gradually broadened and developed into what would now be called an 'independent curator', but I was still very attached to a certain aesthetic, a certain approach to art. In other words, I started out being closely associated and working with four or five artists, and then it became a little bigger, and the exhibitions became more general, more international. The special issue of *Studio International* in 1969, for instance, involved me asking other people to do the selecting. In a way, I just wanted to get away from the problem of selecting great artists. And I wanted to deal with the whole framework, or how society gets the artists it deserves.

JS *But that's a shift that was being played out in the work as well, from work to frame. So in a sense you were following or moving along with what the artists were doing.*

ss Yes, exactly. There was definitely an interaction there. I suppose I thought of myself as a playmaker – like in basketball. Again, not to be a dealer, I never had much success from doing that. Some people do it very well – but not me.

In any case I had a definite predilection towards printing and publishing. That is something that has carried me through my whole life. But at the beginning, I never thought of myself as a publisher. Books were just vehicles, in the way that space was a vehicle for a traditional gallery. But later in my life, after I left the art world sometime in 1971, and moved to Europe in 1972 where I started political publishing and critical research, it became clear that I really liked publishing books.

But publishing also had a specific role vis-à-vis the kind of art that was being produced by these artists – that was a very important nexus. So that's my trajectory, or at least how I see it 40 years later. I didn't start out thinking that we were revolutionaries. It was just another kind of art confronting what I considered – or rather what we considered – basic issues concerning the nature of art, the relationship of the producer to the consumer, and all these kinds of questions. Although we theorised about what we were doing, the dramatic impact the work had probably only became clear 20 or 30 years later. And part of that dramatic impact is related to the next generation of people who, in their own way, picked up on it.

JS *And what is your reading of that reception?*

SS I don't really feel it in the first degree. Apparently, the work has had a very great influence on a great range of art; I think one of the great strands of history, including art history, is this kind of influence through generations. I've become aware of it – probably more so because I'm so distant from the daily life of the art world. I mean, I have art I admire, I go to the Venice Biennale. Occasionally I give a lecture. But I don't really follow what's happening.

JS *What prompted you to reply to Benjamin Buchloh's essay in that first survey 'L'art conceptuale: une perspective' in 1989 at the Musée d'Art moderne de la Ville de Paris?*

SS Buchloh, who I consider – who considers himself – to be a man of progressive intention, wrote a hermeneutically sealed, ahistorical, traditional text which was totally lacking in any feel for the period. That is why I felt compelled to respond. I also felt that his treatment of Joseph (say what one will about Joseph – he is an important figure in all of this) was not very fair.

JS *It was important, I suppose, that the show took place in Europe?*

SS There is nothing surprising about that whatsoever. Most of the interest in the work – in the context of institutions and collectors and money to finance projects – came from Europe. It's only in recent times that there have been one or two exhibitions, particularly at MOCA, Los Angeles, that focused specifically on the project – although one shouldn't forget the 'Information' show in New York at MOMA in 1970. It wasn't a total void, but there was – and still is – a remarkable disinterest in this period in the US.

But to get back to Buchloh's specific text – although I was involved with a certain group of people in New York, there was certainly activity in Europe. I had some contact with it, but I certainly wasn't the same kind of motor or force that I was in New York. And there was also Latin America, where things were going on, too, which I had relatively little to do with. And there were antecedents in Japan. I think one of the reasons, perhaps, for the relative success of the group of people I was involved with had to do as much with the power of American capitalism as with anything else.

JS *What was your take on Alex Alberro's book,* The Politics of Publicity?

ss   He's done more hardcore research into that period than anybody. That is very important because many of the critics who were active at the time are no longer really interested in it. From what I understand of the book, Alex thinks of me as some kind of advertising super-promoter. But he's part of that generation which values the ability to generate publicity and what would now be called 'merchandising' and, of course, I've never really seen myself as an advertising genius promoting artists. I think I do have a certain awareness of the mechanics of the art world and I do try to work with it, but we're talking about 40 years ago: we were just happy to show the work, get some money in, and be able to continue to live and to do work. Alex, I think, gives, not quite a mythological, but certainly a more conscious dimension to my activities than I probably would have admitted to at the time. It is a slightly different reading.

   So, what do I think of it? I remember being very happy that someone had spent time going into this history because, although everybody now has a Conceptual Art book in a series about modern art movements, there are not many serious studies around. And Blake Stimson did a lot of hardcore work on it, too, while Alex spent a lot of time on interviews and conversations to get all the primary material together and the dates right, and who was where and when, and what this one said and what that one said. So I think that's been important. He is the only person who has gone through my archive.

js   *And where is that archive now?*

ss   It is in the US. It hasn't been donated or sold, but Alex used it as a resource, which gave him a certain amount of concrete data for that period.

   You have to remember that I was only in the art world for like six or seven years. The interest people show in the work is obviously flattering, but it is only one part of my life. It is history.

   Recently I found myself in a history of contemporary art dealers where I was referred to as 'Siegelaub Projects'! I mean, I have had a lot of projects but that wasn't what I called myself. It wouldn't even occur to me to think that way. But when this book was produced three years ago, 'Siegelaub Projects' followed on from Deitch Projects, and that must have seemed the logical way to define my work.

js   *Seth Siegelaub as a brand was something that was, in a sense, developed after the fact.*

ss   Yes, I think this whole idea of branding was totally beyond my experience then. It is certainly true that you get known for a certain thing in the same way that, if I mention Clement Greenberg, you think of colour painting – that's his brand, that's what he is known for.

It is doubly curious because the use of branding is like establishing a certain aura and keeping it as stable as possible. In other words, don't move too much, make it clear and put it on T-shirts. It is basically to sell, of course, but also to be known for a certain kind of thing forever – and ever, and ever.

And this is also a problem in artistic creation, too, because capitalist values have infiltrated artistic thinking and artistic development. It is difficult enough to advance as part of your normal aesthetic development or your thinking, but it is doubly so if you have a dealer who just wants you to keep producing what they know, and what you became successful with.

JS *Is that something that, in a sense, precipitated your exit in 1971?*

SS No, my exit was really a personal thing. I went as far as I thought I could go or wanted to go. But it became very clear to me, after having been involved with a certain kind of art-making moment, that the only choice you had was to do it again. I mean, either you stay with it and become the master connoisseur for Conceptual Art and bullshit your life away talking about that, or you take in a whole new stable of artists and, using all your contacts, you try to do the same thing with another kind of art – or what they call a 'second generation' – and I don't think that was really worth the effort. That wasn't fun.

The specific nature of the art I was involved in led me to more political concerns. When I left I was definitely planning to do some kind of journalistic work. The information side really tickled me.

When I left the US, the first project I tried to develop was some kind of news agency, but it became even more hectic and frenetic than the art world. Imagine having to come up with something new every 24 hours. I was still watching the journalist community closely. I was trying to follow what was going on. There was a lot of talk of doing some kind of leftist newspaper – the *Village Voice* wasn't that old – so I was inspired. I was definitely thinking in that direction.

Also, I was very lucky in that the artists that I was involved with were taken on by a very great dealer: Leo Castelli took on all four guys. That was important to me. Of course, I had an obligation to them too. I mean, I didn't bring them lots of money, but I was very helpful in getting their work into the world and the fact that Leo – or anybody

– had taken them on made it possible for me to leave with a clean conscience. There are probably very few people even at that stage who would have been interested in dealing with them, as a group or even individually. Not because they were difficult (through certain of them are) but because they wouldn't 'fit'. But Castelli always had an interest in younger people. He always had his eye open.

That was an important step for me – an important burden for me. It didn't provide me with any money. People think I became rich suddenly.

JS *A finder's fee!*

SS No, no – even Lucy Lippard had the idea that I made some sort of money from Leo by selling my ex-stable of artists. I didn't get anything from him. We had lunch.

They didn't all prosper. I think Lawrence did best of all. I think Joseph did a little bit. Bob had good contact with Leo, but Doug was out in California at CalArts. He certainly got lost in it all.

But Leo was interested and he would do a show every year or two with the guys, and he would try and sell their work – but I don't have the impression he was very successful in dealing with the work. It's not really his thing. Of course, that was perfectly normal because I wasn't successful either. You would think that they would have better luck. I mean, Richard Serra and Bob Morris, they were fine. But the others, I think they had difficult times.

Again, most of the interest and money came from Europe: Konrad Fischer in Germany, Gian Enzo Sperone in Turin and Yvon Lambert in Paris and a few other people. And a few collectors. That was it. There was never a great interest from within the US.

JS *Can you talk a little bit about how your activities found an influence and expression in a second generation?*

SS That I don't know, really. The UK has a teaching tradition, like a studio system, but of the artists I worked with, only Doug taught. He did have a big influence in CalArts on younger artists who have now become famous, like Mike Kelley.

I think it is very difficult to see how artists are influenced by other people. But that they were influential is definite, not least because it has been acknowledged by subsequent generations.

When I give talks from time to time, people say, 'Oh, it must have been great. A free time when anything was possible' making it into some kind of Paradise Lost, or paradigm lost. People romanticise the period as being one of great freedom – May 1968, 'Make love, not war', blah, blah, blah. They have an exaggerated idea of the kind of freedom that we could possibly have under any regime.

JS *But the stakes, in a sense, were different then.*

SS Yes, yes. There has definitely been a dramatic change in the expectations artists have and what they expect art to do for them. And a lot of it has to do with, what I consider, the capitalist integration of the art world.

I used to refer to the art world as a pimple on the arse of capitalism – an object of ridicule. But the professionalisation of art as a liberal profession, equivalent to other kinds of liberal professions, means that today you can be a painter and be a respected member of the community, have two houses and send your kids to private school etc. This was totally, totally, unknown in the 1960s.

JS *I want to talk about the artists you worked with but also some that, in a sense, got away. You mention Carl Andre and how Andre, in some respects, fits in very well – or could have fitted – but somehow it didn't come off.*

SS I've been thinking about this. You have to remember that Carl was much more successful than any of us. He had shown quite a bit and was well known, like Sol LeWitt in a way.

There was a certain element of friendship. If you misinterpreted his work, he could fit in very well. Carl is very definitely a materialist. He believes in, and works with, the specificity of material objects. But on a certain level, I would say he was quite influential in the evolution of what we now call Conceptual Art. It really was a combination of happenstance – particularly between Larry and Carl – and friendships. They would go out drinking – classic artists in a way.

But I also think that, and this is what I have been trying to deal with – at least to contextualise – his influence was probably much greater than his being pigeonholed as a minimal artist would suggest. I think his work is far more expansive than Judd's or Morris's. I mean, philosophically, aesthetically, his work opens up whole areas of ways to make art – what an artist should be doing and how he or she should be doing it. It would be false to say that his work was directly related to work we were doing. I mean, Carl has a definite respect for the work, but it was just not his thing. I think when you referred to people that I've lost along the way, you were probably referring more specifically to people like Ian Wilson.

JS *Yes, exactly.*

ss   Carl – there's no reason to think he fitted in. He participated in shows and he was a close friend, but there is a very good reason why he wouldn't be part of it. Ian, on the other hand, was a part of the activities in the early years. Why he didn't get involved with it is not entirely clear, but he is very much a loner – quiet – he keeps to himself. There was definitely a certain amount of tension between him and Joseph – well, there is between Joseph and a lot of people – and he just didn't want to participate in the 'January' show in 1969. But we were all interested in him.

JS   *And the invitation was already out for the 'January' show?*

ss   Yes, it was well before January that we started working on it – September 1967. It was very clear that he didn't want to participate. I mean it wasn't a last-minute decision. He was basically absorbed in his own work. And maybe he didn't want to identify himself with other people and with the movement – he was somewhat aloof from that. Maybe (and this is speculative) he didn't want his work to be confused with the kind of language questions which all the other artists were involved with in one way or another.

So he is the one that comes to mind as somebody who was there, but went somewhere else or did whatever he wanted to do. There weren't many other people.

JS   *Mel Bochner?*

ss   Bochner, yes, was one of them. I've been asked this on several occasions. I don't know why. Now that I think back on it, there was a problem between him and Joseph at the School of Visual Arts. I mean, Joseph being a student of his – and not being a student of his – and who did what first. Sol wasn't involved either and, eventually, Carl wasn't. You could speak about Allen Ruppersberg, too … I mean, if you look at the period, and you go down the list of artists, you can ask yourself, why not? You could invent a whole story about it, but that's just the way it was.

JS   *And of that core group – Huebler, Kosuth, Barry and Weiner – what, in your mind, was the gel holding them together?*

ss   I don't know exactly. Language has been put forth as the sort of cement, as it were, between their work. But it's all quite different. Lawrence's, at least at the beginning, was about words and things, people's relationship to things. Doug was definitely involved with the relationship between what we see and what we know, or what we know linguistically, in any case. Bob was involved with more spacey things, completely ephemeral ideas. He was thinking of radio waves which couldn't be perceived and things like that.

What is certainly very clear, like with any group of artists no matter who they were and when, is that their interactivity gave mutual encouragement and stimulus. The discussions and debates with your peers, or with your friends, would obviously have a very great effect – especially when you weren't getting any kind of informed feedback from the public or from other people.

So I suspect a lot had to do with the artists being together, talking and drinking together, and planning projects together, which we often did.

js *Yes. But you added something very specific to that sibling culture which was external.*

ss Yes, in a way it was external. It had a lot to do with space – the physical, sociological and cultural space – that we see art in. Remember, it was a time when many of us were attempting to bring art into the world in a much more direct fashion, to take it out of apartments or museums. Whether you want to talk about the beginning of video or street theatre or even graffiti – things which were not directly related to us – these kinds of things brought art out into the public reality.

There were a lot of things that were bubbling around, but it is very difficult to say why, in 1967 – maybe Joseph was slightly earlier – all these artists suddenly stopped making paintings or drawings and decided to develop a whole other, different kind of art.

js *There must have been specific conditions of possibility there to produce that shift from a painted object to information – to the dissemination of information.*

ss The question has been asked many times, why then? There were a lot of factors that fed into an art that became dematerialised, a more ideated kind of art.

But you really started out to say what my situation was. I was an organiser. That's what I was. Because of my unsatisfactory experience with the gallery, I was looking for the possibility of getting out of a gallery situation. There were no models except maybe private dealers – people selling objects privately like dope dealers or book dealers.

So, I was looking around, trying to think of new modes of presenting art which, of course, are related to new types of art that could be shown in other kinds of environments, and in other conditions.

It was my self-imposed job in the group to find these new situations. And once I found them, to then find a way to do them – to pay for them.

In a certain way again, retrospectively, my interests dovetailed very closely with theirs, so I could see my way through to another kind of art relationship, another kind of art dealing or exhibiting practice. It made it easier – not easier for me – but it gave a practical focus for a problem that I was trying to deal with. And I'm sure the fact that I could realise things encouraged them to be able to do things. So the collaborative nature of the exhibition projects formed part of it. It was very complementary.

JS *One of the moves that can specifically be ascribed to you was a move to bring the secondary forward to absolutely displace the primary. For example,* The Xerox Book *with Jack Wendler in 1968 and, further to that, the catalogue – or the interviews – that were put forward in place of anything more concrete.*

SS It was also, in part, to do with the realisation that many people knew art (rightly or wrongly – I would say mostly wrongly) from what they saw in magazines. In other words, more people know art from reading about it, or looking at pictures of it, than they ever do from seeing the physical object. And, obviously, seeing the physical object is absolutely critical – with sculpture it is scale, size, place and that stuff. But also, for my part, it was to do with going some place – I mean, the whole cultural situation.

These people were producing work – other people were too – which wasn't information about something, it was the thing itself. And so you didn't have to go any further. You didn't have to go to a space to see a Huebler, it was presented to you and me in the format of a book – which obviously led me to work on the idea of the book as an exhibition space, if you like.

JS *Also the form of the advertisement. The ad for the Huebler show, combined with the page, is the final form of the piece.*

SS Yes. The idea of the specificity of place got picked up and became a very important aesthetic issue. Before us, to a large degree – maybe entirely, now that I think about it – an artwork was more or less autonomous. Obviously it related to artworks before and alongside it, but basically you could just stick it anywhere. The Huebler ad is a documentation, but it is also a documentation that only makes sense in a certain space, in a certain time, and is defined in terms of that.

JS *It established a radical equality between the work and its publicity.*

ss   Yes, though for me publicity has a negative ring.

JS   *Well, not if it's combined with 'public', in the sense of creating a 'public'.*

ss   Right. But still, the word 'publicity', like in publicity or public relations, always has a hyped-up sense. I was not overwhelmed at Alex's title for the book: *The Politics of Publicity*.

JS   *Your address may have been Madison Avenue, but you didn't consider yourself a Madison Avenue man.*

ss   No. I've said I worked in the R&D department, not in the merchandising, advertising or sales departments! Yes, maybe I did have several tricks that I would use, but I don't think they were super clever – mailing things out and so on. It's not an original idea. Today, I would use the email which, in fact, is exactly what I do. I'm sure in 40 years' time there will be some other means of communicating on an even broader scale. But I never thought of myself as an advertiser.

It kind of has a negative feel to me because I was brought up that way. You know, when I was starting my work life, advertising was sort of for hucksters. It was a very negative thing. I'm sure Alex is being complimentary. He's not saying that this guy was a huckster or a hustler, or a snake-oil salesman, but it is not a term that I would use in a flattering way. If I said so-and-so is a great promoter, I'm being negative. I mean for my generation, that is.

JS   *How did you create some sort of basis on which the work could be evaluated, absorbed, taken in? It couldn't have been easy. It is one proposition to put a piece of Formica before someone; it is quite another to put some information before them and get them to see value in it. Looking back, how do you see negotiating that shift?*

ss   I don't know how much I had to do with it, or what my role could possibly have been in that transition. Really the problem was getting the work seen, getting the work discussed, looked at and, eventually, digested and used or reacted to by the next generation of people. And I don't know how you can really do that in a conscious way.

There's one way that is very clear – it is with money. I mean, you just make enough noise and get the highest auction prices. That is one of the steps towards – short-term – immortality. But other than that, it's kind of like a crapshoot. I was never in a position to think very seriously about how an artist's career is made because there wasn't that kind of interest in the work. I'm sure there are certain steps that need to be followed. You could appear in certain books, in certain kinds of anthology, people have to write about your work, certain collectors have to own you, certain museums have to show you, and things like this – you could probably draw a diagram. But you have to have work that can really get the ball rolling – and I never had the impression that that's what we were involved with at that time. It never would have crossed my mind to create value in that sense. One of the things that I think is really important for an artist is how other artists look at him or her, and especially how the next generation looks at you – how you influence them. This is not given, but I do definitely believe that it is how the younger generation of art makers are influenced by your work that matters, and how aware they are of who they're influenced by.

Basically, it comes down to having other people see the work as much as possible and arguing for it. You really had to claim your intellectual property rights – for lack of a better phrase – especially if you were not building something, or if the work was not some physical object – or at least a picture of it – that everyone can concur about seeing somewhere.

JS *You still have to claim that turf.*

SS   Yes, you still have to. And a lot of that takes place talking in bars and talking between artists. In fact, you make it real even if it hasn't been done, or if you didn't have the means to do it or even – especially – if it was not intended ever to be made.

JS *I'm thinking of the Windham College Show, 'Dissociated Objects: The Statements/Objects of Lawrence Weiner' in 1968. It seems to me that this was a pretty crucial point at which things were established in a tangible way, a kind of staking-out of territory – almost literally, in the case of Weiner.*

SS   Yes, now that you mention it. That was Lawrence's moment of realisation. It's nice you said that. I suppose it's true. Who remembers? It's not like angels come down from heaven or something. It is difficult to understand, or to pinpoint when these things actually occurred. But one thing is very clear to me – that art really is a social activity. It is not just one person who comes up with great ideas and everyone else follows. When you look at it – when you live it – it is a very complicated mess. The question 'who did what first' and all those kinds of art-historical non-questions do have to be dealt with, but it really becomes very, very difficult to appraise. It is very difficult to see who is really making art history – and that's a value too – and it's up for grabs. The work has to correspond to a moment, to a sensibility, to a life 'geist' or spirit of the time.

Part Two: The Contract

SETH SIEGELAUB At any given point in the art world, if you like, I think you come down to ten or 15 dealers who are serious dealers as opposed to businessmen having a gallery, who are more or less at the cutting edge – but I am sure there is no law of requirement.

JOHN SLYCE *There couldn't be in such an unregulated industry.*

SS But there probably are certain rules. Chamberlain once said, 'It is very important you owe money to the right people.' That's like a joke – but there is a grain of truth in it. But I have no idea how you work your way up the food chain.

I never had the impression that that was what we were doing. I figured I had the idea that this is important work; this is work that was asking some questions that had never been asked before; it was doing away with certain presumptions or certain assumptions about what art should be.

JS *And hierarchies.*

SS Hierarchies, yes.

JS *I think it connects to your work around The Contract, a kind of growing radicalisation – after late 1968 into 1969 – that culminates, in a sense, with The Contract.*

SS It's funny you should say that. This was something that a lot of people were talking about and many of the provisions we made, and the kinds of questions we were addressing in The Contract, were things that everybody in town – any sort of progressive artist or museum person or critic – was thinking about. It was not original in that sense. What is original is that I got the fucking thing done and Bob Projansky, the lawyer, and I put it into the world. I'm told that several years later Bob did a very a compressed version of The Contract, which is a smart idea too.

JS *The shift from certificate to contract, in a sense, wasn't so great, but what interests me about your contract is that it connects with your disaffection with the gallery.*

SS In a way, yes.

JS *Because it comes forward as a proposition for doing without a dealer.*

SS It wasn't so much that. The flack that I got – particularly from Lawrence Weiner, and also other people – was that, in trying to give the artist control over his or her art, I was treating the work of art like a capitalist object. Lawrence was very much against this because he felt that, by trying to protect his work, or give it rights, I had changed it into a piece of merchandise – a capitalist commodity – and that was that. There was a lot of resistance to it. Not organised resistance, but a lot of people didn't like it and they felt, in many ways, it would have been like a renunciation of so-called Conceptual Art because it was applying, or trying to apply, the values of capitalist commodities to the artwork and, of course, this was very much against the spirit of Conceptual Art.

JS *Well, it is problematic if you glue The Contract to the form of documentation for inert gas, like the kind of radically dematerialised work Robert Morris was making at the time – The Contract then turns the documentation into the object.*

SS   But that's a problem that is still there. I have a collection of art and I will be putting it on the block later this year, and the auction people are looking at all these kinds of questions.

These problems have been around a while: who owns the work? Can someone sell it? What are they selling? How do you know he or she did it? Authenticity? I don't think we – 'we', 'me', our generation – ever resolved the question of ownership of work. Of course, that was one of the issues that we were questioning in order to circumvent the capitalist system with dematerialised or non-material work. But we still have to come back to certain forms of property rights – that's the world we're living in.

Lawrence has toyed with this through public freehold, which no one can own but anyone can use. There is a whole group of works that pops up at various moments of his life which he has signed the public freehold for, so he can use it for 20 years or something and then it's no longer his to use.

JS *But the works can also be purchased as private freehold?*

SS   No. I don't think there is such a thing as 'private freehold'. I mean, there are works which are labelled 'public freehold' which – if I understand it correctly – anybody has the right to make, and which they can attach Lawrence's name to, but there are no property rights. You can't sell them because you don't own them.

There are lots of ways to get around this issue, but the problems have not been resolved. In the case of a second party – particularly someone buying at auction or through a dealer – the line connecting the artist to the original owner of the work has been cut. Part of what we were trying to do with The Contract was to create that link. We were trying to set up something like a common law, and we were trying to do it privately. In other words, we were trying to establish the same protection of the creator's rights in art that exist in music and the theatre. The question is, is it possible to make a private contract just between you and me – you the artist and me the art collector – that then obliges people to maintain a relationship to you forever?

JS *But the continuing relationship is to the artwork.*

SS   Yes – but the artist's rights are the artwork and, after his or her death, their estate's (for 30 years or whatever the law is in each country) and that, if it is possible, is a very revolutionary step. But that was not the original intention. We were just concerned about how to keep the artist in touch with his work if, and when, it passes hands. We also asked for a share in the profits, which was one of the most visible and most contested parts of The Contract. But we thought of it primarily as a means of keeping track of the work.

JS *Yes, but it seems to me that, in the context of 1970 and 1971, galleries didn't necessarily have inventories and numbers and consignment forms.*

SS   I don't think the management of galleries (or at least the galleries that come to my mind) were that lax. Most of the artists' works were given an inventory number. But still you're just talking about only one step – the relationship between the artist and the gallery. But after the gallery sells it, what happens then? The gallery may want to guard the privacy of the client, or the client may want to remain unknown.

JS *But that could have been a real issue in the reception of The Contract.*

SS   Oh yes. That was why I tried to conceive of it as an entirely private thing. In other words, in exchange for the artist acknowledging the authenticity of the work – and having some rights over it – the value of the work would be greater because you know it was his or hers. So we tried to play off one against the other. I was very much aware that a lot of black money goes into the art world; people did not necessarily want to leave traces. That was the problem.

JS *The market remains highly unregulated to this day.*

SS   Right, it is one of the few big industries that is, and it won't last forever, that's for sure. All the countries are going to get wise to this. I wouldn't call it a racket, but it is definitely an exceptional case that art is just totally unregulated, unlike film or books.

Although I was very careful to try and fit into the existing modes of business in the art world, it didn't take. Bob and I tried to make it into some kind of standard for the industry, an industry which does not recognise itself as an industry even today. But I'd say that this is going to happen soon. I don't know whether it will be tomorrow afternoon or five years from now, but eventually they're going to realise that there are no guarantees.

JS *Do the works in your collection that you are putting up for auction carry The Contract with them?*

SS   No. That was the artists' decision. If they didn't want to use it, I wasn't going to insist. Although, in fact, most of them were acquired before The Contract was drawn up. But that's maybe a cop-out. I could have done it retroactively, as a friend, but none of them had any great interest in it.

The only person who even had a vague interest in using it was Carl Andre, and he did use it – not for pieces that I own which date from 1965-67 – but for a certain period afterwards. He had the idea that the price of a work could be proportional, based on, say, 5% of the buyer's income. If they earned $50,000, they should pay him $2,500. If they earned $10,000, they should pay him $500. Carl was very astute politically, and also socially and economically, particularly about the relationship between his work and a collector or owner. But these kinds of problems of ownership rights, which are related to receipts, documentation and authenticity, are still around. It's not a problem for me, because I'm the first owner. Well, I don't know yet. It may be a problem. But all the works came from artists that I know and worked with. That can't be contested, but the next guy?

I'm still thinking on this, but I certainly have to give them a bill of sale in the way that when you go to a shoe store you ask for your receipt. I am sure there will have to be a receipt. That's a way to avoid the artist having to do it.

JS *So the certificate will come from you?*

SS   It wouldn't be a certificate. It will be a bill of sale. I would state that I owned it, and it was sold to John Doe. But that's capitalism, too. I have no problem doing that. I deal in rare books. I send receipts off. Someone wants to buy a book – I send the book with a receipt and an invoice stating what it is, and my reputation rests on the fact that the book is authentic, as described in the catalogue. I deal in books on Islamic art, particularly Islamic textile art. I am sort of an expert on the subject, so I put my seal on it. It definitely has a value. But even if it didn't have any value, at least it has an economic value in that they own it – they have a piece of paper saying that they are the owners.

If there was a defect in the book that I hadn't mentioned, they could come back to me and try to get their money back.

Lawrence has had a lawyer, Jerold Ordover – you would call him a notary or something – who registers the ownership and comings and goings of the artworks. Carl has a website on which you have to register work or he won't acknowledge it as his. Whether he can do that at all is very questionable, whether the right of ownership in his work is dependent on you registering on his website is a legal question. I can understand why Carl wants to guard the authenticity of his work. I mean, it is very easy to produce illegal copies of his work.

But to return to the problem of documentation – what happens if there is a fire and everything burns down? You're just piss out of luck.

JS *In that case, had The Contract been embraced it would have clarified a number of these issues.*

SS Exactly. And they are coming round to it now. One argument at the time was that the very artists who needed it least would make the most from having a contract. But that's the kind of thing you say about the Beatles too, about them getting 3% or something when they don't need it.

I think because our generation of artists are now heading into their late middle ages (they are in their 60s and 70s) – some of whom have had the good fortune to be relatively successful and have been put on the block several times to establish a market, or speculative market value for their work – we're going to be seeing more and more of these problems. If this auction business comes off, it will perhaps revive some of these legal or even administrative issues – but that's down the line. The situation is ripe for someone to think about some kind of administrative mechanism for dealing with this, something with a semi-official status.

JS *But that will come part and parcel with the regulation of the market and the industry.*

SS As for the regulation of the art industry, I don't think we're there. There are too many people who have too much interest in this. I'm sure it will happen – not in our lifetimes – but at some point down the line. The art industry is an incredible industry now, it is said to touch trillions of dollars a year. It is like a free-for-all.

Issue 327, 228, June and July–August 2009

Omer Fast

interviewed by Marcus Verhagen

Pleasure and Pain

MARCUS VERHAGEN *You regularly use the format of the interview in your work, for instance in pieces like* The Casting, *2007, and* Spielberg's List, *2003. Can you say a bit about how it works for you?*

OMER FAST I don't always start a work with interviews but the interview is one possibility. When I sit at home and have ideas, very often they're contingent on some encounter and on seeing how an idea is activated by people who can start a dialogue with me about it. I've never been happy just making work at home or in the studio – that always feels to me like a navel-gazing pursuit – so there is a collaborative aspect to what I do, and that aspect doesn't necessarily stop with the interview.

MV *That collaborative dimension is something that your work has in common with other forms of production, like film and TV, and you occasionally refer to reality TV in your use of the confession, for instance, as well as to the news media and, of course, to fictional productions. Can you talk about how you position yourself in relation to those forms?*

OF Compared to reality, television is very attractive to me. I'm not at all put off by the reference to the talk show or the reality show, they're obviously very popular forms. But in terms of venue and format what I do is different. When you show work in a space you can play with the installation and the spatial co-ordinates. The other difference is that reality TV tends to develop and ossify into particular formats that are televisual and fairly generic. What I try to do is to articulate the confession on two levels. We take this encounter with a person, we call this person the real person – just like the TV shows do. They bring their guests in front of the camera and I do the same thing. But then the work also begins to narrate itself and to create its own confession, articulating for the viewer something about how it is constructed, the motivations and anxieties that underlie it. I present a kind of counter-figure to the confessing guest in the form of the confessing host or confessing actor-creator-artist-interviewer, who is sometimes me and sometimes an actor playing me. It doesn't even have to be as theatrical as that. The work can also just turn on itself and create inside it a dynamic where the narrative of its own structure is part of the story that it tells.

MV *So you make the confession confess.*

OF In a way it is like articulating the dynamics of the confession. We're bracketing the confession, we're saying yes, there is this content that the work is trying to articulate and you can trace that content to events in the world. But things happen to narratives as they take shape, and those things are explicitly shown in the work to give people an understanding of what may happen to a narrative or a memory or an experience as it is adapted in a short film, say, or in the media.

MV *You are constantly inviting the viewer to consider your technical manipulations, your sources, your groundwork and so on. Is that right?*

OF This notion of manipulation is one that I don't care for. It implies a sinister operation and a cynical understanding of the media and I don't really have that because I accept that the media presents narratives – that is what it does – and in order to present a narrative you have to form it. Of course there are political dimensions and commercial interests that shape narratives but I want to set the notion of manipulation aside. In *The Casting*, when you see the edits in the screens on the back, you become aware that the flawless, fluid narrative that you hear in the space or see in the front is made up of these different bits and bobs that have been stitched together. It is not about removing a veil from people's eyes and suggesting that what they see in the media is constructed. I think people know that, so for me the notion of manipulation is not very interesting, manipulation is part of what you do even when you talk, when you tell a story. When you're editing, you're manipulating footage even when you're trying to make it as linear and honest as possible.

MV *I meant manipulation in a dispassionate sense.*

OF Sure. It is just something I wanted to flag up because it is important to me. I keep getting asked, is this work media critique?

As if that would help in any way: 'Oh yes, it's media critique, let's all breathe a deep sigh of relief.' But that is not what it is. Of course these critical analyses have been important in fashioning our understanding of the media, but I think all that talk tends to obscure something which is extremely important in the media, and that is pleasure. It took me a while to be comfortable with that and to say that I want to make things that are pleasurable, regardless of their relationship to social dynamics and to current events, to history and to the media.

MV *Let's stay with pleasure. In your work you play a variety of different roles. You and your stand-ins figure in* Take a Deep Breath, *2008, and* The Casting, *so you're a participant, but you're also a writer, a director and an editor – and it seems to me that the role of editor is really fundamental and that editing, in your work, is often a means of bringing pleasure.*

OF I think editing is a beautiful way to approach a narrative and I do think of editing as writing, so all the writing I do before a piece is shot and made is a prelude to editing. Editing allows you to deal with words and images and sounds but also to give a temporality to the work – and being able to step out of the conventions of linear time or the time of the body is for me a very pleasurable experience. It is similar to the way people talk about drugs; I mean they talk about being able to step outside of their bodies, being able to travel in time, being able to see themselves from another angle and so on. You have to reach a point where you communicate the high that you have in jumping around in time, in teleporting your way around the narratives you hear or the bits of reality that you record. Obviously the kind of editing that I do is manipulative, yes, but it doesn't try to conceal the fact that the work is edited, so there is a contract, there is an open gesture that is made through the editing. It is like saying, OK, you and I know that these bits have been edited, that they appear contrived, and now that we have got that out of the way, let's see what we can do with it. In order to deal with the pleasure there has to be some understanding of the rules, and for me the rules are acknowledged. They are the rules we use when we consume filmed stories or dramatic narratives or the news. So for each piece I try to look at these rules when I edit and there is a pleasure in breaking them, or at least in articulating them and tweaking them and playing around with them.

MV *What is sometimes overlooked when people talk about your work is the humour. I'm thinking of* CNN Concatenated, *2002, but also of the gallows humour in a piece like* Take a Deep Breath.

OF Very often the black humour you are talking about is the humour of the labourer, the humour of the extremely bored operator of a machine. I certainly don't want to romanticise my job as an artist. *CNN Concatenated* involved recording hundreds and hundreds of hours of television footage and then storing it as single words spoken to the camera by news presenters on the Cable News Network. These are very boring self-assigned tasks, so there is a kind of masochism involved, and the masochist needs to have a sense of humour. The humour is in the desperation, the futility, the ridiculousness of the tasks that are carried out, and these tasks are acknowledged; in viewing a work like *CNN Concatenated* people immediately understand the amount of work that went into it. The work is asking an unanswerable question: why? Why do this? Why would you watch so much TV? Why would you give yourself over to these tasks when you could turn the thing off and take a walk outside and meet people and have beautiful relationships? So I think the humour offsets the more serious desire to reach out to the world beyond the computer screen or the studio. It offsets the desire for reality to come crashing into a process that is obsessive-compulsive, very personal and often very tedious.

MV *Talking about that sense of the real in your work, I want to ask you about the body. Many of the issues you look at – around violence, memory, intimacy, social stratification – get played out on the body. So why, in work that so clearly concerns itself with mediation, with degrees of distance and removal, does the body keep asserting itself in all its materiality?*

OF That is the elephant in the room. As an artist I'm not making autobiographical work in the simplest sense. I'm not telling a story about something that happens to me. I always need someone else to feed on, so there is a vicarious pleasure to it that involves this parading of bodies. It is like a reliquary – you may need to present a body in order to articulate a fact or story and there is something very Christian about that. It is there in the story of Doubting Thomas – you need to touch something in order to experience and believe it.

But in talking about materiality, I'm not just thinking about the social aspect of the work, about my reasons for reaching out to people and talking about certain contemporary events through bodies;

I'm also thinking about the loss of materiality that you have when you are working with recorded footage, found footage, film footage. It is not like sculpture, it is not like painting; it is not tactile, you can only refer to tactility. And that is a source of humour, too, because you can make it sexy but it is always going to be a picture of sex. Okay, it is arguable that a sensual sculpture is also a transposition, but there is a direct pleasure in touching the material which is missing in the kind of work that I do, so through the editing, through the compulsive cutting that I do, I want to make something very sculptural out of the recorded footage and bring that to the viewer's attention. And often I'm dealing with people who have experienced things in their bodies and are then forced at some distance in time to recollect those experiences. So the loss of the experience, the wanting to recapture its immediacy, this is articulated in the work, both explicitly and through the editing.

Also, of course, in *The Casting* or *Take a Deep Breath* you have a parade of bodies that demand attention through their scars, but that is part of the phantasmagoria of film, it is the work of the special effects department. In *The Casting* there is a moment when a woman begins to remove her clothes, and you're thinking, oh shit, what's going on? Then you see her scars and very quickly they become tokens, they become marks to meditate on. I think the scar is fascinating; it is a form of writing, a graphic expression of something that has happened. The scar is something that refers to the past, but by looking at the scar, by probing and poking it, you are releasing the memory, the story behind it and potentially the pleasure that is available when an experience – even a traumatic one – is mastered. I'm often working in that gap between the moment of pain, the moment of experience, and the later moment of capturing that experience by looking at the scar and finding the words to describe it.

MV *Yes, the body in your work is a source of both pleasure and horror, but then it is always on the verge of becoming something else, as it does when the scar becomes a form of writing.*

OF There is a frustration, obviously, that is implicit in that. There is a heightened anxiety in the work around the body, around the fact that your body can betray you. *The Casting* is for me the perfect illustration of that anxiety. I had worked in film before but I had never worked with a team of actors, and my way of dealing with the stress of it was to say, well, I'm not going to be a director, I'm not going to tell people to act, I'll tell them to freeze. So all the acting happened before we shot and, as a director, instead of shouting 'Action!' I would say 'Freeze!' Of course there is the drama and the pathos of the experience that the soldier is recalling, and the horror of what he has done and what he has seen, but it is impossible – and this is clear in the work – to create a direct translation of that; it is not possible to represent it, and so the work proposes a game of substitution. The work is saying, instead of substituting the pathos of the soldier's story with the pathos of actors acting, I'm going to give you the pathos of the body under duress. The director commands the body to freeze, but the body is breathing and twitching and making noises and betraying you at the very moment when you want it to be still. It is like riding in an elevator: you don't want to move, you feel claustrophobic, and all of a sudden your stomach starts to growl. That kind of betrayal is what *The Casting* is about. And you can connect that to the soldier and his recollection (of killing an Iraqi civilian), to the idea that the soldier is obeying an order, but you need to find different ways of articulating that situation.

What I don't trust is when you set up a scene by saying let's find someone to play the role of the soldier and a few Iraqi-looking people and let's pretend to shoot them and let's see how realistically they react. For me that would have been an idiot's way of going about it. I wanted to find different ways of subverting that desire for pathos and identification, but the work is also about finding a release, and funnily enough that release is in bondage, in making the body freeze. So what you get is the drama of the actors resisting the director's requests. Once they have internalised the order and they say, OK, this guy is going to ask us to freeze, then all sorts of weird things happen, people have coughing fits, people inexplicably fall over, the body betrays you, which is funny – unless it happens to you. It is a kind of slapstick.

MV *My sense is that you are not so much concerned with the authenticity or inauthenticity of a narrative but with a taste or need for authenticity that exists in us, especially when we are considering a very loaded or painful topic. And then there is the moral authority of the victim; that is something you probe in* Take a Deep Breath, *for instance, when the amputee uses his injury to flirt with the woman.*

OF Sure, and the authority of the victim is very closely connected to a kind of pornography, to the operations of pleasure. There are psychological operations that are extremely suspect and this desire for authenticity is very complicated. It is a fine line. On the one hand, you can be pushed into a postmodern cynicism that really does look at everything as a whirl of signs and then victimisation and the pain of others are just signs, narratives.

On the other hand, bad things happen to people and injustices are a part of our society, and an articulation of that is a moral responsibility for people working in the media. It is not something you have to do every time you make something, but if you are going to look at contemporary issues you should at some point account for that, or try to. But when you do that you often see that the language you have is inauthentic: it is an acquired language. I know this from editing the piece that I'm working on now for the South London Gallery. There is a sequence where a woman is being attacked by dogs and I thought it would be easy to edit it, to come up with a language. But the stunt dogs don't make a lot of noise when they attack – and this just doesn't come across as convincing on film. Lived experience is often extremely disappointing when you film it, so you have to bring in these dramatic crutches in order to make it work, to make it communicate. And in that desire there is a risk, and my work is often an articulation of that contract, that translation and that risk. On the one hand there is the desire to experience, vicariously, someone else's pain and so to master it, but at some point there is also a desire to empathise, and these desires are all brought to bear when we look at horrible pictures. So very often my pictures resist that complex of desires; they say look, the scars are peeling, the scars are falling off, they won't give you the pleasure that you want, and I think that the amputee in *Take a Deep Breath* articulates that ambivalence. It is about loss and pain, but that pain is denied. It is dangling in front of you like bait, and when you want to consume it, it is withdrawn or just falls off. So there is a bit of a tease there. And that is very much a part of the operations of pleasure.

Issue 330, October 2009

John Baldessari

interviewed by Simon Patterson

Seeing the World Askance

SIMON PATTERSON *I'd like to ask you first about the Cremation Project of 1970. Am I right in thinking that it coincided with you moving out of your studio in a vacant movie theatre that your father owned?*

JOHN BALDESSARI Yes. That was when television became really popular and movies not so popular. The theatre became a lost cause and I asked if I could use it as a studio. I guess I painted for maybe 20-23 years, something like that, and artists didn't sell works back then. So here I was in this movie theatre, painting, painting, painting, and I damn near had it filled up. So I had this idea that, number one: if I was going to go on being a painter, I'd be inundated, and two: did I really have to own them? I'd learned a lot with each painting, and I had them in my mind – I even had photographs of them.

Also I had this growing suspicion that I was on the wrong path. So I decided to be reductive and shrink everything in some way, metaphorically. My first idea was that I was going to change the photographs into microdots and put them under stamps and mail them out to my artist friends, sort of like James Bond, but that was kind of labour intensive. But I liked the idea of somehow atomising things. And then I thought, I'll just burn them all.

That idea grew on me because I thought of some sort of eternal return – the pigments come out of the earth and at some point here they become the painting and then they return to the earth. And then I thought I could push it further in a symbolic act and actually go to a crematorium, taking that idea of a 'body of work' seriously. It was a little hard to find one but I found a crematorium in a low-rent district that needed the business. They said that they could do it at night and

I liked that, and the guy who did the actual cremating was really into it because he had gone to art school.

SP *It's the sort of thing I think most artists would like to do when presented with that sort of situation – what do you do with all this stuff that you accumulate? Should you turn it into a work or just throw it out?*

JB I didn't think of it as art and I still don't think of it as art now. It was just something I did, and the ashes were simply the residue from it.

SP *It was a kind of clearing out…*

JB … a storage solution.

SP *These days the art storage company would probably do the burning for you.*

JB Exactly.

SP *Originally you studied art history, is that right?*

JB Well, I got out of art school and the idea of going out and finding a job was kind of dismal. Living in Southern California then – if you told anybody you were an artist, they looked at you like some exotic flower. So I thought I would have to be something dignified and be a college professor. So I went to Berkeley and did graduate work in art history and I thought I might actually want to write about art. I know exactly the moment I stopped – it was three o'clock in the morning and I was memorising Roman coins, and I thought, I don't want to do this.

SP *In a way that takes me to the way you file your photographic source material. It is a form of obsessive indexing. For example, under 'A' you have listed: Attack, Animals, Animal man, Above, Automobiles left, Automobiles right; and 'D': Dwarf, Death, Division, Door etc. I know that talking about this sort of thing is a bit like trying to explain a joke – pointless in a way – but are you typecasting?*

JB Probably. When I'm looking at photographs of people I've never seen before – a photograph of somebody who looks like the criminal type but who's probably a sweetheart – I'm doing something similar to a person casting for a movie, but then I'm working with those stereotypes to try to convince you otherwise.

SP *Some writers have talked about your work in connection with Sergei Eisenstein, in terms of your use of montage.*

JB I think the easiest way to understand my work, or for me to understand myself, is that I've often said that I think of myself as a writer, but instead of using words I'm using images. I'm kind of building in the same way and, if you go on with that analogy, when a writer finds the right word there's a kind of tautness, a correctness to it. If a word is too loose, or too obvious in its association, then it doesn't work. My old student David Salle compares me with Jean-Luc Godard, and I did go back and look at Godard again and I could see what he was getting at – these unexpected collisions – playing with expectations, and playing with your mind in some way.

SP *Looking at your CV, it seems that initially, although you were showing in the US, your career really took off in Europe. It seems, too, that in the US there was some resistance from the East Coast to West Coast artists, at least early on.*

JB Resistance is too polite a word.

SP *Joseph Kosuth said: 'Although the amusing Pop paintings of John Baldessari allude to this sort of work, being conceptual cartoons of actual Conceptual Art, they are not relevant to this discussion.' It seems like you hit a raw nerve there.*

JB Sounds like it.

SP *And 'Pop' was then used as a pejorative term.*

JB It's a tough one, because we are talking about categories, and how you understand a category. Take Claes Oldenburg and Roy Lichtenstein, both very good friends of mine. On different occasions I referred to them as pop artists, and they both looked at me and said 'I'm not a pop artist, I'm an artist'.

SP *Can I ask you a bit about teaching? You taught for a long time.*

JB Yes, I taught from getting out of school – that was 1957 – but I'm going to preface anything you are going to say about me being a teacher by saying that I only did it to make a living. There was nothing noble about it.

SP *You say that in a very self-deprecating way, but you have been incredibly influential as a teacher. To a degree you also turned teaching into a way of making work.*

JB First of all you need a job and I tried various things, but with teaching the time passed the fastest. And teaching art was not so bad; you had the summers when you could work and a salary – you could live. And then, selfishly, I thought that I could get through the day better if I made teaching a kind of creative thing. I figured that if I was having fun, then maybe the students would be having fun also. It was a good equation.

SP *And you had access to equipment to make video pieces, for instance the*

1972 work Baldessari Sings LeWitt.

JB   Yes. I was teaching at University of California San Diego and I left in 1970 when CalArts started up in Valencia near Los Angeles – I was on the original faculty there. That's when the Sony Portapak came out and a lot of artists got interested in using it. At CalArts we had 26 of them and we didn't have one drawing class – we got busted for that by the accreditation committee – but sure, I didn't have any money and CalArts gave me access to the equipment. That's where those pieces came from.

SP   Baldessari Sings LeWitt *seems like a very affectionate piece.*

JB   Sol was a great old friend to the end and a role model for me. I called him up and asked if I could do this and he said 'Sure'. Of course, any artist who is any good is not going to suffer. The work will stand up, believe me.

SP   *One of the works I saw for the first time in 'Reconsidering the Object of Art' in Los Angeles in 1995 was* A Painting That Is Its Own Documentation, *dated 1968 to the present, which is a kind of inventory of its own exhibition history. What amused me particularly was that it was 'full', so you had added a new canvas.*

JB   That is included in the instructions, and I just added another new one. Maybe I should talk about the genesis of that work, which comes out of studying art history and the continual problem of the work of art and its provenance getting lost or separated. I thought it might be interesting to make the provenance the work of art so that they were never apart. The work starts with the actual moment of the day when I had the idea, and then at the first showing and so on. Each time the work is shown it is documented and recorded on canvas, and as long as it is exhibited it will keep on expanding.

SP   *You used signwriters presumably because you wanted to take away your own hand from the process.*

JB   Yes. Maybe it's too reductive – and yet I abide by it – but when you have paint on canvas on stretcher bars you have a painting.

SP   *And using canvas was quite a radical thing to do then, because it wasn't where people were looking with the kind of work you were doing.*

JB   Let me back up a bit here. A common complaint you would hear back then about first and second generation Abstract Expressionism was 'my kid can do that'. It gets so tiring hearing that, so I thought: change the language, speak the language of the realm. People read magazines and newspapers so I thought, OK, I'll just use text and photographs. The reason that I very consciously put it on canvas was because if something is on canvas and has stretcher bars it is immediately 'art' – trust me.

SP *The 'Commissioned Paintings' series, paintings painted for you by amateur painters, took this idea further.*

JB I always had a fondness for that kind of painting and I'd search them out. A lot of times I would really look at those paintings – forget about the subject-matter – look at the way the paint was put down and they were really not so bad. And I thought, what if I could use that as raw material for work? If I could change the subject-matter and get the paintings into a different context then you could really look at the paintings. So I looked up some of these painters and said: 'If I pay you X amount of dollars, will you paint a painting for me?' Then I had a friend of mine walk around and, any time he saw something interesting, he would point to it and I would document it. Then I offered the painters a handful of those slides and said: 'Pick one, copy it and don't try to make art out of it. Just copy it faithfully and your signature painting style will show up.' Then I found a fairly avant-garde gallery in LA and a fairly avant-garde gallery in New York and showed them, and then the project was over.

SP *There are other works that are formally similar to the 'Commissioned Paintings', the 'Scenarios' series of photographs of 1972–73, where you are pointing at text and highlighting, for example, 'the sound of a pen scratching a quick signature'.*

JB I think in this early period, when I was painting in this ghetto area south of National City, San Diego, I was totally shut off from art. I was trying to figure out what art was for me, and I figured out that it has to be essentially about choosing something, choosing this colour over that one, or this subject over that one.

SP *You returned to painting in the 1980s when you started using paint in combination with your photographic work. You said at the time that there was something 'inert' or 'flat' about the surface of photographs.*

JB Well, I think I started painting into the photograph for a variety of reasons, one because the surface of a photograph is uniform, and you could take another jump and say, 'therefore all photographs look alike'. Then I wanted to change the reflectivity of the surface. But also, I hate categories and what's wrong with painting on a photograph? So it's a hybrid, it's neither a painting nor a photograph.

SP *There is some unexpected anger in your work; I'm thinking of*

Inventory *from 1987.*

JB That's not anger, that's just disillusion.

SP *Going back to that Kosuth comment, do you think the fact that your art can be funny was a factor in it not being taken seriously initially?*

JB I think the answer I've always given to that question is that if I was trying to be funny, I'd be doing something entirely different. It's not part of the intent. I think it is seeing the world askance, or trying to make sense of the world.

SP *In 1988 you illustrated Laurence Sterne's* The Life and Opinions of Tristram Shandy. *In some ways you were an obvious choice as, for me, the book is almost a proto-Baldessari work.*

JB I think of Sterne as my doppelganger, or vice versa. It has always been a favourite book of mine. When I read it I thought 'This guy thinks like I do'. And sure, I just jumped at it. One I'll do eventually is my second favourite novel, *Don Quixote*, which I also feel very close to.

SP *There's a piece that I particularly like that I saw in your show at Marian Goodman's gallery in Paris in 2004: a photograph of a high rise that is part of a series of works using a panoramic camera.*

JB I decided to explore the panoramic camera, which is basically used for landscapes, seascapes, whatever, but in my perverse nature, I decided that no, I was not going to use it horizontally but vertically. But then you've got to find subject-matter and I thought, 'palm trees are good', and then I started doing condominium high rises and it worked perfectly.

SP *The sculptural installation,* Beethoven's Trumpet: In One Ear and Out the Same Ear, *relates to the new work you have made for your show at Sprüth Magers in London.*

JB I was asked to do a retrospective show in 2007 in Bonn with all the works I'd done about music. Bonn is the birthplace of Beethoven, and I visited his house and he had a whole cabinet of ear trumpets that he used. I was really fascinated with them as sculptural forms, especially one that he had designed himself that I thought was quite beautiful. And then for maybe four or five years I've been doing these works about body parts and I think it started out with noses and ears, so ears were on my mind. And then probably there was one of those three o'clock in the morning moments when you are awake and all of a sudden I thought, 'wait a minute – ear/ear trumpet'. I think it was my first venture into sculpture, though it was still on the wall so I don't know if that counts, but it was sculptural. I made six of them because one of my favourite Beethoven works is the six last quartets. And it's interactive – you can put your head into a trumpet and say something into the ear, and it'll play back a section of the quartets.

SP *In 2001, you were invited to make a public project for the campus of the University of California, San Diego –* READ/ WRITE/ THINK/ DREAM.

JB They have something called the Stuart Sculpture Collection that funds sculptural projects for the university campus. They have an international jury that selects the artists and they'd been after me for some time to do a project and I kept on saying 'I'm not a sculptor, I don't do scuplture'. But they persisted anyway. So I had this idea that I would do Baptistery doors, like Ghiberti's in Florence, but instead of the bronze panels they would be scenes from movies, and they liked that idea. And then we looked all over the campus and we couldn't find any appropriate doors. So then they showed me the entrance to the main library and the doors were all glass. It was a pretty challenging piece of real estate, but I took on the whole façade and atrium.

Let me say this about public art projects, I've always pretty much – 99% – said 'no', because you have to go through so many committees, so many compromises, so many lawyers, so many architects that it's just not worth the agony. But the people who run this project are with you 100%. And they have some great pieces – the piece that Bruce Nauman showed at the Venice Biennale, *Vices and Virtues*, was first done there.

SP *One of the components of the work was a series of student portraits taken by a graduate student and selected by you, representing different ages, ethnicities and so on that can be periodically updated. And on the left is a whole row of giant pencils and pens and on the right …*

JB … palm trees etched on the glass and then behind the glass you see a La Jolla beach scene of surfers. When I was teaching art there, kids would come and lean their surfboards against the classroom wall and then come into class. It was very much a part of surfing culture.

SP *The effect is not dissimilar to your piece for the former Italian pavilion at the Venice Biennale, which looked like a classical villa in Malibu. Was that part of your intention?*

JB Very much so.

SP *But it was not your first proposal.*

JB The first proposal was not turned down because of the organisers, really. It was because the signage on the pavilion was going to change, and I had based it on the signage. I had proposed bisecting the building and then, on the right side, there would be a panel like a stage set with a replication of the building, but flipped on its side so it would be upside down. And it worked perfectly with the signage, but then the signage was going to change.

SP *Was that when you proposed the sign that said 'No more boring art'?*

JB I guess at that point I was getting mildly irritated. So then I proposed to place a black panel that would say 'No more boring art' on top of the building, running the same length and about the same width as the strip saying 'La Biennale'. I guess maybe they thought that that would be a comment on other artists. So that was axed. So then I came up with this and I thought yeah, I'll make this like a Roman villa in Malibu.

SP *For Berlusconi, and his 'girls'.*

JB Exactly. You can't argue with it; it's so pleasant – it's a photo op.

SP *And you did in fact manage to show the I* Will Not Make Any More Boring Art *piece in Venice after all.*

JB Yes. It was very sweet of them. I guess they felt obliged that they should hang it somewhere. What I particularly liked was that it was hung right across from the François Pinault building on the Punto della Dogana.

SP *I remember bumping into you at the Duchamp exhibition at the Palazzo Grassi during the Venice Biennale in 1993. It was an amazing show and afterwards you commented: 'It was so well curated that you almost thought you understood it.'*

JB Yes – it was too perfect!

This is an edited version of an interview which took place at the Starr Auditorium, Tate Modern on 8 October 2009. Published Issue 331, November 2009.

Harun Farocki

interviewed by Sophia Phoca

Counter Shot

SOPHIA PHOCA *I would like to start off with your work* Immersion *from 2009 and I was hoping that maybe you could introduce it and briefly describe it.*

HARUN FAROCKI I know the word 'immersion' from language courses, when you go to Paris and stay there for two weeks to be 'immersed' in the French situation. There's also something called 'immersion therapy' which means that when you've had a traumatic experience, you try to recreate the same emotions and then try to talk about it, to repeat it, or distantiate from it. The American army – not only the army, but the navy, the air force and also the marines – they have used this immersion therapy for a long time, but now they do it with digital images – with computer animations.

When we read about it, we thought it would be interesting to make a film or perhaps several installations about this paradoxical aspect: first you use animated images from the war theatre in Iraq or Afghanistan to prepare soldiers for the war theatre and later use them to heal the ailments that follow from the war.

The first base we succeeded in getting access to was Fort Lewis in Washington State. Since then we have also filmed other stuff from the US and there will be two or three little installations which will cover what I'm talking about.

In this installation, or double screening, called *Immersion*, which is some 20 minutes long, we filmed a workshop by therapists working out of different institutions using a method they wanted to sell to the army. It had already been sold, but it had to be demonstrated, so they set up a workshop and a lot of the army therapists in camouflage did this role-playing. The patient always has a headset with digital images like glasses before his or her eyes and you can see this very image on the second screen. It's weird because you really seem to look into the head of the person. It is also interesting that the person who is in this therapeutic process wears something like a mask so that the face is not really visible.

So it is more or less an introduction to the method and we then show how it works. That has, for me, a long tradition because I've always loved to film role-playing games because they've already shaped the structure of your films. If you make a documentary about a person, you ask yourself, 'Should I show him sleeping, eating, talking or whatever?' – and there are no rules. But if you have these prefabricated settings of a game, the structure is already there, and you have an established coding. You don't just see people – you see people playing somebody. It is a bit like in feature films where actors always want to play gangsters and prostitutes because they already have this coded behaviour.

SP *I have actually seen* Immersion *as a single-screen piece and I wanted to ask you about the relationship between the two versions.*

HF I also produce so-called single-channel versions for preview because you can't ask people to watch two images which are in sync. In some cases they also make their way to cinemas and are screened there. In some cases they work quite well, in others it's a bit ridiculous but they still work. We are increasingly accustomed to watching films at YouTube sizes – so there are many approaches at the moment.

In the case of *Immersion*, although the function is really strong – why two screens? – it has nothing to do with a huge associative approach, a different kind of editing. It is mainly that you see what a person sees which you couldn't otherwise see. It's like a specialised counter-shot of the person and, in this case, those works can be shown like a short film and can be shown in the gallery. It doesn't make such a huge difference. Then, of course, all the differences between the cinema and the gallery appear.

SP *I was thinking about the ending – particularly – because the film starts off with the single-screen version that I've seen. It starts off with two screens that are configured with two computer-generated images. And then they move into a reflexive moment where the person who's making up those images is talking about how he's making them, and then we move into the therapeutic context – but we don't know it is a re-enacted therapeutic context – and, finally, there's this reveal at the end where we realise that it's a re-enactment. I find that really effective, seeing it in that linear context, but I was thinking, in the gallery, I might walk in at any time and see it differently, so I wondered how that would work.*

HF Yes, I think that's the case with nearly everything I have done, with few exceptions the films have to be watched from the beginning to the end. In a gallery I have to assume that people watch them in their entirety – but that doesn't happen. Perhaps one could introduce something where, if you come into a space in a gallery, there's a button and then you can restart it if you are the only spectator – but it probably wouldn't work. You can't negotiate all of that, so it is a disadvantage. Often people don't know how long the work is: am I at the end or the beginning; should I come back later – and all those difficult things. Of course, you are totally right – that causes a problem.

Cinemas also started that way. People came in and out and they never knew what they would see – they probably didn't even know what was showing – and the film was shown only once. Then it became standardised, and now we are in a phase where all these standards are vanishing and I'm sure that soon cinemas will have digital devices to show five images in sync. That's not such a technical problem – not such a big deal. At the moment it is still complicated but only because it is not a mass product yet.

SP *You talked about this idea of the counter-shot which is extremely effective. Montage is important, obviously, in your work and in an interview with Kaja Silverman you talked about Soviet montage being ideologically driven while Hollywood cinema is narrative driven. It seems to me that you are using the former to critique the latter in this work, because the narrative falls out of sync. I also wondered whether you were making a comment not only on narrative, but also on the ineffectiveness of CGI representations – that they simulate reality, but they can't actually get to the real. Is that something that you were interested in?*

HF I find it interesting that there is always this resistance to these tools. Now I've learned that CGI is an abstraction, but when I first saw it computer animated imagery was the state of the art. You can represent the war in Afghanistan or in Iraq better with computer animated images than with photographic images or oil on canvas. The British army uses official painters because this monopoly of knowledge is incorporated – it shows that they are technically superior. On the other hand, when you talk to computer people, they always have this idea that the computer animated image should be like a photographic rendition. They are still discontented that they can't produce enough effects of light and shade, all the effects that you have in photographs. Perhaps I'm wrong and perhaps the photographic image is still the ideal, but it should also look a little bit digital – or be digital – and should be artificial because that means, of course, that you have mastered it and you have not just depicted it. You have understood the principle. You can recreate the world that you're talking about. It is not just copying – it is a bit more.

In answer to your question, I don't know what I said during that interview, but I think that American montage, to put it simply, has elaborated a lot of subtleties like the question of silent film versus film with sound. I don't believe that films without sound are smarter because you have to do everything with images because, of course, the opposite is also true. If you just say it in words, you don't have to deal endlessly with the mechanics of narration and establishing a location and a train of thought or whatever.

SP *This leads me on to think about something I've been wondering about your work. You seem critical of 20th-century utopian ideas of progress with regard to science and technology. There seems to be an inherent critique of this idea of progress linked to power, industrialisation, consumer culture – but, at the same time, you use the same technologies, and you're very aware of it, and you reference it quite reflexively in your work. How do you deal with that paradox?*

HF I have quite a minimalistic approach, stylistically, to everything – so I only use a low percentage of the repertory of cinematographic narration, and I try to use it slowly and not overwhelmingly. Also, when using or quoting these kinds of images – let's say technical images from surveillance images, warfare images – I don't use them to show how well they work or what a wonderful emotional impact they have. I try to criticise them, to leave space for critique. I think that's just a different way of exposing them. Perhaps there is some coherence between how I make use of images – normal cinematographic images or photographic images – and how I talk about these advanced technologies.

SP *I was also – in that context – thinking about what could be referred to as the use of human scale in your work. On the one hand you have these macro concerns – political concerns – and, on the other, it seems to me*

293

that you are anxious about how you introduce individual concerns. In
Immersion *that comes out in the human suffering which is re-enacted,*
but at the same time it is as if you can't get to the truth of that moment.

If we go back to one of your first pieces, Inextinguishable Fire,
from 1968, it seems to me that this is a concern that has been running
throughout your work – how to represent things on a human scale. Maybe
you could talk a bit about what led to that film.

HF 'Human scale' is the right phrase for it. In those days we were at
the height of the anti-Vietnam War movement. We talked about it at
the film academy – that there's something self-righteous about taking
a poster with a burnt body and saying, 'Look! I'm on the good side
and you are one of the bad people who are somehow complicit with
these effects as well', and therefore I said that, if you want to show
the effects of napalm to others, then you must also take a risk. In this
case I said a napalm burn was, I think, 3,000 degrees and a cigarette
was about 1,000 degrees, and lying on the table was a cigarette which
I extinguished on my arm in order to show that symbolically, at least,
I must sacrifice something before I can talk about it. On the other
hand, this film is not classically humanistic. It is not talking about
individuals. It tries to have this Brechtian generalisation and to show
structures and not individual emotions. So, it was quite controversial
and I think these two oppositions are strongly at work.

I am also interested in abstraction. About ten years ago I wanted
to make a film about the shopping industry. I had read wonderful
books about unbelievable tests where you had labs in which you had
different carpets to find out which ones made people stop or speed
up. I thought it would be wonderful to make a film about all these
labs, about how people are trying to find out where people are looking
and what they see and how to redesign supermarket aisles. Unluckily
it was not so easy. My hope was to show the phenomenon of shopping
craziness but without humans – of course not *without* humans, but
without the real thing. On this level, abstraction is still a strong
impulse. It is also a very simple reason – if you film a mall it's like
working in a cheap advertising company producing images for junk
mail or whatever. It is difficult to depict them in an interesting way,
therefore it is better to keep some distance.

SP *The human element is also there in how you approach your viewer. You*
seem very generous to your viewer. There's nothing didactic about your
work and I was thinking about the ending of Inextinguishable Fire, *where*

you say that machine guns are interchangeable with vacuum cleaners. You are obviously making certain connections for the consumer – for the viewer – to think about. Do you think about your audience?

HF   I don't think about my audience. I think about the film and I think, 'Is it understandable?' It should be understandable to everybody – even when it's difficult. You don't have to have a degree to see it. I know that there are some strange sociological reasons why some people don't go to the cinema. I can't be blamed for that but if, by mistake, somebody comes into one of my films, it must be possible for them to see and understand it. Yes, it should be possible. Many writers use the same principle rule. Thomas Mann says a book must be accessible to anybody who reads books.

SP   *You have produced over a hundred films, and at the same time you lecture, you write, you are an editor, you were a film critic for ten years between 1974 and 1984 – so there is an enormous amount of work to cover. But I would just like to go back a bit to 1966. You're young and in Berlin. There's a hell of a lot of political activity going on there. The Red Army Faction is very active. What made you think, 'I want to be a filmmaker', rather than going into direct action?*

HF   In 1966 when I went to the Film Academy there were the first critical articles about the Vietnam War. It had not yet become a move-ment. I was, incidentally, with some friends and we knew of the Students for a Democratic Society (SDS) which was the main organ-isation that led to the movement of 1968. It was just a tiny minority. It was really an elitist circle, but within the next two years it changed dramatically and became a huge movement in Europe, and also in Germany – but I think in France it was strongest. Even workers participated and that never really happened in Germany.

So, by 1966 things had happened through the Nouvelle Vague and also through Pier Paolo Pasolini or, in Germany, Alexander Kluge – people who earlier would have worked for the theatre or perhaps written books but could now make films. That was totally new. In those days people made two or three films every year. You can't call them feature films – they were totally new categories of film. They were distributed in perhaps 10, 12 or 20 countries – worldwide – and debated as one once had debated new works by Henrik Ibsen or August Strindberg. So there was a really strong culture in those days. Then a bit later with pop music as well – totally new things became possible. Paul Schrader says the feedback period for film is shorter, that if you write a novel it takes you seven years to get feedback, but if you make a film it can be just next year when you hear terrible things about what you have done.

Then the question came up, often posed in a moralistic way: 'Are you part of the problem or of the solution?' There was no in-between. Some people thought, 'You must really risk something. Only if you *start* something, only then you can have an effect', and that led more or less to the Red Army Faction. Then some of the members totally changed within months, like Ulrike Meinhof, who was a highly recognised writer and had made television films. She had twins she was raising and in interviews she said that it is a very hard thing to be political and to take care of the kids because you can't convey what the politics mean to your kids. That was quite smart, and two months later she liberated Baader and went on to lead a totally different life. Holger Meins, who was one of my co-students and did some camera work in one of my first films, was totally friendly and also very social. He didn't behave this way and somehow he was interested in cinematographic aspects of film, but he also liked formalistic films and the work of Michael Snow. His work had nothing to do with the issues we were talking about, but we admired it. Then within a month or so, I suddenly read in a newspaper that he had gone underground.

In retrospect, I must say that I was never in danger of joining the Red Army Faction because my aspiration to be an artist or to produce films was so strong that, at times, I had to hide it. It was not a good time to talk about it or to have aspirations in those days. Sometimes I hid it so well that I was believed to be interested in building up a collective structure of counter-communication or whatever – which also should include me, of course.

SP *I also read that, paradoxically, you were expelled from film school two years later for political activity.*

HF I was in the bad position where I was expelled twice. After a year five of us were expelled for making bad films or not having enough talent! And then, of course, there was a wave of protest – other students said it was unfair, terrible – and then there was so much protest in Berlin that after some months they changed the rules and we were readmitted for a year on probation. Then, after I had been readmitted (there were totally different teachers so there was no question that they would take me back), we were all collectively thrown out – but at least that was political, which was, of course, better. For ten minutes we were famous so immediately I got a teaching position. Of course, I had hardly learnt anything. It took me the next ten years to learn the most technical things. Everything was reversed in my case.

So, after having made films already and then, at the age of 30 or whatever, joining Film Critique and starting to write and to analyse films – we went back to school in a sense. I even went to courses at the university for the first time – so it was a strange curriculum.

SP *You mentioned Michael Snow. As you probably know, in the UK experimental film and video have been understood (mostly) in terms of the formalist concerns of the structuralist materialists – and that's been a dominant mode in the UK and, unfortunately, essayist film has been quite marginalised. John Akomfrah's* Handsworth Songs *re-engaged with that kind of work in the 1980s as, more recently, has The Otolith Group. This has coincided with a reinvigorated interest in political concerns, which has also coincided with the exhibition of your work in the UK.*

Are you aware of this distinction between representational forms and more formalist/materialist concerns? I find your work extremely formal and rigorous in terms of how you use film – its reflexivity foregrounds these concerns – but it is, obviously, very different work. Formalist/ materialist work resists representational forms.

HF Do these guys still exist – people against representation?

SP *Very much so.*

HF James Benning also once said, 'I'm a structuralist; I'm not a documentary filmmaker'; it's only arbitrary, but he has now changed and admits that his films are also political, that they show how the earth is used by man, not only how the land looks, but also how the land looks because we look at it.

So, for me, that is a more interesting structural approach. I can't talk about it so much because, in Germany, underground film was so unbelievably marginal, with the exception of perhaps two or three cinematheques in some cities. There wasn't much debate about it and, I also think, Michael Snow went into this art circle early on, but it was easier in Canada than in America because then he had some support and could continue producing which you could not do by sending copies around to underground cinemas.

SP *Maybe we could move on to a later piece that was made in 1992,* Videograms of a Revolution. *Talking about formal concerns, this is a much more essayistic film, in a sense, and the female voice-over addresses the camera as if the camera is a protagonist. I found that film extremely powerful for two reasons: firstly those formal concerns I was talking about, but secondly, when I first saw the Romanian revolution of 1998 on television, what I found quite alarming about it wasn't so much the footage, but the way the footage was filmed, by the way the hand-held footage was reconfiguring the world. It seems to me that you picked up on that. Your whole film is set up in that way. Were you trying to talk about the destabilising of Europe in that context through formal concerns?*

HF   I'm astonished that you talk about hand-held cameras. I remember these wonderful bright and sunny days before Christmas. Things probably wouldn't have happened so fast if the weather hadn't been so unbelievable. All these demonstrations were possible until five in the morning because every day was sunny and warm – even in Romania where it is mostly bitter cold around Christmas.

I don't remember hand-held cameras on television. I remember the television crews weren't well equipped. In retrospect, one could say that Romania acted it out for all the other countries. The starting point for me had been that I was so shocked and traumatised by these events around Christmas, and then I read a book by Andrei Ujică, who later became my collaborator on this film. Ujică had talked to the few intellectuals who still existed in Romania about these crucial events like when Nicolae Ceausescu delivered what would be his final speech. Ceausescu had stopped talking, there has been a disturbance – nobody really knows what is happening – but the television continued as if nothing has happened.

I had the idea that one should go to Romania and make a film like a seminar in which smart people debate this footage as you would do in a film school with an interesting Hitchcock sequence or so. We went to Romania and found that this idea of a 'television revolution', which was the slogan of the day, was not true because by definition, a revolution occurs when the people know what has to be done and when.

Then we made something quite simple. We tried to cover the five days of the revolution, which followed in a strange way the cultural model of the French Revolution – only much faster. So, the king was already dead by the fifth day. It follows it quite strictly although the content is different because the people didn't demonstrate for high ideals like 'liberty' or 'equality'. Rather, they were demonstrating for the end of politics. It was perhaps comparable to all those people who had left Europe to go to America just because they didn't want to have any superiors any more. They escaped guilds, governments and kings. This was a strange contradiction. The form was so traditional and the content was so different.

SP *There's a particular scene which captures what you're saying. It's in a car. It is home footage in a car and a woman is talking to a man and at a certain point when she's laughing she covers her mouth, and the man responds, 'Now that we've had a revolution, you can buy false teeth'. I found that so moving because it was the micro narrative. But, again, as you say, they are moving into a different world – into that consumer world where you can buy teeth.*

HF Yes, it's a wonderful scene. We don't know who filmed it. You only see it from the interior of a car which is driving towards the centre of the city where the big demonstration is on the 22nd. Television has not yet arrived in front of the Central Committee. You see all these prefabricated concrete buildings and then you hear the dialogue and they say, 'I really feel an idiot. People had to die to liberate us. That is astonishing.' Then they say to the old woman, 'Oh, you can be happy now. You can even buy new teeth.' That was also a detail. We don't know how it ends. We just found this piece of footage.

That was always a problem. Dating an image, I suppose, is important if you really want to recreate the real order of things.

SP *Your work is highly concerned with the ethics of the image and you often investigate an image over and over again, like a forensic scientist – but it seems that you actually do want to find the ontological truth in the image. You do believe there is a truth in the image if you investigate it enough.*

HF Yes – perhaps it is not very modern, but I obviously do believe that. The image is a reference even if it is not technically a reference – if it is CGI – though that's also a reference even if not a direct technical reference. So, therefore, I always found it a bit strange when, in the early days of Postmodernism, people said the image has no claim to the truth. It was a bit like the structuralist artists who said, 'No representation, it is just an image.' Just an image is true, but in this sense, I believe in it.

This is an edited version of an interview which took place at the Starr Auditorium, Tate Modern on 14 November 2010. Previously unpublished.

Vito Acconci

interviewed by Freee

Changing Spaces

FREEE *Our questions are about how we engage with your work. So if you thought there was an agenda here, there is.*

VITO ACCONCI There should be.

FR *In the early days of your performances you often addressed the public in terms of individuals – following a single person, for instance, in* Following Piece, *1969 – at the borderline between public and private spaces.*

VA That person became abstract. I didn't know this person.

FR *But if your art fantasised about individuals, this is not true in your architectural practice. Hasn't the development of your architectural practice at Acconci Studio changed your conception of the public, perhaps making it more plural? Are there groups involved now in a way that there weren't before?*

VA Those groups are a problem for me, because those groups become representative of something – a kind of abstraction. We try in our projects to do something else. I don't know how you can have intimate spaces in a public project. An intimate space is usually a space where everyone thinks crime is going to happen. You can't really have closed-off spaces but we try to do it.

One of the things I want to talk about is the project for the new Concert Hall in Stavanger in Norway. The concert hall is going to be built and there's going to be an amphitheatre outside. There was a competition and we were asked to do something for the project. What we tried to ask with the project was: could we run something through the amphitheatre? Everyone is sitting in the amphitheatre with a single purpose, all facing the stage. And yet the amphitheatre isn't always going to be used for a theatre event. So we thought, could there be some kind of connection – person-to-person? We took our model from rivers and rivulets and ran these river paths down the bleachers, the grandstand seating. And in the act of running down the banked bleachers they cut through the seating. So, for example, you and I are sitting facing the stage, but the regimented seating is cut so now we can turn to face each other.

I don't know whether that means we are doing things with groups of people but I don't think I understand people enough unless they're individuals. That's why I hate words like 'public', which gives the impression that there is one single body with a single purpose and a single motive. The word 'multitudes' might be better, it gives the idea that there is a swarm of people that, if left on their own, would be fucking each other or killing each other. But somehow they don't. Somehow there's this rule of civilisation.

FR *If we connect what you say about the bleachers with historical designs for theatre architecture, and in particular the relationship between the mass of seats on the ground floor containing the multitudes, and, above them, the boxes which allow for the possibility of someone to turn and speak to somebody else, it is as if what you have done is taken that logic and spilled it out over the bleachers. Now the multitudes get a chance to turn around.*

VA Sure. When I was a child I went to the opera a lot with my father and I always wondered: 'Who are those people, those families separated from the others?' I didn't quite understand.

FR *In your architectural practice, you said at the beginning that you were interested in 'working in the cracks' which, we assume, is at least partly because you had no architectural career and were offered 1% for art projects rather than the whole building.*

VA But strangely it still is. It hasn't changed very much. It's changed a little, but not much.

FR *We wondered whether you now had to find the cracks within bigger projects.*

VA Well, for example, that amphitheatre project is a public art project. We weren't asked to design the concert hall, nor were we asked to design the amphitheatre.

FR *So do you still work on public art projects?*

VA For a while we were trying to say no to them, but we don't get enough real architecture projects. I think people still don't consider us architects. I find that a big failing. Part of the problem might be that – and I don't know how many people know this – we don't have a registered architect in the studio, so it's difficult for us to apply for a competition. We have to make some connection with another architect who would then be the head architect. It's disturbing for us that the public art aspect is always an extra element. There is a certain amount of money for the architecture but only a tiny fraction of that for public art.

FR *And the architect gets in earlier.*

VA Totally. In this case, with the amphitheatre project, it is interesting – not that we had this in mind, what we had in mind was how could we use this public space and make some kind of insertion of the possibility of more private relations – because we are really not adding much, we're mostly just removing. But it costs money to take away too.

FR *You have moved from poetry that addresses the page to performance that addresses space to architecture addressed in terms of squeezing, stretching, folding, twisting – all things you can do to a page, and most of which you have done to your own body in your performances. Do you think there has always been an emphasis on the physical as a driving force behind your critical position?*

VA Yes. I was very struck a long time ago when I thought of myself as a writer. A very important poet for me was the American poet William Carlos Williams and his statement about 'no idea but in things'. It's not that I'm against abstractions; I'm against abstractions that begin as abstractions. If you use words like 'belief', 'faith', 'trust', 'honour', it's all preacher's language, politician's language. Whereas if you start with 'no idea but in things', you start with something that you might think of as an example of something but then other people might think of it as an example of something else. And the great thing about that is that people have a chance to think for themselves. I went to Catholic school for too long – I shudder at abstractions, start to go into a wooze. It's like when you read a contract for a project and you realise this is lawyer's language.

I still want to believe that if people are given a chance to think for themselves and they are given these physical spaces then maybe they can do something unexpected. In some ways they always do something unexpected. The great thing about architecture is that you're kind of always wrong. First of all, it takes so long to do it. You make a conjecture about what might be appropriate for this place at this time but then it might take you seven years before the thing is built so it's already too late. But even when it's not too late – and of course you try to anticipate, you know, we try to imagine what can people possibly do here that they couldn't do anywhere else – ideally we'd like to give people a chance to change the space. What I hate about architecture is that when you design a space you are designing people's behaviour. Architecture is inherently a totalitarian activity. Obviously we try – like a lot of mostly younger architects, not the most established architects – to find something abhorrent in that.

FR *Do you think there is a relationship between your architecture and practices of dissent and critique?*

VA I don't know how obvious this is and maybe it's not obvious enough, but when we do public art projects rather than architecture projects, I always used to make the assumption that if a project gets built it is because the institution has allowed it to be built, whereas when the public art project comes in maybe not as much attention is paid to that as to the official architect. So maybe you can sneak something in. You can sneak something in that maybe gives people a chance to think: 'Here's the space that's kind of turned upside down. If this space is turned upside down, maybe I don't have to believe that space is as implacable as I thought? Maybe I can turn some other space upside down?' And turning space upside down, it seems to me, is the beginning of dissent.

FR *In a previous interview, you said that you prefer to be in the corridor rather than the main space. Is the corridor a space that is less monitored?*

VA It's less monitored but also a corridor is a circulation space, whereas a room is like an end. You went through the corridor in order to get to this room – it's like a node, it's a rest. We're more interested in the unrestful places, the spaces between things, the spaces on the way to other things. We'd love to give people a chance to make their own space, sure, but for the time being what we'd love to do is give people as many choices as we can. Not one way from here to there. They might get a little lost but that's OK. They can find their way around, make their way through space.

FR *There's an element of trust in that, just as when you said once that, if people want to sit down, they'll sit down on a step, so you don't have to design seating for them that tells them where to sit.*

VA I don't know. Sometimes I think that that trust is misplaced.

When I think of the US – and I don't think of New York, Los Angeles and Chicago – all these other people, can they really do this? I don't know. They seem very, very happy to have it all done for them. Why do they want it done for them? I hope it's because they haven't had a chance to think for themselves but I don't know if I can say that. I would love to believe, in spite of the fact that I've seen so much of the opposite of this, that if people have choices they at least have the chance to make a choice that's not the usual choice.

In the US, in the late 1960s, we used to think nothing could be as bad as Richard Nixon. We were wrong. And we're probably wrong about George W Bush.

FR *In resisting the technocratic ideal of the architect as an expert on the built environment and by opening up space for people to do things for themselves you have, in fact, left yourself without an architectural career because what commissioners and funders want from the architect is technocratic expertise.*

VA As you know, I might not be that much of an expert at all on the built environment, but what I like about working with a group of people – I admit it's a small group – is that each one of us knows something that the others don't. This might be a deterrent to somebody asking us to do a project, but I believe that four or five people might not think better than one but they certainly think more than one. And the great thing about the way a group of people work is that there is always a second part. Just as you are about to finish a project, one of you says: 'Isn't there another way this could go?' In some ways we could probably go on doing the same work for a long time because there is always another way to look at it. We'd love to give those other ways a chance to happen. This does not make a city organisation very happy. In some ways the most interesting US president since I've been alive was Jimmy Carter. People were so against him because he changed his mind. Presidents aren't supposed to do that.

FR *A lot of architectural schemes these days carry with them a very loose idea of who the public is, and very often when the public aspect of an urban building project is discussed it is restricted to ideas of retail and leisure, and often as secondary and adjacent to the primary development of business and residential property. Does your work establish a different set of relations?*

VA It establishes a different relation, I hope, but at the same time we have been asked to design a clothing store and there is probably very little public space in it. We were asked by a US developer who was interested in buying abandoned strip malls – apparently lots of strip malls are going out of business – and he approached us about a strip mall makeover. 'It still has to be 60% or 70% retail,' he says, 'but then surprise me, mix it with something else.' I thought this was a kind of interesting directive, you know. I think it is unreasonable to believe that someone who is going to spend money on something is going to say he wants no return. But the idea of a mix, even if we have to sneak it in, even if it's only 20% or 30% ... I hope there's still a chance to do this; the developer seems to think now that this isn't as great a project as he first imagined.

FR *One of the problems with public space is that it is so instrumentalised, but another is that it is so often bland.*

VA There's an example of that in New York right now. There has been this unused space for years, an elevated space called the High Line. It used to be a railroad system for freight. There was a body that wanted to turn this High Line into a public park. It was done relatively quickly for an architecture project in New York, with somewhat interesting landscape architects called James Corner Field Operations, working with architects Diller Scofidio + Renfro. This thing is done now, and I thought: 'Is this all they could have done with it?' Sometimes the great fear we have is, do you start to censor yourself? You start to think, 'they won't let us do that, so let's not even try' – internalising the values of the developer. It's so scary. The High Line Project is nice, it's OK, but the best thing about it is that here's this park, three storeys above the street.

FR *Do you ever try to reconceptualise those things? So, if someone asks you to design a public park do you go into the studio and say 'let's design a park for the multitudes'?*

VA Yes. We had submitted an initial general proposal – they didn't pick ours – that said 'let's have a moving park'. So you go walking down 18th Street, and you do a double take because you see these trees moving. They're moving slowly, just slow enough that you can get on. They didn't even consider us. The other thing that's funny about the High Line is that it is very narrow. We would have tried some way of making it so that every once in a while you walk in a circle, you don't have to continue the straight line. As soon as there's a straight line, there's a beginning and an end. You have to try to subvert that in some way. But also, if there are ways to go down, couldn't there be an intermediate park? Maybe these people proposed things like that and were told, come on, just do this basic park. Even though I heard it cost $900/sqft – which is a pretty big budget.

FR *You left poetry, then you left art ...*

VA Writing is still in the background, probably more than art.

FR *Yes, but do you think that the world of architecture is more satisfactory? Is it where you want to be?*

VA I don't know if I can say architecture, but if you use a more general term – the field of design – if you think of yourself as a designer, you can design for all the occasions of everyday life. Sure, we'd love to do a building but we'd love to do a cup, a glass, a bottle. But this is an assumption that I make that people get more out of something that they're using than something that they're contemplating in a museum – contemplating is already a loaded word – but they're being a viewer. As much as I love books, I always want to get something from books, I always think of them as raw material to get something from. It's not that I'm so sure that people don't get something out of studying something, contemplating something, but at the same time I'm convinced – and this goes back to one of the first questions you asked – that they get more when they are in the middle of things, when they don't have the space and time to contemplate the whole view. Sure, the whole view is a great way to learn something but you're always above it all, as if there's a diagram. You can't see the whole thing – when you get lost in the trees, you can't see the forest. That's a situation that kind of jolts you because you can't see where you are.

FR *So, you're a kind of William Carlos Williams architect?*

VA I kind of am, yes. Though apparently he, like a lot of American poets, had fascist underpinnings. Not as much as Ezra Pound. It's funny, these people you think of as the most social-minded, most liberal, they are also – Americans especially – very conservative. I don't know if this is true but supposedly Neil Young voted for Nixon.

Issue 332, December–January 2009–10

Artur Żmijewski

interviewed by Daniel Miller

The Politics of Fear

DANIEL MILLER *Let's start with* Democracies, 2009, *your films of political demonstrations. Demonstrations are also identity parades: they are shows of political force, and shows of force by political brands. You filmed both right-wing and left-wing demos across Europe.*

ARTUR ŻMIJEWSKI Demonstrations show the level of political importance of the event – you can literally count the number of its supporters and the number of its ideological opponents. Manifa, an annual feminist demonstration in Warsaw, is a good example. It started in 2000 with 150 people. But in 2010 Manifa assembled 4,000 participants. It is a very visual presentation of the growing significance of equal rights in Poland. For some people, participation in a Gay Pride parade can be a public coming out – even if they are heterosexuals – because they exhibit their protest against the domination of so-called heterosexual normality in public life. I mean, if you take part in a demonstration it can be a political coming out. I also filmed demonstrations in Israel and the West Bank. If you take part in anti-war demonstrations in Israel, you automatically become a member of a minority. Being against occupation in Israel is a strongly nonconformist attitude in such an obedient and heavily militaristic society. When people demonstrate, it is a symptom of something having gone wrong – demonstrations are the critical mass of democracy. Some Israelis are fed up with being occupiers, but their government doesn't listen to them and they are forced to shout their demands on the streets. Israel and Europe are moving to the right. In my country, Poland, abortion is illegal because the law is infected by rules of Catholic morality. Poland is also involved in the war in Afghanistan, with all the colonial terms that are applied to this situation: there are no soldiers, but 'terrorists'; no battles, but 'traps' and 'ambushes'. And of course it's not a war, but a 'stabilisation mission'.

There is a lot of aggression in the relationships between peoples in Europe – even when they protest against NATO. Anti-NATO protests in Strasbourg in 2009 were conducted by violent groups of anarchists – they burned two buildings in the city.

DM   *What do you think is the relevance of 'identity' to political demonstrations generally?*

AŻ   I'm not sure people fight to confirm and to keep their identities; rather they want to feel safe. They don't want to live under siege. I live in a strongly patriotic country in which people were dying to defend our national symbols, to keep the Polish language and so on. But I think that more interesting than identity is the desire for a safe life, a healthy body, no hunger, no military threat, no occupiers, no racial rules, no anti-feminist policy.

Them, 2007, documents the process of dismantling identity. At the end of the movie the protagonists are without all these ideological limits – all symbols were burned. They were not satisfied by these symbols and were looking for a less limited reality. In *Democracies* we see not diversity of symbols and political aims, but a single strong demand to be a part of real democracy. We the people want to take part in political decisions. And you can check reality using art – you can find out what people fantasise about, what they really want.

DM   *One of your early works was the machine sculpture* Fear and Trembling *of 1994, which Adam Szymczyk describes as 'an organic gelatinous blob ... set on a mechanically-driven base ... which unpleasantly quivered and, in addition, rotted, oozed and mouldered'. What were the thoughts and intensities which went into this work, and how would you say that they've informed your later work?*

AŻ   It was a 'fear machine'. It was a student exercise, a study of the nude. There were naked men posing, but I decided to extract one function from the body: emotion. Fear is quite basic to the human condition – we live in a culture of fear. Every day we are confronted with crises: the swine flu pandemic, al-Qaeda, minarets represented as the spears of radical Islam, Ahmadinejad, immigration and so on. We keep this fear in our bodies – I was trained to be afraid of 'unknown' threats rather than to enjoy pleasure. But there are other works that are more important for me than this one. For example, I made an 'executing machine' – a big hammer – which functioned a little like a guillotine. This object was closer to the kind of cynicism which allows people to talk without shame about issues such as 'ethnic cleansing', the so-called repatriation of immigrants and the destruction of Palestinian communities.

DM *Would you place any importance on the formless aspect of* Fear and Trembling*?*

AŻ The beginning is always chaotic, formless. It is the principle state of reality. So, I like to start from this point – it is very productive because I don't try to be smarter than reality itself – and this formless beginning will produce order and knowledge.

DM *You are perhaps still best known for* Repetition, *2005, which in some ways introduced the strategy of the experiment into art.*

AŻ Strategy sounds rational, and it is – even if the strategy means to be obedient to your deepest fantasies and pure intuitions. I think that art tries to escape its autonomy, its loneliness, and joining universal rationality is one way of doing this. You suggest that I work in the field of so-called 'aesthetics' – whatever that is – but I don't want to be part of this doxa. I repeated the Philip Zimbardo experiment because, unlike scientists, I can do this, because in art it is still allowed. It doesn't mean that there is more freedom in art; it just means that there is cultural permission for rebellion in art. *Repetition* was the experiment and, like the original, produced knowledge – even if for Zimbardo my work was just a pop culture event. Let's be serious: I don't want to produce a paradoxical art piece. I do not use art merely to elevate myself to a higher level in the social hierarchy but in order to be one of the 'actors' in the field of knowledge, in the field of social practice, in the field of politics.

DM *On the question of doxas: what about your relationship to* Krytyka Polityczna, *the left-wing Polish journal, and how is this different from a doxa?*

AŻ What is artistic doxa? It is presenting the autonomy of art and keeping a distance from society, presenting art as a shamanistic activity. The artwork must present ambiguity and polysemy. Synonymy is forbidden, as stated by Jacek Suchecki: 'Unsolvable riddle is a model of a question – paradox is a model of an answer.' Whereas in politics it is important to try to be as dependent on society as possible, to reduce distance between different communities. In using the language of reason and emotions, I am not only attempting to identify problems but also to produce proposals for solutions. Questions are expected, but also answers. So, I prefer this set of principles taken from politics, which are also represented by *Krytyka Polityczna*. Both art and politics are ready to take risky decisions and to create new realities – this is something they have in common.

DM *Both* Repetition *and* 80064 *of 2004 contained aspects of sadism. Your works generally seem to deal with the dark side of human nature. There is a quote from Henrik Ibsen that comes to mind: 'Zola descends into the sewers to bathe in them, myself, to cleanse them.'*

AŻ The dark side of human nature sounds so poetic. What if we try to treat ourselves more seriously and not use the language of literature? In both works I was repeating the situation in which people were changed into objects, their former personality erased and replaced by a new one. In the case of *80064* it was the personality of a slave. Do you think that the man with the tattoo ever went back to his original personality? People suffer when they watch this movie because they are confronted with a man who doesn't protest enough. Is it really so easy to make us slaves? Yes, it is. That is the aspect of sadism that confronts the viewer in this movie – this specific knowledge. Why do people usually laugh when they watch *Repetition*? It is a nervous reaction because they can't believe that it is so easy to break down any protest, any resistance.

DM *The 2009 trial in Germany of John Demjanjuk began on 30 November. It seems to connect to many of your themes. I wonder if you have thoughts on the case?*

AŻ He is one of the last survivors – the very last identified Nazi murderer. I fantasised about being among the journalists reporting the trial. But at the same time I do not like the idea of revenge without end, even if in the case of Demianiuk it is right. I'm afraid of this idea of endless punishment which exists in our collective fantasy, and which is justified and vindicated by the law.

DM *Would you say there's a comic streak to your work?*

AŻ People laugh when they watch *Repetition* or *Them*. Spectators transform shame into laughter. In *Repetition* everything goes so bad – prisoners want to keep their dignity but they become obedient to every shitty order they are given. In *Them*, political groups want to make the situation better, but in the end everything is burned.

Participants in both movies had really good intentions and diverse aims, they felt like free individuals, but finally they too were subordinated, becoming obedient to commands and instructions – as in *Repetition* – or possessed by some destructive desire – as in *Them*. Spectators can observe and recognise the mechanics of the situation, which are so commonplace, so very ordinary. Paradoxically, that is what makes people laugh, what appears first as comical. But this comicality covers something more fundamental: shame.

DM *Is shame a more fundamental expression than comedy for you?*

Aż Yes, it is. Shame means self-control, internalised social control. It is difficult to break social rules – to break this order of muteness. Opportunism is probably the most fundamental choice in all societies, because opportunism means internalised shame. In *Them* and then in *Repetition* we were working with both shame and opportunism.

DM *Could you say more about the privileges of the artist? You drew a distinction between artists who work mainly in isolation – the art proletariat – and your own status as an international artist. There is a quote from Heiner Mueller's play* Hamletmaschine: *'I am a privileged person. My nausea is a privilege.' What does this line say to you, if anything?*

Aż I am privileged, because I can use my position as a tool in the cultural/social/political struggle. There is this website – Artfacts.net – with its never-ending ranking of artists. Each artist has a number, a position in the art hierarchy. The lowest number I found was 56,569. The number of registered artists is 224,323. This means that most of them float freely outside of any classification. They are the so-called art proletariat, the underclass of artists.

The art world has different faces; it is the place where art activity is commercialised, but also the place where ideas are presented and exchanged for free. It produces useful knowledge, but also 'art pollution'. It offers some freedom, but also subordinates its employees. It has tools to criticise western cultural domination, colonialism, the hegemony of science and so on, but it also produces a lot of idiocy. It offers visual experiences, but also makes people blind. With all these galleries, museums, art schools, magazines, critics, collectors, collections, sellers, art fairs, websites, books, catalogues – with all this collected knowledge and collected idiocy, including of course, artists – it is huge, global and powerful, a cultural machine.

DM *Do you want to mobilise this art proletariat?*

AŻ To revolt? No. Their significance is different. They copy the most effective art languages and translate these usually difficult languages into easier ones. Their 'slow reactions' and art conservatism stabilise the art field. But do you remember what Walter Gropius said about them? Let me read you the quote: 'Academic training, however, brought about the development of a great art proletariat destined to social misery. For this art proletariat, lulled into a dream of genius and enmeshed in artistic conceit, was being prepared for the "profession" of architecture, painting, sculpture or graphic art, without being given the equipment of a real education – which alone could have assured it of economic and aesthetic independence. Its abilities, in a final analysis, were confined to a sort of drawing painting that had no relation to the realities of materials, techniques and economics. Lack of all vital connection with the life of the community led inevitably to barren esthetic speculation.'

You can replace the words 'painting', 'sculpture' or 'graphic art' with 'performance', 'photography', 'street art', 'net art', 'video' and so on, to make the text more contemporary. This is the army of creative people – do we really need them to produce ridiculous art objects? Or maybe we want them to produce something more useful? As Gropius also points out: 'The fundamental pedagogic mistake of the academy arose from its preoccupation with the idea of individual genius and its discounting the value of commendable achievement on a less exalted level.' He was thinking about how to make them well-educated workers who could survive in the labour market.

We still keep this naive fantasy about artistic genius, the creative act and so on. But something really changed: a part of art started to be directly social and political. There is a cognitive delay in art and we haven't noticed this fundamental fact, that the end of art has already happened. 'The end of art' doesn't mean that the former paradigm of art was replaced by a new one, for instance mimeticism by abstraction. It's not to do with the language, but a different model of authority and power. There is this word 'writing' which describes the activity of people who write books, but don't produce literature. So, if some 'artists' are socially, politically, therapeutically, critically, cognitively active – why use words like 'art' and 'artist' to talk about them? What they produce is the equivalent of the activity called 'writing'.

DM *It is valuable to conduct political experiments in art. But what if at*
some point an artist crosses an ethical line and begins making works
which are not just about exploitation, but are themselves exploitative?

AŻ What do we need to live successfully in society? Empathy? No, we
need indifference and distance. We are trained to keep our distance.
That's why it is easy to be passive when you see people suffer. The
ethical challenge is to activate your empathy. *Repetition* was an
investigation as to where in this social hell is the proper moment to
activate empathy. But art is innocent if we compare it with politics or
with science. Artists don't conduct wars and don't construct weapons.
Art is not directly responsible for poverty and terror. But of course
art has cultural power – and sometimes political power too. It has
enough power and enough visibility to criticise politics, culture,
science, religion and so on.

It is not my aim to cross ethical borders. My aim in the case of, for
example, *Repetition* was to discuss dangerous knowledge produced
by science and to question its authority. The idea was to maintain the
position of a noble, moral person, but to use the same language as
scientists use so that *Repetition* cannot be simply dismissed as pop
culture entertainment. The most dangerous and the most attractive aspect of science is its ability to transform knowledge into technology. Art doesn't have this ability – art only fantasises about it.

DM *You have been explaining your work in terms of its critical social and*
political dimensions. Let's say I'm suspicious of this rhetoric. It seems
superficial. The novelist Jacob Shabtai, describing one of his characters,
says: 'Caesar could only see life as a crushing meaningless defeat or a
freakish joke to be enjoyed as much as possible.' Isn't this a fine summary
of your work to date?

AŻ Is it your final conclusion that 'social and political dimensions'
are not a part of the human condition? Tell me then, what is the
content of the human condition? I could invert the interview process
and ask you a question: don't you live in Israel, a country in which
political issues produce powerful feelings, a country which continues
to occupy Palestinian territory and doesn't respect the human rights
of its populations? Is there anything 'superficial' in this political and
social situation? Could you describe this situation as 'a freakish joke
to be enjoyed as much as possible'?

So, this is my quote [from an interview with Pablo Picasso by
Simone Téry for *Les lettres françaises*] and – I can say – also my

conclusion: 'What do you think an artist is? A fool with only his eyes if he is a painter, ears if he is a musician, or a lyre in every corner of his heart if he is a poet, or even if he's a boxer, just his muscles? On the contrary, he's at the same time a political being, constantly attentive to the heart-rending, fiery, or happy events of the world, moulding himself in their image. How ever could one take no interest in others, and by virtue of what ivory-clad nonchalance live at a distance from that life which they so generously share with you!'

DM *There is an intensity to this conflict which generates pleasure at the same time that it generates suffering. We have to acknowledge this – our complicity at this level – and perhaps we should even be looking to deepen it. I see this in your work and I respect it, but it seems to me now that you're ducking it and adopting the more comfortable position of moralism.*

AŻ Your question was mostly about 'political and social rhetoric', and in my opinion there is nothing superficial in it. I spent the whole of January 2009 in Israel – it was not a pleasure for me; I went back to Poland depressed. Israeli society is morally devastated. I did not go to Israel because I'm fascinated by war; I was invited by Galit Eilat to go there as an 'expert'. She asked me to do something very direct, very particular. And I did. I visited my Israeli neighbours to talk about the attack on Gaza and to film these conversations. One woman told me: 'This war will change the life of Palestinians for the better.' In her opinion killing changes life for the better. So, Eilat and some people like her are trying to rescue this society. Art is weak, but why not use it?

DM *Throughout the interview we have been talking about political and social issues, so it seems to me to make sense to reflect on this rhetoric, its powers and its limits. I believe there are aspects of human experience – life and death – which in some way escape these dimensions. You may not be fascinated by war but you are clearly fascinated by power, and what is war except power mobilised? This isn't meant as a criticism. I share the fascination. But on this basis – and, again, perhaps I am speaking more for myself than for you – I think that the 'expert' line, or the 'I only went because I was invited', is evasive and problematic because it kicks the political question into a moral dimension.*

AŻ In literature there exists the convention of the narrator, he/she is not a writer personally but an abstract person who represents possible opinions and occupies 'possible positions'. It means that the writer is not necessarily personally responsible for what is narrated.

Can I really say, 'of course, in the movie *80064* Artur Żmijewski appears and behaves like a perpetrator forcing an old man to agree to the re-tattooing of his camp's number from Auschwitz, but this Artur Żmijewski is not a real person, he is merely a narrator who recounts to us the story'? In art the author – the artist – is directly and personally responsible for the content of the artwork. It means that there is something more real in art than in literature.

You said: 'I believe there are "socio-political" aspects of human experience – life and death – which in some way escape these dimensions.' Yes, sure, but this is not what is at stake in my work and not my issue. I'm also not interested in so-called existential fear and many other issues. But what you said represents a general strategy. If an artist tries to talk directly about politics, for example about the cruel policy of Israel, or about the colonial policy of the US, art critics can say: 'This artist is superficial – the work could be valuable but unfortunately the artist didn't include life and death as important aspects of human existence. We expect artists to talk to us like a human being, not like a reduced political entity.' Such gobbledygook discredits the artist's aims.

As to the last issue, 'you are clearly fascinated by power'. No, I'm not – I work with power. I want to know what power means, how it functions and how to defend myself. You noticed the word 'expert', but you didn't pick up on the word 'rescue'. There are people in Israel who are desperate to stop this state paranoia and rescue people – Palestinians and Israelis. Eilat takes part in this activity. But let's go back to the word 'expert', which is also interesting. Artists are experts – like professionals from other fields. If we leave behind this naive, romantic idea of the role of the artist as one who presents us with what it means to be 'a pure human being', then we can use all of our professional skills, knowledge, strategies, power of engagement, political opinions and political position, social status, visibility and access to the public. All these attributes don't describe political impotence. On the contrary, they describe potential political power.

Issue 333, February 2010

Kimsooja

interviewed by Maxa Zoller

Mirror/Needle

MAXA ZOLLER *Your work is concerned with boundaries between the self and the other; cloth, the needle and the activity of wrapping, sewing, walking and breathing have become not only methods but philosophical tools by means of which you investigate the liminal space of where the self ends and the other begins.*

I would like to start this interview with one of your recent works, the multi-channel video installation A Needle Woman, *and then work our way backwards to your early* bottari – *the Korean word for bundle – sculptures. In a way, this interview will work like a Russian doll in which the largest part includes the smallest which, in turn, already anticipates that in which it is nesting. As your work is non-linear, but cyclical and interconnected, I thought that this would be an appropriate way to gain insight into the relationship between content and method in your complex practice.* A Needle Woman, *1999–2001, and* A Needle Woman, *2005, are eight- and six-channel video installations respectively, showing a woman standing still in a crowd in different metropolises around the globe.*

KIMSOOJA Yes, the first series of 'A Needle Woman' was performed and filmed in eight different metropolises around the world beginning with Tokyo, then continued to Shanghai, Delhi, New York, Mexico City, Cairo, Lagos, and London.

When I travelled around the world performing this work, I learned a lot about the reality of the political and cultural differences. When I was invited to present a piece for the 51st Venice Biennale in 2005, the whole world was facing conflicts caused by the Iraq war that created tensions between Muslim countries and the US, and this conflict contaminated the rest of the world. I felt the urge to do the same performance focusing on the cities in conflict, to witness the world while keeping the same formality of the performance and the frame of the video documentation with *A Needle Woman* in 1999-2001. I decided to place my body in the middle of conflicted cities that are suffering from poverty, violence, post-colonialism, civil war and religious issues. This is how I chose six cities including Patan in Kathmandu Valley, Nepal during a Civil War; Havana, Cuba; Rio de Janeiro, Brazil; Sana'a, Yemen; Jerusalem, Israel; and N'djamena, Chad. I performed and documented them all in a few months in 2005. The last performance was commissioned from France and I decided to focus on different realities in Paris, performing in three neighbourhoods that represented multicultural communities such as Barbès market place – a typical Parisian community on Rue Montreuil – and a tourist location such as Champs-Elysées.

MZ *I would like to quote the German curator Volker Adolphs who very eloquently wrote about* A Needle Woman: *'Like a pin, she pricks into the colourful social tissue of the cities, sews different societies together. Kimsooja sees the pin as an extension of her body; she overcomes inbetween spaces and disappears again. The thread remains as a binding and mediating trace of the ghost in the tissue's weave. [...] But it is also possible to see this the other way around. In this case the unceasing, endless wave of people is the stationary and enduring part and the artist is the existence that is in motion, who will go on, pass away, decompose and disappear.' Can you talk about how you developed this extraordinary series of videos?*

K Before I started making videos as a medium for my practice which included performance, I was painting using Korean bedcovers and traditional clothing. I have always kept my artistic position as a painter. All of my experiments in using different media have been a continuous evolution of my painting. I've always been aware of western art history and I have been writing my own painting history by contemplating the larger social realities and conditions as a Korean woman. I have been searching for a methodology that articulates the questions that I have about the structure of the canvas, nature and the world – focusing on horizontality, verticality and duality – but at the same time questioning the self and the other, and to unite these in oneness. I continued my sewing practice from 1983 to 1992 – almost a decade. The documentary video that I made about my daily life and practice of working with Korean bedcovers in nature happened to be the first video when I discovered that my body functioned as a symbolic needle that weaves the big fabric of nature, which is why I titled it *Sewing into Walking – Kyungju* in 1994. That is how I started to use video as my medium for my work – not because I was particularly interested in image-making, but because of the idea that the camera lens is a gaze that weaves the reality of the world, and the video frame is an immaterial way of wrapping objects – a *bottari*.

In 1999, when CCA Kitakyushu commissioned me, I thought that I might experiment with performance pieces by using my body – one in the urban fabric, and another in nature. I thought that I could do a walking performance. So, I began walking a couple of hours in different areas of Tokyo City, but I couldn't find the right moment and energy to define it, and the precise methodology to film it. At last, I arrived in the Shibuya area where hundreds of thousands of people were coming and going. I was completely overwhelmed by the huge crowd and its accumulated energy in my mind – I was screaming inwardly and had to stop walking and stand still right there. At that very moment, I realised the meaning of my hours of walking: I decided immediately to continue to perform standing still and to document the performance behind me.

MZ *So you are saying that* A Needle Woman *is not so much about being a global citizen, but that it actually developed out of a moment of personal crisis?*

K Yes, it was a very personal encounter, a contemplation of myself and others, and of humanity. At first I didn't think about the global citizen. I started the performance more as an existential question, but I've been more and more engaged with the world since this first performance – contemplating the destiny of all humanity and feeling compassion for it. In the beginning of the performance it was very difficult for me to resist all the energy coming from others on the street and I was totally vulnerable, standing still – as a woman – totally naked, psychologically. But then in the middle of the performance I found my own space and time and I learned how to breathe, how to be still, how to relax different parts of my body, and how to focus. It was like being at the centre of a vortex that creates enormous silence and noise within it.

I experienced an amazing transformation and transcendence while performing *A Needle Woman* in Tokyo, because in the end my mind was full of love, happiness and peace and I was enlightened with peace in mind while looking at the waves of people coming and going. Then I perceived a white light coming through from behind the horizon of waves of people, like the light coming through the void in the needle. After the powerful experience of that performance, I was eager to continue the same performance on every continent and to meet everyone in the world.

MZ *In these performance videos you stand in for the needle that stitches all these different pieces of the world together, your long black hair becoming the eye of the needle. Over the many years of your sewing, wrapping and performing art practices you have developed your own philosophical topology of the needle.*

K In the first performance video I used my body as a symbolic needle that weaves the big fabric of nature, but I was also conscious of the needle as an object that has many different kinds of dualities. A needle is a tool that is used in healing practices, but it's also used in connecting separated parts together – both actions performing pain. The needle is a hermaphrodite, and then it also has the void that is the eye of the needle which allows the thread through the other, which in a way represents our soul and spirit. At the same time, a needle is definitely an extension of our hands and body – so it combines the body, the spirit, the physical and the void, the material, and the immaterial.

MZ *In what way is the second version of* A Needle Woman *from 2005, which was presented at the Venice Biennale of that year, different from the first?*

K This time I chose cities in conflict. Patan in Kathmandu Valley, for example, was caught up in a civil war at the time; I saw soldiers with guns everywhere and heard many gunshots. The recent history of Havana, another city I chose, is related to the US through colonialism – which blocked free travel between the countries. Rio de Janeiro has problems with violence and poverty as well as postcolonial issues – I visited the favelas and experienced severe violence and threat there. N'Djamena in Chad, another city that I chose, is one of the poorest countries in the world that also has post-independence issues. Just as Sana'a in Yemen, which has political and religious conflicts with Israel. I had to travel from Sana'a via Jordan to Jerusalem, as there was no other way around. We believe we live in a global society and that we should be able to travel freely, but in fact it is more and more difficult to travel freely in the world and we have to risk our life to live our life.

In this second version of *A Needle Woman*, I considered my body more as an axis of time, whereas in the first version I considered my body as an axis of space. I weave in different societies and economies, and different cultures, by positioning myself at a zero-time zone – and slowing down the speed of the movement of people on the street in relation to the real time of the audience. In this way I created three different positions of time: real time where the audience locates, zero time where I stand still, and a slowed down time zone where passers-by move around my body. I am still questioning what it was that happened when I stood still at that 'point zero', and I keep thinking about permanency within it.

MZ *I wanted to talk about the relationship between the passers-by and the camera. Sometimes the people approach the camera directly and look through it directly at us, the audience.*

K I think that is what is interesting in terms of photographic perspectives in performance and video, it's like having a third, hidden eye. Before I made *A Needle Woman* in 1999, I did another video piece called *Sewing into Walking – Istiklal Caddesi, Istanbul* in 1998, in which I positioned the camera within a fixed frame and just allowed the people on the main street Istiklal Caddesi in Istanbul to come and go without manipulating them. In a sense, the camera itself was my body, and the lens was my eyes. I wasn't aware of it when performing the first *A Needle Woman*, but that was one of the origins of the *A Needle Woman* piece, which I might have to revisit at some point. I tend to go back and forth, to and from the centre question. I think this enables me to relate my eyes and my body to the audience, and to the location, creating different layers of meaning and different viewpoints. It is interesting to me to place my body both as a centre and as an observer.

MZ *Let's talk a bit about the role of your body in these performances. By positioning your back to the viewer rather than facing the camera you complicate the relationship between yourself, the stream of people walking towards you – the camera – and the viewers. In a peculiar way it is through the reaction of the passers-by to you that we come to identify with you, that we 'see' your face.*

K By positioning the camera against the audiences – I was able to stay anonymous, but at the same time the audiences could enter my position and focus on what I was experiencing. For example, in Lagos I performed in the middle of the marketplace and there were kids and adults carrying items on their heads, and they stood still, watching me from beginning to end. It was an interesting mirroring reaction of what I was doing. At the same time, the actual audiences in the exhibition space, when viewing this performance/video, could also enter my body at a certain moment and experience what I am performing.

MZ *In other words by becoming the mirror and the needle between the audiences and the world, you remove yourself.*

K In a way, I objectify myself as a needle: I am a needle to the audience as well as the surface of the mirror, the canvas. I believe that painters, all through their lives, try to find their own mirror on the surface of their canvases in order to find their own identity. I was also trying to question where the boundary is in *To Breathe – Invisible Mirror, Invisible Needle*, a video and sound installation piece at the La Fenice Theatre in Venice. We can never stop resting our eyes on this endlessly transforming colour field because we cannot truly measure the depth or define the surface of it. This is also related to my early painting practice. While the *bottari* represents a physical, material, wrapping practice – just as the fabric of a canvas, an object, and a sculpture. I use the mirror as a physical and a symbolic material, having similar functionality to video-making in terms of framing the images. There are materialised and dematerialised elements in my work and, in the end, they are one.

MZ *I recently read Jean-Luc Nancy's text on the* Noli me Tangere *story in the Gospel of St John in which the resurrected Christ encounters Mary Magdalena and says to her: 'Do not touch me; I am not from this world'. In* A Needle Woman *you serve almost as a sort of apparition. You produce difference by inserting your body in these particular environments. This results in reactions that range from indifference to rather threatening curiosity, but nobody touches you. It is as if you are saying: 'Noli me Tangere.'*

K I think it has to do with the transcendent element in performances dealing with time. This is also true of *The Laundry Woman* performance I did in Delhi in 2000 on the Yamuna River bank right next to a Hindu cremation site. The floating debris that you see is from cremations from the nearby bank– burnt parts of bodies, flowers and pieces of wood slowly float and pass by my body. I was contemplating human destiny and the purification of the burnt bodies, and of myself. In the middle of the performance I experienced an unbelievable confusion – I couldn't figure out whether it was the river that was flowing, or whether it was my body that was flowing. But then, after a while, I found myself back in the centre of the flow, and away from the confusion. After this performance, I learned from the confusion – my inner and physical gaze was so focused that there was no boundary between myself and the other. Much like a needle point that has no physicality but a location, which is open to the void. It was not the river that flows, but my body in time, which seemed a solid, physical entity that flows and that disappears.

MZ *I think that this experience also translates to the viewer of your work. At least I can say for myself that I entered a trance-like state in your exhibition at The Baltic in Gateshead where you presented both* A Needle Woman *installations.*

K Yes, there is a kind of hypnotic element in the duration of time – in fact, time is a repetition of each moment of breathing, inhaling and exhaling, and this repetition creates a hypnotic state of mind. I was so concentrated and focused on one point – which is nowhere, actually. There are no references around at the very point of the needle so that you cannot relate yourself to anywhere, but at the same time you are everywhere. I learn from each performance and that offers deeper questions and that's why I cannot help but continue my work.

MZ *The needle then is like a threshold or an interface – like a skin, if you like.*

K Yes, that's why I also consider the mirror to be an unwrapped, unfolded needle because it has a certain similarity to the needle in its nature.

MZ *You mentioned earlier the work* To Breathe – Invisible Needle, Invisible Mirror *that you made for the Teatro La Fenice in Venice in 2006. Could you talk to us about the needle-mirror relation in this particular work?*

K I find the needle and the mirror very interesting in the way that their own identity is not revealed. A needle always functions dually as a medium that connects things together, but at the same time it can hurt the other. But only by hurting the other can it heal, and that's when its function is completed – a needle leaves the site at the end. Like the needle, a mirror is also an interesting object in terms of identity because it reflects everything but itself. I find this very intriguing in a similar way to the needle.

The mirror also creates a boundary that reflects the self, and the illusion of the self – the real and the illusory self. That is very similar to the surface in the practice of painting, which I was always aware of because of the way I used sewing. As I mentioned earlier, the reason why I started sewing as a painting practice was not because I was particularly interested in sewing, or because I was a woman artist, or a good sewer, but because I was interested in the question of the surface, and in questions about the relationship of the other and the self. The whole process of questioning and answering by pushing a needle into the fabric (canvas) and pulling it through as a repetitive action – this circular movement of sewing as a dialogue led to my wrapping *bottari* pieces as a three-dimensional form of sewing. The moment I discovered *bottari* as a new object was a very intuitive and astonishing moment. I experienced it as a new encounter when staring at the ordinary *bottari* that I kept for a long time in my studio. All of a sudden it presented itself as a new painting, as a sculpture and as a new object. The journey with the *bottari* truck piece in *Cities on the Move – 2727 km Bottari Truck* 1997, and the whole idea of the mirror has to do with a mirror representing a borderline. I spent much of my childhood near the DMZ (Demilitarised Zone) area where I heard about casualties on the border; this must have influenced my attention to the idea of borders. That is also related to how I came to create this constantly transforming video colour spectrum painting: *To Breathe – Invisible Mirror, Invisible Needle* in Venice in 2005.

When I was originally invited to create a piece for La Fenice, I was aware that it is an opera house, and discovered that singing is all about breathing. I wished to emphasise that element but I also realised that breathing is the same as sewing – inhale and exhale – and it can be the moment of life and the moment of death. So this notion of breathing related to sewing and defining the depth of the surface was what I wanted to examine in this piece. And, in a constantly changing colour spectrum, I also wanted to incorporate the audience's breathing with my breathing within the architecture, so that I could embrace the architecture as my body breathes.

MZ To Breathe – A Mirror Woman, *also made in 2006, is obviously related to the La Fenice piece. Can you say something about this large-scale intervention in this extraordinary space?*

K This was in the Palacio de Cristal in Madrid and was organised by the Reina Sofia Museum. When I saw the space I was stunned by the beauty of it; I thought it was an absolutely beautiful object in itself that didn't need anything added to it. So instead I decided to empty the space in order to push the void outwards all the way to the very skin of the building. I covered the entire glass façade with diffraction-grating film which diffused the light into a rainbow spectrum, and placed mirrors on the floor to reflect the structure of the building and create a virtual space.

I also added the sound of breathing from La Fenice Theatre installation. There are two different stages – the sound of inhaling and exhaling, and the sound of humming. The result sounds like a chorus of my own voice echoing and bouncing onto the mirror floors of the space. Depending on the light and the time of day, the colour spectrum changed endlessly and amazingly around the clock. For me it was, in a way, the *bottari* of light and sound that completes all the different concepts of needle, mirror, breathing and wrapping – all of these elements together in one space.

MZ *I wanted to return to the work* Sewing into Walking – Kyungju, *a key work that connects your architectural installations and the colour and video projections of the 2000s with your early* bottari *works. In this piece you use breathing and walking as an extension of the sewing and wrapping practices of the* bottaris.

K I didn't originally intend this to be a video piece. I just wanted to make a daily documentary record of how I relate to fabric in my daily practice, so it was very naturally done. But when I reviewed the video, especially in slow motion, I discovered the amazing transitional nature of the performative element in my daily life practice.

The fabrics I use are mainly used as bedcovers for newly married couples in Korea, and are given to the bride and groom as a gift by the bride's parents. The performance ended with me wrapping all the bedcovers together and tying them into bundles and then leaving the site.

The site of the bed is our frame of life – where we are born, where we dream, love, suffer and die. So wrapping and unwrapping the bedcover has a symbolic meaning for me – wrapping life and death, in the end. When unfolded, the bedcover signifies a couple – a family, love, settlement – and also location. When wrapped into a bundle, the bedcover suggests a totally opposite concept, one that signifies separation and dislocation. It also signifies migration and the status of refugees. When a Korean woman says, 'Wrap the bundle', it means a married woman is about to leave her family to pursue her own life – so it has a feminist element too in Korean society. In a way, by working with the boundaries of wrapping and folding, I have been able to create different perspectives and dimensionalities in my work. When unfolded, the bedcover signifies a couple – a family, love, settlement – and also a location.

The first *bottari* I made (or rather discovered) was in 1992 at PS1 studio in New York. *Bottaris* were always with me in my studio and as part of a Korean household, I used them to store things and fabrics from the beginning of my sewing practice that started in 1983 – but I wasn't aware of it until later. I was looking back at my studio and lying there was an unusual object that looked so familiar but yet totally distinctive. It was a unique painting, and at the same time, a sculpture made with one very simple knot, and a ready-made/ready-used object.

MZ   *There is also the modernist question of medium-specificity in these* bottaris *such as 'What is a canvas?'*

K   *Bottari* is very much linked to our body and our daily life. I consider our body as the most complicated *bottari*, so the bedcover fabric is like a skin for me. Without that kind of close link to reality, it would be less meaningful and more abstract for me, and I wouldn't have been able to create a broader concept for my work.

MZ   *Earlier you mentioned your upbringing close to the demilitarised* zones. *Would you share a few more details about this part of your life?*

K   My father was in the military from the Korean War until he retired as a general. We were moving from one city to another, one village to another, every other year wrapping and unwrapping. As a nomad who spent much of my childhood near the DMZ, I have always been aware of the border – not only in my own work, but also physically and psychologically. I always felt a certain kind of awareness of the other, or a danger around me when I lived in that region. Since I was little child I have been very sensitive and vulnerable to the pain of others which could have to do with my experience near the DMZ. I was always aware of other places (The North of the DMZ), outside of my own places (The South of Korea), and that is not unrelated to my use of fabric and boundaries in different practices. I guess without realising it, I began to discover more and more about my own history and destiny through my work. At the Venice Biennale in 1999 I installed a full-sized mirrored-wall in front of a *bottari* truck and dedicated it to the Kosovo War refugees. In fact, the mirror opens up the virtual exit, but it's the road that you cannot get through – so, in a way, it also represents the frustration of all the conditions of the refugees.

MZ   *Travelling also features in your two videos* Cities on the Move *for the exhibition of the same title.*

к   I was very inspired by the title of the exhibition, which was linked to my life. The distance travelled over 11 days in *Cities on the Move: 2727 kilometers Bottari Truck*, the piece I made for the exhibition in 1997, was quite meaningful to me – the *bottari* truck and myself as another *bottari* sitting on top – endlessly moving like a line on a graph, in time and space. At this time I was very much aware of the notion of time in my practice. Looking back at my past and looking forward to the future and drawing lines along the journey onto the topology of the South Korean land.

мz   *Is that why it is in slow motion?*

к   Not necessarily, but I think a slow mode could reveal much more of the realities around us that we don't often gaze at with much attention. In a way it resembled my inner rhythm or the wavelength in my mind.

This is an edited version of an interview which took place at the Starr Auditorium, Tate Modern on 20 February 2010. Previously unpublished.

Sturtevant

interviewed by Coline Milliard

The Power of Repetition

COLINE MILLIARD *From your very first solo show at the Bianchini Gallery in 1965 to* Vertical Monad *and* Cold Fear *at the Anthony Reynolds Gallery in 2008 and 2006 respectively, your exhibitions have always been conceived as installations in their own right rather collections of objects. Will this thinking manifest itself in your exhibition, 'The Razzle Dazzle of Thinking', at the Musée d'Art moderne de la Ville de Paris?*

STURTEVANT Yes definitely. In my show at the Museum für Moderne Kunst in Frankfurt am Main, the installation was devised in terms of tonality, movement and transition. It wasn't about the objects per se, but more about how the objects move in relation to each other. The installation demonstrated what the work is about, which is giving visibility to thoughts. My piece *Vertical Monad* of 2008 is most certainly making thoughts extremely visible. In the Paris show, the first part of the wall text, 'Wild to Wild', is about the reversal of hierarchies. For example, it is image over object. There is not much to look at but there is much to think about.

CM Vertical Monad *really stands out in your production. The installation is completely grey, including a monochrome grey video, and a voice intones in Latin from Spinoza's* Ethics. *Your other recent works are often brash, sometimes verging on the aggressive – I'm thinking for example of* The Dark Threat of Absence, *2002, which combines the reenactment of a Paul McCarthy performance with filmic collages of TV footage – but here you seem to be opening up a space for introspection, or even meditation.*

S No, no, no – not meditation. Absolutely not. I do not want people to meditate. During one of my lectures, someone said: 'What do you want people to think?' The work is not about what to think, but rather to engender thinking. 'Triggering thinking' is what I am going for. For instance, if you are put in a situation that we could call 'displacement', it brings discontinuity into play and that in turn should – with the gaps and the jumps – bring you to a different place and a different space.

cm *Anthony Reynolds told me that you were thinking of repeating* Vertical Monad *three times in the Paris show. How do you think this will affect the way the piece is perceived?*

s It becomes something else other than a total installation. How will it change the way it is received? I'm not sure. How is that going to work? We'll have to wait and see. It is about taking risks. And if it doesn't work, the first thing you say is, 'Wow, how did that happen?'

cm *In 2008, your 'philosophical musical'* Spinoza in Las Vegas *was played at Tate Modern. It involved dozens of dancers and actors and some of your video works projected in the background. You even performed as the philosopher and Anthony Reynolds was the ventriloquist.* Vertical Monad *and your 'philosophical musical'* Spinoza in Las Vegas *seem to be two faces of the same investigation, one inward-looking and another one outward-looking, more fiesta-like. Do you agree with this reading?*

s *Spinoza in Las Vegas* really has a strong interior structure, so even though it looks festive, if you read the script – it's really hard to pick up everything when you are looking at the theatre because the action is pretty disturbing – you'll see that it has a very profound under-structure. It is a critique of Spinoza and of the cybernetic world. I was on Spinoza at college and I just couldn't stand him – he's so logical, he's so tight and so rigid – I always wanted to get on his case. Basically, what motivated this work was the fact that if you want to open new space in your head, you tackle Spinoza. It's an enormous challenge. *Spinoza in Las Vegas* brings a more profound level to something which is basically amusing, like a musical or a play. But it's really a severe critique of Spinoza, not heavy-handed and yet very accurate.

cm *The under-structure – what you call the 'silent power of art' – has been a concern of yours for many years.*

s Since forever.

cm *I suppose the problem some people had when trying to engage with your earlier work, such as your* Warhol Flowers, *1969–70, or your* Johns Flag Painting, *1964, is that instead of seeing them as a critique and a challenge to the functioning of art as a whole, they only saw individual pieces in relation to works by specific artists.*

    s   This is a way of looking. People look at an installation and they see only objects. Many exhibitions are about objects, which is a reversal of what is happening now, because imagery is much the higher power in today's society. It's a big move to simulacra.

CM *Staying with this distinction between art on the one hand and mass communication on the other, I have read that you are very keen to be always 'of your time', that it is important for you to be technologically up to date. This contemporaneity manifested itself in the 1960s. The artists whose work you selected have since been validated by the 'canon': Frank Stella, Roy Lichtenstein or Claes Oldenburg. Now your work is more concerned with image and the simulacrum. Do you think that today the impact of digital and cybernetic technology is a more pressing issue than authorship in contemporary art?*

    s   Yes and no. Firstly, the initial work was about the extreme power of repetition. It worked and lasted. People began to realise what I was talking about even though they didn't really understand the dynamics of repetition – we still have people who call my works 'copies', but I suppose that will forever be the case.

CM *That's your cross to bear.*

    s   It's not my cross, it's their cross. But in order to move forward, action was needed. So then of course you go into film. The first video that I did was *Dillinger Running Series* in 2000, and after that *Greening of America* the following year, in the reverse sense of course. It is a four-frame video of 'excess', 'limitation', 'transgression' and 'exhaustion'. This is our digital world.

CM *In the cyber world, when so many things are reproduced and shared, the notion of signature seems irrelevant. This new reality has very strong connections with issues present in your work since the beginning. Is this what triggered your interest in the digital world?*

    s   The cybernetic world has been with us quite a while. It is becoming louder and nosier but I was always aware of its progression. It brought me away from repetition to this other dynamic, which is a mode of thinking, amongst other things.

CM *What would you say is the biggest challenge in this information-saturated society?*

    s   The biggest challenge? I have no idea. Probably it is trying to maintain a self, and an identity related to the self and not to the exterior world.

CM *This duality between exterior and interior is also the key to many of your recent works, like the three-channel video* Blow Job, *2007, where your mouth blows air behind what looks like a silicon skin.*

S Well, yes, of course. The 2002 video *The Dark Threat of Absence* – the first one, presented on two screens – is also very clear about that. The camera on the right represents how you behave outside when you do not recognise what's going on in the interior. The camera on the left is about how the exterior is folded to the interior – how painful all that is. This work is a very clear example of exterior/interior dynamics, links and connections.

CM *In 2006, at Art Unlimited in Basel, you produced an interactive installation,* Digital Click, *in which people were invited to pose on moon-shaped pedestals with a couple of inflatable sex dolls. Interactivity seems to be playing a more important role in your practice, and this will probably culminate in the Paris exhibition with your ghost train,* The House of Horror. *Why did you feel the need to bring the audience literally into your work?*

S That is true, I do bring them into it. That's very clever of me, isn't it? But I don't think this is the main force of the work. One of the things that brought me to *The House of Horror* is the museum space itself. *Wild to Wild* is incredibly beautiful from front to back. *The House of Horror* is dark, there is no light, it is also sheer entertainment, in total opposition to *Wild to Wild*. I think it is through this idea of opposition that the piece came into my head.

CM *What about the nine-monitor piece* Elastic Tango, *2010? It has been in the making for quite a few years.*

S It was first conceived for Tate Modern, but we never made it, and in the meantime it has been through 12 different transformations. I have a huge stack of storyboards, drawings and collages. It is structured as a three-act play without narrative – the presentation of the problem, the escalation and the resolution of the problem. And the resolution of the problem is the higher power of simulacra – bang! It will be presented on nine monitors arranged in the shape of an inverted pyramid: 2, 3 and 4.

CM *Your reputation is still much bigger in Europe than it is in the US. How do you explain that?*

S Well, the US is coming to grips with my work now.

CM *Some critics have suggested that you decided to use only your surname as a way to escape gender specificity. Do you agree?*

s   No, the dynamics are not about gender. The name Sturtevant is
strong and very powerful.

cm   *You started your career in New York in the 1960s, a period which has
been mythologised, and I don't mean only in art history books but also in
mass culture, with films like* Factory Girl *in 2006, it is very much part of
popular consciousness. How do you remember that time?*

s   It was great – martinis, parties, discourse. It was a super time,
a superior time. But around 1965 on, I had a big battle. It was very
difficult because the dialogue surrounding the work was totally
negative, the understanding of it glued to the idea of the 'copy'. Then
the appropriationists came along in the 1980s and they were crucial,
they gave people a hinge to my work. Of course, people tried to block
me into appropriation, but although I am not an appropriationist, it
provided me with negative definition – a strong force – and it clarified
the work.

cm   *Do you ever get nostalgic for those times?*

s   No, I'm very much on top.

Issue 324, March 2010

Phyllida Barlow

interviewed by Colin Perry

Why Things Are The Way They Are

COLIN PERRY *Since your earliest exhibitions you have quietly avoided the commercial art scene, showing at museums and non-profit spaces such as Cornerhouse, Manchester in 1986, the Baltic Centre for Contemporary Art, Gateshead in 2004, and the Kunstmuseum, Basel earlier this year. Your forthcoming UK shows, at the Serpentine and Studio Voltaire, are similarly in non-commercial spaces. You are known as a teacher as much as an artist, having worked as a tutor at art schools in London for 40 years before retiring last year. To what degree was this non- or anti-commercialism a deliberate choice?*

PHYLLIDA BARLOW My work has always been about the physical and material process of making and how this relates to space. I have not considered whether the work is going to sell or not. It has never been about commerce or the idea of the product. I think that gradually, over the years, my work has established itself as sort of non-commercially viable, not through any politicised motivation, but just through happenstance.

CP *Did you deliberately avoid commercial galleries?*

PB I don't think that I have consciously avoided them. I simply never had that opportunity. But, of course, it would be disingenuous to say: 'No, I would love to have had a commercial gallery.' It's more a kind of mindset that some of my generation grew up with in the 1960s; reacting against getting signed up by a gallery was the fulfilment of a different ambition. In the mid 1960s, the big hitters were the Robert Fraser Gallery, Kasmin Gallery and Rowan Gallery, and they were all very much about selling work. Then, when the 1970s kicked in with the recession, a very different attitude began to emerge. Suddenly, artists started finding alternative spaces, and they started enjoying the freedom that such spaces enabled. But at the same time there was incredible hardship. Obviously the gallery has to be somehow connected to politics. Therefore, artists like myself were, on that front, politicised.

CP *But it was a muted type of politics?*

PB Yes, it was politics with a small 'p'. We did not want to be answerable to that system where the selling of work was prioritised over other ambitions. Having said that I don't think I would ever underestimate how enabling galleries can be of highly experimental and ambitious work.

CP *What differences are there, in terms of circumstance and attitude, between your generation and the current generation of emerging artists?*

PB Really, I think my generation was quite lazy, and I think there was a laziness in my so-called 'career'. I was very lucky to get two teaching jobs: one at Chelsea School of Art and another at Bristol, and being amazed that each month there was this income coming in that enabled me to buy material and keep going and not have to think about exhibiting. By contrast, young emerging artists today are highly professionalised in very strategic ways. For them, it's a form of survival to have ambitions focused on selling work and aligning themselves to galleries.

CP *You have recently worked and exhibited alongside artist Jess Flood-Paddock at the Russian Club in London. What kind of dynamic does working with young artists bring to your work?*

PB I invited Jess to take part in an Arts Council project called 'What do Artists Do?', a project that took two years to work through. Then Matt Golden and Nat Breitenstein, the curators at the Russian Club, invited Jess and myself to make one of their 'double shows', which always feature two artists showing together. An immediate response to your question is more about how we generated a dynamic rapport between our working methods regardless of age. I think we energised each other in different and contrasting ways, not through one of us being younger or older than the other. We had six weeks in the space. But it was a time when I had a run of other shows to work on and it was quite difficult to find the time to work together in the space, so I wanted to make a decision very quickly. I asked Jess if she minded if I brought into the space these huge cylindrical structures left over from the show at Baltic, and said that I wanted to screed them in cement. My intention was to make them disappear into the concrete floor of the Russian Club gallery space. During our discussion we were thinking of keeping it open and light, but in the end I put these two huge concrete towers in the space – I think it must have been complete and utter hell for her!

Jess has an extraordinary way of working which is absolutely opposite to mine, where she collects and culls quite disparate items – whether it's Freud's couch, an Aztec sculpture or a cartoon cat – and I'm trying to join up the dots of how she's thinking. For me, being in contact with someone who had that kind of mental agility was absolutely extraordinary. I feel my sculptural process is quite broody and melancholic. But with Jess's work, you have no idea where it's going to come from, or, more importantly, where it's going to. So it's not only interesting but surprising and challenging. She's not afraid of all sorts of clashing histories and very disparate intellectual approaches, and absorbing copious amounts of theoretical material, whereas I'm still very much involved in the psychology of why things are what they are, and the space, the here-and- now. Something has happened to art history where we see the 20th century through binoculars. The juxtaposition of things is no longer problematic. You can put Meret Oppenheim's furry teacup next to Donald Judd. But in the 1960s, you wouldn't have learned about those two things simultaneously, they'd have been boxed differently. Now, there is this extraordinary bran tub of ideas, the influence of the internet, this great pic 'n mix from the 20th century.

CP *You will soon be showing at the Serpentine alongside Nairy Baghramian. What are the similarities between your work and hers?*

PB I think it is something to do with edges and touch, those two things. Importantly, her work and mine demand this interaction with space as if there is a question being tested out as to how much ownership the work has on the space. But Nairy's work is very wired – you feel there's a danger in getting too near it. It's almost warding you off, and I think my work draws you in, in some way. I describe it as like stuff left behind on the moon, stranded in an anaesthetised vacuum, sanitised and sterilised, in the aftermath of space exploration. But air and light flood through it, opening up the interior space into the exterior space so you cannot tell which is which. For me, that is where the political qualities inherent to her work reside, as if it reveals all, offering transparency to refute secrecy.

CP   *What I see connecting your work is a concern for the everyday, objects that you could potentially handle or relate to in an everyday sense.*

PB   To me a lot of my works are born out of the urban environment and become like surrogates or bad copies of those things. The process of making allows the change to happen. It might begin with seeing a barrier or a bollard on the street that I'm attracted to. Then, by the time I make my drawings, at the initial stage of the process, memory starts to manipulate them. Then, as I work, the choice of materials has an effect. The way something loses its original identity is very important to my work – it involves a gradual erosion away from the original in the hope that it becomes its own autonomous entity.

CP   *For her contribution to the 5th Berlin Biennial in 2008, Nairy collaborated with the legendary left-wing designer Janette Laverrière. In a recent interview, Laverrière said that useless objects are actually very useful. Do you see a connection here between your 'useless' objects?*

PB   I think their 'use' is also the function they have psychologically within the everyday. That intrigues me. Paul Auster wrote about it in one of *The New York Trilogy* books where he asked when is an object no longer the object by which it is named? For example, when the waterproof hood of the umbrella is no longer there, and you're left with these spikes, you still call it an umbrella. That collapse of the use of something really fascinates me, where the evidence of the object is still there. Like the piano without its notes, but the hulk is still there. Once something is a named thing, we are all at one with it. But remove the thing that gives it its name and I don't know what it becomes, and that, for me, is where the sculptural object is. It becomes an uncertain object.

CP   *Does this concern with uncertainty and subversion also connect with your idea of 'risk' in sculpture?*

PB   I have just finished a huge work in the Kunstmuseum, Basel, a show that was organised by the Berlin-based gallery Silberkuppe. It was a nerve-racking experience, not least because I had no real control over whether the materials were going to be the right kind of materials when we got there. When I work like this, I've got to give very clear instructions to assistants because I'm handing my method over to them. It excites me that the idea has to be got rid of and replaced with the whole process of production.

What I have been trying to look at is how we try to give the notion of action and the process of making, and all the actions that go with the process of making, the same kind of credibility as this thing called an 'idea'. I am interested in the point where the action completely eradicates the idea. For instance, the idea might be that I want to bisect the space, or I want to create this very narrow passageway, as was the case in Basel. There, the idea was of creating a building within a building, squeezed into the gallery space. The resulting work eventually overwhelmed the space and proposed an impossibility, like a ship in a bottle – an object that is too big for the space it inhabits. It's my way of challenging the authority inherent to institutions and politicising the processes of making and the resulting physicality and materiality work. I suppose during the making of the Basel work, anything that it might have been just went, because of the sheer power of the quantity of stuff to be used, organising five people to build it and keeping that momentum going. It just became this very different thing. What it is, I'm still trying to work out. I think that's where the risk is – my loss of a sense of knowing what something is.

CP *Is it work that can fail? Can your work fail?*

PB I think that it can fail, absolutely. I feel vulnerable and uncertain about the Basel piece, and I need to revisit it in my head because it was one hell of a job to do it. Whether it's a failure or not, I'm not sure. How would you define a failure?

CP *I ask about failure because of comments you have made previously about experimental studio-based practice allowing for a certain degree of necessary failure. When you use the exhibition space as a studio to construct a work, you invite and risk failure – but what would failure be like in this context?*

PB Well, for one, I think one of the problems with placing big things in exhibition spaces is that there are always much bigger things out there in the real world. Also, I think theatricality can get a bad press – it can become a form of emotional blackmail, and the viewer understandably can say, 'Actually I don't want to be emotionally blackmailed'. I think that a lot of the works in Tate Modern's Turbine Hall can do that. They seem to have 'Tate' written all over them. There's something going on there that is very politicised. It must be incredibly difficult to work in that space, because either you go huge or you go invisible. But it's always theatrical.

CP *But you continue to work on a large scale?*

PB As an artist, I make things on a large scale not to create heroic objects but because largeness takes me into that area of making where there is that risk of losing control. I'm excited by making physical stuff that isn't definitive from the outset, and I try and find its definition through a process of making. I'm often working beyond my reach and beyond my height, so the object is constantly eluding me, even though the physical stuff is accessible and handleable. That contradiction really is what drives me with these big objects. Therefore, whether it fails or not is a complicated question. It may fail formally, but the actual process was enormously thrilling – this journey to make work that is beyond our control the whole time.

I think that this is something that sculpture has been able to take on. It has been part of the history of 20th-century sculpture that it can go well beyond its former orthodoxies, the public or heroic.

CP *Does the disruptive power of post-minimalism still have the charge it once had? Or has the paradigm changed?*

PB When Nicola Dietrich, the museum director in Basel, saw photographs of my work she said she felt bewildered because so much of the work looked as though it could have been done in the last five years or so. But, of course, it wasn't; it was done 20 or 30 years ago. Over the years I've seen the temporary – here-today-and-gone-tomorrow – as psychological, emotional and political. It's one of those paradoxes. Having been trained in a very rigid kind of way as a sculptor, learning all these rigid disciplines, and then in the late 1960s realising that sculpture could just be a piece of paper thrown on the floor. The whole question of how you might define the status of object just suddenly opened up – and this was absolutely thrilling.

When something is losing its sense of being an object and becoming something else, that 'something else' is a source of fascination for me. Whether that is a cloud evaporating in front of one's eyes or smoke disappearing, or the weather changing. For instance, is rain an 'object'? What is it if it isn't? I'm interested in how spaces are altered by different kinds of things, whether it's temperature, smell or dampness. Observing these things has made me aware of how things last in a different kind of way.

CP *Your work is usually demolished after the exhibition finishes. How does your work relate to temporality or duration?*

PB This temporariness relates to a fascination I have with the idea of syntax, the tense of a sculpture. The tense of how we are looking at something. Take Nairy's show at Studio Voltaire and compare it with my building structure at the museum in Basel. My show was very much in the present tense – it was 'now, now, now'. And it seemed to retain that 'nowness' for quite a few days, before ultimately it became another tense – perhaps the past tense. And perhaps that is where I'm critical of it. By contrast, Nairy's work was almost in the future tense. Her works were almost like things that will happen or are going to happen. I find it fascinating how the act of making and the result of that can have a grammatical tense.

CP *Why did you start to use colour and paint in the early 1990s when previously you had been content with the relatively drab colouration of found urban materials?*

PB I think a sort of rebelliousness. I want sculpture to retain this absolute sense of action. If I tie something around it, it's the act that holds it. Or if I paint something, the paint kind of seals it as an action. I was looking for a way of bringing together all my previous ways of making which had been quite ad hoc and all over the place. This new way of working involved compressing these concerns into quite simple tactics. And oddly enough, this use of paint involved not worrying about the image of the work. Rather, it was like building up a vocabulary. Whether it was the 'Objects For Objects' series – placing a huge 'thing' on top of a piano, or an ironing board or a television – the act of doing that felt very complete in itself. These acts of tying or throwing, pushing or stuffing could have gone on forever, but at the same time they could be looked on as a closure. I think it was like a form of frustration finding its way into the work and then understanding that as a subject of the work.

CP *But they are also fun – even funny – works.*

PB Yes, although I think making art that makes people laugh is just awful. But I think unintentionally an action can have its comic side. I'm interested in those kinds of unforced moments. Like when you see a bag placed by the local council over an inoperative belisha beacon, but you can still see it flashing inside. I don't know how you better those moments. They are just incredible.

CP *As an artist with an established practice and a certain way of working, how do you face making work that's still relevant, that addresses the present time?*

PB After working for so long as an artist, it's almost like the resources are there and juggling with those resources is enough, and that the struggle to be innovative is a waste of time. But at the same time, I have this endless craving to try things out. So I have this peculiar argument with myself about wanting to use this archive of stuff, but also wanting to retain this sense of unfamiliarity and surprise. The territory is already quite well explored, but there are still things to revisit in a totally different way. As artists, what we're all left with is retreading the 20th century. How do we stand on the shoulders of Duchamp? Really, I think the 20th century is blocked up. Can we ever do Robert Morris's late 1960s works using felt again? Or can we redo Gordon Matta-Clark's work with buildings? And if we want to, how do we do it? I think those things do pose quite challenging questions. In real terms, these questions are often answered as tidied-up versions of those works, spectacular intellectual quotes or huge commissioned pieces. How we deal with innovation now has become a really exciting challenge. It's almost as though art history has got to become personalised and made much more intimate.

Issue 325, April 2010

Fiona Banner

interviewed by Patricia Bickers

Tooth and Claw

PATRICIA BICKERS *My first reaction on walking into the Duveen gallery during the installation was – apart from 'Wow!' – a feeling of confusion, as though I had walked into the wrong museum, perhaps a natural history museum.*

FIONA BANNER I do see these planes as part of nature. The first time I saw a Harrier I was walking in Wales, aged 7. It was a perfect pastoral scene – then bang, it came out of nowhere – and then it was gone. It was totally overwhelming, so beautiful, but such a monster. Both these models are still in active service, so there is a sense that we are implicated in them. They do not really belong to another time, though they might look like dinosaurs. It is ironic that, because fighters and bombers can't fly over built-up areas, they fly over the most peaceful parts of the landscape. Air bases sited next to National Trust properties – it makes a kind of sense. There's a sort of parallel between the idea of the rarefied art object and the military object. When I made *Tornado Nude*, which was shown at Frith St Gallery in 2006, I upended the left wing of a Tornado and inserted it through the floor, so that it spanned two galleries, turning it into this totemic object, an object of worship.

So in thinking about the piece for the Duveen, there was already that relationship between the two worlds of art and the military. They both have a closed circuit of language and reference, and this very intense relationship to objects, the art object and the military object. The whole element of display, and of the trophy, seemed to cross over. As objects these planes are so potent that people behave peculiarly around them, not only because of their horrific function, and possible histories, but also because people find them exciting.

They are seductive. That contradiction has been apparent throughout the process of making this work when people come into contact with them the face-off between an intellectual and an emotional – perhaps primitive – response, is evident. One is to do with language but the other is the very opposite of language. In the case of this installation, the two come together. Planes – military stuff – are displayed all the time in military museums, so there is a way in which they exist as radical sculptures already, but the presentation is always an attempt at heroising or historicising the machines.

PB *Spread-eagled and hanging upside down by its tail fin, framed by the neoclassical architecture of the Duveen Gallery, the Harrier is like an upended version of Leonardo's drawing of 'Vitruvian Man' standing, arms outstretched, within the perfect forms of the square and the circle, which seems doubly appropriate, given his obsession with flight and flying machines.*

FB The proportions of Tate Britain are grand and churchlike but they are related to human scale, whereas, for instance, the Turbine Hall in Tate Modern is an industrial space, it would be like putting planes in a hangar. The neoclassical architecture works exactly because it was never designed to accommodate a piece like this, there is no mammoth loading bay here. The planes had to be broken up into small parts to be brought into the gallery. Though the planes seem to fit perfectly, and to reflect the belligerent symmetry of the space, they feel misplaced. There is a sense in which they are 'exactly wrong'.

PB Harrier and Jaguar, *'nature red in tooth and claw', and yet the Harrier looks strangely vulnerable – the hunter hunted.*

FB Both planes are trophies, but in different ways. The Harrier takes its name from a bird of prey, the harrier hawk. It has feathers painted on it, the cockpit – the eye of the plane – becomes the eye of the bird, the nose cone becomes the beak, and so on. The nose cone hovers inches from the floor. It is still an astonishing object, but there is a forlorn sense about it, like a trussed or captured bird. The Jaguar, on the other hand, lies upside down, supported by the wings and tail fin. It just lies there, belly up – a fallen trophy.

PB *Kenneth Clark wrote quite honestly about being 'seduced' by the nude in art, and to me, while the dull grey Harrier suggests a naked body, the polished Jaguar is redolent of a nude – an odalisque.* Harrier and Jaguar *obviously relates to those works of yours that directly address the*

341

body, albeit the body displaced, as in Tornado Nude *of 2006 or the nude performance pieces.*

FB The planes themselves are built around a human scale, and the forms are naturally anthropomorphic. The Jaguar, stripped and polished, reveals itself to be luxurious and tactile, a fetishised object. Everyone wants to run their finger down its skin. One is adorned and one is stripped, but both planes are naked in a sense, separated from their function, grounded, no payload. They are out of their element, and they have been placed in a critical space where questions will be asked of them.

I have presented both objects in a way that I think they might exist in the subconscious. There is always that tension in making a work between absolute control and the confidence to let objects reveal themselves.

PB *The space shuttle may be a fantastic piece of engineering but it doesn't have the charisma of the fighter, the killing machine.*

FB There is always this paradox. When people look at these things they say, 'God! It's hard to believe that these things are designed for function because they are so beautiful ...'

PB *... when in fact it is the other way round, they are beautiful because they are designed for function.*

FB They are designed absolutely for function, and when you think what that function is ... that reveals something very contradictory about the politics of beauty.

PB *Clark described the nude as a confident form, while the naked form suggests the opposite, and to my mind, at least, there does seem to be a correlation here with the Jaguar and the Harrier.*

FB The Jaguar had a heroic history, while the Harrier was a duck. I looked into the histories of both planes and the Jaguar was active in Desert Storm, in the 1991 Gulf War, saw action in Bosnia and was decommissioned a couple of years ago. I couldn't get any information from the MoD, so it all comes from the public domain, internet chatrooms etc. The Harrier crash-landed on the deck of an aircraft carrier pretty soon after it was upgraded in 2002 – whenever I say that it gives me a really weird flashback to *Top Gun*, the first line is: 'The flight deck of an aircraft carrier ...'

PB *Which takes us back to your 1994 work* Top Gun, *a verbal description of the film from beginning to end.*

FB Yes. In Desert Storm this Jaguar, the xz118, used to be known as

'Buster Gonad with unfeasibly large testicles', after the *Viz* character. It had some nose art including mission symbols and an image of Buster pushing his vast balls along in a wheelbarrow. The nose art was removed after Desert Storm.

PB *It is your largest work to date. And yet, paradoxically, despite their scale, both objects disappear: the grey Harrier absorbs the light, while the shiny Jaguar reflects it. The mirror-like surface of the Jaguar also, of course, implicates the viewer, drawing them into the complex ethical as well as aesthetic dilemma it presents.*

FB The Harrier is the original military grey, the colour of shadows, the colour of the sea, the sky, the non-object, the default colour of camouflage, so in that respect it disappears, but also it becomes part of and naturally echoes the architecture.

The Jaguar is like a giant Airfix model; stripping it has revealed all the structure and also the anomalies in the surface. It feels like a radical object but, at the same time, polishing it makes it into a non-object because it disappears, the reflective surface constantly updates itself, it refuses to be static. And you as the viewer cannot separate yourself from it, you see yourself reflected in the work, there is a literal collapse between subject and object.

PB *Like Brancusi's 'birds in space', the polished surface makes it appear to move, but unlike Brancusi's sculptures, the Harrier and the Jaguar at some level remain themselves. Going back to* Top Gun, *it is strange how things connect – you have just completed a narrative text for a wall drawing for the South London Gallery.*

FB It is a text I began in 1994, and I just finished it last week. It's a description of the film *Black Hawk Down*. It is a cataclysm of language, in a way, the text that gets crushed by its own weight until you can't read it any more. There are various partially erased attempts at description on the wall, revealing the struggle to translate not only from the visual to the verbal, but from history to myth, and myth to history, and the slippage that involves. The shape of the text on the wall, and the image it makes, is like a spilt screen, it has bust out of the frame – it looks a bit like a blown landscape.

The film is all about a hopeless incident involving a Black Hawk helicopter in Somalia, the film came out a few years after the incident so it was all quite close, a sense of reporting history, but the basic situation in Somalia hasn't changed that much – I keep hearing about it, on and off – and that is why the piece finally got made. It wasn't a linear process, as the work itself reveals.

PB   All The World's Fighter Planes, *1999–2009, is a work that was also made over a long period. Does it function something like Gerhard Richter's Atlas of source images?*

FB   I was halfway into this process of accumulating newspaper clippings of fighter planes and helicopters before I actively turned it into a collection. Forming a list of what was in service and what was not was a key element, and researching the nicknames of the planes. Eventually they ended up in a vitrine, not only because it is a traditional way of sealing off a collection, but also because it has these references to a natural history collection. And the names were really important: Eagle, Cheetah, Puma etc. They are presented like a butterfly collection, each plane with its label.

There is a kind of twist when what you think of as being the reference material, part of the back-story to the work, becomes the work. In the end I wanted to represent the patheticness of the images. It is through these tiny transient – ephemeral – newspaper images that we most often see them, and there is this quality that newsprint has, of changing colour over time.

PB   *It is like an old family album with fading photos of deceased relatives.*

FB   Yes. When I finally vitrined this collection in 2008, it was a full archive of all the world's fighter planes. There was an element of it being an 'unedited document', subject to the same process as the 'total/unedited' accounts of films.

PB   *In your studio you have a stacked column of bound copies of* Jane's All The World's Aircraft, *the aviation industry's manual that is annually updated. Is it in the process of becoming a work?*

FB   I got hold of a few of these books 20-odd years ago. I always thought I would use the images as source material for the paintings that I was making then, but I never did. I have spent a lot of time looking at these books and trying to work out what they mean. Recently I started collecting them furiously, so now I have nearly a complete collection dating from 1909 to the present day. I've got 13 to get. The stack is the sculptural equivalent of a list. To me it is the most simple, 'makeable' sculpture. In an odd way the books go back to being to being a tree, or column, or tower – a very literal transition from being a collection, or a library, to a sculpture.

I always enjoyed the name – *Jane's All the World's Aircraft* – it sounds so ridiculous but charming, this super- male compendium with a cute girl's name on it. Like an album that got totally out of hand. For years I didn't realise that it was so called because the book's founder was Fred T Jane. And then there is the Second World War cartoon character, Jane ...

PB *Who was often depicted in nose art.*

FB Indeed.

PB *Talking about how works come to be made,* Mirror Fin, *2006, with its polished mirror-like surface, looks like a kind of vanitas. Did that work lead directly to the Tate piece?*

FB I had that fin for ages before I knew what to do with it, then rather than add to it I decided to subtract, to strip it and polish it. I polished it to within an inch of its life and it revealed a luxurious mirror surface. Then I began to think of it as a self- portrait – not of me but of whoever was looking at it. Somehow the form of it – it is a Harrier wing – the way it slouches in the corner, took on this shape or shadow of a person. Of course it now feels like it was leading up to the Jaguar in *Harrier and Jaguar.*

PB *Is there a connection with the 'Full Stop' sculptures?*

FB I suppose they are like the 'Full Stop' sculptures, they animate you, you animate them.

PB *You can't help saying that they punctuate space.*

FB Those sculptures come from a position of being stuck, that scenario of not knowing where to go – in a different discipline it would be described as writer's block. Moments of breakdown are the key motivating moments.

So the 'Full Stop' sculptures speak of a lack of language, or a lack of content. They are, on the whole, really visceral and physical abstract manifestations of a space where words don't work. And in that way they link to the fighter planes, too.

PB *It is often how scientific breakthroughs are made.*

FB Ultimately, art is an experiment, and it is an experiment that is eventually carried out in public.

PB *Could the work be shown in Iraq?*

FB Maybe it should be shown in Iraq.

PB *Oddly enough, it is more likely that actual nudes, including your own 'Performance Nude' series, would be more controversial. You are also working on another project that involves a Tornado fighter plane with* Locus+ *and* The Great North Run.

FB I have bought a Tornado, which has been stripped and smelted down, and from the metal I will cast a bell.

PB *Turning swords into ploughshares? If so, it is in stark contrast to the Americans, who cast 7.5 tons of scrap steel from the twin towers into the bow of the new warship USS New York, named in memory of 9/11. But I imagine that this simple idea of turning a negative into a positive would be too obvious a reading of this work.*

FB A bell is the simplest object of communication that I could think of. It is a marker of time, and space. The bell is an instrument that doesn't require music, a communicative tool that needs no words. In a sense the bell is an object that exists outside of itself. In a way it's a non-object. A tornado is a phenomenon of nature, a massive centrifugal wind that connects the earth to the clouds, whilst the Tornado aircraft is possibly the most important and vicious European aircraft of the past 30 years.

The idea came out of not being able to sleep. You know as you lie awake and you hear bells or sounds in the distance – it all gets quite abstract. Fairly recently I remembered a bell that my grandfather had in his flat in Birkenhead, a bell that came from a warship – though I didn't know that at the time. He had a lot of military memorabilia, including a clock set into a spitfire propeller. One day I decided, as an act of rebellion, to climb up on his chair and ring that bell. The sound was so exciting and empowering, but scary. Every fluid in my body jangled. I remember being on the edge of some weird physical transformation. The object kind of dissolved into sound. That was my first sculptural encounter. It's funny that, until now, I had never recalled this memory, but then I had never forgotten it either. We still have the bell in the family.

PB *Are you using the Whitechapel Foundry?*

FB No. They won't do it. They are purists. They will only work with bell metal, which is the heaviest and densest of metals, whereas this bell is made out of aluminium, the exact opposite kind of metal, strong and light. But there is one other great bell foundry remaining in the UK, in Loughborough, that is willing to do it. They made the bells at my local church, Shoreditch, which I hear all the time. The actual bell is going to be called *Tornado* and will have the serial number of the airplane written on it.

PB *On a different note, so to speak, I couldn't help noticing on your 'bell' drawing that the clappers on it look like a pair of balls.*

FB You've been reading too many *Viz* comics! There is something hilarious about the clappers, though I call them dongers, myself. You will be able to dong it, too – the bell is so big that it makes a strange physical space.

PB *Publishing, under your own Vanity Publishing imprimatur, is a central part of your practice. Will there be an associated publication to accompany this project?*

FB Yes, it is called *The Naked Ear*. In a way, the whole business of publishing to begin with felt like finding a way to distribute ideas outside of the formal expectations and distribution methods of the gallery. So, works like The Nam came out of that, in 1997, and later the fighter plane books. And then I think publishing moved more and more into the centre of the work, sometimes becoming and 'act' or performance even. The recent ISBN works are one-off published works.

PB *What was so special about the summer of 2009?*

FB I don't know, it got lost ... Last summer I went away and left a piece of paper outside my studio with a stencil of 'Summer 2009' on it. When I returned the paper had got sun burnt, the text appearing on the paper like a kind of bikini of words. This work was subsequently published with its own ISBN number.

PB *Was it photographic paper?*

FB No, just cheap drawing paper.

PB *Like an early Fox-Talbot photographic image on exposed paper before he was able to 'fix' the images?*

FB Exactly. And then I put them in light-safe frames.

PB *Which brings us back to what you were saying at the start, that sometimes works 'make themselves' – literally, in this case, while you were in absentia.*

FB Yes, but it is also about encapsulating time, like those early film text pieces. I suppose they are 'text photographs' of time. Then also they were about mythologising that time, because I published and titled that period of time. *Summer 2009* was also about how do you not make work.

PB *And, of course, you have your own ISBN number, which you depict on the spine of your own body on the cover of your book* Performance Nude. *I suppose it is a self-portrait, or should that be 'autobiography'?*

FB I have my own personal ISBN. I am officially registered as a publication – Fiona Banner. It is a sort of portrait as book – but it is also an open-ended performance. It is not really about branding, but

how works of art act as mirrors. It is also about stories and biography
– the conspiracy of narrative, and how we make and recycle myths.
I was thinking also about copyright and publishing in a jokey, but
serious way. There is a copy of the image in the British Library.

PB *I saw in the courtyard of your studio a marble slab carved with an
ISBN number.*

FB I purchased the ISBN and later published it under the title of
Sleep.

PB *Eros, Thanatos and so to Morpheus, the god of sleep?*

FB There is a rubbing of that stone, part of a series of facsimiles,
which is going to form part of a dossier called Legal Deposit because,
under the 1911 copyright act, you are required to make a deposit of any
legal publication with the British Library.

PB *So you have been interred in the British Library?*

FB It beats Westminster Abbey.

Issue 338, July–August 2010

Jorge Pardo

interviewed by Alex Coles

The Parallax View

ALEX COLES *The interest your generation – Atelier van Lieshout, Tobias Rehberger and Andrea Zittel et al – has in design and architecture is not so much in the disciplines per se, but in how the language developed in these fields enables you to establish a dialogical relationship with the viewer. Would you agree?*

JORGE PARDO So much has been said about my work's relationship to architecture and design but most of it is bullshit. It's not so much that my work contains references to architecture and design but how those references are made to work within an art context that is important.

AC *Exactly. Spending time in your micro-studio in Merida, the Yucatan, and your main studio in the Alhambra district of Los Angeles, has given me an insight into the way you run your practice. One thing that stands out compared with the other practitioners I've visited, where there are often discourse workers – critics and art historians – working alongside archivists in the studio, is your lack of care and caution when it comes to the critical discourse on your work. Given how this completely frames everything you do, isn't it crucial that you grapple with it?*

JP Up to now I've always resisted it, but recently I've been thinking that I actually need to introduce some sort of discursive platform within the studio to add a density to the discussions we have there. But at the same time, to produce both the work and the discourse with which to interpret it, means that you're fencing something in – that you're scared of what people may really say about it.

AC *How would you introduce it? By having a discourse worker on the payroll?*

349

No, that's too creepy. I'll leave that to others. It would be more like having someone conduct occasional research in the studio, perhaps allowing students to pass through it – anything that really opens things up and prompts a richer dialogue between the studio members and myself and the work.

AC *Let's focus on your new project which has been privately commissioned in the Yucatan – no one has heard anything about it yet. Due to be finished at some point next year, and with an as yet undefined programme, the project consists of an interpretation of a ruined hacienda in Techoh, in the jungle about an hour from Merida. The centrepiece is an enormous building with a grand staircase that takes you from the ground floor, which is at the foot of the jungle, and onto its roof, as if you are sitting on top of the jungle. From the roof you have a vantage point onto the six outer buildings and the numerous swimming pools that are dotted around the site. In both scale and ambition the project seems to be on a par with Rirkrit Tiravanija's* The Land, *1998–, and Andrea Zittel's* High Desert Test Sites *project.*

JP In a way. It's all about controlling the frame, and each of us has a different way of doing that. But the essential difference between our projects is that Rirkrit and Andrea strive to establish a dynamic that includes presenting themselves as a part of the picture. As a result, their work, and those projects in particular, are highly emotive and at times even narcissistic. Channelling the point of entry and exit in this way is a deeply problematic gesture as it prescribes where the discourse on the work begins and ends. I think of what I do as my job – a job I very much like and one I get very well remunerated for. I clock in at nine in the morning and clock out at six in the evening. There is no big romance about it. If I need romance, I have a relationship.

AC *As you were making your way down to the Yucatan on this trip in your small airplane you stopped off at Donald Judd's ambitious project at Marfa, Texas. It seems like a very pertinent visit given your current project here.*

JP Rather than modelling what I'm doing on Marfa, I was looking at Marfa and using it as a model to try and understand what I'm doing in Tecoh.

AC *But Marfa is so problematic …*

JP Absolutely. In part, it's a generational thing. To take the artwork out of the world and build high walls around it like Judd did is one of the deadliest moves you can make. One of the things I want to do at Tecoh is to think through the programme – and that means interfacing with a public of some description. My work is nothing without a public and you need a programme to bring them in. What that will be I don't know yet. Judd's relationship to this issue is very complicated. As everyone knows, Marfa came out of his frustrations with the way gallerists and curators controlled the frame and there-fore the viewing conditions of his work, which he felt were seldom optimum. What I particularly like about Marfa is the way Judd kept his autobiography to a minimum. As a result, there are many points of entry and exit from it. If there is one thing I take from Marfa then it is that.

AC *Can you say something about your studio model? Compared with someone like Judd, it is very different.*

JP Judd is someone who had his work fabricated using post-industrial methods. At the same time, he felt the need to isolate himself in the overpowering natural landscape of the desert. The landscape of Marfa became a kind of object in his studio. This happens with me in the Yucatan. The difference is that I'm interested in how my work has some sort of relationship to the place that can be thoroughly embedded in the studio and its output. Judd's sense of place and location was much more puritanical than mine. He left New York and established himself in Marfa because he found the city and the art world too stifling. The Yucatan is not a place of escape for me, but more a place where I can get things done – things that couldn't happen in LA. Once those things are up and running then an audience is crucial.

AC *Where Judd farmed out almost all of his production to specialist fabricators and eventually turned his studio into a design office and archive, you strive to ensure that the production process remains within your studio in order to understand precisely how it operates. This allows you to manipulate it further.*

JP Precisely, it is crucial to my work that all of these skills and pro-cesses are embedded in the studio model. Without them, the work would be very different. After a while, it would become static.

AC *What surprised me about visiting the studio in LA is how you often make major alterations to the work once it has been fabricated – even sometimes at the very last moment just as it is about to be shipped out – and insist on bringing it back to the design process. The changes I witnessed all centred on the three palapas structures used in your*

exhibition at K21 in Düsseldorf in 2009. This is in sharp contrast with
the often tightly planned process designers and architects work through
during the design process – first refining a design, then a prototype, and
only then moving on to fabrication. Using the studio as you do offers a
greater degree of flexibility, and the ingenuity this introduces into the
studio model expands your vocabulary and working methods. So why
do you think Judd chose not to situate the process of fabrication – his
primary means of production – in his studio when he stopped making
them by hand?

JP   Probably both the machines and expertise weren't so widely available to the degree they are now and at the price they are now. At the
time it would have appeared like a more radical gesture to turn your
studio into an office and so completely displace the traditional model
of production by situating it physically somewhere else. That may be
part of it. Because Judd made the gesture back then there seems little
point in repeating it now.

AC   *John Baldessari is often held up as being a crucial player in the*
generation that developed the next crucial studio model in the 1960s, that
of the 'post-studio' artist. Since you have lived and worked in the same city
as Baldessari for decades you must have a take on this.

JP   Baldessari is representative of a particular period and that period
still plays quite large today. Basically, the guys in his generation were
hippies and they really believed that by changing the representation
of their studio model they would change art. Their naivety has led
to the total recuperation of their original project. Where previously
I felt that the notion of the post-studio practitioner was bullshit,
now I think this concept is actually the only thing interesting about
the work. At its core is an attempt to resolve the moral issue of not
making something yourself. If you look at post-studio art from
that generation, it is always about legitimising being an artist who
doesn't actually make things with their hands. If you are in a culture
and place where you are actually surrounded by manual work, that
is much less of an issue and there is no need for such theoretical
gymnastics to legitimise your feelings about it. At root, this version
of the post-studio artist, with all of its hang-ups, is very southern
Californian.

AC   *While being aware of the various ways the issue of the studio plays*
out in art, did architecture and design studio models – whose skills and
technologies you draw from – also have a bearing on this?

JP   No. As my work began to develop it was obvious that I needed to introduce an infrastructure – including new technologies and skills – that would complement it and then eventually push it further. So I started to collect people together who could work in the studio on the understanding that I would direct their particular skills and biases. This happened very gradually and in many ways I wasn't superconscious of it.

AC   *You must have been: for a start, you have someone who has a background programming at NASA.*

JP   In the beginning there was a guy who worked in the studio who was technically brilliant. With his guidance I bought my first machine. I wasn't so much interested in it as a thing but in what it could do – how it could push the studio's capabilities further. Then I hired people who could operate it at a more sophisticated level and interpret what I wanted. Eventually this led to John, who has the NASA background, coming on board. As I say, it was a gradual process.

AC   *In little more than a decade you have built a series of houses: 4166 Sea View Lane in LA, in 1998, The Reyes House in Puerto Rico, 2004–08, your private house in Merida, 2003–08, and the living quarters at the hacienda in Tecoh. What strikes me when I see your buildings – and I think they are by far the most complex and dynamic aspect of your practice – is how they operate like self-reflexive sculptures first and as buildings second.*

JP   In many ways I'm a very traditional practitioner. From the beginning I chose to think of myself as a sculptor – and not even a modern one. Really what I run is an old school-style atelier.

AC   *What is the relationship between the micro-studio you have in Merida and your main studio in LA? After repeated visits to both, it seems like they are in parallax with one another.*

JP   I'd actually like to use the work I'm doing here to enable me to become a part of the fabric of the culture, both fiscally and socially, by opening a real business, a bar like I did in LA – The Mountain, a bar above which I actually had one of my first studios – and later maybe even a restaurant. Basically, I love it down here. If Cuba had been available to me then I might have gone back there, but instead it's the Yucatan.

AC   *Why the need to branch out in the first place? Was LA becoming too limiting?*

JP   No, but having an axis like this can be dynamic. Things produced in the studio in Mexico can serve as a portal through which to view the studio production in LA. Initially I came to the Yucatan over a decade ago and then just kept returning. At that point my principal interest in being here was to figure out why I wanted to be in a place like this so much. Then I began to import the things I usually did when I wasn't here – my work – so that I could be here more. It's as simple as that. Now LA has become the place where I produce things for exhibitions like the recent ones at Friedrich Petzel in New York and Gagosian Gallery in Beverly Hills, whereas Merida is somewhere I produce much larger, more comprehensive things, such as the detailed interiors and furniture for the hacienda.

AC *I've noticed that your vocabulary has expanded since you have been spending more time in the Yucatan – as if subtly registering the rhythms of the culture here. I'm thinking of the large paintings exhibited at K21 in 2009 and also recently at Gagosian Gallery, Beverly Hills. There has always been a 1950s–1960s Verner Panton-type aesthetic underpinning your work, but now it has become even more formally elaborate, florid even. Again, this must be connected to the way the micro-studio is embedded in the culture of fabrication and production of the area.*

JP When you interact with a place in this way it has to have some effect. To not register that the work was made here instead of in LA would seem like an odd thing to do. At the same time, I would never want it to become the single and explicit subject of the work. That would close it down to too great a degree.

AC *First you produced things to go in rooms – such as your early lamps at Thomas Solomon's Garage in 1993 – then the spaces in between these things – the four bedroom suites at Patrick Painter in 1998 – followed by the buildings that contained them – Pier at Munster in 1997 – and now the space between these buildings and, eventually perhaps, an entire mobile community in the Yucatan. With the development of your practice over the past two decades there has been a constant increase in scale. Many of the things you produce are associated with a wealthy lifestyle – a sailing boat for Chicago Museum of Contemporary Art in 1997, a glass house for MOCA, Los Angeles in 1998, a speedboat for Haunch of Venison, Zurich in 2005, designer furniture from your earliest exhibition at Neugerriemschneider in 1994, and further houses like* The Reyes House. *Have you ever interpreted your development in this way – especially now you have much more space and resources in the Yucatan?*

JP Remember that I grew up in a very working-class environment like you and so was always fixated on accessing material things associated with classes above mine. I like rich people's things – I just don't like the forms of etiquette and the general weirdness that so often accompany them. Look, in terms of the Yucatan, my presence here is very simple. I'm here for the same reason Coca-Cola are – to bring the unit cost of production down. The difference is that I actually like it here.

Issue 339, September 2010

Gregor Schneider

interviewed by Gilda Williams

Doubling Doubling

GILDA WILLIAMS *The spaces you create seem to invite secret activities,
taboo occurrences not meant for the public eye – kidnapping, illicit sexual
encounters, murders, imprisonments, torture. This kind of violent secrecy
then seems weirdly connected in your work with the secret or forbidden
places of childhood, and childhood's own set of fears. And then the act of
art-viewing itself seems in your work to become another of these secret,
perhaps shameful moments.*

GREGOR SCHNEIDER Anything is possible in a child's playroom. Usually
a secret is based on the fact that there is no secret. I have created
rooms which are literally secret and inaccessible, but the question is
not whether my rooms are secret, but whether you recognise yourself
in them. In my work it is as though I'm wandering through the
layers and enclosures of my own brain, following the mechanisms of
perception and knowledge.

I'll explain how I work – my work is easy to describe – I place a wall
in front of a wall, a room inside a room. It's as if parts of rooms are
replayed. While an unsuspecting visitor sits on a sofa before a coffee
table, the whole ceiling slowly rises and falls by 5cm well above his
head – so slowly as to be unnoticeable.

My working method is always one of doubling. A double just in
front, just underneath or just inside what already exists, or a plausible
double placed at another site. So there is no invention. What little
I invent is barely noticeable and unobtrusive. Doubling is a gesture
which confirms what already exists in the present, not in the form of
a statement or proof but like evidence in a court of law.

I'm interested in free-wheeling action. My work is an addition –

something extra or superfluous in the sense that it does not state, or express, or refer to anything new. On occasion I have remade a room within another identical room, but always I make an exact duplicate or double of an original room that exists elsewhere – I've just transported it, exactly as it existed, to another place. My working method has not really changed over the years. Most of my rooms may seem imaginary or unreal in a museum or gallery space, but they are just normal, real rooms, or parts of real rooms. And my figures are cast from family members or from my own body, so the figures duplicate an original too.

cw *Why is it so important to you that there is an original? This need for an original that you describe seems surprisingly to connect with the traditional role of art-making as mimesis, of traditional art setting out to mimic reality in detail and as faithfully as possible.*

cs In the end you don't have the question any more – why build a duplicate room? In the end you cannot recognise the built room any more. I once visited a psychiatrist, and he said he couldn't help me understand this need of mine to build a duplicate room. I choose to rebuild a room in order to really analyse the structure of it. By rebuilding a room, I truly understand the room. What is exciting for me is that from the moment I rebuild a room, the original room that lies behind it becomes hidden, and the newly built room is accepted as a room that has always existed. For me, this emptiness is a part of the work. The more one continues to rebuild the same room, the more inexplicable the layers between the original and the copy become. When movement is then introduced into the process – whole rooms begin to turn, or ceilings move up or down – one finds oneself imperceptibly within a completely alienated time frame. I am sitting in an ordinary-looking room that happens to be built inside another room, and I can no longer remember the original. For this reason *Haus u r*,

begun in 1985 and ongoing, the recreation of my childhood home, today has great significance for me as a long-term work. I have actually built room-sculptures in this house that I can no longer access, and therefore can no longer photograph or measure. All that remains is a room number – and a feeling – but you can't really talk about the rooms as if they still existed normally.

The doubling of what already exists legitimates the work in the simplest possible way. This resolves the question of legitimation, or your question about 'what my art does', for example, without giving it great importance. My work is focused in on itself. I don't think much of psychologising artworks. Visitors' reactions are always very different – an example for me would be the 2007 black cube *Cube Hamburg*, which is actually just a simple wooden black box made with a steel structure inside, cloaked in black fabric on the outside. Censored for political reasons in Venice and in Berlin before it was realised in Hamburg, *Cube Hamburg* provoked fears of terrorism in people. But when it was finally built in 2007 everyone just thought it was beautiful – psychological reactions to art could not be more diverse.

As human beings we carry ourselves and our repressed or forgotten memories. I carry my whole house on my back like a snail. Artistically, what my work has done is to shift so-called installation art into recreating actual rooms.

cw *I'm interested in the history of museum access and entrances, and how the transition from everyday life ('the street') to an institutionalised encounter with art ('the museum') has literally been shaped by artists and architects across history. This varies from, say, Schinkel's post-Enlightenment Altes Museum in Berlin of 1823–30, where visitors first pass through a domed, church-like space to be elevated to art-viewing, to Maurizio Cattelan's performance in 1998 at the Museum of Modern Art in New York, where an immense Disneyland-style Picasso figure – a literal embodiment of modern art – actually breaks out of the museum to greet you in person and usher you off the street and into the museum. Your extraordinary 2008 work E N D turns the museum entry into a long, black, disorienting canal – a kind of hellish descent into art, rather than Schinkel's elevating entrance.*

cs *E N D*, which is sited in front of the Museum Abteiberg in Mönchengladbach, is for me an alternative design for a museum – it is not bright, light and white but dark and black. For me, black represents nothingness. Black describes the absence of light. The black funnel was built so that it would absorb the light like a vacuum, from there death can flow. *E N D* developed out of the desire to enter the black cube. It is a pedestrian path which at first goes nowhere, like a wedge shoved into the museum. The gallery rooms housing the collection inside the museum were also painted black, so Hans Hollein's architecture for the building became invisible. In these rooms a different architectural context could be glimpsed, independent from that created by the architect. The blackened rooms in the exhibition made the existing architecture invisible, so I could be free to position rooms, or parts of rooms, outside the frame of the original museum structure.

How a visitor reaches my rooms and how the rooms are built within the museum have varied over time depending on the specific gallery space. *Haus u r* was for me a counter-move to the museum – a compromise, or a refuge, or an alternative to the museum. In 1992 I made an exhibition of empty rooms in a gallery – which puts into question whether it could even be considered an exhibition at all. It took three months to rebuild the whole gallery in replica inside the first. Visitors stood inside an empty room measuring 10 × 5.7 × 3.25m without having any idea that they were standing in a room which existed inside another room, and which was identical to it. On one hand you were completely immersed in this double construction, but at the same time you had no sense that you were in anything other than an ordinary, empty room. Later on, other artists had exhibitions there, but still you could not recognise the real nature of the space you were in.

With *Dead House u r* at Portikus, Frankfurt, in 1997, I completely ignored the usual workings of the interior space. I took possession of the entranceway directly inside the main entrance, where visitors usually walked past the information desk and the toilets to get to the gallery. Instead, visitors found themselves inside *Dead House u r* as soon as they passed through the main glass doors at the front.

In *Haus u r* at the German pavilion at the Venice Biennale in 2001, the modest front door which you might find in an ordinary suburban rented house was framed by the pavilion's threatening Nazi architecture and formed a new entranceway to the pavilion. In 2003, in the old and treasured rotunda of the Hamburger Kunsthalle, I made a replica of Strasse Steindamm in Hamburg, the street infamous for child prostitution and also the site of a mosque said to be frequented by sympathisers of al-Qaeda. 24-hour access to the work was available through a new passageway created by breaking through the Kunsthalle walls; inside, authentic, uncontrolled street life went on round the clock.

Another example would be *517 West 24th Street* of 2003. The title describes an address in Chelsea, Manhattan, but at the time that particular street number was not used as an address, and again I built a room that could be accessed 24 hours a day. The space looked as though it had always been there, like the garages or empty buildings that existed in Chelsea before the galleries arrived. Nothing could remind you that this was once the Barbara Gladstone Gallery. Again, the work was an open, uncontrolled space. In 2003 my *Dead House u r* was constructed for MOCA in Los Angeles and was on view there for a whole year. For this project a new entrance into the museum was knocked through the existing walls, making the artwork accessible from the outside for the whole year.

GW *You are literally breaking down walls between the museum and its public – accessing art becomes an almost criminal act of breaking and entering. Again, you seem to be equating art-viewing with some kind of secretive or criminal activity.*

GS Since 2002 I have been concerning myself more and more with socially relevant topics. But now, as always, I am concerned with rooms that I cannot physically access, which are unknown to me. An example was *4538km* in Museum Dhondt-Dhaenens, Duerle, a replica of the high-security complex of Camp V of Guantanamo Bay. Rebuilding it myself was the only way I could physically come close to the place.

GW *I see you adopting and updating a lot of the ideas from the gothic and horror traditions, such as ideas of doubling, labyrinths, prisons and haunted spaces, which were important in the 19th-century writings of Edgar Allan Poe, Mary Shelley and others, to conjour similar reactions of fear. Your work is especially extraordinary to me in its ability to stage horror in modern spaces – not the usual spooky old house, but the bright lights and clean spaces of modernity, as in your work* 4538km *from 2006.*

GS The exhibition 4583km is about 'white torture', cruel practices endured by prisoners which do not leave any physical marks. The rooms in 4583km show no traces. Everything is highly designed, glossy and homogeneous. The sleek and self-mirroring aesthetic of the bright chambers enhances their destructive, self-referential existence. The metaphors of bright light and clarity, which became a commonplace in the presentation of art in the 20th century, turns in *4583km* to the very opposite. The clarity of the museum room turns to weirdness. It becomes an expression of terror itself. The beloved clean and bright qualities of the museum space, of the white cell or white cube, are transformed into a critical résumé of conventions of cognition. I haven't discharged myself from the history of art, as it were, I have just transferred installation art into real, rebuilt, rooms.

We are thrown back to our own feelings when we enter completely darkened rooms and we become aware of ourselves. We enter dark rooms like the 2010 installation at Sadie Coles gallery very carefully, slowly, unsteadily – we charge the room with powerful emotions ourselves. Every visitor brings with him his own being and his own feelings. I don't think the rooms cause visitors to recall actual personal memories, but each room is so strongly loaded that the visitor believes that he is remembering his own experiences. When we are confronted with our own unknown inner life, we become frightened, we slip into a frightening underworld.

For the twin houses in *Die Familie Schneider* in London in 2004, visitors were instructed to visit the twin East End houses all by themselves, and visit them one after the other. The experience of visiting these two identical houses – with rooms occupied by identical twins, behaving identically in each room – caused unpredictable and extreme responses. Visitors found it especially awful to encounter what seemed the very same room, with the very same people, a second time in the second house, and to re-experience the very same uneasy feelings again. The experience of visiting the first house was deadened when visitors had to go through the second house and live the experience a second time. The twin houses of *Die Familie Schneider* showed how imprecisely we remember the details of places and the singular events that took place there. Some visitors actually ran screaming from certain rooms, even though nothing terrifying had ever actually happened in the house. In the first and in the second house, visitors met identical-looking rooms and people, and they couldn't recognise a difference. This was what was terrifying them.

cw   *I recall some early performance works of yours which were quite wonderful, though not as well known as your installation work – for example one performance in particular where you rode a bicycle through the city streets at night, covered in plaster and looking quite monstrous.*

cs   I also make amateur films, but I never go to the cinema. Given the choice between a cinema or a pub, I'll always choose the pub.

Marina Abramović

interviewed by Iwona Blazwick

The Artist is Present

IWONA BLAZWICK *I want to go back to a moment in Belgrade when it was still part of Yugoslavia. I wanted to start by asking you about a radical move that you made as early as 1970 that was a response, in a way, to the prevailing ideology in communist Yugoslavia of Socialist Realism. You proposed a realism of a different order. The first work I wanted to ask you about with regard to this is called* Cloud and Shadow. *What was the origin of this work?*

MARINA ABRAMOVIĆ I was living in this really political, communist environment and, in 1968, during the student demonstrations, we were given this student cultural centre as a kind of present from Tito so that we could start doing experiments and try to figure out some other way of seeing art. The director of the institute invited us to bring in something that inspired us.

In those days I was painting clouds and I brought in this peanut and just pinned it to the wall and called it *Cloud and Shadow*. Another person brought the door of his own studio because there is something inspiring about opening the door and going in to make the work. Somebody else brought his own girlfriend, saying: 'I always make love to my girlfriend before I make the work.' And so on. It was a really important show. It was in 1971 and the title was 'Little Things'.

IB *I know you were part of a group – another member, for example, actually taped you to the floor …*

MA Yes.

IB *This was, for me, a kind of paradigmatic moment where you see the idea of the artist's body as both subject and object. Another aspect of your work which comes out over and over again is the idea of removal, a kind of freeing or evacuation of something, for example in* Freeing the Horizon. *Can you tell me something about this work?*

MA First of all, I really felt like I was in the wrong place at the wrong time. I felt really suffocated. I had an idea that I'd like to travel – though I could not actually go anywhere – and so I would take photographs of different parts of Belgrade and then make slides and literally paint the buildings away – freeing the horizon – so that I could see as far as the eye could see.

At the time, in 1973, I made an installation with these works using eight slide projectors to create a 360° panorama of Belgrade without buildings and the most striking thing is that, 35 years later, because of the American bombing of Belgrade some of these houses actually no longer exist.

IB The Airport *is also, perhaps, a work about a kind of leaving, a fantasy about potential destinations.*

MA This work also took place at the Culture Centre. There were six artists – I was the only woman – and we were there every day, trying to work. One of the spaces was this big hall where I created this kind of utopian airport. I put speakers with the sound of my voice, very cold and very distant, saying: 'Please, all the passengers of the Jat (the Yugoslav airline) airline go immediately to Gate 345 (in those days we only had three gates, now we have seven) the plane is going immediately to Tokyo, Hong Kong and Bangkok.' Every three or four minutes this voice would remind you that you could go on this imaginary journey.

IB *We're talking now about the realm of the conceptual. I think that, throughout your work, this idea of immateriality has been a very important aspect of what you do. Having left Yugoslavia – now you are travelling – you moved to the Australian desert near Ayers Rock. Can you talk a little bit about the experience of being there, and about living in a non-western kind of society or community?*

MA When I left Yugoslavia I was 29 years old and I literally escaped. Until then, all my performances were very difficult and physically and mentally consuming. I had to do everything before ten in the evening because by ten I had to be home because of my mother's iron discipline. When I eventually escaped she went to the police to announce my disappearance, and the police asked, 'How old is she?' and when she said, '29', they said: 'It's about time.'

First I went to Amsterdam and there I met Ulay, the person with whom I made performances for 12 years. The end of the 1970s was somehow the end of performance art – the galleries, the dealers, the museums – they just could not actually deal with something that was so immaterial like performance. There was nothing to sell and there was real pressure on artists in those times to create objects, to create paintings, to create – you know – things. I and Ulay didn't feel like going back to the studio to make anything two-dimensional, so we decided to travel. Buddha went to the desert. Mohammed went to the desert. Moses went to the desert. Jesus Christ went to the desert. They all went as a nobody and came back as a somebody – so we were definitely thinking it had to be the desert.

We went to the Thar Desert, to the Sahara Desert, to the Gobi Desert and to the Great Australian Desert. We spent one year living with the Aborigines – literally without any money – with different tribes and moving through Central Australia and the Northern Territory. This was the most important and life-changing experience I ever had. First of all, we were confronted with a nomadic culture that doesn't have any possessions, they just move as the songlines move – from place to place. Theirs was the most immaterial culture I have ever encountered and they influenced our way of thinking about performance.

IB *One thing that is striking is that it seems to coincide with an impulse in other artists at that time towards the idea of land art – not only going to the desert to escape the white cube but also to escape certain aspects of western society. The other aspect, I think, was the allure of alternative ways of being, of other societies, which seemed to coincide with a kind of anxiety about the affluence of consumerist society and so forth – the Beatles going to India, for example. How much did you feel that you were part of a bigger impulse?*

MA I don't know. Coming out of Yugoslavia I did not know about the Beatles or the Rolling Stones – I was listening to Bach, Mozart, Brahms or Russian composers, so I wasn't really aware of this impulse. To me, going to the desert was really about looking for ways to take performance beyond physical limits. At the end of the 1970s, my generation of performance artists – from Chris Burden and Dennis Oppenheim to Gina Pane – had stopped performing. They were making objects or dealing with architecture or painting, but not performance, whereas I felt that performance was far from over. I was looking for different ways to use the body and to push it beyond the limits of our culture.

IB   *To get back to the idea of 'nomadism', you were living in Amsterdam in a van – in fact you even made works with this van, did you not?*

MA   Yes. It was not like an American luxury camper van, it looked like a sardine can. It was a French police type of vehicle with no heating, no bathroom, nothing. I mean it was just a box – and second-hand at that. You could hardly live from performance work, but by living in the van we didn't have to pay electricity and we didn't have to pay rent, and if we needed gasoline we just cadged it with an empty mineral bottle from the gasoline station – we lived in the countryside and I knew every bathroom in every gasoline station in Europe where we could wash. It was really a happy life because we didn't compromise. We were taking risks not just in the work but also in our way of life.

IB   *Also, I suppose, you could never predict what was going to happen the next day or who you would encounter – so that must have been part of the risk-taking.*

MA   Totally. After we sold the vehicle at the end of the 1970s to go to the Australian desert, we completely lost track of it. Then, about ten years later, we were approached by Paul Schimmel, the curator of MOCA, Los Angeles, who was working on the exhibition called 'Out of Actions'. He wanted to include relics left over from performance art, like the golden nails Chris Burden used when he crucified himself on the Volkswagen, and he came to see us in Amsterdam and asked, 'Where is that vehicle?'. We didn't know, but he put in some work and traced it to the south of France – somebody was keeping chickens inside it. So we had to clean this car of chicken shit – which is very difficult – and bring it to Los Angeles. When I had my retrospective at MOMA last year, this vehicle was there and its arrival was very emotional for me. Our entire life was captured in this piece.

IB   *A very profound aspect of your practice is the idea of time and duration. I wanted to ask you about the shortest piece and the longest piece. The shortest piece – I believe it lasts four minutes – is* Rest Energy, *first performed with Ulay in Ireland in 1980.*

MA   Yes. I have made two pieces in my life that were most dangerous for me. The best pieces are the ones where I'm not in control. In the one called *Rhythm 0* the public was in control – they could do whatever they wanted with me. The other one was this piece which was based on trust – if either of us lost control, the arrow would go straight into my heart. It was simple. We held the bow and arrow with our weight until we really could not hold it any more. We had to release at the same time.

IB Rhythm 10 *is also a very simple work where you ended up cutting yourself quite seriously. This idea of risk – of pain – has been a consistent element in your work. What do you think motivated that work?*

MA This was very different because I was not risking my life. In *Rhythm 0* there was a pistol with a bullet and people could have used it if they wanted to, and in *Rest Energy* there was the bow and arrow.

Dealing with pain is an interesting subject. We are always afraid of pain, of dying, of suffering – the main concerns of human beings, basically. Many artists deal with this theme in different ways. I was always interested in how various ancient peoples worked with this in ceremonies – the ritualisation of inflicting a large amount of pain on their bodies – even to the extent of being clinically dead. The reason for this is not to do with masochism. The reason is very simple: to confront pain by taking this kind of risk in order to liberate yourself from fear and, at the same time, to jump to another state of consciousness. That is a really important thing.

I could never do this in my own private life, but if I stage the situation in front of an audience – and the staged situation is dangerous – I can take energy from the audience and use it to give me strength to go through that experience. So I become like your mirror. If I can do this in my life, you can do it in yours, and through that I liberate myself from fear.

IB *One thing I hadn't understood is that something as simple as sitting very still for a long period not only involves endurance but is also very painful.* The Artist is Present, *which you made for your retrospective at* MOMA *in New York in 2010, is your longest piece, is it not?*

MA One other piece was the same length – 'Walking the Wall'. Ulay and I walked the Great Wall of China from two different ends to say goodbye. But in that piece the audience was not present, which is a very different matter. For the MOMA piece the audience was present and the situation was extremely simple. In the first two months I had a table and two chairs, then in the last month I actually removed the table and left just the two chairs, and that was it. It was a very simple structure. The idea was to sit motionless during the entire time that the museum was open – seven hours a day and ten hours on Fridays. The museum only closed one day a week – Tuesdays – and that was my free day.

IB *At the beginning, I think, there were the expected number of people*

but over the final weekend there were 20,000 participants – it was
extraordinary. There were 850,000 participants in total. It seems that,
given a lived reality which is often virtual – Facebook, social networking
– and the frenetic nature of everyday life, this idea of actually connecting
with somebody, and being asked to do something as simple as sit and look
at the face of a complete stranger, somehow really spoke to people.

MA You know, to me the most important thing is to do with how the
public is always perceived as a group. We never perceive the public
as individuals. This was an opportunity where everybody could have
a one-to-one experience with an artist, and this really makes a huge
difference.

It was also very important for me to deal with the museum atrium
which is really the most difficult space because it is in permanent
transition – people are moving from ground floor to second floor to
different types of galleries, and there is also a library and a coffee
shop – so there is nothing but a kind of hectic feeling of movement.
It is like a tornado. But in every tornado there is a stillness in the
middle – the eye of the tornado – so I tried to make this eye of the
tornado the stillness of that moment of sitting.

IB *It must require a lot of training – I mean, all of your performances*
require a great deal of preparation even though they look intuitive and
spontaneous – but to be able to endure sitting in a chair for seven hours
must be tremendously punishing on the body.

MA When you do any kind of artwork – or work generally – I think you
have to put in an enormous amount of preparation, but the results
have to look effortless. That's the magic of it. It really looks like – well,
here I am just sitting, what is the big deal? But it was hell, literally
hell. If you just try it for yourself, sitting motionless for three hours,
you will find that already after an hour and a half your muscles will
want a change and you get this incredibly painful feeling that in one
second you are going to lose consciousness. And yet you still don't
move – willpower is very important – you keep still, not moving, and
that's when something really interesting happens. When the body
understands that you're not going to move, the pain disappears and
you really start having an out-of-body experience, which sounds
mystical but it's true. You leave the body. But then the pain returns
again, but you just have to keep going. For two years I trained for
this piece, like NASA trains astronauts. You can be trained physically,
just like for the Olympics, but if you don't have the determination

or willpower you can't do it. The mind is the biggest obstacle to everything.

The idea of this piece was to be in the present – absolutely in the moment. Not in the past which has happened. Not in the future that hasn't happened, but just in that moment. Your mind doesn't go anywhere else. You are in the here and now – and not only the here and now in yourself, but also in the person sitting opposite you. It was amazing what happened to people. They came to sit opposite me – I didn't limit the time – and they would become anxious, or they would become angry because they had had to wait for a long time or they would become suspicious or timid or self-conscious. Then, after a while – maybe six, seven, eight minutes – they would enter this zone where sound disappears, I disappear. They become the mirrors of themselves. And these incredible emotions surfaced – I heard so many people crying. The last month was the most difficult one, when there were just two chairs and nothing else.

IB *Why did you remove the table?*

MA There were many people in wheelchairs so, to accommodate the people in wheelchairs they would remove the chair. In the middle of looking at this person, I figured out that I didn't even know if he had legs or not. I just saw his eyes. I felt that I didn't need the table, I didn't need the structure. So I decided on 1 May to remove the table. But the strangest thing was that, after removing it, I still saw it like a grey shadow. It was as though I was going crazy, but I realised that when you are in stillness an entire parallel world opens up to you which is normally invisible because we're always moving. When you get into this stillness you start feeling things you could never imagine feeling normally. And the public started feeling what I was feeling. Why was it so emotional? I can't explain it to you. You have to experience it.

IB *Has MOMA captured the anecdotal reaction of the sitters?*

MA One of the most moving experiences for me was when the museum guards came on their free day to wait in line to sit. The longest time a person sat there was seven hours, and then he came and sat another 21 hours. There was also a group of 75 people who sat more than 15 or 20 times with me. There was a group of people who met once a month. There were people who didn't have any idea what is a performance, who don't even like performance, who came to the museum like tourists come to New York – just to see it – and something clicked for them and that really matters to me. You know performance really has this kind of power to change not just the performer's life but also the one who is witnessing the performance. I truly believe that only long durational work has that kind of power because if you do a performance for one hour, two hours, five hours – you can still pretend. You can still can act. You can still be somebody else. But if you do something for three months, it's life itself.

IB *I suppose also the structure of the two chairs – the one facing the other – one could read it as being in some way sculptural or domestic, but one can also read it as a mirror of psychoanalysis. Does that interest you, the idea of a therapeutic encounter?*

MA You know, performance can be seen in so many different ways. Of course there's a therapeutic element. I always believe that a good work of art has to have many layers of meaning. It can be political. It can be social. It can be spiritual. It can be just a sculpture. There are so many different ways that it can be taken by every person who experiences it.

I also believe the context in which you do something is very important. If you bake bread, however good it is, you're still the baker who makes the bread, but if you bake this bread in the gallery – like Joseph Beuys – it becomes art because the context has changed. So I really believe what I'm doing is art.

Finally – after 716 hours of performing – they removed the chairs and there were just little crosses on the floor that marked the spot. Later on people came and started kissing the floor as though they were visiting Lourdes – I don't know what happened. It was overwhelming.

IB *I want to talk about some of the very sophisticated aesthetic strategies that you use. Your use of systems and seriality, for example, in works like* Rhythm 0, Rhythm 1, Rhythm 2, Rhythm 3. *At the same time there is an absurdist element and a poetic element, especially in some of the titles. For example,* Nightsea Crossing *is a work which I would say was a prelude, perhaps, to* The Artist is Present *where you and Ulay sit opposite each other across a table. In* Boat Emptying/Stream Entering *there is this idea of symmetry and of a negative and a positive. Then there is* The House with the Ocean View, *a performance piece that you made at the Sean Kelly Gallery in which you lived inside the gallery, an idea that relates to* The Artist is Present, *whose title is taken from the convention of the private view card.*

MA For me the title is incredibly important. I always believe that when an artist puts *Untitled* on a work, it is like leaving children without names. I don't know how you can do that. I really love titles. *The Nightsea Crossing* title was a really important title. It is not about crossing the sea by night, but about a subconscious crossing.

Boat Emptying/Stream Entering was made after 'Walking the Wall'. It was like ending one period of my life. It is like when you have so much luggage on the boat that it will sink. What you have to do is throw everything out and only then can the boat take you to safety. So that was really a way of marking the change in my life and my work.

The House with the Ocean View was this long durational performance of 12 days without eating, just observing the audience and living in the gallery. Of course there was no ocean – the ocean was the public. That was the idea. *The Artist is Present* is literally like when, in the old days, you had an opening of a painting show and it would say that the artist would be present for the opening. I really was there for three months. I was present.

IB *The use of colour is very important to you, particularly in a number of tableaux that you made in the 1980s. Could you say something about that?*

MA In the early works – in the early 1970s – everything was black and white. In the 1980s we paid a lot of attention to colours and the meaning of colours. We studied the Vedic square and how colour changed you. We had this experiment: we took seven pairs of white trousers and seven pairs of white shirts and we just coloured them in the washing machine because it was too expensive to buy new ones. Then we would wear the bright yellow one month, the bright green one month, the bright red one month – all the spectrum of colours – and see how our behaviour changed. It was very interesting. Yellow is the colour that really works on your nervous system, you become completely nervous and crazy – that's why they use it in advertising. Blue calms you down. Green – everybody talks to you when you wear it because it's a communication colour. And so on.

Then we went much deeper into a sense of colour. In Modus Vivendi: Pietà, for example, Ulay is in white and I'm in red. In Chinese mythology – ancient Chinese mythology – the world was created by a red drop of menstrual blood and a white drop of sperm. We used this element in our work for a long time – the white and red.

In *The Artist is Present* I wore three colours. During the first month it was blue, the second month red and the last month white. All three colours have to do with energy – I really needed to calm down to get into the piece with the blue. By the middle of the piece in April the energy level was so low that I had to get energy back, and so it was red. White was very much to do with a complete purifying feeling at the end of the performance.

IB *Geometry is another unexpected aspect of the work. Could you talk about your use of the star, in particular in* Lips of Thomas*?*

MA I think that geometry, generally, was very much in our work, especially the early work. It was very important to me how things looked in a space and how they worked with the architecture – not just outside but inside with the architecture of the body.

The five-point star I cut on my stomach when I was in Yugoslavia was not the Jewish star, it was the communist star. I was born with that star, it was on my birth certificate. It was on every book at school. It was in every celebration of communism. It really was something that I felt that I wanted to get rid of – that symbol.

I cut two stars on my body, though you just see one. The first star I cut had two points at the top, which is actually the negative aspect of the pentagram. Twenty-five years later I cut another star with one point at the top. Somehow these two stars neutralised each other and so I was free from the concept.

In another early work, with Ulay, *Duration Space*, which we made for the 1976 Venice Biennale, we used our bodies in a very minimal kind of way, though it was still in an architectural way. It deals with two bodies passing and colliding with each other. The idea was how two energies – male and female – can come back together and make something that we called 'Dead Self'.

We were also invited to make a performance at the Bologna Modern Art museum, and we had the idea of the artist as a 'door' because, if there were no artists, there would be no museum. So we became a door, and when people entered they had to make a choice: left or right. We were supposed to be there for six hours but after three hours the police arrived and asked us for our documents, but as we really were naked we had no passports to show them.

IB *That symmetry is seen again in* Light/Dark *of 1977.*

MA We only used one hand and we slapped each other as fast as we could – slow at first, then as fast as we could until we could not increase the rhythm any more. Again, it is a very simple structure using the body as a drumming element with amplified sound.

IB *Another iconic piece that again has to do with this idea of symmetry is* Relation in Time, *also of 1977.*

MA This is an important piece because we had 16 hours without the public and then, when we were at the end of our energy, the public arrived. We took energy from the public to enable us to sit one more hour – making it 17 hours in all. Normally we would take a performance to the point of exhaustion and then it would be finished, but here we actually got to the point of exhaustion before the work was completed.

IB *Do you want to say something about the work to do with the levitation of Saint Teresa in this context?*

MA I love this piece. I just found, in the north of Spain last year, the abandoned kitchen of a monastery where the nuns made food for 8,000 orphan children. It was abandoned in the 1970s. I decided that I wanted to make this levitation dedicated to Saint Teresa of Ávila because I was fascinated by her personality. I read her memoirs and many people in her time believed that she really could levitate. In her diary she talked about levitation. One day she levitated many, many times in her church while praying to Jesus. When she went home she was very hungry and wanted to make soup before taking a rest because she could not stand any more of this levitation. But, in the middle of making this soup, she found that she could not control the divine power which took hold of her again and she was so incredibly angry because she couldn't finish her soup! I love this disadvantage of her divine power.

IB *One of the key aspects of performance is that its longevity depends entirely on documentation. You have made a very important decision, I think, about the way that your work is documented. Can you say something about the filming of this particular work?*

MA Up to 1975 I never filmed my work. There was no video at that time, especially not in Yugoslavia, nor was there enough money for any 16mm or Super 8 camera – nothing. So the only documentation was done with a simple camera. But in 1975 I went to Copenhagen to do the performance *Art must be beautiful, Artist must be beautiful* and there was the possibility for the first time of making a video. It was the big new technology, but I didn't know anything about it so I asked the man who was making the video to record the performance without giving him any instructions at all.

After the performance I was very eager to go to the backroom to see the material, but when I saw what he had filmed I was incredibly upset. He had used every possibility of the camera – zooming in, zooming out, looking left and right – it was not a document of my work. I asked him on the spot to delete his tape immediately and he did. Then I said to him: 'OK, I'm going to do the entire performance right away, in this backroom, with only the camera – the camera is my public at this moment – you turn on the camera and please go out and smoke a cigarette.' He did.

From that point on I understood the importance of documentation, and the importance of giving clear instructions to the photographer or cameraman as to how you want to present your work after the work is no longer performed. So this was a really big lesson.

IB *Bruce Nauman came to the same conclusion, as did a number of other artists who realised that it was not about making cinema, that it was not about theatre, and that it was not about drama – it was about making a completely indexical record of a performance or event.*

MA It is not about editing and cutting and all that stuff. It is just one forward shot – and, of course, in 1970s video it is always grey and boring. In the 1970s they made great performance work but the lousy documentation makes it look like shit. Whereas you now have great documentation of very bad artworks. The technology has developed so well that everything looks glamorous. But, when you're talking about performance art, if possible you should always show the video material because it is still so much closer to reality than slides. A frozen slide is just mystification.

IB *Which leads into the question of re-performance and whether it is possible to restage a work – something we actually did at the Whitechapel Gallery a few years ago in 'A Short History of Performance, Parts 1 and 2'. What does it mean to show a work that was conceived and made 30 years ago in the here and now? You took this as the subject of a work called* Seven Easy Pieces *at the Guggenheim Museum in 2005 in which you actually re-enacted iconic works of art by other artists as well as your own.*

MA First of all, the reason why I did that was that I was so angry. Oh, God, was I angry! You know in all these years performance was nobody's territory. Photography and video had been nobody's territory but then they became mainstream art, but not performance. But now everybody – I mean everybody – was taking from perfor-mance. Even Lady Gaga – you name it – and without really referring to the original material. If you take a piece of music, or you take stuff from a book, you have to pay for it. And you have to acknowledge the composer and the author. But not with a performer. I was so angry with young critics who praised young performance artists doing things as though it was the first time ever when it was done so many times before that. My generation has really been damaged by that.

I felt that, as my generation of artists is almost not performing any more for different reasons – and I respect that – I felt it my duty to put things straight. This was my idea: to teach a lesson. And so I made this performance called *Seven Easy Pieces*. It was, of course, very metaphorical – *Seven Easy Pieces* was not at all easy to do. But I asked the artists – those who were living – for permission. In the case of those who were not alive, I paid their foundation for the permission. Basically, I respected the entire structure of each performance. The only change I made was the time I gave to each piece.

The first piece was *Body Pressure*, which was interesting because Bruce Nauman never performed this piece himself. He only had piles of paper which you could take home where you could read the instructions and perform it if you wanted. But I actually recorded the instructions and for seven hours I performed the piece.

The second piece I performed was Vito Acconci's *Seedbed*, where he masturbates under the floor of the gallery. This one is very complicated because men produce sperm but a woman produces something else.

The next piece was Valie Export's 'Genital Panic Machine' – an open vagina with a machine gun. It is a timeless piece that can function in different periods, and I was really happy that she gave me permission to perform it.

The Gina Pane piece was very difficult. Her estate gave me permission to perform only part of the piece, the part where she lay on the candle bed. It was originally 28 minutes but I decided that I would perform it for seven hours.

The next one was Joseph Beuys talking about art to that hare. This was very complicated because his wife told the Guggenheim that she would never give permission. But if somebody says 'no' to me, it is just the beginning. So I took my suitcase and I went to Düsseldorf in the middle of the winter and rang her bell. She opened the door and she said to me, 'Bravo, but my decision is still "no". But you can have coffee.' And I said to her, 'But can I have tea?' Five hours later I had permission. So that was *Seven Easy Pieces*.

Then came my retrospective. I thought it was very important that I choose five major historical pieces to be re-performed by young artists for the entire three months' duration of this exhibition. There were 29 artists who re-performed these works in two and a half hour shifts – *Point of Contact*, *Imponderabilia*, *Nude with Skeleton*, *Luminosity* and *Relation in Time*. I didn't give permission for any piece that would endanger lives or would injure the person.

Many artists are absolutely against the re-performance of works. But I'm very willing to give permission for re- performance. Performance is a live form of art, a time-based art, and if it is not re-performed – even without the original artist's charisma, even if the piece is changed – it is still better than mere documentation in books or video.

IB *Do you acquire the rights to restage a performance piece or do you acquire the documentation for it? You have cited a number of artists as offering precedents as to how a collecting institution can acquire a work of performance – Yves Klein, for example.*

MA One of the most beautiful works by Yves Klein in the 1950s was when, on a bridge of the Seine, he sold *The Artist's Sensibility* to his collector. The collector signed a cheque and gave it to the artist, and the artist took a match and burned the cheque and let the ashes fall into the river. So there was a kind of immaterial transmission of the artist's sensibility. This was a wonderful act, I think.

The second one is Gino de Dominicis who, I think, is a really important artist. I knew him in the 1970s, when he sold *Invisible Piece* to a collector. This was a really interesting event that was very important to me in thinking about art as an immaterial kind of thing: the collector gave Gino the cheque and thought no more about it but, three weeks later, the collector got a phone call from a well-known transport company saying that they were going to deliver the invisible piece to him. He was very surprised, and asked when. They replied: 'Next Wednesday at ten o'clock.' So, the next Wednesday at ten o'clock the truck arrived with six people in grey coats and white gloves carrying *Invisible Piece*. When the collector opened the door they asked him, 'Where are you going to put it?' The collector said, 'Next to the window.' They said: 'No, no, no. It is very sensitive to light. You have to put it somewhere else.' And that was it. And now, so many years later, I went to see his retrospective at the MAXXI in Rome and the collector had lent *Invisible Piece* to the museum. I almost stepped on it. There was just a piece of tape on the floor and that was *Invisible Piece* right there.

Tino Sehgal is the only artist – he was an economist, by the way, before becoming an artist – that I know who has actually figured out a way of selling re-performing rights to a museum. He does it by whispering the instructions into the ear of the curator. The curator has to memorise it and if he leaves his job, he has to whisper it to somebody else. And this is how he sells his work. There have never been any photographs of his work.

Performing rights – that is the only way. But then you have to change the entire mentality of the collectors because, you know, the collector buys a painting, he puts a nail in the wall, he hangs his painting and he has it forever. But when you buy the rights to a work you have to choose the right person to re-perform it, and each time you have to pay for it.

IB *Can we talk about a future project, which is the Institute of Performance that you're conceiving in America – in New York?*

MA Right now there is a hole in the roof that I'm going to repair from the money from the work we hope to sell from the show at the Lisson Gallery. The money will all go into this place. It is in Hudson, two hours from New York. It's an old theatre built in 1936 – it can hold about 1,500 people. It later became a movie theatre where they showed regular movies, then it became a storage deposit for an antique shop, and now I've got it.

At this point of my life, I want to leave a legacy of my life. I want to make a centre for performing art, but also a centre for the preservation of performing art. This centre will address different types of art – not just performance as I am doing – but also dance and theatre and opera and music and video and film. The difference between this kind of performing centre and any other one will be that it will concentrate on long-durational work – nothing less than six hours – because I truly believe that long-durational work is the most important type of work right now. Because of the way we live, our lives are getting shorter and shorter, so art has to get longer and longer.

We also have to educate the public to see performance work that is long-durational, to experience something that is 20 hours long and where nothing much changes – maybe just the light. So that's the legacy.

This is an edited version of an interview which took place at the Starr Auditorium, Tate Modern on 16 October 2010. Published Issue 349, September 2011.

Alfredo Jaar

interviewed by Kathy Battista

Models of Thinking

KATHY BATTISTA *Could you describe your work for the Liverpool Biennial?*
ALFREDO JAAR I have created a new piece titled *The Marx Lounge* and
it is sited in a large empty storefront in the centre of Liverpool.
There are too many of these around, it is quite depressing and sad.
It consists of a salon painted all red, including a red carpet, black
sofas and a large 8 × 2m table that contains 1,500 books by Marx as
well as subsequent writers, theorists and philosophers. As you know,
there has been a renewed interest in Marx because of the financial
crisis. I wanted to offer a larger audience the extraordinary amount
of knowledge that has been created in the past few decades. I believe
an intellectual revolution has been going on for the past 20 or 30
years, but I also see an extraordinary gap between this intellectual
revolution and the real world. So I wanted to ask, why is this? Is this
gap a symptom of the difficulty of apprehending this new knowledge,
or is it in the interests of the status quo to keep it the way it is? I am
afraid it is a little of both. Besides hundreds of books by and about
Marx, you will find political theorists and philosophers like Žižek,
Hall, Rancière, Butler, Laclau, Mouffe, Jameson, Bourdieu, Fanon etc.
For me these writings offer us models of thinking the world. And that
is what I try do as an artist – I create models of thinking. I view *The
Marx Lounge* as a space of resistance, or as David Harvey would call it,
a space of hope.
KB *It resembles an architectural model of a city.*
AJ I was thinking about an architectural model, what might the
architecture of knowledge look like. But in the end it is a reading
room, a very focused library.

KB *Do you think your work is most appropriate in a biennale context rather than a commercial setting?*

AJ I consider myself an architect making art and most of my practice is site-specific. In the past 30 years I have divided my work into three distinct areas and only one-third of my practice takes place in museums, galleries, what we call the art world. But because of its extraordinary insularity – it is a small world in which we mostly talk to each other – I decided to get out.

That is why in another third of my practice I create public interventions. These are actions, performances, events that take place in places and communities far removed from the art world where the audience is not well-versed in the vocabulary of contemporary art. So you have to create, to communicate using a new language, a different language. I like the challenge of talking to a different type of audience.

The third part is teaching. I give talks and direct seminars where I share my experience with the new generation from whom I learn enormously. It is a real exchange. I feel complete, as a professional but also as a human being, only by doing these three things at the same time. The Liverpool Biennial context, like most biennales, has the potential to go beyond our little art world and reach larger audiences, and it has a strong education component.

KB *The three categories implode in* The Marx Lounge.

AJ Absolutely. This is clearly a work where these three categories/ audiences overlap in the most perfect way.

KB *Was the work acquired by the Liverpool Biennial or by Tate?*

AJ The economics of my strategy have always been the same with all institutions. Liverpool Biennial paid for the production of the work but I own it. If it ever gets sold, I will return the production money to the Biennial. This way they can finance another work by another artist. Money must circulate.

In the case of this particular production, because there are three copies of each title, in a way I potentially own three Marx Lounges and what I do with these three sets afterwards is a fundamental aspect of the piece.

Because of the reckless funding cuts being implemented now in the UK, there is a great deal of resistance but also some initiatives in England to do with creating places of study. In Liverpool there is a group of intellectuals trying to create the Free Liverpool University.

I am planning to possibly donate one of the Marx Lounges to this new young institution, where they will hopefully recreate it and make it grow – a living library. For the other two sets we are looking at poor, underfunded libraries in marginalised communities.

KB *Is there a special arrangement for the books, such as alphabetical or chronological?*

AJ What I did was try to place Marx in all areas of the table and then organise some 'short circuits' between titles and authors, suggesting different connections or oppositions. We also included the *Communist Manifesto* in all the languages of the so- called 'minority populations' of Liverpool.

Parallel to *The Marx Lounge* I have organised a series of public discussions, encounters between a political theorist and someone from the art world. David Harvey and Ivet Curlin participated in the first dialogue. Then we had Chantal Mouffe and Mark Sealy.

I also created an advertising campaign in Liverpool streets with posters and billboards that say 'Culture = Capital' and announcing *The Marx Lounge*. I believe we must insist that culture is the real capital. If the state can produce money to reward irresponsible, criminal banking, then it can and should produce money to create culture. A living culture is one that creates. If the UK has any visibility in the world it is thanks to its artists and intellectuals and cultural institutions and universities. It is not because of its banks.

KB *Do you think this relates to your Documenta piece?*

AJ I think all my works relate to each other one way or another. The Documenta piece focused on the blindness of our society. Here in a way it is a reverse situation – I am confronting the audience with this huge body of knowledge that exists, but that we do not know how to use. This is the dilemma we face as cultural producers or artists – we speculate, we dream, we invent, we create and then there is this huge extraordinary gap between our productions and the real world. How do we close that gap?

KB *How does your background in architecture play a role in your art practice?*

AJ Architecture is a tool that I apply in every single work to articulate the ideas of the project. For me a project is foremost a thinking process. Perhaps 90% of the process is about thinking and the last 10% is about articulating that into a visible work. That is when I use the language of architecture – scale, light, movement, space, tension.

379

As an architect, I look at a site not only as a physical space but most importantly as a political space, as a social space, as a cultural space.

KB *Was studying architecture in Pinochet's Chile part of a dream of transforming society?*

AJ I always wanted to be an artist. My father thought it was a very bad idea. So the compromise was architecture because he thought I might be able to make a living that way. My father never in his wildest dreams imagined that I could make a living as an artist and, in Chile 30 years ago, I didn't believe it either. But I feel extremely lucky that I never studied art and became an architect instead. In a way I don't know what art is. And this pushes me in creative directions trying to invent it. Working with students I have realised how they have been inserted into a preset framework of thinking about what art is. They tend to naturally follow certain existing aesthetic formulas.

I have this extraordinary freedom. If you look at my work of the past ten years you might think these are 100 works by 100 different artists. I am not seeking to have a branded look. I am more interested in developing and articulating ideas. Of course that makes the work quite difficult in terms of its marketability.

KB *Yet you do work with commercial galleries.*

AJ I have a very slow relationship with galleries in that I show with them every three, four or five years. It is not the normal commercial rhythm and this has to do with the slowness of my process and perhaps my resistance to that world. I think I have always had a schizophrenic relationship to the art world. But I do not reject that audience at all. It represents a third of my practice. I think we have to use every space available.

KB *One element I was interested in concerning your work is the concept of beauty. You deal with so many topics – from genocide to gold-mining – yet the visual remains paramount. Is it ever a concern in your work that it could become too beautiful?*

AJ I am not afraid of beauty. That upsets a lot of my critics. On the contrary I think beauty should be part of the language we use in order to communicate our ideas. It is an essential constitutive element of my work. But I am not referring to visual beauty only. I think that concepts can be very beautiful. Sometimes the truth is incredibly beautiful. The artist defines what is beauty. The artist invents it. What is difficult is to find that perfect balance between content and spectacle. Most of the time I fail and the work is either too didactic or too beautiful. Hopefully so far in very few works of mine the audience gets everything at once – they are informed, they are moved, touched, illuminated and they will leave changed. That is a lot to demand of a single work and that is very difficult to achieve, almost impossible.

KB *Beauty is also an abiding issue in photojournalism, which is something that you have been interested in throughout your career. I thought of your work when the trapped Chilean miners were in the media recently.*

AJ The rescue was absolutely controlled and manipulated for political gains. The government took over all aspects of the operation to an extraordinary degree. If you followed the rescue on TV, you could see the government logo on the top left corner of the screen. I had never seen this kind of blatant ownership of the image. It was totally unnecessary as we knew the government was in charge.

But everyone involved tried to do the same. The company that did the final drilling to reach the miners – the day before they completed the passageway that would finally bring them up – sent T-shirts down with their logos asking the miners to wear them. So when they filmed that extraordinary moment, all 33 miners were wearing the same T-shirt with their logo. Thankfully – and ironically – when the government saw these images and understood what had happened, they wouldn't release that footage. There are no public images of the miners celebrating. I would give a lot to get that tape.

When the miners suffered this accident, the relatives spontaneously put 33 flags in the desert near the mine in commemoration of their lives. They didn't know at that time if they were alive. Each flag was dedicated to one of the miners.

In 1981 I did a piece called *Chile 1981*, before leaving, where I divided the country with a thousand flags from the mountains to the sea. The line divided Chile in half. I wanted to articulate the dramatic division of the country under Pinochet. At the time half of the country wanted the return of democracy, but the other half was perfectly happy with Pinochet. The two sides were brutally divided and I was suffocated by the military dictatorship and I wanted to leave with a powerful public statement.

The flags end in the sea as I wanted to articulate the idea that the country was practically committing suicide because no communication was possible between the two sides. This work also had another connotation. There were rumours at the time that the Pinochet regime was killing its opponents, by throwing them alive into water with weights at their feet or burying them alive in the desert. Unfortunately, later we learned that it was true. So that piece had a certain reading at the time, but it acquired a different reading when we learned the truth.

When this mining accident occurred – and the flags were back in the desert – people couldn't believe it. But the beauty is that they were found alive and they were brought back to life, something we couldn't do with the Pinochet victims.

KB *Would it have been frowned upon to make a work like that in Chile in 1981?*

AJ During the military regime we learned as artists how to speak a poetic language. We practised self-censorship. We knew if we crossed a line we would be in danger of being 'disappeared'. The regime killed almost 4,000 people. If we wanted to participate in exhibitions we had to learn how to express what we wanted to say, but in a way that would be unreadable to the authorities. My use of metaphors and poetic devices started in those years in Chile. I also had no choice.

Another work of mine is a memorial for the victims of the Pinochet regime in Chile. Michelle Bachelet, who ended her mandate in March of this year, was the first female socialist president of Chile. As part of her legacy she created the Museum of Memory and Human Rights where the story of the 17-year dictatorship is told. There was an international competition and a group of architects from São Paulo won. It is a very striking building with a façade covered in copper, which is what the miners were looking for in the north. The entire economy of Chile revolves around copper.

The building is a huge volume that sits on two reflecting pools. It creates a large plaza where one can walk underneath the building. I was commissioned to create the memorial for the victims of the regime somewhere in the plaza. When I studied the proposal and saw the space they had built I thought I couldn't compete with this building and that whatever I put outside would be totally ridiculous. So instead of going up like the architects I am going to go down.

The entrance to my space is 20m away from the entrance to the museum. People walk down 33 steps to reach a level of 6m underground. So the title of the work is *La Geometria de la Conciencia*, which means *The Geometry of Conscience*. The piece consists of the subtle graduation of light. You first reach a 5m-square plateau. Even though it is still in the open air the light is filtered by the depth. Here you face the entrance, which is minimal. Once you enter the second space, which is also 5m square, there is nothing – just concrete walls and floor. The only light is indirect, coming from the two side doors. There is a museum guide who welcomes you and explains that you will enter a third cubic space where you will spend three minutes inside, that the door will close automatically, and that you have to turn off your phone and remain silent. A maximum of ten people are allowed.

Finally you go in and the door closes automatically behind you and you find yourself in full darkness for one minute. (The guard has explained that there is a panic button if there is an emergency and you need to get out.) After a while your eyes get used to the darkness and you start seeing silhouettes on the back wall. The silhouettes are all different. There are two kinds – half of them are victims of the Pinochet regime, the others are anonymous Chileans whom I photographed on the streets of Santiago. But they are mixed up. People can perfectly recognise relatives or loved ones, other people just see silhouettes. After 60 seconds of darkness, the lights come on and gradually intensify. It takes 90 seconds to go from 10% to full intensity. When you get used to the blinding light you realise that both side walls are mirrored, which creates an infinite wall on both sides. You are illuminated historically, conceptually, physically and emotionally by the faces of the living and the dead.

I wanted to suggest that this monument was not only for the 4,000 people who died under Pinochet. This is a monument for all Chileans. Instead of marginalising the victims like most memorials do, I wanted to integrate them into a collective narrative. We are all together, I wanted to suggest. This is a monument for 17 million Chileans alive and dead. I thought hard about how in memorials the victims are always marginalised. We create these crypts or mausoleums and bury them there as if to get rid of them. Logically there is always resentment from the relatives who feel that society has never really understood their pain. I wanted to suggest another paradigm for memorials.

KB *It also implicates the viewer.*

AJ Yes, because we are absolutely part of it. After 90 seconds the lights go off again and you remain in the dark for 30 seconds before the doors open. During that time you will experience an after-image effect and you still see the silhouettes in the dark as they are imprinted in your retina and that is a possible way to take them with you. It is a permanent memorial. I felt free because the museum is there and will tell the official story. They have the faces, names, stories, documents – the historical narrative.

I am now designing a memorial for the victims of the genocide in Rwanda so I have had to visit a lot of memorials. Most of them are grey and depressing. That is why I wanted to invite the living into these spaces and the light. That is why I dared to shift the paradigm and hoped that it would go somewhere. I couldn't sleep for months. I have made maybe 60 public interventions and most of them are ephemeral – you use the city as a laboratory and if you fail it goes away after a while. This was going to stay forever.

KB *How much do you identify yourself as a Latin American artist? Do you feel that being from Chile allows you a platform to deal with issues that a western artist might not be able to?*

AJ Well, I feel incredibly free, not because I am Chilean, but because I am not afraid to express my point of view and invite people into different worlds that I create. You have asked a fascinating question because when I arrived here in New York it was a huge disadvantage to be from Chile. Thirty years ago the art world was incredibly provincial and an international exhibition included a few Americans and a few Germans. It was very difficult to break in and nobody really cared about artists from other places. We were totally invisible. So when you ask me if it is an advantage I want to believe that things have changed. For me the world of art and culture is perhaps the last remaining space of freedom. And I exercise my freedom fully. We must because we don't know how long it will last.

KB *It is interesting to see how mainstream institutions today are embracing Latin American artists.*

AJ I think there are extraordinary artists in Latin America – like everywhere else – and of course the establishment needs new blood. I'm glad that these institutions have opened their doors to artists and intellectuals from other places, but the change is only on the surface. We need more radical, structural changes. The canon is still one and the same – the practice and production of these artists are seen as just adding to it. But a lot of progress has taken place.

KB *Latin American art has such an impressive body of scholarship around it already.*

AJ Latin America has always been there. We were just invisible. If you look at the development of conceptual art there were extraordinary concurrent developments there and here and sometimes we were the Avant Garde, but we were ignored because history was written here in the US. There are people trying to change that, but it will take perhaps another generation to create structural changes.

KB *Can you comment on your work with film and video?*

AJ When I was completing my fifth year of architecture studies Santiago was being redeveloped in the most horrible way. A lot of ugly apartments were being built as part of the neoliberal economy that Pinochet was imposing without any possible resistance. I abandoned architecture and went to study filmmaking. After I completed my film studies, I decided to go back and complete my architecture degree because I had discovered how connected film and architecture were.

I am a frustrated filmmaker. All my works have this filmic quality that I can't avoid because I am thinking about film all the time. I have managed to create quite a few short films. I released a film last year, *The Ashes of Pasolini*, at the Venice Biennale. If someone would give me the funding I would immediately stop everything and do my first film. Film is perhaps the most complete language in which to express yourself. I envy the communication that you reach with an audience in a cinema. As you know, in the art world the average time the spectator spends with an artwork is three seconds. We work three years on a project, we finally install it somewhere and people walk by, casually. That is a tremendous frustration.

KB *What kind of film would you make?*

AJ I have written a few script ideas. The ideas are fictional films, but of course based on reality. It would be in the same spirit of what I do as an artist but trying to reach a large audience because I don't want to make a film seen by 30 people.

Issue 342, December–January 2010–11

Andrea Zittel

interviewed by Alex Coles

A-Z

ALEX COLES *I know that at A-Z West – 35 acres of land in Californian high desert next to Joshua Tree National Park – you have a number of shipping containers currently being used in lieu of a studio. How did that evolve?*

ANDREA ZITTEL Those containers are really a pain in the ass! They get superhot in the summer and very cold in the winter. We can never fit a full eight-hour workday in. The containers have really been more of a stepping stone towards building a larger space out here. The new studio will have 4,000sqft of interior space, which will allow me to work in advance of exhibitions – it will be great to be able to edit installations before actually installing them in galleries.

Having said that, I also have to admit to feeling more grounded when working in my home – you can always turn a room in a house into a studio for a few days and then flip it back afterwards. There is something about the studio space being a part of my habitat that I really like.

AC *There is an obvious link between these containers and the series of works that you are perhaps most known for: the 'A-Z Travel Trailers'. Was your decision to use them driven by a need for conceptual continuity or was it something really pragmatic?*

AZ I have always been into the modular aspect of shipping containers – they are in everyone's backyard out here in the desert. Whenever someone has too much stuff in their house they get a shipping container and dump it all in there. They look pretty junky, but I'm often drawn to a kind of vernacular architecture that is junked up because you have to make a real effort to get it to look good.

When I first moved out here I was trying to avoid having to get permits of any kind. I didn't want to build a building as a studio because I was in some way ideologically opposed to having to file for building permits from the Building and Safety Department. Later I found out that, technically, I was even supposed to get a permit for the containers, and since I didn't go through this process I got in trouble anyway ....

AC   *What, do officials cruise around the desert on a regular basis checking for illegal architecture?*

AZ   No, I think the guy down the road turned me in.

AC   *Tell me a little about the development of your studio and the path that led you to these containers.*

AZ   From the beginning I have always had a series of what I would term 'spaces' rather than professional studios. In the early 1990s I had a little storefront space in Brooklyn where I lived and worked. In early 1994 I moved into a larger loft space a few miles away where I also lived and worked. At the time, this space didn't have any running water or heat. All my work from that period – *A-Z Dishless Dining Table* and *Prototype for A-Z Cleansing Chamber*, both of 1993 – addressed the physical needs of the body. Later in 1994 I moved into A-Z East, a little storefront in Brooklyn, which soon became an exhibition space and testing ground for my work. When we built things in Brooklyn we often had to use the sidewalk in front of the building because there wasn't enough space inside. Following this, I had a short stint living in a suburb in Los Angeles where I worked in a trailer in the front yard, and from there developed A-Z West in the desert in 2000 – a further exhibition space and testing ground but with a lot of outdoor space. This is where the shipping containers come in.

AC   *How is the space you have at A-Z West playing out in terms of the production of the work for the show in Berlin? Is it because of the demands of the Sprüth Magers space that you are feeling the limitations of the containers so acutely at the moment?*

AZ   Yes, though I have been feeling this way for a while. For the Sprüth Magers show we are making a large series of interconnected wall sculptures that also function as shelving units. The units are too big to work on in the containers, and it is winter here right now, too, so we are working outside in rain, hail and wind. Almost all of the galleries I show in started out small but are getting bigger and bigger now and really require a lot of production in order to fill. Sometimes this can be frustrating because I don't necessarily think

I'm that kind of studio artist; however, I do like the challenge of a big space. What interests me in this relationship is how the architectural development of the gallery has directly affected the studio model of the contemporary artist. In the last few years galleries have been getting bigger and bigger and I feel that in many cases this has really forced artists to supersize and professionalise their studio practice. Art has become more production oriented and in many cases less contemplative or philosophical.

AC *At A-Z West do you fabricate the relatively modest sized mobile vehicles and 'A-Z Wagon Stations' yourself? What happens when you do something much larger in scale like Indianapolis Island of 2010?*

AZ Often I work with assistants. But sometimes I work with fabricators – this was certainly the case with the *Indianapolis Island*. The 'A-Z Wagon Stations' are now mostly fabricated here: one person welds the frames off-site and then they are powder-coated and transported here where we get all of the panels in place and trick out the interior. This kind of assembly isn't actually that complex, it just takes time and demands space.

AC *I didn't realise that you did so much fabrication in-house. I remember the special issue of* Artforum *in October 2007 devoted to the subject of production and your article in there focused on a fabricator you worked with. I just assumed that was the case for much of your work.*

AZ In the late 1990s I started working with Callen Camper Company – a custom trailer outfit that mostly makes trailers to haul off-road vehicles that they call toyboxes. They made the large trailers for me and also the 'A-Z Escape Vehicles'. The issue of production also depends on the budget and the deadline. Sometimes we'll get things done outside because it is so much quicker, but this means it costs more too.

AC *In terms of the notion of the post-studio artist, what is your take on that legacy given the way you work?*

AZ I don't know if I consciously position myself in relation to that category. From time to time I think about it – lightly. I think I'm really stuck between the 'post-studio' generation of the 1990s and the mega-studio syndrome that is happening right now. What sometimes strikes me about the difference between most artists who I'm often compared with in the post-studio category is that they usually have large studios and entire production facilities. By contrast, I still work alone most of the time. Sure, I have part-time people that come in for a few days a week – they float in and out and usually are friends – but it doesn't feel like a real industry. I just find it's impossible to think when there are five people hanging around waiting for me to make a decision. Perhaps a large studio would be more efficient, but in my world privacy is the ultimate luxury.

AC *Can you take me through the process by which your production model works? For instance, do you develop the sketches and prototypes before passing them down the line?*

AZ I am not very good at drawing and I certainly don't know how to use any kind of 3D computer program – yet. I generally think about a new work for several years before deciding to move forward. Once I feel it is time to realise the project, I'll do materials experiments in private and then teach my assistants how to help me take it full scale. Or if I work with a fabricator we will meet up several times and go through a lot of contortions – including mental telepathy – in order for me to communicate my ideas.

AC *Another area I wanted to ask you about is the subject of 'lifestyle'. The first time I saw your work was at the Münster Sculpture Project in 1997 when it was side-by-side with works by Atelier van Lieshout, Tobias Rehberger and Jorge Pardo. The exhibition gave the impression of a generation that was using the vocabulary of design as a point of access into an investigation of lifestyle. This is especially so in your case.*

AZ Right. It's true it all came together at once in the 1990s. In part, I think this may have been influenced by the industrially fabricated art of the 1980s – Haim Steinbach and Ashley Bickerton et al. The vocabulary and production methods of design lent their work the appearance of gaining access to the tangible real world – and that kind of access was something that my generation really jumped on. When I first became interested in design I spent a lot of time researching it and its links to fine art. I thought that if an art historian of the future were studying the art of the 1990s they would have to take design into account. I remember being frustrated by how most fine art hinged on trivial observations or certain topics – but that design dealt with broader issues of how life is lived within a set of wider societal conditions. At the time, this was a big part of my rationalisation for wanting to use the language of design.

AC *The historical Avant Garde's use of design as an instrument to organise everyday life was premised on various forms of utopian thinking. Other artists of your generation, including some of the ones in the Münster* exhibition in 1997, have also been interested in this subject – leading them to create micro-utopias of their own: Atelier van Lieshout's 'free state' AVL-Ville *in a port in Rotterdam; Rirkrit Tiravanija's* The Land *project in Thailand; and Jorge Pardo's haciendas in the Yucatan jungle. Do you see a point of correspondence here between these projects and your* High Desert Test Sites (HDTS), A-Z Pocket Property *of 2000, and* A-Z West *in terms of scale and ambition?*

AZ Definitely. I think there are many overlaps and also, of course, many differences. For instance, the islands that I construct are meant as utopias for one person – a bitter-sweet idea. A number of my works touch on the societal construction of individualism as a way of discussing how individuals are not able to live within the construct of a collective any more. I remember being really interested in Tiravanija's *The Land* and its ability to pull the art world out of its centre by creating other centres. I feel an affinity with this project since creating a centre outside a centre has also been a long-term goal with the project at A-Z West.

AC *This is something you are also trying to do with the HDTS, the series of experimental art sites that includes Pioneer town, Joshua Tree, 29 Palms and Wonder Valley. At what point were you in your practice when a project of this scale and breadth seemed like something that was viable?*

AZ I have always been interested in what happens when the work of art is placed in the world at large. The idea of art having a real, lived experience outside institutions and galleries is very important to me. In the mid 1990s I remember thinking that it would be interesting if I could be part of a community that wasn't an art-world community, and I began wondering about where that could be and how it could come about. That place is A-Z West. It's very comfortable for me here, partly because I have been visiting the area my entire life. I felt it was a small but diverse community where I could experiment and test out ideas of contemporary art having some sort of larger social function or meaning.

AC *How has the project evolved since you first arrived? Has it become much more structured and professionalised now – or is it just the blog and website that makes it appear so?*

AZ A-Z West started in 2000 with 5 acres and a cabin, and since then I have been trying to add one large project/property a year. There is a camping area, wagon stations that people can stay in, a guest-house, main house, the studio, growing areas etc. The long-term plan is to turn everything into a large interconnected organism. I don't know if it is professionalised – but I'm definitely continually working on it as a structure. Of course, because A-Z West is also my home and personal space – and because I am by nature a private person – it isn't really intended as a fully public interface.

HDTS, on the other hand, is a project that is more inclusive and is always open to visitors and participants. There are several large parcels of land set aside for the projects, a home base 'headquarters' in downtown Joshua Tree, the website, and we also have a lot of volunteers and interns and collaborators who help pull everything off. Because there is so much activity and so many different people involved, there needs to be a lot of organisation and structure – though within this framework we still try to leave some wiggle room. And we still have trouble keeping up with the email.

AC *There are other platforms you have generated too – including the Smockshop and, of course, the Group Formerly Known as Smockshop.*

AZ Yes, I really enjoy creating these structures and then setting them in motion. Not necessarily controlling them too much once they are actually up and running, but organising them well enough in the beginning that they can take on a life of their own.

AC *Do you still think they would work – creatively and economically – if you totally faded into the background?*

AZ That is the eventual goal. Creatively, yes, I think they would, once I have pulled the right people in who generate the right energy to keep them in motion. Economically it is more difficult. Much of the time I'm trying to come up with a solution that will sustain these platforms without the need to apply for grants. I have been avoiding non-profit status and funding because I want to see if I can create something that is fully self-sustaining in its own right. Though for now I have to admit that most of these alternative practices are funded by income that I make through my commercial practice.

AC *It would be difficult to transfer the HDTS project effectively into a gallery or museum context.*

AZ That is why I haven't attempted it. To extract and re-present it in the right way would be really difficult. My show in summer 2010 at Sadie Coles was me attempting to speak precisely about this, the difference between having an experience and representing an experience. I find that I am always struggling with the various ideological constraints of representation. Over the past few years

I have definitely covered some ground here but it is never an easy process.

AC *The key paradox would seem to be how to transfer the hot social dynamic of the group effectively into the tepid walls of the white cube.*

AZ Yes. The way I have broken down my practice is that, generally, I make structures that can be used in relation to lived life. I do everything I can to ensure that. When these structures are on the verge of falling apart I extract them and aid their transition to an institution that will look after them and archive their history. If an object has as long and circuitous a trajectory as some of the 'A-Z Vehicles', then, when you see one of them in a museum, you get a sense of something that has really passed through time and has a story to tell. But I only figured that out recently. Many of my earlier works felt too hermetically sealed because they weren't allowed to play out a full lived life.

Of course, gallery shows are always more difficult as usually they are presenting new works that don't have a history. I think of the things in the gallery shows as being made for export. The works in these shows tend to be a little more reflexive or philosophical in nature – reflecting on the different structures I'm playing with that are more integrated into the direct experiences of lived life.

AC *Frequently I find problems with your gallery shows, but seldom with the museum ones. I guess there are a number of different strategies artists have used to either attempt to get around or draw attention to this paradox, like making the exhibition the site of the documentation of an activity that took place elsewhere or staging a performance in the space, turning it into a temporary workshop or social space of some kind; or, like Robert Smithson with his series of 'Non-Sites', drawing attention to the impossibility of the very thing you are trying to do.*

AZ That's interesting. I think that Smithson's approach, from *Partially Buried Woodshed* in 1970 at Kent State to the 'Non- Sites' within commercial spaces, was often dead on. I wouldn't ever perform lived life in a gallery since that would just be contrived. But I do like the idea of a physical energy of some sort running through the space.

AC *The Smockshop exhibitions were engaging – partly because the activity was displaced from you onto a collective, which fabricated the garments live in the gallery space. In the most literal way, this introduced the dynamic we have been speaking of, and the one I witnessed in London at Sprüth Magers was one of the best shows I have seen of yours in a commercial gallery space.*

AZ That was a really exciting project, but I have to admit that I feel uncomfortable claiming the smockers' energy as my own. Although I'm flattered you liked the project, unfortunately I don't think that Smockshop was really a show by me.

AC *How has the art/life equation that so much of your practice turns on developed over the years – not just as a thematic but as a continuous series of personal experiences?*

AZ Well, I think that my work has always evolved directly out of the act of living. Many things have changed: for instance, I have a kid now – and having responsibility for another human means I can't live full-time in some of the living experiments that I used to subject myself to. But my work has always addressed freedom – or the illusion of it – and I think I'm now coming face to face with the moment where one has to accept limitations and create structure and meaning out of life as it is.

Issue 343, February 2011

Bethan Huws

interviewed by Mark Wilsher

Time to Reflect

MARK WILSHER *The new exhibition features a group of text works that reveal new and unexpected readings of work by Marcel Duchamp. How far back does your interest in him go?*

BETHAN HUWS Duchamp was more and more present in my thoughts, starting from *Singing for the Sea*, 1993, although that wasn't directly influenced. After doing that I saw an overlap with my own work.

MW *In what way?*

BH It was this construction thing of putting the singers in relation to the sea, so you have two blocks and then something happens between them. In Duchamp's *Fountain*, 1917, the readymade is the urinal itself, it is the point of view we are seeing it from, it is his title, it is the context – it is all these tiny little things that Duchamp uses to structure his work. *Singing for the Sea* was very similar, with all these tiny little details of language and facts. When we are constructing things from scratch, there are too many details even to see the details. When using things straight from the world you are using bigger building blocks. You are seeing the details blown up – fewer elements, but more precise.

The serious study began when I was doing a Henry Moore fellowship in Rome between 1999 and 2000, next door to the National Gallery. Arturo Schwarz has donated most of the big editions to the gallery, and they were in a kind of corridor space upstairs. *Fountain* must have been there although I can't recall seeing it. I used to go walking in Rome, which is full of fountains. And, as you do, you just say these things to yourself: 'I'd like to say something about *Fountain*, and film many different fountains of Rome and put them in relation to Duchamp's *Fountain*.' So I started to look at *Fountain* and to write. The more I looked at it, the more mysterious it got, and I couldn't get all the facts by looking at *Fountain* alone so I started to look at more works by Duchamp. Eventually I bought the catalogue raisonné and went through all 700 works, and this is how I started to go deeper and deeper into Duchamp's system of working. So we filmed the fountains in 2001.

MW *But you left it for a long time before completing the film in 2009.*

BH Yes, because I had to write something about it, and that is more difficult than filming fountains. In the end the whole affair became so complex, I discovered so many things I hadn't expected, and many things that completely oppose what is said about Duchamp. I have been overwhelmed by what I have discovered.

MW *It is certainly a new way of reading Duchamp.*

BH I think that maybe what is specific to what I am doing – how it differs from the art historians – is that I look at Duchamp's work and then I listen to what Duchamp says. That is all I do. I don't read texts on Duchamp. I have, actually, but they are secondary.

MW *Do you find that he writes quite clearly about what he was doing?*

BH When I say I listen to what Duchamp says I am speaking about interviews. The notes of Duchamp are something else. They are quite mysterious, quite enigmatic; it is Duchamp trying to figure things out or setting out his future work plan. There are about 50 interviews existing with Duchamp in the last 10 or 20 years of his life and I have read about half, and that's OK. I mean, we always think we need to know more but the problem is not there.

I was going to speak about *Fountain*, and then I ended up speaking about *Étant Donnés*, 1946–66, and in fact I spoke about it in a very minimalistic sense, speaking about this sequence of idiomatic expressions simply because they are like the big beams in a house, they are the things that stick out. And I chose to do that because Duchamp has been using idiomatic expressions as big chunks in his work since the large glass, really consistently, from the beginning to the end. It is uncontestable. I mean *Étant Donnés* is more complex and rich than just idiomatic expressions, but what is interesting with Duchamp is that it is not his personal meaning. He keeps to the original dictionary definition of a word and doesn't divert from it. It is only what he tells us with this that is personal. Sometimes I wonder, maybe everything in Duchamp's work is a readymade. It was quite overwhelming and upsetting to discover these things.

MW *Why upsetting?*

BH Because he is one of the artists who is the most written about, and then discovering things that are clearly evident in Duchamp – and yet nobody ever observed even one of them. I mean in *L.H.O.O.Q.* and *Tiré à quatre épingles* the idiomatic expression is already directly in his titles. Duchamp is very precise. Maybe that is the affinity I have with it. The method is scientific. It is all intentional. What is there, he puts there. Each piece in his work is like a machine, it is a functional mechanism, like a clock. *'Entrer par la grande porte'* – we still hear this idiom on French television. Most of the idioms are still in use: to enter by the big door, the good door. When we listen to Duchamp speaking he is a very noble soul, he is out for justice since the injustice of 1912 when his colleagues asked him to change the title of *Nu descendant un escalier no.2* (*Nude Descending a Staircase no.2*). The 'large door' is the court door in Paris, so if you were pronounced innocent you came quite literally out of a large door. You can also say *'belle porte'*, or 'beautiful door'. There is this idiom *'avoir les yeux en face des trous'*, or 'to have eyes in front of holes', that in French means to see things straight. It is very French, very Cartesian, very geometrical, no distortion – it is about seeing things clearly.

MW *There must have been a point when you decided to make Duchamp more explicitly the subject matter of your own work?*

BH That's not really a decision; you fall into these things. It is a patch of ground or whole continent that I am continuing to explore but I wouldn't like it to take over my whole spirit either. I work on other things. It is a killer task to study Duchamp because it is always to do with cross-referencing and you really need to study all 700 works to understand the system that is within each work. He dissected everything. He took everything away until he got to the human soul and that's what is so important. His mission, I think, was to reflect and to fight for the purity of the human soul.

MW *Let's talk about the other room upstairs at the Whitechapel Gallery where there is one of your raised floors, which was your breakthrough exhibition at Riverside Studios and that you have remade on several occasions since.*

BH It was my first exhibition in London in 1989 and it was an important piece for me.

MW *It set the tone for the critical reception of your work in that you are often said to be an artist interested in how art is experienced.*

BH If we don't want to fall into the trap of theory we have to check it out with the body. That is to do with the human soul again and the purity of what touches us. Not theory – inside. That is where my interest in Duchamp lies. If Duchamp had only produced theory I wouldn't be interested in him. His work is much deeper. It is to do with human truth. This experience thing – we always have to check out how we feel.

MW *Does this relate to something you said nearly 20 years ago, 'My work is not a concept, not an idea, it's not theoretical, it's just there'?*

BH Having reflected on it, my work is conceptual – it isn't perceptual – but in a very different way. I wasn't at all related to what we know as Conceptual Art from the 1960s. Because the colleges I went to didn't have very efficient art history courses, they weren't really engaged in educating us in Conceptual Art. The Riverside Studios piece had taken me one year to make and it was a very slow conceptualisation and a very personal way of conceptualising, fighting with myself, saying 'What the hell do you want to do, Bethan, now you've been given this space and you have to make something?' Then I would go away and take time to reflect away from the space. The time of reflection was just as important as walking around the space and getting to know it inside out. Knowing the space enough so that I could see through the walls, knowing exactly where everything was, and the limits of the audience. What we encounter, when we encounter it, how we encounter it. And coming to this conclusion: 'OK, I'm going to make a floor the size of an ordinary step. And that's all I'm going to do, raise the floor.' I thought it was dead simple. I hadn't even thought that it would entail tons of material.

That working process didn't work with ideas because they are immaterial. I work by drawing on all my resources, using all five senses and using everything I have, my memory, my knowledge. In the floor pieces I can see very much my education on my parents' farm, because I knew the farm inside out. My principal knowledge was spatial, I spent my childhood outside.

MW *There is a very interesting resonance here at the Whitechapel, walking into the upstairs gallery where there was a Carl Andre exhibition in 2000. The large open spaces and the experience of your own self-awareness standing on these floors, looking inwards. Andre has talked about his experience of the flat landscape of the US.*

BH   Carl Andre was definitely an influence. I admired his work, it was one of my models to work with. The difference is that Andre's floor pieces are solid blocks. My floor has a space inside, it is a volume with a chamber inside it. For me that relates to language and communication, it is a space for something to resonate like a musical instrument.

MW   *You often talk about language in this physical and architectural sense.*

BH   For me it is poetic. Painters do it with colours and textures, and poets do it with the sounds of words. You have a tremendous joy not only in what you're saying but also in the sound of what you're saying. Shakespeare, Joyce, Beckett – they are often reflecting on the sound phenomena of speech. Linguists used to study written language; and believed that it was a superior form to spoken language; now they have reversed the story because written language is fundamentally based on speech and not the other way around. The human soul is a linguistic soul. It is terrible that we sometimes have to underline this.

MW   *The first text work you presented at the ICA,* The Lake Writing, *in 1991, was in fact transcribed speech rather than writing per se, since you spoke the words into a Dictaphone.*

BH   Because I had no experience in writing I had to find a strategy to be able to write. The first thing I did with the lake piece was to sit down on a stone, look at the lake and start speaking, writing down what I said. And it was awful. It just sounded absolutely awful, nothing to do with what I wanted. So I went down to Bangor and got a Dictaphone and I started to speak, which was better than writing, but it was still not satisfactory because I was stalling and thinking too much. I was too self-conscious. So I started to walk and it is that classic thing: because the scene was changing, I had plenty of things to recount. It is like riding in a train. Everything I was seeing I was forcing myself to say, to externalise, which is something we would have been doing more quietly if we had been walking round the lake. So I was artificially forcing myself. It was very exhausting, to make more intense something that happens naturally.

MW   *You have said that another impetus for using text was that you disagreed with what people were writing about your work and you wanted to take control of the writing around it.*

BH   It was nothing to do with taking control. I was simply shocked at what was said of how I was working, little of which was in fact true, and I took it very seriously. I felt 'Shit, I made all that work at the Riverside and now it is all undone and ruined.' Because speech is always going to be much more powerful than an artwork because it is us, it enters our bones, it touches nerves. I began to feel kind of useless. I felt 'OK, I've done all of that and now the critics are thinking I was really well studied in Minimalism and well read.' I mean, I had seen a few Andres, maybe one Sol LeWitt – one Sol LeWitt is enough of an injection for me for life. When you see something that really corresponds to a human spirit, it never leaves you, you don't need much. There was the influence of Michael Asher, there was Andre and there was the influence of my upbringing in Wales, and I thought it was important to readdress this. It is not just that you make works of art and then they are talked about in a misleading way. That is not the truth, and, for me, the only thing that really interests me is the truth.

MW   *There is something that I detect in several pieces of your work, and that is a kind of suppressed frustration or even annoyance, and I'm not sure if it is with the critic or the audience. Works like 'What's the point of creating more artworks when you don't understand the ones you've got?'* (Untitled, *2007), or 'Do we accuse the cook of not being an artist; because she did not make the vegetables? She makes things with her vegetables'* (Untitled, *2009), or even 'Piss off I'm a fountain' (*Untitled, *2004).*

BH   I think we have a right to be angry. I don't go to many dinner parties but sometimes when I am talking with art critics or art histor- ians, it is as if I have no right to disagree with what is said. I have a perfect right. Everybody has a right. It does make me angry, the way the artworks are spoken about, because as artists we don't have a public stage, the stage is taken away from the artist and it is the museums, the museum directors, the curators, the boards explaining the works and all of this. It is then repeated indefinitely. We should be educated just to go and read the works themselves. We don't need loads of literature. Everybody's perfectly capable – with a few tools – to read works of art. There is nothing difficult about it.

I get angry because life is short, it is precious and we are not here to play around with it. And I think a work of art, when you do it properly, is very complex. It is a universe, it is a life itself and for me that's what is interesting about what artists make. It is an external-isation of a person's thought. An artwork has distinct limits; it is saying this and not that. There are certain things done within an artwork that are facts, and other things that are totally inside our heads.

It is a good exercise for me to work with Duchamp. I try my best to keep my own system out of it. I know what I'm speaking about in touching another person's work. You can say that I'm only saying all these things about idiomatic expressions, but I have checked, cross-referenced, I have files and I could prove it in court. It is not just play. I mean it gives me a stomach ache to deal with Duchamp because I'm putting a finger in another person's work and for me, as an outsider, I have to be respectful, that is the first thing. It is not my artwork. And I think that is what interested me with the rush boat – it is not my concept. The conceptual content of the boat is not mine, and that is what I wanted to learn, that a certain person picked out a single rush and made something out of another thing, and conceptually that is so beautiful, seeing a rush to be a line with a beginning, a middle and an end. To be respectful, to keep a distance with the boat or with Duchamp. It is not ours.

MW *How long have you lived in Paris?*

BH I moved there in 1991, since *The Lake Writing*, and I'm just about to move to Berlin.

MW *Do you feel a much stronger affinity to the European art centres of the early 20th century?*

BH I went to Paris because of my partner Thierry Hauch, but I had wanted to leave the UK because of its island mentality, and it tended towards a US system which I don't like – that we are only given credit or status when we have money. I think France is still less like that. I was conscious also of living in England – Wales didn't have any independence then – and if you have been educated to believe in the independence of Wales, you could have told me anything, you could have told me that you adored me, but coming from an Englishman it would still have been suspect. That was because of my upbringing.

In 2009 I made the film *A Marriage in the King's Forest*. That was my way of making peace with the English. I know it is difficult to believe, but I came from an area in Wales where we were treated with little respect by the English community and these things run deep.

MW *That was a real wedding that you filmed?*

BH We went to visit the big sites in Margate, and one site was the Winter Gardens, and one thing that goes on there is weddings. I said, 'That will be wonderful, we will film the wedding of a couple from Margate', and then we projected it in King's Wood. Funerals and weddings are the last rituals we seem to have in the West.

MW   *You have spoken quite a lot about purity and the soul. Are you a religious person?*

BH   No, not at all. That is in Duchamp too. That is what I am interested in within Duchamp. It could be Agnes Martin or Robert Ryman using the colour white to its end. It is an experience inside. It is the white page of Mallarmé. It is a clearing out of your house – get rid of the Welsh, get rid of the Welsh language, get rid of the English language, get rid of everything you have learned and try to feel the house we have inside, the interior. That is what the human soul is. And we can see that human beings suffer when the soul isn't nourished, and we lack care. It is to do with love in fact, isn't it? Human beings need to be loved, need to be cared for by other human beings, and nourished in an intellectual way. And for me that is the purity of the human soul. We don't need to go to colleges to know what humanity is, you just look at another human being and you recognise our spirit.

So I am not religious but we can say that when you read religious scripts it is to do with a certain experience – even God. It is a description of a certain experience inside. It is the thought externalised, and we can relocate it inside the body.

Issue 344, March 2011

Roman Ondák

interviewed by Martin Herbert

Time Capsule

MARTIN HERBERT *You have made two new works for Modern Art Oxford, your first major UK solo show. The first,* Time Capsule, *references the Chilean mining incident of 2010. You have installed in the darkened gallery a precise replica – almost like a displacement of the original – of the rescue capsule that was used. And directly above it, through which a connecting rope dangles, is a tube, its far end illuminated, that suggests the shaft to freedom.*

ROMAN ONDÁK At first, the Chilean accident was just a news story to me. But later on I followed the discussions among the rescue teams, and when I heard about the capsule – as an object that could raise all the miners up from this distant place – I was attracted to that. My interest wasn't so much in the event itself or the publicity around it, it was in this object with the potential for transformation, moving between ground level and a distant place that was mentally much further than people could imagine. Not the literal 700m, but a place of total inaccessibility. And then this idea of the 'time capsule' came to mind, that it is not only a physical transference but also a transfer that we could perceive in terms of an enormous span of time, one that could be expanded to infinity in terms of the imagination.

MH *That immediately makes me think of* Measuring the Universe, *2007, where you invited gallery visitors to be measured against the wall, as a growing child would be, creating a cloud of height marks that grew during the exhibition's run. In both cases, a very literal, specific starting point serves as a vehicle for the kind of metaphoric expansion suggested by the title.*

RO Absolutely. In the case of *Time Capsule*, I thought that this could be an interesting issue to conceive in the form of a sculpture or installation. And as I came across more detailed information about the mining rescue, I thought the best idea would be to replicate the capsule as closely as possible – which makes the work also about a kind of doubt, whether this kind of experience can be represented or replicated. You could understand this, too, as a reverse situation.

You could imagine – given that in the darkened gallery there is only the capsule and the shaft, or the idea of the shaft – that the gallery has been transported down 700m underground. So what this image, this installation, brings to the mind of the visitor is left open. It activates the memory of those pictures in the newspapers, but also it relates to the physical experience of being somewhere so far down that it defeats the mind.

MH *You have made meticulous duplications before, like the scaled-down model of Tate Modern's Turbine Hall in 2005-06.*

RO I would compare this new piece to *Spirit and Opportunity* of 2004, a section of the surface of Mars based on newspaper and media images. As with *Time Capsule*, it is a replica of something which none of us has the real experience to compare against.

MH *That suggests a fathomless mental expansion, and it seems like you frequently want to create that kind of leap, from a focused – and often very simple – proposal, to the most extensive ramifications.*

RO Stretching the potential perception, I'd say, while not changing much of what we have seen, or what we are confronted with. For the other work in Oxford, *Stampede*, we put out a public call for participants. Around 300 people showed up and they were all led into the last gallery, which was dimly lit. They filled the room like black ink on paper, like a slow avalanche; an enormously interesting image to watch. The room filled up, and then everything went backwards – everyone went back out again, down a narrow constructed corridor connecting the two main spaces.

MH *A constricted release: shades of the miners' rescue.*

RO Yes, a very compressed space. As a viewer, you pass through this corridor from the room containing *Time Capsule*, and then it opens out again and you see projected video documentation of the performance, and you watch the film alone or with just a few people in the room. *Stampede* was again inspired by media images, which I'm constantly collecting and archiving. In this case I thought the reference shouldn't be directly revealed, but it was inspired by some events with worse endings than the Chilean mining accident: stampede situations, overcrowded moments where people died, in Cambodia or in Germany at the Love Parade. But I was interested in the other extreme, which in one way could be compared with the one in the mine where there were only a few people, totally isolated, for 69 days, and they were concentrated on the idea of escape. You could feel the same if you were in an overcrowded situation in the open air. If you are in the middle and there is no escape, it could be the same as being trapped in the mine.

MH *This reminds me of your works involving queues of people, such as* Good Feelings in Good Times *of 2003. Malcolm Gladwell noted recently that, in organising political demonstrations via Twitter etc, it is easy to get a lot of people to do something quite small, but the political pay-offs are small too. Within art, you seem to make the low-stakes invitation work.*

RO I am definitely interested in this kind of performative work that involves a large number of people, sometimes more than you can count – in *Measuring the Universe* it could be 10,000 – and seeing how people choose to behave in such situations. I don't want to manipulate people, I don't want to 'use' them, but I am interested in what could motivate people to take part, via a small proposal. And there is a kind of ambiguity, too, in the potential failure of these proposals – whether people will be attracted or not. I believe, though, that people can somehow refer to their memories in these situations, and they like to be confronted by those memories. The idea of being measured in the gallery is absurd, but if you see that it is part of a group event, that it is not only you who is being measured, somehow you can be pulled into this stream of obsession, and I believe the same thing was happening with Stampede.

MH *If Duchamp turned life into art using the gallery, and Allan Kaprow et al sought to merge art and life, it seems that you want to oscillate between the two. You create situations where viewers are not sure which side they are on, as in* Loop *at the 2009 Venice Biennale, where you brought the flora of the Giardini into the Czech-Slovak pavilion, either making it into art or eliding the gallery and the external world, or the Turbine Hall piece* It Will All Turn Out Right in the End. *In such a situation, the audience might have felt like they were the work.*

RO I like this shift, and also this doubt, between the real and the represented. With *Loop*, you might think a lot about sculpture but the end result was only an extension of reality into the pavilion. What

I am very interested in is the open end of the form, of the artwork, perhaps in a performance – thinking about a queue, say – which the viewer does not so much complete as contribute to by accepting certain rules. Even with sculptural works that have been completely finished or brought to a perfection of form in terms of competition with nature, with the real – such as in *Loop* – at the same time the work is only finished when people step in and accept this perceptual trick. So somehow this open-endedness, whether in three-dimensional works or performances, is always there. I aim for art that is beyond the physicality of an object that we observe, and I believe that art – talking about conceptual or post-conceptual art – is not what is inside an object but between an object and your mind. And it is more and more difficult to use this capacity within the gallery space.

MH *But you want to stay there.*

RO It is the place that has the strongest references. It is filled up with the history of art. Yet at the same time you can always forget that, because the place has a social aspect. Such a potential is like a small model of society, so to speak.

MH *I did wonder about this idea of the exhibition space as a model for a larger structure. Your work is hardly free from reference to vexed external situations – your 2008 video* Across that Place, *for example, featuring people skipping stones on the Panama Canal;* Snapshots from Baghdad *two years earlier involved the display of a camera containing undeveloped film photographed in the Iraqi capital. Do you intend this upending, reversing and displacing that features in so much of your work to allegorise change in a larger societal way? Or, to put it another way, is there a politics inherent in your work?*

RO It is always very personal. When I was an adolescent, for example, I couldn't travel [Ondák grew up under state communism in Slovakia]. This didn't have a strong political impact on my mind. I was too young to understand it. But it did have an influence. Thinking about geography and space, how one can be confronted with space in general and the limits of space – what is considered public or private – informs most of my work.

MH *Over the last decade, there has been an increase in the amount of participation-themed, open-ended art, accompanied by a certain amount of rhetoric about the liberating capacities of such work, its privileging of the viewer's agency. How do you see the potential effects of such art on the viewer?*

RO   I started working with participants, friends, relatives, people who surrounded me, because in the 1990s there was no real audience for either my work or that of my colleagues. There were no institutions. And creating an audience could happen through involving some people in the creation of an artwork. I didn't want to escape from the museum because that wouldn't be a solution, but I did want to disperse my authorship, my hand, my language. In terms of the viewer, there is always a desire for change – not in terms of a utopian vision but in terms of potentiality – in this openness. Something isn't finished, but you can think of the step that can come later. This is what I have always been interested in, something that can be constructed in such a way that the next step can be made by someone else.

MH   *So, I don't want to be prescriptive, but your experience of collectivism, say, hasn't shaped your interest in involving groups?*

RO   Not directly. I did observe that the generation of artists above me was critical about late communism and somehow I thought that the next step from this would be forgetting it. So my references are subtler. But something that stayed in my mind from the 1970s and 1980s was that, in that society, you always had the feeling that something was slightly manipulated. You didn't know what was really true and what was an image you should believe in, and this kind of play with reality was, for me, stronger than direct references.

MH   *Again, the real and the represented. Given that your process involves throwing viewers into a space of uncertainty and the unexpected, how would you characterise your working process? It seems you would have to start afresh every time.*

RO   A decade or more ago I realised that if I was going to refer to the real, to the nature of reality, it couldn't be based on style. It really had to be taken as a whole, and not be me taking a certain part of reality and saying 'this is my reality'. And in that way, I wondered how much it would be possible to expand, not in form but in terms of topics, and still feel that it was my work. I thought that in every work I made, I could erase the one before, or just jump from an installation, say, like *Spirit and Opportunity* of 2004, to the queue pieces, and there would be doubt as to whether it was the same artist making it. But in a way the whole system has been constructed as a kind of network, so what people might get from coming to my next show could be an erasure, but also a challenge to step further into this experience. In practical terms, I am going through a lot of materials every day and critically dividing potential sources from things that couldn't work – 99% nothing, 1% that attracts my attention.

MH *I am interested in the idea you mentioned earlier, of the potential for failure, particularly when you work with participants.*

RO It is not that I would create things with failure at their core. But if there is something that is almost entirely constructed and controlled, yet leaves a small percentage for someone to finish, it can change the thing entirely. That percentage can break the whole thing down. I am very interested in this marginal yet potential-filled role, which also has a political or a social resonance. You don't have to measure it, but it is really important to leave this space for potential. I leave something for the viewer, and all the imperfections that are added to the work could enrich it, but also suppress it. It is this kind of risk that I am interested in.

MH *Making a piece that is, say, 95% you and 5% the viewer, is that for you the difference between a piece of art that is alive, that is an organism, and one that is not?*

RO Yes, exactly. I am very interested in how that can be transferred to fluid forms, like those that involve people, but I am also interested in this fluidity in real objects in terms of their openness.

MH *Once that is part of the conversation about your work, that fluidity, it seems like it can reappear in places where it wouldn't otherwise be there.* Time Capsule *sounds like it should just be an object, but actually it is a dynamic: between the particular, nudging, physical form and the viewer's vaulting thought. It is a kind of sculpture-plus.*

RO It is not a performance but, thinking about your body or other bodies – the presence of someone in the capsule, the transfer of the capsule into the shaft – something makes this work open enough to be not only an object. It is a dynamic process, an additional step. Maybe it won't happen in the gallery, but the potential is there.

Issue 345, April 2011

Mary Kelly

interviewed by Maria Walsh

Corpus

MARIA WALSH *You have said that in your 2010 work,* Habitus, *you go back to your own primal scene, the Second World War. In some ways your work is a primal scene for me. I came to it late, at the end of the 1980s to be precise, and have always been backtracking through it. The only work I saw in my chronological lifetime was* Gloria Patri *of 1993, but* Corpus, *made between 1984 and 1985, has been a really informative work for me. I wanted to start by asking about feminism and delayed time and narrative. Apart from the fact that within each work there are different narratives, it is almost as if the show itself, which is a retrospective, is plotting a narrative.*

MARY KELLY I called the exhibition 'Projects' because the idea of a project-based practice is very important to understanding how the work comes about in relation to a discursive field as an ongoing process of questioning. In terms of medium, I have been interested in extending the definition of 'technical support', as Rosalind Krauss puts it, to include different discursive sites – the Women's Movement, for example – and then seeing psychoanalysis as a set of procedures generated by it. So the exhibition captures the narrative, as you say, of my engagement in that discursive site, and the urgency of the inquiry that leads me from one work to the next. My first questions were about femininity, maternal femininity in *Post-Partum Document*, made between 1973 and 1979, and then in the work you were talking about, *Corpus*, I asked what falls outside of the reproductive paradigm, questions of object- choice, ageing ... It seemed logical after this to ask about masculinity, and *Gloria Patri* came out of that. Then, it was a question of what was behind the shield, about the victims of war, which lead to the *Mea Culpa* series in 1999, and *The Ballad of Kastriot Rexhepi* in 2001.

I didn't do any work that was explicitly about feminism until 'Love Songs' in 2005-07. That was the first time I looked back to see where my practice came from and, really, to say that the idea of interrogation, or *les enquêtes*, originated in the events of 1968. Most of the women I collaborated with on restaging the archival images were born around that time. Maybe your age group is in a no-woman's-land in relation to that, but I don't think of generations as literally chronological. For those born from the early 1960s right up to the early 1980s, it started to occur to me that they get drawn into the orbit of 1968 as an object of fascination much in the way that Freud talks about the primal scene – the sexual scenario that informs the child's question: where do I come from? Well, I wanted to consider how the family saga is linked to the grand narrative of social change. I mean, how the child deciphers parental desire as the political primal scene.

MW *For women who have this fascination with that time, even though we were children then, it is as if we have no memory of that time. I felt quite traumatised by the exhibition, in the sense that Hal Foster talks about trauma in Freud, that we can't understand things in the present…*

MK Deferred action.

MW *Yes, I was alive then, but I wasn't 'there'. It is not until much later that the event becomes real but then you can't experience it. Moving to a different question but remaining within the framework of the exhibition, the idea of cinematic time, the sequential nature of it and how that might operate in gallery space has always been important in your work. The newer works* Multi-Story House *of 2007 and* Habitus *seemed to have more of a sense of simultaneous time and space. Even though you can go into* House, *and we follow the narratives around the work, it is very different. It is so much object-based. I was interested in your decision to make this shift.*

MK Both of those works are collaborations with Ray Barrie, who is a sculptor. Film culture has been key for my work, and I worked in film collectives on *The Nightcleaners* in 1975, and other works, though I didn't take that route. I wanted to see how durational elements could be explored in an exhibition context. When Peter Wollen saw *Post-Partum Document* in the 1970s, he said 'that's diegetic space' and now I have realised, after the fact, that this was, more precisely, what I was interested in. I have spoken many times about how I was influenced by the long take in Straub and Huillet's film *Othon*. But in my work, I present narrative prose that unfolds in time, creating a sense of something accumulating over time in the gallery space. At the extreme end of the sequential or real-time experience there is *Post-Partum Document*, with its warts and all diary style, and then *The Ballad of Kastriot Rexhepi*, which involves the viewer moving through the work using the idea of a 360° pan. *The Ballad* is about 200 linear feet, which is the length of an old film reel. And it took time to produce. The lint casting process for this work took over six months and 10,000 pounds in weight of washing to finish. I think simultaneity becomes a focus with *Gloria Patri*. I became interested in what was happening on the periphery of the viewer's vision, what enters the space where you're reading from the places you cannot see. In that work the trophies are slightly out of your range of vision while reading the text on the shields, but you're aware of them inflecting that experience. But even with 'Interim', when it was shown at the New Museum in 1990, I had *Historia* in the middle of the installation, so there was something happening across the space between these objects and the wall works, not just in a formal sense but also as a kind of historical dialogue. Perhaps this marks a move towards a different kind of space, not simply 'narrativised', as I used to say, but dialogic. And this is what predominates in the three-dimensional work.

MW   *While the text in* Habitus *is reflected in the mirror below in a kind of loop, I noticed that there are also other reflected layers of the text occurring, giving the work another dimension.*

MK   It changes with the light in the gallery. Unlike *Multi-Story House*, which is illuminated from the inside by fluorescent lighting under the glass floor, drawing you into the work and into a process of identification, *Habitus* doesn't give you that kind of access. Memories are reflected, distorted perhaps. It is based on the Anderson shelter of the Second World War, and could be considered in some sense an extension of domestic space, but it doesn't have the intimacy of *House* and the structure itself is less like an assisted readymade.

MW   *I wanted to ask you about monuments and trauma. We are constantly subjected to the portrayal of war trauma stories by the media. We do not have time to process them or remember them. But then, memorials sometimes cover over the site of trauma, monumentalising it in a way. In* The Ballad, *what is really interesting is your use of an everyday waste*

material – lint – in which, while it is transformed into something aesthetic,
something beautiful, you can still see bits of hair and flecks of dirt. I'm
interested in the link between this everyday waste material and this
traumatic story.

MK I wouldn't want to make monuments.

MW *We need them to remember but the question is what kind of*
memorial?

MK It was so difficult to think about how to make a work dealing with
the victims of war-related atrocities. I had been working on this for
a few years, getting nowhere, and then I had my epiphany. There is
always washing to be done and, well, I was doing the washing when
I heard a woman giving witness at the Truth and Reconciliation
Commission on the TV. I didn't see the image, only heard her voice,
and I thought that the ephemeral quality of the lint in the filter screen
of the dryer captured, in an almost unconscious way, the affect of that
moment, and I wondered if I could make a reliable casting process
so that units could be combined to form a continuous narrative
relief. That resulted in a series of works in 1999, 'Mea Culpa', based on
incidents in South Africa, as well as Lebanon, Buenos Aires, Sarajevo
and Cambodia, that had been reported to the War Crimes Tribunal.
In *The Ballad of Kastriot Rexhepi* I use this process for a larger installation and then, of course, there's the Michael Nyman score, so it is
a memorial but not a permanent one.

MW *Why did you have the music commissioned?*

MK Earlier he had asked me to write something for him, but I
didn't want to get involved in musical theatre. But when I started
the lint works, there was something inherently rhythmic about
the organisation of units and the panels – they could be arranged
in groups of two or three or four, like time signatures in musical
notation. And then, with *The Ballad*, Kastriot's story is written
as a parody of the national allegories that abound in traditional
ballads and I wanted to present it in a more performative way, so
it just seemed right to have it sung. Michael's film scores, for Peter
Greenaway especially, are often very emotive and parodic at the same
time, so I felt it would be perfect to have him write an original score
for the exhibition. I also liked having the musicians perform in the
middle of the space, so that people could walk around, listening to
them and reading the 'libretto' at the same time.

MW *Could you say something about the importance of psychoanalysis in*

411

your work? Psychoanalytic theory was a dominant discourse in art in the 1980s and 90s. It was like a tool for questioning subjectivity, sexuality, identity etc. Interest in it seemed to wane after that, although I think there is a renewed interest in it currently. Does it still inform your work?

MK   Psychoanalysis has a long connection with art throughout the trajectory of Modernism – Surrealism obviously, but it is not always the Freudian unconscious that we find there. For me, Freudian psychoanalysis, and Lacan's reading of it, in particular, is more relevant. Its linguistic emphasis allows you to deal with the psychic structure of difference in ways that address sexuality in relation to other issues such as race and class. Language is the interface between the social and the psychic; as Maud Mannoni says, 'The specifically human environment is neither biological, nor social, but linguistic.' That was my mantra for *Post-Partum Document*. In more recent work, I have been trying to combine the Lacanian account of the unconscious as 'the effects of the speech of the Other on the subject' with the Benjaminian idea that 'there is a secret agreement between past generations and the present one', that is, something missing in the past that bears on the present and the future. I see this collective project emerging from the symptomatic exchanges of childhood, so 'working through' that archive, in Freud's sense, is very important to me. I would say that those are the two theoretical poles around which my ideas revolve.

MW   *Funnily enough, it was my encounter with your work that led me to do an MA in psychoanalytic theory.*

MK   Where?

MW   *With Parveen Adams at Brunel.*

MK   How wonderful! We were both in reading groups in the 1970s. Parveen was in the family group, I was in the history group, then we were both in the Lacan reading group. Initially, psychoanalysis was very attractive to us as a discourse that could address sexual politics via a Marxist notion of ideology. There was so little translated at that time. Well, Ben Brewster had just translated *The Mirror Stage*, so we had that. But, mainly, it was the reference to Lacan in Althusser. In the movement, we were convinced that this new discourse of psychoanalysis could make sexuality pass into the grand narrative of social change, though when I first started talking about Lacan in relation to my work, it was like a freak show. During the exhibition at the ICA in 1976, Parveen Adams, Laura Mulvey, Sue Lipschitz and myself led – or tried to lead – a seminar defending our use of Lacan against accusations that is was just male-dominated theory. Parveen always says that she started writing about art because of my work.

MW   *In the* Corpus *section of* Interim *you said that you were daring the female spectator to ask the question: am I a man or a woman? The hysteric's question and, of course, the discourse of hysteria features so much in that work, creating a kind of hyperbolic femininity. Do you still think of it in that way?*

MK   Well, what I was trying to do in that work was create a space for the woman, or the spectator in the position of the woman, to send herself up, like the joke, a space where she could laugh at herself and gain a certain distance from that hyperbolic femininity you noted. As psychoanalysts say, the obsessional neurotic's question is: am I dead or alive? And the hysteric's question: am I a man or a woman? So, miming the hysteric in *Corpus* seemed to be a way of releasing the woman from that moment of narcissistic identification that pertains to sexual difference. That is still relevant, though in another way for me now, because I think that being a woman is only a brief period in one's life.

MW   *How do you mean?*

MK   The structure of femininity, its heteronormative aspect, doesn't last very long.

MW   *That question – am I a man or a woman? – reminds me of the child's questions about the differences between men and women in* Post-Partum Document. *I have always understood that your use of the first and third person is between fiction and documentary, that you put conversations into fiction and that the use of the 'I' is a kind of collective sign. But reading the text in* Documentation V *in this exhibition, I must say that I felt the child's questions were, dare I say, 'true'.*

MK   Fantastic. I want them to be 'real' – not realism – but in Lacan's sense of the Real, the object-voice. Do you hear that in the voices in *Multi-Story House* too?

MW   *I hear them, but not in the same way, as I am very much aware of the form of the work, of looking through and walking around it. The voices are more simultaneous – a polyphony perhaps – as opposed to that sense of something unfolding sequentially in* Post-Partum. *But I guess that is my spectatorial positioning at this moment in time.*

MK   When I talk about the voice, I have the Lacanian *objet petit a* in mind, that aspect of the real that is always already lost. The effect of

413

these voices, not simply what is said, is there in my memory and I try to evoke it through the specific materiality of the work. In *Documentation V*, the units are so tiny, aren't they?

MW   *Yes, I had to peer in at them and then stand back with the jolt of this 'real'.*

MK   Scale is part of that experience, certainly.

MW   *I'd like to quote you back to yourself. This relates to what we were talking about at the beginning about feminism and time. In 1995, as a response to the 'Bad Girls' exhibitions, you coined the fantastic phrase about what you thought women artists were doing: 'A woman mimics a man who masquerades as a woman to prove his virility' and that this, in zine-speak, was 'A girl thing being a boy thing being a girl thing in order to be a bad thing'; a great way of putting it that relates, I think, to the final panel in* Gloria Patri. *There seems to me to have been a shift from this aggressive posturing, and I was wondering what you thought of the current resurgence of interest in feminism in art.*

MK   Yes, it does relate to the final shield in *Gloria Patri*, where I was thinking about the fascination of masculine display for the woman and asking, how do you take up that position? You try to pass, you wear it on your sleeve and, with the 'Bad Girls', you do it better. Since that work, I moved away from that concept of masquerade, and looked more at questions of power and the way it is encoded, which is less visible. It was really people in the LGBTQ movement who went on to do something interesting with the legacy of anti-essentialist feminism. As one of the narratives in *Multi-Story House* says: 'In the queer/ trans movement, we're trying to sort out stuff that was started then … to continue the legacy of activist feminism, but still be flexible.' I see a return to feminism here, and my thinking about generations stemmed from being surrounded by these women who seemed to have a connection to that moment of the Women's Liberation Movement.

MW   *Your students?*

MK   Yes, mostly. If you think of this in terms of what I have called the political primal scene then they are really asking about their parents' desire, trying to decode it. And I thought their questions implied a kind of failure: 'Why didn't you finish the job?' In the war series, if you want to call them that, I was considering the event, primarily, in Freud's terms, as traumatic. But with 'Love Songs' I began to think of my experience in the Women's Movement more as an epistemological event, closer to Alain Badiou's notion of 'event' as the instigation of a truth procedure. Something unexpected happens and it changes your life, right? You have to decide what it is about the event that you are going to be faithful to, what was missed in the past that bears on the present and the future. Perhaps that is what it means to have a 'project'.

Issue 346, May 2011

Thomas Struth

interviewed by Mark Prince

Paradigm Shift

MARK PRINCE *In the 1970s, you were taught by Gerhard Richter then, later, by Bernd Becher. In your early photographs of Düsseldorf, the serialism of the compositions relates to the work of the Bechers, while the generic subject matter recalls Richter. You have spoken of your perception of the distance between the artwork and the artist's experience and, in your first Düsseldorf street pictures, the repeated centralised perspective has an impersonal quality, yet they were of your own home town. Did they seem personal pictures to you?*

THOMAS STRUTH I grew up in the city. When I was six months old we moved to Düsseldorf, and then, when I was ten, we moved to a small city near Cologne where I went to high school, until the age of 18 or 19. For nine years I was not in Düsseldorf, but I was never far away. So Düsseldorf is my home town. But I think all my pictures are very personal. To make a picture requires an interest, an investment, a curiosity, a personal empathy.

MP *In the same room in your exhibition at K20, there are pictures of streets in New York, Tokyo and Paris which were taken in the two or three years following. Structurally those pictures resemble the Düsseldorf pictures, except that many of them are continents away.*

TS When you are becoming an artist you need to find a subject matter that interests you long enough to spend time with it. It is the same in painting – that is why there are a lot of Rembrandt self-portraits, and why Gerhard Richter has made so many abstract paintings. In order to develop something you have to spend time with it. I began with the subject of the street when I was still studying with Gerhard. When Bernd Becher came to the academy, he introduced me to large-format cameras – before that I had photographed the streets with 35mm – and that was a revelation. I did 300 streets in Düsseldorf and then I got a scholarship to go to New York. I liked the central perspective because it was more conceptual.

MP *It was less aesthetic, more generic?*

TS Yes. Anti-compositional, in a way.

MP *Which is very Richterish. Whereas with the Bechers, it is a socially specific subject matter.*

TS At the time I was thinking a lot about questions of responsibility. Why do things look like they do? Who made this?

MP *In terms of the architecture?*

TS In terms of the atmosphere. With the architecture you have someone who pays to erect a building, the architect, the city planners, building laws and whatnot. But still there is something else, which is a general atmosphere, and I was fascinated by that question of what is the common, unconscious energy.

MP *With the streets you can analyse the history of the architecture. And yet in the same room at K20, you have the 'Paradise' series which, in contrast, seems unanalysable.*

TS That was why I wanted to put them together in one room.

MP *The subtitles are very specific about the remote locations and yet it seems they have become very flat, almost abstract, like a decorative surface. Consequently, the viewer loses a sense of specificity.*

TS You wrote to me about how it seems that I react to the subject and include material that was not initially part of my idea of the subject, that I didn't intend to include. That's true.

MP *In the taxonomical sense?*

TS Yes. Some of the 'Paradise' pictures are quite far from what I initially wanted. They came about after my first few trips to China. There were a few preconditions. I went to a forest near Winterthur in Switzerland, and made some pictures of complex tree and branch arrangements. When I had photographed streets in China, there were some pictures which were very crowded, full of detail. I become interested in the idea of more dense pictures.

MP *But aren't photographs always full of detail, even if you photograph an empty floor?*

TS I mean pictures that you cannot completely decipher. For example, when you look at one of the street pictures, you can see that here is a VW Beetle, here is a Ford Capri. You can break it down.

Whereas with the forest pictures, you see immediately what it is, you don't even have to think about it, and through the title, 'Paradise', it becomes clear that it is not about botany.

MP *It is an allegorical title.*

TS It's a humorous title which came about because it fell together with the change in the millennium, and for ironic political reasons – and also because I was, for a time in the 1990s, very interested in the question of stillness, in being calmer. It is not so much a question of the stillness of the jungle as what looking at something does to you mentally, with your position as an observer in front of the picture.

MP *When you described your work as 'a tool for psychological research', is this what you meant?*

TS It echoes back to you as an observer. I am the first observer; I make the observing plan. I want to observe something in a way that has a particular effect on subsequent viewers.

MP *For me they are buzzing, intensely active images – not peaceful.*

TS I felt I wanted to make pictures which were very full, and the forest seemed the ideal subject matter. They deal with depth of field – with a large-format camera you can go to F32 or F45, and you get an amazing interlaying of structures, and it takes a lot of time to look at all the detail, and you have to surrender to it. I think the 20th century was the first time – with Sigmund Freud and Wilhelm Reich and others – when the psychology of human beings was studied and evaluated more systematically. I grew up in Germany with its complicated history, and psychology has always played a very big role for me. To ask myself why I became who I am, what are the conditions. When you make a painting there is a very direct psychological conclusion; it is a form of handwriting.

MP *A trace.*

TS But the camera is like a robot, a tool being used by people who have a gaze. It responds to decisions which include, consciously and unconsciously, your psychological conditions.

MP *You said that when you originally approached the idea of being an artist that it seemed a vague pursuit. It seems you consciously try to counteract that perception with ordering processes: the work groups which span many years, each group analysing a certain problem. The museum pictures are a departure, in that they lay themselves open to accident in a way that is consistent with the idea of photography as a spontaneous capturing of something unpredictable. Was it a conscious decision to threaten the order you had created?*

TS I spent three months in Naples in 1988 where I made a photo of restorers working on paintings at San Lorenzo. Aside from giving me the idea of making photographs in a space where there were other pictures of human figures from another time, the time in Naples changed my life. I discovered a different side of myself. I was always very much determined by my strict upbringing but in Naples, I thought, this is my city. I discovered something about myself that I didn't know before, that I was only partly such a strict person. It was a way of dropping a link with system and order. It was very liberating. Those three months changed my life.

MP *How did that experience lead to the situation in which you set up your camera in museums and waited for something to happen?*

TS Photographing the restorers in Naples brought me back to painting. The restorers have to go deep into the surface of the painting and analyse what the artist did from the ground up. I knew I was not going to resume painting myself, but I was thinking about this process as a form of resurrection. Famous paintings in some museums are almost like tombstones in cemeteries. When people approach a Turner or a Delacroix they have so much anxiety to connect with them directly. I thought I would do something to remind people how great painting is.

MP *The museum pictures capture a contrast, a direct comparison, between past and present. You have the schoolgirls in front of the Infantes of Velasquez. There is a doubling and tripling of spaces – that of the painting, the museum in which it is displayed and the museum in which we are standing looking at the photograph. These works have a different take on the art of the past than much other art photography, such as that of Louise Lawler, Sherrie Levine, or, more recently, Rosa Barba's films. Their work is elegaic. In your work, it is as if something is being recalled, brought back to life. Did you have to fight to create a frame in which this art could be seen again?*

TS There was a lot of uncertainty. I would stand in front of one work for five hours, not knowing what was going to happen. There is one picture from 1990 of an old man standing in front of two Rembrandt portraits at the Kunsthistorisches Museum in Vienna. This was just before the wall came down and the borders to Hungary were open. The city was full of Hungarians and Bulgarians, and because it was winter the museum allowed everyone to come inside. I took a lot of pictures contrasting the Rembrandts with their modern clothes and then, at one point the gallery was empty, and a man came in who, it turned out, was a well-known German writer and I took a few pictures of him which, in the end, were more interesting than what I had been expecting. I was looking for a context, a new narrative between that of the painting and the observer. People often remark that there is no abstract or contemporary art in the pictures, but that is because this time-tunnel method doesn't function with abstraction. I made some attempts at photographing Mondrian or Rothko.

MP *Why did that not work for you?*

TS There is no visual connection between the painting and the visitor.

MP *Is it to do with the figurative content?*

TS Yes, this particular pictorial strategy only works when there are figures in both picture planes: in the painting and the photograph.

MP *There is a contrast and a connection between the narrative structure of the photograph and that of the painting, but I think even when there isn't an obvious antecedent, when for example you photograph a family, there is not the sense of it being random, like a snapshot. It seems to have been composed to measure itself against a traditional iconography of portraiture, overwriting existing models.*

TS Those pictures refer much more to all the family photographs in photo albums. I think about what a photograph can tell, what truth it can offer. It is a process of taxonomical or comparative analysis. Establishing certain patterns improves the chances of getting a result – that is not to say that the resulting content is not a debatable entity. I saw the family portraits as a portion of the street, taking the street as the society, as the larger culture. The family is a basic group, in which the subjects' community, knowledge, behaviour and psychology are all visible.

MP *It is a standard section of society.*

TS A primary group, in the language of psychology.

MP *So you are gravitating towards these subjects as archetypes. It is the opposite of photography as a model of contingency. And yet some of the most recent photographs of industrial complexes and scientific research facilities seem exceptionally non-archetypal. It is relatively difficult to categorise them. Were you trying to break out of your own taxonomical frameworks? What do you see as the common thread in that series?*

TS For me it is held together by the question of what is happening in the minds of the people who designed these things. What most immediately comes up for me when I think about this is the connection between nature and politics. It is the body of work of mine which arose in my mind the most quickly, at a time when I was at a point of not knowing what the next chapter was going to be. I sat in the studio with my assistants, and I said, 'Let's give it a work title.' This is how I have always worked; the street pictures were originally called 'Unconscious Places', the jungles were called 'New Pictures from Paradise'. How you describe something to yourself matters.

MP *You are defining the parameters.*

TS Yes, what the frame is. So that it is not so literal and indicates what I am interested in. So we called it 'Nature and Politics', which I didn't use because I thought it would be better to leave it open and let the public find a name for it. I find these are places of entanglement, where people get deeply involved in the desire and the strategy to solve a large problem, something they are fascinated by. The space programme, for example. At the Max Planck Institute for Plasma Physics they are trying to find a new and better method for generating energy through permanently running collisions of hydrogen atoms. One of the factories I photographed produces the base substance to make plastic. I was in a laboratory in Edinburgh – I am not sure exactly what they were studying.

MP *That is the image with the balloons. It is a funny picture.*

TS The balloons and the writing on the glass. It is funny because it shows a kind of tunnel vision – these workers are so entangled in solving particular problems that they are removed from the larger questions of what will happen in the long run, what might be the consequences of what they are doing. There is a picture of a wave tank filled with green water. It is a place in Edinburgh where they test which objects will, when placed on the surface of the ocean, pick up most energy from the waves. They are wave-energy power stations.

MP *Many of these industrial processes have idealistic purposes. They are trying to do something admirable, environmentally.*

TS Some of them. There is a picture of a nuclear power station in Germany that is being dismantled, but they began dismantling it in 1996, and it will take 25 or 30 years to take it down. There are a lot of dimensions to this, but my main picture of it all is of what I call entanglement.

MP *It is always clear that the industrial machinery the Bechers were photographing were relics from the past, whereas your pictures of industry present it as a living process the outcome of which remains in the balance. The processes you are picturing are always active.*

TS When I was a student I was not only very interested in the philosophical kernel of this problem but I also experienced it very personally, and thought about it a great deal. In general terms, how do you digest the past, what sense do you make of it, what is driving us in the present and what would be an ideal future? How would you define what you want to participate in? If you say, politically, I want to contribute to improvement in this or that direction, how do you motivate yourself? There is an essay by Walter Benjamin called 'Theses on the Philosophy of History' in which he uses a painting of Paul Klee, *Angelus Novus*, as an image to describe his perception of history. An angel looks at all the disasters that are piling up behind him in history as he is flying backwards towards the future. Despite all the disasters that the angel sees, there is some energy in the future that draws the angel forwards. Call it an idealism. Of course in recent German history there has been a gigantic disaster and I felt very close to it although it was in the era of my parents. When you consider that, it is unavoidable that this question of past, present and future is such a strong presence. As a primary school child I was surrounded by this atmosphere of destruction. You didn't see so much actual destruction, but you saw few old buildings. It was a view of disrupted history.

MP *You felt that you needed to articulate for yourself a strong purpose in order to forge forward, away from that past?*

TS Exactly. In my working mode I have always liked the idea of doing something orientated to thought of the future. In a way this is a contradiction of photography, which is a means of recording something immediately, which then belongs to the past. What drives me is the idea that maybe I can contribute something by showing that this entanglement will one day become more open and less conflicted. So you are always looking ahead of time into a different mode of existence.

MP *The photograph becomes a problem-solving device?*

TS It is like a springboard. It could be a transformative tool. It is a very high ambition, but I need this idea.

MP *But many of these recent photographs are apocalyptic. They seem to ask, What are we doing to nature? It is as though nature has been erased from the picture.*

When I looked at the photographs, there was a feeling of exhaustion. Our ambition and greed have manouevred us into a situation in which we have to believe in constant growth. It is difficult not to panic if we find we are in the same position as five years ago, that we don't have 3% economic growth.

MP *In making a big, beautifully produced photograph of this technology, does the spectacle of the image itself function as a confirmation, a value judgement of its subject? If you are photographing something you find morally ambiguous does that ambivalence enter into your techniques?*

TS In the 1960s and 70s, there was a lot of accusatory photography of big apartment buildings in the Marzahn area of Berlin. They were photographed in an ugly manner to enhance a sense of their ugliness, and I always felt that this failed as a strategy. I thought it much better to photograph very ugly buildings as immaculately as I could. I wanted to understand the fascination of the scientists who are working in these places. You see their investment. But since the reason you come to look at my photographs is nothing to do with that, you get a change of paradigm, a taste of both sides. I would be horrified if someone reacted to the series by saying they thought I was heroising these subjects.

MP *The pictures are varied in tone – some seem celebratory, marvelling at the extent of human ingenuity while others, of rusting dilapidated basements, look like you have descended with your camera into the bowels of hell.*

TS When I visited Cape Canaveral I was struck by the political implications of the space programme, which I hadn't thought about so much before. They are selling it to the US public as a tourist attraction, as a fascination with space, a marvel.

MP *Like Disneyland?*

TS Yes. The rocket garden. But when you really look at it, what shook me up was the immense dimensions of the project, the immense investment involved and the idea of world dominance bound up with it. There is a famous speech of Kennedy's, which I hadn't heard until then, in which he says, 'We choose the moon!', like an army general. Because we have the money and we have the guts. Very possessive. I thought, I have to do something with this. So it took a long time to get permission, but when I was there, I found it was something you could not really put in a photograph.

MP *The power structure, the sense of entitlement? You felt those things couldn't be depicted?*

TS They offered me the opportunity to photograph the repair of a
space shuttle. What I found was this utterly hand-crafted object. It
is all very advanced, but everything was handmade. All the tiles, the
washtub, the bathroom. For me this shows that the perfection is
not what it seems. When new technology is offered it is done in an
idealistic, clean, unproblematic manner without a full sense of its
implications – otherwise people wouldn't buy it. The taxpayer would
say, 'We're not paying for that, we don't need it.' But you wonder what
the costs are, the side effects. You see how high they can be, what
with all the problems around nuclear energy and the sinking of the
oil rig off the Gulf of Mexico. The space shuttle photograph is also
an image of restoration. They are replacing some of the tiles. And it
looks so much frailer than you would expect, which brings you back
to the bombastic, glitzy promises and reminds you that most of the
time these objects are made by you and me – by us. The object itself
is much softer and more human than the aggressive promotion that
comes with it.

Issue 347, June 2011

Christine Borland

interviewed by Rosie Lesso

Ghosts

ROSIE LESSO *Your 2011 exhibition at Camden Arts Centre, 'Cast from Nature', is the culmination of work completed during nine months in residence at Glasgow Sculpture Studios (GSS). I understand you encountered a sculpture at the Royal College of Surgeons (RCS) in Edinburgh which would become the starting point for your work during the residency.*

CHRISTINE BORLAND I had visited the Royal College of Surgeons some time before and encountered a figure which is a centrepiece in the exhibition space at Surgeons' Hall, a fibreglass cast sculpture of a flayed, partially dissected figure. There are several labels on the sculpture, one of which reads, 'Cast from Nature 1845', and which attributes the dissection and presumably the sculpture to Sir John Goodsir, who was head of anatomy at Edinburgh University in the mid 19th century. Another label indicates that the fibreglass replica of the original plaster cast was commissioned by the National Museums of Scotland in 1986. I made some initial enquiries about the original sculpture – where it was, who made it, who the subject was and if any original moulds existed. The short answer to all those questions was: 'Don't know!' So the initial enquiry led nowhere.

RL *But you persevered, in spite of the lack of information?*

CB I left it for a while, which is the way I like to work; to be intrigued by a subject and have it sit at the back of my mind while I work on other things, then to revisit it again after a period of time. That process suits me really well. I was invited to do a production residency at Glasgow Sculpture Studios in 2010, which I started working on in August, with a show scheduled for November. Originally I thought my starting point could be the plaster-cast heads from the 'SimBodies' and 'NoBodies' series, which were shown in 'An Entangled Bank' at the Talbot Rice Gallery in Edinburgh in 2009, with a view to trying to cast on a more ambitious scale. But when I moved into the empty studio space it seemed to offer the chance for a clean slate, so rather than bring previous work out of storage I decided to start afresh. In looking for new starting points, I went back to see the sculpture at the RCS and followed up on my initial questions, but without any better outcomes.

RL *So why were you still attracted to the work when it seemed to be leading nowhere?*

CB Perversely, that missing information, and therefore the inability to contextualise the sculpture, was definitely part of the appeal. If all the information had been a given, I think this would have just become a footnote work, leading somewhere else. The fact that it is such a striking statement in the centre of a large museum yet nobody officially seemed to be able to tell me anything about it made me want to find out more. If the purpose of the work was as an educational dissection demonstration, why choose such an extreme pose? I suspected it would have been made with an exhibition in mind but, again, for what purpose?

RL *So where did the research process lead you?*

CB To Edinburgh College of Art (ECA), where they have a great cast collection, including an écorché known as 'Smugglerius', which had recently been the subject of a research project, and a cast of the Christ figure from Michelangelo's *Pietà*. The positioning of the body looked very similar to the sculpture at the RCS, so I wondered if there was a chance that maybe the artist who posed *Cast from Nature* could have seen the ECA work, if not the original *Pietà*, and deliberately positioned the body in the same way. What also intrigued me about the ECA cast was that it is really just the front face which has been cast, so it doesn't have any depth. You can go right behind the beautiful, smooth, idealised surface replica and the caster's hand marks are clearly visible. In complete contrast to the front, they are really quite rough and violent, and an intimate signature of the anonymous person who made the cast.

RL *So there is a hidden element to the work which is actually very awkward and uncomfortable, but far more real than the perfect surface of the replica, the only element we are meant to see.*

CB Exactly. This reinforced my interest in pursuing the *Cast from*

Nature original and the possibility that in making a cast, a replica, there could still be room for me in there as an artist too. As it often works out, the time spent researching this project gave me the space to develop more ideas around where I wanted it to go.

RL *Was it a difficult process trying to track down the original* Cast from Nature *sculpture?*

CB There wasn't much to be gleaned through official channels in the museums but I eventually became a right pest, asking everyone I could think of about the work. A conversation with the collections' manager at the RCS who knew all the collections in Edinburgh revealed that a similar sculpture had once been on display in the University of Edinburgh's medical school. Following up this lead, I found out that there was a vast basement in the medical school, full of specimens which had been damaged or withdrawn from display.

RL *The sound of that place must have been very enticing to you, given that this kind of subject has informed so much of your practice over the years.*

CB Well yes, and almost a cliché in that it was so exactly what you might expect. Behind a creaky wooden door was a dingy basement full of cobwebs and corridor after corridor filled with body fragments preserved in all kinds of ways – an amazing sight. At the end of a labyrinth of corridors was the damaged plaster sculpture of the *Cast from Nature* body. I am sure this is not the one that the fibreglass was made from as there are no traces of the process of fibreglass casting, which is quite invasive.

RL *Do you think more work might come out of the experience in that basement at the university?*

CB Absolutely! I really had to put blinkers on to try to stay focused on the original subject, but it was so full of possibilities. The medical school is relocating, so it is unlikely that this unloved collection will stay together. Before it goes, I would at least like to document it.

RL *I am particularly interested in how you set this casting process up as a performance, a live feed, so viewers could watch the painstaking process of making the mould over a number of months, screened in front of a tiered seating arrangement resembling a traditional anatomy lecture theatre.*

CB Normally artists would have a three-month residency with a five-month exhibition at the end of it, but the first three months were really spent sourcing the subject, so the format of the residency had to be changed to fit my project. The work you see in Camden Arts Centre existed here, in Glasgow, but only for a few weeks as the end result of what became a nine- month residency.

RL *So you changed the making of the work into a performance in itself. Was this approach something you had tried before?*

CB No. But that kind of process is something I am interested in. Take the research I do in medical schools. I have long been intrigued by the ways in which they teach communication skills now, and how the performance elements of that link to the early anatomists and the notion of the surgeon as a performer. I haven't done anything nearly as direct as the set-up here but it was born out of experience in a way.

RL *The nature of your project sounds as if it grew and changed quite a lot during this process.*

CB It did. And knowing the way the GSS building is used – that it is primarily a production space, studios and workshops – I felt it would be great for the artists there to encounter a project which evolved through a sculptural process. There is always a feeling that, however good the exhibitions are at GSS, you can't help but be intrigued by what is going on behind those closed doors, where the work is actually being made.

RL *Your residency was therefore remoulded contextually to suit the creative and evolving nature of what happens in the rest of the building, which seems like a natural evolution.*

CB Yes, that's right. If the project had always been destined only for Camden I wouldn't have built that element into the work. It is entirely appropriate here as this is a production space, but if I was to do something similar in another venue without this context then it wouldn't sit quite so easily, it would be in danger of becoming a 'mock-up'. I would still like to unpick further elements of the theatricality of the anatomy lesson. The live feed also makes a direct reference to contemporary medical education, which is something I'll continue to explore.

RL *It must have been strange to have been working knowing people were watching you, especially if this is something you aren't used to. Didn't you find that off-putting?*

CB The *Big Brother* element was there but I was surprised that I could quickly accept the situation and be completely natural. I purposely built an arena with a sculptural presence because that was to be the main exhibit for the majority of the time. It wasn't a replica anatomy theatre but it was resonant of those kinds of spaces.

RL *The relationship with medical education in this project makes me think of your exhibition at Ormeau Baths Gallery in Belfast in 2009 that you referred to earlier, 'SimBodies' and 'NoBodies', in which there was a series of works exploring the use of 'simulated patients'.*

cb   Yes, observing the teaching of communication skills in the 'safe' environment of medical schools really spoke to me of the kind of audience catharsis possible in the seminal performance pieces by artists like Chris Burden, Yoko Ono and Marina Abramović. I observed the students responding to scenarios with actor patients, like breaking the bad news of terminal diagnoses from test results.

rl   *Did the medical students you worked with find this acting part of their training hard work?*

cb   Yes, it is very stressful, and not only in a way that is inevitable as training for the real situations. These scenarios operate on so many levels. After viewing a live feed of the role play, the class hear the actor come out of character to give feedback on how they felt as 'themselves', and as their character. Within their own context no one is able to step away and see through all these layers of simulation. The students themselves are aware of these contradictions, of being taught to 'act' empathically, and usually have a desire to be themselves, to be real. It related a lot to Hal Foster and Jean Baudrillard's theories which were so much part of the discourse in which I was interested when starting out as an artist in the early 1990s.

rl   *So was that project the first in which you really explored medical teaching in any depth?*

cb   That exhibition was the starting point of using medical education as a part of my work but the research really goes back further to 2001, when I was making a commissioned public artwork installed at Glasgow University when the new medical school had just opened. I was doing research as part of the development of that project and spent time looking at the new aspects of the building, including a whole floor of suites with surveillance cameras and sound equipment transmitting live action via camera from one room to another. I also became acutely aware of the use of simulated patient manikins, which students use for the practical, clinical aspects of their training They are nasty figurative sculptures, so difficult to relate to that the students generally have a good laugh when working with them.

rl   *Do you then see more personality in the Victorian educational medical tools that have been used so often in your work, including* Cast from Nature?

CB   Since many of them were made by skilled artists, I'm certainly more drawn to them, but the problems with many of them are similar to those reflected in *Cast from Nature*, they are overtly aestheticised and emotive. I haven't found the answer – it is more about the importance of raising the question.

RL   *To move on to your exhibition at Camden Arts Centre, how did the final display come together?*

CB   Although I work with many different materials, I usually pass the final production over to someone else, so I wouldn't normally have such a long experience with the process in the way that I have had here. So many of the discoveries made during that experience are evident in the final presentation of the work. Maybe without the oppor-tunity of the residency I would have given the cast to someone else to do and the work would look completely different.

RL   *What kind of discoveries are you talking about?*

CB   Well, for one, the decision to show two sculptures – one facing up, one down.

RL   *What happened in the process of making which led you to this outcome?*

CB   During the mould-making you have this strange experience of creating negative space, such a long process to create a void which then needs filling. You can't help but form a very personal relationship with the subject. The positioning came from the purely practical act that to get the plaster into the mould, everything was lying face down and I instinctively knew that this different perspective was doing something very powerful.

RL   *Yes, the two Camden sculptures each trigger their own set of emotional responses just by straightforward inversion. So there is an element of simplicity, but also the complexity that the viewer brings to the work and the comparisons they intuitively make between them.*

CB   There is this allusion to freedom in the one on his front, which accentuates the deadening effect of the other pose, on his back. The swathe of fabric also accentuates this dividing line between the two sculptures. That came about because I wanted to investigate the drapery which was part of the original. In the original *Cast from Nature*, the drapery was used to preserve some kind of modesty when the most intimate details were already revealed by the dissection. My work on the fabric evolved in a very traditional way, the artist working in a studio, experimenting with sculptural materials – all quite 19th century. But this is not a way of working that I have had much previous experience with.

RL *Would you say a less rational end result came about from this project as a result of the residency, in contrast with some of your previous work which you have made without a specific, designated studio space to work in?*

CB Yes. But it still makes some kind of rational sense too, although the conceptual elements came together during the process.

RL *How did you find the experience of working across two sites so closely towards the end of your residency, particularly as the work at Camden was initially shown at GSS?*

CB The black box situation at GSS is very different from Camden's space, with all its period architectural detail and natural light. They both had a very different dramatic tension. In its current context at Camden the work is released from the very direct physical link to the process but still seems quite complete. But I didn't feel the need to show, say, slides or a film of the work being made alongside it because the process was so built in and remained visible, as evident in the hand marks and casting lines, which were left rough.

RL *Are the materials you use always considered an important element of the final work? I am thinking about the austere white plaster in your current project, and plaster's ghostly qualities, as well as its ability to replicate.*

CB Plaster has such a historical reference that just by choosing it as a material you can say a huge amount. The sentiment always sticks in my mind from a piece of carved marble by Ian Hamilton Finlay in Kelvingrove Museum in Glasgow, which says 'clay the life, plaster the death, marble the revolution', which sums up how I read those materials. The fact that plaster comes from the earth and has this amazing chemical ability to change from rock to liquid and back to a hard material, and this ability to create a ghost – a second life through death – makes it work in so many ways for me.

RL *And I suppose the film you made for the RSA Morton Award, which documented elements of your* Cast from Nature *sculpture being made, also exploited the unique properties of plaster, with condensation gathering on the glass next to it as the plaster warmed during the setting process. It was as if it was breath coming from the sculpture.*

CB That original idea came about by accident when I was working in a freezing old church as a temporary studio on head casts for the 'SimBodies' and 'NoBodies' series. I could feel the plaster was still warm when I took it from the mould, so I put a glass jar over it.

431

The obscuring and revealing that came from those works, slowing the viewer down to engage with the subject, is something that I am always trying to do, both in the film and in the sculpture.

RL *There is a real tranquillity in the film and I think that is the most important element of what divides your work from direct medical research – that stopping, slowing down and making people take time to look.*

CB It is quite clear that people involved in medical research do not have the luxury to take the time that I have, so I see it as an important role, going into these situations and asking questions which they aren't able to, opening up that space for reflection which they don't have on a day-to-day basis. I used to feel that I didn't know enough and was shy about asking uninformed questions, but I now see real value in it as it is becoming clear that people in those situations have themselves gained something from the work that I do. I don't want to be the person investigating the value in the work that they do: I would rather start a process of positive questioning.

RL *It is clear to see the kinds of questions you have raised in relation to medical education which could then have a hugely positive knock-on effect somewhere down the line. Can you give any examples of the more recent kinds of questions you have raised within the medical establishment which might incite change in a similar kind of way?*

CB In relation to *Cast from Nature*, I have had a number of discussions with anatomists at Glasgow University who realised that they always dissect bodies in the same position, so they constantly see the anatomical structures in the same way. But they are now considering what would happen if that could be changed, even in a small way. So it is possible to open up different ways of looking and seeing. Traditions can get entrenched so quickly and if no one questions them they can really narrow possibilities for seeing things anew. Along with this exhibition at GSS it was important to organise a programme of talks and events and include the voices of people from medicine and science who have informed what I am doing, to come and share their experiences with the audience.

RL *I was just thinking back to your work* Phantom Twins, *1997, and wondering what role the Gothic still played in your work. In* Cast from Nature *there is this grimace on the man's face which is very unsettling.*

CB I am drawn to the Gothic; maybe it helps stop the work being too cold or clinical. I have made quite a number of works that reference Mary Shelley's *Frankenstein*, so I do indulge occasionally.

RL *I suppose you don't want it to become gratuitous.*

CB No, but making artwork allows the freedom to indulge or pull back as I choose. What makes me feel OK about *Cast from Nature* is the fact that the more Gothic element was already there. When we looked together at the cast I showed you how the wooden false teeth had probably been inserted under the gum to rebuild the structure of a sinking face, creating this grimace. I am revealing it, but I am not actually creating it – these rules I set for myself control how far I can go with this type of imagery.

RL *So why do you keep returning so often to the Victorian, or Post-Enlightenment period of medical education, as you have done with this current project?*

CB I do keep going back to that era for many reasons. Discoveries were so urgent and exciting at that time, scientists were steamrolling forward and the discoveries made paved the way for the future of medicine, but they set aside or ignored ethical concerns for the 'greater good'.

Issue 348, July–August 2011

Ryan Gander

interviewed by Alex Coles

Happenstance

ALEX COLES *I'm particularly interested in your collaborative works with designers – they seem to expand the already broad discursive territory that you move around in. But I find it curious that, given your general interest in triggering discourse on your work and producing work as discourse with the ongoing series of 'Loose Association Lectures', you don't have a discourse worker on the payroll in your studio.*

RYAN GANDER What's a discourse worker? A clever bod?

AC *Kind of...*

RG What would they do in my studio? Blog about me?

AC *Perhaps, but they could also read books that you don't have time to read and generate seminars and conferences about your work – generally accumulating discourse on it.*

RG Would you have to pay them more because they're clever?

AC *I'm not too sure, but I can try and find out for you. One thing a discourse worker would do is ensure that interesting essays and interviews were strategically commissioned for books and catalogues about your work. I noticed that the book you did with the graphic design collective Åbäke,* Ryan Gander: Catalogue Raisonnable, Vol. 1, 2010, *doesn't have any new texts in it at all. Your discourse worker could have plugged that hole for you. But I guess that the book doesn't need any new essays: it is already textually dense because of the way Åbäke designs. In fact, it is really unusual for an artist to have such an open attitude towards collaborating with graphic designers.*

RG Do you think?

AC *Definitely. Most artists probably wouldn't view it as a collaborative process at all – or at least not to the extent that you do.*

RG   I studied interactive art at Manchester Metropolitan University so there were playwrights, ballet dancers, computer animators, furniture designers as well as graphic designers on the course. They were just people I would talk with.

AC   *Maki Suzuki from Åbäke walked me through the design process of your book a little in preparation for this interview, explaining how at the beginning of the research for the book you personally selected the pieces you did and didn't want to include, and how as a result this made Maki want to include everything you had ever done in the book.*

RG   But not everything is in there. There is an erratum that lists the pieces that have been taken out – mainly for political reasons.

AC   *Like what?*

RG   You know – when you've made something and then you make another one but give it a different name. Anything that could make me look like a trustafarian trying to generate cash was taken out. Works that I remade afterwards but didn't want to delete from history were also taken out and works that I generally felt were rubbish. Basically, everything is in the book, but not everything is glorified.

AC   *Were Åbäke the first graphic designers you collaborated with?*

RG   No, that was Stuart Bailey of Dexter Sinister and The Lending Library.

AC   *So it was always important for you to be in dialogue with graphic designers?*

RG   Yeah. And when I was in Amsterdam for three years, Stuart lived down the road. We were like the expats and would have dinner together every night.

AC   *What year is this?*

RG   1999 to 2001. Stuart was teaching and starting up Dot Dot Dot and I was at the Rijksakademie.

AC   *When was your first collaboration?*

RG   We worked on the book *Appendix* for two years before it was published in 2003. There are probably 150 pages in it but it felt like we generated something like 500-odd. In 2007 we did a sequel *Appendix, Appendix* and laid it out at Marc Fox gallery in Los Angeles while I was having a show there.

AC   *So for you a graphic designer was always another form of practitioner?*

RG   Yes. I've designed a few books myself but I don't feel so comfortable in this role. That 'jack of all trades master of none' thing always worries me. I prefer someone else to do it.

AC *When you are working with Stuart or Åbäke or the young graphic design collective Europa do you intermingle your studio cultures to help the collaboration?*

RG No. The collaboration with Stuart happened in our respective apartments and then later in a little side room in the gallery in LA. The big book with Åbäke was designed and edited at my house in Suffolk: three laptops, a printer and a very large table with lots of readymade meals – that's all you need.

AC *It was interesting talking with Maki: the art galleries funding the book obviously wanted the section with the colour images of your work. Then for you and Åbäke the rest of the book was the pay-off for having to do that.*

RG It was a bit like that. Artists are always down on cataloguing things they have made. The preference is to make an artists' book, but I've done almost ten of them now and actually wanted something more detailed. At my studio we use the book every day as a reference – it's so handy because we know everything in it is correct. In a way it sets things in stone; there can be no more fluctuations.

AC *What informed your choice of Åbäke as collaborator on such an important project, one that represents what you do?*

RG They are friends and it's nice to work with different people each time you do something. Many graphic designers have their own stylistic signature but I don't necessarily think they are good graphic designers. The good ones go into a project open and generate something that interprets the specific situation they are in. And with Åbäke you know this is what you are going to get. They take a long time trying to understand the situation before they design anything.

AC *Their designs seem to operate in parallel to their subject, whereas the designs of someone like Experimental Jetset do the exact opposite.*

RG Exactly – traditionally graphic design is about economising information.

AC *What do you think of someone like M/M (Paris) from a generation earlier who also work closely with artists like Pierre Huyghe and Liam Gillick?*

RG I don't see what they do as graphic design. It's stylistic brand-making or something. Their contribution to the 1999 *Ann Lee* project was its branding.

AC *But don't a lot of designers traditionally do precisely that?*

RG But then a lot of artists do watercolours. M/M (Paris) have an ambition to be artists, which was obvious to me when I met them for a chat in Paris. But you are only as good as what you make. If the first thing that comes into someone's mind when they see something you have done is whether it's design or art, then it's probably shit to begin with. If it's something good, you are just blown away by it no matter what it is.

The whole thing about the current design market is odd. This year I went to Design Miami/Basel. Everything there looked like art that did stuff: here's an Anish Kapoor with a light on top; there's an Antony Gormley with a rug attached to it. So strange! It's all so compromised in its integrity by needing to have a function or be shiny and unique. I thought it was awful. What did you start with that book [*DesignArt*] you did?!

AC *In your works that appropriate product design you enter into a different form of collaboration – an involuntary form of collaboration. I'm thinking of the way you use Konstantin Grcic's* Chair_ONE [*Attempting to Visualize the way in which one's work would appear..., 2009*] *or Gerrit Rietveld's crate chairs in your Rietveld reconstruction series of 2006.*

RG The Grcic is just a little tongue-in-cheek thing. Those chairs are not comfortable for everyone – you need to have a very particular physique otherwise sitting on them gives you a pain in the bum. At home we have eight different chairs around our dining room table and one of them is Grcic's but it has a cheap IKEA cushion on it. We have one in the studio too – I placed a cardboard box from B&Q on that one. They are two variations on how to make a wonderful looking thing actually work.

AC *How did the Rietveld series come about?*

RG They had his crate chairs at the Jan van Eyck Akademie where I did my postgraduate course. I sat on them most days. I asked the woodwork technician to cut me the bits to make two chairs and a table so that I would have some appropriate furniture in my studio space there. But the technician just gave me all the bits with no plan of how to assemble them. Someone came into my studio space and saw me with all these bits and asked why I hadn't been able to assemble the furniture yet – they said it was so easy it was like child's play. That got me thinking: what would happen if a child tried to put this together? Perhaps there is this inherent modernist quality to the wood – maybe it's like magic dust and the children will automatically make Tatlin's tower. So there were ten experiments with ten children to see if that modernist magic was actually in the wood. One child made a table and chair but the rest made crazy compositions.

AC *How come there is no record of that one successful version,* Rietveld Reconstruction – Cosimo, *2006, in your book with Åbäke?*

RG There is, but instead of an image there is just the title and a blank space. I didn't take an image of it at the time. But volume two will have some stickers with images of the work missing in the first one so that you can go back and add them – if I can track down the work, that is.

AC *How did this year's recent project with the product designer Michael Marriott* Ernó Goldfinger v Groucho Marx *at the Russian Club come about?*

RG We've known each other for years through friends. Michael's 'Mies Meets Marx' exhibition at the Geffrye Museum in 2002 was amazing. In terms of what we were saying earlier, the way I see it is that people like Michael aren't really designers or artists: they are conceptualists. They instigate something and it doesn't really matter what area it's in. Åbäke are the same: they edit an album or a book and they stage an installation or a dinner party – it's all about instigating concepts.

AC *I know what you mean, but even when you pay no regard to medium and context those things are still there.*

RG Maybe, or maybe not. With Michael his ideas can come out in a mug or a bedside cabinet, and it doesn't matter which because it's about generating ideas and posing problems and solving them. The object or thing that results is just a by-product, it's not a thing in itself. On the bookshelves in Maki's old apartment he turned the spines of all the books he'd read against the wall. That's a thought process being visualised, it's not a thing in itself. In their kitchen, Maki and Kajsa Ståhl have stuck jam jars to the underside of rows of shelving – instead of sitting on the shelves they hang under them. When you want a jar you simply unscrew it. Actually, Maki did this one wrong: he pierced the lids with a screw to attach them to the shelf instead of fixing them with Araldite. Now they aren't airtight – that means soft pine nuts. A design flaw!

AC *Was the Russian Club collaboration with Michael your first one together?*

RG Yeah. They sometimes do two-person shows there. Michael had done a previous one with them and one day Matt Golden and I were talking about how much we admired his work and I mentioned that

I'd love to do something with him.

Our installation looked at Ernö Goldfinger's Trellick Tower from 1966 and his house at 2 Willow Road from 1939. Michael and I are both big fans. I've even written a children's book about him: *The Boy Who Always Looked Up*. The great thing with Goldfinger is that he was someone who saw a need for something and then acted on it. The two things that we took a slant on in the show were both lifted from Willow Road. Mine was a viewing device – a big box on a stand with a bookshelf that was originally used by the surrealists for loose association collages. Michael's addressed a table Goldfinger made out of an old iron base. We also had text: a transcription from one of my associative lectures and the catalogue that the graphic designer Alex Rich designed for 'Mies Meets Marx' were laid out along the gallery wall.

AC *Wasn't there another project that you wanted to do with Michael that involved building a series of studios?*

RG Yes. There is an Isokon house about five miles from my house in Suffolk. It's a small one-story holiday home built on the same principles as the company. Michael stayed there once. One day we were talking about it and I was looking at plots of land in the area – just thinking, really. Then I found an old derelict school house in our town and was considering doing a summer academy or something. I thought that if I built five of these holiday houses in a row then I could turn it into a project, selling a few and keeping one back for Michael and one for myself. Each of the houses would be quite different: the one for a writer would have good views, the one for the typographer good skylights and so on. They would all appear the same from the outside, like a row of traditional cottages, but if you viewed them from above each one would look completely different. This also relates back to 2 Willow Road because Goldfinger designed the living room with his wife Ursula Blackwell, who was a painter, in mind. Towards the back of the living room there is a studio-like space for her: a stage to paint on with massive skylights.

AC *Returning to your collaborations with Åbäke for a moment, I have seen a rough proof of the second collaboration you did together – the forthcoming catalogue for your exhibition at the Villa Arson in 2009, 'The Die is Cast'. Where* Ryan Gander: Catalogue Raisonnable, Vol. 1, *was more of an equal balance between you and them, the catalogue is quite different.*

RG   I sort of left them to it with this one. It's more like a book about me by them. The way they did it was to consider me as a fictional artist: 'Ryan Gander' [spoken with a heavy French accent] rather than Ryan Gander. The CV that's in the back of the catalogue only lists the things I've done in France, so it's actually quite misleading if you don't know much about what I do. Åbäke had picked up on the methodology I use when making works to edit and design the catalogue. That takes some balls for a designer to do because the results can be difficult for people to accept.

AC   *This notion of the fictional does of course underpin a large portion of your work – including the* Locked Room Scenario, *2011, completed for Artangel. While you have used this strategy before, the extent and scale with which it is played through in this work feels like something new.*

RG   It's weird because when people see the installation they comment on the architecture of the piece, even though this is only 20% of the piece. It only being this 20% is important: most of the works are hidden.

AC   *By way of a put-down, one review used the title 'Ryan Gander: An Underwhelming Scenario', which I really liked because I think they are right but not in the way they intended. Your work requires the spectator to meet the work more than half way; it is much more discreet than the installations of Mike Nelson and Gregor Schneider which it has been compared with. In this sense, it's underwhelming – but strategically so.*

RG   Maybe.

AC   *Or perhaps* Locked Room Scenario *is the exact opposite. Compared with some of your other work, it is actually quite stage-like – it dramatises the situation of being a spectator.*

RG   That is precisely what I didn't want. It is not really staged. It is insofar as it's constructed but the devices it uses are very much things we associate with the everyday world: it's not like I'm making a space station or something. More than anything I was trying to create an air of uncertainty, pressing the spectator to ask what is real and what isn't. In some way your life feels staged when you leave – that was one of the motivations for doing the piece. The work uses fiction but as a catalyst in the mind of the spectator. It doesn't present a completed scenario that has been targeted.

One of the problems I have with the piece now is that nobody understands how much bloody effort went into making it! The install alone took five weeks: four weeks building walls and the rest developing the devices in it and doing the workshops with the actors.

AC   *This is where your discourse worker could come in: they would have forcefully put that across for you.*

RG   Probably, but I'm not sure my need to communicate a definitive message is that strong. That is not to say that the work lacks meaning, it's just that meaning is appreciated more when you discover it by happenstance rather than having it spoon fed. I can't be too grown up about it – that would take the fun out of it.

Issue 351, November 2011

Judith Barry

interviewed by Omar Kholeif

Cairo Stories

OMAR KHOLEIF *Your latest body of work, ...Cairo stories, 2011, which was presented in two different forms first in Sharjah and later in Munich, took you almost a decade to complete. How did it evolve and why did it take so long to produce?*

JUDITH BARRY I represented the US in the Cairo Biennale in 2001 and I fell in love with the city. In March 2003 Scott Bailey, then director of the American University in Cairo Gallery, invited me to make a project and that is when I began what became ...*Cairo stories*.

Coincidentally, this is also when the US began the second Iraq War. I was interviewing women on the streets around the AUC, then located in downtown near Tahrir Square, and, when rioting broke out, my project was deemed seditious and I was 'escorted' out of Egypt. Subsequently I made many trips to Cairo, progressively expanding my contacts, to reach the 214 women whose stories inform the current iteration of ...*Cairo stories*. As I wanted it to be an in-depth examination of women's lives across the many strata of Cairene culture, I never conceived of ...*Cairo stories* as something to be finished quickly. What was much more important was that it should reverberate with the women whose lives it was about. In many ways ...*Cairo stories* found me. When I was first in Cairo, many women I met casually revealed very personal things to me about their lives, possibly because I was a 'foreigner' and they could speak more freely with me than with someone from their own culture. This piqued my interest in the lives of women in Cairo and I became interested in the specificity of how women negotiate the daily existence of their lives.

OK *In Sharjah the work was presented in the public realm as large-scale*

outdoor projections, while in Munich the work was far more intimate
for the spectator because it was presented as six individual installation
experiences in the gallery space. What was the reason for positioning the
work in these two different ways and which is the ideal scenario?

JB   I see the exhibition spaces that constitute the art world as open-
ended and allowing a certain kind of freedom, in terms of the
questions of representation, especially compared to the commercial
realm. Hence, I cannot say that there are only two ways to present
...Cairo stories or any of my works. I often redesign my installations
and the content in relation to the exhibition context. For *...Cairo
stories* in particular, both the form and the content – to go back to
an early proto-semiotic formulation – produce meaning. Stories
in particular lend themselves to many types of formulations and
iterations. I can imagine it in many forms – including in written form
or aurally. I am sure there are ways of presenting it that I have not yet
thought of.

There are, however, several conditions that I like to insist upon
when presenting this project. I seek to locate the work somehow
within Middle Eastern and North African communities. In Munich we
projected out of the windows of Import Export, an alternative space
in the Arab part of the city. To make a context for the work, we also
screened the film *Microphone*, 2010, which attracted a mixed audience
of Turkish, Arabic and German speakers during the time that we
were projecting there. While the stories were initially shot using
actors speaking both Egyptian Arabic and English, a voice-over in
German was included because reading subtitles takes away from the
emotional impact of the stories.

I also insist that the stories appear and then disappear when they
are projected or shown on a plasma screen. That the stories appear
and disappear is central to the overall concept of the series of works
of which *...Cairo stories* is a part. I wanted to find a way to underscore
what is unexpected in the way a story might be told, as well as to
give a presence to that which might be unknown or unrepresented.
In a sense a kind of 'magic' occurs when the stories are projected –
suddenly on a blank wall a face materialises and then, during the
storytelling process, the face becomes the person whose story it is.
This also distinguishes the stories from television and news. Hence,
there is a 30-second pause between stories where the wall is blank,
and then a 30-second dissolve. This provides a separation between

the stories so that they don't blur together for the viewer.

The first iteration of the project, *first and third*, produced for the 1987 Whitney Biennial, was shown when few women or minorities were presented in that museum. I located the project – which was about hopes for an American Dream among recent immigrants – in disused spaces in the museum and disguised the video projector so that it disappeared into the space, hence to the viewer it appeared as though the walls themselves were speaking.

OK *There is an obvious desire to unpack the mechanisms of representation in this work, not only of Arab women but, more specifically, Cairene women. What interested you in this?*

JB There are a lot of stereotypes circulating about women in the Middle East and North Africa (MENA) region, yet the cultures of the various countries that make up the region are different. Cairo, being a place that many people visit because of the pyramids, is also one of the loci of 'Orientalism'. As Edward Said discussed, the construction of the terms 'Oriental', 'Arab' or 'Middle Eastern' to describe people in this region is the attempt in occidental discourse to impose the hegemony of the West over many disparate cultures with the specific aim of devaluing them for subjugation – hence, not western is not rational, not trustworthy and not capable of self-government – and the specificity of any and all differences is erased. One antidote to this erasure of difference, as Said argued, was to employ narrative rather than visual strategies as a means of both empowering local voices in particular places and representing the complexities of specific experiences throughout a region – in this case Cairo. I use the documentary tradition and artistic licence to reconsider a conundrum posed by Ludwig Wittgenstein – that ordinary language is unable to convey the extraordinariness of existence.

The stories we tell each other – and ourselves – bear witness to how what is subjective and what is objective in our own histories also intersects with larger historical narratives and how all are partial and, simultaneously, each offers a multiplicity of representations. Do the stories we tell each other more accurately reflect who we are than the facts of our lives? I think so.

OK *What was so culturally specific or unique about women from Cairo?*

JB Many things! Initially, I interviewed women from privileged classes, and I was shocked to realise how little freedom these women have to determine the trajectory of their lives. Yes, they have money, but they have much less freedom than women in the middle and working classes. Their parents determine who they marry, what they study, where they live and so on. Their rueful understanding of their actual situation was often a by-product of our interviews. Although across MENA parents do suggest marriage partners, Cairo is less sophisticated than cosmopolitan Beirut, or so they told me. As I met more women from the middle and working class I began to see how less parental and societal pressure among these classes allows women more freedom to reinvent themselves. Also, the paucity of jobs in Egypt often means that working-class women are the breadwinners in their families as there is less of a stigma attached to a woman doing 'menial' work than would be attached to a man doing such work. The money this generates gives women agency both within their families and in society. Family is what matters most. Women as the primary earners can assert their power.

Meanwhile, the culture itself was becoming seemingly more conservative and, simultaneously, more liberal. In 2001, it was extremely unusual to see a woman in a niqab and very few women wore a headscarf. Gradually more and more women became 'covered'. Yet, no matter what the class and background, when asked, each had unique reasons for adopting it. Sometimes women would wear a headscarf in one part of the city but not another – for instance, downtown. In a sense it functions like a uniform to ward off harassment.

That Cairo has become more liberal is reflected in the agency of the educated classes, men and women – university is free – and also in the increased agency of many of the working-class women.

As I heard many times during the revolution: poverty does not produce revolution, agency does, and this includes the hopes and dreams that reverberated through Tahrir as we were filming ...*Cairo stories*. Revolution is born from those aspirations.

OK *Your project was initiated after a trip to Cairo at the beginning of the new millennium. Did you ever feel conscious of the imperial connotations of your 'American-ness' while producing this work, especially considering the fact that you were working on the project during the start of the second Iraq War?*

JB I felt my 'American-ness' most during the Cairo Biennale as these events are so nationalistic.

One reason I fell in love with Cairo was because of the bantering – the jokes and storytelling I heard while wandering the streets. Cairo is polyglot, particularly downtown. Teashops and vendors blend with the sidewalk, and pedestrian traffic threads through labyrinthine passageways. Everyone talks to you, everyone has something to tell you, and after a while you realise that this storytelling, this form of engagement, is central to the social fabric and identity of the city. It is how you negotiate the city and also how you find your place within it – although for young women, this can often be rather difficult as they are the most distressed by the harassment.

After war broke out, I noticed the mood of the city towards me, a western person, change radically. Suddenly, taxi drivers no longer bantered with me, even the 'harassment' was noticeably subdued. The mood was wary, solemn, and I felt I was being watched more but no longer engaged with. This did not extend to the women I was interviewing as I had close relationships with my translators and this eased any tensions that these women felt, I think. Nonetheless, I always felt safe walking late at night – something I don't always feel in parts of New York City, where I live.

OK   *The use of actors in the different presentations creates a theatricality that emboldens the work. For me, at times it could feel like an uncomfortably mediated experience. What was your intention in this?*

JB   There are many reasons – especially for *...Cairo stories* – that I use actors for these 'as-told-to' stories. Most women would not agree to have their photograph taken, much less allow a video of themselves to be shown. The non-linearity of the interview process means the stories don't often come out in a linear form, there were many digressions, as well as many people in attendance: translators – a crucial element in this process – family members, friends, neighbours, children. So that is the practical answer to your question.

More importantly, I have long been engaged with questions of 'what does it mean to image someone', to take their photograph or video them? How can you give the subject of the photo or video control over their image? How are you, as an artist, responsible for the use to which their image is put? These are all questions that were circulating within the art world in the 1980s and became part of the discourse of Postmodernism. My strategy for this series as a whole, and especially for Cairo, has been to pay people fairly throughout the process and to protect their privacy. All the interviewees and translators were paid, as was everyone else, including my team of Egyptian women advisers with whom I vetted all the stories.

Additionally, these women were telling me their stories because they wanted their stories to be heard. Having actors embody their stories enhanced the emotion of the stories and, after viewing the acting in other iterations of the series, they all agreed actors were the best solution to the issues raised above.

OK *How did the community that you were working with evolve and change over the period of your research?*

JB It grew and grew. I began with the undergrad students in the art and theatre department at the AUC. Throughout this process William Wells at the Townhouse Gallery was a crucial adviser. Gradually I extended the interviews across a network that included many other classes and across many parts of the city – from Cairo to the areas surrounding the city where the undocumented workers live and finally to parts of New Cairo.

I have kept in touch with many of the women – especially the translators and advisers whose work was obviously crucial to the success of the project, as well as the interviewees. I mean it when I say that ...*Cairo stories* is a collaboration.

OK *I take some issue with writers, organisations, artists, curators etc who piggyback this notion of the Arab Spring, professing some grandiose prophecy that they were able to surmise through their practice. But still, I can't help but ask, did the recent dissidence encourage you to read or interpret some of the stories any differently in retrospect?*

JB No. I was ready to shoot the project when the revolution began in Tahrir Square, hence I had already written and vetted the stories with my team. When it became clear that it would be very difficult to shoot in Cairo – this was mid January 2011 before the revolution began – I moved the shoot to NYC where there is a large cohort of Egyptian-Arabic actors. We began shooting in late January and I was able to include two stories from women at Tahrir Square.

These were relayed to me by my team of advisers and I included them almost verbatim, quickly casting actors and rehearsing them with the Egyptian dramaturges we had flown in for the shoot. During breaks in shooting we were glued to Al Jazeera on the computer – at the time not on TV channels in New York. You can imagine the mood on the set: elation mixed with excitement, and also at times a great deal of fear. We wrapped two days after President Mubarak stepped down.

OK *Representation of the Arab world has been perpetually mediated by mainstream news media, at times defacing it, distantiating it, rendering it*

devoid of intimacy. You, on the other hand, dig deep into the heart of the
human. This makes me curious as to what your relationships with your
female subjects were like. Did you feel an obligation to narrate their story, or
was narration not at the fore of your consciousness when producing the work?

JB   Yes, I felt a responsibility to be true to their stories since the truth
of their stories – and the communication of those truths, however
they are defined – is one of the most important issues that this
project addresses. Many of my preconceptions about women's lives
in Cairo were incorrect – often the opposite of what I expected from
my US perspective. During the interview process, and especially as
the interviews were always translated during the actual interview, we
often questioned if our translations and understandings were correct.
We often discussed with the woman whose story it was what she
thought her story meant, her reasons for telling this story and who
she wanted to reach with her story. The whys of this telling. Often we
made more than one interview. We also discussed the intent of each
story in the vetting process.

OK   *Is it a work of fiction? How did you marry together the fictive and*
documentary?

JB   Isn't every story a fiction? Yet aren't they also true on some level?
Every story implies a listener. I thought of the urban geographer
Arjun Appadurai and his exploration of the cultural efficacy of the
'imagination' as enabling desire. He calls this activity 'the work
of the imagination'. He is one of the few writers around so-called
'globalisation' who values culture and imagination. In describing
how storytelling constructs not only affect but effect, he describes
how the stories people tell themselves of getting from here to there
actually aid them physically to get there – the process of telling these
stories, again and again, makes it seem possible, then plausible.
I have certainly witnessed this in these stories.

There is also something else about the role of the listener in these
projects that I want to mention which is that people like to tell their
stories to strangers – yes, to embellish them of course – but also to
imagine another possibility, a different outcome. And they will often
tell or imagine things with strangers that they dare not imagine with
anyone from their own culture. All this was on my mind as we decided
on the final form of the stories.

This process reminded me of Jacques Derrida's notion of
hermeneutics as a living tradition moving along a horizon that is

ever-evolving and continuously rearticulating the very processes
of human thought. To aid the actors in embodying the stories,
I encouraged them to make the stories their own any way they
could, which included changing the language if they thought it was
wrong for their character. I gave them access to the translations and
recordings. Throughout the casting, rehearsals and shoot, there were
two dramaturges from Egypt working with the actors.

OK *The representations in ...Cairo stories transcend your individual
artistry – and I mean this as a compliment – because the work diverges
from everything that I have seen before, insomuch as it avoids the
tendency to overtly fetishise its subject. Was this intentional? Were you
attempting to avoid the paradigm of Orientalism?*

JB I was aiming for something contemporary in the visual style that
was also capable of representing the specificity of Cairo. We had a
number of discussions about the headscarf and how to frame women
wearing it. We decided on a portrait mode with no cropping of the
scarf or the women's faces.

In Galerie Karin Sachs, I also wanted to stage two different kinds
of representation – the photographic portrait and the video portrait
– as the juxtaposition of the two together enunciates some of the
differences between these two modes of address. Each delivers
crucial information to the viewer and yet each is very different.

It was important that the portrait would occasionally be of one of
the women telling her story, but not always. I wasn't trying to produce
a one-to-one comparison, but more to ask that the viewer recognise
and hopefully think about the differences between these two forms.
I noticed that once a viewer saw these two modes of representation
align – meaning the woman in the portrait was also the woman in the
video – then an aperçu effect would occur where suddenly the portrait
not being the woman in the video made you think differently about
both the portrait and the videos that you had already previously viewed.

OK *Do you feel that the work is politicised – not merely because of
the context that surrounds it but bearing in mind how it will also be
'appropriated' or 'interpreted'?*

JB For me every act is ideological and this includes the political,
both directly and indirectly. In my view there is nothing that is not
potentially political. Whether it will be politicised overtly is another
issue and often a question of who the audience is.

Lis Rhodes

interviewed by Maria Walsh

Structural Slips

MARIA WALSH *Your film* Light Music, *1975, was exhibited in the oil tanks at Tate Modern as part of its Expanded Cinema event in 2009, but mostly your work has been seen at film festivals and programmed screenings. How did the idea for a solo show in a gallery like the ICA come about? Is it a first for you?*

LIS RHODES The ICA suggested it. Actually I did exhibit at the ICA in 1976 in the Festival of Expanded Cinema. I was working with Ian Kerr and we did a series of expanded works at that time. We were running two 100ft loops of film, one of which was black leader, the other was transparent. The idea was to change the two forms over, so we used black chinagraph to darken one and scraped off the other. We had a xerox machine and every now and again we would run the film through the machine and take a xerox of it and pin it on the wall. By manipulating the film strip's optical soundtrack in this way, from almost silence, we created quite a racket which was then supposed to resolve back into silence, but that would be impossible. With the xeroxes, we were setting up a series of notations right around the wall of the gallery. I think the relationship between filmmakers working in galleries and in the cinema was pretty fluid.

MW *It is interesting that you mention notations as there is a series of notations – stills from your films – that lead one to the upstairs space which is presented as a gallery film installation. The particular installation format of the new work is very unusual. There are two juxtaposed screens which we are used to seeing in galleries, but you have chosen to juxtapose an earlier film,* A Cold Draft, *1988, on one screen with the two new films,* In the Kettle, *2010, and* Whitehall, *2012–, being shown in sequence one after*

the other on the adjacent screen with the soundtrack from A Cold Draft
*operating between all three films. Could you say a bit about your decision
to present the new films in this way?*

LR   The actual imagery in *In the Kettle* and *Whitehall* is very local to
the ICA. It was something that one was very aware of. It was really a
question of not so much the length of time between the films as the
conditions that underlay all three films – conditions that had simply
worsened over the 24 years. My first thought of how to present it was
almost as a book, just a sense of 'bookness'. It was more a way of
thinking about it for a moment. I was interested in the years when
there was no let-up of pressure in increasing inequality. There were
various economic changes made during those years that would
ensure that this is what would happen.

MW   *The reference to the bombing of the flour mill in Gaza in* In the Kettle
*adds another element to this constellation of local moments. Is it because
we are all interconnected now and feel the impact of global events?*

LR   I think I'm very clear in my own mind that *In the Kettle* is seen
from here, from London. It is the kettling, the besieging, that one
was looking at. We may think of ourselves as global, but I see myself
as a filmmaker artist who works in London. In that sense it is not
a document about Gaza.

MW   *Is that why you used written text, reported facts about the bombing,
which is very different from your use of text in other films?*

LR   It is taken exactly from Justice Richard Goldstone's report of the
hearings (*Human Rights in Palestine and Other Occupied Territories*,
report of the United Nations Fact Finding Mission on the Gaza
Conflict, 15 September 2009). I wanted to show the ordinariness of
violence – the phoning up to see if it could be avoided, being re-
assured that it would be avoided – so, in a sense, a feeling of a certain
kind of language used in the presenting of something 'illegal'.
The underlying concern running through the films is the question
of legality, of 'official' actions.

MW   *The soundtrack from* A Cold Draft *is your voice. It is very evocative,
referring occasionally to an absent woman, a trope that also occurs in*
Light Reading, *1978. So I wondered about the juxtaposition between this
voice and the images of oppression and violence – in the midst of all that,
there are these moments, could one call them feminine?*

LR   I'm never quite sure about the word feminine. But if one uses the
word feminist, then yes.

MW *Yes, I have problems with the term too. I guess I'm using it here as shorthand for the gendered subject, the 'she' that is evoked in the soundtrack.*

LR I think one is trying to listen so that it enters into the writing. After all, how does one know that except in relation to other women? Would you know how to speak if it weren't for shared and exchanged experiences over time?

MW *Speaking in one's own voice as a woman is a problem for women in a way that is not quite the same for men.*

LR It is not a matter of finding your own voice. It is more a matter of making connections and that is where one really begins to have some understanding. It has to be wider than oneself, or one is led into the possessive pronoun very quickly. I think what we are saying is, there are a lot of voices that we are hearing, listening to, possibly arguing with, listening very carefully to. That is what I'm trying to hear and to write.

MW *I was outside the kettle at the student protest in 2010 when the horses started charging. Even though I know that media news manipulates imagery, I was still shocked when I watched the footage on the news that night and how it distorted events. Some of the moments of synchronicity between the two screens in your installation made the experience of being there very palpable, the images were speaking to that body that was actually there.*

LR The curious thing is that one didn't plan it. Some of those camera movements are because I was being pushed very hard so they weren't calculated. You have no time to calculate. I was one among many. It was shot not from outside but within the kettle which is physically very different. People have done absolutely nothing except be present. It is false arrest and it is indiscriminate. One could connect this to the disturbances in the summer of 2011 and the enormously punitive measures involved later. Understanding the background as to why that happened brings up some serious problems, such as stop and search.

MW *Can you say a bit about the importance of drawing to your filmmaking?*

LR I find that drawing and writing are rather close together. I don't know why, but it is as though when you are writing, you are seeing something, and when you are drawing, you are seeing and writing something. They are connected in my mind. I find drawing a useful way of thinking. For most of my films, I do the sound work, the drawing, the photography, the writing and so on, so I see all of those as interrelated. One could begin writing at the same time as one is doing some drawings, trying to find out how something might work. Sometimes a film starts from the sound rather than from any visual material. I might consider them both in the same relationship – and I do. I don't divide things. I think that is why I have trouble with the objective/subjective separation that I actually don't see. There isn't a separation. I find language quite difficult in that sense. It seems to depend on dualisms which I don't think are altogether useful.

MW   *Your newer films are more digitally manipulated. Digital technology allows for more films to be distributed and shown on curricula, but also I think the resurgence of interest by younger artists in the experimental work that came out of the Filmmakers' Co-op and expanded cinema relates to a desire to make digital surfaces expressive in some way.*

LR   I suppose I came to digital not through the image but through sound. Editing sound on film is very time consuming. I got some very early sound software, which was wonderful, just for minute sound files. I think there are very particular characteristics about film. *Light Music* cannot be shown except on film. One of the major differences between when the Filmmakers' Co-op was starting up and now is that there were places in London that you could go to and do things that would not tie you down financially. I think patronage has a lot to do with what is allowed to happen and what is allowed to be said. When I was running the cinema, the Musicians Collective had another space next door and there were interesting crossovers.

MW   *From this point in time, the utopian dimension of the Co-op seems somewhat enviable. It seemed possible to think that you could have this control over practice, its production, exhibition and distribution. There was a commitment to this.*

LR   There was. I worked a bit with the GLC. We weren't allowed to support individual artists, it had to be groups – eg Aphra Video, The Poster Collective, Women in Sync – which I found was a very good system of funding. Things actually got moving and people who perhaps wouldn't have applied to the Arts Council found a space, a place.

MW   *It is so different today. You mentioned that you don't like to make a distinction between what might be considered documentary and a drawing as a document. I'd like to talk about* Light Reading – *which is screened in the other gallery space in a sequence with* Dresden Dynamo, *1972* –

*in this context. There is a strange kind of forensic quality to the film which
is different from the forensic voice of the media where the closer in you get,
the more readable the image becomes. In your films, the image becomes less
readable, as if the search for evidence is being continually undermined in
some way. Reading Felicity Sparrow's programme notes on* Light Reading
*for the package you distributed through the company Circles, 'Her Image
Fades as her Voice Rises', she also talks about evidence ...*

LR   You have reminded me of a piece of Gertrude Stein's writing
called 'Forensics', from her 1931 book *How to Write*. In *Light Reading* it
was a search for evidence of the way grammar is arranged. Stein did
it particularly in *How to Write*, the question of the relation between
a sentence and a paragraph. What I am searching for are structural
slips that then accumulate into a whole way of separating subject and
object, distributing them according to power relationships, which
happens in gender and politics. On the question of documentary, one
could make an argument, or at least I could, that *Dresden Dynamo* is
the most documentary film I've ever done because it had no camera
or sound recording – in a sense, there is no illusion. The sound is the
image. The further away you get from that, the more chance there is,
if you like, of making a separation between fiction and documentary.
I don't think things separate that easily. What representation isn't an
abstraction? And you were quite rightly talking about the news on TV,
which is extremely abstract and sometimes rather fictive. It reflects
back on language and the idea of dualism, and 'whose' truth and
'whose' history, and the use of these possessives as question marks
rather than as 'givens', as we were talking about earlier on.

MW   *Your essay 'Whose History?', in which you discuss the importance of
researching women's film histories, was published in the catalogue of the
seminal exhibition at the Hayward in 1979 'Film as Film'. I'm probably
being a bit literal minded here but I wondered if the whole controversy
and discussion around that event spurred you on to explore the more
narrative voice in your films. Prior to that, you could have been classed as
a formalist filmmaker.* Light Reading *puts that under question doesn't it?
If the film were silent, it would be so completely different.*

LR   In many ways that probably has a sense about it. Actually much
of the film was made about five years before, but not the soundtrack,
which was 1978. The investigation into language had started with
a very small film that I don't really show very much, *Amanuensis*,
1973. It was a set of experiments. I was trying at that point to get an

equivalent sound out of actual letterings. I was using typewriter tape that had been perforated and was printing that onto raw film stock. I was slipping it so the letters became rather sculptural on the surface of the film. I wanted the surface of the letters from the tape, which had been written by someone else, so there was a history to the questioning of language. Those experiments formed part of *Light Reading*. I think these things happen gradually. It didn't suddenly happen in 1978, so many things feed into one's filmmaking.

MW *Your new films seem bleak. Do you see hope for the future?*

LR Immensely, yes. Anything is movable, changeable. I think things will change, definitely. Nothing is immutable. They tell us capitalism is immutable, but it is not. I'm absolutely certain of it.

Issue 354, March 2012

John Smith

interviewed by Mark Prince

Waiting Game

MARK PRINCE *One of the things that makes your films currently so distinctive is that you return to primary experience for your material. You walk the streets or look out the window and film what you see. You are not looking through a filter of received references that backs you up. I associate this return to first principles with the spirit of early British conceptual art. Would you say that was your original context?*

JOHN SMITH It was. Conceptual Art was formative but also, when I began making work, it was within the world of structuralist, materialist filmmaking, and also the world of semiology, looking at the construction of meaning. But I'm glad you mentioned that there aren't many references in the films.

MP *Which is unusual now, at least in films made within an art context.*

JS Absolutely. Most of my friends at the time weren't at art school. I wanted to make work that you didn't need to have a background in art or experimental filmmaking to appreciate. That has remained important to me. I'd be as interested in showing my work at a library film society to a group of old-age pensioners as I would to an informed art audience.

MP *Although many of your methods seem structuralist, you tend to work in the opposite direction: to begin by seeing film as hampered by its literalness and then to go on to create a space for fantasy within it. A new potential for illusion is opened up from a position of disillusionment.*

JS I am trying to work backwards and forwards between an involvement in the illusion and making you aware that what you are looking at is a construction. Unlike many of my contemporaries in the 1970s, I have a love/hate relationship with illusionism rather than just a hatred of it. I am wary of the power that mainstream cinema has but I'm also fascinated by storytelling and the psychological involvement it asks of you. I like work in which you have that experience of identification while being regularly reminded of its artifice.

MP   *Entertainment is a great resource.*

JS   It seems such a shame to throw that away.

MP   *Now that the digital modification of films can be done on an iPhone, we are generally more aware of how artificial images can be. Do you think that invalidates Structuralism or makes its project more urgent?*

JS   I think it is still very relevant. Despite the fact that we know images can be constructed we still look at them as if they were evidence. We can't help it. In the same way, when we're given verbal information that we know to be nonsense, we still half believe it. That is really what *The Girl Chewing Gum* of 1976, and *The Black Tower* from 1985–87 are about. You are given these obviously false narratives but the power of the word is such that it is all too easy to imagine them. You are told there is a man in a long raincoat with a gun in his pocket who has just robbed the local post office. If that is funny, it's because it is so easy to imagine that it is actually the case, although you know it isn't.

MP   *We need to imagine a film is happening before our eyes for it to remain engaging. In* The Girl Chewing Gum, *your voice-over makes it difficult to maintain that illusion. Your films seem to express frustration with the limitations of the medium by manipulating our sense of time in this way or by extreme cutting – radical juxtapositions between documentary and fictional modes, and between still and moving images. Do you find the limitations of film frustrating?*

JS   Not at all. Sometimes I think there are too many possibilities. I often deliberately set up limitations. For example, a film has to be a single shot, or it is going to be exactly one minute long, or the camera is not going to move. I like limitations and I am interested in suggesting what might be going on outside the imposed structure that I'm putting around the work.

MP   *But do you see the solipsistic narratives of* The Girl Chewing Gum *and* The Black Tower *as metaphors for the insularity of a film's world?*

JS   I find it interesting when people see *The Black Tower* and ask if I have suffered from mental illness. Well, not as far as I know. For me, it is a playful engagement with constructing these worlds.

MP   *How did* The Black Tower *come about?*

JS   Like most of my work, it was made over quite a long period, over two and half years. It could have been four different films. The sequence in which monochrome colour fields turn into representational images was originally an idea in itself. The part in which the seasons change on the street and the cars appear and disappear from behind a tree was also planned as a single film. I am interested in making hybrid work which goes off in unexpected directions. To me, one of the exciting things about filmmaking – and particularly about editing – is how you can bring disparate elements together and create a seamless flow from one kind of engagement to another. But essentially *The Black Tower* came about because I moved into a house in Leytonstone in East London in the early 1980s. From the bedroom window was the view that you see at the end of the film of the black tower from across the graveyard.

MP *There was actually a black tower?*

JS Yes. You are looking at completely undoctored images of the same building from different angles. It was a water tower in the grounds of the hospital.

MP *I assumed it was a little model you had made in the studio and somehow superimposed onto the 16mm film.*

JS Someone else said that to me recently. That's the last thing I would have expected people to think when I made the film, especially because things like that were so much harder to achieve convincingly then. I guess it relates to your point about our contemporary awareness of the constructedness of photographic images. Coming back to *The Girl Chewing Gum* and how the voice can determine how we see images, it was a formal proposition for me to make a film in which you are told that this building is in different places and then to make that convincing simply through careful framing. The narrative came out of the places the water tower was visible from: across the graveyard, so I knew it was going to have death in it; the grounds of a hospital, so there was going to be sickness in it; behind high walls, so there would be a prison; over some trees, so I could place it in the countryside. I wrote down what the locations suggested. The film was about the power of language. I was quite shocked when people started saying they found the story scary. I simply wanted to write a pastiche of a mystery horror story, the sort of thing I used to enjoy reading as a teenager.

MP *Many of your films are based around East London, where you live, and determined, like* The Black Tower, *by the features of the area.*

Perhaps there is a connection to London-based painters, such as Frank
Auerbach and Leon Kossoff, who have worked in the city over the past
half century and treated it as a field for empirical artistic research, even
though their work can be almost abstract. Would you agree with Auerbach
that the greater the familiarity with the subject, the greater the freedom to
invent from it?

JS Absolutely. You can draw whatever meaning you want out of something if you dwell on it for long enough. You become aware of detail.
With *The Black Tower*, I became fascinated, in an aesthetic sense,
with what the tower looked like in various lighting conditions.
On a sunny day, it was like a hole cut out of the sky, an absence of
image on a plinth. The film is about encompassing polarities – there
is illusionism, narrative, conventional cinema and, at the other
extreme, something completely abstract. The black frame could be no
image at all, or could be the wall of the black tower, or a night sky.

MP *When your films stray from London, they do so rhetorically, as though*
to point out the absurdity of the exotic when the familiar is so strange.
There is the exile to the field in Hertfordshire at the end of The Girl
Chewing Gum, *or the last imageless frames of* Lost Sound *which tell us*
we are in Palermo, when the rest of the film has taken place in a few square
miles around Shoreditch. In the 'Hotel Diaries', 2001–07, you are in a series
of foreign cities but always confined to the four walls of the hotel room.
Vienna, in Worst Case Scenario *of 2001–03 – mostly shot in black-and-*
white stills from another hotel room – seems an alien territory. Does being
elsewhere dictate a different method?

JS It is important for me that the work is rooted in the mundane.
So even in the section of the 'Hotel Diaries' set in Palestine, when I
look out of the window and over the Separation Wall, I deliberately
don't show the dramatic events I am talking about. Although I
shot a lot of video footage when I was there which could be seen as
reportage, I am more interested in showing ordinary things and
investing them with something which makes them extraordinary.
So much of cinema is about spectacle that you become immune to it.
I find it hard to look at a sunset in reality because it makes me think
of shampoo adverts. Our pleasure in the natural world can become a
cliché because of our overexposure to it through media.

MP *Your longest 16mm film,* Slow Glass *of 1988–91, taps into an archive*
of footage of the same London sites filmed over several years. It gives us the
impression of watching the city altering before our eyes, which produces

a sense of nostalgia and loss. A shopfront switches its sign several times within seconds. Does deconstruction, which is usually thought of as a dispassionate process, have an emotional meaning for you?

JS I think it's both. I'm a bit of a sucker for the optical effect – for example, switching between an image of something by day and night. I find that very seductive. Sometimes I get a bit annoyed with myself if it begins to feel gratuitous. I first got involved with making films through doing light shows for rock bands so I was really interested in the optical effects of imagery.

MP *In your 2011 show at* PEER *in London you began looking back to previous work. You were qualifying not just the representation of the Dalston site in* The Girl Chewing Gum, *but the film itself as an established cultural artefact. Was there a sense of trepidation in tampering with a film which has become a classic of British experimental filmmaking? Or did you feel it was yours to tamper with?*

JS I felt I had every right to do it. But a few people were a bit shocked. I thought I would treat the film with the irreverence it deserves. I show these older works all the time. They are so familiar to me that I don't have the distance of someone seeing them for the first time. But it did really shock me when I superimposed the new onto the old images.

MP *What seemed staged in* The Girl Chewing Gum *takes on a documentary status. The new colour images push you and the 1970s passers-by back into a black-and-white world which is definitively past. It has become an emotive autobiographical document.*

JS I think that is something that runs through a lot of my recent work. Maybe because I am still showing those early films. It is a constant reminder of how long ago things were and how much things have changed. Not least because I am actually in a lot of the work. I am seeing images of myself or hearing my voice and, of course, I am getting older.

MP *In the series 'Hotel Diaries', it is a looped process of watching yourself filming yourself watching yourself filming etc. The political theme seems to arise serendipitously in the first film,* Frozen War. *Did you then seek it out in the subsequent parts?*

JS *Frozen War* was made in 2001. The second film, *Museum Piece*, was set in Berlin in 2004 and ends with me talking about 'Schindler's Lift'. The film had a serious political motivation but I was a bit concerned that people would think it was all a cheap trick, leading up to that pun. So I wanted to make another one just to qualify that. The third part, *Throwing Stones*, I made only a month after *Museum Piece*.

MP *That is the one in which you mention the possibility of a trilogy.*

JS Yes, but the reason for making that one was that Yassar Arafat had died the previous day. That is how it has been with the remaining parts. They have always been triggered by events relating to the conflicts in the Middle East and Afghanistan that have occurred while I have been travelling.

MP *How much foresight do you have? Are they scripted at all?*

JS They are not scripted, but I know what I am going to talk about and in what order. It is important what the camera is looking at while I am saying something. I have to get myself into a certain frame of mind because it is quite difficult to film and talk at the same time, and I don't allow myself to edit. Occasionally I have done two or three retakes until I get it right.

MP *When you look out over the city in Palestine, there are specks of dirt on the camera lens. At the beginning of the next film you comment on how you found this regrettable. But you didn't go back and reshoot it, you chose instead to incorporate the mistake into the narrative of the next film.*

JS And that also enabled me to give the film the title *Dirty Pictures*.

MP *What are you working on at the moment?*

JS A commission that is going to be filmed in Margate. I am simply going to film the sea.

MP *There are those lines from* The Wasteland: *'On Margate Sands. / I can connect / Nothing with nothing.' In your film* The Waste Land, *T S Eliot reads part of the poem, but I think not those lines.*

JS That's funny, because the film is going to be very much about nothingness. I am interested in looking out at the vista from the window, and all you see is sea and sky. It should look like a completely naturalistic image but I'll use the same device as in *Worst Case Scenario* where it gradually becomes apparent that you're looking at the same place at different times of day within a single image.

MP *How long would you give yourself to make such a film?*

JS In this case it is dependent on the limited periods I am able to use the office from which I am planning to film. Usually it is flexible. There is a lot of sitting around waiting.

MP *Like waiting for the ceiling tiles in the hotel room in Palestine to start flapping around again?*

JS Or waiting for the unexpected. The waiting around usually pays off in the end. Making *Lost Sound*, for example, Graeme Miller and I would find a strip of tape to film and I would set up an interesting shot, but then be left waiting for things to happen in the background.

MP *It seems amazing that coherent sound could be retrieved from those bits of chewed-up tape found on the street.*

JS You are hearing the content of the tape that you're looking at. It might have had almost all the magnetic coating washed off, but we are so familiar with music that when you play it, your mind fills in the gaps. The type of music is very quickly identifiable. But we also wanted to draw attention to the musical qualities of natural sound – sometimes you are not sure whether what you're hearing is on the tape or ambient sound. So the stop/start of the eroded material creates its own rhythm, or the ambient sound fills in the gaps.

MP *It is a speculative process.*

JS And a solitary one. Waiting for sound as much as for pictures. The clock nearby is going to chime on the hour, or there are some workers on a building site putting up scaffolding, they stop, and you are waiting for them to start up again.

MP Blight *was filmed at a building site along the route of the M11 Link Road in East London. As in* Lost Sound*, there is a musical component. The voices on the soundtrack seem to derive from found recordings but they are looped and set to music, so they seem like incantations. How did those different elements come together?*

JS It was a collaboration with the composer Jocelyn Pook, who also lived in that part of Leytonstone. Both our houses were being demolished – the house you see being knocked down was next door to my house. I recorded interviews with people who lived in the area, exploring memory and loss – recurring themes in my work. I asked them, for example, what they remembered about the houses they had lived in. Fragments of the interviews were chopped up quite ruthlessly, given that those people had often been baring their souls to me. Jocelyn noticed the musical qualities of some voices, which played a big part in what we selected. You are looking at discarded objects in a wasteland, an old vacuum cleaner or record player, as you hear the words 'Blue' or 'Grey with a little pink'. Or you see the rings of a tree trunk while hearing numbers, which could be someone's age, the number of the house they lived in or how many brothers and sisters they have. The question is what a number or colour can convey without being given a specific context in which its meaning declares itself.

MP *There are various lateral associations between word and image, or image and image, such as between the map of the motorway network and the spider's web tattoo on the arm of a builder.*

JS I came home one night and the house next door had been partly demolished. A wall was exposed revealing a poster for *The Exorcist*. So I decided to construct the beginning of the film in such a way that you wouldn't see the people involved in the demolition, so it looked as though there was a poltergeist in the house. Some unseen force. And then I started filming the workers, and one of them had the spider's web tattoo on his elbow, which looked like the motorway network around London. Then in one of the first interviews, I asked a woman what she remembered about the house she had lived in as a child. They had an outside toilet which she hated because it contained lots of spiders, and she would have her father go in first and kill them. So the theme of the spider emerged from these separate sources, completely by chance, and became a motif in both the image and the soundtrack. All of a sudden something like that happens which you realise you can build on. That is also why I tend to work over long periods. I'm afraid that things will not come through unless you give them time. You have to wait to find out what you need. Things radiate outwards from that serendipity.

Issue 355, April 2012

Mohamed Bourouissa

interviewed by Anna Dezeuze

Protocol

ANNA DEZEUZE *When I wanted to describe the characters of your 2011 film*
Boloss *in my review of the 2011 Venice Biennale, I couldn't find a word
to translate the term* beur – *a syllabic reversal of the word arabe which
describes a French citizen of Arab origins. How do you define yourself?*

MOHAMED BOUROUISSA Beur is a very 1980s term ... In any case I don't
like this kind of subcategory. I define the young people I work with as
French, with different origins, different stories – I was born in Algeria,
for example. The people I photographed in my series of staged images
in 'Périphéries' in 2007-08 were just guys from those neighbourhoods
on the other side of the *périphérique*, or Paris ring-road. I even prefer
the term *banlieusard* [someone who lives in the housing estates on
the outskirts of the city] because it includes everybody – white, Arab,
black people – who all share the same state of mind, just like a guy
from the countryside is a *campagnard*, a country guy.

AD *Did you stage the 'Périphéries' photographs in the neighbourhood that
you are from?*

MB Not only my own. The kids I was at high school with in Paris came
from different banlieues – Sarcelles, La Courneuve, Pantin. I made
friends at school and one thing led to another. I met their friends, we
got talking. The relational system involved matters a lot.

AD *'Périphéries' was associated with the 2005 riots in the banlieues. Over
seven years later, how do you perceive the relation between this series and
what happened at the time?*

MB I think that my early professional success was obviously related to
that. I had started to work in the banlieues before the riots, although
the photographs were not really exhibited until 2007–08. During the

riots I was actually in Algeria – I experienced them via the prism of television. This confirmed my intuitions and allowed me to pursue the work with a certain conviction, even after the riots. One of the most emblematic and best-known photographs from the series, which I titled *La République*, was staged in Clichy-sous-Bois on 25 December 2005, after the riots had calmed down. I was working above all on the feeling of tension, an invisible tension. That is what I was trying to make visible rather than what happens in riots, because riots are only the visible part of this tension. By the way, I think that we will have new riots in the next three or four years if things don't improve.

AD *When I saw* Boloss *in Venice, I perceived the characters as exclusively 'North African' – as* beurs*. Only afterwards did I realise that they were from Marseille. In one of your interviews you even describe* Boloss *as a 'franco-français' or super-French film. What do you mean?*

MB I liked the idea of showing a film in Venice that was about a specific place, with no universalist ambition. I decided to make a film about the specificity of a city, with its culture, and obviously a strong North African culture. Those guys in the film are assimilated, they speak French with all its 'mixes', with Arab slang made in Marseille that nobody would understand in Algeria. In an earlier conversation you said that *Boloss* reminded you of the well-known 'card game' scene in Marcel Pagnol's filmed play *Marius*, 1931, which takes place in Marseille. Well, you can't get any more French than Marcel Pagnol's films, can you? The atmosphere in *Marius* or *Boloss* is very French.

AD *I was thinking of Pagnol because* Boloss*, like 'Périphéries' and another film you made in between,* Légende *from 2010, involve some staging, they are quite theatrical. In* Légende*, which is filmed through mini-cameras worn by illegal sellers of American Legend cigarettes – among others – at the Paris underground station of Barbès, you even had the participants replay some everyday scenes that you had observed. Why?*

MB At the beginning I thought that I would let the cameras do their own thing and see what happens – which I hadn't done before in my staged images in 'Périphéries'. But the space in *Légende* was too fragmented. The guys working in that space work for hours, they run around in all directions, they talk to everyone. It is all very fast, their bodies move, so I had to ask them to move less and I had to structure the space in order to make it legible, even as it remained unstructured. The only way to visualise their movements in this chaotic space would have involved setting up multiple cameras and

465

creating a screen. But that is not what I wanted to do because I was trying to give an account of what was going on – and of some scenes that I had been able to witness earlier – by choreographing them.

There is a real filmic construction, which is visible. I'm playing with this way of reusing visual codes from television – hidden cameras worn by journalists – and trying to create new forms out of them. In *Boloss* as well, with the hidden surveillance cameras, I was trying to appropriate those principles and use them as elements for a film. I try to use the documentary form as a fictional tool.

AD *But for* Boloss, *for example, what kind of instructions did you give to the friends that play in the film?*

MB At the start I told them, 'play a game of poker in which one of you will cheat and another will lose all his money'. And I told others to hang out in the hallway and go back and forth and be a bit of a nuisance for the 'grown-ups'. So we had fictionalised a document, but we hadn't really been able to show that in the video. It made me think of bluffing because nothing was happening in the video and you couldn't understand much from looking at the guys coming and going or the guys playing cards. So I went back to the documentation and added a commentary. I reconstructed the film by interviewing each player, asking: 'who was the cheat at that table we keep talking about?' I constructed this film as a bluff. Actually I could have called it *Bluff* rather than *Boloss*, but I like '*boloss*' because it is very French.

AD *And the* boloss, *or 'sucker', ends up being the viewer, because we can't understand anything. I was wondering if the fact that you don't help us understand what is happening reinforces a division in your public between the* banlieusards *and other social classes. Especially since the general climate of suspicion in the film could confirm general prejudices against the* banlieusards *in relation to questions of illegality, crime and so on.* Légende *also raises this problem.*

MB As an artist, I'm not here to try and give a better or more positive image of people. What I'm trying to show is my generation's general way of living, of thinking. I don't want viewers to have an empathetic relation with the men in *Boloss* but rather that they simply consider them as their equals, and you don't always completely understand an equal. What is positive is that, rather than the creation of an image, the film is the creation of a fiction with people who tell a fake story. In fact it is funny, it is a joke where you don't understand a damn thing. And in the end you realise that you are getting everything wrong, including maybe your prejudices.

AD *On the other hand, in* Temps Mort (Time Out or Dead Time), *which you made in 2009 before* Boloss, *an affective relationship with the characters sets itself up very naturally.*

MB *Temps Mort* was above all a story with a friend who was in prison. My first work about prison was a series of photographs. One of my friends who had helped me make 'Périphéries' went to prison and we were in touch via mobile phone. I would send him refill cards and one day he sent me a photograph. At the time I really felt like moving away from 'Périphéries' and as soon as I saw his photo I thought to myself that here was another way of creating a protocol, a way of creating images differently. After developing a series of photographs about prison with him, I realised that what was interesting was the relationship we had kept alive, this relationship that worked through images and text messages. And in order to give an account of that work process maybe I had to film it. By that time my mate had left prison and I had to contact someone else he knew in prison, whom I had to audition via mobile phone.

AD *But isn't the use of mobile phones banned in prison?*

MB It is banned, but at the same time it is tolerated. And there is a difference between remand centres and prisons. So I contacted this guy who my friend knew, and who was in a remand centre, and I offered him the same deal as I had with my friend: 'In exchange for certain images you send me, I'll send you others, and at the same time you can get refills and that is how we can communicate.' And gradually we started to know each other and the film developed on its own. I edited and scripted the final film by selecting and ordering the exchanged text messages and videos, but it was the result of an experience. It feels intimate, though we were separated by all these grids – of the phone, the text message.

AD *What do you mean by 'grid', exactly?*

MB The idea of the grid comes from the artist Jean-Luc Moulène, who was my teacher and who often quoted this sentence by Antonin Artaud: 'The grid is a terrible moment for sensibility, for matter.' For me grids are forms of language – you have the prison grid, the grid of the institution. Phones have a grid but they allow a free circulation of information, even if it is also a surveillance tool. 'Périphéries' also used a grid: the language of painting and photography. I wanted to question representations of the *banlieue* youth of the hyper-sociological kind by introducing them within a painting grid. That was partly due to my university studies.

AD *Did you study art history at university before going to art school?*

MB Yes, and I realise that it was also a big influence on my work. For 'Périphéries' I would build my images in space – I was inside the images, I would be experiencing a place. With the photographs and the film for *Temps Mort* I could only work with the surface of the images and someone else's testimony. I was working with the document without making a documentary. In *Légende* or *Boloss*, maybe the grids are less obvious.

AD *Your new project* L'utopie d'August Sander, *2012, seems very different. What was your starting point?*

MB It was a work that I had presented at Le Fresnoy, a postgraduate art and media programme. They were asking me to use very expensive technology, to make super-clean works, a little like those I had made for 'Périphéries'. But after *Temps Mort* I didn't feel like making very clinical images any more. So I decided to use new technologies, but they were open source, or at least much less expensive: a 3D printer, which I was using with a 3D scanner that I had built myself. With this home-made scanner I was losing information and image definition but the posture, the weight of the scanned human body, would be visible in the sculpture produced by the 3D printer.

AD *At what point did you decide specifically to scan the unemployed?*

MB I wanted to do a project around the idea of work. But when I talked to a mate in Marseille, where I was planning to do the project, he said to me, 'over here we talk less about work than unemployment'.

AD *And why recruit the unemployed at a* Pôle Emploi, *a Job Centre?*

MB I didn't want to talk only about individuals, I wanted to talk about this relationship between individuals and the systems in which they find themselves, and how individuals try to exist inside these systems. In 'Périphéries' I was showing individuals in their environment, in their architectural spaces. *Temps Mort* was about prison space. This time, I am trying to talk about individuals in the space of the Job Centre. Some advisers there strive to get individuals to fit into boxes. This confrontation – yet another tension – is what I am trying to visualise.

AD *Why did you choose to sell the statuettes that you produced with the 3D printer at the Arnavaux flea market?*

MB   People who go to that market may be the same as those who go to the Job Centre to claim their benefits. I liked the idea that the same kind of person could buy my sculptures. We have sold around 20 or 30 of them, at €2 each. Right now we have only produced 80 of them, but we are going to continue making and selling them. My business plan is to sell at a loss.

AD   *By developing a project at a loss, are you suggesting that the role of the Job Centre is ineffective? I am thinking of the film you have made at the flea market, where a fixed camera gives the perspective of the statuette waiting – mostly without hope – to be bought.*

MB   Today there are more and more unemployed and fewer and fewer of them find work after having been on the dole. It is an economic game, a mechanism. This sale at the Arnavaux market reflects that mechanism: there is a system, and there are visible and formatted individuals whom we then try to reintegrate into the economy.

AD   *Can you talk about the project's title,* L'utopie d'August Sander?

MB   Sander photographed, for a long time, workers, craftsmen and so on. And I have taken up this rhetoric but in a reversed form. I only 'photograph' the unemployed – people who cannot be recognised through their work. When I discovered Sander at the École des Arts Décoratifs, I was struck by the way that he photographed his subjects – he gave them a kind of nobleness, in their posture, the position of their bodies; often he presented them head-to-toe.

The word 'Utopia' refers to the impossibility of representing your time. It is an absurd project, like my attempt to represent the unemployed, to visualise this reality. This is a work doomed to fail: it is impossible to visualise reality in its totality.

Utopias are also related to ideologies, sometimes humanist ideologies, that are very western. What bothers me about ideology is the way it negates experience. And I am suspicious of the humanist discourse. Coming from an Algerian family, I feel there is a real resonance between humanism and colonialism, for example. The hidden face of humanism's benevolent gaze.

AD   *A similar dichotomy can be found in Sander's project.*

MB   Yes, exactly. The desire to categorise people through pseudo-scientific classifications can often serve to erase their identity. You can look at Sander's work from a negative as well as a positive perspective – you can choose. And my project can also be looked at from this double perspective. You can see in it a kind of monumentality, with this 'army' of the unemployed, and you can see in it the misery of the individual I am scanning as part of a series and selling at the market. Sander helps us understand his times and give a face to that specific time, that is what is important for me.

Issue 357, June 2012

Tino Sehgal

interviewed by Jennifer Thatcher

Descending Tate Modern's ramp on the first public day of Tino Sehgal's Turbine Hall commission, *These Associations*, it is hard to tell the performers from the audience. As my eyes adjust to the swirls of people, I notice that the interpreters – the preferred term – are performing a choreographed movement that looks like footballers practising marking techniques. A few moments later, the whole group walks slowly towards the entrance. The deliberate, focused pace suggests political resonances (a protest march), but I can't help also thinking about the zombies in Michael Jackson's *Thriller* video. Later, I catch the end of the work's sequence, when the lights are dimmed and the group starts chanting like a medieval Gregorian choir, repeating the hypnotic chorus 'natural, natural, natural!' and singing declarative lines about channelling voices into the work. Sports pitch, public square, horror movie, cathedral – the piece evokes a range of group situations and the conventions that determine behaviour within them.

But what I have really been looking forward to is my one-to-one encounter with the interpreters. Having read the first online reviews of *These Associations*, I know that I can expect to be told intimate stories. Unlike earlier projects I experienced, such as *This Progress* at the ICA in 2006 (where you were met by a child at the start of the work, who handed you over to progressively older interpreters) or the German pavilion at the Venice Biennale in 2005 (in which interpreters bribed you into a discussion about economics with the promise of a ticket refund), the scale of the Turbine Hall means that there is less of a sense of inevitability about the encounter and I find myself lying in wait for someone to break from the group and single me out for a confession.

Sehgal himself, however, will not be divulging any secrets to me. In the Tate cafe that afternoon, he says: 'I think artists' intentions – I'm not sure that's so relevant. They are important to generate the piece but then I just don't feel that I am the authority to speak about it any more.' He asks me not to transcribe the interview as a straight Q&A, anxious that once an artist has expressed their thoughts on a work it becomes impossible to interpret it in any other way. 'I'm more interested to hear what other people have to say because I don't trust myself that much that I can translate my intentions 100% into some reality that I communicate perfectly. Even in written language that wouldn't work, I think.' Indeed, the written information around the piece is characteristically scant and, as always with Sehgal's work, no official visual documentation will be produced. This is refreshing in an age when the press release has become so dominant: the blueprint of an artist's intentions on which critics have become overreliant. Warming up, Sehgal expresses his bemusement at the current cult of personality that means the media are more interested in him than his work: 'Even the big newspapers, they all write portraits. Like I remember the *New York Times* doing this massive thing on me, then there is this column on the show.'

Instead, Sehgal grills me about my three encounters. It is clear that, although the interpreters must have been given certain guidelines, he can't know all their stories let alone dictate their interaction with visitors like a megalomaniacal spin doctor. There is a gospel singer who confesses her nerves at going into the recording studio for the first time ('Jamaican?' Sehgal asks. No: white, middle-aged) and a young man who describes the burden he felt at being given a car by his grandfather on his 18th birthday ('And that was more banal to you, somehow?'). Sehgal interrupts me as I describe the more abstract, philosophical chat I have with a third interpreter: 'How did he look?' I sense I may be getting this guy in to trouble, when Sehgal repeats 'Short, grey hair? Talking about interaction? And what was his point?'

I am starting to feel guilty for having encouraged a meta-discussion of *These Associations* with the man, so I am relieved that Sehgal laughs when I ask whether the interpreter might have gone off-piste. After all, that is the first rule of being an interpreter: you can't speak about the piece, and neither should the visitor. For the artist, it is a 'confusing of the place where it happens'. So how free are the interpreters in their interaction? The young man of my second encounter broke off our conversation about social burden just as I was warming up to the subject; I had felt a little slighted, like I had been boring him. Was there a time limit on conversations, I wondered? 'It is not about the amount but if it goes into chit-chat, then they have to break it off.'

It is debatable who has the most power: interpreter or visitor. The interpreter offers a degree of vulnerability, yet the visitor's curiosity or emotional vampirism is only indulged to the extent allowed by the interpreter. The juxtaposition between private and public realms is something that the scale of the Turbine Hall makes particularly striking: 'What they tell you, it's like it is happening at the Tate and there are thousands of people here per day but, on the other hand, they are just telling it to you,' Sehgal says. Unlike our name-badge culture of faux-intimacy (Hello, my name is Bob, how can I help you?), these interpreters remain anonymous. Yet that anonymity 'paradoxically allows for greater intimacy', Sehgal argues, 'because normally you would think, you can't bring strangers into an intimate setting. And so doing the work I realised that it is almost mechanical. When you meet a stranger on a train, you can always say more; to a distant friend who is not part of your life, you can say more.'

Yet there is still necessarily an element of risk when you delegate to a group of strangers. There is the risk, for example, that the encounter might have consequences outside the piece. A friend I had met in the Turbine Hall had imagined derailing *These Associations* by coming on to the interpreters, while another acquaintance had found herself talking to an interpreter who taught on her university course. There is a fictional quality to the interpreters that relates them to the worlds of film or literature – I imagine a Paul Auster-style scenario of coincidences or subsequent real-life encounters. Sehgal indulges my fantasy: 'When that happens it can produce social consequences. But here the probability is very low. That would be more the ICA or something.' I suggest instead parallels with reality TV programmes, or those scripted reality programmes like *Seinfeld* or *Curb Your Enthusiasm* in which the protagonists play a fictionalised version of themselves. You cannot tell the boundary between real life and fiction with those actors, because you don't know them in the first place. Sehgal hasn't seen these shows but he allows that the lack of explicit distinction between interpreters and the public can generate unexpected scenarios: 'I have heard rumours that visitors also have gone up to other visitors,' Sehgal says approvingly.

The recruitment process was rigorous. Sehgal says that it took a year and that each individual was subject to a two-to-four-hour meeting. One thing he learned from his earlier pieces at the ICA was that he could work with a wide range of people. 'At that time, I was – I still am – very, very interested in the kind of more intellectual discourse but, being a sociology nerd, I realise that often when people talk about things which are issues for them, without mentioning them explicitly, I could relate it to broader sociological issues even if they don't. And that one could also work with a housewife from Southwark just as much as a chair of philosophy at LSE.'

In her recent book on participatory art, *Artificial Hells*, Claire Bishop argues that there is a masochistic quality to this genre and that, rather than simply focus on the hierarchical relationship between artists and their delegates and the moral ethics of exploitation, we should consider that both participants and visitors might perversely enjoy their subordination to an artwork. I ask Sehgal what motivates his interpreters to sign up to work with him. He mentions that, for many, 'it is just doing something else; it is a different mode of speaking'. For others, it was curiosity. He mentions a woman moving to a small town in Israel: 'She said she wanted to do one thing that she could only do in London. An experience, I guess.' Shifts are four hours long. The physicality of *These Associations* had made Sehgal anxious that it would be less appealing to academics, whom he has favoured in many works. 'We were worried because it involves a lot of moving,' he says of the current piece, 'and then we realised that was exactly attractive because maybe the separation of the more intellectual from the embodied is something that they are not necessarily happy with. So to combine that ...'

I ask him whether he felt the weight of such a large, high-profile commission as the Turbine Hall; after all, there had been quite a build-up to the piece – he had received the first email proposal from Tate curator Jessica Morgan in 2008 and began the workshops a year or two later. It took him a week, he says, to get used to the scale and initially tried out a few ideas that didn't work. His experience of showing *This Progress* at the Guggenheim in New York in 2010 (the museum actually purchased the piece) helped him prepare for a wide audience: 'I really understood that it is a very different thing when you engage with a larger, more touristic audience. It is very different from doing a show in a Kunsthalle place like the ICA. It was also interesting to move out of this inner art circle. These places like the Turbine Hall and the Guggenheim, they are really global crossroads.' In fact, tourists might even be more responsive: 'These people have left their homes to give time to another place,' he says. 'They are more open; they are ready to experience something not necessarily art-related.'

The number of people to involve was a big issue, not least in terms of budget. Who would have thought that dematerialised art would get so expensive? He knew already last August [2011] that he wanted a large group but had to keep whittling it down – 'OK, now five people less, five people less' – until he found the 'smallest number that would give this kind of, not regular group, but larger group feel'. For Sehgal, a larger group has an 'inherent' or 'archaic power' – the 'sheer power of presence'. He makes a connection with the Arab Spring and the power of 'people just gathering on a space'.

'Think of Tahrir Square,' he offers, 'they didn't really do anything, did they? Just their sheer presence was enough. This is potentiality. Doesn't even need to be to set into action. They did set into action at times in Cairo but not that much.' Sehgal's argument is provocative given that the violence of the protest and the sule were not 'just there', but I can see his point in relation to other recent political activity, like the Occupy activists, who unnerved government and media by seeming to fight more for their right to occupy public (or, what turned out not to be so public, like St Paul's) spaces than any concrete demands. At the time, Slavoj Žižek wrote an approving article in the *Guardian* titled 'Occupy first, demand later', arguing for the importance of remaining 'subtracted from the pragmatic field of negotiations and "realist" proposals'. And certainly the act of gathering is a freedom that totalitarian governments notoriously curtail and, even on an everyday level in the UK, we are confronted with constant checks on the power of groups, whether kettling demonstrators or not allowing more than two school children in a sweetshop at any one time.

I ask whether Sehgal could imagine working outside the museum context in a different type of public space – a train station or shopping mall, perhaps. But Sehgal is clear that his work needs to be contextualised within the history of art institutions, and specifically in the context of objects. 'My work always deals with the question: what can you do instead of producing objects?' he says. 'This "instead of" is really important. You only get the instead of by placing it in a gallery, because immediately – although there are no objects – you think, oh, but where are the objects? You have this comparison going on.' This approach could evoke the kind of zeitgeistian ecological anti-materialism that Nicolas Bourriaud analysed in *Postproduction* when he reframed the artist as a recycler of pre-existing cultural elements. But Sehgal is clearly wary of having to defend his work as militantly anti-capitalist – after all, he isn't against selling his work: 'Not that I am necessarily against objects. Or that I am necessarily trying to prove some point. But I think just the sheer comparison is interesting. In our culture we are really attached to and focused on objects.'

Sehgal's work seems closer to the idea of the late 1990s' 'experience economy' model of American business analysts Pine and Gilmore, where experience itself is in fact the product to be bought and sold. 'I think that my work totally mirrors or goes along with that shift', he agrees, although he points out that the German sociologist Gerhard Schulze coined the phrase 'Experience Society' six years earlier than 'those guys from Minneapolis' but that he hasn't been widely translated. He sees art history in the same terms, linking the establishment of museums as a 'new ritual for individuals' with the rise of bourgeois society and contemporary market democracies. 'Then you can trace how they shift according to economic orders,' he argues. 'So at the beginning you see lots of objects, then you have the white cube that is more focused on this one object – how it relates to the materiality of the artist, this one particular subjectivity. Then minimal art already goes more to the body and the situation. I would say my work is definitely in this line.' I mention Tate Modern's new Tanks, built to accommodate the rise in large-scale performance and time-based work. I ask him how he thinks institutions are coping with shifts in art-making like his and how he imagines his work will be dealt with historically given the lack of documentation. But he fixates on the comparison with performance art, a tradition with which he prefers his work not to be associated: 'Mine is more in the tradition of sculpture and installation in the sense that it happens all the time.'

I have the feeling that, like his relation to performance and theatre, Sehgal will be dismissive of the trendy term 'participation' despite featuring prominently in Bishop's book. 'My opinion on this discourse on participation, at least on a theoretical level (maybe not on a practical level), is complicated,' he confirms, 'because I would say if you behold a painting then that is also a way of participating. Contemplation is also participation. So even saying "participatory art" – even if I know what people mean – is tautological because any art only becomes art if it becomes public, if someone participates in it in a kind of active beholding.' The idea of the spectator as an always already active interpreter is an argument Jacques Rancière explores in *The Emancipated Spectator*, in which he also challenges the assumption that theatre has a privileged relationship to the notion of community over people watching TV or going to a gallery.

Aside from the issue of hierarchy, one of the main critiques levelled at participatory art or relational aesthetics is that they have a predetermined outcome, that viewers are not really free to interact – I know I am not supposed to ask an interpreter to continue our conversation in the cafe, for example. But Sehgal is adamant that the artist needs to retain a strong sense of aesthetic control. 'I think it is a question of composition. It needs some rules or it is not art or it is not artificial.' He pauses to think of an example: 'It would be like, say, a composition by Mozart. It would be a bit like critiquing – it didn't include all the notes that exist because some notes were not possible. But that is exactly the nature of composition. The composition is that you select a few notes and then you arrange them, and that makes something specific. If you just include everything – that for me is a problem.'

For Sehgal, aesthetics – or what he calls 'the craft of composition' – are a vital part of art-making and he is disdainful of the Duchampian conceptual tradition that relies on declaration as a mode of designating art. 'If you declare something art – I think that is a very un- generous and actually ethically problematic thing. If I say, "I declare this chair art", that puts me into a position of absolute authority. Who am I to declare that? It was maybe OK for Duchamp at that time, but even he turns the urinal upside down or hangs something … there is still a composition, even in a very small way, although I do find it a little bit problematic. Also John Cage,' he adds, 'I find it a little bit problematic the older I get. There is too little composition going on. I mean, maybe for their time, it's great.'

Sehgal seems very much an artist for our time. In London this summer the Olympics have made us hyperaware of the power of crowds – their negative effect in terms of security and the city's creaking infrastructure, but also their positive effect on morale and business. At this time, however, Sehgal seems satisfied that I have enough information: 'I think there is a lot you could write for your text: the emancipated spectator, Experience Society, television – all of those are interesting topics which are coming from you and not from me,' he says encouragingly. He explains that he needs to go and give his interpreters a break. It turns out that the Turbine Hall will unexpectedly be open until 8pm tonight, and he and his team haven't organised the new schedule. 'I want to slow down the piece a little bit.' He spots someone in the distance – 'I'm wondering if that is one of my people; she looks similar' – which gives him the excuse to break off our chit-chat. The encounter is over.

Issue 359, September 2012

James Welling

interviewed by Kathy Battista

Picturing

KATHY BATTISTA *Can you talk about the decision to focus on the period of the 1980s for your show?*

JAMES WELLING I was in 'The Pictures Generation' exhibition at the Metropolitan Museum of Art in New York in 2009. The show was a 1980s show. The idea of a Pictures aesthetic originates in a couple of places earlier, simultaneously, and the curator Doug Eklund started the show by looking at what was happening at CalArts in the mid 1970s. I was part of that group of artists along with David Salle, Jack Goldstein and Matt Mullican. David and I were actively looking at and thinking about repurposing images, using images from media, magazines and books. We shared a studio for a year and a half and we would look closely at what each other was doing.

In 'The Pictures Generation' Eklund included two of my very early photo appropriation collages – some are in the Milton Keynes show – work I made in the mid 1970s with magazine images. The Milton Keynes show follows roughly the same period as 'The Pictures Generation', from 1974 until 1988. Director Anthony Spira asked me to do a show that looked at my evolution from an artist who started with images of media and moved to someone who took a concentrated look at abstract photography. I think Anthony got this idea from a show Donald Young put together in 2009 of a number of very early works of mine. So, how did I make that transition? What were the things that I was looking at, reading and listening to? I pulled from my archive material from that period and we made a show using the photographs that I exhibited and the archival materials and ephemera that surrounded those shows. At Milton Keynes we

479

recreated six exhibitions: two shows I did at Metro Pictures in 1981 and 1982; one that I did at Cash/Newhouse in 1984 in the East Village; two shows that I did in 1987 – one at Christine Burgen Gallery New York and one at Feature in Chicago – and finally an installation that I created in 1990 at the Kunsthalle Bern of work from the 1980s.

In the MK Gallery exhibition there are vitrines with written notes, press releases, watercolour studies for photographs, memorabilia and ephemera. There are also two vitrines with tapes, records and posters from the NoWave music scene in lower Manhattan in the late 1970s to the mid 1980s. The musical material focuses largely on Glenn Branca and his circle, including Sonic Youth and a few other bands that were active in the early 1980s. Music was extremely important to how I thought about making photographs.

KB   *There hasn't been as much focus in the UK on 'The Pictures Generation' so it is important to show that body of your work.*

JW   I'm happy to be included in 'The Pictures Generation' but I always felt a little bit of an outsider to that grouping. My work is not really about media imagery, it is more of an epistemological questioning of photography as medium. You could say that some of the Pictures artists who work with photography, such as Cindy Sherman, Louise Lawler, Sherrie Levine, Sarah Charlesworth and Barbara Kruger, asked the question 'what is a photograph?'. But my trajectory is a little different.

KB   *I was wondering how much you identified with The Pictures Generation.*

JW   In the late 1970s I was very close to Sherrie Levine. She lived four blocks away and we were always talking about work. I was also friendly with Barbara Kruger, Louise Lawler, Jack Goldstein, Matt Mullican, Erika Beckman and David Salle. We were always going to the same openings and parties.

KB   *Were you affected by the landscape and the light when you moved to Los Angeles? Did the city have an effect on your work?*

JW   The ironic thing is – and this idea has only just occurred to me – that I have always been very attached to the East Coast but in the west I found my way as an artist. My show up now at David Zwirner in New York is about my early influences, notably Andrew Wyeth. I grew up on the East Coast, lived in New York for 20 years and still make work about the East Coast landscape. But it wasn't until I came out to Los Angeles that I found my voice as a photographer. I live in Los Angeles, but I still identify strongly with issues from the East Coast. But, as I just came to understand, I was able to get things together only when I moved west, away from my upbringing. So, yes, Los Angeles is a place that instilled in me certain ideas and a lot of the conceptual underpinnings for the work in the show.

KB *And do you think it was through the colleagues and teachers like John Baldessari that you were able to come to complete aesthetic fruition in LA?*

JW I don't want to minimise the importance of my teachers because I now teach and spend a lot of time with my students, but I have to say that when I was 20 I was a loner when it came to how I thought about work. So while Baldessari and my peers were important, when I left school I looked inward at what I really wanted to explore.

Between 1974 and 1979 I became interested in the poetry of Mallarmé and Rilke and books by them and on them are in the exhibition's vitrines. This period was an intense five-year reading period, when I began to imagine a new type of photograph that I could make.

KB *Could you say something about your engagement with New England, and Connecticut in particular?*

JW I think one of the benefits of moving to Los Angeles and studying there was that when I returned to my parents' house in Connecticut, Los Angeles stood in absolutely stark contrast to it. I remember making some very early videotapes at CalArts when I was homesick for Connecticut using objects that I brought from home. So in a way, my understanding of New England and Connecticut was intensified by moving to California. The strangeness of the Los Angeles landscape allowed me to then go back to the East Coast and see that landscape in a new way. And that phenomenon continues to this day. I live in Los Angeles and I return to make work on the East Coast. I'm going to Maine soon to photograph. It is a very intense, special feeling to be back in that landscape that I love so much. I might not have that same relationship if I had lived there continuously.

KB *Speaking of your family, I was going to ask you about your engagement with history and your fascination with the 19th century.*

JW I like looking at things that are distant in time but still with us, the way that vestiges of the 19th century were present in the landscape of Connecticut in the 1950s and 60s. At CalArts in my early 20s, I was extremely interested in the art of the now; but after art school, I became aware of this other idea about the 19th century – a sense of time as a hundred-year-long span. 'Old' as an idea began to impress me when I would return from the East Coast to Los Angeles where the structures and the roads were set down years earlier. The alien-ness of the East Coast – because I was living in California – allowed me to access my sense of the 19th century.

My father's Aunt Elsa lived in a house in Hartford that was built in 1910 and had furniture from her grandparents' home which dated from the era of Abraham Lincoln. Elsa was a formal, imposing woman and my siblings and I would go visit her twice a year. When we got to her house we would time travel back into the 19th century. So my great-aunt was an important portal into the past. When she died in 1976 my father came into possession of the diary of her grandmother and I began to photograph that book in 1977.

So there is a continuum with my great-aunt and her grandmother's diary from 1840. That project was started in 1977 and I worked on it until 1980. By then I wanted to make work that referenced some of those same ideas about the past but not tied directly to family history or even to any visible monuments. After some thought I began to photograph aluminium foil and then later drapery, both of which evoked my sense of the 19th century. The foil and the drapes were evocative without physical attributes. I wasn't photographing buildings or diaries or landscapes. I tried to create this place abstractly as an evocation of my sense of the 19th century.

There are two other bodies of work in the exhibition from the mid 1980s, the 'Gelatin' and the 'Tile' pictures, which don't follow on this continuum away from 19th-century references. These two bodies of work are concerned with process and procedures more than historical time. With these later series I became very interested in the formal properties of photography.

KB *And would you say that there is a dialectic in the work between the abstraction and the more documentary photographs?*

JW I don't think I make purely abstract work for any long period. After the abstract work of the mid 1980s I began to photograph architecture and railroads. Both subjects return to the explicit content of the 19th century.

In these final parts of the show, I look at chance and randomness. And for the first time I have included the actual objects that I photographed – the aluminium foil, the drapes and the tiles – as relics in the show.

KB *You have worked a lot with cameraless photography. Do you have a relationship with cameras? Do you always have one with you?*

JW   I always have a camera now. But in the period we're talking about, 1976 to 1987 when I was intensely involved with photography, I was not with a camera all the time. It was a studio practice. Now things are reversed. I take a lot of documentary pictures outside the studio. In the 1970s and the early 1980s I did not have much money and photography was expensive. Even though I made a lot of photographs in this period, I was very careful about my finances. And now that I have more resources, I'm not working in the studio as much.

KB   *How do you feel about mobile-phone cameras? Do you ever use one?*

JW   I use my cell phone mostly to send someone an image of an artwork. I don't use it as a replacement for my digital camera.

KB   *There is talk of iPads and mobile phones as new media for artists but I don't know if they can ever replace a real camera.*

JW   There is no reason why they can't. I just don't work that way now. However, I use a scanner quite a bit. I do much more scanning than I take pictures. I made Xerox art as an undergraduate and a photocopy machine is nothing more than an early form of scanner. I loved going to the library and making copies of things. The diary photographs use the camera as a photocopying machine.

KB   *Do you feel that the boom in the art market since the 1980s has become a factor in your production?*

JW   Some of my work sells fairly well but with some bodies of work I have never sold a single example.

KB   *What are the abstract pictures that look like liquid?*

JW   They are called 'Fluid Dynamics'. I made them in 2009 by immersing chromogenic photographic paper in water and then exposing it to light as water ran off the sheet. I scanned the prints and added colour with Photoshop by taking samples of colour from my Wyeth photographs. So there is a two-step process involved: a monochrome photogram is turned into a colour image using Photoshop.

KB   *Do you have a darkroom somewhere where you do this?*

JW   I made some of them in my studio darkroom and I made some at UCLA where I teach. In the summer I am able to use the darkroom for a couple of weeks a year.

KB   *I want to ask you about teaching. I wondered how you find your role as a teacher and how that fits into your artistic practice.*

JW   I didn't teach until I was 44. I supported myself working as a short-order cook then by working in museums as an art handler. I was very lucky to be considered for the job in UCLA without prior teaching experience. I was hired to run the photography area and to teach graduate students, and I now share some of those responsibilities with Catherine Opie. Teaching is important to me, it allowed me to have a more open view about photography. Before I taught, I was fairly intolerant of certain kinds of photographic practices. As a teacher I'm now much more interested in a wide range of work, and I want to see what everyone is doing.

I really enjoy exploring creativity and in challenging the students and myself to make every day, every crit, every class an opportunity to go deeper into the creative process. So my teaching is a laboratory. The most important thing is to be very encouraging with my students. My teaching philosophy is that there are no bad ideas in art. Every idea is a fantastic one if it comes from somewhere deep inside you. I try to be open as an educator and that is something that I learned from studying how Baldessari taught. John is a very open and generous teacher and if you look at the students who came out of his programmes, they are amazingly diverse artists. But I couldn't have done this when I was younger. I was a very quiet, uptight, nervous person when I was younger. Age helps.

Issue 361, November 2012

Jonas Mekas

interviewed by Gilda Williams

Remains of the Day

GILDA WILLIAMS *The title of the central filmwork of your recent Serpentine Gallery exhibition is* Out-takes from the Life of a Happy Man, 2012. *This year you celebrated your 90th birthday. Is this exhibition a satisfied reflection on your long life, one spent immersed in art and film?*

JONAS MEKAS *Out-takes from the Life of a Happy Man* really is made up from out-takes, the footage I did not use, that did not fit into any of my completed films – ends and bits. I discovered I had a lot of it; time was passing and the films were slowly fading. It will all be gone soon and I was worried about it. I thought on this occasion, on the occasion of the Serpentine Gallery show, I will do something with all these remains.

GW *When you returned to these out-takes and were re-editing your footage after perhaps 30 or 40 years, could you remember most of it?*

JM I know exactly where I shot every bit, every little piece. I remember where I filmed it and every different circumstance. Yes, I remember every moment of it.

GW *Is your filmmaking a kind of prosthetic memory for you; is it part of your memory?*

JM Not the usual memory that people talk about, or what we usually mean by 'memory'. I do not work with 'memory'. I work with actual material, physical material, film – that's very real. I don't think of myself as working with memory but with real recordings of moments in the past, with whatever we have left. I work with concrete pieces of film that happen to contain moments from a certain place and a certain time, a certain situation. It is very real. And I don't think they are just personal. I think they are universal.

cw *In contrast to the art gallery, in a cinema your sense of the actual space you are in disappears.*

jm Yes, of course. To be cinema, it has to be that way – just you and the screen.

cw *How do you choose when or what to film? Do you always carry a camera with you?*

jm Oh yes, always. I have my camera with me right now, in my bag. But I don't make rational decisions about what to film, I don't plan. Whatever I film is a moment when something happens that triggers something – suddenly I have to take out my camera and film it. There is no explanation, no planning. The reasons I choose to film are invisible, they are never rational.

cw *Obviously, sound is added afterwards. How do you decide how to join sound and image?*

jm In this case the sounds are from my sound library. Just as I have collected images, I have collected sounds – thousands and thousands of cassettes. The music in this film is actually my wedding music. My wedding took place in Kremsmünster Abbey in Austria, a very old abbey, like 1,200 years old. You can hear the monks singing, the nuns singing – these are from my recordings. The piano is played by a Lithuanian musician and painter Auguste Varkalis, a very good painter and a very good friend. Everything in this work is part of my life.

cw *You write in one of the wall texts how your life has witnessed so many tremendous 20th-century events – the rise of Soviet power and the invasion of the Nazis in your homeland of Lithuania, your subsequent imprisonment in a forced labour camp near Hamburg during the Second World War, then your time in displaced persons camps across Germany after the war.*

jm Unfortunately – or fortunately, perhaps – I was born shortly after the communist revolution and shortly before the arrival of Hitler. I went through all the horrors of the 20th century. Yes, that was my fate, what can I say?

cw *Yet you always seem able to focus on the redemptive moments of your life, the happy episodes of your everyday life.*

jm Yes. I don't remember the unhappy parts – I don't try to remember. That's my nature. I don't remember for very long the horrors that were close to me. I could, I suppose, spend my time brooding on or remembering the horrors of the 20th century, but I'm not interested in that, that's not my nature. I concentrate in my work and in my life only on the celebration of life. That's what I am all about. I am celebrating life and having a joyful relationship to life. I am a propagandist for happiness and beauty. This show, this exhibition, is my manifesto: a manifesto for the celebration of life and happiness and beauty.

I think that too much in contemporary art – too much time, too many exhibitions, too much space – is dedicated to horrors, to the darkness of our civilisation. If you surround yourself with darkness it begins to affect you, those images start to affect you. When you go into a cemetery, you think about death, it has an effect on you. When you visit the Museum of the Inquisition ... you are affected by those horrible things. You leave depressed, you need a drink. But if you are in a field of flowers, you are affected by the flowers – you smile.

CW *You were relocated by the UN Refugee Organisation with your brother Adolfas to New York in 1949, and by the early 1960s found yourself at the centre of the Avant Garde, working with filmmakers like Jack Smith, Maya Deren and Kenneth Anger, with poets Allen Ginsberg, William Burroughs and John Giorno, and with artists including Andy Warhol, George Maciunas and so on.*

JM You didn't mention music, which was also at the centre – John Cage, La Monte Young and others. All the arts were being reinvigorated at the time, so much began in those years, or was brought up to date. But maybe we have been stuck too long on the 1960s. For decade after decade the interest was always on the 1960s, but now I think attention has moved forward – people are discovering the 1970s. Maybe that is good.

CW *You have always worked independently, securing your own funding and working outside established institutions – in fact often inventing your own institutional models. I am interested in the strategies you invented to finance and organise your many ventures –* Film Culture *magazine, from 1955, or the Film-Makers' Cooperative, which you founded in 1962 and which was funded by the artists themselves.*

JM Luckily, for my own personal work, I did not need money. My kind of films do not require money. But my struggle and all the fundraising – oh all the fundraising! – was always directed towards other projects. *Film Culture* magazine, the Filmmakers' Cinemateque (now Anthology Film Archives) – that is where all my work and effort in fundraising was needed. Film preservation, for example, takes quite a bit of money. I have spent much more time, many times more time, on fundraising than on making my own work. Fundraising is not easy for us independents – it never was and still isn't. We have always had very little support from the city or any official bodies. I'm still fundraising.

cw *Did you fund your projects through co-operatives or through individual donors?*

JM Mostly individuals. I have spent a lot of my life writing letters, making calls, trying to persuade rich people to support us. It is hard work. Fundraising is hard work, it's no joke. Some artists supported us too, by donating their art, which we sell. I bought the Anthology Film Archives building from the City for $50,000 in an auction in 1968 or so with an outright donation. But to fix the building cost me $1.8m. To transform this former courthouse and prison into a film museum … you can imagine what it cost! I spent ten years of my life raising that $1.8m but I needed to create the Anthology. It was a nightmare. I still have bad dreams about it.

cw *Were you surprised when film and video moved massively into gallery and museum spaces from the 1970s into the 1990s?*

JM No, I wasn't surprised. I thought it was natural. It was hard work to convince some galleries and museums to embrace film, but not all of them. For example the Museum of Modern Art included film right from the start, since the 1920s. The Pompidou also included cinema from its very beginnings in the 1970s, thanks to Pontus Hulten, who was a visionary. But in the private galleries, it was really the introduction of video art that marked the change, mostly for practical reasons. It was much easier to present a video on a monitor than to project a film, which requires a projector and someone who knows how to operate it. Film projection is a much more complicated business than a video show. For the galleries it became very simple to show moving-image art because of the video cassette. The simplicity of the technology opened the door first to video and then to film.

cw *In your films, you are not interested in staging events but in recording the everyday events going on around you.*

JM That is my challenge. The everyday, the invisible, life around us, the daily life which we don't even notice – especially the art world, which seems to be totally uninterested in reality. They aren't even interested in colour. The art world seems to like things that are so boringly black and grey. But I crave colour. When I walk into the art opening I search for colour and most of the time I don't find it. So I'll go back to my movies. My challenge is how to see and record moments of daily life that pass as if invisibly. That is my challenge. So much of the contemporary art-making I see around me – it's all an artificial, invented reality, with artists trying to be 'creative'. I'm very old-fashioned in that sense. I am interested in living things, like an anthropologist who is going with a tape-recorder and recording old songs that humans, somewhere, are still singing or dancing to. I'm interested in catching these moments of contemporary humanity, recording it. I don't need to create it.

GW *Today everybody carries around with them in their phone a fairly sophisticated digital camera, recording daily minutiae, and we can instantly distribute this imagery over the internet. Would this have been the ideal means for your 'everyday' films? You have a very comprehensive website, jonasmekasfilms.com, and in 2007 you created there the internet project* 365 Day Project *in which you presented a new short film every day, like a visual diary.*

JM The internet, to me, is just an extension of the telephone. It continues the history of correspondence, of having conversations by other means than face-to-face talk. This history is as old as the world itself, and the internet is just an extension of that history. It is a very vague thing for me to try to define what my art is, or what film art is. In fact it is hard to define what any art is, or how best to distribute it. I'll give you an example: a friend of mine from Naples, Giuseppe Zevola, worked in the Banco di Napoli, which is about 400 years old. He showed me stacks and stacks of ancient records in the bank – you know, cheques cashed, that sort of thing. And the bank employees from long ago, obviously very bored with their work, doodled in these books. These bank registers are full of doodles, hundreds and hundreds of these improvised little drawings, which Giuseppe collected. They look like the work of many contemporary artists that I see everywhere today – in fact they are often more interesting than a lot of what I see in the galleries.

So how can you say what 'art' is and what it isn't, or where best to show it or to find it? Where would you place these doodles? What's being exchanged today on YouTube or other websites is part of the everyday exchanges and conversations that have been documented in the past in other ways – why do we need to call things 'art'?

GW *Do you call your films 'art'?*

JM No! I am not an artist! I refuse to call myself that. I am not an artist. I am a maker, a filmmaker. I make films. I film with a camera or I videotape. To decide what is 'art' and what is 'not art' makes no sense. We must always remember that what we have left of art, what we call 'art history', is just what managed to survive. It is not the whole story. We know only about what religious fanatics and political fanatics did not manage to destroy, to say nothing of the earthquakes, fires and wars that destroyed plenty more. We call it 'art history' as if this history is complete but in fact very little is left. I was just told that Botticelli destroyed almost all his late work, something like 20 years' worth of works, hundreds of paintings, only because the religious fanatics around him told him it was sinful to paint the works he did. Botticelli was said to have been pressured into destroying much of his work. What is left of Botticelli, like all art, is just a fragment. What we see in the museums or what is written about in books, what we study in schools as 'art history', in truth is only the miserable leftovers that happened to survive the horrors of the past.

The same is true now. We have this visual flood of images, produced by all the tools at our disposal for recording and disseminating moving images. What will remain of it all will be only random pieces, fragments. Consider how quickly technology is changing. Already it is difficult for me to see material I recorded just five years ago. Recording formats become obsolete, the machinery dies out and vast quantities of recorded material turn invisible. They are only as permanent as the technologies that support them.

You have to remember that decisions about formats are made solely by businesses, making business decisions not artistic ones. Motion-picture film is disappearing purely for profit-driven reasons. Business people realised they could make more money with video than film, so everything moved to video. The production of celluloid has been discontinued and you can no longer find film labs, which are all closed. Business determines formats: it is certainly not the artists who are making decisions about dominant formats. Every two years or so, formats have to change for business reasons only – for money, for profit. We all have to buy and change everything. We are spending a lot of money now at Anthology Film Archives to transfer video art from the 1970s and 80s to new formats. We have to do all this work because we can no longer watch these works on the original machinery, which has disappeared. And of course this is bound to repeat itself as even newer formats will replace the current formats.

CW *And there is always a loss in quality in any transfer of this kind.*

JM Of course, there is always a loss. If a painting is made in oil, the content could only have been captured using oil paint. There are different contents that can only be caught in watercolour or inks. The exact same thing is true with moving image – what you can do with 35mm you can't do with 16mm, and what you can do with 16mm you cannot do with 35mm – much less with video or digital recording. The tool you use to make the image and the result are inseparably connected, you cannot transfer film to video and think it is the same thing. You are no longer seeing the film, you are seeing something else. The texture is different, everything is different – it is a completely different thing. All that is left is 'the story'.

CW *Were you appalled when the Museum of Modern Art showed Warhol's films on video, as they did in 2010?*

JM Yes, I called it a crime. It is a crime! For the Museum of Modern Art – and other major museums – to show films like Andy Warhol's 'Screen Tests' on video when it is still possible to show them as films – to project them – was criminal. In ten years' time it really will be very difficult to project them but in 2010 it was still possible to screen them properly. To present Warhol's films as videos really was a crime.

CW *I would credit you with being among the first to take Warhol's art seriously – not just in the light-hearted context of Pop. Already in the early 1960s you understood him as a radical artist and filmmaker.*

JM Of course we should take Warhol very, very seriously. The 'Screen Tests' are incredible: hundreds of portraits, unique in the history of portraiture. Warhol's early silent-film period, I think, is especially important. But even the sound period – I mean, *Chelsea Girls* is a monumental work, its complexity and richness still hasn't been understood. We still haven't understood enough how important that film really is.

CW *Do you remember the circumstances behind the making of Warhol's* Empire, *1964?*

JM I was walking with my friend John Palmer, carrying *Film Culture* magazines to be mailed. The post office happened to be in the Empire State Building. We stopped and we looked at it from a distance, and Palmer said, 'Ah, this is a perfect subject for Andy Warhol!', because Andy was interested in iconic images. 'Why don't we tell Andy?', I said, so we did. John Palmer's name appears in the Premiere announcement of the film.

CW *That is very rare in Warhol's lifetime – he didn't like to openly share artistic credit, especially in writing. Despite all his assistants and collaborators, the art was always signed 'by Andy Warhol' alone.*

JM Andy actually thanked John later for giving him the idea. Marie Mencken, a filmmaker and Warhol friend, worked at *Time* magazine in the Rockefeller Center, on the 40th floor or so. She let us in at night – without permission, of course. We went there with some sandwiches. I did most of the work. I set up the camera and loaded the film. We waited until each reel ended, then I changed immediately to another reel of film. It was quite boring, we just sat there nibbling at our sandwiches. But the film – it's a great movie. That kind of idea – duration art – was in the air already. La Monte Young had already made music by extending one single note into four or five hours, for example, and, of course, Andy had already made *Sleep* the year before *Empire*.

CW *You have always been a writer alongside your image-making work – you wrote anti-Soviet and anti-Nazi propaganda, then you were a journalist and a poet, and text is often interspersed in your films. Are they parallel activities for you, writing and filmmaking?*

JM Yes, but I wear many different hats, not just those of writer and filmmaker. They are all me.

CW *A word that comes up often in your writing is 'paradise'. You use that term to describe your early childhood in a farming village in Lithuania, for what you found in New York when you arrived in 1949 and, later, in the 1960s.*

JM Paradise means 'innocence' – where there are still patches of innocence, of nature, an innocence that has not been destroyed by any of the poisons produced by our civilisation. In every area you pick – what you drink, or what you eat, what you dream – you can find little that hasn't yet been poisoned. Whenever you find something that is still pure, where you know that what you are getting is not contaminated, by chemicals or whatever, that is innocence, that is paradise. There are still some fragments of paradise. And some of us are still trying to protect them, to see that they remain. That is what I am trying to do. Preserving films – it is like keeping seeds for the future, when maybe they can grow. There are still some fragments of paradise around us, but they are being eaten away, attacked, all the time. Like the corals in the ocean, eaten away by the pollutants.

I think we are doomed, actually. I think our civilisation is doomed.

cw *You have said that in Lithuania you are mostly a poet, in Europe a filmmaker, in the US a kind of maverick promoter, supporter, enabler and friend to avant-garde film.*

JM That is still so. In Lithuania I am a national poet. When I work on my films they think I'm just wasting time. In the US some institutions have started recognising me as a filmmaker, but mostly they think of me as an organiser, a writer for the *Village Voice*, founder of *Film Culture* magazine. They admit and recognise now my contribution to the development and changes in cinema. In Europe, I would say they recognise all those aspects, in Paris especially. But now other countries in Europe are beginning to see my work too and accept me as a filmmaker, like here in the UK.

cw *Do you have a favourite way that you like to be described?*

JM One description of me that I liked was coined by Vincent Canby in the *New York Times* who said, 'Jonas Mekas does everything with the shrewdness of a farmer.' It's true, I grew up in a farming village and I am still a farmer. I plant many things. I water them, I see that they grow. I defend them – I see a lot of what I do as defending. I function as Minister of Defence, Minister of Finance, Minister of Propaganda. I do all those things, out of necessity. No one else was doing any of this, showing our films, preserving them, protecting. It had to be done – and it still does. I have done all those things without stopping since the 1960s. I did it all for the glory of cinema.

Issue 363, February 2013

Michelangelo Pistoletto

interviewed by Alex Coles

The Minus Man

'I was born in Biella in 1933. I live in Turin. I have experience in
making dentures, cultivating fields, designing ads, restoring
paintings, marriage, painting, cinema, theatre and literature.'
  Michelangelo Pistoletto, *The Minus Man, the Unbearable Side*, 1970.

ALEX COLES *I'm interested in how your studio has developed over the
past six decades – both literally and conceptually. In the early 1950s
you worked in your father's restoration studio in Turin, moving to your
own studio in the city in 1956 and to a new one in 1958 where you began
developing what became the 'Mirror Paintings'. In 1965 came a move
to a typesetting workshop studio in Turin while working on the 'Minus
Objects'. This was followed by the dispersal of the studio during the period
of The Zoo, 1968 to 1970.*
  MICHELANGELO PISTOLETTO The studio is an individual place where
you work and develop your activity. It is a kind of institution for me
because it is in the studio that the activity is created and things are
made. But at the same time it can also be a public place, a place the
artist looks to the outside from. Let's say that the studio is a passage
– from the work itself to the outside. For example, working with
my father I had the opportunity to learn about the art of the past
because he restored paintings. The process of restoration gave me the
opportunity to witness how the world was changing immediately after
the Second World War. During this period, with Italy transitioning
from having an aristocratic economy to an industrial one, the wealthy
people were selling their art collections to the new rich. Many of
their paintings went through restorers' studios. The studio became

witness to the transformation of the balance of the Italian economy. Observing this shift was very meaningful for me at the time.

After the period of working with my father I moved to the advertising industry and began to understand how broader forms of contemporary creativity could also be transformed by these societal changes. At that time, advertising was an attempt to create a future for a particular place at a specific moment in time. Following this experience, I founded my own personal atelier and began working on paintings, including the 1960 *Silver Self-Portrait* and *Man Seen from the Back – The Present* of 1961 – eventually leading to the 'Mirror Paintings'. The 'Mirror Paintings' were a reflection of not only what was happening in my studio but also what was happening outside in the street. The mirror was a device that allowed me to open the door of the atelier. This had significant repercussions, some of them political, especially in works such as *The Trap*, made between 1967 and 1974, in which viewers found themselves in a gallery transformed into a prison. While to begin with people would come into the studio to experience the work, eventually the work took place outside on the street. From this time onwards I have not had a real studio, so to speak. I activate the space where I am.

AC *Looking at archive pictures, it seems that from the time you moved into the typesetting workshop studio in 1965 in Turin, when you were generating works such as* No To The Rise of the Tram Fare *of 1965 and* Two People Passing By *the following year, you selected your space and operated in it in a very particular way.*

MP At this point in time I used the studio as a place for an activity that encompassed both the fabrication and the reception of the work. This way the traditional system of the art world was probed and the place the gallery had previously assumed in it was usurped. The new work could be seen in the studio at the same time as it was being made. In this sense the studio was activated; it was a live, open social space – not a closed private one.

AC *Though prefigured by the performative dynamic that* Walking Sculpture *of 1966 triggers, when the activities of The Zoo started in 1968 with performances such as* The Trained Man*, did you find that the studio became completely obsolete?*

MP Yes, definitely. The Zoo could only take place on the street: the street was the place where music, theatre, dance and performance could come together in my work. The reciprocity between the different languages taking place on the street generated the capacity for a recreation of the rapport between the different languages of the arts in my work. The Zoo, in name and function, was also a reaction to many societal pressures. In 1969 I wrote of how 'so-called civilisation had relegated every animal to its cage. The less dangerous, more docile and submissive had been placed in large fenced-in areas: factories, housing projects, sports stadiums. Artists were isolated in the Venice Biennale, in theatres, museums and organised events.'

AC *Because your concern to open up the studio as an interior happens so early on it is interesting to note how, as your studio is turned inside out as a real interior at the end of the 1960s, you begin to create fictive interiors in the form of installations –* The Office of the Minus Man *of 1970 comes to mind.*

MP *Office of the Minus Man* was an attempt to metaphorically open up another space that is usually closed: the office – to open it up, like my studio, to exchange. Years later this led to Cittadellarte: Fondazione Pistoletto, an attempt to create an open institution. Instead of continuing to try and operate outside the institution like The Zoo did – for there really is no outside, I realised – I wanted to create a new, more dynamic institution of my own.

AC *Following the radical experiments of The Zoo, did you return to an earlier, more traditional studio model, for the remainder of the 1970s?*

MP I maintained what we could call a studio throughout this period but its role in my work changed significantly. Between 1972 and 1978 I had a studio in the countryside in San Sicario, in Val di Susa, as well as maintaining my studio in Turin. But no longer was the studio the primary place where the work was made. Instead the studio became a place where I both literally and metaphorically stored past works. The studio became a meditative space, an archive that could be accessed through memory.

AC *Due to the scale and labour-intensive feel of many of your works from the 1980s, especially the polychrome series, the role of the studio must have changed again.*

MP 1981 to 1985, while I was making the black polychrome series, the studio did indeed become important again in a more literal way. The matt black surfaces of works like *Black Polychromy* and *Polychrome Volume* of 1985 seemed to suck the studio space in. So the studio was activated again but in a completely different way to the 1960s and 1970s.

With the development of Cittadellarte in the 1990s, the role of my studio moved on again. I try to keep my activities at Cittadellarte distinct from my personal work as an artist. But since it has all my files and books, the offices of Cittadellarte – which are connected to my private house – became the place where I often conceive of my work. Both their fabrication and reception happen elsewhere.

AC *In one reading, Cittadellarte replaced your studio by co-ordinating your broad interests – performance, object making, installation, photography etc – together under one umbrella. Did you begin thinking about Cittadellarte early on in the 1960s?*

MP Not really. It only began to gain true momentum at the beginning of the 1990s when I was working with the students at the Viennese Academy of Fine Arts where I was a professor from 1990 until 1999. I was always telling the students that art is not just something you produce in order to make money, art can be used in a more thoughtful way and make a broader societal impact. It was only while at the academy that I began to develop Cittadellarte, a place that could be simultaneously independent and yet still dependent upon it. I chose the name Cittadellarte precisely because it incorporates two meanings: the citadel, where art is protected, and the city, with its openness.

I bought the old factory here in 1991 and soon I began to reactivate it. My plan was not only to join together the different artistic languages and creative disciplines, but also to bring different sectors of society together. So politics, economics and sustainability all became key elements in our collective research.

AC *Your teaching in Vienna was obviously very important to those who witnessed it – particularly someone like the furniture designer Martino Gamper, whose project* One Hundred Chairs in One Hundred Days *brings to mind your* Mobile (Furniture) *of 1965–66, and his series of 'Total Trattoria' events your* Painting for Eating *of 1965.*

MP Yes, Martino is a good example of where these ideas can lead in a different field.

AC *In relation to this, the transformation of the artwork at the end of the 1960s found a parallel in the worlds of design and architecture – with so-called radical design, especially in the work of Alessandro Mendini and his 1975 performance* Little Monument for the Home, *where a chair is set alight, and Carlos Caldini's Space Electronic nightclub in Milan. Were you in dialogue with these figures at the time?*

MP Not so much. Only with Ettore Sottsass Jnr.

AC *There was a small essay by Sottsass on your show at Gio Ponti's Sala Espressioni–Ideal Standard in 1965.*

MP Yes, but that was the extent of my dialogue with designers at the time. There was never any direct rapport with any of the other figures.

AC *In the late 1960s and early 1970s your works that were associated with Arte Povera such as* Orchestra of Rags *of 1968 and* Little Monument, *also of 1968, use objects of design – found everyday objects like kettles and shoes. So design, or the appropriation of design, does play a role in your practice even if you weren't in dialogue with your contemporaries from design.*

MP But when my works use design elements – tables, sofas, doors and windows – they do so as extensions of the human body. I use them in a way that is fundamentally different from the designer. In design you adapt your ideas to a necessity. What I do is the exact opposite. In *Double Ladder Leaning Against the Wall* of 1964 and *Green Pyramid* of 1965 – or even *Upside Down Furniture* of 1976 – I use design as a conceptual extension of the human body by transforming these practical objects through their appropriation.

AC *With your return to the mirror in the mid 1970s in* Division and Multiplication of the Mirror *of 1976, and in lesser-known works from the late 1970s and early 1980s such as* Wedding-Trees *and* The Etruscan, *you incorporate reproductions of classical sculptures into your work. There is a further correspondence here with the leaders of radical design as they moved into a fully matured Postmodernism. How do you feel in relation to the Alchimia and Memphis groups?*

MP Their work lacked any poetic dimension. Of course, by definition it included the viewer, because the viewer used the objects – be it a chair or sofa – and thereby became a user. But never was this reflected on in the work in a deeper way. Never were these objects and their uses transformed.

AC *But in his* Monument to the Home *Mendini saw himself as doing precisely that ... Leaving designers aside then, I'm also interested in another area of dialogue of the period: between yourself and theoreticians such as Umberto Eco with* The Absent Structure *of 1968, and also an activist and theorist such as Antonio Negri and his articles for Quaderni Rossi.*

MP Eco? No. There was no special relationship, but it was interesting later to read what he wrote about the mirror.

AC *So his 'The Mirror as a Prosthesis and a Channel' in* Semiotics and
the Philosophy of Language *of 1984 was more important to you than*
The Absent Structure?

MP Yes. I knew Eco was interested in my work but the essay on the
mirror was the only thing that felt relevant to me. To be honest, I
was not so interested in the theoretical positions of the time and nor
was I interested in more aggressive political positions like Negri's.
In many ways, the aggressive politics of the time were as suffocating
as the continuing onslaught of capitalism. As I said in 1969, 'art is
dead because it is crushed on the one side by the superstructures and
on the other by the war against the superstructures ... But creativity
has nothing to do with these things, it is essential in the same way
as food or shelter. The only political action open to artists today is to
unshackle themselves from this pincer movement.'

AC *To bring us up to date, following on from the travelling retrospective*
'Michelangelo Pistoletto: From One to Many, 1956–1974', first in Rome
and then in Philadelphia, can you tell me about the 2013 exhibition at the
Louvre – will it be an extension of this travelling exhibition or will your
earlier works be brought into focus through a different optic?

MP There will be two parts. The first part is a retrospective of sorts,
from the early 1960s up to the present. The second consists of a
series of interventions in the Louvre spread out between its various
galleries. I spent a good deal of time considering which works to place
where and in what departments.

AC *Could you give me some examples?*

MP Some of the 'Mirror Paintings' will be placed in the rooms devoted
to Italian art – the *Mona Lisa* will be paired with *Red Flag (Demon-*
stration 1) of 1966, for instance. There will also be a presentation of
Cittadellarte and a related work attached to I M Pei's pyramid. Further
works will be mixed up with the Roman sculptures.

My interventions will be a mirror of the Louvre's collection – a
mirror of the past but also a mirror of the present because the viewer
will be included in the work through their reflection. The museum
will become a place of live interaction.

AC *This is interesting in relation to what you said at the beginning about*
the many historical paintings passing through your father's studio in the
1950s and how this passage reflected a societal shift in Italy. Now with the
Louvre again there is a change in the relationship between the paintings
and their audience.

499

MP Yes, we are in a time of large transformations. The exhibition at the Louvre is in many ways premised on the idea of transformation: the reflection of the past and the projection of the future through the mirror of the present.

Issue 365, April 2013

Mark Boulos

interviewed by Jonathan Harris

Love Stories

JONATHAN HARRIS *Can you describe your new work* Echo*? On the face of it, this piece is very different from* All That is Solid Melts into Air *of 2008, which is concerned with Niger Delta anti-oil corporation activists and Chicago commodity traders, and* No Permanent Address *from 2010, whose subject is the Philippines' Marxist group, the New People's Army.*

MARK BOULOS At a surface level *Echo* is rather simple. It is a video installation: you walk into a black box and you see a spotlight on the floor. When you step into the spotlight a movie appears in front of you and your image is standing in the centre of the movie. It is strange because there is an apparent 3D effect that you see with your naked eye. It is something of a mirror – everybody has a fascination but also a discomfort with seeing themselves. It plays with that. You see a kind of holographic video image of yourself, an unusual, ghostly 3D image. As the video unfolds, optical and audio effects change the background from being a straightforward documentary cityscape to something quite strange.

JH *There is also a sound element to it.*

MB There is an echo – a delay on the sound that serves as an echo, because there is a live audio feed. So there are two sound elements: a recorded soundtrack and a live-feed – sometimes the live-feed is synchronised and sometimes there is a one-second delay, which becomes an echo. When you step into the spotlight and the video first appears, the sound echo stops and you are in sync with your own image on the screen. Then there is a Hitchcock zoom – a 'contra-zoom' effect – and through the period of the contra-zoom your image slows down and so does the soundtrack. Then the audio-feed

returns with a one-second delay – now in sync with your image –
which is also delayed by one second. The piece is about a movement
between synchronicity and asynchronicity. This effects a feeling of
identification and then of alienation.

JH   *Did you build those technical elements into the work, or is it just the
way the technology works – that there is a delay?*

MB   No, it is all intended. It was one of the forms inspired by neuro-
scientific research conducted by Olaf Blanke. That work was about
trying to understand what patients with neuro-pathological problems
were calling 'out-of-body' experiences – a sense of disembodiment.
Blanke and his team were trying to reproduce that sense using
perception manipulation, particularly through the use of 3D video.
One of the ways of disorienting perception is to show people images
of themselves in 3D but then to alienate them from that image by the
use of a delay, for example.

JH   *Could you say something about the broader philosophical and
theoretical background within which that piece was located – Marxism
and psychoanalysis? How do your projects relate to that conceptual
apparatus, before being realised in a context like* FACT?

MB   I had been exploring ideas of alienation and the fragmentation
of subjectivity that might be called, in psychoanalytic terms,
jouissance. However our sense of self is structured, it is not so
stable that it can't be undermined. The structure itself can be an
ideological prison because it is constructed by things like law and
language – the Lacanian 'symbolic'. So I had been making pieces
that represented people whose life's work was to undermine that
through revolutionary or spiritual transcendence – they were saints or
mystics, or were political-ideological militants – and who would even
sacrifice their own bodies in order to materialise and make an idea of
liberation manifest.

I also was trying to elucidate that everyday life that seems self-
evidently material is actually infused with ideology in a way that
is alienating – and I mean that term in a specifically Marxist way.
Making capitalism strange again, then – because it is. That's what
I was doing with *All That is Solid Melts into Air*. The strange language
of these Chicago commodity traders – signing to each other – and
these strange commodities – 'futures' and 'derivatives' – that kind of
alienation as well.

And then more formally I was trying, through the use of a

multi-screen, large-scale, immersive installation, to present this hyperrealist documentary and to effect a sense of dislocation of the body in space – to transport you somewhere else and to divide you internally. With *Echo* I was trying to readdress the body. It was interesting to me because I thought my work was becoming too discursive. I was interested in how to make an entirely visual piece of work – or visual and audio – without words.

JH *What was your organising principle for how the show as a whole would look or be understood?*

MB It was about how these screens, which are basically planes of images, interact with and charge the space, becoming sculptural. The function of the video screen in the past has been as cinema screen or television – either a window or a stage – but my interest was in how the works can create an interstitial space. So with *All That is Solid Melts into Air* the idea was to have a film that was both two individual films and at the same time one. But then it became about the space between the two screens – both physically and in audio terms. But it is also the way that the light on one screen reflects on the other. This wasn't something I necessarily anticipated – it appeared when the work was installed. Then I became interested in what is a sculptural issue. For someone who was trained initially as a filmmaker and afterwards as an installation artist, it was a new discovery as I had been thinking about it in cinematic terms. With *No Permanent Address* of 2010 I was thinking that, instead of having two opposing films, they could be a singular unified film that was internally divided (on three screens) so that it could be about totality and fragmentation. I was trying to preserve the totalising worldview of practical Marxism but at the same time recognising that it is certainly not 'total' any more.

JH *Would you say that you are a Marxist filmmaker? How would you elaborate what that means in formal, material terms?*

MB 'Formal terms' is difficult and interesting. Futurism and Constructivism could be both fascist in Italy and communist in Russia.

JH *You are not a 'montage artist', not a classical Brechtian in that sense, are you? The documentary film tradition is very different, isn't it? The problem with documentary is that it creates a narrative and the realist codes that are built into that are so explicit in the broader culture that it is very hard to turn it over. The content can be turned over – the ideological message – but it is less easy to overturn the actual formal construction of the reality code, the set of tropes and visual conventions that operate within documentary. You are not a constructivist.*

MB   I think the internal division, the fragmentation of screens, is a minimal form of Constructivism – the use of the three screens, sometimes synchronised and sometimes not. My inspirations have been communist filmmakers from Dziga Vertov to Jean- Luc Godard, from Pier Paolo Pasolini to the propaganda films I saw in Vietnamese war memorial museums and the activist films from both the third world and western activist groups from the 1960s and 1970s. I hope my films find resonance there. I don't think I'm trying to duplicate the kind of shocks that the constructivists were making at their most extreme but on the other hand none of my films are straightforward narratives. I employ their constructivist montage strategies to make them more strange or more lyrical rather than expositional or explicatory.

JH   *In a way* Echo *is quite different from the earlier works because of the attempt to bring the viewer directly into the image stream. Would you say it represents a break?*

MB   I think it is a rearticulation. My films always try to destabilise the assumed difference between subjective and objective positions and points of view – the opposition between the viewer and who they are viewing on the screen. They try to elicit on the narrative level some kind of deep sympathy where the viewers can identify themselves with a totally different, radical other on the screen. The work addresses this issue of how an observational documentary-style work can still be expressive, and how I represent myself by means of the other. The issues I choose are both personal and universal, although I never show my face and I edit out my voice from the interviews. But I ask some very direct and intimate questions of other people.

JH   *What is very dramatic and disturbing at the beginning of* All That is Solid Melts into Air *is the Nigerian fisherman who is wielding the large machete. Is it true that when you were filming that you didn't know what he was saying?*

MB   That's right – he was speaking a local dialect of English that was hard to understand.

JH   *What did you think was going on?*

MB   It took a while for me to process what was happening. It was exhilarating.

JH *He was on the edge of threatening you, wasn't he?*

MB Yes. I didn't take it personally because I hadn't met him before. At first I didn't know whether he was talking to me or my camera. The only thing I could do was to try to turn it into a performance rather than a personal confrontation. I accepted it as that. I didn't know what he was saying and as it unfolded it became really dramatic and maybe I was scared but also I was very happy to get that image.

JH *It is a classic moment in documentary film when the outsider arrives and is understood as a threat by those the camera is turned at, whatever the actual purpose of the film is. You are invading someone else's space.*

MB Yes. That was an issue I was really worried about before I went to Nigeria. How am I going to represent this in the work? It turns out that I didn't have to worry about it because they – the oil rebels – addressed it directly. And that is what the work is about. I filmed in Nigeria first and then edited it. Then I filmed the Chicago merchandising exchange. Then I re-edited them both so that they worked together. The Nigerians were much more welcoming to me and my camera than the financial institutions.

JH *The FACT gallery space affords a certain kind of experience compared with other spaces where you might show the work. What about the art context for these works? FACT is a hybrid organisation, somewhere between a conventional art gallery and something else which isn't fully realised yet. One of the historically determining causes for contemporary art being so depoliticised is that the 1945 postwar settlement generated the idea that art had to have a level of indeterminacy or ambiguity for it to be taken seriously. This begins with Abstract Expressionism, then Pop Art and the way Andy Warhol is understood. So, in an art context, it is really hard to make work with a direct, didactic, propagandistic purpose. But* All That is Solid Melts into Air *is that: propaganda for Marxism in the most positive and historically most important sense – yet the work is in a venue where all the other signals about contemporary art are about ambivalence, indeterminacy and 'creative ambiguity', which is the way contemporary art has been dominantly understood since the 1950s. How do you deal with that issue when you think about yourself as an artist?*

MB I don't think this is exclusively an art issue. It is an issue across all the humanities and it is a general retreat of the left into a kind of postmodern liberalism. This work was inspired by Alain Badiou and Slavoj Žižek and their reclaiming of a strident leftist programme. It is a mistake to cede so much ground that it becomes impossible to say what we believe. What interested me about the Movement for the Emancipation of the Niger Delta was that these people were able to say declaratively what they believed because they were living it. One of their leaders said they had 'declared total war on the oil corporations' – a 21st-century anti-colonial revolution. I thought, 'these people are geniuses, and they look great, so I have to go film them'. A lot of artists are afraid to take a declarative political stance because in our position, as western European political subjects – specifically artists – we are bourgeois and our production is bourgeois, and we are complicit in imperialism.

JH *I agree with you, but it is not a view that goes down well with a lot of artists – left-wing artists.*

MB Of course there is going to be a certain amount of hypocrisy in my work. It is where I am sometimes criticised – I am making work about these issues but making them in a bourgeois art gallery context. So there is an impurity about the films. I feel that this is what the work is about. Putting Maoist propaganda in a commercial gallery is a self-critique but it is also a critique of the art system as a whole. Still, it is unavoidable because how else are these images going to circulate?

JH *There is a difference between that propagandistic, narrative base and the fragmented documentary quality to* All That is Solid Melts into Air *and* No Permanent Address, *and* Echo, *which is about interpellation in a much more direct way because you have the person in the spotlight actually seeing themself in the film.*

MB I think *Echo* embodies many of the ideas that I started with in *All That is Solid Melts into Air*. When I was filming the Chicago exchange I wanted to represent capital and capitalism in their most metaphysical and alienating mode. There is a moment in it when an image of the exchange is pulled apart, first through a contrazoom and then the background kind of pulls away, a Brechtian effect addressing the constructed nature of documentary video. Both works model the destabilising aesthetic events of capitalism, not just in the political effects of how it makes us feel, the vulnerable body in that world of steel and concrete, but also in the world of abstracted economy that we don't understand but which controls us with its hidden laws.

The two scripts for *All That is Solid Melts into Air* and *Echo* started out being very similar. *Echo* is basically a two-screen installation –

a documentary and a self-portrait, or a landscape and a portrait. I looked at the Watteau paintings where you have these landscapes – a 'tunnel' of trees – and a weird portrait inserted into the space where it doesn't really fit. Even though you experience *Echo* as this strange 3D image, it is as much a two-screen installation as *All That is Solid Melts into Air*. It is two screens plus a mirror – three screens if the mirror is counted as a screen. It also becomes about the space between them. Then the portrait is a self-portrait. If it is about the uncanny then it is about alienation – and the financial city centre location makes sense because of that.

JH *Less informed viewers are perhaps not going to think through the same lines that I have gone through to try to make sense of* Echo. *How does that figure in your concerns? Are you bothered about aberrant readings? Do you think there are aberrant readings?*

MB My first concern as an artist is not about reading, it is about creating a visceral or aesthetic experience. I hope that viewers like it. What I am provoking first is a feeling, not necessarily an appeal, but a fascination and a disturbance as well. *All That is Solid Melts into Air* and *No Permanent Address* are propagandistic and polemical and anyone without Marxist theory can understand very clearly what the situation is. Though there is a critique of capitalism in *Echo*, it is not the primary intention or necessary reading. It is much more about the uncanny, the disturbance of self-perception, recognition.

JH *Your work process and the films produced are humanistic, aren't they?*

MB They are about fragmentation and alienation but there is a humanism in showing the social relations between people and groups. That comes out particularly in *All That is Solid Melts into Air* and *No Permanent Address*. They are concerned with the destruction of human life that capitalism brings about. That was the project of *No Permanent Address*.

The greatest taboo in contemporary art is a discussion of love, which is surprising for people outside the art world – that we can't have images that talk about or represent love. We will happily talk about sex or perversion or any amount of abjection, but not human tenderness. So I wanted to explore love from feminist, queer as well as psychoanalytic perspectives. Love is the basis of queer politics, for example. The necessary ethics of communist politics, beyond Marx, may be something that comes from Christianity and other elements: love and agape. I first became interested in the New People's Army when they performed the first gay wedding in the Philippines. That love could suture a gap in theoretical Marxism, a gap in its ethics. Materialism doesn't offer enough reasons for why we should support it. With Marxism, feminism and Christianity, the common denominator is love. The problem with love is that it can turn violent and destructive. How can the decision to become a terrorist be born out of love?

JH *The social relations of that love are demonstrated in your films. The man threatening you with a knife in* All That is Solid Melts into Air *is doing it because he can't feed his family because all the fish in the river have been killed by oil pollution.*

MB Then I show his family. His kids are standing right there. *No Permanent Address* is about love and *Echo* is about self-love. Maybe that is why my work remains very cinematic – because in art the two big taboos are narrative and love.

Issue 371, November 2013

Danh Vo

interviewed by Jennifer Thatcher

We The People

JENNIFER THATCHER *Here, at* PEER, *you are showing 26 elements from a total of over 200 that together make up a life-size replica of the Statue of Liberty. Titled* We The People, *the first line of the United States Constitution, the work is like a gigantic jigsaw of which the public will only ever view a small section. These pieces at* PEER *are mostly taken from the pedestal that Liberty stands on, apart from three figurative elements – an ear and two pieces of hair – which are not immediately visible among the more abstract elements. You are also showing some more figurative elements in a group show at David Roberts Art Foundation. How do you choose which pieces to show? Is it a practical decision based on where the pieces are located in the world or are there site-specific reasons?*

DANH VO Yes, in the beginning the project had to be practical, and so at PEER the decisions basically came down to the size of the doors.

JT *Were these pieces shipped directly from China, where the work has been produced over the past two years, or have they been exhibited before?*

DV They have been exhibited before. The first place I exhibited the project was the Kunsthalle Fridericianum in Kassel, and these pieces have actually been in storage since then. If I had been more courageous I would have exhibited these much more.

JT *So did you choose to show the figurative pieces more often?*

DV In general I never choose the pieces. I want people to participate in the sense that I think the project is also about projection, how meaning is produced by what other people bring to it. It was not a conceptual piece where I could understand it from the beginning and say, 'OK, now we will exhibit this or that'. It was a co-operation between exhibition spaces, even collectors or museums which bought pieces.

JT *Were some people adamant that they wanted a certain piece, like the crown or the torch?*

DV That was always the problem. That was the only time when I would say no, because people always thought of the figurative parts.

JT *Let us rewind to how you started the project. Did you work from drawings of the statue by the original sculptor, Frédéric Auguste Bartholdi?*

DV We had no drawings. To go further back it was a very stupid idea – it came from an invitation by the curator Rein Wolfs to exhibit at the Fridericianum. The space is quite big so usually he would have two or three solo exhibitions at the same time. He came to me and told me he would love me to do an exhibition in the whole space. At that time I hadn't exhibited much but he told me that he loved the way that I was able to deal with big spaces, in that I didn't necessarily fill them up. I was always against the idea of being boxed in by anyone – I react by going the other way – and I think this was one of the times when I thought: I'm going to fill that fucking space. And the first thing I came up with was the Statue of Liberty. That is what I referred to as a stupid idea – it was the result of a resistance to things.

JT *So you decided on the idea, then figured out how to do it?*

DV Yes. But when I first thought I could do something with the Statue of Liberty, it could have been anything. I started to research and found out that the skin of the Statue of Liberty is just 2mm thick – I think that triggered it.

JT *Did that research involve you going to the Statue of Liberty?*

DV Yes, I always thought it was this massive monument, but finding out that it was only 2mm thick presented a contradiction: it is quite fragile, it's not what you think it is. I didn't know that 'she' was standing on a copper pedestal on top of the stone pedestal before I was working on this project; there are all these elements to be discovered. I also wanted to make a project with an icon that was immediately familiar to most people. I think it was very important to me to deal with objects or imagery that are arbitrary in relation to most of my interests. I'm interested in weird stuff as well as icons like the Statue of Liberty. That is actually how people function – we have these arbitrary interests.

JT *Were you aware of the number of sections in which the original statue was shipped from France to New York?*

DV No.

JT *So you just came up with this arbitrary figure of about 200?*

DV Yes, because then all the other practical decisions came. This piece is produced in China, but I wish it would have been anywhere because the location emphasises a certain meaning.

JT *So why did you pick China? For financial reasons?*

DV Financial, but also because the workshop was one of the few that would take on the job. The Statue of Liberty was restored between 1984 and 1986 by a French company, so we asked them. But the French doubled the price because it was like patrimony – they had the right knowledge. In Europe you still have workshops doing repoussé – the technique of pounding copper that was used to produce the Statue of Liberty – but more to repair sculptures than to build new ones, so the workshops are much smaller. But in China and in Thailand they still build gigantic Buddhas, so they have the right workshops. A Swiss company oversaw the production and outsourced the manufacturing to China.

JT *The original title of the Statue of Liberty is 'Liberty Enlightening the World'. It seems very neoliberal today.*

DV I would not have been able to make a project like this without the war in Iraq or September 11 – how the western world has been using 'freedom' in order to enter into war. On the other hand, the project is not about that, but it is a seed that has been sitting in all our minds. The US has been protective over the Statue of Liberty after September 11 because of fears that it would be a target.

JT *It was closed to the public during much of the Bush administration. Barack Obama opened it up, but only to a limited number of people per day.*

DV That was why I couldn't get the scans from the National Park Service. They were the ones who had the statue scanned. I was reading a lot of texts from people who were writing about the statue, for example Lauren Berlant argues in *The Anatomy of National Fantasy* that the Statue of Liberty had to be a woman. Her argument was that it needed to be a classically passive character in order to function as an 'empty', vessel-like monument onto which everyone could project whatever they wanted. I thought it was such a beautiful way of looking at it.

JT *Is it provocative for Americans that you, with your Vietnamese background, have made this project?*

DV No. Although it might be, but most people who see it are in the arts. It totally suits the system for criticising the US. But I would love to hear arguments and reactions from more right-wing people.

JT *The press release mentions the term 'virus' – a term associated with Félix González-Torres, whom you have previously cited as an influence – in the sense that the pieces might be said to be acting as a virus spreading liberty or democracy around the world.*

DV It is the idea of imitating something you are not. The perfect virus – the one that Félix González-Torres used – is the AIDS virus. He was really perverted: using the same strategy as the virus that was killing him. The quality of the AIDS virus is its ability to imitate something that cannot be detected, eventually destroying the thing that it attaches to. I wish I could make works like that but I'm not Félix González-Torres.

JT *Do you find a personal parallel with these pieces of the Statue of Liberty that are sent out around the world – the life of the nomadic artist?*

DV Definitely.

JT *Can you see your work being read through the discourse of globalisation? In his new book,* Anywhere or Not at All, *Peter Osbourne summarises the contradictory position that contemporary art finds itself in. He talks of art being a kind of passport that 'figures the market Utopia of free movement while in actuality it embodies the contradictions of the mediation of this movement by capital'. So, on the one hand art seems to be – like the Statue of Liberty – spreading a utopian ideal of universal freedom, but on the other hand is dangerous precisely because it masks the neoliberal ideology behind this supposed freedom.*

DV Exactly. That is why I have problems with it.

JT We The People *embodies these contradictions.*

DV That definitely is a part of it but I wouldn't emphasise it. One of the best destinations for *We The People* was the National Gallery of Denmark. They wanted the project so much that they had to start thinking how to get around the bureaucracy. So they proposed to host the project as a storage space for two years. Otherwise, I would have – together with the galleries – needed to find a storage space when certain pieces were not being exhibited. In 1995 the museum built an extension with a gigantic atrium for sculpture. But there was always something wrong with this space, so it never really functioned. And that was the space they offered for us to use. It is these kinds of things that made the project so interesting because it was bending rules. The whole institution had to rethink its role and be creative.

JT   *You had to sell certain pieces in order to fund the rest of the project,
like Bartholdi did. Did this mean that production was stop-start, based on
the funds coming in?*

DV   More or less. Qatar was the project's sponsor. We basically told
them that we could cut off Liberty's arm – they could have that if they
funded the project or at least gave us the amount we needed to start.

JT   *In theory, a curator could want to exhibit all the pieces together and
recall them from all the various spaces around the world. Could you
imagine that happening?*

DV   Well, I tended to think that this was not possible but, actually,
Qatar wanted them all. That was too scary. That's why we said, no, you
can take the arm to start with.

JT   *Do you know where all the pieces are?*

DV   No. I don't even know how many pieces there are. But that is
because sometimes I could just cut a piece or break it in two.

JT   *Do you see each piece as an individual work, or a detail from the larger
artwork or project?*

DV   I think the beauty is that they function in themselves but they are
also part of a bigger piece. They have these double agendas – like life.
Like with the letter that my father is doing, 2.2.1861, 2009-.

JT   *This is the tragic last letter written by the French Catholic missionary
to his father on the eve of his execution in Vietnam, which you ask your
own father to meticulously copy out each time someone orders one until
he himself dies or is otherwise unable to continue. You showed a version
of that letter recently at Xavier Hufkens gallery in Brussels, where you
chose to present it against what might seem like inappropriately erotic
wall texts, including the phrases 'Take My Breath Away' and 'Fabulous
Muscles'. Do you always try to present the letter in a different way?*

DV   It is more of an examination of how things can reappear in and
be inflected by different contexts. It is also related to the fact that I
travel a lot, so I don't have a studio that I can do these exercises in.
So the exhibition space becomes a place for trying out different ways
of putting things together.

JT   *At Xavier Hufkens, there seemed to be a real disconnect between the
garish outside, which was a riot of sexual graffiti and apparently bloody
handprints, and the more subdued interior. If you didn't know, you would
think that these were exhibitions by two different artists. Is this a way
of trying to make sure that the narrative is not too straightforward, too
logical for viewers? You also showed simultaneously at a project space in*

Brussels, L'Etablissement d'en face, where you turned the lights off in the
main space so that it looked as though the gallery was between shows.

DV   Yes. In Brussels, there was no connection between
L'Etablissement d'en face and Xavier Hufkens. I think it is very
important to play with the choices one makes: it was a choice to
exhibit in both spaces, which was a kind of schizophrenic idea.

JT   *Tell me about the postcards that you have included in this show at* PEER.

DV   I don't know where that idea came from – maybe because the post
office is next door. I have never really made postcards.

JT   *You have collaged dictionary definitions in French for various*
anatomical parts (nose, rectum, cunt, foot, hand, face, nipple) on to
reproductions of Ingres' Grand Odalisque *and the anonymous painting*
Gabrielle d'Estrées et une de ses soeurs, *which infamously depicts*
a nude woman tweaking her nude sister's nipple. There is the French
connection between the painters and Bartholdi, but also a connection in
the way that both the postcards and the Statue of Liberty fragment the
female form into fetish symbols.

DV   Of course there is a relationship, but these postcards – or rather
these collages – were made some years ago before I started the
Liberty project. I made them for a friend of mine when I lived in her
apartment. To thank her, I filled up her refrigerator with flowers
and dead animals – and collages. But it was a choice I made to put
the postcards and sculptures together. Things are just around, and
at a certain point it makes sense to combine them. It was also a
way of learning French, not only the language but also the cultural
inheritance.

JT   *So how many languages do you speak?*

DV   Just Danish and English.

JT   *What did you speak at home?*

DV   First it was Vietnamese and then Danish. In Vietnamese, if you
speak with women it would be in a certain way and if you speak
with older people you speak in a different way. You identify yourself
with the way that you speak to people. Basically, my Vietnamese is
like children's Vietnamese. Girls got so offended when I started to
travel to Vietnam, which was very late in my life – when I was 30 or
something – because I would speak to them as if they were old ladies.
I had to quickly relearn Vietnamese.

JT   *Do you still have family out there?*

DV   Not really.

JT   *How did you make contacts in Vietnam? Did you make connections through the art world first?*

DV   No. I knew a lot of people from the art world in Thailand, so after my studies I would go there a lot. And then at a certain point I thought, Vietnam is so close so I should go there as well.

JT   *Did your parents ever go back?*

DV   No. I really did it on my own. I had a friend who knew a lot about indigenous people in Vietnam so my first travels would always be to the region where they send indigenous people.

JT   *Can you tell me about the project you made for the 55th Venice Biennale? The Catholic church that you brought back from Vietnam, Hoang Ly church, Thai Binh Province, Vietnam. It is interesting to contrast this found relic with the replica Liberty statue that you made.*

DV   I mostly work with found objects, so the Statue of Liberty was unusual. The project for Venice started with a trip I made to see the late paintings of Caravaggio. There was one that I was particularly interested in, which was in Syracuse, the *Burial of Santa Lucia*. What I love about the place is that the Caravaggio is not there any more. I never understood the history of these things, and that is when I started to read about Constantine the Great, that he Christianised the Roman Empire and moved it to Constantinople, now Istanbul. He took all these relics with him from the Roman Empire. Then when the Venetians conquered Constantinople, that was how all the relics came back to Europe. And I only knew that because the people in this church in Syracuse told me that since the unification of Italy they always ask Venice to return the painting. They never did, of course. But instead – because this church has really nothing – they have this Murano chandelier, which I thought was so beautiful. I have never had a desire to have things be in the right place. When Massimiliano Gioni asked me to participate in the [2013] Biennale last summer, I wanted to do something with this notion of how Venice was the first creator of the East. I had this stretcher for the stolen Caravaggio from Palermo and that was what triggered it. I wanted to have all these weird things related to Christianity. One of them was the skeleton of a wooden church, which today are mostly protected inside concrete churches in Vietnam.

JT   *How did you find this church?*

DV   It is from Nam Dinh, which was a very Christian region. I always knew about these churches. In the beginning of Christianity in

Vietnam, which would have been the mid 19th century, they would first build big houses as churches, inspired by Chinese architecture. When the religion grew in popularity, they would keep the structures but just enlarge them. These early buildings became very rare because churches would mostly demolish them to build bigger ones. Of those that remained, a lot were bombed during the war or decayed with time, so you now find them inside concrete churches. The tourist industry buys them, mostly, when they want to build resorts that have an ancient feel.

JT   *Your work contests the ahistoricism and universalism of global culture, the fact that we are all supposed to relate to one another.*

DV   You propose an image that everyone recognises – like the Statue of Liberty – but there is no real communication, no direct message. You just have an object that you circulate whether you are the author or the viewer. I never thought that my works were a bridge or a communication.

Issue 372, December–January 2013–14

Hito Steyerl

interviewed by Jennifer Thatcher

No Solution

JENNIFER THATCHER *The intersection between art, the military, labour and popular culture is one to which you always return. You don't seem to have to look very far to find provocative coincidences where these areas collide, like* Guards *of 2012, whose protagonists are ex-military and law enforcement personnel now working as museum guards. In the 2013 lecture* Is the Museum a Battlefield? *you uncover a persuasive chain of evidence leading from the Istanbul Biennial's sponsors back to the defence companies involved in producing the bullets that killed your friend Andrea Wolf on the battlefield in southern Turkey. And yet you managed to weave Angelina Jolie into the narrative. I was at the live version of this lecture you gave in Istanbul. In the questions afterwards, people really wanted to know what to do with this information: how can we in the art world operate in a way that is not tied to the military, to financial operations, to these compromising scenarios?*

HITO STEYERL I'm not a good person to ask for solutions. I wouldn't recommend following them.

JT *That's the answer you gave in Istanbul.*

HS Because it's true.

JT *That is obviously a direct contrast to Andrea Wolf, who took the opposite path and went into action as a PKK activist.*

HS What would you know about her had I taken the same path? Actually, many people are finding solutions all the time. It is so difficult to speak about it in a general way because all these solutions have to be tied to the conditions they happen in. But look at the case of the Sydney Biennale [2014] from which several artists have now pulled out because of its corporate ties to the company that

517

actually runs offshore detention centres. Another case: the Gulf Labor coalition. The Precarious Workers Brigade, Ragpickers, ArtLeaks and WAGE are other examples. All these people are doing wonderful work. Ask them, not me.

JT   *Is art always already compromised? Is it enough for artists to just point out what's wrong?*

HS   But I never promised to solve any problem. It is interesting that people keep expecting me to anyway, as if I had signed a contract. But I didn't. It's fine for people to have expectations to this end, but why should I fulfil them? People also expect me to represent Japanese culture, foreigners as such, the internet or to wear size zero. Let me repeat: I am not a social engineer and I don't want to be. And I don't think there should be any prescribed role for artists just as there shouldn't be any for mothers or secretaries. Why should artists be boxed into rigid templates? This is late kitsch Marxism.

JT   *It depends on whether you split the role of the artist and the citizen. Perhaps this has a parallel with the discussions in your essays about splitting the body and the metaphorical body politic. You provocatively suggest that women should embrace their objecthood, for example, to avoid being subject-ed. Likewise, you suggest that we go on image strike and allow spam to take the place of our own representation. Where does the subject lie in these thought experiments?*

HS   It doesn't make any sense for me to talk about object and subject as separate entities. I think that they are so intertwined that it is a continuum nowadays. Every organic body is plugged into hardware and software. Not only that, but also into infrastructure – all these material supports. So in that sense, how are we going to separate that? The new work *Liquidity Inc.*, 2014, has a dialogue about water as essential for sustaining human life. So, am I going to say that 60% of my body, which is water and fully exchanged every few weeks, is an object and the rest is a subject?

JT   *I meant on the level of representation.*

HS   Well, every representation is an object, right? It might be an immaterial object, or institutional body, but it is definitely mostly not a human body. So there is always a sort of, what used to be called 'alienation' involved in representation. It seems a fact to me that once anyone or anything is represented it goes into the realm of materialising differently. And by being materialised differently, it can never be a correct representation. Because there are always going to be some errors of translation, some form of displacement, something that will go wrong in that process. And I think one should look at the process instead of constantly being frustrated about representation being a misrepresentation. Whether it is political representation or aesthetic representation, it will always go wrong – and come out in the form of objects, too. The simple answer is: I am embracing alienation, period. I am an alien just like the water that came from the depths of the universe. The question for me is not how to avoid alienation, but how to wrest control over it from various kinds of exploiters, like Hegel's slaves do. But that bunch of former slaves would not become new masters, as in Hegel's narrative, but would storm supermarkets.

JT *In* Lovely Andrea *from 2007 you went back to Japan to find a physical, paper representation of yourself as a bondage model – a photo in an* S&M *magazine – 20 years earlier. Was it a surprise to find it after only three days?*

HS It was quite a surprise. Everyone told me that it wouldn't happen. But this started a very important shift in thinking. It began during a discussion in Paris with Elisabeth Lebovici. I think it was something she said about precisely the relationship between object and subject and representation, and it became completely clear to me that this representation of myself had an existence in its own right. It was a piece of paper. It was printed – something produced within certain modes of production. I couldn't control it ultimately. It was a version I didn't want to control either. I just followed its trail.

JT *What did you do when you found it?*

HS You know the first thing I thought was, OK, could I just pretend never to have seen it, just close the book, put it back in the row of S&M magazines and keep on pretending to look for it. But there were all these eager people I had enlisted to help me and they were so overjoyed that I had found it. It would have felt like cheating.

JT *One might have imagined that people would be nervous about being involved in your project, especially given the dodgy circumstances in which these types of photographs are taken – the coercion, lack of payment, Mafia connections – but they appeared to be supportive of your mission and accepted your filming.*

HS Oh, I think some of them found it really strange. Some of them were puzzled by the idea that anyone would come because bondage is hugely associated with shame. They were so puzzled that they went into an enthusiastic mode irrationally.

JT Lovely Andrea *was considered one of the highlights of Documenta 12 in 2007. For many of us it was also the first time we encountered the name of Andrea Wolf, who continues to crop up in your work in unexpected ways. You reward your followers in the way that clues as to why you insert her in the various films often appear in previous works. For example, in your 2004 film* November *you discuss the disturbing scenario of seeing a martyr poster of Andrea, following her death, next to posters advertising erotic movies. This, then, gives us some understanding as to why you might have chosen her name as your alias when making the S&M photos in Japan. What was the reason for using her name in* Liquidity Inc. *in which it appears as a weather front?*

HS In Germany, low-pressure fronts are named after women. First, it was going to be Ulrike Meinhof, and then I changed it to Andrea Wolf. Also, seriously, this is not about a reward system for anyone. I am going to keep mentioning this case because it is not solved, and probably cannot be solved.

JT *You mix elements of ambiguity and fiction into your representations of Andrea. Is this due to a fear of being seen as a 'sensitive' director, in what you describe in your writing as 'the pose of the sensitive director'? Is this one way of defending against an easy empathy with the horrific events that led to her death – one that could take over all readings of your work?*

HS This is certainly one reason. You know, I have never claimed to have done a film about her. But I deal with the images of her that continue to circulate, and these are very different from what she might have been. In the case of *Is the Museum a Battlefield?*, it is not the images but the objects. It is about the circulation of objects from the battlefield: of a bullet flying in circles from the battlefield to the museum and back. The longer I have been following this issue, the less I know that person at all – she disintegrates.

JT *Even though the story keeps evolving? In the way, for example, evidence was recently found regarding her remains?*

HS It was very important for me to go to the location where she was presumably killed because this forever changed my perception of who she could be, or who she is now. Because she is there in a mass grave with about 40 other people, and those bones are all over the place. It is a pretty interesting feeling because the standard impulse is to reconstruct the skeletons and assign them identities and so on, but I realised that this wasn't what these people wanted. They went into that situation together and if we want to reconstruct a body it would be a body with five legs and seven arms, a couple of skulls maybe: a collective future body, nothing that would fit into any category of personalised identities and humanitarian kitsch any more. Oh really, you are handing me a fully reassembled skeleton of Andrea? And you think this solves the problem? It was very important for me to realise that the veneration of Andrea Wolf as a martyr is something truly disgusting. I mean, 12,000 women died in that conflict and nobody is talking about the vast majority of the other ones. So, Andrea Wolf as a person is not my concern, it is about what to do with the debris, how to see through all these fragmented bodies-as-objects, how to see all of them in the first place.

JT *Were there any issues about showing* Is the Museum a Battlefield? *in Turkey? You also chose to present a lecture rather than an artwork. Was there a reason for this?*

HS The issue for the whole Istanbul Biennial was time pressure and political volatility. This is why I did a lecture because I was able to change it up until the last minute.

JT *I am interested in your ideas around mass art production. Like Susan Boyle, whose rendition of 'I Dreamed a Dream' you include in a 2013 lecture of that same title, everyone seems to have a life dream, and that dream is an art project. It wasn't so long ago that being an artist was an exception, not a mass occupation. Now we are constantly being fed the idea that the creative industries are the fastest growing sector of our economy, in the UK at least. Students are willing to pay huge fees for arts degrees.*

HS The art-education industry is a huge Ponzi scheme. The fantasy of the art career has become very similar to the fantasy of doing an MBA 20 or 30 years ago. This idea of striking rich quickly, the pyramid-game fantasy, bankers behaving like mad creative geniuses creating an apocalyptic Wagnerian-type Gesamtkunstwerk.

JT *You studied film originally. At what point did you realise that you were more involved with the art world?*

HS Well, that's not a decision I made. I wanted to be a film director but the industry was changing so dramatically and radically that it was just not possible.

JT *Changing as in becoming more commercial?*

HS Oh yes, absolutely. I mean the lack of funding for independent, documentary filmmaking, the cutting-down of television sponsorship. I found myself in limbo because I was doing work that wasn't going anywhere on that circuit. Then people from the art world started showing it and at first I was bewildered. And people were talking about philosophy and theory, and I had no idea what the fuck they were talking about. So I got really angry and started reading up on philosophy.

JT *Your essays are filled with philosophical references. For example, you frequently mention Walter Benjamin's reading of Paul Klee's 1920 print* Angelus Novus, *the Angel of History, and the image often comes up as a motif in your films, as it does in* Liquidity Inc. *Do you still feel that we are hurtling towards the future, unable to turn away from the horrors of the past?*

HS *Liquidity Inc.* suggests that the poor creature has been thrown into some kind of wind tunnel, blown all over the place. The wind has turned – perhaps because of climate change – now the blast is coming from a future hell and the poor thing is being blown in the other direction, towards the past, eyes wide open. I think that is where we are at right now. We are no longer hypnotised by a past we can't change and which is a sort of trauma. The real task is not to be engulfed by that past again. I was so happy to leave the 20th century.

JT *I think it is strange for my students, for example, to appreciate the paranoia of the end of the last century. The fact that we thought the world might end when the clocks changed. That we talked about an 'end of history'.*

HS I am trying to write a new essay about the temporalities of the present that Sven Lütticken called 'Junktime', which is basically imploded time, a time of the impact of Hellfire missiles on time and space. Is there anything left?

JT *Like Rem Koolhaas's 'Junkspace'?*

HS Yes, it is epitomised by these microloops, by a lack of duration, lack of attention, things going on simultaneously all the time.

JT *I was interested in your relation to psychology and psychoanalysis. Your writing does seem to have some Lacanian influence, particularly in your thought experiments: the way you are able to flip ideas.*

HS Oh really? I hope not. He's such a dickhead. I mean, Sigmund Freud is a terrific writer, lucid in communicating as well as having all these fantastic anecdotes. Having said that, I don't think that this idea of the psychic apparatus holds any longer for contemporary people. I think the psychic apparatus is an iPad nowadays with standard issue backdoors, not a magic writing pad. We should think of it in terms of a wired contemporary technological object, basically. The dreams and case studies in Freud's writing are so tied to the European bourgeoisie of the fin de siècle. To take this as an ahistorical template that would apply to anyone at any time is an unlikely idea at best, no? I think even now the ways that people's sensory apparatuses are hardwired across the world are very different. On the other hand, technology definitely acts as a connecting factor. You know, I don't want to use the terms 'psyche' and 'psychology' any longer, because I'm not really sure what they mean and if they still apply to what is going on inside people's minds.

JT *Except perhaps that the longer we are living, the greater the chance of developing psychological or nervous malfunctions.*

HS That is true. The way the nervous system – my nervous system is being wired into wider networks of course causes all sorts of physical effects.

JT *This is why you chose to give yourself the role of 'Nervous Breakdown' in the final credits of* Liquidity Inc.*?*

HS Absolutely. It is one of the effects of neurocapitalism: depression, nervous breakdowns, neural conditions. I think the context for these conditions has changed a lot since Freud, Jacques Lacan or feminist psychoanalysis described them. The composition of the mind has changed. Bifo and Mark Fisher have started describing these developments brilliantly. I recently had the feeling that my nerves had started picking up emails. In fact they did.

JT *How much pressure do you feel to keep up with technology? Your films have increasingly moved into the realm of post-production: CGI graphics etc. Do you work with a bigger team now?*

HS There is one technician, Christoph Manz, who I have worked with for the past ten years now, and he is crucial for every single project. Other than that, production is plagued by an eternal lack of funding, so a lot of my teaching salary goes on funding the films. And we are keeping up with technology but always with the cheapest and crappiest parts of it. I want to use consumer technology. I simply don't feel attracted by blockbuster technology at all, or by corporate aesthetics. Anything that is expensive to make, I don't get the point, but it is not that difficult to keep up with the degraded parts of technology. This is the frontline of what is going on today in terms of labour conditions, but also in terms of political configuration. Apart from this, the teams are shrinking rather than expanding.

JT *It seemed to take a long time for artists to explore digital technology* and its associated issues without being relegated to the niche category 'media arts'. Claire Bishop talked about this in the Artforum article 'Digital Divide' in 2012. I feel that the same thing happened in the 2000s with 9/11 and the Iraq War: it seemed to take a few years for artists to react on any large scale. This wasn't true of writers. There always seems to be a delay in the art world's responses. Why do you think that is?

HS I don't know why that is. The infrastructure of the art world has been digital for such a long time. It wouldn't exist in its present form without the digital.

JT That is in terms of facilitating production. I am talking about the digital as a subject.

HS I'm not an art historian, and I shouldn't be talking about it because I don't really understand it all, but when industrial factories were portrayed in painting, I think it was really late. Examples in the 19th century are few and far between. So when did the factory, when did industrial production finally enter art production? I think it took until the 1920s to be fully integrated, to be a motor of how art is being defined. Probably we are seeing something similar right now. It is like the awareness of the social factory finally entering people's minds.

Issue 375, April 2014

Yvonne Rainer

interviewed by John Douglas Millar

Running Dance

JOHN DOUGLAS MILLAR *So, let's start at the beginning.*

YVONNE RAINER God, that's a long time ago. So, I was born in San Francisco in 1934, to an émigré father who was born in a little town in northern Italy and came to the States in his early 20s. Family lore has it he had a fight with his father and never went back.

My mother was born in Brooklyn of Jewish émigrés from Warsaw. Her father was a tinsmith, and her mother never spoke English, only Yiddish. My own father had been a stonemason in the old country and he knew of people on the West Coast, moved out there and became a housepainter. There was this mix, in those days and up through my early adulthood, a mix of bohemians and Italian anarchists up in the North Beach area.

My mother became a vegetarian and she had these girlfriends who had hitchhiked across the country in the early 1920s writing her letters saying, 'Oh, the weather is great and we're meeting all these great Italians, come out.' So my mother went across the country and, family lore has it, met my father in a raw-food dining room. They were both vegetarians, which was a big attraction. My father, actually, had stopped in Chicago on his way out and had visited a slaughterhouse and became a vegetarian as a result of that.

JDM *I'm interested in that anarchist milieu you spoke of and what impact it might have had on you. I know your father was involved in politics and your brother too.*

YR Well, there were a lot of social evenings throughout my childhood involving the anarchists. In the fall there would be a picnic. An old anarchist had a farm east of San Francisco, and there would be lots of barbeques and there were grape arbours and a band with violin, banjo and accordion, a very *gemütlichkeit* environment. But I became more aware of anarchism, not as a practice but as an ethos, when my brother dropped out of college and became a carpenter and began to socialise with some New York anarchists who had come west and who had been activists against the Second World War; they were pacifists. There were two couples in particular, older than my brother, who had driven across the country and who had this kind of salon in their home where poets and radicals met. There were also Friday night events at a place called the Workman's Circle, which was a kind of social club. Almost every Friday night from the age of 12 I would go with my brother – and my parents too, especially my father. One week you might hear Kenneth Rexroth, the poet, or George Woodcock, a British writer who was living in the States. That was my first real exposure to anarchist ideas and culture.

JDM   *Primarily literary culture at that point?*

YR   Not only literary. This was the early 1950s, before the Beats. I had one year of college in San Francisco, I dropped out and hung out in North Beach and bought books. That was when I was 18, and then I ran away to Chicago.

I got picked up by another dropout, a guy who had gone to the Art Institute of Chicago after fighting in the Pacific in the Second World War – by the way, it was not so uncommon in those days to drop out of college. I knew a lot of people like this, also women who were a throwback to my mother's generation of wild women hitchhiking across the country. My lover and I drove from San Francisco to Chicago having various adventures on the way. In San Francisco I had worked at odd jobs. I worked in a factory at a machine that stuffed coupons into envelopes. I did that kind of thing and also my parents helped me out a bit. Then, when I got to Chicago, I got a job in place called Hibbard, Spencer and Bartlett, a wholesaler in Evanston Illinois that occupied five city blocks full of bin after bin holding every kind of hardware and kitchen appliance. You pushed a cart on wheels and to fill a quota you had to be pretty fast, so it was all these young black girls who wore roller skates clambering up these bins to fill their order. That lasted six months.

JDM   *Did those experiences working in factories influence your political outlook at that time? I mean was there any involvement with unions?*

YR   No, I wasn't that savvy then and nor were the people I worked with.

JDM *Was it in Chicago you met Al Held?*

YR No, I came back to San Francisco and with some renewed confidence I got a typing job in an insurance company. I rented a little three-bedroom house in North Beach. Then a year or so later I met Al Held, a Bronx-born New York painter, and I met other abstract expressionists – Ed Dugmore and Milton Resnick. Al moved in with me but he wanted to go back to New York and so I followed him and that was the beginning ... Well, I had started to study acting in San Francisco at The Theatre Arts Colony on Washington Street, a beautiful building since torn down.

JDM *Was it very Stanislavski orientated?*

YR Oh yes, very much so. I took classes there and they did these small productions. My first experience on the stage was in Robert Penn Warren's *All The King's Men* and I had several parts. As the mother of the judge I was on this raised platform wearing, well, I guess you'd call it a peignoir, screaming at the top of my lungs 'YOU KILLED HIM, YOU KILLED HIM' and the lights went out and I was stage-struck. I realised I really liked it up there. So, when I got to New York I immediately enrolled at the Herbert Berghof School of Acting and my first teacher was Lee Grant, who had been blacklisted in the McCarthy period. I was not successful in class. They said, 'we see you thinking'. Obviously the Stanislavski method never took with me.

JDM *So you hadn't had any experience of Bertolt Brecht or Brechtian ideas at this point.*

YR In San Francisco I became aware of Samuel Beckett, *Waiting for Godot*, everyone was reading that at the time, but no, not Brecht at that point. I landed in New York in 1956 and by 1957 I had taken my first dance class and realised that dancing was for me, naive as I was about the limits of my anatomy, whether I was fit to be a traditional dancer. I started studying with someone called Edith Stephen, who had danced with Limon, and an African dancer, Asadata Dafora. Stephen had an eclectic philosophy. We did all kinds of things with technique and improvisation. She said of me, 'Yvonne uses everything she has learnt.' I mean, I was just gobbling up everything.

Then there was a crisis. I became pregnant, carelessly. I wrote to my mother that I wanted to study dance full-time and she was able to give me a small amount of money every month to help me out. In those days you could live in New York for $45 a month for a three-room apartment. I left Al after three years and it was then that I

527

began seriously to take classes.

In those days – people don't do it now because they can't afford it – I took three classes a day. I went to the Martha Graham school in the morning, I took a ballet class around noon and then I went back to the Graham school for another class. That was around 1959 or 1960. In between I would go to the Museum of Modern Art and watch movies. So I was getting a film education and a dance education at the same time. Then in 1960 I started studying with Merce Cunningham.

JDM *How did that come about?*

YR I had gone to see a concert and been impressed. Actually, in 1959 already, I was taking a Cunningham class. Somehow I knew I would end up there.

I was studying very seriously at this point. I became friends with Simone Forti who was studying there and had come from Anna Halprin in California. In the summer of 1960 she was going back west to take some summer classes and I drove over the country with her and her then husband Robert Morris, and we took this month-long course. On returning to New York, Robert Dunn, who was an acolyte of John Cage, was giving a composition course for dancers in the Cunningham studio, which was above the Living Theatre, which in those days was a hotbed of activity. By 1960 the happenings were going on – Allan Kaprow and Claes Oldenberg, and Jim Dine at the Reuben Gallery. The art world was much smaller then – you saw the same people in the audience everywhere you went, whether it was dance, art, happenings or music.

So, for two years this Dunn class took place with more and more people participating – there were only five of us at the beginning – and by 1962 we realised we had a body of work and a number of us, including Trisha Brown, Steve Paxton and a couple of other people from the course, had auditioned at the 92nd Street YMCA, the more conservative venue for showing modern dance, and we were all turned down. They had never seen the kind of thing we did before and they weren't interested. They thought it was bad dance. Years later, one of the jurors came to a rehearsal of mine – he knew a dancer I was working with – he sat behind me and he leaned over and he said 'we were wrong'. Well, you can imagine how that felt.

So, I had been going to the Poet's Theatre, which took place on the balcony of the Judson Church, and I knew Al Carmines, who was the cultural minister there, and four of us auditioned for him. Later he was to say that he didn't understand what he was looking at but that he sensed that it was important. So we were in! It was free; all we needed was postage to send out flyers. We could use the gym once a week for a workshop and to show new work and anyone could come to the workshop and whatever happened in the workshop would be shown in the programme.

JDM *Let's skip forward a little and talk about* Trio A. *Can you talk us through its composition and perhaps what your ambitions were for it at the time?*

YR I worked on it for about six months, the last six months of 1965. I presented it at Judson a year later. How it came about? Well, I don't know. Forti and Morris had split up, Forti had married Robert Whitman and I got involved with Morris and we shared a loft in what became SoHo, a big barren space that we divided – he had a studio in one side and I on the other – and I just began to fool about. I began to get a sense of the gamut of movement phrases that had different kinds of energy but appeared to have the same uninflected continuity. I just made little bits and began to put it together: I knew that ultimately it would be the first part of a full-evening artwork, *The Mind is a Muscle*. So before it became *Trio A*, it was called *The Mind is a Muscle: Part I*.

JDM *I'm interested in the way music has featured or not in the perfor-mance of the piece over the years. In that early performance, slats were dropped from above as a kind of soundtrack. Was that a self-consciously Cagean decision?*

YR You know Merce Cunningham always said we were John's children, not his. Certainly music could come from any source. I mean it was a kind of osmosis the way we absorbed Cage's ideas. We went to all his concerts, his lectures.

JDM *Because then there was also the use of popular music* – In the Midnight Hour, *Jefferson Airplane.*

YR *The Mind is a Muscle* had these interludes between the movement sections. That's the way I used Jefferson Airplane, as a kind of alter-nating viewing experience: now you look, now you listen.

JDM *And there was the John Giorno piece,* Pornographic Poem.

YR Oh yes, you've done your homework. Well, the Giorno piece was one of those listening interludes in *The Mind is a Muscle. In The Midnight Hour* came a year later, when I shared a concert with Deborah Hay at the Billy Rose Theatre, which is in the Broadway/

Times Square area. I had taught *Trio A* to a group of untrained people, or people with very little dance training, and they performed it, and then those of us who were more professional, who had more training, did it to *In The Midnight Hour*.

When was that? 1969? Let's see, in 1963 I had done a running dance. Steve Paxton and I always used to joke that he invented walking and I invented running. You know, one part of my reputation is that I'm a minimalist, but I was never a purist. The running dance, for example, had a grandiose section from a Berlioz requiem accompanying it. So all the Minimalism was in the running, and the drama and excess were in the music. This contrast was what I was after, radical juxtaposition I came to call it – a Susan Sontag term. That's what I was interested in and I guess I'm still interested in.

JDM *Could we talk about the place of democracy in your work? It's a word that is often tied to it, the idea that your dance work is 'democratic'. Yet, for me, there is something interesting in the way you maintain authorship, there is a tension there.*

YR OK, well let's go back a notch to *Trio A*. For me, originally, I thought it was a piece that could be taught to anyone and I thought I could accept any rendition of it. I was in residence in 1969 at the Connecticut College, which then was the home of the American Dance Festival. We were there for a month making new work and a West Coast painter called Michael Fajans learned *Trio A* from Barbara Dilley, one of my dancers. He went back to Oberlin, he was a student getting his BA or his MFA there – I don't remember which – anyway, he taught it to 50 people and they performed it to *In The Midnight Hour*. Now, one of those people came to New York and looked me up and she showed me her *Trio A* and it was almost unrecognisable – in just two or three generations. I realised then that I had to get tough with it. I'm very authoritarian with that dance.

However, the dance I was working on in 1969, which was eventually called *Continuous Project Altered Daily*, had set movement phrases but the order of things was left up to the performer – they could initiate different modules throughout the performance. We toured with that and it took many different forms. One of the dancers who had danced with Cunningham was Barbara Dilley (in the Cunningham company she was known as a troublemaker – a dance of Merce's called *Story* featured boxes of costumes and things the dancers could put on and take off and Barbara, well, she came out nude, which was a no go in that company). So, Barbara came to me and asked 'why don't we include some of our own stuff?' Well, I was at a point where I was working with these extremely talented, brilliant people and I didn't feel I could make work fast enough to keep them interested and, also, I was questioning my own authoritativeness and I was showing things in unpolished form. Some things we would rehearse they were set. Other things we would hold in a rough kind of condition, which necessitated talking about it. This was a revelatory kind of thing – to talk about something that was unfinished and raw – so my notebooks are full of these lists of possibilities for unformed work up through polished work, and I realised that this was a very interesting combination of things, another juxtaposition, this time of casual behaviour with stylised dance work.

That led to starting to let go of the reins. It took all forms – me opening the stable doors and letting the horses out and then trying to rein them back in over a period of two years – and it led to the formation of what came to be known as the Grand Union, adding Trisha Brown and Nancy Green and, for a short time, Lincoln Scott. The Grand Union lasted from 1971 to 1976 and I dropped out after two years. I was moving towards making film. Also, we never rehearsed. We tried to rehearse and basically it was a group that didn't always get along very well, so we would go on tour and take our records and props and our this and that and make a show with no preparation. Well, the strain on me of doing this resulted in the fact that I couldn't do it without getting stoned and I realised it was an untenable situation. They went on, though, and one of the attractions for people who came repeatedly was that the audience never knew what kind of explosive psychological thing would go on among the members. There was a lot of talking, a lot of slack moments and then something would happen that would be riveting. Very uneven. Very adventurous. So, that's the story of my experience with democracy.

JDM *In your autobiography* Feelings Are Facts *you say that reading feminist theory by writers like Shulamith Firestone and Valerie Solanas made you feel like an 'intelligent and intelligible participant in culture and society, rather than the over-determined outcome of a lousy childhood'. At what point did that feminist work become important?*

YR By 1970 I was aware of the second wave of US feminism that had begun in 1968, and some of my peers and I started a consciousness-raising group that kind of petered out. I was reading all the literature,

Sisterhood is Powerful, Firestone's *Dialectic of Sex*. I mean my dances in the early 1960s unconsciously reflected that – women picking up men, everyone learning the same moves in an anti-balletic, non-hierarchical mode – I mean the clichés of ballet were very much on our mind, which also characterised Cunningham's work to some extent.

A feminist consciousness was subliminal, I suppose, but it didn't reveal itself or manifest itself until maybe my second film, *Film About a Woman Who*. Getting into fictionalising autobiography, that certainly was the main influence of feminism and the feminist movement. I felt my experience as a woman and as an 'oppressed' person could be legitimate subjects for film and language. Certainly language was the attraction of filmmaking – subtitles, inter-titles, voice-over. So, for me, writing and feminism came together.

JDM Feelings Are Facts *is your largest text-based work, a significant work in its own right. The tone is unique, humorous, but really avoiding all sentimentality. That seems to be a continual strain in your work. I'm interested in the way you use emotion though, it's there but not in any classical Aristotelian sense where an audience or reader is meant to find catharsis.*

YR Certainly I'm not interested in catharsis either for myself or for the audience.

JDM *Yes, the audience made active, forced out of passivity.*

YR As far as the audience goes, I like to say that I don't give a shit about them, but that's not entirely true. I mean, I'm not interested in getting them out of their seats. There is all this talk of immersion now, having them go to sleep or whatever. I was slow to pick up on this stuff. There is a theatre group now where you lie on sofas and go to sleep. I don't get that at all. No, I mean I am very Brechtian in that sense. In filmmaking, especially in the later films, I used cinematic techniques for creating empathy and then destroying it, pushing it away. So there is this push and pull, this unpredictability where the audience has to stay on its toes, not send their minds away, as Pauline Kale used to say. As a spectator you have to keep hold of your critical faculties.

JDM *What about the place of analysis and psychoanalysis in your work and life?*

YR Aside from a few seminal essays, like Laura Mulvey's *Visual Pleasure and Narrative Cinema*, I never went in for the way feminists use psychoanalysis. There is such a gap between theory and practice. I was in therapy from the age of 16 to 60, it saved my life.

JDM *Can I ask which kind of therapy you experienced?*

YR It wasn't psychoanalysis, it was talk therapy with various people who had had an eclectic range of training. You can see it as an influence in the films, certainly – the way people (including my narrative voice) psych out each other.

JDM *Can we return to the question of feminism, but feminism as it stands now. It seems that there is a renewed interest in the second wave, people who are in their 20s or 30s or 40s who were not there then but who are trying to get their own grasp on their relationship to it, either actively or in a more archival sense.*

YR I feel really removed from that these days. If you look at the texts I currently use in my dances, I'm much more involved with social and economic inequality and history. In my last dance, called *Assisted Living: Do You Have Any Money*, there is a classic adagio by a male dancer and a female dancer and he describes Keynesian economics while they are performing these classical *developés*. Psychoanalysis was historically important for film theory, but I'm not very attuned to it as a choreographer.

JDM *Do you feel your work can be viewed as a totality or do you think your dance and film work are two entirely separate domains?*

YR I'd say my dance and film work are quite separate, other than the fact that they share occasional political themes. My formal concerns in each are so different that they seem like entirely different enterprises.

JDM *What about pedagogy? Are you still teaching regularly?*

YR I'm retired from the University of California, but I still do a yearly seminar at the Whitney Independent Study Programme. I used to teach a course in California called Materials for Performance and the students were a mix of dancers, visual artists, people from comparative literature. I taught an experimental film survey course as well.

JDM *So the last film you made was in 1996?*

YR Yes, *MURDER and murder.*

JDM *Was there a conscious decision to cease making film?*

YR It was kind of forced upon me. I never felt comfortable in the production side of it. I liked writing the scripts and editing, but I felt like the dog wagged by its tail in dealing with the labs and the camera. I'm a techno-dummy. Also, I just couldn't raise that kind of money any more. Each film got exponentially more expensive and I'd gotten all the big grants. I love working with dancers. They know the meaning of work. You see what you get – it's very immediate and material. So I was very pleased to return to dance.

JDM *Choreography has become quite a fashionable topic in contemporary art and I wonder how you feel about your own work being viewed as a 'foundational text', as it were?*

YR There is too little documentation of my early work for it to be viewed in that way.

JDM *Am I right in thinking* Trio A *has been notated using Laban?*

YR Oh yes, I'm afraid it is not the best method for notating *Trio A*. Most of the people here at Raven Row have learned it from Laban notation. Pat, my assistant who is here with me, had to undo a lot of errors. I mean, it is really hard to get it right from Laban notation. Melanie Clarke, who notated and teaches it at the Laban Center, does her best, but it just doesn't adequately represent the precision of the dance.

Issue 379, September 2014

Pablo Bronstein

interviewed by Jennifer Thatcher

Oddballness

JENNIFER THATCHER *We are standing on the beach below your new project for the Folkestone Triennial,* Beach Hut in the style of Nicholas Hawksmoor. *Is it a beach hut or a lighthouse? It looks quite sinister.*

PABLO BRONSTEIN It is definitely not a beach hut or a lighthouse. You can't go in, and it doesn't warn ships. It's a sort of emblem, a folly that is more of a landscape scenic device. It's not a pleasure house.

JT *Why did you pick Nicholas Hawksmoor, who is better known as a church architect?*

PB Well, he never designed a lighthouse, at least not a proper one, and there is a gap in the historical market here in Folkestone: there is no early-18th-century architecture. But I'm being a bit cheeky: it's Hawksmoor seen through the eyes of 1980s postmodernists. But there is also a good deal of Victorian architecture involved. I make reference to Hawksmoor but it's a mishmash.

JT *It is well documented that you spent three weeks studying architecture but decided that it wasn't for you because of the oppressive client/architect relationship. What makes art commissioning more acceptable to you?*

PB That's a very good question. I think that, fundamentally, your artistic persona is your principal client: how the project represents you as an artist. Is this pushing the work forward? Is this representative of what you are interested in?

JT *Many practitioners now blur that distinction between artistic practice and architecture or design.*

PB I don't have much sympathy with that stuff. There are very sophisticated architectural professionals who are perfectly capable of doing interesting things. The joy of being a goofy artist is that you can be a goofy artist!

JT *You don't find yourself drifting towards architecture via a different route? Do you ever get asked to collaborate with architects?*

PB All the time. They are excited by the oddball-ness of my practice. When an architect sits down with a brief, 90% of the architects come up with nearly identical solutions, and it is within those minor variations that competitions are played out. With art, there is no client, there is no brief. Inventing your own brief is something that artists are excellent at and architects have no idea about.

JT *You have talked about your love of drawing buildings as a boy. What did you draw?*

PB When I was a child, an image I would return to again and again was of St Basil's Church in Moscow, with the onion domes, which was reproduced on the cover of a set of Russian classical music records my parents had. I was obsessed with the architecture present in cartoons, leaning towards evil: so Gargamel's castle, Skeletor's castle, the Gothicky house in the Wacky Races.

JT *The styles that you now appear most drawn to – 18th-century and postmodernist – are they ones that you admire aesthetically or do you choose them as a provocation? Do you genuinely enjoy them?*

PB Yes, I do. I have always enjoyed them. I've grown up with post-modern architecture and never aspired to living in brand-new, spanking neomodern developments – or loft conversions, which I think artists aspired to in the late 1990s and early noughties. It sounds a bit romantic, but I was formed in my own little bubble. I grew up in an extremely boring suburb and my upbringing was odd because my parents are Argentinian – I was essentially an upper-middle-class boy going to a mostly working-class state school. There is a kind of landscape that I think is outside the acceptable areas for artistic production. People think that artists should either grow up in really shitty, grim northern towns or weird bits like Hastings, or that they should be very cool bohemian urbanites. The sort of bland, semi-detached Victorian houses that I walked past every day weren't worthy of high praise or angry commentary.

But, going back, this question is interesting. It is a blurred line where you are being double-edged: so you like the stuff that you are critiquing, or you secretly like it. As I get older, I want to replicate it less and less, but what I replace these things with is quite difficult to pinpoint.

JT *If you often look at the 18th century through Postmodernism, you also throw in modernist references too. That is true of your performances, such as* Constantinople Kaleidoscope *at Tate Modern in 2012, in which you not only referenced the Renaissance quality of sprezzatura but surely also recent figures like Dan Graham and Bruce Nauman.*

PB Yes, again, consciously so. The people that I was interested in when I was growing up were people like Peter Greenaway and Derek Jarman, people that were ...

JT *... doing the same, mixing eras?*

PB Exactly. And so what I did was simply point at part of visual art history, architecture history, that had been ignored, perhaps because it was too close. So they are being reviled. Perhaps because their political associations were not cool.

JT A Guide to Postmodern Architecture in London, *2008, is one of my favourite artist books. In your introduction, you equate Postmodernism with high finance and Margaret Thatcher, but you don't let the left or the liberal establishment off the hook. The first entry is James Stirling's Clore Gallery extension at Tate Britain.*

PB I find that postmodernity has its use in signifying a particular moment in time that people of certain generations understand, that there were very serious changes to how we organise ourselves socially. Since its writing, there has been a revival of interest in postmodern architecture within the architectural profession and that has had a very positive effect on assessing what is good and bad along traditional, architectural judgement lines. I still think that the architectural intelligentsia leans towards the worthy, and so the big, flabby slagheap palaces on the Thames by Terry Farrell are pretty marvellous things. They are important buildings for London's architectural history but they are also important popular buildings. There is an extremely irritating connection between a liberal, left-wing stance within visual culture and a romanticised, ruinist-modernist aesthetic. It absolutely drives me mad!

JT *I thought I detected some overtones of Robert Smithson's 'ruins in reverse' idea in* Postmodern Architecture in London. *Is this something you read when you were studying?*

PB No. You can point at any 20th-century architect and they are interested in ruins, so I am not particularly into Smithson if I'm being honest. If I was looking at certain things, it would be people like Carlo Scarpa, people who are involved in a sort of crystallised ruin.

JT *But Postmodernism isn't really dead. If you go to places like Dubai, that is still the predominant style.*

PB The postmodernity that I'm interested in has a particular focus on reworking classical detailing. I think classic postmodernity, with a couple of exceptions, is never particularly spatially complex, certainly not complex in its construction techniques. Very often, they are steel frames; nothing to do with the technologically obsessed Zaha Hadid architecture. But I keep thinking about this question of left and right wing. It figures in my head a lot, which of course is a generational problem because I don't think that 25-year-old artists have that classical spectrum in their heads.

JT *Do you think that your background gave you a particular licence to talk about issues that British people might find uncomfortable?*

PB What happened in my case is that I came with a lot of visual culture baggage from Argentina. For example, my grandparents' house in Argentina, because they were pretty wealthy, had an old-school, John Fowleresque decoration scheme with ivory tusks and prints of parrots and silver tables, and these sorts of things were definitely not within my peers' frame of reference.

JT *Your mother is a psychoanalyst, and I thought about this in relation to the kind of language you use in* Postmodern Architecture*: the erotic charge or jouissance of postmodern architecture after years of austerity.*

PB That's right. Writers really did describe these things as explosions. I am very excited that I live in Deal now and that Sue Timney, of Timney Fowler, also lives there. Timney Fowler was this big decoration firm in the 1980s. It was the Terry Farrell of interiors. I was conscious of them because I loved interior decoration magazines as a kid – exuberant interiors with a kind of French-print sexuality. They were looking at bordello prints and things like that.

JT *Has this influenced the decoration scheme for your Deal house?*

PB My Deal house transcends all explanations. You will have to wait until the *World of Interiors* 2018 for it to be fully revealed!

JT *Your London flat has already featured in the* World of Interiors.

PB Bethnal Green, yes.

JT *It showed you to be quite a collector, and that you make little concession to Modernism, let alone to the 21st century.*

PB Oh, the Deal one is ten times worse than that. It is really extreme: there are only a couple of LED lights in the whole house, that's it.

JT *Deal seems the perfect place for you to have settled – the well-preserved*

Georgian houses and the history of subversion, people hiding away from the prying eyes of morality.

PB   The joy of Deal is, well, it's a queeny town. It has got a big dyke and fag community that goes back decades and decades. One thing that's good about Deal is that, when we moved there, it was already gentrified. We didn't have this annoying crusading spirit that these shabby-chic wankers have when they move to, you know, Margate.

JT   *I wanted to ask you about your latest show at Herald St, 'Recent History', which deals mainly with 17th- and 18th-century history. Why did you pick that title?*

PB   In 2014 I had done a show at REDCAT in Los Angeles about the origins of architecture according to Enlightenment thought, 'Discourse on the Origins of Architecture', and so I was looking at architecture way, way, way back and, within larger historical briefs, the late 18th century is extremely recent architecture and already about the formations of institutions. Public institutions today were formed not only politically but also visually in the 18th century. Courthouses were refined as a concept architecturally, parliaments – anything that we still take for granted as linchpins of our architectural world. But this is a way of looking at architecture that is already gone. It is absolutely retro to design public buildings in architecture school. God, if you go in and see what architecture students are looking at and designing now: designing a water park for a dwarf or designing a marshmallow factory on a boat in the Bahamas. Nonsense that is entirely – I mean, not nonsense, 'exercises' – that are ephemeral, abstract, removed from the grander row of architectural moments where society and stones that form it arise together somehow.

JT   *How much historical research do you do before starting a series?*

PB   Not that much, to be honest.

JT   *Do you go to Italy, for example, to do your research?*

PB   Not really, it's pretty bookish – books and online. I'm not that interested in real space and real humans and real things.

JT   *Do you use assistants?*

PB   Sometimes on large projects, but less and less now. Mostly because of the problem of the hand of the artist needing to be neces-sary in the actual drawing. That is what people assume a drawing is: it is a sort of ideomap, historically. You are not sure what Leonardo painted, but you're pretty sure what he drew. It would be very difficult to pass that on to assistants.

JT *You went to three different art schools, is that right?*

PB The Slade and Goldsmiths. St Martins, I only did Foundation there. The Slade was wonderful; Goldsmiths was a bag of shit.

JT *In what way?*

PB They were miserable bastards – bitter, twisted wankers that didn't have a clue about contemporary art. Extremely pedestrian and by the book. A bunch of awful, competitive students who were desperate to sell to Saatchi. It was what you would expect, and it was true. The Slade, however, was really fantastic.

JT *Which department were you in at the Slade?*

PB Painting. But far less neurotic than the kind of freedom of Goldsmiths, where people pseudo-question you on things in the most retarded way possible – those interminable crits.

JT *Were you already formed, in the sense of working the way you do now? When did you become comfortable with your approach?*

PB It was quite complicated, thinking back. I turned up at the Slade as a fully formed cubist, thinking that was really current, and it wasn't. People were doing photorealist paintings and weird, sloppy New Neurotic Realism paintings, and my work was quite laboured. It was awful. In year two, I became unashamedly PoMo and 1980s-ish. But I was in danger of becoming a sort of 'School of Ken Kiff'. And so I started reducing and making very detailed paintings of architecture and so on – very, very condensed. At Goldsmiths I started feeling embarrassed by all that stuff, and I started to do ironic film posters and fuck knows what.

JT *Did you keep any of that work?*

PB Yes, but only in the way that people who have gone on successful diets keep pictures of themselves from before.

JT *Can you imagine showing them in a retrospective?*

PB I will burn them before that! And then there was a moment of revelation. I was sharing a studio with Olivia Plender, and she was a breath of fresh air, along with Lali Chetwynd and other people. Goldsmiths was extremely constricting, and these girls, they were really doing their own fucking thing. It sounds romantic but they weren't so bonkers, they managed to phrase it within interesting conceptual constructs. And so I followed their example and pursued my very, very particular interests. I bought myself a book on Borromini, and I started making these Borromini-style drawings, and it was good. Luckily my gallerist, Nicky Verber – well, he wasn't my gallerist at the time – was starting Herald St and he liked them, and I met Catherine Wood, who became a close friend and supporter, and she liked my willingness to be weird and that the subject matter was outside the ordinary. And one of the things that I think made my work seem different was that there was such a strong weight in favour of looking at the decay of Modernism. And it's still going on with these dumb kids: you know, a triangle on the wall, a hexagon on the floor, a zigzag, a pin-up photo of some sort of brutalist council flat. Done! A bit of glitter ... There was also a lot of the sort of Stephen Willats – you know, 'I can't get my shopping trolley up those council flat steps' – type of art. It felt so naughty, this interest in the baroque and postmodernity.

JT *You didn't feel any pressure having a gallery?*

PB No, because at that point work sold for three hundred quid. The gallery meant you got to hang out somewhere. It was nothing like the kind of hysterical pressure on hot young painters who cannot fuck up a show with their blue-chip gallery.

JT *Tell me how you came to do performances. What was your first performance?*

PB It was at the Tate Triennial in 2006, and Catherine Wood asked me to activate this piazza that Celine Condorelli and I had conceived. This idea of perfection is – I mean, I'm not quite there on it, but I'm interested in public space without people as an idea. There was this grid on the floor, there was a square and a cross, which is the architectural symbol for 'void', and there was a baroque dancer, a Laban dancer riffing off the baroque movements, and then two other dancers riffing off each other to a metronome with some choreographed interchanges that were randomly encountered. In ballet there is a space around the dancer that places the dancer in a focus or a central position – I flipped that backwards and forwards. In the Hayward arch I did, *Magnificent Triumphal Arch in Pompeian Colours* from 2010, the dancer is there just to eulogise this big lump, and other times the architecture is there to enclose and formulate the dance.

JT *Did you have any training in dance?*

PB No. Well, I was interested in dance. I liked Michael Clark as Caliban in *Prospero's Books*. I have always liked formal baroque re-enactments. I always loved the entrance of Louis XIII in *The Devils* by Ken Russell, and the *Birth of Venus* ballet that I did at the ICA in 2011 derives from that.

JT *Do you teach at art school?*

I don't teach in art school. I rarely get asked, almost never. I haven't had a request to give a tutorial for the past five years. Shocking, isn't it? I mean, for fuck's sake, I'd probably do it for free! But they don't want me.

JT *The requests might start rolling in now ...*

PB That's right. But I teach a lot in architecture school. The art world often reaches out to people that it sees as parallel and brings them in for a brief period. It does this with film, fashion, dance, whatever. And so I think at the moment I'm having a time like that within the architecture profession. Since the *Postmodern Architecture* book, a lot of people, such as Sam Jacob of FAT, were aware of my work on conceptual grounds. Now there is interest within the architecture profession in my visual work. I don't know why that is. Perhaps because it is so anti computers, because it is so recherché, at the same time so personal. Because I think architects have a real problem bringing in quirks. It's not dissimilar to the interest that architects have shown in the past to Madelon Vriesendorp. Of course, someone like her is very connected with famous architects, so it is different, but there is a tentacle drawing me in. Unlike dance. I mean, dance I've been working with for a long time and they couldn't give a flying fuck about my performance work. I am going to be designing a ballet for Rambert in 2016. So in terms of the stage design there is some progress, but architects get me to teach a lot, and sometimes judge competitions, which is always extremely fun. It's nice to be a bitch and judge without knowing what you're talking about – or rather to judge with your own criteria. Adam Caruso got me to teach recently at ETH, which was wonderful, mostly because these kids in Switzerland grow up with the expectation that they will actually build a fucking building. Can you imagine how that would affect an architect?

JT *Have you noted any interesting reactions from the architects mentioned in* Postmodern Architecture?

PB None of them have read my book; they couldn't give a fuck. They are old men and they're essentially in robo mode where they stand up and tell their five jokes and then sit back down again. Either that, like Piers Gough who is unashamed about talking about the early stuff, or if not that, people like Terry Farrell, who would probably kill you if you mentioned their early works – if you mentioned the words 'TV AM'. I tried to get the TV AM building listed recently, to no avail.

Oreet Ashery

interviewed by Larne Abse Gogarty

Irreplaceable

LARNE ABSE GOGARTY *Thinking about the exhibition at Waterside Contemporary in London, how do the live and gallery-based elements of your practice relate?*

OREET ASHERY To answer this, I have to refer back to my childhood. I was brought up in an area of Jerusalem that was like living in a cinematic, micro-regional cliché. Leaving the small tower block I lived in, you could cross one side of the road and come to the valley leading to the Palestinian Arab neighbourhood Shu'fat. On the other side, you would find yourself climbing up the trenches and bunkers of Ammunition Hill, overlooked by an oversized flapping flag. Further up the road were the gated walls of the strict Orthodox Jewish community. As a young girl I spent time drifting in and out of those territories, in a kind of beginner's dérive. I was already acutely aware that my body produced a disturbance. I was stared at because of my gender and my age – I was too young to be walking alone – and I didn't belong in any of those places. These were probably my first public interventions. During those walks I also collected things – ripped posters, rusty nails, degraded signage, mutated colourful plastic utensils – which, together with drawing and other crafts, like macramé, were made into hanging mobiles, assemblages and collages.

Meanwhile, back indoors, I was so inspired by a book I read about a girl who was a witch that I was convinced that I was one too – a good witch, I hoped. As part of my witch-practice I believed that I had hypnotised friends and young relatives in group-rituals that I conducted. Years later, as an adult, I realised with some guilt that those taking part were by no means hypnotised but rather sought to please in these rituals that involved performing various actions. Once, I ground down a chalk stick, taken from the classroom, into a cold chocolate drink for a friend who struggled in school, believing the concoction would work miracles with the right kind of incantation. It ended badly with a stomach pump and so too ended my career as a witch. I did produce at the time a set of props to help my performances as a witch, alongside a body of crayon drawings. I guess this was when my awareness of the difference between props and art objects began to form.

One of my favourite interventions as a non-artist happened later on as a teenager. I became frustrated with people looking at my growing breasts and, at times, even grabbing them in busy public spaces. Riding on the back seat of a moped one time, I spontaneously asked my friend to stop on the curb of this really busy curved high road where I performed a strange strip dance. Cars were swerving, screeching and hooting, risking their safety to my great irresponsible adolescent satisfaction. These early experiences informed how my future practice incorporated the performative and fictive, the body in deterritorialised public contexts, objects and assemblages and the potential group.

LAC *Can you say something about the title of the current exhibition at Waterside – 'Animal with a Language'?*

OA It comes from Theodor Adorno's writings on self-mutilation and self-annihilation of the animalistic or the debased that resides inside ourselves or that we project onto others.

LAC *What kind of languages run through the show?*

OA There is an overall lineage between the work and modernist movements such as Dada and Bauhaus which are associated with resistance and socio-cultural change. In the exhibition, humble cleaning materials are elevated through the display system. The figurative assemblages or totems that inhabit the space yield a collective reading – due to their stylistic similarities – yet each of them has its own unique language of objects and text. On one figure the stuck-on text reads: irreplaceable. It is an open-ended word, but for me it connects to the flat-lining effects of some conditions of labour, where everyone and everything is replaceable, for example zero-hour contracts.

In the video *Winking Series 1*, 2014, people from groups that I recently worked with are simply winking. Winking at someone is like sharing a secret knowledge, but it is so quick, you are not sure if it really happened. In relation to participatory work this has particular resonance, as it gives the participants the benefits of 'knowing'. Also in the exhibition are two deep-red cotton hammocks which are quite womb-like. It was important for me that people will watch a short video as well as the rest of the show sitting and swinging on the hammock. Having two makes it more sociable and intimate. The hammock produces a somatic viewing experience as another form of language. At first, you are not sure that the hammock can take your weight, but once you relax into it more, you are continuously reminded of your body and gravity while absorbing the work.

LAC *Recently you have also produced large-scale participatory works,* Party for Freedom *last year and* The World is Flooding *this year. Both these involve groups of people, but unusually in comparison to your earlier work – you are not performing in them or appearing on screen.*

OA After years of making discreet public interventions, intimate one-to-one performances and more elaborate live works – one involving a memorial party for 300 guests, for example – I decided in 2011 to stop performing myself. This was after performing *Hairoism* a number of times, and I felt overexposed both physically and emotionally. I also felt that audiences were watching me as empathic witnesses because it was my body on the line, so to speak, as well as the imagined biographies attached to this body. There was something essentialist about this that made me feel too fixed. I wanted to explore different modalities of audience experiences, as well as different ways of working with myself. Looking back at the past three years, I actually feel more exposed through these new works where I am not performing as an individual.

LAC *I was particularly interested in how with* Party for Freedom *you had a history and aesthetics of sexual liberation being played out in conjunction with an address towards the rise of far-right populism in Europe. The film and performance unwound these two poles towards a point where it often seemed like the work would totally fall apart. Yet as soon as the mess and chaos almost completely collapsed, the film and/or performance would snap back into focus. Why did these two ideas become important for you to address, and what was the meaning of that formal approach?*

OA The sense of antagonism, collapse and slippage was like a guideline for me in the making of the work and in thinking of its

545

possible reception and audience experience. When I started to think about the work in 2011, I became aware of the rise of right-wing and far-right populism in Europe, and a lack of a clear alternative – what has been termed the failure of the left. The effects of neoliberalism and hyper-capitalism, as well as other historical forces, continue to blur the boundaries between the right and the left. So what I wanted to communicate was my own sense, as well as a general feeling, of not knowing and of political disillusionment – a western, post-liberation, apolitical feeling, if you like. A certain lack of coherence was therefore absolutely important, and my version of the political unconscious became paramount. There are no goodies and baddies in the work and it does not tell you what to feel or think. In fact, the work scrambles any sense of political certainty.

Really, I was interested in exploring unconscious motivations, eccentricities and somatic experiences that feed political policies and military actions. For example, in researching *Party for Freedom*, I read an article by Ferry Biedermann that mentioned how Geert Wilders, the founder of the Dutch Party for Freedom (PVV), went to visit Egypt and Israel as a schoolchild and contracted a stomach bug in Egypt, which contributed to the formation of his low opinion of Arabs and Muslims. Wilders notoriously posits Islam and non-western immigration as a threat to the pillars of western freedom, such as the rights of women and gays. In *Party for Freedom* the meshing together of leftist performances of liberation and far-right apparatuses was filtered through trash aesthetics. I looked at trash aesthetics in relation to populism, far-right blogs and other mediascapes. In parallel, I looked at trash aesthetics in three 1960s and 1970s cultural and artistic groups who were engaged with the ethos of liberation and freedom – 'Naked as a Jaybird', a nudist Californian group, the Russian avant-garde group Collective Actions and the enigmatic UK-based Scratch Orchestra. I chose these groups to explore a self-made axiom of bodies – nakedness collective action and democratic sound.

LAC *Can you say a bit more about what you call 'trash aesthetics' and how it functions in your work?*

OA The trash aesthetic has always been a big part of my visual language. I was brought up surrounded by unfinished buildings and broken pavements and a huge amount of plastic furnishing and household goods. My parents' flat was filled with posters, really bad paintings made by a distant uncle, and cheesy memorabilia alongside stacks and stacks of books and carefully labelled colourful folders touching the ceiling. Later on, when I came over to England my visual experiences were late 1980s Leicester with its textile factories, home-grown music, bleakness and flocked wallpaper in garish colours, which still makes me panic when I see it. The post-industrial desolation of Sheffield was where I did my first art degree and, later on, coming to London in the early 1990s, I took part in various countercultural moments, such as rave as well as transgender, queer, camp and Dada-like environments. All those various forms of trash aesthetics came to hold their own cultural and political value and have embedded themselves in the visuality and materiality of my work.

LAC *You have always traversed between working in collective ways, often with groups of people who may not self-define as artists, and then your own production as an individual artist and performer. In terms of* The World is Flooding, *your performance at Tate Modern in July 2014, how did this work?*

OA *The World is Flooding* was a project I planned while making *Party for Freedom*. Although they are both based on Vladimir Mayakovsky's revolutionary 1921 play *Mystery-Bouffe*, *Party for Freedom* was incredibly nihilistic and antagonistic by comparison. For *The World is Flooding* the Tate call-out went to non-professional performers from groups such as the UKLGIG (UK Lesbian and Gay Immigration Group), Freedom from Torture, which works with asylum seekers who have suffered torture or threats of torture, and Portugal Prints, an arts and mental health project, as well as Morley College in south London. The participants didn't know each other but, despite my initial concerns, the group developed fruitful dynamics. The schema of the play involves a world inhabited by 'The Clean' and 'The Unclean', which worked very well for both projects as explorations of freedom and regulation, desire and repulsion.

The World is Flooding was conceived from the outset as a project that values the specificities of collective and personal knowledge formations. Catharine Grant speaks beautifully on Bertolt Brecht's concept of learning-play, *Lehrstücke*, and learning through participation. The theatrical performance at the Turbine Hall involved giant low-fi banners, an up-beat catwalk displaying vivid ponchos and headgear made of cleaning materials, and was accompanied by a spoken script that was reprinted in a zine.

In contrast, *Party for Freedom* antagonistically and insistently questioned the notion that we might know anything, or possess any political agency as artists and audiences. *Party for Freedom* involved professional artists and performers, responding to a call by Artangel and Performance Matters. Apart from being incredible artists, dancers and performers with diverse practices, the participants in *Party for Freedom* were all white except for one Asian. They were also all young, 'beautiful', slim and able-bodied. This was antagonistic in itself, apart from for those viewers who took the lack of diversity for granted. I wanted the work to speak of white privilege in the context of freedom, and of the fascist fantasy and nightmare of homogeneity. It is important to note, however, that this reading of a group of white bodies on stage does not represent the invisible realities of the performers, or performers of any race for that matter, and how class, life circumstances, sexual and gender orientations and mental health issues are hidden from view.

LAG   *The lack of nihilism in* The World is Flooding *was striking in comparison to* Party for Freedom. *To me, it was far clearer how you were working with the Mayakovsky play, mostly because the politics we associate with that history are affirmative rather than nihilistic. So, in a way,* The World is Flooding *contradicted that history far less than* Party for Freedom. *Nevertheless, moments of antagonism did spill out during the performance, and those were the parts I found most interesting. How much were those moments also about laughing at the Mayakovsky work and questioning the point of returning to earlier moments of utopian thinking?*

OA   Mayakovsky's play is not without its own ironies and absurdities. It is about class and celebrates The Unclean, the proletarians who survive a worldwide flood, and their victory over The Clean, the privileged. It is emancipatory and utopian, but also perhaps aware of its own grandiose morals and ridiculousness. Yet it is certainly not a postmodern play, and is wholly sincere in its intentions. So the notion of sincerity was something that I grappled with. Devices such as absurdity were projected into the legal and administrative system we live in. There is a part in the performance where the audience is asked to read aloud accounts of struggles with the system only to be laughed at by the performers. This laughter, as well as being directed at the carelessness and crudity of the system, was also directed at the actual performance itself, undoing its own sense of importance and seriousness. The script we wrote has some funny and dystopian sentences that I really like, such as: 'If you cannot control your weight how can you control your life?', 'Middle Class wanted to become a journalist or a filmmaker, but realised that he was just ordinary', and 'Rich children read *The Economist* at the age of 6 or 7.' There are similarities between those elements in *The World is Flooding* and Brecht's notion of the epic theatre and its various alienating and critical devices. For me, there was also something absurd about the large-scale theatrical feel of the performance involving a chorus and a large number of people performing, which was a bit of a nod and a wink towards the original production.

LAC *I think those differences are important since perhaps returning to the historical Avant Gardes is only successful if there is a formal antagonism – political antagonism is always there when there is a disjunction between two historical moments.*

OA Often in turning back, or referencing historical Avant Gardes, contemporary artworks are simply elevated by default through the cultural value attached to certain historical moments. In and of itself, it is a challenge to take a politically or culturally utopian moment and make it bounce in the present. In *Party for Freedom* we went to people's houses and workplaces and performed there – it was very important that we were inside those spaces. With *The World is Flooding* it was about working directly with a group of people who are often the mediated subjects of other people's artworks. There is something about an immediacy of connection in the present in both projects that balanced the historical referencing.

LAC *What does the use of cleaning products and the ponchos refer to in* The World is Flooding *and the exhibition at Waterside?*

OA I wanted to use ponchos as they work on different registers. They are seen as ethnic or indigenous and hence have been subjected to cultural appropriations. They are also seen as the simplest form of dress – a blanket with a hole, used as a basic form of protection from rain at festivals, for example. They are also made for cardinals as an official high-status symbol, so they really traverse a rich territory. Crochet and knitted woolly ponchos are generally condemned to remote village craft shops, and seen as shapeless and lacking in style. The fashion designer Walter Van Beirendonck has successfully saved ponchos from their fate and created some brilliant ones that I have looked at for inspiration. Cleaning materials also tend to oscillate between the cheap, mass-produced recognisable ones, such as the classic blue-and-white J-cloths, which I'm sure will become a collectors' item soon, and the more design-oriented products which are a rapidly growing industry. More specifically, the activity of cleaning as a job has associations with cheap and unpaid labour, related to ethnicity, gender and economic bracketing.

LAG *Can you discuss the use of music in your work?*

OA Music features regularly in my work. I was a percussionist in a failed band in the 1990s called DogRack. In 2005, I dressed as an orthodox Jewish man to dance in a religious festival in the north of Israel that centred on Mizrahi and Ashkenazi music, documented in the video *Dancing with Men*. Similarly, going to rave clubs in the late 1990s and how they formed part of a counterculture has also been important and informative for my practice. In *Semitic Score* of 2010, the performance explores sites of gender and orientalism through a dance score and drumming, and I always used a live drummer.

With *Party for Freedom* and *The World is Flooding*, I was interested in an idea of democratic sound and producing sound through clapping, speaking or just improvising. I was also interested in the idea of a democracy of sound in terms of using different musical registers. *Party for Freedom* included all newly commissioned music – classical music by Finnish composer Timo-Juhani Kyllönen, punk and noise music by Woolf, and Morgan Quaintance playing jazz-fusion with other players. The structure of *Party for Freedom* was conceived as an album with ten tracks and Woolf punctured every title preceding each track. I wanted to contain the indecisiveness, or the falling-apart quality of the album with women's voices and sounds that are direct, angry and very succinct.

LAG *How does the episodic shape of these works function – as in the structure of* Party for Freedom *being presented like an album?*

OA It is a way of arranging the world. The research for *Party for Freedom* was based on ten incidents of barely conscious thoughts or images that hover just at the edges of your mind or memory. With *The World is Flooding* it was important to have a structure for editing volumes of material that had been produced collectively into a script. I use scores, or episodic formal devices, in order to establish a kind of anti-narrative or a structure with its own internal logic.

LAG *What about the concept of Utopia in your work – how do you relate to, or mobilise this?*

OA The direct experience of having seven naked bodies in *Party for Freedom | Party for Hire* activating the space inside people's living rooms was important to me in terms of mobilising some notion of a politically utopian moment in art. Elements of self-organisation, on behalf of the performers who had to adjust every time to a new space, and on behalf of the audience who had to absorb and interact with the peculiarity of the situation in an otherwise familiar environment, were interesting to me. The somatic experiences of nakedness, as well as the kidnapping and auctioning off of an audience member, for example, resonate with what I perceive as an unconscious political experience of symbolic nakedness and questions of participation or non-participation. As I mentioned before, there was a didactic and dogmatic side to the homogeneity of the bodies, and some of the content of the work, which is also a part of historical Utopias.

LAG *That seems politically astute as a negative articulation of the utopian moment. I see this as related to working with Mayakovsky and the necessity of not holding earlier aesthetics and ideals aloft, but not getting rid of them either. In that sense, the attention to the somatic, the unconscious and the questioning of sexuality perhaps stand out as qualities which fell through the cracks previously.*

OA It seems unfashionable to talk about 'the body', or the somatic, when so many of our experiences are virtual, simulated, capitalised upon or otherwise flat-lined. But for me, somatic experience and narratives often make the most interesting political moments in the most surprising ways. And, in terms of minority discourses, there is still no escape from the body.

Issue 381, November 2014

Richard Tuttle

interviewed by Mark Wilsher

Equal and Opposite

MARK WILSHER *In conversation with Chris Dercon at Art Basel Miami in 2012, you explained that your initial interest in textiles derived from wanting to understand your own work, specifically your early octagonal canvas pieces, which had no front, back or particular orientation, in your frustration that presenting them on the wall meant losing the ability to experience the hidden side.*

RICHARD TUTTLE I'm going to refer to my new friend William Hogarth. People who admire him admire him for what is called 'getting beneath the surface'. So there might be caricature involved, there might be character involved, but one thing people miss is that when you look at a Hogarth you are actually looking at the observer observing. He is completely honest, he is completely available for anybody who chooses to look at his work that way. But of course most people look into the work and look at the subject matter. The relationship that's interesting is that, as an artist, he got under his own surface as well as getting under the surface of the world. This is what the textile showed in a way that interested me. I think it is quite important that on the whole the world seems to be highly invested in destroying the ambiguous, whereas we have art on the other side that actually protects the ambiguous. I think that is why art as such – music and poetry or whatever – has this position as protector of civilisation and culture, ultimately. So with the textile, this aspect of mystery was extremely exciting because looking at one side, the wall condition, there is everything you need to know about what the other side looks like, and yet your experience is that you don't know the other side, and this created a tension or an edge that was ripe for exploration.

MW *As someone known for small-scale, intimate, tactile works that create a very close relationship with your audience, it was perhaps surprising that you took on the huge unruly public space of the Turbine Hall, which necessitates presumably something big and powerful and the opposite of all these things that you have previously worked with. I was intrigued by how you had handled this – was the appeal something to do with the chance of having such a vast audience come through and encounter your work?*

RT   A vast audience is quite, shall we say, scary. Vast audiences have not usually been supportive of my work. And yet I have changed fairly recently. I used to be the person who thought my job was to do my work, and now I think that I do my job when people see my work – and that is quite a difference. So now I feel I should look for every opportunity for people to see my work. It is just my sense of how I as a person am supposed to do my work. A mature artist, if you will, has a different job to a mid-career artist. I do believe that when we are in our senior years we are supposed to make the world. You know you have learned the world, you have destroyed the world, and now you are supposed to make the world. And part of making a world comes from people seeing what you have made.

   Recently I have been thinking that I'm an example of a kind of artist who is mystical and individualist, and I can see very well that the world tolerates that type for brief periods, but you cannot expect a huge or lasting interest. So in that small window I should do what is appropriate.

MW *In fact you have worked on large-scale pieces a couple of times in recent years. I am thinking of the ceramic wall piece* Splash, *2004, for the Allison Island Aqua development in Miami, and the very long paper banners that hung outside the Wolfsonian as part of the 'Beauty-in-Advertising' exhibition you curated in 2004.*

RT   One of my starting points was when my first dealer, the great Betty Parsons, who was an artist herself and a poet, said that this group of artists – the New York school – were trying to paint the expanding universe, and she would wave her arm. I just looked at her and thought in my mind that there must be an equal and opposite universe that is coming this way. If they have done that then I as a young artist should do the opposite, as the pendulum swings. But at the same time this energy that is going in as opposed to out has as much importance, as much vitality, as the energy going out, so there is a combination. Even though I do a thumbnail-sized work on a 40ft wall, people who experience the work experience the full 40ft wall. It is just my way of making large work, I guess.

There has always been a part of art that it should be an accounting for the infinitely large as well as an accounting for the infinitely small and, if you are ambitious in art, you have to address those. You don't have to be ambitious in art, there are plenty of places in art for everyone, but I find I like being ambitious in art. I have no ambition in the world.

MW   *Do you think you are more ambitious now than when you started out?*

RT   Probably, yeah. And it is partly because art is about the spirit, and the spirit is the one part of us that can grow, that in fact needs to keep growing when everything else is collapsing. Even from youth I thought that it is not that interesting to be creative when you are young. Who is not creative when they are young? And even in middle age. But where does creativity come from in the senior years? That is really interesting to me because it defines what life is, what human beings are, the interface between nature and art and all these things. Every artist is challenged by things that are more attractive or less difficult than their actual work and seem to offer greater rewards. Betty Parsons was a real nurturer and she used to say, 'for the real artist the slowest way is the best way', and I still believe that today. Part of the tension is to stay slow – to go as slow as possible.

MW   *Could you say a little about the experience of taking on the Turbine Hall commission? How did the piece originate and develop?*

RT   Chris Dercon, Tate Modern's director, came forward with this notion of the textile, this kind of brotherhood of the textile – because most 'men' are not supposed to like textiles. Shortly after he approached me, I knew what I wanted to do – and it did not seem large. It was confined to six inches or something like that. It had this aspect of strength and believability and yet it couldn't prove itself until it was executed. In a way it is the genius of the work that knows that, because how is anyone supposed to keep a focus for three years – or as long as it takes for these projects to happen? Everyone wants a big project, a major work. But I'm not complaining. It is fun to bring something into dock, you know through the icebergs and the rocks and the tides, and we all feel satisfied. I'm proud, actually, because the starting point is a real vision of Chris's, but it falls on me to understand his vision first, and then I have to figure out how to realise that vision and then I have to make a Richard Tuttle show. So it is quite an undertaking. What is the likelihood of understanding someone's vision, what is the likelihood of realising it, what is the likelihood of coming through all that and making a real artwork, you know? It is worth taking on.

MW *When we were talking earlier you said that you had been surprised by the view from above the piece now that it is installed, and that this was now one of your favourite views. You also compared it to a human body, an abstract form that has the kind of integrity that a figure has but without referring to it.*

RT I do like to study artists and creative people, and I like people who do know something about human creativity. I had this great Swiss-German friend who died and, as he was dying, his investigation of creativity and artists increased. We had a conversation and he said several unforgettable things, one of them was that when artists lose themselves, the first thing that's lost is their idea of death. And I think that he is definitely right, more so now than I used to think.

The interesting part of human beings is our struggle with mortality, and art has been thought to be a way towards immortality. You can be like Rembrandt, he is immortal. But my work, which emphasises fragility and is not particularly lasting, shocks people, I think, because it steps outside that path towards immortality. I think in the top there, it is almost like you can see the dream of immortality, and then you can understand that it comes into a rational place which is quite beautiful because as it comes into that rational place you reach your immortality. All of us have the immortal in us, we just don't know it.

It is funny because it's not the most dramatic, the most catchy, the most beautiful part of the piece, but it has this aspect of a single artwork. Technically, an artwork has to be a unity, in fact that is one of the dangers of suddenly making a big piece like this because you lose the unity factor, and that is one of my stresses. But the view from above has a place in unity that is different to the view of the piece from below. Why make something big like this? I have said many times, 'why make something big if you can make it small?' And so it was thrown back to me that if I did make something big it had to be worth making it big. I mean, I believe in contradicting myself.

MW *Your work generally seems to take its cues from art history, from a certain kind of abstract formalism, and yet I have come across a couple of intriguing instances when you have pointed more to specific events in the world as subject matter. I am thinking of some comments you made a few years ago about your early paper octagonals, which you said had a certain sense of peace to them that was in opposition to the Vietnam War. You have also said that the public piece in Miami was your response to the 9/11 attacks.*

RT   I think I am constitutionally loath to dishonour the actual world. I think I must have been Islamic in my last life because somehow the separation of this abstract world is not in any way a step over a line. At the same time I am very busy trying to make a cosmos that is the same, or potentially the same, as that other side, and it is a way to say 'thank you' to that other side by imitating it, or something like that. I'm thinking of poets who do a similar thing, for example someone like Yeats who is famous for his drafts. Every single poem has hundreds of drafts, each draft could actually touch something in the real world, some sort of event that made it a draft. But in the end they were all polished out – there was no need for these references.

To answer your question – this is the mystic side of things I see that work as a living entity that speaks to me verbally, that puts concepts in my mind. The paper pieces came about because I showed them in 1970 or 1971 and I went to the opening – it was a group show – and all the artists came running up and said 'we're going to close the museum' and I said, 'close the museum? Great!', but then they said 'as a protest against the Vietnam War'. And I said 'what?' And then we had a meeting the next day and I realised that, you know, my work is what I have to say about that, and that they were reduced and austere and full of values which I felt were the values that life should be operated under as opposed to those values that were in operation in this war. The idea of closing the museum was absurd to me, and I was shocked because I assumed that for the other artists, their work was intrinsically an embodiment of their feelings, what they had to contribute as artists to society about real life.

One of the things I find I think about recently is this notion of 'what's your relation to other artists?', and this morning I came up with a very good idea: that I am happy when an artist does their work. I am just thrilled when an artist does their work. Any artist is thrilled when another artist does their work, and conversely not happy when an artist doesn't do their work. Unfortunately, I think I'm mostly unhappy with artists because you know it is hard to do your work.

It is hard to find your work, it is hard to do it, it is hard to keep the energy. In our family we use a phrase: 'Are you a man or a mouse?' I think that is one of my greatest gifts: as a child I sort of knew profoundly that I would not have an easy life and, in terms of my work, whenever there is frustration or confrontation I just say to myself, 'well, you never thought you would!'

MW *It is now almost 50 years since your first solo show in New York. You referred to yourself earlier as a 'senior artist' and you have had many career retrospectives in the past 20 years or more internationally. What is it like now to go back and install some of those earlier pieces from the 1960s and 1970s? Is it hard to recapture that original feeling or impetus? I am thinking perhaps of a piece like* Ten kinds of Memory and Memory Itself, *1973, which is very much a gestural, bodily moment captured through the action of throwing the strings on the floor.*

RT   The wire pieces? Sometimes I call them my life insurance, but it is strange because they are commercially not valid at all. I love them, but in order to make them I have to stay pure, I have to protect myself as an artist. But even more than that, they are set up so that they can become better through life. They are a challenge – to keep their simplicity or purity – but also I get excitement because I know how well I have made them in the past and I can tell if I am actually making them better than I have made them in the past.

The wire pieces raise the issue of thread as opposed to textile. When the issue of textile is raised then the behind area is about mystery, but if you raise the issue of thread, the behind area is then about unknowability – vast, endless, infinite unknowability. It is about your comfort: how comfortable are you with mystery? How comfortable are you with the unknown? You find more people reach comfort with mystery than with this unknown element. But I think the wire pieces do address the comfort of the unknown, and when people look at those works they breathe a sigh of relief.

And the string pieces, we are going to make those for the White-chapel Gallery. It is something different but they do have to be made again, and we will have to see. I just wrote a little mystic text on them and realised there is something about their nature. I keep learning about my work as the years go on. I always say there is an informal side and a formal side and I get very excited and overenthusiastic about the informal side, and 40 years later I can revisit a work. But there is the other pattern, where a work I made when I was 23 or 24 –

it's gone, it's on the other side. I know I made that, I know I had the sensibilities, but it is like a diary entry when you can revisit yourself partially but never completely, and that is very odd and touching, I find.

My wife and I are very much New Age people and there is always this question of a redefinition of what the human being is. One of our favourite definitions at the moment is that we are genetic material that is constantly being changed from one thing to another and of all the things that help us, mosquitoes are at the top of the list because they take and give so much with every bite we are given. In that scenario you can no longer connect with the soul that made that work. If you want to discuss the soul, there are real things and then there are not real things, and the real things you can expect to change, I don't have a problem with that. But the unreal things – truth, the soul apparently they change just as much as the real things. It is wonderful to have some way to experience these unreal things. I have always loved that famous Robert Browning line when he was asked the meaning of a poem and he said that when he wrote that only God and he knew what it meant. And now only God knows.

Issue 382, December–January 2014–15

Lynda Benglis

interviewed by Virginia Whiles

Going with the Flow

VIRGINIA WHILES *The clarity with which you articulate your practice demonstrates your hands-on approach, so why did you strongly resent being classed as a process artist alongside Robert Morris and others in the run-up to the 'Anti-Illusion: Procedures/Materials' show in 1969?*

LYNDA BENGLIS There were closed systems of thinking then and process was hip in the 1960s. They spoke a lot about anti-formalism but I hated to be labelled and there was a lot of labelling. I prefer to be open-ended. When I arrived Pop Art was playing ironically with advertising, they were being ironic even with themselves, they were not shy and mocked the material way in which art had to do with advertising, seen as once removed, and the way that minimalists were simplifying material. Context was very important as I saw it. I presented it to my students at CalArts and I saw feminism as a con-text to be dealt with vis-à-vis Miriam Schapiro and Judy Chicago. The head of the department had initiated an introduction and had invited me to teach there saying 'you're really doing something' – as if they weren't. I saw that I didn't want to think things through in just one way. I wanted to ask questions within the context of materials linked to spatial issues around architecture. Before teaching there, I had also been the recipient of a Guggenheim scholarship and, because it was a lot of money at the time, I was able to cast certain works in metal. *Come*, 1969–75, was conceived as I came back to New York to work at the Modern Art Foundry and cast one of my first in-the-round pieces. *Eat Meat*, 1969–75, was another. All are now being presented at the Hepworth Wakefield. Prior to going to CalArts, I was performing in situ, so to speak, in museums all over the country: *Phantom* was created in 1971 at the Union Art Gallery at Kansas State Art University in Manhattan, Kansas. This is the only work still in existence and it was reinstalled in my recent retrospective at the Rhode Island School of Design Museum, the New Museum of Contemporary Art and the Los Angeles Museum of Contemporary Art. *For and Against, For Klaus*, was created at Vassar College, as per Linda Nochlin's invitation. I made *Adhesive Products* at the Walker Art Center in Minneapolis, *For Darkness (Situation and Circumstance)* at the Milwaukee Art Center and, finally, *Totem* at MIT – all in 1971. There was no way of storing the works as they were so large. I also had a chance to do one in Buffalo at the Albright Knox and the MOCA in Chicago, but I felt I could not wear art on my sleeve.

VW   *How did the rapport with architecture evolve? Your ceramic pieces have an effect you have described as 'making an architecture of gestures'. They evoke another scale.*

LB   In the 1960s Barbara Rose spoke of two worlds and asked if easel painting was dead. Well, painting isn't like architecture, we need illusion and straight lines but not the rules, they need to be broken. I was always involved with different sorts of spatial environments. I grew up in museum spaces and used them as my studio. I worked in situ and was very ready to do that.

VW   *So that adds to your number of studios – already you sustain one in Manhattan's Bowery district, one on Long Island, one in Santa Fe, New Mexico and a fourth in Ahmedabad in India. This is quite extraordinary and you evidently navigate between them quite easily, even taking your dogs along with you. Can you expand on how site influences the work? Are there distinctive links between place and artworks?*

LB   They are distinctive but the objects are individualised through their process and through the phenomena: the natural formations surrounding the site of the studio. There is always a sense of time that is stabilised by the materials. There are so many different issues. For example, my ceramic work is inspired by New Mexico – the landscape, the earth, natural phenomena. My studio is built in adobe style. I was at Newcomb where George Ohr produced some of his best work in New Orleans, however I was not familiar with it. The environment of New Orleans – with its large oak trees and Spanish moss, and the cypress trees with their large 'knees' – evokes Art Nouveau, which was very popular at the turn of the century in Newcomb pottery. There is something specific in each material.

I believe that people identify proprioceptively directly with the material, whatever image I was making, whether it be bronze or, as I'm making now, natural sheets of wet paper, stretched over forms and painted. My latest work is in paper, and I am sensually involved with the process, with making and playing with it, using powders and pigments and gold leaf and coal tempera – organic materials that relate to the body.

vw   *Your forms are biomorphic and geological, and you take a phenomenological approach in your work – spraying, pouring, twisting, 'womanhandling' your stuff. Can you unpack proprioception?*

LB   I am asking basic questions about the way we see – I experiment with light, with phosphorescence. Above all, I am interested in gravity, the sense of the body when you look up at something. I remember Clement Greenberg was said to have provoked Morris Louis with the question, 'What's up or down? What's correct?' But for me there is no up or down. I depend on gravitational pull – Greenberg couldn't turn my floor pieces upside down! Our perception happens through our bodies; I controlled the pourings by using gravity to work out the amount of pigment. Body perception happens even with materials such as stainless steel and aluminium that I used in the 'Pleat' pieces such as *Scarab* and *Raptor* in the 1990s. I am especially interested in the buoyancy of the body in water and our memory as embryos in the womb.

vw   *You draw upon childhood memories of being in Greece on the island of Kastellorizo with your Greek paternal grandmother and once used a portrait of yourself at 11 wearing the traditional Greek uniform of a soldier for the invitation to a 'Sparkle Knot' show in 1973 – a nod to androgyny a year before your satirical pin-up invitations masquerading as both male cool dude, 'macharina', and as female sex symbol in your dildo ad. Why do you think your early work raised such a debate about taste in the US? It has been described as kitsch, camp, vulgar and, in the immortal words of Donald Kuspit, as 'cosmetic transcendentalism'.*

LB   Well, there was puritanism in New York at one time. It no longer exists. I think it depends on how we value art. Important ideas are classic and beyond a sense of time. It depends on what an artist has to say – sensibility and pleasure can work together, art can deal with pleasure and pain. I was riding a wave and have absolutely no regrets about my provocations.

vw   *Other reviews either ignored or suspected the craft aspect, and even as late as 2001 you were called a 'closet-craft artist' on account of your work in glass. Your work is based on collaboration with technicians and craftspeople in diverse local cultures, particularly India. How do you consider 'traditional' practices and this continuing split between fine art and craft engineered by colonial art education and sustained in a neocolonial discourse on contemporary art?*

LB   Even before going to India in 1979 I was interested in Asian art through certain museums and galleries such as the Doris Wiener Gallery, where I saw her collections of manuscript paintings as well as sculptures. I was invited to Ahmedabad by the Sarabhai family, particularly by Anand Sarabhai, who had been inviting artists for years to participate there in workshops within the family house designed by Le Corbusier, as well as in the Gandhi Ashram nearby. They included artists such as Alexander Calder, Isamu Noguchi, Frank Stella, Robert Rauschenberg and John Baldessari. Ironically, my work had even been described as looking Indian before I went. All traditional art is collaborative and I just felt it was quite natural to work with artisans in India and in New Mexico in the same way that I co-operate with technicians in the various foundries where I work. In Ahmedabad in 1995 I worked on two carved red brick works. I had seen a digitised wave of brick and thought it a good idea to do something with brick in motion. I created a trapezoid wall with bricklayers and then employed a temple carver to carve out my drawing 20ft long and 12ft high. It was made up of the head and body of an elephant, a Grecian urn and buttresses, and was called *Chimera*. Then I did the snake wall (*Eve, Naglia*) around a dying neem tree. Worship began to take place there at Vasant Panchami – the spring festival – and local villagers drew snakes on the well with different colours. All my work with paper prior to this at the Gandhi Ashram had confirmed as well my sense that my pieces were about exchange. This was a very good feeling.

vw   *It is curious that in view of almost 35 years of contact with the Indian art world there has not been more attention to your work there. I know that you showed with Peter Nagy and had a commission from the US Consulate in Mumbai but that was a while ago.*

LB   Those were different times. My partner Anand Sarabhai was personally intent on promoting the arts through international exchanges. He was ahead of his time. Now, there is less of a sense of nationalism and even more exchanges with younger artists. I have shown in group shows and have very warm contacts with certain artists. I was particularly close to Bhuphen Khakhar and Amit Ambalal, two artists who had a strong understanding of the miniature painting we were both so interested in. All of the artists, including Mithu Sen, have taken the traditions of craft and Indian miniature painting as well as folk sculpture, in the case of Rajeesh Sagra, into the contemporary realm vis-à-vis their production, material and scale.

vw *I saw one small catalogue of your work entitled* Drawings in India *with some intricate diagrams for motifs, mixing mandala forms with Kandinsky-like patterns, and this was a surprise to me. How has drawing figured in your practice?*

LB Those drawings were in a group show at the Chemould Gallery, one of the oldest galleries in Mumbai. The drawings were done with many of the workers collaborating with woodblocks that had been collected by Anand. I can remember I even had the driver of the car make drawings on the Ashram paper. Others were men who happened to be seamsters. It was an experiment on my part to see the organisational power of a culture that I was finding out about. These weren't trained artists, they had different roles in the layered society there. It was kind of an exercise, an education, my education as well as theirs. It is true that I have not often shown drawings but I feel I draw with gesture and materials – with cotton, latex foam and even bronze. I have been interested in images of the brain since my mother had a stroke in her 90s and I made the link with underwater sea corals that I had seen in my scuba diving. I made drawings of sea creatures, not to illustrate them but to give a feeling of both illusion and allusion. I like things that feel and look like other things.

vw *Your fountains, which you started in the 1980s and are still working on now – for a big show at the Storm King Art Center in upstate New York – go right back through the first cast aluminium cantilevered works of the 1970s to your early pouring pieces: the pigmented rubber latex paintings on the floor of 1968. How do you see this pattern?*

LB Yes, in a way I keep repeating the same damn thing. These works all link to my idea of the frozen gesture. With the pourings I would wax the floor to slow down the work. With *Night Sherbet* in 1968, I poured polyurethane foam and let it set but it was still flexible.

The Graces from 2003–05 involved drawing before making moulds and casting in a kind of polyurethane that looks like glass. It was a frozen gesture and suited its aim to become a fountain – it appears purple under electric light but is clear in daylight. I wanted to put light into the flowing pieces to give the sense that they are floating on water within a landscape. I really want to push the envelope with the materials at Walla Walla, one of the foundries where we are doing the new work. With phosphorescence, a sense of gravity is easily displaced and that is the fun element that comes through, like on Mardi Gras or Guy Fawkes night.

vw *Talking of fun, an image of your 2009 fountain in Dublin,* North South East West, *was lying on my desk when it was grabbed by a grandson who cheekily put it next to his latest Ninjago vessel by Lego – both share flying buttresses.*

LB That's terrific, I must look at them. I want my fountains to be played in by kids.

vw *The notion of play seems important in your work, and one aspect is seen in your Patang silk banner inspired by kite flying in Ahmedabad. You looked at Henri Matisse's cut-outs while making this work. Did you know that his granddaughter, Jackie Matisse, also came to Ahmedabad for the kite festival? Two years ago she had a superb exhibition of her work on kites at the Chateau-Cambresis Matisse museum in France.*

LB I think everything we do is about play and pleasure. It is important to play with kids and animals – even animals have the desire to participate. The only thing that is not playful is crossing the street! I met Jackie Matisse at her mother Teeny Duchamp's house long ago near Paris but I did not know of her show of kite works. She did a work for Anand when I first met her and she made a kite string of her long, fine red hair.

vw *Dave Hickey once described you as possessing 'subversive grace'. You are quoted as saying: 'I am a permissive artist, I allow things to happen.' Would you say this links your practice to John Cage's ideas on chance?*

LB No, with me it is not about chance or giving permission. I am in control and I permit the making because it is a collaboration between me and the materials in a kind of dance. Stylistically, it is very different from others who use chance such as Cage, although I did a series in the late 1990s called 'Jacks', which were direct castings of plant materials such as turmeric roots and a wild cactus grown in India for fencing to corral livestock. I did many castings on their variations of form and they could be piled or thrown. The turmeric works could be thrown as jacks and the cacti could be stacked high. These works were called 'Jacks' because they could be arranged in any way. Cage's work has a different context. His work was linked to Surrealism and played with associations. I am taking a context and changing it. Nothing is permanent as I move with the flow of materials and make configurations that are images to identify with, images for others to identify with.

vw   *You often refer to rhythms of breathing in describing certain works, especially the pleated works. Do you practise yoga?*

LB   I have done but I try to do it through my work. I try to be as active as I can and often stand for eight hours a day. I do use the Alexander technique developed from yoga, I perform it for my dog and she loves it and copies me, she has good muscles – she even does the yoga roll. But maybe the most important thing is to have a good bed.

vw   *This prompts me to acknowledge a play with the erotic in your practice that might be compared with the Hindu notion of 'Lila', meaning 'divine play'. It is a term that even occurs in contemporary Indian art criticism – are you interested in Indian philosophy at all?*

LB   I am very interested in the cyclical notion expressed in Jain texts. I relate to this strongly and use it in my work because Jainism is very pragmatic. Anand, my partner, was Jain and had a great sense of play. His mother was a Montessori-trained teacher and it is part of that understanding that made me gravitate towards that household. India was so different and yet I felt at home – all arrivals were welcome. There were people and animals everywhere and my dogs individually always travelled there with me.

vw   *You once said that 'art has the value of having no value … like a gift or an object'. This might seem like another irony today as we hear that the highest price ever for an artwork has just been paid for a Paul Gauguin (*When will you Marry, *1892), sold at auction for $300m [February 2015].*

LB   Wow! This recalls the very first painting that I remember, which was a Gauguin reproduction on my mother's chest of drawers. She was undergoing shock treatment at the time and was being told to draw portraits by her nun-nurses – something she resented strongly, as she came from a Protestant family. Gauguin used to be my favourite artist, but I think I've grown a little bit since then.

vw   *Concerning your comment on value and art, could your analogy with a gift or object be related to a proposition by the anthropologist Alfred Gell that an artwork can replace the gift in the Maussian sense: as an object that mediates social agency, or as a kind of prosthesis, an extension of the body?*

LB   I like that idea very much, it sounds close to my practice. The gift notion is important but there has to be equality between the giver and the receiver.

VW   *Working with artists in South Asia, many often tell me that they find it hard to comprehend the anti-aesthetic discourse that has permeated much postwar art in the West. They say they feel the need for beauty in order to counter the pain in their daily lives.*

LB   I would say that beauty is as real as tragedy. Sometimes dying can be a beautiful experience, we can participate in that process and be beneficiaries of pain. It is not always ugly. There is a tension between the will to live and the end of life. If one can witness it, give in to it, it is extraordinary.

VW   *Your work is at once comic and tragic, it is theatrical and suggests a narrative –do you ever write?*

LB   No way! I will leave that to you.

Issue 384, March 2015

John Hilliard

interviewed by Patricia Bickers

Cover Stories

PATRICIA BICKERS *One of the themes of your recent show at the Richard Saltoun Gallery was the recurrence of certain ideas in your work over the years. I wanted to start by asking you about new work – at least new to me – using digital technology: the 'post-scription' pieces. You talk in your own essay in the catalogue about an article you once wrote concerning the role of pre-scriptive drawing in your practice. What is the relationship between the two?*

JOHN HILLIARD Pre-scription means, in this case, a prescriptive drawing. It may sound a bit odd, but it's the way I always work with photography. I effectively draw, or sketch out, or make a diagram for a photographic image before it ever exists, before I even take up a camera – so that's always a preliminary stage for me. The post-scription, instead of being a drawing for a photograph, is a drawing from a photograph. There is quite a history of artists doing that, going right back to the 19th century, but I think the difference, in this case, is that rather than being a transcription of a work by somebody else, it's a transcription of my own work. Part of the intent, initially, was to make up for a perceived lack that I see in photography – a lack of a particular kind of definition that you get in painting and drawing. It is something, if you like, very tangible, something that you might see in painting as brushstrokes or in drawing as a line – in the case of a lot of Renaissance painting, the drawn line is a feature, particularly where hands or faces are being described. Photography, normally, is a much smoother medium without that particular kind of definition – so, I was trying to import some of those properties that I value in other two-dimensional media.

PB *You have described the process succinctly as 'a photograph of a drawing of a photograph from a drawing'. As in all your work, you constantly remind the viewer of these processes or stages in the making of the work, forcing the viewers to think about these processes and not to accept the surface as a smooth – to use your word – given.*

JH It is a kind of modernist inheritance, really. Whatever medium you use, one of your tasks is to engage with the medium itself and to articulate it on its own terms. Having decided very early on – in the latter part of the 1960s – that the photographs I took of my own sculpture would, in some way, displace it, so that photography would become the primary form at that point, part of my obligation was to discover and draw attention to the medium of photography itself – which is what I have done subsequently. Part of what I do is also a kind of critique of photography as it performs to represent things in the world. It's a mixture of those two things, I think – having some kind of critical appraisal of that function, but at the same time having a sort of positive embrace of all the properties of photography.

PB *Yet you have you have always expressed a certain necessary ambivalence towards photography. You often return to this as a theme in your work. One of my favourite early works that was included in the show is* Seven Representations Of White *from 1972. It poses both a painterly question and a question about colour perception, but presumably it also addresses photography's unreliability in respect of representation.*

JH I think it is a mixture of unreliability and specificity. One of my favourite quotes is from Jean-Luc Godard, speaking about film: that what is important isn't the representation of reality, but the reality of representations. I am always very aware of that. Whatever your purpose, it is what you end up with – and the reality of that – that is important. That is what one has to deal with.

PB *In your notes in the catalogue you say that you described your early sculpture as being about 'presentation' rather than 'representation' and that, in a way, is what you are doing with photography.*

JH I think it is partly what I'm doing. It's always problematic because however much you wrestle with what I think of as the problem of the image, it is also something very seductive. I think the word 'ambivalent' is the right word to use in terms of my own position. I'm seduced by the medium I use, but at the same time I have some critical distance from it. Between those two seemingly opposite positions is where I function.

PB *In the selection of works for the show there was much emphasis on*
your use of abstraction, in particular your use of what you have described
as 'evacuated zones'. But these voids are also an interruption – the action,
to use a movie term, appears only on the periphery. That is a kind of
refusal of the seduction of photography, a refusal to allow the viewer
to entertain the illusion of entering the image space. At the same time
you could be said to fill the void by reference to other media: to painting
(the blank canvas in Debate (18% Reflectance), *1996), to cinema (the*
empty screen in Off Screen, *1999, or the curtain in* Main Feature, *1995),*
or mirrors. But in every case, by interposing this flat plane between the
viewer and the work, you stop the viewer from crossing the proscenium,
so to speak – though there is nothing to stop viewers from projecting their
own ideas onto them.

JH Well, as I said, I think it betrays a continuing modernist sensibility
on my part. At the same time that one is drawn into, let's say, some
kind of narrative or some kind of illusory space, one also has an
enforced conscious awareness of the means of production and of the
presence of the medium itself. It is a mixture of those two things.
Like a lot of artists, I am trying to have my cake and eat it. I am trying
to have the best of those two worlds.

PB *Your work puts a lot of responsibility on the viewer. It is possible, of*
course, to engage with it on the surface level – literally, since at one level
the works are about surface – but if you choose to take the time to unpack
the work, it will deliver a great deal more and result in a more equal
relationship between the artist and the viewer.

JH Those particular pieces that you are talking about are part of a
body of work – whatever its antecedents in much earlier work of my
own – from, let's say, 1994 until about 2000. They were intended to
be quite aggressive towards the spectator, I think, and even towards
the medium itself. They were intended as a refusal, at least in large
part, of photography's conventional illusionism – so, in that respect,
they might be an affront to the spectator. But if they also make the
spectator do some work, I think that's a good thing.

PB *Speaking of 'affront', one of the most aggressive works from this*
period that was included in the show is Study For Miss Tracy *of 1994.*
The work is highly problematical in the same way that Marcel Duchamp's
Étant donnés *is. In both works a woman lies spread-eagled on her*
back, legs apart, in a pose suggestive of rape. In this instance the image
of the woman is overlaid by another, which is blurred and out of focus,

so that the violence suggested around the edge is not confirmed by the superimposed photograph.

JH I'd say the aggression is actually not towards the woman in the image. I think the aggression is towards the convention of pornographic or even simply erotic images because what it refuses to deliver is what someone might most like to access, which is the unadorned view of the model herself, and that's exactly what you cannot access.

PB *When you address these kinds of issues, you are walking a very difficult line, obviously.*

JH When I first started making images which were potentially provocative in the 1980s it was partly because, having worked my way through a lot of the facets of the medium of photography to do with picture editing or choice of film stock or choice of camera settings and so on, I began to think also about the subjects of photography and among those subjects are areas like the pornographic, the erotic, things like war photography and so on – images of sights which might not otherwise be easily available to us that we have some desire to have access to. I felt I wanted to have a look at that territory because it was there; because it seemed as much a part of the medium as anything else and, if you like, I wanted to dismantle it.

PB *Do you think that in* Balance Of Power *(3), a work of 2010, you were in part redressing that imbalance in that the Three Graces – the three nudes in the photograph – confront the male photographer in an image that is made up of more than one exposure, more than one 'take'?*

JH There are two exposures from two exactly opposing points of view. It is an image which has no right way or wrong way up. It can be right way up or wrong way up depending on what you decide – but the normal relationship between the photographer and the models is intended to be subverted. All the models are in the process of rebelling against or even attacking the photographer – they are not compliant. The photographer, the male photographer, depending on which way up you decide to have the image, might even be turned on his head. That was the kind of thinking behind that work. It is about power relations – hence the title.

PB *Two works, both of 2000, that were also included in the show, operate very differently:* Panchromatic *and* Untitled Interior *(15.7.00 and 18.7.00). They appear to invite the viewer to enter a shallow space in seemingly conventional perspective, but then entry is denied or baffled by the edge or periphery.*

JH The space is both three-dimensional and two-dimensional because the lines of perspective are actually ruptured as well as continued by the overlaid image. In respect of *Panchromatic*, the overlay is a completely black-and-white rendition of the otherwise coloured central part of the picture. In *Untitled Interior (15.7.00 and 18.7.00)* the figures refer to two dates. It is a timelapse image. The room was at first in a derelict condition and, over a period of two or three days, I restored the space to a kind of white cube perfection and then rephotographed it from exactly the same position. All this time the camera just stayed in place on its tripod without being moved so the second shot is identical to the first shot except for the fact that the room has now been redecorated and, as with *Panchromatic*, the restored central part of the image is overlaid onto the background – quite literally, one photograph is glued on top of the other – so there is definitely a rupture. You have a sense of being able to enter, as you say, but at the same time there is a two-dimensional panel across the image, which is now both accessible and blocked.

PB *The black-and-white 'inner' image in* Panchromatic *is framed by what appear to be* CMYK *colour bands.*

JH It is actually a mixture of CMYK and RGB. It's a kind of hybrid which is impossible to achieve because the blue of RGB isn't quite the same as the cyan of CMYK and so on. Rather than being a precise equivalent of the two systems, it's an approximation.

PB *Together they form a kind of diptych since in* Untitled Interior *the image of the white cube is superimposed on the paint-spattered wall of what looks like a studio wall – photography superimposed over painting.*

JH In both cases, and in numerous other works, I hand-painted the interiors, so my connection to painting isn't entirely without substance! In *Untitled Interior* the wall had been graffitied and then sanded down, which is exactly what gives it that rather colourful painterly effect.

PB *It suggests an abstract expressionist painting, and abstract expressionist painting is usually masculinised; its macho character has been critiqued by artists as various as Mike Kelly and Cheryl Donegan.*

JH Of course that's a feature of *Miss Tracy* as well. I've written about that work and I say the background sheet is like a butcher's cloth because it is so bloodied, but it is also like an expressionist painting that has been splashed and stained in a very energised way.

When we started talking about *Miss Tracy* you referred to it as *Study For Miss Tracy* – but actually, the original work was quite large. It's about 2 x 2.5m – the size of a certain kind of large-scale painting – and it is also printed in ink (this is an early form of inkjet printing) on to a vinyl substrate and stapled over a wooden stretcher as you would a canvas. I mention that because it is not just the expressionist application of theatre blood that has a painterly reference, it is also the scale and the means of printing and the substrate itself which references painting. Speaking of the masculine affiliation of Abstract Expressionism, *Miss Tracy* has attracted a surprising array of interpretations, one of which identifies the subject as male, not female.

PB *I noted in the show you had a piece from 1998 called* Fallen (Into The Light). *It looks like a deposition or entombment or lamentation – or an amalgam of all three. I couldn't identify it, though the lighting made one think of Michelangelo Caravaggio.*

JH There is a reference specifically to paintings of the deposition but not to any particular painting. It is a generalised reference to the genre.

PB *What draws you back, again and again, to painting and to art history?*

JH As a fine art student, even though I was making sculpture, I always had a great deal of interest in contemporary painting and I wasn't working sculpturally in a figurative way – quite the reverse. As you said, I referred to my sculptures as being presentational, not representational – so they were wilfully far away from any kind of figurative depiction.

The paradox of using photography, for me, is that I was employing what's actually a representational medium to record and then displace non-representational work. Photography, after all, is also largely a figurative medium, so when you begin to compare photographic work with other kinds of figurative two-dimensional work, you are likely to generate an interest in figurative painting from throughout history. With regard to Renaissance works – from frescoes to easel painting – I do have an interest that is partly born of a desire to make that comparison: what can, and what does, photography do? What are its assets, but what are its deficiencies? What can figurative painting do? And, similarly, what are its assets, what are its deficiencies? I had obviously decided there are some assets that

I would like to try to import into photographic work. Hence those pieces we talked of which I think of as being transcriptions and which all have in their title the designation 'after', a classic way for photographers or, for that matter, printmakers, to indicate images that are copies of existing works by other artists.

PB *There is a great deal of work at present that is the result of commissions to work with archives. Some of the work is, quite frankly, less interesting than the contents of the archives themselves. You have recently made works based on the plaster collection in the Royal Academy Schools in which you have brought your own aesthetic to the project, treating the archive simply as a subject like any other for your photographic interrogation. And yet, in so doing, you have achieved exactly what such a project should ideally do, which is to animate something that, in the case of the RA collection, was literally about to be (albeit temporarily) relegated to the vaults of history – out of sight in the cellars during scheduled rebuilding work. This is one of the things photography can do other than simply to record. Was this the result of your own initiative, or were you approached by the Royal Academy?*

JH Oh, no, it was my initiative. I was probably just a nuisance, I think, but they were incredibly tolerant and helpful and I'm very appreciative of that. In the past I've done one or two works which were commissions but experience now tells me that my practice doesn't lend itself easily to those sorts of constraints. I'm much happier working entirely on my own initiative – so I haven't done anything like that for quite a long time. Now, even if I do go into some kind of institutional context, it is almost certainly going to be because I have developed my own need to be there.

PB *One of the works I particularly admired in the exhibition was* Four Monochromes Not Registered (Cyan Over Yellow Over Magenta Over Black) *of 2004. Again, this relates to some of your earliest works like* Red Coat/Blue Room *and* Green Trousers/Red Room *of 1969, both of which dealt with complementary colours. In* Four Monochromes *you use all the colours to negate colour and, in so doing, you create the ultimate modernist icon – the black square. When did you begin making these works using multiple exposures?*

JH You were talking earlier about works which I described as being aggressive towards the spectator in which the largest and central part of the picture, where you would expect to find the intended centre of your attention, was screened out one way or another and rendered as an opaque plane with all the 'interesting' events only to be found in the periphery. Having reached a point where I felt that I had done as much as I wanted to do with that idea, I suddenly decided to do almost the opposite and return the identifiably interesting element of the image to the centre and actually have the periphery now more confused – but not just to return that central element to where it belonged, let's say, but to do it emphatically – not just once but again and again and again.

Actually, the very first work I made of this kind had that as its title: *Again And Again And Again*. I think that was in 2002 – so let's say that's the starting point of those works which, you could say, are about point of view. They asked the question: should I photograph this object from here, or over here, or possibly over here? Because, actually, even if the object is wholly symmetrical such that at any point of view facing towards it from around a 360° periphery it's always going to look the same (at the same height and distance), it will register differently from different positions because, almost certainly, whatever surrounds it and is behind it will vary. So, those works were based on that idea.

PB *Another work related to that is* Division of Labour, *also of 2004, and it, too, lays out the tools of the trade all around an apparently blank canvas or unprinted piece of paper.*

JH It is exactly that – it's a *tabula rasa*. The studio, which looks like a real mess in the finished image, is recorded using a quadruple exposure. Actually it was very ordered so that one entire side of the studio was filled only with the media and tools of painting, and another side only with the media and tools for making film or video, and so on, with photography and also with sculpture. The only thing that retains its coherence is that *tabula rasa* which is a metre-square sheet of – well, we don't know what. It could be blank photographic paper, it could be blank paper or canvas, it could be a blank element for a sculptural construction, or it could be a projection screen for film and video. It is intended to reference all those things. It is waiting for its subject and is surrounded by the various means by which that subject could be introduced.

The thing about *Four Monochromes Not Registered* is that, rather than being an exposure of a fixed object at the centre of surrounding viewpoints, there are actually four monochrome prints – black, magenta, cyan and yellow – placed at the centre of the four walls of a print studio so the camera now is actually in the middle of a space pointing outwards towards the periphery – that's the difference. But otherwise it's still a quadruple exposure and, of course, those four colours are the CMYK colours that we spoke about previously and the room itself is white – so, altogether they should be capable of delivering every colour and, of course, they mixed to a sort of muddy nondescript sludge which I particularly enjoy.

I didn't just make one shot; I made several shots, but I made them in different orders – so magenta might be over yellow over cyan over black but, equally, yellow might be over black over magenta over cyan – and, depending on the order in which you make those superimpositions, you will get a different colour.

This is partly a tribute to monochrome paintings by Bob Law, and I mean that quite seriously. I always had a great interest in the paintings he made which, seemingly, were black monochromes but actually were arrived at in the kind of way I've described but through painting, by painting layers of different colours on top of each other to get, in the end, what might have been a plum black or a green black or a purple black. You didn't really see that so easily until you saw a collection of them in a single space and then they hummed, vibrated, with these colours.

PB *You started out by saying that your interest lay not in the photography of objects but in photography as an object in itself which, as you say, is a modernist stance. But in our conversation we have roamed through film, photography, sculpture, painting, art history – all seen and discussed through the medium of photography. When you asked yourself, 'what can photography do?', it seems it can do a hell of a lot. What other things would you like to do with it? In other words, what are you working on now?*

JH I'm working on some pieces that actually stem from a reflection on photography as a medium which, as a rule, is repetitiously consistent in its structure. I mean, starting with analogue photography, with the simple fact that a photograph has a grain structure which is present all across and throughout the whole image. The same is true with digital photography in terms of pixelation. But more than that, I think most photographs which depict something in a particular way – let's say in soft focus, for example, or maybe a picture is taken with the camera in motion, or maybe a picture is taken with everything dramatically overexposed or underexposed – in each case those features will usually apply throughout the image. It interested me to try and make works which have built into them a certain kind of variety. Some of the elements I have just mentioned might be co-present within a single picture space. I made one or two works where, either within the camera itself or in, if you like, post-production, two or three shots of the same subject have been combined. I tried to make works so that a variety of features existed within a single work and one of the features I became interested in was that of enlargement, where you might discover, even after the fact of taking a picture, some content which wasn't noticeable to you when you made the picture in the first place and, perhaps, wasn't even noticeable to you when you first started looking at a print, but something you discover subsequently.

PB *I see on your bookshelf right in front of me the catalogue for* Blow-Up. *The movie came into my mind as you were speaking.*

JH It is especially pertinent to point to that because it's actually a catalogue of an exhibition of works relating to the film *Blow-Up* that was initiated by the Albertina Museum in Vienna. I had two works in that exhibition but, in fact, the works of mine that were first considered for the show were pieces that did, indeed, enlarge from a single photograph a particular detail, possibly to the point of oblivion and, as you know, that's a central feature of Antonioni's film.

The works of mine I'm referring to are actually from 1971. We started off with you talking about the repetition or recapture of certain ideas throughout a lifetime's work. I certainly do find that sort of recurrence, not really deliberately, not really consciously at the outset, but certainly on reflection one notices these things and that's an example.

PB *Could you talk about some specific works dealing with enlargement in this way?*

JH Well, for example, there is a work called *Cover Stories* which takes details of an image of bookshelves, in this case bookshelves filled only with crime fiction, and enlarges monochrome areas from the book jackets – from the spines of the books – where there is no text; there is simply a single colour, and because of the shape of the books, those enlargements tend to be vertical rectangles, narrow to the point of being describable as stripes. I have taken not just one enlargement, but a number – let's say 20, for example – and put them all together into a single block. So you have now got something which is deliberately referencing hard-edge striped painting and this is overlaid on the image of the books. The books themselves are really only accessible around the edge of the whole image, but with enough information to allow you to cross-reference and discover from where some of these enlarged details have originated. But between the background books and the central block of coloured bands there is a real difference in the structure of the image. I was talking earlier about the granular and pixelated homogeneity of the photograph. Well, the grain and, indeed, digital 'noise' are discernible now in these works, simultaneously present in dramatically different scales, resulting in very different readings.

PB *We talked earlier about Modernism and photography and there are purists who wouldn't touch digital – but this is not where you stand at all.*

JH I think if we talk about Modernism, there ought to be purists who will only work with digital photography. When I was teaching at the Slade, I used to talk about the 'toolbox'. There are many methods and devices which allow for different ways of working – it could be charcoal and sugar paper or it could be acrylic paint and canvas or it could be bronze casting or it could be digital video. My thinking always was that whatever came along that you could add to the toolbox, you add it – but you don't throw anything out. You still leave yourself that entire range of options. With photography, when I first started using the medium, the only option was film. As digital photography has entered into the medium and invaded it and, for many people, completely displaced analogue photography, for me it's not something to be resisted. It is something to be considered and to make use of, and there are certain areas where it is actually more efficient, more practical to do a certain job digitally. So, even though I still shoot everything on film in the first place – or almost everything – I do frequently use digital means to progress things in particular ways. My feeling is that hybridised works usually throw up something interesting – or perhaps this is just another example of wanting to have one's cake and eat it.

Issue 386, May 2015

Pavel Büchler

interviewed by David Briers

Honest Work

DAVID BRIERS *The name of your exhibition at Ikon – your largest exhibition in the UK to date – is '(Honest) Work'. How did you arrive at that title?*

PAVEL BÜCHLER Putting the word 'honest' in parentheses is meant to act like a kind of question mark for the viewer: what do artists do when they work or what is art when it is 'work'? As a society we somehow assume that work is honest by definition – honest people doing honest work. So morality, honesty, a sort of trueness or duty are associated with work. But the artist's function in society is, if you like, to avoid honest work and do things that in an ethical sense don't need doing. The working mode of art is not honesty but insincerity. Marcel Broodthaers announced his intention to become an artist by saying that he 'too wanted to do something insincere', John Baldessari in his film *The Way We Do Art Now* was 'insincerely offering a cat a carrot' as a way of doing art and Kierkegaard wrote something to the effect that if sincerity was the point in art, then the most popular artistic medium would be akvavit.

The idea of 'honest work' came out of my recent rediscovery of letterpress. I was trained as a typographer, which is a long story that doesn't need to be told here, except that I could never find any use for typography as an art form and hadn't given it much thought for 20 years. Then a couple of years ago, I inherited all this letterpress printing equipment from an old man who gave it to me under the condition that the first print I would make would be this little poster commemorating a common friend, a fine typographic designer. So I did that the moment I set it up, but it came out like your first print would and I sent it to him with an apology, saying it will get better. He replied: 'Don't worry about it. It's honest work.' It was like an epiphany, like a little gem you chance upon. Honest work, absolutely – letterpress is extraordinarily honest.

It struck me that unlike any other language technology that we know, from the clay tablets with cuneiform script to word processing, letterpress is the only one which will not enable you to say everything you may eventually want to say, because at any point in time there will only be so many letters A or B in the universe – you will run out of a letter one day. And so that idea that a million monkeys with a million typewriters over a million years will inevitably write all the works of Shakespeare does not apply to letterpress – you cannot do it. And that is where the word honesty comes into it: whatever you do with it, it will always in some way reference the medium, it will always be true to the way it is made and will necessarily acknowledge its own limits and its own limitations.

DB *As part of its general coverage of pre-election issues regarding employment, the* Guardian *asked a number of British creative people 'at the top of their field' about their first jobs, their big breaks and their next jobs. David Hockney's reply was, 'I never really had a job. I have always just painted. It's what I'm still doing.' Is what you are exhibiting at Ikon the outcome of your job, or of a number of different jobs, or of no job at all?*

PB That's a very good question. It's all three. We live in a culture of jobholders (and jobseekers) where almost all identity is derived from what you do for a living. Within this culture the ambiguity of artistic practice as a job is what really creates a space for it and what gives the artistic production a meaning as a kind of idle protest against the way things are, including the ways in which our professional and personal identities are formed, seen and understood. And one form of that pro- test may be the insistence on the recognition of your labour as a 'job'.

The work in the exhibition is also an outcome of a number of different jobs, because in my own case that professional identity is made up of different components. I describe myself as an artist and a teacher and a writer to account for different ways of working with the same basic material, which is visual images, words or texts and so on. These three jobs (and one could certainly identify a few more over my lifetime) don't overlap very much but they do have a bearing on one another. The methods and ways of doing things that you need for teaching and for writing are very different from what goes into the studio practice, where there is no method, but it is precisely that difference that defines the results.

So the artwork is an outcome of three different jobs, or perhaps more. Or is it none of them? Yes, it is none of them, because I am not even sure if I have a practice. I cannot really say that I make artworks, all I can say is that they come into being, usually by accident, by chance, and of course whatever happens by chance in the course of just living in the world can hardly be described as a job. It would be very nice if there was a job like that. I would apply for it. Just hanging around and watching.

DB *Nevertheless, your artworks often derive from carrying out repetitive actions methodically. The writings of Samuel Beckett are regularly referred to in your work. The characters he created in his fiction are frequently caught up in repetitive actions from which they cannot escape. Is there some sort of attraction of opposites there?*

PB It's not an opposite. I am maybe like a Beckettian character – trapped, if you like, in daily routine. There is nothing creative in it and yet it is the catalyst of creative production. I think there is a lot to be said for boredom. Boredom is the most powerful starting point for something creative. We get bored with our everyday life, we get bored with seeing the same things, we somehow try to look again and find something new in them. Without boredom there would be no art. My everyday life is the most banal, boring thing that there is. I am like the Beckettian character who can never get out of this loop. Yes, I think the treadmill of repetitiveness is what drives creativity, indirectly.

DB *Certain words or short phrases are often employed in texts about your work, and some of your own texts about your work, and they might be said to characterise your work. These are things like 'found objects', 'visual puns', 'obsolete technologies', 'repurposed things', 'the text', 'the page', 'appropriated material', 'art historical references', 'absurdist humour', 'understatement', 'economy of means', 'gaps', 'by-products' and 'purposeful uselessness'. They are all there in your work, but you could equally use them in relation to the work of other artists, such as the Fluxus artists and their predecessors, some of the concrete poets and a few of the early conceptualists, for example. But I don't see that what you are doing is simply reiterating what has gone before, though I couldn't work out for myself what it is that distinguishes your work beyond these traits. Am I responding to the craft element present in your work? Say, compared with an artist like Robert Filliou, who was exactly the opposite in this respect, strenuously avoiding the acquisition of any artists' craft skills whatsoever and making a feature of this lack. I think that, very subtly, you do the opposite.*

PB   Yes, maybe it is Beckett again – you know, the better failure. I often tell students not to worry about whether someone has done something before. If an artist notices something in the world that is worth doing something about, that doesn't diminish the potential of that thing to be taken up by another artist. It raises the hurdle, it raises the challenge, it becomes even more interesting to look at it again. And so you could think of it in that kind of Beckettian sense of 'fail better'. There is a pleasure and thrill and some degree of pride in noticing little opportunities in places where so many artists have gone before – even though I don't actually go out to look for these gaps. They just present themselves, just as I would think of what you call 'found objects' as objects that have found me.

So that's one thing. Another is to do with keeping things around for a long time. That seems to be the reality of my life. Look around in this studio: every single thing here is old, including the two of us. It's just how I am, I am that kind of a person. Look at my car, look at the jacket I wear, look at my hand-me-down mobile telephone. I am unable to let go of things until they completely fall apart, and in a way the art making is a bit like that. You have something in front of you that is staring you in the face, and it has to reach a point where it collapses, implodes or disappears in a kind of puff. I do have a nostalgic streak in me, but it is not nostalgia that makes me hold on to things that should really be thrown in the bin in order to see whether something that has reached the threshold of obsolescence can yield some last drop of meaning. You quoted the phrase 'purposeful uselessness', which I think is the definition of art's function – art is useless on purpose, its function is to be useless. And so somehow working with these things, with ideas and objects, with technologies or techniques that are of no further use in the practicalities of daily life, gives me a sort of head start. I don't have to do the rather tedious legwork that some artists who start working with a blank sheet of paper or canvas have to do. A blank sheet of paper is a potentially useful thing and so they need to paint on it to put it beyond use outside of art. Nobody paints anything for any practical end – why would they?

As for the craft aspect that you mentioned, that is quite interesting because I do have a whole side to me, a line of work I have recently started, where I work in ways I was trained for – observational drawing, watercolour and so on – just to see how much is left, if I can still do it and whether I can make some use of it in just the same way as I can make use of some practically obsolete machine or a piece of technology. But if the craft is indeed there, it is only there because it is difficult to unlearn. It is like swimming or cycling which you are supposed never to forget once you have learned. Fortunately, I never learned any craft very well and I'm not very good at those things and so, unlike Filliou, I don't feel any need to avoid the traditional artistic skills 'strenuously' and I don't feel that they get in the way. The very idea of a skill is to avoid strain, and if I have any craft then it is probably something to do with knowing how to keep things simple. And that is something that I learned from life. You know, the way we used to live in the old country demanded that kind of skill, of keeping things simple.

DB *What you might call some of your sculptural works are often very small. They require the sort of attention with which you would study a postcard, or peer at a small object you have noticed on the pavement. And you don't only make work for gallery spaces. Am I correct in sensing that there is no hierarchy within whatever forms you may choose to use? A small booklet would be as important to you as a display in a gallery the size of Ikon?*

PB Yes, absolutely. There is no hierarchy of materials or forms or media. Ultimately, every material or every procedure has its own criteria, and different things fall into place in different ways. In the Ikon exhibition there are some works which are on a huge scale. *The Castle*, for example, the biggest ever version of it, is an enormous thing with over 150 loudspeakers, each one almost the size of a person – huge things. Or *Idle Thoughts*, the overwritten diaries that I have been writing almost every day since 2003, or *Work*, my photographs of 1,200 cigarette breaks that I have taken in recent years when installing exhibitions. But there are also works that were produced in an instant, that came together as a result of some fortuitous encounter with readymade things in everyday life: a diamond in an ashtray, for instance, a copy of *Art Monthly* with its masthead cut off by a bookshop assistant, or an old slide projector with nothing in it – you can't even say that I made that. I didn't, it was just there and it left me nothing to do. And I hope that somehow I can let these different things show what they can do together when I leave them to their own devices. So there is no hierarchy of any sort, just as there is no key work or indeed a central motif or a common theme.

What is important in all art, I think, is what the work does, not what it is. A text work of three words cannot have the complexity of a novel or a feature film. It would be difficult to stand in front of it and stare at it as if it were a painting by Jackson Pollock. But then again, three words can do things that a novel, film or Pollock can't do and they can have the capacity to hold your attention long after the object is out of sight.

DB *How important is it to you where you place your work in the world, literally? You have shown* The Castle *at different times on different continents. Does it remain the same work?*

PB Our encounters with art – with what used to be called the visual and plastic arts – don't take place strictly speaking in the world at large. They take place in environments which are more often than not specifically devised, maintained and equipped for that purpose – typically galleries, museums, art fairs and so on – and to that extent every work of art is as much autonomous as it is context-specific. On the one hand, *The Castle* is the same piece now as it was when I showed the first modest version of it in an obscure group exhibition in London in 2004. The work is based on a fragment of Franz Kafka's text which is put through the treadmill of a synthetic text-to-speech computer programme. This alienating contemporary technology is married awkwardly to antiquated technology from Kafka's day: loudspeakers that were patented by Marconi in 1926, the year of the first publication of Kafka's novel. The tension between the two is at the heart of the work and holds it together no matter how the work has grown in scale and developed through its various adaptations or where it has been shown over the years.

On the other hand, the effect of using the public-address speakers was quite different in a gallery remodelled from a former gas works in Sweden, the cradle of social democracy, and then in a ramshackle kind of space – an old tobacco warehouse – in Istanbul, and it was different again a year later in Kunsthalle Bern. All these places are galleries, but like the loudspeakers they have their own histories and offer different opportunities. When I took the work to Greece I changed the soundtrack, adding some 1970s Greek film music.

When I took it to Prague, I did part of it in Czech and in Shanghai I tried to do it in Mandarin. Prague is the place where Kafka wrote *The Castle* and where it in some sense belongs, but it equally belongs to China since, quite interestingly, *The Castle* was apparently the first western novel ever translated into Chinese. In Birmingham, in the context of a survey exhibition, the work is probably going to do something else once again – I hope so, anyway – and it will be interesting for me to see what it does as much as how it resists the specifically local context.

DB *Do you ever feel marginalised from the contemporary art mainstream? You have lived in the UK since 1981, but always outside London. In 2009 you won the Northern Art Prize, which you deserved to win, but there is something rather curious about having that particular appellation conferred upon you.*

PB I am not sure where or what the contemporary art mainstream is. The geography of the art world and the geography of what is interesting in art at one time or another are not the same. Right now we are doing an interview in Manchester for a magazine published in London that, much to its credit, seems to ignore and often question the London-centric idea of contemporary art in the UK. The interview is about my exhibition at Ikon, a gallery in Birmingham whose programme places it among the great European kunsthalles. It is true that there is something provincial and even provincialist about such tokens of recognition as the Northern Art Prize, but a paranoic distrust of the local and a deference towards anything international are equally the traits of provincialism. In the end, I feel just as uneasy about being described as the Northern Art Prize-winner as about being labelled an international artist. What makes me feel comfortable in Manchester, the suburb of the art world as it may be, is that the city seems to have enough self-confidence not to care too much about such distinctions.

Issue 387, June 2015

Amikam Toren

interviewed by Patricia Bickers

Re-Toren

PATRICIA BICKERS *When I was looking back over several decades of your work, I found myself using a number of words beginning with the prefix 're', as in 'reconstruction', 'reconstitution', 'recuperation', 'restitution', 'representation' – or re-representation – and, more recently, 'reproduction', a word used in the title of a new series of works.*

In one of the first series I remember, 'Simple Fractions' of 1975, you addressed sculpture by breaking – fracturing – milk bottles and, as though they were precious archaeological objects, you reconstructed them, in each case mapping the breaks in a drawing displayed alongside the reconstructed object. So you broke the source object down in order to reform it and make something new, a metaphor perhaps for the creative process, one that is necessarily preceded by a destructive process.

Similarly, in the 'Of the Times' series begun in the 1980s you addressed painting by pulping newspapers and mixing the resulting material with PVA medium to form the paint, displaying the finished painting – depicting a form derived from a single letter – alongside The Times *logo with the date. The newspaper is thus reconstituted as a painting, as art. But in the most extreme series, the 'Pidgin Paintings', you treated the painting/canvas as a patient, pulping canvas cut or torn from the stretcher, mixed with a medium and applied to the support – treating painting by painting, so to speak.*

It seems appropriate, then, that in 2006 you made a work called Deus Ex Machina *that I like to think of as a kind of dramatic rescue of sculpture by painting: a white towel – a cypher for painting – is draped (protectively?) over a collapsing concertina drying frame which is reinforced by a steel armature.*

AMIKAM TOREN A crutch – yes. Destruction-as-a-metaphor is well established in art. But I use destruction practically, in a non-

585

metaphorical way. My approach to making art is aided largely by 'tactile' thought, it forces action first and then reflection – or analysis – follows. Though I see my output as propositional, the thinking is largely tactile, and that is the case even with all the text-based works I have ever made, and there is a good deal of text in my work.

The 'Simple Fractions' series was an important moment in the history of the making of my work. Mapping the reconstructed bottle enabled me to see how much precision there was in the destructive process. And more importantly I realised how vital the possibility/ impossibility of representation was to me as a subject. It gave me the green light to paint without it being a return to painting. Traditionally, representation was the domain of painting. I wanted to bring to the practice the lessons I had learned from my work with fragments and give it a propositional option – painting with a question mark.

PB *It is a commonplace of art criticism to write of the crisis – even death – of painting but not of sculpture as a category. Perhaps this is because it has morphed into installation or other forms?*

AT Yes. Over the years sculpture has been able to acquire a wider brief. Work that was defined as performance, installation or video installation and so forth came under the category with comfort because it was handled within space – which is the domain of sculpture.

Painting, though, was excluded from those explorations, and it seemed smug and conservative. It was a kind of category unto itself – always on the wall or within a frame of some kind. It needed to be reapproached – not in terms of image-making, but in terms of questioning everything about the process of its making: what is painting made of? What is paint? What is the relationship between painting and the rest of the world? Where do you place it?

The interesting thing to me about this process of reapproaching painting was that it enabled me to use representation (which itself is a very traditional form) as an axe with which to demolish painting and reinvent it. I ended up reversing the maxim that representation excludes its subject. This opened up everything and paved the way towards a fresh practice.

PB *You re-presented painting?*

AT Yes, but this was an extension of the way I was already working with other objects – chairs, teapots, windows or whatever – the rest of the ordinary world. Painting was there, just one of many items, like newspapers, cardboard boxes and so on, part of what I saw as a non-hierarchical order of things, all of which were available to me.

PB *And yet painting does enjoy a special status, particularly in the market, and when you began to make the 'Armchair Painting' series, a riff on Henri Matisse's paintings for the bourgeoisie, you seemed to be taking on painting's special status – I'm thinking here of* Untitled: Worship Here *of 2007, a seascape which, unusually for the series, is in a gilded frame. The cutting of the words directly into the canvas support could be construed as an act of aggression towards painting.*

AT I did cut them lovingly.

PB *Yes, paradoxically. You have said that in creating real space through cutting into the surface you are attacking illusion in a manner that relates perhaps to Lucio Fontana's 'Concetti spaziale' paintings, in the sense of cutting through to the other side.*

AT Yes, but my other side isn't a metaphoric 'other side', it is the immediate wall behind the paintings. Fontana had this receding black space on the other side, which I don't believe in. I wanted the immediacy of the ordinariness of it. In other words, that little space which is trapped between the wall and the painting is a real space and it deals with light and shadow in a very particular way, which affects the rest of the painting. That clash, or uneasy link, between real space and illusionary space creates an ambiguous kind of presence that holds the gaze of the viewer as they interrogate what it is they are seeing. Very often people don't understand immediately what it is they are looking at because they imagine the text is either a light projection or even something painted on top.

PB *That is the very essence of illusion – our capacity to be deluded, you might say. But whereas in the 'Pidgin Paintings' you cut or tore the canvas and used it to 'bind' painting's wounds, in the 'Armchair Paintings' the cutting is more aggressive. How do you respond to that?*

AT I don't think of it as aggressive. On the contrary, I give it a chance. I make art. The aggression I use may be compatible with the kind of aggression you would find in most kitchens up and down the country, where people use a sharp tool that cuts. All making involves some form of aggression, so it's there – but in the scale of aggressive acts committed upon earth, I think it is a minor offence, really.

PB *We were talking earlier about the position of painting in the hierarchy of art and it could be said that in the case of the 'Armchair Paintings' that the source paintings, or I should say 'found paintings' ...*

AT   ... Purchased paintings.

PB   *The 'purchased found paintings', then, are mostly by amateurs, and are usually seen as being of less value than, say, paintings by recognised artists in museums. For instance, the slashing of the* Rokeby Venus *in the National Gallery is seen as an act of vandalism whereas Robert Rauschenberg's erasure of a drawing by Willem de Kooning is seen as an artistic act.*

AT   'Armchair Paintings' can be made from the work of professional artists as well. I don't have a case against amateur painters. I am able to afford their work whereas Monet is out of my pocket.

PB   *But you would if you could?*

AT   Yes. I don't think any work would be destroyed by my action. The image is still there. You can still see what the painter painted. In some cases, what I do gives the work another chance, an upgrade. In others, it would just give you a bit of a jolt, if you like. And re-engage your seeing.

PB   *The original painter might not agree! Do you think that in the recent 'Memento Paintings' series you make amends by painting your signature under that of the original in the corner of the purchased found painting, which is all that remains of the original? Is this a form of reparation?*

AT   It's a kind of acknowledgment. Not exactly reparation but a non-patronising, non-hierarchical gesture – this is my signature, this is your signature. I'm not trying to wound or diminish anyone else's art at all. Nor elevate my own. These are just opportunities to explore new propositional paintings, which are as economical as a Japanese haiku. There are many things you could do with a painting: put it on the wall, bin it, burn it or put your own name on it. I include my own work in this, of course.

PB   *In the more recent works using found paintings, the 'Reproductions' series, the figurative painting, referenced in the title, is almost entirely obscured by your 'abstract' painting, which literally consumes the original. At the same time, all the colours turn to a kind of grey, though when seen together the range of greys is subtly varied so that references to the original subjects remain in the overall tone: forests, grass –* Reproduction No 8 (Green Park) *– sky –* Reproduction No 60 (The Sky's the Limit), *both from 2013 – urban scenes and so on.*

AT   All reproductions make reference to the original. This series does that, of course, but here each individual painting is consumed so that it becomes its own reproduction. You actually get a lot of colour variation when you see a group of them together. This particular process denies the image but reveals the colour of the painting. It also unlocks the viewer's imagination. The titles are very often a description of what image was in the original painting. And often, if a title was written on the back, I will reuse that.

PB *I particularly liked the play on words in the 2013 work titled* Reproduction (Three Men and a Pregnant Woman). *You have literally generated a new work from the old.*

AT I have reproduced it. I became a woman!

PB *Indeed, a kind of parthenogenetic birth. This series, like others related to it, could be said to have been born out of the 'Armchair Paintings' – the longest-running series in your work so far. You return again and again to painting as a suitable case for treatment. There is one,* Untitled: In use Night and Day, *1991, which suggests simultaneously the longevity of the painting tradition but also that it is 'parked'. Another, from 1996 and depicting a black female nude half-length figure, carries the – again 'found' – text: 'Penalty for improper use'. Obviously, that has political and gender applications but, equally, the accusation could be made against you.*

AT That is an important observation – I take full responsibility for my improper act. Art does not exclude the political. Mine is a reflection on the political rather than being agitprop itself. For instance, in *Untitled: Kill Rushdie* from 1990, a political point could have been scored simply by printing the text on top of the painting, if that was the sole message. Leaving aside the politics in the text, the painting is constantly at work, negotiating its existence as an object/painting. This exceeds the merely political.

PB *Has* Untitled: Kill Rushdie *ever been shown in the UK?*

AT No. Though it has never been 'censored', it has always somehow been 'excluded' from being shown in the UK.

PB *In the 'Actualities' sculpture series the body is more obviously referenced, the chair being its surrogate. In the case of* Actualities No 2, *1984, half the chair has been pared away – including the seat whose stuffing spills out like its guts – right down to the joints. All your work deals with, yes, destruction and re-creation but through it all is this sense of vulnerability – not just of the human but, perhaps, of the category of art itself.*

AT This group of object/sculptures came out of my attempt to make a presentational painting of a chair. In 1979–80, I was filing down a wooden chair, producing paint out of the filings in order to make a painting of the chair with itself as pigment. The one chair yielded nine paintings, all the same size and bearing roughly the same image of a chair. Because I wanted to keep the remaining structure of the chair intact, I left more body around the joints. Eventually the object of a skeleton emerged but it was never planned. The work that resulted was *Neither A Chair Nor A Painting*, 1979–80.

Once this was done I realised the potential of the 'object as a skeleton' and some time later began to make the 'Actualities' series. While I will not argue with your observation, it is important to admit some innocence – I only initially wanted to paint a chair out of itself. I have no idea how to approach work that deals directly with 'the human condition' or 'the condition of art'. Those shoes are too big for me.

PB *The window has often been a subject in your work and, of course, the window as a metaphor in art goes back to Alberti and perspective: the window on the world, this constructed illusion of three-dimensional space that you have attacked. But more particularly, in your case, it is a reference to Marcel Duchamp's 1920 piece* Fresh Widow.

AT Regarding *Fresh Widow*, one of the works that I have made with windows that has never been shown is actually titled *Slash Widow*. And it has the same colours as the original work by Duchamp – so, the reference to Duchamp in my work is certainly steady over the years.

PB *The 'Burglary Pieces' that involve using broken glazed windows and doors, are overtly threatening.* Safety Regulation Painting *of 1989 in particular, in which the remains of two sash windows are strung up, held in a precarious balance, like two opaque eyes, the glazing obscured by whitewash. Unlike the 'Armchair Paintings', which you can see through, this work actually prevents you from looking in.*

AT Yes, it forces you to look at, rather than in or through. I go around the town and see those kinds of whitewashed windows in shops and so on. To my mind they are remarkable paintings. I enjoy looking at them.

PB *So a preoccupation with painting runs throughout the work, even though it may not be so obvious in some of the works using other media – you have worked in all kinds of media from photography, film and collage to sculpture and installation. Even the move to video is in your mind something to do with painting, is that right?*

AT Storytelling is a form of representation which needs a certain amount of de-banalising. Both *Carrots* and *Refreshments* tell autobiographical stories. The possibility or impossibility of that was handled by turning the location into a protagonist which created a gap between what the viewer saw and what they heard, and which supported both the narrative and the moving image.

PB *I was particularly interested in* 16 Evelyn House, *which you made in 2009, because it addresses so many of your themes to do with destruction and reconstruction, with restoration and recuperation. At the time, your building was being renovated. It was almost as if you had commissioned the builders to make an Amikam Toren work and the result, to use another traditional art category, is to my mind a self-portrait. Would that be fair?*

AT Yes, indeed, it became a self-portrait. And the fact that I had to pay £13,000 (my share of the building work) did make me feel as though it was work I had commissioned. I videoed different kinds of jobs that were being done on site and coupled this with a voice-over reading letters that I received while living at the same address. It produced the same kind of discomfort, maybe, that you have with the text and image in the 'Armchair Paintings'. The connection between what you saw and what you heard was a bit uneasy – unpredictable.

PB *It is very intimate, too. Your private world is made public in a most unusual way, appropriate to the fact that it was your home.*

AT It is – the gamut of letters ran from the intimate to the professional, and official things that you receive from the gas board, the NHS or stuff like that.

PB *This ties in to what you were saying earlier about the fact that you don't want art to be a special category. It is part of life, part of politics – it doesn't operate outside those things.*

AT It is political in the sense that art operates within the political system under which we live – but I wouldn't categorise it as social realist. The kind of art I make needs to be completed by the viewer and every viewer may do that in their own way. Hopefully, the work is able to engage with the condition of life in a wider field.

PB *Looking back at your work it is possible to trace certain themes and connections between artworks, but the first time I saw* Golem, 2002, *I was totally unprepared. I had absolutely no idea what to make of it. How did that work come about?*

AT I can't make it out either! In that sense I'm in the same position as you are. In the 1970s I made a decision never to censor myself. To do, if at all possible, everything that came to mind. Though some of my sculptural work is closely linked to my practice as a painter, the rest is often entirely spontaneous. *Golem* is one of these spontaneous eruptions. Though I'm not a visionary kind of artist, I woke up one morning with that image imprinted on my mind. As I was having coffee, I drew it and wrote the word 'Golem' underneath. Very quickly I felt compelled to produce this object and I thought, 'Well, if I can find a way of making it, I'll do it'. And there it is. Though I made it there is not much more that I can say about it.

PB *I now see it as another way of addressing what you might call the burden of art: the spindly legs of the John Lewis ironing board, albeit clad in stainless steel, supporting this massive half-ton weight of Kilkenny black marble, the thin aluminium membrane of the cover – standing in for painting – in-between, takes one back to the chairs in the 'Actualities' series. There is the same sense of taking something almost to breaking point before bringing it back from the edge.*

AT That's something that happens again and again in the work – that sense of vulnerability, of being at the point of almost being unsupported, but just being there.

PB *Do you ever feel, as an artist, that the struggle is sometimes unsustainable? I know you taught for years and that, apart from what you may have got from teaching, you also had to teach to live.*

AT You have to do what you have to do. It kind of felt as though there was no choice about the matter. I did all kinds of jobs to make money. Teaching was one of them. And though I never earned enough, I somehow managed to make it work. My accountant often told me that my life didn't make economic sense, he thought (wink-wink) that I had some cash income that I was not disclosing … I wish. But what can I say? It's a life priority. You take responsibility for doing what is important to you. It is so simple that it is almost impossible to say.

PB *Was teaching sustaining in other ways – intellectually?*

AT Teaching in itself was intellectually engaging, at times. It has some parallels with making art – you are engaged with giving. Attempting to support young artists as they struggle to emerge is also a process of teaching oneself, there are quite a few unexpected by-products along the way and that feeds into your own practice too.

PB *In a strange way certain things have come full circle in that you were born in Jerusalem and lived in Tel Aviv before coming to the UK. You are about to participate in a show about painting at the Jewish Museum in New York, which, of course, has a distinguished reputation for showing challenging art – particularly in the 1960s. How do you feel about that?*

AT Well, I have lived in London since 1968 and, like it or hate it, it is my home. This is where I have matured and made my work over the past 50 years. The upcoming exhibition in the Jewish Museum is a survey, making important links between a number of artists who approach painting in an unorthodox way – of course I'm delighted to participate.

PB *One idiosyncratic series of works that we haven't discussed is the orange peel works, the first of which,* Black Hole, *1997–2006, was developed over a long period. How did that come about?*

AT It has to do with my diet. I guess, being born in Israel, it's just too predictable. I peel them by hand, and then I put them on the windowsill to dry and enjoy having the odd look as they are drying, how they twist and turn into these strange spirals and then, also, the scent – the slight marmalade scent. Once they were dry, I would throw them away. Then, at one point, it occurred to me that I was throwing away really beautiful objects that have very significant sculptural values and so I started to collect them in black dustbin liners – after all, they're rubbish.

PB *The titles –* Black Hole, Quarks *– suggest some kind of revenge of the organic and the natural against science and reason. Is that possible?*

AT At one point I had to put the bag of orange peel into an exhibition and it had to be titled and, being bored with untitled work, I just gave it the first title that came to mind – so, *Black Hole*.

PB Plan B, *2013, is another apparently idiosyncratic sculpture.*

AT It was made with readymade sculptural objects – wooden objects. You could call them airport art: small statues made out of wood that come from all over the world. I amassed them in a cube-like shape on top of an architect's drawing board, suggesting a 'plan B' – a new possibility. Like *Golem*, the cube is big, oversized, too heavy for its apparent support.

PB *Back to the drawing board?*

AT Back to the drawing board, yes.

PB *Conversely, the 2006 work* Received Wisdom *– the lecture chair whose wooden armrest for writing on is repeated in the form of an unfeasibly high stack – like* Plan B *can be related, at least retrospectively, to* Golem, *but neither is like* Golem. *They are more explicable.* Golem *still remains a mystery.*

AT Mystery is not a way of pulling wool over the viewers' eyes, it is a by-product of dealing with the unknowable. That mystery is important. Without that, there is no point in the work being there, really.

George Barber

interviewed by Maria Walsh

Shouting Match

MARIA WALSH *Your recent work overtly addresses political issues – Drone attacks in* The Freestone Drone, *2013, and the migrant issue in* Fences Make Senses, *2014, currently on show at Waterside Contemporary. Yet your early work, the 'Scratch' videos especially, seems in high contrast to this. I'm curious about this shift.*

GEORGE BARBER Yes, it is a big shift but even though I was making videos, and consciously getting into postmodern recycling of style over content – actually, I always wanted to be a writer – it just seemed that maybe the 'Scratch' stuff was a blip because I realised it was a way of making something visual fast and I precisely didn't want meaning at that point, because it was music-based and I wanted it to be immersive. My interest in having conversations with people about the world and projecting that in art was always there, but I can see that it might seem as if I was bumbling around with materials and then became this thinking, issues character.

When I was a student at Central St Martins they used to preach this doctrine about not thinking in terms of metaphors, that you should concentrate on what is in the piece – nothing else. I couldn't stand all that. Basically, they were telling you to stare at the pattern, the material, the frame, but you would need a lobotomy to keep that up. They also seemed to dislike the idea of a sort of bourgeois discourse: 'we are just talking about the mechanics of film; we hate narrative,' they seemed to say. It was a complex moment, but in the late 1970s there was a certain fashion that it was bourgeois to be very discursive or link ideas to a wider field. For a short while, lots of key artists wanted the surface, the medium and the mechanics to be centre stage. The structuralists held great sway in art colleges then. I wanted something else.

MW *It is interesting that you have segued into this as I did want to ask you about your relationship to structuralist film. I always thought of the formalism of their discourse as bourgeois. They looked down on the popular – Hollywood movies were seen as indulgent cultural illusions.*

CB Yes, their great discovery was that boredom was political. A film with nothing going on made you a radical – yeah, right. I felt it to be a profound censorship, something totalitarian in spirit. But what I meant was that, say you have a literary critic on the BBC talking about a new novel, they can précis it and interpret it with all sorts of literary frameworks and modes of analysis that seemed revolting, stuffy and old-fashioned in the art world of that time. The structuralists were looking for something revolutionary or tough in their discourse. It was anti-bourgeois in that sense.

The irony about this is that years later after 'Scratch', I realised that I was doing something quite similar. I was doing what I had been taught, only much quicker and perhaps more pleasurably. But in the end I was asking the viewer to fall into the image and just look at it – I hadn't travelled that far from them really – though I did add these meaningless mantras from Hollywood films, pop choruses and music with a beat. Ironically, it was a version of Structuralism, even if it was edited in television time rather than art time.

MW *What do you mean by that distinction?*

CB It used to drive me nuts as a student – the arrogance of most of these makers – and it still goes on today. For example, there is a Richard Serra piece I remember where you sit in a room for about 45 minutes to watch somebody placing different coloured paper in front of a rostrum camera, and that's it! It annoyed me, the sense in which you were supposed to just chill and go willingly into this zombie world. I didn't think art should be like this back then. I mean, look at literature – there is no book that does that and sees it as an advantage. Art is quite bewildering today, too. A lot of younger makers do use durational time because that is actually what television doesn't have, so it is another marker of saying this is 'art'. A lot of contemporary work looks like rushes to me; the tentative, unfinished nature of it. So it is almost like participation for the viewer to think: what does it mean? What is it about? I'm more of a classicist. I still edit and, if it begins to get boring and it is not producing a thought in my head, the chances are it won't produce one in anyone else's either, so I go back to where it seems to work.

The Freestone Drone, at 12 minutes, is a concise piece. I think the times and the experience of time have changed – you can't make work like Chris Marker or take time like Jean-Luc Godard any more, people are a bit more fidgety. One thing that breaks my heart also, in this discussion about time and duration, is that you are not taken seriously if you make short work. Most artists want to take up space and take up time. I have been to many screenings where the 40-minute work is seen as important and the three- minute one is seen as a joke, or as slight, when often the longer work is just very slow and repetitive.

MW   *In another context, I think there is a shift towards the short, albeit shared rather than screened. Some of your early 'Scratch', particularly* Absence of Satan, 1985, *and* No Frank, Yes Smoke, 1985, *has a contemporary feel with a* GIF-*like use of repetition and surface materiality. Other work seems more dated because of the imagery, like watching old cult* TV. *People look different, dress differently – I'm especially thinking of* The Venetian Ghost *of 1988.*

CB   That is my elegy to LA. I always thought that video picked up on the emptiness of LA, which is pretty timeless. It looks terrible now, though. The image is harsh in a way that modern cameras aren't, but they were the best professional video cameras at the time. Now it looks like a Brazilian soap opera. I think at the time I knew that but it was what I could afford. My *Taxi Driver 11* of 1987 is like that too.

MW   *The humour of the historical references, for example, Gaddafi and Clearasil, Arab terrorists and portable food, is quite prescient in that video.*

CB   If you think as well about the Robert de Niro acting classes in the video – that was really prescient. There is a funny story about when it was shown. Colin MacCabe, who gave me the money to make it, showed it at a very nice plush cinema in Piccadilly. The film on before mine, which had cost thousands, was a ponderous romance. My little thing came on and the audience loved it. Colin was very pleased so he gave me a bit more money to get the ending right – I needed to hire a convertible for the day and get the star a Mohican haircut. Then Colin used to forever get calls from South America saying: 'This *Taxi Driver 11*, when can we have this new sequel?' And he had to tell them it is only a seven-minute British video art work. The world always thinks of me as 'Scratch' first and then with add-ons, but what I said about being literary can be seen in both *Taxi Driver 11* and *The Venetian Ghost*. In fact, the last piece of 'Scratch' I did was in 1985 but I was already working with actors in 1987 and 1988. I was always working with writing. I have just put together a collection of short stories, too, which will be in gallery bookshops soon. I was always doing literary things at the same time. Actually, I was always capable of working with actors and dialogue.

MW   *The people who appeared in previous shorter works, such as* Beyond Language, *2005, and* Shouting Match, *2004, were non-actors and executed a set of simple instructions, whereas in the current work you have hired actors and you are directing more.*

CB   In *Taxi Driver 11* they were acting students, as they were in *The Venetian Ghost* too. Those works, and others like *Walking Off Court* of 2003 and *Withdrawal* from 1997, are about the common pain that people feel about existence. In my latest work, *Akula Dream*, they are professional actors. The captain, Richard Leaf, has acted in Shakespeare productions and he played Hannibal Lecter's father in *Hannibal Rising*. He really liked the project as we shot it on a real Soviet submarine near Rochester. The great thing about modern cameras is that you don't need a lot of power, so we were able to get all the lights we needed, powered by a tiny generator. Anyway, he has that great animism, that presence. In *Fences Make Senses*, the participants are experienced improvisers. I thought they were very talented at running with an idea and acting out the refugee scenarios. Of course, in their tradition they veer towards humour, but so do I. If you look at the greats – Shakespeare, and I was reading George Eliot's *Middlemarch* recently – they do combine seriousness with humour. Today, there is a tendency to think you can't have both, especially in politics.

Anyway, the long and the short of it is that I wanted to travel between two registers. I know my way round video art and I just slip in enough to keep it attention-grabbing so you know that is where I have come from, but at the same time the narrative keeps you wondering how it will end. It's a good combination. *Akula Dream* was shown at 'Transmètic' at Lewisham Art house recently and the audience loved it. The art bits are just the length that you don't walk off, and the narrative gives it drive. It is quite a satisfying piece in that it represents the two sides of me coming together after all these years. They are going to show it at the London Film Festival. This link between registers seems to be acceptable now. What video art does well is that it allows you to dream and drift into the image. It is primarily a visual form. So I'm partly back to what they were telling me at St Martins, but in the context of *Akula Dream* you still have an umbrella of sense and development: you know that it is about a bloke on a submarine, and the dreamy moments punctuate the narrative. They are the shamanic journeys of the crew.

MW *In relation to what you were saying before about being literary,* Akula Dream *is such a contrast to your use of the guttural aspects of language in* Beyond Language *and* Shouting Match.

CB I think I have three categories: the narrative poetic stuff, then 'Scratch' works, which are material and quite fashionable now – the younger generation love all that stuff and there is tons of it on YouTube – and also my middle period, which is conceptual. When I did *Shouting Match* I was consciously thinking that the best video art was made by the early crowd – Vito Acconci, Bruce Nauman, Marina Abramović – they were performing simple animal-like actions connected with language. *Shouting Match* is another iteration, but of course the camera works differently – I had tracks and used dollies – but I would admit that it somehow comes from the founding greats of video art. *Automotive Action Painting*, 2007, which is one of my hits with lots of views on YouTube, is the same.

MW *Where would you place your monologues?*

CB There came the point when I was a bit short of cash and I was struggling, so I made a piece called *Waiting for Dave*, 1994, which was about waiting to come alive so that 'Dave', David Curtis, at the Arts Council, would give me a few bob. If you adopt a confessional mode and you have quite insightful things to say about your own life, that is the best an artist can do because you can't have fancy sets but you have your own body and your own mind. My monologues attempt to get at what it feels like to be alive in quite a personal and extreme subjective mode. You can construct imaginative scenarios of what it is like to be on the airport disaster plane – *Passing Ship* from 1994 – or these kinds of things. It was a stimulating moment I picked up on then, the slacker ethos that I affected. But even though this work had a genuine insight, it was digging me even more into this thing where you had to be an English person to get it. I became worried, especially in the 1990s, about being associated with – a terrible phrase – 'English whimsy', and that put me off. Videos like *Walking Off Court* cannot be appreciated unless you have very good English language. The reach of your art is limited if it is so language based. *The Shouting Match* series was a further response to that.

MW *I wanted to ask you about your use of props and installation space in recent and current work. Was* The Freestone Drone *the first time you exhibited in this way?*

CB I had done a few, but not so well developed, so it is a new shift. I began to see that if you just do screens, it is not much of an event. We walk past screens all the time at stations so I began to think of simple ways of staging the piece. Thematically, the centre point in *The Freestone Drone* is about drones watching the washing-lines. It didn't take much to turn it into an event. I like the notion of staging the work. I don't mind phrases like 'dressing a set' either. They have a function. They reinforce key points within the video. The hanging washing alerts you – I like crap, haphazard washing – because it is non-aesthetic too. We took it to the Istanbul art fair and it looked very untidy in the space, like an unloved show. Wherever it goes, I have to find dumped washing to put on the lines.

MW *When people write about your work, they say you are critiquing television. Is that how you see it?*

CB That's a big question: whether anyone's critique has any effect. I was to some extent critiquing television because I wasn't taking good stuff, but B movies and cheap adverts and travel shows. I wanted to take that material and put it together in a way that the sensibility of what it produced was a million miles away from the original maker's intention. I wouldn't make any great claims for it but at the time I think it was subversive in that I was taking recognisable bits of culture and transforming them. Then pop culture liked it, record companies liked it, so in a way the critique must have worked because commercial culture saw that it was a change in perspective. Obviously it was recuperated in the old Marxist sense soon enough.

MW *Critique has become such a calling card in the art world now.*

CB Yes, who would have thought that research would become so popular at Basel, that university art would become such a scene-setter? If you have a piece of work that connects with the world and connects with famous theorists like, say, Slavoj Žižek, you cover historical ground in a way that gives people lots to talk about and it gives the work great intellectual and critical provenance. You can include my new work in this, though I didn't make it like that as I am not a cynical person. Art has drifted away from being a formal thing. It is a good time to have a repertoire of issues that you situate your practice within.

MW *Like the migrant issue currently?*

CB I didn't know it was going to get as big as it has. *Fences Make Senses* was made last year [2014]. It was a different issue then. I'm not sure it would be a similar piece if I made it now. Now, it is a bit like 9/11 – one doesn't want to turn on the TV. It is a bit like we are watching the 21st- century Jarrow March and it looks as if it will be going on for some time. I think that artwork is rather good because it seems to have hit on something, but I am in no way offering a solution. Every country has a definition of a refugee but they don't set up a booth in Somalia to see who fits it. They let them climb mountains, swim seas, walk miles, get to you illegally and then will decide. There is madness to it. The West has its rules but, deep underneath, the true fact is that we all know that if we are going to share everything, we are going to be a lot poorer. And it would seem as if Iraq and Syria are going to become a large military exercise ground without people, like a super large Salisbury Plain for military powers to try things out.

MW *I think your use of found footage in* Fences Make Senses *has an oblique relation to the 'documentary turn' in the art world. I was put in mind of Nicolai Bendix Skyum Larsson's* The Promised Land *from 2009, also on the migrant issue.* The Promised Land *is a very powerful piece using documentary images that are beautifully shot and make one ask oneself: 'is this an aestheticisation of misery?' Art can't but be aesthetic and I'm not saying one way is better than the other, but your poetic – and as you were saying earlier, personal – voice-over makes for a non-didactic way of accessing material that in an art context could seem quite gratuitous.*

CB I probably spent too much time watching Godard. I was told at the Slade by Tim Head, my tutor there, 'George, you are always searching for this big meaning, you should just make simple things', because it does actually work. I think art that has the potential for a conversation with you and seems to indicate a mind at work behind it – you, the viewer, can interpret it and you can think, 'I've thought that' or 'I can get that' – is a lot richer than that lonely feeling which is quite common for a viewer today.

Issue 390, October 2015

Rosalind Nashashibi

interviewed by George Vasey

Gaza Stripped

GEORGE VASEY *Could you give a brief context to the commissioning process behind your new film for the Imperial War Museum,* Electrical Gaza?

ROSALIND NASHASHIBI I was asked to propose a new work on the subject of Gaza, so the impulse came from the IWM curators initially – they asked other artists to propose who weren't connected with Palestine, as far as I know. I had thought I hadn't been to Gaza but my mother reminded me that we had visited once with the family when I was very small, four or five years old, and she showed me a photograph of us having a picnic on the beach.

CV *When did you shoot the footage?*

RN The filming took place in June 2014 during the run-up to Israel's latest war on Gaza, 'operation protective edge'.

CV *Wow, I'm always struck by the abstraction of militaristic language. I understand you have a Palestinian father – do you view the film as, in some way, biographical?*

RN My family is from Jerusalem. I don't view this film as biographical, but when I work in Palestine I'm always seen in relation to my father's side of the family, and it helps me to move around and to be trusted there. The names of your parents and grandparents are more important to the Palestinians and the Israelis than your nationality, citizenship or language.

CV *And the title, how does the word 'electrical' operate in this context?*

RN The word came from a book I was reading a while back about grief, where the writer described the air around him at the beginning of his grief as being electrical. He meant highly charged, tense, artificial and even exciting, but a million miles away from the rush of happiness and life that fresh air can provide. The implication is that you cannot live permanently in that 'electrical' air without becoming damaged and exhausted. That made sense as a description of Gaza.

CV *When I was in the gallery, a young couple came in halfway through a screening and one of them asked the other where the film was shot. They had obviously missed the title of the show, yet large parts of the film do feel curiously placeless. The conditions of Gaza only become apparent at particular moments. In the context of the IWM, the film countered the typically journalistic representation of Gaza. It refused to depict the place and the subjects just as victims, which unfortunately tends to be the norm.*

RN It was important to me to depict what I saw and felt there as accurately as possible – in terms of a mix of how I remembered it and how I understood it when I got back, in reflection. I have tried to depict Gaza as an enchanted place because that is how I experienced it. I understood this a week after returning to the UK when I was watching an animated kids' movie. I realised that I could present Gaza through the language and eyes of childhood as an enchanted place, because it exists on a different plane of reality to everything that surrounds it, especially to us here in the UK. You cannot enter Gaza without complex dealings with different authority groups. Most of that process is hidden and opaque and the outcome in-secure. To enter Gaza through Israel is to pass through a process that takes place in a brand-new-looking military facility where you are controlled and surveilled at every step by Israeli guards that you cannot see or touch. The place itself is deserted. Once entered, it is not clear how easily or when you will be allowed to leave Gaza. And this is all before experiencing the peculiar and wired stasis of Gaza and its layers of social protocol. So to go back to the question of victims – that's not how I experienced the place or the people. My experience was much more contradictory and layered, of a culture reflecting of and on itself, rather than in relation to the world outside.

CV *It is interesting that you mention the children's film because throughout* Electrical Gaza *there are moments when the film is translated into short animations that depict the same scene in the film. Often you insert elements that aren't there in real life. I wonder whether this technique connects to one of your earlier films, 2005's* Eyeballing, *where you collate all these anthropomorphic elements from architecture – a doorbell becomes a smiley face etc. There seem to be two ways of seeing the same scene, first through a form of indexical representation and then also through this other filter of the imagination – a childlike eye.*

RN Yes, the comparison with *Eyeballing* makes sense because both use strategies to show something that is not visible in reportage or *vérité* style filming alone. They are attempts to dig under the images to see what effect they have, to see the moment of cognition taking place. Here the animation was a way of investing much more time and thought into the scenarios than the moments of film alone can offer. The experience of each moment was, of course, multi-layered, and that is something that cannot be easily portrayed through contemporaneous filming. The time of the film is multi-layered, as is my memory of the events: each time animation is used it relates to a live-action scene that we shot, yet it portrays some of its elements faithfully but enhanced and altered, and, as mentioned earlier, suggests another time/space experience of the same moment.

CV *Yes, in one animated scene a group of soldiers appear who aren't present in the filmed scene. Also, I was particularly struck by an abstract black dot that starts to grow over one scene, forming a redaction – it is striking because there is a sudden shift in representation.*

RN The two scenes you mention visualise elements that weren't there at the time of shooting. The militants/soldiers/guards were around us but behind the camera on that street and the circle or hole that grows over the scene is an abstraction, yet both anticipate the violence that was coming and that was always there, under the surface. The black circle can be a rupture in the fabric of the film and in the fabric of the place – it's a sign of death and destruction to come.

CV *Most of this film revolves around the depiction of men. There are only a couple of scenes where women appear, most prominently about halfway through when a group of women are seen looking after young children. In previous films, such as 2009's* Jack Straw's Castle, *you have similarly focused on masculine identity, why is this?*

RN Gaza has a more traditional Muslim society than the West Bank or Jerusalem. Like any society that is sealed, it is no melting pot, and it isn't influenced much by the world outside. This means that women are less visible than men in public life. Taking care of foreign media – almost always men – is a job for men in Gaza, and so those around us were men. I felt that the most free people in Gaza were the little boys. They were always out in the street and not yet burdened by the twin responsibilities of family and resistance that weigh on the older boys. The girls weren't so visible – they were on a shorter leash.

CV *You have explored closed and isolated communities numerous times before, of course. I'm thinking of films such as* Bachelor Machines Part 1 *from 2007, which depicted life on a cargo ship. What is it that draws you to these situations?*

RN It is always hard to say what draws you to the things that you do, it's a big question. I think I must be drawn to patterns being revealed or structures exposed. I like to look into things in detail by filming, to see how they are made. Closed communities have to be self-sufficient as best they can, each role needs to be fulfilled from within or the machine doesn't work – which it never completely does, like the bachelor machine. So on the ship or in Gaza, there is a walled universe in each case where the structure of society and of the institutions is closer to the surface. Nevertheless, many things remain mysterious and opaque.

CV *I was wondering what your relationship was to the people in the film. There is one scene where someone making food seems to offer it to the person behind the camera. It is quite a subtle gesture.*

RN The men and women that you see in the film were all brought together to work with us by the 'fixer'. They were drivers, translators, the family of the fixer and some who were around us for reasons that weren't made clear. They became familiar to us and every time we were in public it was noticeable that they walked in front, behind and on either side of us in a kind of formation. This was all unspoken. They were working for us, they were buying us ice creams and falafel but at the same time they were protecting us and keeping us in sight.

CV *I really enjoyed the soundtrack, which seemed to move quite effortlessly between ambient house, electro and, finally,* Fanfare, *a piece of music by Benjamin Britten taken from* Les Illuminations. *What do you see as the music's function in the film?*

RN The musical tracks operate as fictional screens. Usually they come in strong and end abruptly in near silence or against some contrast of non-music, so they don't transform the film into a passive experience for the viewer or a friction-free cinematic ride. They are there to channel the strong reactions I experienced in these moments and in memory. Footage shot on the streets of Gaza is not enough when the job is to direct the viewers' attention to an inner experience of place and time. One of the tracks is there to transmit the sheer joy and triumph we felt to have finally entered Gaza after years of trying different tactics, and to be bumping along in a car, actually there in

Gaza itself. Everyone was smiling and sharing that moment, even the fixer and the taxi driver. That was the experience of the first moments, the short-lived high when Fatah and Hamas had united and before war seemed inevitable.

cv   *Later in the film, Britten's music is layered over a shift in perspective. The camera switches to a surveillance viewpoint. There is a curious conjunction between the previous topographies – homes, markets and alleyways – and this sudden panoramic, colonialist-like gaze.*

rn   There are two panoramas that run into one another where the Britten music starts: one is shot from a tall tower in a media facility in Gaza City, and the other is shot from a rooftop in Rafah, looking over the tunnel area and the border with Egypt, a spot for surveillance and from which we were visible to soldiers watching from the Egyptian side.

cv   *The scene reminded me of Eyal Weizman's writing on the 'politics of verticality', the sense that Gaza is controlled through the sky, via surveillance, and the ground, by asserting historical sovereignty through archeology.*

rn   This is a moment where the conditions of Gaza are made more explicit through a colonial eye that controls through surveillance, but it is also a sweeping look from the sky that could be an overview of an almost religious sort, an epic view, taking in a whole landscape of history and of destruction. That viewpoint often precedes destruction.

cv   *The film is not subtitled, and language is treated as a somatic and musical element, a recurring motif of your film work – the gesture rather than the voice is foregrounded. Do you see your films as a form of portraiture?*

rn   I don't see them as portraits. I'm usually trying to understand something that I don't have language for yet, by making comparisons or juxtapositions so that I can read the friction that occurs between things/times/situations I encounter. People come and go in these scenarios, work their rhythms, and it is part of the weave of what I am both looking at and constructing. What is said is a small part of what happens, equal to glances and movements. In this kind of investigation, words can stand as they are but translating – supplying text – changes their relative importance and introduces reading into the viewer's cognitive process.

cv   *There is a compelling edit in the film where the scene of a group of*

young men sitting around singing quickly cuts to a Hamas march. Both
scenes represent, in different ways, forms of collectivism. The depiction
of institutional power is something you have explored in previous films:
the police force appear in a number of your films, for instance. Could you
expand on this representation of militarism?

RN I have been looking into our institutions, how we both internalise
and navigate them and they navigate us, since I started making films.
Cops/soldiers/guards/militants are powerful archetypes that stand in
for the control that comes from without rather than within. The men
sat together singing. It was a beautiful and harmonious moment,
but they were nationalist and resistance songs – some were moving,
others were violent. The songs and the joining of voices in a domestic
space were acts of resistance and power-building, but also about
the simple joy of connection. When that scene meets the one of the
Hamas Youth march, I'm thinking that, though there are political
divisions in Gaza, resistance to the occupation is a universal cause,
and militancy and hospitality are two pillars of Gazan existence.

CV *At the start and near the end of* Electrical Gaza *we see a group of*
people transiting through the Rafah border crossing between Palestine
and Egypt. This is where the conditions of Gaza become most apparent.

RN The film starts and almost finishes with chaotic scenes at the
Rafah border crossing. The border had been closed for a long time,
and, while we were there, the Egyptians opened the border for
three days or so. Only a few thousand Gazans were authorised to
leave, those who were sick and needed medical treatment outside
or had other such urgent situations. But many more flocked to the
border to try to leave.

CV *In relation to the border, I was interested in your depiction of the sea,*
which appears through the film and is often filmed at a distance. In one
scene it appears framed on either side by buildings while children play
in the foreground. This seems like an important metaphor for me: the
sea is often depicted as a site for escape and travel, but here it becomes
constricted.

RN Gaza is locked, and the sea is a beautiful vista but, in some way,
false. It was exciting to be at the sea in Palestine as the West Bank
always feels so hemmed in by Israel, by the checkpoints and the
separation wall, and by the settlements inside. You are never far from
the sea but the coast apart from that of the Gaza Strip was all taken
by Israel in 1948. In Gaza, however, Palestine is on the sea all the way

down. It was breathtaking to have that expanse to look out on, but try taking a boat out for more than a few kilometres and you will be shot at by the Israeli navy that routinely patrols the limits of its blockade. So these features – the sea and the impenetrable borders – define Gaza's limits and they are in everything and everyone all the time.

Issue 391, November 2015

Mark Leckey

interviewed by Jennifer Thatcher

Moon Child

JENNIFER THATCHER *Your latest video,* Dream English Kid 1964–1999 AD, *premiered at the BFI London Film Festival in October [2015] and was also showing at Cabinet Gallery. Can you tell me about the title? It's a change from the one you gave an earlier trailer,* On Pleasure Bent. *I am also interested in the specific dates – will there be a sequel?*

MARK LECKEY *Dream English Kid* comes from a children's programme on YouTube that I was watching with my daughter April, and it's called something like *Dream English*. You know in the 1990s when you used to get those Japanese translations of English phrases that were slightly off? It puts a bit of distance. It is my dream, but it's not. The syntax isn't right and that is the same analogy as the video. And the dates? 1964 is when I was born and there are a couple of reasons to end it in 1999. One, it's the end of the millennium. There was a very particular type of pop culture that existed between the postwar period and the end of the 20th century. And then, things changed for me personally after 1999. That was when I started making art. I made *Fiorrucci Makes Me Hardcore* in 1999. In a way, the new video is like the non-dancing bit of *Fiorrucci*: it is everything else that was going on at that time. And also, on another level, it just gets too close then to be able to untangle whatever was going on for me in the early 2000s. I don't know how to depict marriage and kids. I kind of want to but I don't know how to do that. That's the in-family joke: that I'll make something about April and my wife Lizzie and me.

JT *And why did you include the 'AD'?*

ML To make it feel more archaeological – it is an artefact.

JT *The video is bookended by images of the moon, which is one of several motifs that appear throughout.*

ML I was born in June, so I'm Cancer, a moon child. I was also born in the moon age, the Space Age. And the other thing is, I wanted the shots of the moon to be from the periods that they depict in the video. So the first moon you see is from 1966, shot on film, and at the end there is a VHS moon, and then at the very end there is an ASCII moon. They all have a different texture because of what they were recorded on. So, it is not just the moon, it is the recorded moon.

JT *Your use of a countdown at the end gives the work an apocalyptic feel. In retrospect, it is amazing the fear that we were made to feel in anticipation of the Y2K bug.*

ML It is all about fear, that video – fear being fed to you. I'm resentful about the kind of trauma that as a kid you suffered because of the fear of nuclear war. TV programmes like *Threads* or *The War Game*: in depicting nightmarish scenarios, they gave you nightmares. And I don't know if they were entirely justified. So it is something about that apocalyptic bent that gets amplified by media.

JT *It is a very dark film, considering that it is autobiographical – there is not much let-up. There is a scene with a boy kicking leaves that seems more light-hearted.*

ML Well, that's a clip from a film about autism. He's autistic.

JT *There is also a striking animation sequence about an autistic boy.*

ML Taken from a 1950s study of an autistic boy by the psychologist Bruno Bettelheim, who wrote a lot about autism and is now maligned because he came up with this theory of the 'refrigerator mother' – the idea that autism is caused by a cold, indifferent mother. Anyway, he studied this boy he called 'Joey the Mechanical Boy' who believed he was a machine and that he had to surround himself with automative devices to keep himself alive. I was fascinated by that, and by the idea of the boy as a kind of cyborg. That's the thinking approach. The non-thinking approach is that everybody is on the autistic spectrum in some way. There was a theory that it was to do with an 'extreme male brain' – it's a very masculine tendency to pattern and to order.

JT *Is that something you recognise in yourself?*

ML Yes. Throughout the video, apart from the moon, there are a lot of grids, these patterns that are the way that images are produced through pixels and line scans. A trait of autism is to be obsessed by patterns to the detriment of everything else because essentially it is about an inability to deal with oversensorial input. So you focus on something particular to cancel out the noise. It leads to obsessive, narrow interests – such that I have. That marries up with the fetishism aspect that I have as well. So when you get that cross detail of a pair of fishnet tights in the video, that to me represents a cross between autism and fetishism. Those traits I find are amplified by technology. I might not have those traits inherently but they seem to be a kind of underlying structure to technology. Does that make sense?

JT *On a basic level, that this technology is created by people with autistic traits?*

ML That's my theory: that a lot of people on the spectrum write the code that then creates the algorithms that we learn by. So we are inadvertently absorbing autistic behaviours. There is a lot of thinking about autism now that the condition is not about being closed off from the world but rather about inhabiting the world in a different way, and that's fascinating.

JT *In the video, there is an unsettling sequence set in a small, windowless room. Does that part represent a particular episode in London?*

ML That is to do with when I was squatting and taking a lot of drugs. All the way through the film there are these kinds of hermetic spaces or cells. I think that is a feedback reflection: that's where I am when I am making this thing. In editing the video, it is just me and the computer. I go into my hutch.

JT *Another trope that comes up is the empty highway and the flyover.*

ML The whole film started off as an attempt to try to assemble my memoirs from all this stuff out in the world. So I started by trying to find for each period an instance that had lingered or even festered. That's basically the motive to doing it: things that have been playing in my head, to manifest them in some way, to be able to look at them and see what they are. As if that could somehow transform them. But it can't.

When I was a kid, about eight, we used to sit under the flyover and eat sweets and be a bit naughty. At one point, sitting under this flyover, I thought I saw a pixie. And I had this very vivid memory of a pixie underneath this bridge until I was about 19 and I had to go back and do English O Level. And I wrote a story about seeing this pixie and I realised as I was writing the story that up until that point I had believed it. But as I wrote it, it kind of fell apart; it became unbelievable.

Anyway, there was no way to introduce a pixie into the film. I couldn't get it to sit right. But it did end up as a bridge, literally. And the bridge goes through transformations. It's quite a crude narrative device: it starts off in the 1960s as this white heat of technology, this kind of clean, brutalist concrete bridge, then it gets graffitied in the 1970s and becomes this recognisable dystopic image. In the 1980s, it is subjected to nuclear attack. And then in the 1990s it is repainted in this New Labour graphic design. I remember, in the 1990s, that through Britpop and young graphic design companies, Britain sort of rebranded itself. It's that rebranded bridge of the 1990s.

JT *I was thinking of you in relation to Mark Fisher's autobiographical book* Ghosts of My Life. *He has some interesting ideas about nostalgia, influenced by Jacques Derrida. For him, we are undergoing a formal nostalgia so that today's pop culture references the past in terms of style but not substance. He thinks nothing has been as interesting culturally since that period from the 1960s to the 1990s.*

ML No, I don't agree. There is a shift away from that drive towards authenticity, which I think that period was about. Now we're in a period of understanding inauthenticity. That's partly what the new video is about. They're not authentic memories in the film. In order to get to something, you can't approach it as if it is an authentic thing. You have to approach it through a cloak of inauthenticity. You have to enhance the artifice in order to generate a sensation that feels in some way genuine. For the period that we are talking about, the greatest artist would be someone like Patti Smith. Now, I don't think Smith is authentic; I think it is still showbusiness, and she has a persona, it's a kind of drag. But today we are fully mediated beings and we understand the world in a much more complex and unreal way. And I think that makes this period really interesting – we are in a whole different matrix.

JT *You were saying you have a knack for finding images.*

ML Well, I do have a knack. In music they call it crate-digging. I used to run a clothes shop. I used to go to charity shops. So I have that kind of knack – for shopping. I'm a good shopper and it's the same thing. I think everyone can do it now. It used to be a preserve of the artist; artists used to have collections and *objets trouvés*. I only began to make art because I got access to editing. Before that, I went to art school. I tried to paint, I tried to sculpt – I couldn't. It was only when I used video that I could make things.

JT *Were you ever tempted to look for actual images of yourself to use?*

ML I always look for myself on the internet, that's all I ever do. I love Googling myself.

JT *You didn't want to use those images?*

ML There is nothing that goes back to that period. The idea of the video was to have all these surrogates that could take my place. I mean, I look like that kid dancing. There are other lookalikes within the video that stand in for me. There is a bit with the band Joy Division but it is taken from the 2007 film *Control* – everything is a substitute.

JT *I don't think we have yet grasped the extent to which new technology has affected our memories and the way we think. Your work spans both pre- and post-internet time periods. How do you think the idea of 'self' is changing today? I was reading a book by Jeremy Rifkin called* The Age of Access *in which he argues that access to services has overtaken ownership. In it, he talks about the postmodern self as one that constantly edits and updates itself, which he contrasts with the 19th-century idea of man as an island, unchanging.*

ML It is easier to say than to experience.

JT *You could say it manifests itself in the pressure we feel to better ourselves, whether through exercise or eating better, or improving our minds or by changing jobs.*

ML Let's come at it another way. There was an idea at the beginning of Postmodernism that this self was fragmented and mutable, that you could be somehow disinterested in that self and analyse it or understand it critically. What I'm trying to do is find a way to feel more involved or within something, rather than trying to step back.

JT *Your work seems to be about experiencing the things that you are thinking about. So, for the performance of* Mark Leckey in the Long Tail *at the ICA in 2009, you did actually wear a long tail (Reviews AM324). You go right into the metaphor and inhabit it.*

ML Yes, it's that. But I don't know who I am as I do that. I can only understand myself as a series of impulses or drives or desires. I make work to understand those drives. That is how it starts out but it never gets resolved.

JT *Going back to* in the Long Tail, *what made you borrow that idea, which is essentially an economic theory about the internet. The author, Chris Anderson, had been at the ICA to talk about his book* The Long Tail *when it was first published in 2006.*

ML   His theory has now been discounted, smashed to pieces by Amazon and Google and all the rest of it.

JT   *His was a utopian idea that favoured niches over conventional mass markets. Was that what you were attracted to at the time?*

ML   For me at the time – and still now – the internet felt wholly magical and I was trying to understand the material reality that was generating that magic, but also wanting to go with the magic as well. And what interested me about the idea of *The Long Tail* is that there was a sexual dimension to it. What the internet does is use pornography as an engine. This 'long tail' idea was about catering to niches, and then producing niches within those niches – perversions and peccadillos. Any whim could be not just met but amplified and extended. That
was what I liked about the long tail thing: this weird economy of perversion.

JT   *You use the term 'bachelors' a lot in relation to your work, with its Duchampian reference.*

ML   Yes. You know I'm married, and I have to negotiate my marriage and my desire to enclose myself in Leckeyness, and to be in that bubble. I think always the thing with art is: what is the ignition for anything? Because the ultimate artwork for me is something like a perpetual motion machine: you just set it up and it runs on its own and takes you with it. It is the mechanical element: that somehow Marcel Duchamp's bachelor machine is just feeding itself and repeating over and over again the same actions – but also that it grinds its own chocolate and is productive. And you can get really locked into that, but it comes with all sorts of problems and is essentially unhealthy. It is like the thing you were talking about before with the self that I couldn't answer. All you've got is your pathologies. All you can do is uncover your pathologies and make them productive rather than debilitating.

JT   *Can you tell me about 2010's* GreenScreenRefridgeratorAction *as an example of how you deal with our relationship to machines – the beauty of machinery, but also how we exploit machines and are exploited by them?*

ML   It is back to that sensation of things appearing magical – like your phone. I remember one of the first experiences I had like that: Lizzie was in a wood in Sri Lanka and I was in Epping Forest. Now this seems mundane but we were in these geologically riven places and we were having this conversation. And that was astounding.

Just to think of the satellites that were in place making that happen. But at the same time it was impossible not to think of it as magic, which brings a whole other set of questions.

JT *A kind of spiritual dimension?*

ML On one side there is that, yes, but on the other side there is the idea that it is a completely cynical exercise in what they call 'black boxing'. Everything is hidden, obscured, and that is what produces this magical effect. I'm between the two poles. The gallery is a very awkward space to ask these questions – a 19th-century environment in which you are trying to place these questions of dematerialisation and image production. But the gallery is a place where thigs can happen in a ritualistic way. You can make objects that people can gather around. So the *GreenScreenRefridgeratorAction* was a ritual because it begins with a performance when I'm in the green screen with the fridge, and I'm puffing this coolant that is running through the fridge's system because it gets you high a little bit. I had read about shamans in South America: if they want to take sap from a plant, they don't just snap the tree and extract the sap, they mimic the plant, they dress like the plant and they rub themselves in oils and then they sing to the plant in order for the plant to give up its essence. And that magical aspect of technology throws you back to those more aboriginal rituals or animistic ways of thinking. That was what it was about: to be like the fridge.

JT *Did it work in the moment?*

ML Yes. It was exciting. I recently read someone defining ecstasy: to be beside yourself and at the same time to look at yourself and experience yourself taking pleasure. There was a moment of ecstasy with the fridge.

JT *I want to ask about your interest in galleries and display in relation to the Hayward touring show that you curated in 2013, 'The Universal Addressability of Dumb Things' (Reviews AM370). I saw the version at the De La Warr Pavilion and my daughter thought we were in a shop. She really wanted to touch the objects, they looked so tempting. You know: gallery, no touch; shop, touch.*

ML I have never heard anyone say that but I like that idea. That is more my experience of display than it is in museums. I think that was what was so wrong with that show, that you couldn't touch it. The objects were all on loan from museums and galleries, and I couldn't touch them either. For example, there was a Richard Hamilton computer and that was just ridiculous – I wasn't allowed near it. I found that really frustrating. It led to me making copies of those things so that I could not only touch them but now they are mine. They are fetishistic objects and, as with any fetishistic object, the drive is to be able to touch and stroke and fondle.

JT *Are you interested in the new theories about object-oriented ontology?*

ML I don't understand them. When I made the fridge, I did read some of that stuff. But what I was more interested in was magic and animism and autism. This was my problem with college because to understand object-oriented ontology you need to have read Immanuel Kant. I went to art school, I didn't do philosophy. I still think it is a crazy idea that art students should try to make work and at the same time understand philosophy at that depth.

JT *Tell me about your blow-up* Felix the Cat *at Frieze London – do you see him as your avatar?*

ML Exactly, he's an avatar. To be honest, at Frieze, Galerie Buchholz asked, 'Can we show the cat?', and I was so surprised that I said yes. Usually Buchholz is quite tasteful and discreet. And then when I first got in there, I was like, 'oh shit'. I immediately thought of people going, 'this is how dumb Frieze is – it's just a giant, blow- up cat'. And then I also thought, it's an Instagram. I was a little bit embarrassed. But it is like having your avatar there representing you in the hope that people take an interest in what you do. I have a fascination with Felix because, as well as being my avatar, he is an avatar of the electronic image. I saw some references to him and people were filling in that history that he was the first image ever broadcast – that's enough, I was satisfied.

JT *He is just an inflatable?*

ML Yes, it is like literally you are inflating something out of its own scale. Also, that is how he looms for me as a figure. I have this line that sounds a bit too clever but he is as real to me as God and John Lennon.

Issue 392, December–January 2015–16

Jordan Baseman

interviewed by David Barrett

Blackout

DAVID BARRETT *A number of your films, such as the new piece showing at TAP,* Blackout, *utilise documentary conventions but then swerve off in other directions.*

JORDAN BASEMAN My interest is not in documentary or reportage, journalism, sociology or anthropology. I think about creative non-fiction, like Truman Capote's *In Cold Blood*, Dave Cullen's *Columbine* or Haruki Murakami's book on the Tokyo gas attacks, *Underground*. In all of these, information is heavily manipulated and readers receive it differently to how it has been captured. Same with *Blackout* – while its account is not inaccurate, neither is it totally accurate, in that it was recorded over a couple of months and the hours of raw interview recordings were boiled down to 11 minutes.

DB *When the credits appear, we see that it has been recorded in Omaha, Death Valley and London, which suggests that the whole thing is a construct.*

JB It is important in all my work that there is this obviously constructed nature. In *Blackout* some of it is clumsy, so when she first says the word 'blackout' the screen cuts to black, which is kind of hokey but it establishes something, sets something up. I think of the films as portraits – artworks – not as testimonies. They may be truthful but they are not the truth, because there are multiple truths. With *Blackout* there was more than a year between when I made the recordings and when I returned to edit it, and that gap gave me the opportunity to be ruthless with the material. The interview process is emotional, speculative, spontaneous and out of control. Yet the editing is an intellectualised assertion of ideas that may not have been as evident in the original recording. So with *Blackout* she mainly talked about getting sober and I didn't want to talk about that. I was interested in this perception of time when it is beyond memory and cannot be reclaimed.

DB *So during the drink-induced blackouts that the narrator is describing, she is not unconscious, she just has zero recollection of what she did during those periods, is that right?*

JB She has no memory of them whatsoever. She gets told about what she did but she has no recollection. During the interview she talked in detail about what she had apparently done, but I cut all that – I feel protective of the participants. That is a delicate line to walk: do you protect the participants from being judged too harshly or do you allow that judgement to play out only to be undermined, which is what I think happens in *Blackout*.

DB *She talks as if it is someone else that takes over, like Jekyll and Hyde, although she then expresses remorse over her actions.*

JB There is this clear schism. It was filmed a couple of years ago and she has been away from alcohol ever since, so now she has no desire to see the film because she doesn't want to revisit that time of her life – I mean, five years is a long time to lose, especially in that period of adolescence and early adulthood. The interviews were recorded in Nebraska but she has left all that behind, including her family, and moved to New York to reinvent herself as someone who doesn't drink alcohol. She had judged herself to have behaved pretty badly and wanted to escape that person. One thing that I try to be careful about is potential disparagement that might be cast on participants through the work. That is why at the end, when she talks about moving on to Ecstasy and not allowing her issues to define her, I think it is a really strong position to hold.

DB *At first, it seems to be a familiar story of redemption, but then it becomes clear that she is still living a wild lifestyle.*

JB Exactly, it is just that she now avoids alcohol because it has this one specific effect of causing blackouts, which she can't control. It was important to me that this work wasn't evangelical or promoting temperance.

DB *Is she the only interview subject who has remained anonymous?*

JB There have been a few. I knew that I would anonymise her when making the work. I also modified her voice very slightly so people she knows might not be able to identify her. She didn't ask me to do that but with all the interview-based participants I do feel a responsibility towards them because I am hijacking their experiences for other ends. They all know I am doing this. They are all complicit.

DB *But the ends you are working towards are yours. The schism in her character, for instance – you highlight this to make the artwork more compelling. The version of reality you construct is not only different from an objective reality but it may also present the protagonist in a way that is at odds with their own self-perception.*

JB That negotiation is interesting. It is definitely an exaggerated state that I present to the world, and I sometimes worry that the films are too compact and contained.

DB *I am thinking in particular of the 2010 work* The Dandy Doctrine (A Delightful Illusion) *with Sebastian Horsley, someone who attempted to control his image and had a quite specific view of himself. I understand that he was surprised by what your approach revealed.*

JB That was one of the last works that I made where the participant was visually central. There is always a moment where I deliver the work and go 'ta-dah', and the response is often one of surprise. No matter how much I have talked about portraiture or the creative process or creative non-fiction, or how many previous examples I have shown, there is always surprise. With Sebastian, his surprise was at something that I hadn't even noticed myself, which was his drug use. He saw himself in the camera's mirror and what was reflected back to him was a heroin addict. I was really naive – I didn't know he was using at the time. I think what he saw in the film was a functioning addict, and he was concerned that other people would see that too because he had said he wasn't using drugs any longer. He didn't really care about the work itself so much. Making that work with Sebastian, he was so used to answering questions about himself that he had stock replies to everything. It was almost impossible to get him away from that, and that was why it was interesting to locate that rote response as the centre of his perception of himself.

DB *The hollowness of the stock reply?*

JB He says so himself, he says: 'I love meeting new people because they haven't heard this tired old thing.' So he was very self-aware in that regard. The most difficult thing is when people want me to watch the film with them. This only happened once, with Steve 'Krusher' Joule and the 2010 film *Jump*. He was a heavy metal DJ at GLR but was sacked, he said, for refusing to play Def Leppard. Anyway, I returned to his dope-filled flat in the tower block in Millwall where *Jump* was filmed and sat with him as he watched it. That was awful. There was a long silence afterwards. Then he just said: 'I've never seen myself like that. That's not how I see myself, but it's obviously how I am.'

DB *While some of the works play with this idea of documentary truth, others make the constructed nature of the work really clear, such as in 2006's* Ask for It, Ask for It *where you mic-ed up a youth football coach and we hear everything he said before, during and after a match. But you removed the pauses so it only lasts five minutes – the editing is front and centre.*

JB A lot of people don't get that. I used to work with a guy who would ask in crits, 'where is the art in this?' A horrible question, but a good question to ask. For me that is where the art is, in the construction, the edit.

DB *The power of editing was made clear in a comment by Francis Wells, the surgeon who performs the heart transplant in 2003's* Under the Blood.

JB Yeah, he said that the experience of watching the film was more visceral than performing the operation. But in many ways the film theatre is more dramatic than the operating theatre. There is no dramatic lighting in the operating theatre, for instance – it is really bright.

DB *And the soundtrack you used featuring the preacher Billy Graham – that wasn't playing during the operation either.*

JB Definitely not. A different kind of evangelism was going on in there.

DB *As well as documentary conventions, you also utilise structuralist filmmaking tropes: the projectors are visible, the leader tape is visible etc. You demonstrate film's materiality.*

JB There is a directness I aim for in the presentations. That is echoed in the films, too, where I try to present the least amount of information. But those compact moments are, I hope, conceptually expansive.

DB *Documentary makes a claim to narrative truth while Structuralism makes a claim to material truth. You co-opt them both to show the plurality of truth.*

JB Whatever it takes, that's my attitude, I'm not precious about material. When I studied at Goldsmiths, people talked a lot about truth to materials and I never got it – it's all fake anyway, it's all artifice.

DB *You use the materiality of the film not as an appeal to literalism but instead to produce a further imaginative leap.*

JB Yes, absolutely. The structuralist thing – I'm not really interested in anything that is purist or totalitarian. I don't have such extreme rules.

DB *In* Perfume Disco Coma *from 2007 we see the dots from the filmstrip but they are a metaphor for this imaginary disco that is being experienced by the narrator at the edge of death.*

JB I like the material of film and I like the physical aspects of cameras, both video and film, but it is not meant to be literal and I don't think about it as illustration. In the new work *Veil* there is a bubbling kind of visual effect which was made by layering together three pieces of film, spraying them with sugar and wine and then pulling the film through the projector in real time. The film is burning and losing its integrity, so the visual effect is the material failure of the film itself. I want this visual abstraction. I am abstracting things in the narrative anyway, and sometimes I think abstraction is the only way to represent things that are happening in the film. The visual filmmaking, at the point of capture, shares the unpredictable nature of the interview process, but through editing I can reclaim something useful. In *Blackout*, the stuttering effect is me jamming the camera and pushing it forward, so I didn't really know what I would get when the film was developed.

DB *In the 2009 film* A Hypnotic Effect, *where the protagonist is rehabilitated after being attacked and set on fire, there seems to be a shot of a swimming pool but it looks as if the film itself is moving.*

JB The camera jammed but I didn't notice at the time, so all that streakiness is the film wearing itself out as it goes through the camera, burning out. Recently, I have only recorded audio from the interviews and have produced all the visuals separately. The result challenges the viewer more, makes them less passive as they try to understand what the work is doing.

DB *I guess nowadays your practice would be defined as 'moving-image work', but when I watch your films the image is moving not in the sense that the picture is animated but rather that the medium itself has velocity – you are aware not only of the camera moving through space but also of the film moving past the aperture or the projector's bulb.*

JB That sense of movement is important along with a sense of time. I'm propelling a narrative forward. I'm also really interested in the optical thing, so you see streaks from road lights captured in long exposures and other such effects. Funnily enough, I have recently been struggling with my eyesight, which must have been the case for a while, and that might also explain why a lot of the work is abstract.

DB *Well, one history of art is a history of ophthalmic pathologies –*
Modigliani, Monet and so on.

JB True, but I am drawn to an optical quality in the work where you
are not sure what it is you are looking at. In *Perfume Disco Coma,*
the fleeting nature of the images is meant to leave the viewer with
an after-image of the woman in the footage. Same in the 2009 Alan
Wakeman work, *Nasty Piece of Stuff.* I'm really interested in that
retinal thing both as an idea but also as something that has visual
impact. The narratives are quite impactful, I want them to have
potency and meaning, and the visuals are used to reinforce that while
also keeping the work fluid so that it cannot be entirely pinned down.

DB *Your early work from the 1990s was object-based. Tell me about that*
transition from physical to optical work.

JB I still make things, I just don't show them. The special effects in
Veil and *Blackout* are the result of physical experiments in the studio
but I don't want to present those physical things to the world.

DB *So what precipitated the shift from sculpture to film?*

JB I had a series of epiphanies all in a row, back in 1998. I had some
not great experiences with commercial galleries. I was confused
about how to progress because I didn't want what was happening to
continue to happen and I was unhappy with that model.

DB *In terms of the commercial art market?*

JB I was unhappy with it in every way, that model where I make
something then give it to somebody else and they are responsible for
its delivery in the world. I had never really challenged it, and then it
was challenged for me because of some negative experiences where
people were not entirely honest with what was happening with the
work. Why I originally wanted to be an artist was changing and I
didn't want it to change. The money was great. It was great to sell
work – but at what cost? I'll never forget that I had a gallerist saying:
'I've got people who would buy ten of those.' And that's fine but it
was not why I wanted to be an artist and it was not why I wanted to
continue to be an artist. Then I got a job at the Ruskin School of Art
just as it bought a whole load of Macs. I had never used a computer
before so I just spent about a year and half reading computer manuals
and learning to edit instead of making work. I had made films as
an undergrad, but that was pre-digital. So I was trying to figure out,
and I'm still figuring this out, how to be the artist that I would like to

be. I don't think that's a static thing – if you are lucky, it is a series of investigations and questions. So I think I'm making the same work as I was when I was making sculptures but the films are more expansive and ask other kinds of questions. For me, the sculptures I made were so singular that they didn't allow for any kind of expansion in the viewer. I might be deluded but I'm much more interested in the work I'm making now. I never show that sculptural work and I never mention it when I give an artist's talk.

DB *That's why I'm asking about it, and because you are now head of sculpture at the Royal College of Art.*

JB Those early sculptures are not a secret, it's just that, you know, I have a lot of more recent work – I've been around a while.

DB *Me too and I remember those early works!*

JB I have had a few people say to me, 'you know what, I don't like your films but your sculptures were great'. Thanks. But I think part of an artist's practice needs to be a constant questioning of what you are doing.

DB *Questioning is also a theme in the work, where questioning perception becomes a question of belief insofar as we sometimes see what we believe we are going to see. This, in turn, leads to a strand in the work about belief and faith.*

JB I'm from a really religious family. I don't practice or believe but my parents and my brothers are religious. I went to Hebrew school four days a week and I hated it. But it has created a real interest in the way that we structure our world and what is important to us. We're lucky because we live in this city where you can do anything, more or less. You can be anything and you can believe anything. But I'm not from that kind of background. I'm from a background where you either believe in one thing or you don't, and if you don't then you are excluded. I have always been in it but have always felt outside because I have never believed. I never hid my lack of faith from my parents and that infuriated them, especially when I was a child. I blew out the Sabbath candles when I was seven just to see what would happen. And nothing happened. I wasn't struck down. I just relit the candles and nobody knew. But I did.

DB *In* Perfume Disco Coma *the narrator is talking about the lights that she saw in her coma, which she interprets as a disco. Yet someone else in that situation with different cultural baggage might have interpreted it differently.*

JB   True, and the visuals I hope allow that openness. That is where abstraction is useful, it is a form of representation but it isn't strictly representational. In the 2003 film *1 + 1 = 1*, where the transplant patient is talking about his surgery dream, the image could be the light at the end or it could be a scan or it could be something you are moving through. I want things to feel as if they are fleeting – not that they are moving away from you or towards you, but rather that they are out of your grasp.

DB   *I'd like to ask about conflict, as you seem to end up in a few. I remember you once talked about a commission that ended up as a racism row in the press.*

JB   Yes, *I Hate Boston and Boston Hates Me* back in 2009. The narrator worked for the local council in Boston, Lincolnshire. She had worked there for five years and is probably still working there. She was originally from Portugal but became part of this long-standing, stable Portuguese community in Boston. Lincolnshire also has casual agriculture workers coming over from Portugal every summer to pick cabbages and the like. So I interviewed her about her experiences of living in Boston and she talked about the racism that she encountered daily for being different. She walked her daughter to school every day and they would get abuse every day – for being from Portugal. She told a friend that she was participating in this project, and her friend told somebody, and somebody told somebody else and then they threw a brick through her window. The police got involved. She wanted the work to go ahead and the Portuguese community wanted it to be shown, but I was anxious about her safety and I didn't want to be responsible for her getting hurt, so I pulled the film and never showed it. And yet it got all this attention because it was August and there was nothing else in the news. For something that was never seen, it got a lot of attention. But that wasn't because of the work, it was because of issues around migration.

DB   *There is often a sense of the complexities and fragilities of human interaction in your work. In the 2009 piece* Dark is the Night *you even went to great lengths to film Soho without really showing any people.*

JB   The process of capturing interview material is often the same, sitting down and talking with people, so I try to make the work visually different each time. *Dark is the Night* has no people, other than some homeless people asleep in doorways, because I made that a semi-formal rule when capturing the imagery in order to change

623

the visual parameters of the work. The people are ghosts that move through it.

DB *You often take on commissions and residencies in unfamiliar communities and institutions which put you in the position of being an outsider.*

JB Back in 1998 when I stopped presenting physical works, I wanted to take more of a proactive role in how I was going to exist in the world. I didn't want to have a commercial thing but I still wanted to make work, so I started to look at residencies, commissions and grants. Also, I really wanted to get out of the studio, to look at the world and to be located in it. Making work out in the world feels really risky, genuinely frightening and exhilarating. It is never boring or static, always unpredictable.

DB *You feel responsible for the representation of the participants in the film, but how do you avoid the instrumentalist do-gooding that commissioners might be looking for?*

JB There is often a three-way tug of war between my idea of the work, the participant with their expectations and also the expectations of the commissioner. My allegiance is more towards the participant than the commissioner. Some funders know that what they are going to get will be unpredictable, and recognise that the final product needs to stand on its own as an artwork first and foremost, whatever else it might also do. The Wellcome Trust understands this, commissioning *Deadness* in 2013 when in the past it had previously turned the proposal down. A counter example, though, might be *Perfume Disco Coma*, which was commissioned by a European housing development programme for the regeneration of Widnes and Runcorn. The interview subject, Wendy, is a librarian from Widnes. I went to speak to her because someone told me that she had seen a ghost in the library, but when we were talking she started telling me that she had once been in a five-week coma following an illness – I was way more interested in that. I asked all kinds of questions and buried within them were the things that I was interested in. That is often the case: it becomes clear to the interviewee that I am not interested in the ghost in the library, for example, at least not for the film. And at that point they either continue with it or they bail out of the project, and that has happened a few times.

DB *And were the Widnes regeneration commissioners interested in the ghost or the coma?*

JB   The focus of the work was supposed to be the library and the social experience of the library.

DB   *That wasn't the focus of the film you produced.*

JB   No. I presented it to the commissioners at a meeting. I showed the work and there was silence in the room. Then they were like, 'this has nothing to do with what we wanted it to do'. And I said, 'well, she lives here and this is her experience of living here – it's not what you wanted but there you go'. They distanced themselves from it at that point. It has never been shown in this country. But I never go back to refashion something for the agents that are funding the work. Sometimes the participants are disappointed in the work because it is not what they wanted, and sometimes I will make them a film that does what they want just for them. This is a private transaction, a gift which is not an artwork or part of my art practice.

DB   *Is this to avoid the charge of exploitation that documentary or photojournalistic practices can struggle with?*

JB   The working process is mutually exploitative, I'm up front about that. The participants want to take part for their reasons and I want them to take part for my reasons and we have agreed on that early on. I'm really fortunate in that my survival does not depend on me selling artworks and I feel very lucky to be liberated from that whole thing. I would love to sell something, not in a mercenary way but because money is not a bad thing to have – it offers freedom. But if I did that, I would need to be able to look at myself in the mirror. I told Alan that if I sold *Nasty Piece of Stuff* I would give him half the money. We paid Sebastian but he sent the cheque back.

DB   *I think the Widnes regeneration team were being shortsighted because in* Perfume Disco Coma *what struck me was Wendy's story of her birthday, which told me everything I needed to know about the community in Widnes.*

JB   Me too. At the library, Wendy spent most of her time chasing kids with their cans of Kestrel Super out of the building, but it was still the main community hub there. And in the film she describes how all the other librarians showed up at hospital on her birthday and she couldn't figure out how – had all the libraries been shut? The staff had arranged for teams of temps that day so that all the librarians of Widnes could come and celebrate her birthday in hospital after her coma. I was really moved when she said that. But the story wasn't about the new homes they were building in Runcorn, so the commissioners didn't want it.

DB *One final thing: for some reason, I feel that I should ask you about clowns.*

JB Yeah? Go on then, ask me about clowns.

DB *They seem to crop up a few times. You have made clown shoes as sculptures, your avatar on Vimeo is a clown.*

JB There are a couple in *Blackout* as well, at the very end there are two fleeting shots of clowns. You know what it is? My parents didn't have any art at home but they did have pictures of clowns by this guy named Louis Spiegel. He was a clown painter from Cincinnati, Ohio and my dad loved clowns. I hate clowns, can't stand the damn things. My dad dressed up as a clown as a surprise for my younger brother's fifth birthday. I went with him to buy the costume. My dad was a frustrated entertainer – he was a door-to-door encyclopedia salesman, so it was the same talent. He had my little brother on his knee and my brother didn't know it was dad, and my dad said: 'Hey, sonny, where's your dad?' And my brother replied sadly: 'He's in jail.' My dad was devastated. I don't know where my brother got the idea from but it floored my dad. I remember looking at my dad and I kind of laughed, and my dad got really upset and very angry. But he was dressed as a frickin' clown.

Issue 394, March 2016

Copyright Notices

First published in 2017 by Ridinghouse

Ridinghouse
46 Lexington Street
London W1F 0LP
United Kingdom
www.ridinghouse.co.uk

Distributed in the UK and Europe by
Cornerhouse
c/o Home
2 Tony Wilson Place
Manchester M15 4FN
United Kingdom
www.cornerhousepublications.org

Distributed in the US by
RAM Publications
2525 Michigan Avenue Building A2
Santa Monica, CA 90404
United States
www.rampub.com

British Library Cataloguing-in-
 Publication Data
A catalogue record of this book is
 available from the British Library

ISBN 978 1 909932 42 5

For the book in this form
©2017 Art Monthly and Ridinghouse

Editor: Patricia Bickers
Project Editor: Chris McCormack
Copyright Clearances: Daniel Griffiths
Proofreader: Penny Williams

Designed by Mark Thomson
Set in OT Arnhem
Printed by Samhwa Printing Company,
 South Korea

Acknowledgements
The editor would like to offer sincere
thanks to all of the artists and their
interviewers who have enabled us
to create this book, as well as to Art
Monthly's co-founder Jack Wendler,
to David Barrett, Chris McCormack and
Penny Williams of Art Monthly, and to
Karsten Schubert and Daniel Griffiths
of Ridinghouse, and the designer of
this book and former deputy editor
of Art Monthly Mark Thomson.